The Comp[

ALASKA FISHING

1995-1996 Edition

by René Limeres & Gunnar Pedersen
with contributions by
Kenneth T. Alt, Thomas Cappiello, Gary Souza, Steve Wottlin

ISBN 0-935701-27-3

Foghorn
Press
BOOKS BUILDING COMMUNITY.

Foghorn Press
555 DeHaro Street #220
San Francisco, CA 94107
415-241-9550

Foghorn Press titles are distributed to the book trade by Publishers Group West, Emeryville, California. To contact your local sales representative, call 1-800-788-3123.

To order individual books, please call Foghorn Press at 1-800-FOGHORN (364-4676).

Library of Congress ISSN Data:
March 1995
Alaska Fishing
ISSN 1079-6916

Printed in the United States of America.

The Complete Guide

ALASKA FISHING

1995-1996 Edition

by René Limeres & Gunnar Pedersen

with contributions by
Kenneth T. Alt, Thomas Cappiello, Gary Souza, Steve Wottlin

Foghorn Press
BOOKS BUILDING COMMUNITY™

CREDITS

Managing Editor—*Ann-Marie Brown*
Associate Editors—*Howard Rabinowitz, Julianne Boyajian*
Maps/Layout—*Michele Thomas*

Illustrations—*Thomas Cappiello, Willliam Hickman,
René Limeres, Mark Whitfield*

All photos are by René Limeres, except:
•Color photos of arctic grayling, cutthroat trout, halibut,
northern pike, sockeye salmon—*Tom Cappiello*
•Color photo of sheefish—*Ken Alt*
•Pages 199, 234—*James Garrity*
•Page 216—*Paul Allred*
•Page 261—*Tom Cappiello*
•Pages 226, 286—*U.S. Fish and Wildlife Service*
•Page 467—*Gunnar Pedersen*

Dear Anglers,
    We are committed to making *Alaska Fishing* the most
accurate and detailed fishing book ever published. We welcome
your comments and suggestions. Please mail in the enclosed
postcard or write to us at: Foghorn Press, 555 DeHaro Street
#220, San Francisco, CA 94107.
    Please enjoy and protect the outdoors—

Ann-Marie Brown
Managing Editor

PREFACE

This book joins quite a few others on the subject, written over the years by many authors of varying backgrounds. Each has attempted, in his or her own way, to describe the remarkable and vast sportfishing opportunities in the state of Alaska. More subcontinent than state, with diverse terrain and a bewildering variety of fish species, the Last Frontier places some very real limitations on any one writer's experience and resources, a fact which must be taken into account when reading most of the guides currently available.

The idea for this project began a while back with a dream of creating a complete reference on Alaska fishing, written collaboratively by a diverse group of guides, outdoor writers, biologists and hard-core sportfishermen, each bringing a particular expertise to create together a comprehensive, insightful and (hopefully) flavorful guide that can be of use to readers of all backgrounds.

Like others before us, we relied heavily for our baseline information on the research data and experiences of personnel within the Alaska Department of Fish and Game and other agencies, both state and federal. However, we placed a major emphasis on the input of guides, outfitters, air-taxi operators and lodge owners, for as fellow members of this profession, most of us well know (and cherish!) the unique and abundant opportunities for hands-on observation and experience that our work allows. In the course of a typical summer season, we witness hundreds of angling encounters, under every condition imaginable, in a dozen or more watersheds, and for a whole gamut of species. This experience—along with that of biologists, local fishermen, river runners and others "on site"—represents a most significant and relevant component of knowledge on the subject.

In the development of this book, we departed from the standard approach to the subject. We begin with a rundown of the important Alaska sport species—their distributions, life histories and habits, popular fishing methods for them and best sportfishing locations. We then focus on Alaska's six major geographic regions and their particular sportfishing highlights, including specific location information for more than 250 of the state's best rivers, lakes and marine areas. With region-by-region analysis of conditions, highlights, weather, access and available services, along with appendices and a completely cross-referenced index, this guidebook, to our knowledge, is the first of its kind to attempt a thorough and integrated account of Alaska and its fishing. We hope you find it enjoyable and useful.

René Limeres & Gunnar Pedersen
Anchorage, Alaska—January, 1995

TABLE OF CONTENTS

MAP 1   MAP 2   MAP 3

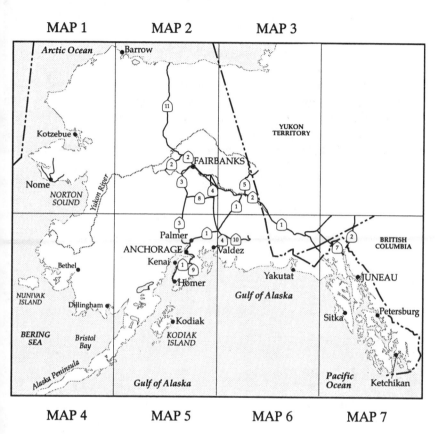

MAP 4   MAP 5   MAP 6   MAP 7

How To Use This Book

You can search for your ideal Alaska fishing spot in three ways:

1) If you know the name of the fishing hot spot you'd like to visit, or the name of the corresponding geographical area (town name, national or state forest name, national or state park name, lake or river name, etc.), use the index beginning on page 591 to locate it, and turn to the corresponding page.

2) If you'd like to travel to a particular part of Alaska, and want to find out what type of fishing is available there, turn to the Alaska Regions chapters to read about your area.

The state is divided into six separate areas, more or less following the standard physiographic "provinces" recognized by the state's geographers, according to terrain, climate and conditions:

•Arctic—the north slope of the Brooks Range to the Arctic Ocean, from Point Hope to the Canadian border, pages 201-226

•Northwest—Norton Sound drainages, including the lower Koyukuk and western Brooks Range lakes (southern slope), pages 227-262

•Interior—the central part of the state between the Alaska and Brooks ranges, bounded by the Middle Fork of the Koyukuk River on the west, pages 263-300

•Southwest—the Alaska Peninsula and Aleutians, Bristol Bay and lower Kuskokwim and Yukon River drainages, pages 301-370

•Southcentral—Gulf Coast drainages from Cape St. Elias and Shelikof Strait, including the Kenai Peninsula and Kodiak and Afognak islands, pages 371-476

•Southeast—the "Panhandle" from Dixon Entrance to Icy Bay (and coastal streams to Cape Suckling), pages 477-590

3) If you are interested in a specific type of sportfishing, and want to find out what geographic regions provide good fishing for a certain species, turn to the chapter on the Alaska species you want to fish. Major sportfishing locations are listed in the final pages of each chapter.

In the Alaska Species section of the book, we chose to emphasize only the 13 major species of importance to anglers, and have omitted or only casually referenced several other fish of lesser interest—burbot, whitefish and lingcod, for instance. This does not imply that the opportunities for these species in Alaska is lacking. Readers who want more information on any of the minor sport species available in Alaska should contact the Alaska Department of Fish and Game. Overview maps are given at the beginning of each region section, along with locations of the hot spots detailed within. In addition, map references (U.S. Geological Survey, topographic contour 1:63,360 or 1:250,000 maps) are given for each hot spot listing; addresses for purchasing USGS maps are given on page 630 in the Appendices. Please read all the species sections and refer to them frequently in your trip planning. We have referenced in their text the best locations and the best times for fishing certain species, as well as other pertinent details which you can use to access more information in the regional descriptions and hot spots listings. Local contacts for information and services are provided; consult them for the latest conditions and up-to-date information.

In our hot spots descriptions, we list the major species of interest that occur in fishable numbers, enclosing in parenthesis those that are found only infrequently. The fishing is rated from fair to excellent, using a variety of adjectives, such as "outstanding," "superb," "great," "decent" and "good," that hopefully will be meaningful and not too subjective for most folks. Keep in mind that this is Alaska, where even "fair" fishing can far surpass anything most people are used to in home waters.

ABOUT RIVER RUNNING

In our hot spots descriptions for rivers, we frequently give information pertaining to their suitability for floating, using the following international scale for rating their degree of difficulty:

•*Class I:* Moving water with some riffles and waves, but few or no obstructions. Beginning river runners can negotiate it, usually with no problem.

•*Class II:* Small rapids with standing waves up to three feet high; clear channels can be negotiated without scouting, with some maneuvering required. It is recommended that boaters have some river experience.

•*Class III:* Rapids with high waves, some irregular, capable of swamping a canoe or other open craft. Some passages may require scouting or difficult maneuvering. Intermediate whitewater skills are required for safe passage.

•*Class IV:* Long, difficult rapids and turbulent waters. Passage may be severely restricted and complex maneuvers are required. Scouting and "lining" boats from shore is commonly required. Safe passage by canoe or small open boat is generally not possible. This water is for boaters with a high level of whitewater experience only.

•*Class V:* Extremely difficult and hazardous whitewater, with long and/or violent rapids, chutes and difficult passages, requiring complex maneuvers, scouting, "lining" and even portages. There are significant hazards to life in the event of a mishap, with difficult rescue conditions. Expert whitewater skills are required.

•*Class VI:* Extreme whitewater encountered usually only in floodwater conditions and rare locations. Dangerous and life-threatening, this water is for top-notch experts only.

Keep in mind that the above scale is a very general rating applied to rivers during normal water levels. Conditions can change dramatically and swiftly on most Alaska rivers, so caution is the rule for safety.

FISHING RULES OF THUMB

•Respect the rights of property owners along rivers, streams and lakes by contacting them, if possible, before you trespass on their lands. Some of their addresses are given in the hot spots descriptions.

•Keep only the fish you intend to eat or take for mounting; practice proper catch-and-release techniques whenever possible.

•Be courteous to other anglers.

•Tread lightly and please don't litter!

DISCLAIMER

•Use the information given for locations only as a general guide for trip planning. Conditions vary from year to year, even from month to month, on many of Alaska's waters. Consult with local sources before making any definite trip arrangements.

•Check with the Alaska Department of Fish and Game for the latest regulation information and any restrictions that may apply.

INTRODUCTION

Alaska has been a challenge and source of wonder to generations of adventurous people. Every school kid knows that the 49th state is more than twice the size of Texas, has America's tallest mountains, deepest wilderness, largest animals and most frightening extremes of weather. It also has a coastline longer than that of all the other states combined, along with some of the wettest, iciest and snowiest places on the continent. But what's most important—to anglers anyway—is the abundant water that all this snow, ice and rain give rise to... countless rivers, streams, creeks, lakes and ponds drain the state's prodigious runoff, in an amount that yearly equals or surpasses the combined annual surface water flow of all the states east of the Mississippi!

Much of this water is glacially silted, too swift or shallow, or otherwise inhospitable to fish. But enough of it is perfectly suited, by its location, size, purity and the divine grace of Nature, to support an abundance and diversity of coldwater gamefish species such as exists nowhere else on Earth. Five species of Pacific salmon—king, sockeye, chum, silver and pink—along with rainbow, cutthroat and steelhead trout, charr, arctic grayling, northern pike and sheefish, all await the angler in unheard-of numbers.

This staggering amount and variety of water, and the amazing gamefish it holds, is the essence of *Alaska Fishing*. For the angler contemplating a vacation here in Alaska, knowing what species are available and when, where and how they may best be encountered, not to mention the logistics involved, has always been the most daunting aspect of the planning process, even for longtime Alaska anglers. This book can help readers sort through the confusing claims, blatant hype and gray areas that exist in the popular literature and tourist publications.

As a fishing destination, Alaska is different than most any other. It is still very wild, with most of its better waters free from the intrusion of hatcheries. The occurrence of species here follows the broad, uniform pattern of Nature, instead of the random and artificial distributions seen most elsewhere. This guide should help you develop your own sense of what the Alaska fishing scene is all about and some of the better ways to access and enjoy it.

Keeping in mind that a fishing vacation in the Last Frontier is much more than just catching fish, we hope readers will use this guide as a starting point, an invitation to explore the most awesome destination there can be for the sport angler. A timeless land, where the frantic pace and contrived needs of the human world are lost in vast distances and magnificent, untouched landscapes, Alaska is a refreshing antidote to modern civilization. And once you've experienced the country and its stupendous sportfishing, life will never seem the same. Another trip and another river always beckons. May it always be so.

Happy angler with spring steelhead.

GETTING READY TO GO

ALASKA TRIP PLANNING

In today's busy world, with time and money at a premium, folks are demanding the very best in service and value from the travel industry, and the Alaska fishing vacation business is no exception (just ask any guide or lodge owner). Yet, despite the best intentions of everyone involved in the planning and delivery of the great Alaska adventure—the visitor information people, travel agents, lodge owners, guides and outfitters, air taxis, not to mention the folks footing the bill—every summer brings its share of disappointment and frustration, when fishing trips somehow don't measure up to expectations. A certain measure of the blame lies with the industry itself, which sometimes fuels unreal expectations with hyped-up literature, glossy brochures or big talk over the phone. Alaska tourism is a competitive business, and many in the industry are pressed to "make the sale," even if they have to bend the truth a little. But misrepresenting services (and fishing possibilities) just to snare peoples' business is plain fraud, not much different from the old snake-oil salesman who took the townsfolk's money and ran. Fortunately, the overwhelming majority of people in Alaska's tourism industry are sincere, dedicated professionals who would just as soon poke themselves in the eye than sell you a trip or service you won't be happy with.

As a consumer, however, the ultimate responsibility for getting the kind of Alaska fishing vacation you deserve is yours alone. No one can read your mind or know your heart in order to deliver the arrangements and the fishing that are right for you. Like shopping for a car or a home, planning a successful Alaska fishing vacation is a process that begins with identifying what you want, surveying the available market, asking some serious questions, "tire kicking," and then bargaining hard with a few prospective businesses. The end result is a signed contract and two satisfied parties—hopefully. What follows are some fundamental points to keep in mind before you begin, which can make the whole process more efficient and ultimately more satisfying:

KNOWLEDGE IS POWER

The fact that you've got this book in your hands shows that you recognize the importance of educating yourself before planning your fishing vacation in a place as diverse and immense as Alaska. Read this book in its entirety (and any other similar publications you can find) and pore through the sporting magazines to find articles on Alaska fishing. Contact the information agencies listed in this book for materials they may have to offer. You should also try to talk to folks who have fished Alaska before, and make a point of attending one of the winter trade shows in the major cities to meet and chat with lodge owners, guides, air taxis and outfitters. You may even find a worthy TV special on the Last Frontier. The more general background you have on Alaska—its geography, climate, rivers, lakes, etc.—the better you can decide exactly what you want to do up here, how and where you want to do it, and with whom. It's the ultimate trip insurance.

SEEK AND FIND

Once you have a fairly good idea of the what, when and where of the fishing you're after, you can begin to narrow your choices and save tons of time, instead of shooting in the dark. There are services and facilities that cater to every whim and desire imaginable as far as fishing in Alaska goes, and usually you can eliminate quickly the ones that don't have what you're after with preliminary contact by phone, mail or in person. Magazines, vacation planners, travel agencies, sportfishing organizations, trade shows and word-of-mouth are usually the standard avenues for finding organizations that specialize in some aspect of the Alaska sportfishing industry you are interested in.

ASK QUESTIONS

It is vital to ask the questions that need to be answered in your selection process. Make a list of the important things you want from your vacation—such as the species and type of fishing desired, preferred accommodations, meal requirements and budget constraints—and work through each and every item as you consider possibilities. When talking to lodge owners, guides, air taxis and outfitters, don't be shy. Get answers to your satisfaction for anything you may have questions on. And don't consider doing business with anyone who hesitates to give you the facts or tries to intimidate you in any way. Most reputable people in the business enjoy talking with someone who knows enough to ask questions, and wouldn't think of putting them off because of their inquisitiveness or meticulousness with details. Some important points to remember when you deal with people in the industry:

•Are you talking with the owner, manager, guide, booking agent or someone else? It is important to deal directly, whenever possible, with the people who will be personally responsible for your arrangements, as they are best capable of answering any questions or concerns you may have, and will be most committed to seeing that you get what you've bargained for.

•Make sure you discuss exactly what is to be provided in the way of transportation, accommodations, meals, guide service, alcoholic beverages and gratuities. Don't assume anything.

•Be certain to explain exactly what kind of fishing you're after and the services, accommodations and prices you had in mind. See how closely what they have to offer matches what you want and ask plenty of questions. Be prepared to compromise somewhat.

•Listen and learn from each and every person you contact along the way about local fishing conditions, available services and accommodations, as it can certainly prove useful later on, no matter who you decide to do business with. Be open to suggestions and advice about your trip planning from those who know more.

GET REFERENCES

As part of the narrowing down process, be sure to ask your prospective guide, outfitter or lodge owner for a list of former clients to contact for reference. Any operator who balks at this request should be dismissed immediately from consideration. Some of the questions to ask former clients are:

•Did you receive the services you were promised?

•Did the accommodations, fishing and services match expectations?

•How many times have you done business with the operator, and will you do business with him in the future?

Naturally, any hesitation or negative response to any of the above should be cause for concern and doubt as to whether this is the person or organization with whom to do business.

GET IT IN WRITING

When it comes time to narrow it down and lay your hard-earned green on a particular lodge, outfitter, guide or what-have-you, be sure to get a contractual agreement in writing for all services, equipment and/or arrangements to be provided and the fees charged, to the specifications previously discussed and your satisfaction. Read the contract over carefully before signing and immediately discuss any discrepancies or unclear areas you find in the wording. This is most important, as the written agreement is the legally binding document that holds the provider to deliver everything specified. It's your guarantee of getting what you bargained for.

TIMING CONSIDERATIONS

Despite what you might be inclined to believe from some of the travel literature, Alaska's fishing is not a continuous "fish in the bucket" cornucopia of angling opportunity, at least not in any one location. The fishing, even here, has its ups and downs, with some very real and distinct advantages to each part of the season, from early spring to late fall, some of which have little to do directly with fishing but which can affect your vacation significantly in other ways.

The big question, of course, is one of fish availability and how it fits in with your schedule and desires. If you've never been to Alaska, it's probably wise to plan a trip for early summer (late May to early July) so as to enjoy the best of the chinook salmon fishing. Then again, if you could care less about the king of salmon, you might be happier stalking spring rainbows or even fall coho salmon for your first Alaska angling experience. Seasoned Alaska anglers can fine-tune their timing to partake of the best trophy fishing or peak period for a particular species (early October for Alaska's biggest rainbows, for instance). The choices are many, and certainly not easy to make, but here's a summary of the best times to fish the major species throughout Alaska:

Rainbow Trout: Late April to June and August to early October
Steelhead: Late April to June and late September to November
Grayling: Mid-May to mid-September
Northern Pike: Late May to early October
Cutthroat Trout: May to June and August to October
Charr: April to June and August through September
King Salmon: Late May to early July
Red Salmon: Mid-June to late July
Chum Salmon: Early July to early September
Pink Salmon: Mid-July to mid-August
Silver Salmon: Early August to early October
Halibut: Late May to early September
Sheefish: May to October
Lake Trout: May to early July and late August to early September

Keep in mind that wide variations in run timing exist from region to region, even among certain streams within an area, so it's wise to inquire with reputable sources, like the local Alaska Department of Fish and Game, guides or air taxis, for accurate details. Many anglers will plan their trips to fall on the cusp between different runs or peak periods, like late July or late August, for instance, in hopes of sampling some good angling for each. Though it certainly can be done, especially with broadly overlapping species like pinks, silvers, rainbows and charr, don't expect to stretch it to include all the salmon that run during the season, as the general condition and availability of "stragglers" from the end of a run is not desirable from an angler's standpoint. (The notorious "grand slam" for the five species of Pacific salmon is an almost impossible and ridiculously expensive feat to achieve.)

OTHER CONSIDERATIONS

There are some other things to be aware of that can affect your fishing vacation, things they don't mention in the brochures or the splashy color layouts in the magazines, for fear of turning people off—bugs and bum weather. Alaska has its share of both. But did you know that there is a "peak period" for each? The notorious Alaska mosquito and its allies generally come out in greatest force during the warmest time of year, in the weeks surrounding the Summer Solstice (from June until mid-July, usually). A fishing trip in August or early September, while offering some of the best fishing of the season, also has the advantage of being virtually free of the swarming hordes that plague anglers incessantly earlier in the season.

Weather, always a factor in Alaska, has a historical tendency to be more benign (drier and calmer) in the spring and early summer throughout most of the state, deteriorating through late summer and fall, although it can vary dramatically from year to year. If you're planning an Arctic or Northwest trip, keep in mind that the season is effectively over by mid-September or even earlier in some years.

Another very important thing not to overlook, especially if you're planning a camping or floatfishing trip, is the extreme variation in daylight throughout the season. A trip in June or early July will offer exhilaratingly long hours of daylight, for almost nonstop fishing and leisurely camping, while the same outing in late September will have 12 hours of legitimate darkness, making for a much different pace, with considerably less time for fishing and setting up camp. These great fluctuations of light and dark are even more pronounced in the Northwest and Arctic regions.

GUIDES & OUTFITTERS

Alaska's guides and outfitters have often been cast as a maverick lot, reputedly drinking and swearing too much, lying outrageously and otherwise not presenting very high standards of professionalism. While this may have been true years ago, today's guides and outfitters are astute businesspeople, professionals in an industry that demands much in time and personal commitment.

You'll find them to be an extremely diverse and likeable bunch for the most part, eager to share in their knowledge and love of Alaska's incomparable fishing. The many different services they provide cover the full range of visitor activities related to fishing, but can be summarized briefly as follows:

SHORT-TRIP GUIDES

Far and away the greatest number of guides currently operating in Alaska offer services that cater to the shorter, flexible itineraries of today's visitor. Usually hanging a shingle in the more populous regions, like Southcentral's Kenai Peninsula or the larger communities of Southeast, these guides offer a variety of short-trip options ranging from a half-day to several days fishing, usually by boat or small plane. Accommodations, if provided, are simple, often at small cabins, bed and breakfasts, hotels, tent camps or on-board vessels. Some meals and gear are usually provided. This group includes the many charter boat captains, river fishing guides and small air taxi operators across Alaska, many offering unguided outfitting options as well. Advance reservations are preferred, but walk-ins and last-minute inquiries are usually welcome. Prices range from $75 dollars per half day per person to $250 per day per person, depending on the location and the services provided.

WILDERNESS GUIDES

The real thing, the hard-core, seasoned cadre of the Alaska guiding profession, wilderness guides generally represent the highest level of training, education and commitment within the Alaska sportfishing industry. Many have college educations, wilderness emergency medical training and other qualifications. Most of them operate out of the major hubs—such Anchorage, Fairbanks, Dillingham, Nome, Kotzebue and Bettles—and offer trips that range in length from 5 to 14 days (or more). They handle everything from float trips to spike camps, usually offering unguided outfitting options as well. Reservations generally must be made at least two months in advance, although, if room allows, they can fit folks in at the last minute. The better operations certainly can provide some of Alaska's finest wilderness fishing experiences, with personalized service, outstanding professionalism, and itineraries in some of the state's best locations, like Katmai, Iliamna, Bristol Bay and the lower Kuskokwim. Prices vary from $250 to $400 per day per person, all-inclusive (covering transportation, meals, guided fishing and anything else from the point of departure).

Guides and outfitters are eager to share their knowledge and love of Alaska's incomparable fishing.

LODGES

Rustic fly-in fishing lodges are a celebrated part of that potent Alaska fishing mystique. While the best of them can certainly deliver an experience that is hard to duplicate any other way, there is a wide variety of services and accommodations available to suit the different needs and budgets of fishermen of all persuasions. If you're considering a lodge stay, it makes sense to know the main types of facilities available, what they offer and their range of costs.

DELUXE LODGES

These are the cream of Alaska's lodging and service facilities, usually located in remote stream or lakeside locations in the best parts of Bristol Bay, Southeast and Southcentral Alaska, with awesome fishing out the door or not too far away. These custom operations usually feature plush accommodations, daily fly-outs to Alaska's best fishing locations, knowledgeable guides, gourmet food and some rather exclusive clientele to rub shoulders with. Some go even further with on-site flyfishing seminars or personal instruction, European chefs, in-house tackle shops and fly-tying benches, an open bar and more. Itineraries and schedules are usually fixed, with regular hours for fishing and dining. Expect to pay for all the luxury and service, however, usually from $2,800 to $4,500 per week per person.

FAMILY-STYLE LODGES

These lodges are a step down in luxury from the big glamour establishments, but they still offer outstanding service and accommodations, without all the frills. Some of the better ones pride themselves—and rightfully so—on delivering more real fishing time than any custom lodge. Located in remote or semi-remote areas, many in Southcentral and Southeast, these less-costly facilities usually offer fly-outs or boat fishing packages, bunk-style or small, shared cabin accommodations and informal, family-style dining with plenty of good, home-cooked food. Fishing can be outstanding, depending on the location, time of year, quality of the guides and other factors. Research and referrals are generally the best ways to locate a good operation. Costs vary from $1,800 to $3,000 per week per person.

FISHING CAMPS/TENT LODGES

These are the real basic, streamside or lakeside facilities catering to hard-core anglers, with accommodations that range from a bunkhouse to small cabins to heated tents or even large boats or barges. Fishing is usually done from banks, by wading, or from skiffs. The rustic fish camp ambience is enhanced by plentiful, home-cooked food, and lots of fishing opportunities (24 hours a day if desired) in some of the best fishing locations in Alaska. Some of these operations are truly unique, set in areas far off the beaten path and run by remarkable individuals, locals usually, who can deliver more than your money's worth in abundant fishing and overall quality of experience. Many also offer unguided packages as outfitters, providing camps already set up in choice locations. Again, as with the family-style lodges, the best way to locate a reputable operation is by word of mouth and research. Prices vary from $1,500 to $2,400 per week per person.

The U.S. Forest Service maintains public-use cabins throughout the Southeast region.

BUSH PILOTS & AIR TAXIS

If you had to pick the most romantic figure in all of Alaska's wilderness fishing scene, it surely must be the intrepid soul who braves Alaska's skies to shuttle the people and supplies that make it all happen—the bush pilot. Steadfast and reliable through thick and thin, he keeps everyone on schedule during the busy summer season, which is not an easy job in a place so vast and primitive. Your average Alaska bush pilot also knows the local fishing locations like no one else you'll meet, so it is definitely to your advantage to get on his good side and cultivate a working relationship with him, especially if you plan on returning for more adventure.

Most air taxis bill by the hour, which can vary from $125 to over $600, depending on the size of plane used (fees usually include return flight time). A variety of interesting craft is in service all across Alaska, but the real workhorses are the single-engine Cessnas, Pipers and DeHavillands, which have proven their versatility and reliability over the years in the most challenging conditions. Since most of Alaska's better stream and lake locations involve some flying to reach them, air transportation is usually a significant part of total trip costs. If you are planning a do-it-yourself excursion, some of the ways you can keep air taxi costs down are:

•*Travel with a small group.* Usually two to four people is an ideal group size for lowering per-person costs and achieving higher efficiency, not to mention the time saved in spreading the work load. You'll also have much more fun if you go with a group of buddies.

•*Use scheduled commercial flights whenever possible.* You can buy a ticket to just about any village or town in even the most remote parts of Alaska on the regular scheduled flights offered by the major air carriers (shipping your gear as cargo), then contract with local flight services for arrangements to and from nearby fishing locations. Careful planning and research are required, but this can save you a bundle over chartering small planes from major hubs like Anchorage or Fairbanks.

•*Shop around.* Have a definite idea of the number in your party, the kind of trip you have in mind, and the rivers, lakes or bays you wish to fish before you contact anyone for preliminary arrangements. If possible, get quotes from at least two other services. Air taxis have different planes and rates vary; some can even save you money on the "back haul" if they've got flights already going to the area you're interested in.

•Go light. The number-one mistake seen among tourists in general and the bane of every bush pilot has to be the excessive amount of gear most people bring for an expedition. Limit yourself to 40 pounds of personal gear—such as clothes, sleeping bag and camera—and streamline your equipment list to a bare minimum. (If you're traveling with a group, coordinate your planning to avoid duplication of gear.) You'll save money (cargo costs these days are in the neighborhood of 50 cents per pound one way from Anchorage to the state's better fishing areas), and enjoy your trip more with less gear to lug around.

Bush pilots and air taxis can take you where you want to go in Alaska.

HELICOPTER FISHING

by Robert Farmer

All across Alaska, virgin streams await discovery. The most exclusive of these lie along the coast, from Kotzebue Sound south to Unimak Island, then east along the Pacific to the Southeast Archipelago. The upland reaches of these coastal areas, mostly inaccessible, hold immeasurable beauty, along with untouched fish populations and some of Alaska's last great wilderness fishing, and they are now open for serious exploration by helicopter.

"Heli-fishing," still quite new to Alaska, is limited to three lodges currently offering this unique experience. Crystal Creek Lodge in Southwest fishes upland streams in the Nushagak drainage, Talaheim Lodge on the Talachulitna River in Southcentral fishes the upper stretches of this famous trout and salmon run on the west side of Cook Inlet, and Deshka River Lodge near Mount McKinley in Southcentral offers an ambitious heli-fishing program that covers an area from Katmai National Park in Southwest to Wrangell-St. Elias near the eastern border of the mainland.

The advantages of heli-fishing go beyond the obvious opening of formerly inaccessible fishing sanctuaries. Because of high costs, the experience is exclusive and limited, especially suited to flyfishermen and catch-and-release fishing. Those with physical limitations can reach prime waters with little or no arduous hiking or demanding boat rides. Perhaps most importantly for the future, the exclusivity of heli-fishing virtually eliminates exploitative angling whose primary measure of success is "price per pound." The few reputable lodges who operate helicopters in Alaska only select environmentally conscious anglers who appreciate this international treasure.

Rates are steep, however, and openings are limited. Costs average $700 per day to $4,600 per week. Crystal Creek Lodge is limited to 20 guests per week, Talaheim takes only two guests per week and Deshka River Lodge can handle 12. The experience is rated quite high by all who have had the exclusive opportunity to fish this way. It promises to be more popular in the future as more accessible waters become visited more often and anglers seek the peak experiences that only truly wild waters can provide.

FLOAT TRIPS

Perhaps the most unique and exciting way to experience Alaska's wild rivers and their fishing is to float down from headwaters in lightweight rafts. While certainly not an option for everyone, float trips offer some distinct advantages over fly-ins, camps and lodges. For one, the float trip offers an intimate river experience, traveling through remote headwater sections which few can access by any other means. The entire length of the river can be fished, and schedules and streamside camps allow for convenient, 24-hour-a-day access to prime areas like salmon-spawning redds, where the rainbow trout, charr and grayling are abundant and hungry. Variety and catch rates on float trips are unequalled.

Since neither motors nor mechanized equipment are used, the entire trip is one of peaceful immersion in the sounds and sights of the wilderness, with wildlife frequently sighted during the downstream journey. The downside to the float-trip experience can be the weather, with particularly foul stretches hampering comfort and overall enjoyment. High-quality equipment, including tents, raingear and footwear are essential, as are maps, bear protection and wilderness survival and boating skills. The services of an experienced guide are highly recommended, and fees charged range from $250 to $400 per day per person, all-inclusive. The price generally depends on the location, as some trips require extensive travel by small plane. The best rivers for float fishing in Alaska are in the Bristol and lower Kuskokwim Bays of the Southwest region.

SPECIES

1
CHINOOK:
KING OF SALMON

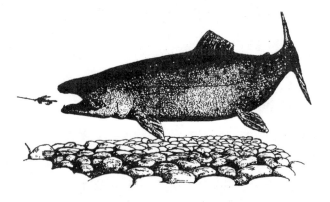

You may find yourself someday—in your wildest fish dream come true—on the wind-whipped tundra of the Bering Sea coast, at one of a handful of small native villages that lie at the mouths of the great rivers there. A kindly old man with sparkling eyes and a face like shoe leather waits to greet you warmly, then listens intently to your strange request. With an affirmative nod and a toothless grin, he motions to his youngest son to fetch the skiff and run you upriver. The smiling boy quickly takes you around a few bends to a big fork in the river, where he deposits you and your gear on the gravel and is gone in a flash. For the next few days and sleepless nights (there are no nights dark enough for sleeping this far north in June), you are caught up in the magic of one of the greatest miracles to yearly befall these desolate coasts—the stirring arrival (in numbers undiminished) of the first and most awesome of the Pacific's five salmon of summer. It's a fish prized through the ages for its size, gaminess and good eating: the one they call chinook, the king of salmon.

Not given to recklessness like his cousin the coho, and certainly not the same class of fighter as the exalted steelhead, the chinook, in sheer size and strength alone, supremely outclasses any of his peers. Husky from summers out in the rich North Pacific, he'll tip the scales at 40 or

50 pounds or more—a formidable adversary, especially when fresh from the sea. When an ocean-bright 30-pounder slams your fly and rips into half your backing with lightning speed, you'll swear you've snagged a whale. The ensuing grudge match can last hours (a Minnesota man fought a monster Kenai River king for a day and a half), during which the brawny lord of all salmon will test you and your gear to the limit. But if you're tough—and lucky—enough to slug it out with him to the end, you'll stagger ashore with a prize definitely worth the trip to these waters. For the only thing more impressive than the fight of a big king salmon is the magnificent sight of one up close: immense, full-bodied, with sides of buffed platinum tinged with purple, and muscular, tapered flanks. His is a countenance that suggests both power and grace, one of nature's most exquisite creations of a sea-roaming, fish-eating, river-running machine.

INTRODUCTION

More than an angler's prize, the great chinook *(Oncorhynchus tshawytscha)* has been an inseparable part of Pacific Northwest culture for centuries. The fish was first encountered by white men over 250 years ago on the epic voyages of Vitus Bering, and was later written about by explorers Lewis and Clark and Alexander Mackenzie because of the elaborate rituals the native coastal tribes performed for the chinook's annual return. (In the mythology of these people, the great salmon were the embodied spirits of supernatural beings from the sea, who ascended the rivers to sacrifice themselves for the survival of their captors.) The chinook has managed to survive the ravages of man, and today, in Alaska at least, he retains a measure of his former glory.

Here in the Last Frontier, the mighty king salmon has become almost a pop icon. We have made him our state fish and used his name and image shamelessly in countless business promotions, names of streets and subdivisions and works of art. As the focal point of a multimillion dollar sportfishing industry (and prized commercial and subsistence species), the chinook's significance and stature is elevated beyond any measure. Hooking and landing a big king salmon has been and probably always will be the quintessential Alaska angling experience for the thousands of folks who travel from the world over to fish here.

DESCRIPTION

Chinook salmon are the largest of the five species of Pacific salmon, routinely reaching weights of 30 pounds or more, although their average weight in Alaska is around 18 pounds. The IGFA world record is a king of 97.25 pounds from the Kenai River in 1985, although fish of well over 100 pounds have been caught in commercial fishing nets. Their length at maturity is usually 30 inches or more. A mature chinook fresh from the sea is full-bodied, with sides of bright silver, a deep blue-black back, and large, irregular cross-markings across the upper sides and fins. Its belly is white; its tail is broad and moderately forked, with spots on both lobes (this, along with a black gumline on the lower jaw, helps distinguish smaller king salmon from the similar coho salmon, *O. kisutch*). Teeth on mature chinooks are well developed, especially in breeding males.

Spawning fish undergo moderate changes in physical appearance. Both sexes turn dusky red to copper or brown (sometimes with blackish or purple shading), while males develop hooked jaws, ridged backs and more dramatic coloration. Juvenile king salmon are hard to distinguish from other small salmon, trout or charr, but normally have wider parr marks, tinted edges on the adipose fins, and moderately forked tails.

The flesh of a king salmon is usually a deep red color, but it can vary to pink or white in some locations, depending on diet and other factors. Its meat is prized for eating, as it is rich and flavorful—perfect for the grill, smoked or canned. King salmon ranks along with the red or sockeye salmon as one of the North Pacific's most valued food fishes.

RANGE, ABUNDANCE & STATUS

King salmon were originally distributed coastally from Hokkaido, Japan to the Anadyr River in Asia and from Kotzebue Sound to central California in America. The least abundant of the Pacific salmon, they have historically been most concentrated in larger river systems (the San Joaquin-Sacramento River system of California and Washington's mighty Columbia each supported runs in excess of a million fish at one time). Today, king salmon are found in greatest numbers from British Columbia north to the Yukon River. In Alaska, chinook runs occur along most of the southern and western coasts, from Dixon Entrance in Southeast Alaska to Point Hope in Northwest Alaska, with the most significant populations found in the state's great rivers—the Yukon, Kuskokwim, Nushagak, Susitna and Copper.

Though the chinook has not fared well by man throughout much of its range (the Columbia and other once-great salmon rivers of the Pacific Northwest have runs so decimated that they are now under protection by the Endangered Species Act), the chinook's status in Alaska remains remarkably stable. Commercial catches have been above 600,000 fish in recent years, while sport fishermen annually harvest more than 120,000. The greatest threat to the future of Alaska's wild chinook seems to be the proliferation of hatcheries and creation of "mixed stock" fisheries that fuel an insatiable and unrealistic public demand for more angling opportunity. (Hatchery releases of kings now contribute to a significant percentage of the commercial and sport harvests in certain areas of Southeast and Southcentral Alaska—up to 50% or more.)

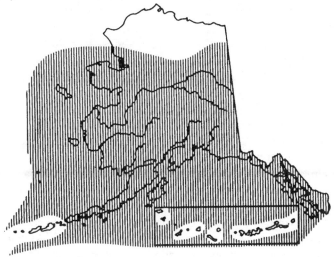

Shaded area shows range of chinook in Alaska.

LIFE HISTORY & HABITS

Chinook are in many ways the most ecologically diverse of the Pacific salmon. They are the longest lived, and can return sexually mature at anywhere from two to nine years of age, which allows them to attain the greatest size of any salmon (to 100 pounds or more). In Alaska, they generally spend a year or two in freshwater as fry, then three to five years at sea before returning in early summer (May through July) to their rivers of origin. Their wanderings are potentially among the most extensive of any fish species, involving forays into the far reaches of the North Pacific and river migrations of over 1,500 miles in the Yukon River.

Eggs hatch usually in late winter or early spring, with the alevins remaining in the protection of the gravel for two to three weeks until the yolk sac is absorbed and they emerge as fry. Newly emerged fry feed on insects, plankton and crustaceans. They school in pool edges, under cutbanks and around aquatic vegetation and logjams for protection from predators and strong currents. In the spring of their second year of life (or occasionally their third year), Alaska chinook will "smolt up" and proceed *en masse* to the sea. Remaining close to shore, these adolescent, estuarine chinook feed on small fish, crustaceans and molluscs, rapidly increasing in size until they are large enough to venture into the open sea. Some stocks, particularly those found in Southeast Alaska, may spend their entire lives in protected inshore waters, providing the basis for year-round local fisheries. These are called "feeder kings." Others will make extensive migrations into the North Pacific and Bering Sea during their third year of life.

While in the open sea, chinooks feed almost exclusively on other fish—herring, sandlance, eulachon, pilchards, pollack, smelts and anchovies—with seasonal binges on squid, crab larvae, euphausiids, and amphipods rounding out their diets. Chinook salmon have been found in a great range of depths, from just below the surface to over 250 feet, depending on the season. Chinook are subject to the same predation as the other members of the Pacific salmon clan. Fry get eaten by charr, rainbow trout, coho, terns, mink, etc. Older fish in the sea are at risk from larger pelagic fishes, marine mammals (seals, whales and sea lions), and of course, man.

A king's final year in the ocean brings a substantial size increase, and for Alaska fish this can occur anywhere from two to seven years of age or more. Precocious returning two-year-old fish, called "jacks," are a well-known, frequent phenomenon in many river systems. Generally, however, in Alaska, most returning fish are four to six years old. Mature Alaska kings begin showing up in freshwater in May (earlier in Southeast), with peak periods of river migration occurring in June and early July. Generally, fish that show earliest will complete the longest migrations, which may be considerable in systems such as the Yukon, where a significant number of chinook travel the entire river length to spawn in Canada (a journey of over 2,000 miles). Actual spawning takes place during July and August (later in Southeast), and, as with the other Pacific salmon species, is instigated by the female's digging of the redd. Nest location is influenced by a variety of factors, but kings seem better able to utilize the larger substrate and greater stream flows of main channels, probably because of their size.

Kings have some interesting habits that should be noted by anglers. Like the other salmon, they'll frequently show themselves in tidal waters and in lower river sections, making it easy to pinpoint their location. They can hold in bays and off the mouths of rivers for days, even weeks sometimes, until conditions (water flow, temperature and wind direction) are just right to make their in-migrations, at times even making extensive movements into freshwater and back out to sea (some fish tagged far up certain rivers have been recovered in ocean nets miles away!). Because of their size, they are inclined to move and hold deeper than other salmon, preferring the main channels of rivers, though they do at times use side channels and sloughs. Another chinook habit very noticeable in freshwater is their sensitivity to light; they prefer the low light of late or early hours and cloudy or windy days for most of their activity.

FISHING ALASKA'S KING SALMON

Sportfishing for the king of salmon has become serious business in Alaska. On Southcentral's Kenai River, the state's most popular fishery, visitors are often shocked to find a scene more reminiscent of New Jersey than any idealized image of the Last Frontier. On a typical day in June or July, a mad army of anglers swarms the river, engaging in aggressive, no-holds-barred combat for the Kenai's world-famous run of giant kings (to 80 pounds or more). Further west and north, the action is generally more subdued, but it is still a far cry from peaceful wilderness. It is only in the far reaches of Southwest and in isolated bays of Southeast that one can enjoy any measure of real solitude along with abundant fishing.

In Southeast, nearly all chinook salmon angling effort occurs as a saltwater intercept fishery, targeting returning salmon bound for Canada, the Pacific Northwest states and parts of Alaska. Major spawning occurs in only a handful of large river systems in Southeast—the Taku, Alsek and Stikine, with about a dozen or so lesser rivers supporting small runs of several thousand fish or less. Hatcheries and enhancement efforts have augmented the fishery considerably in certain areas. Most chinook fishing there is done by trolling or mooching from boats, with either bait or lures, with some jigging (see page 43 for details). Non-breeding, immature king salmon, called "feeders," can be caught year-round.

Further north into Southcentral are found the state's most popular and intensively managed king salmon stream fisheries—the fabulous Kenai and the clearwater tributaries of the Susitna and Copper rivers. There, most effort is spent drift fishing or back trolling from boats, with a significant amount of bank fishing in some areas. Saltwater angling for kings occurs in lower Cook Inlet, Kachemak and Resurrection bays, and to a lesser extent, Kodiak Island and Prince William Sound. The remote, clear-flowing streams of Southwest's Bristol Bay and lower Kuskokwim Rivers hold Alaska's most abundant opportunities for shore casting and stalking the mighty king on a fly rod, although a significant amount of boat fishing occurs on the larger rivers (Nushagak, Alagnak, Naknek, Togiak and others).

FRESHWATER METHODS & GEAR

From northern Southeast to Norton Sound, most of the fishing effort for Alaska's king of salmon involves drifting, trolling or casting lures or bait in freshwater. In the big rivers, this is most effectively done from boats, but significant innovations in gear and increased access to prime waters have made shore casting (with spinning, baitcasting and flyfishing gear) more popular than ever. Here's a rundown on the more popular techniques used:

Drifting & Trolling

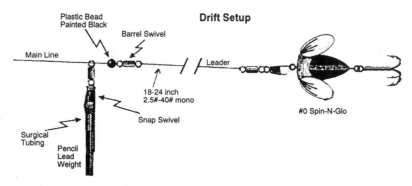

Alaska's most deadly chinook lure is nothing more than a bright, buoyant plastic whirligig, commonly called a drift bobber. Rigged off a swivel on a 24-inch section of 25- to 40-pound leader, with a lead dropper ($3/4$ to three ounces lead), and drifted along the bottom, the bobber or Spin-N-Glo (as the most popular style is called for its spinning action and bright color) is deadly for all salmon, as well as trout and charr. The larger sizes (#0 to #4 and Super Spin-N-Glo) and brighter fluorescent colors (red, orange, chartreuse, yellow) are the standard for kings on all major Alaska chinook rivers from the Gulkana to the Unalakleet. The addition of flashy hook skirts, colored yarn, drops of fish scent or cured salmon roe (attached with an egg loop hook snell) considerably enhances their appeal.

You can fish the Spin-N-Glo from shore with a "quarter" cast upstream and a steady retrieve to reel in slack as the rig bounces downriver along bottom (you can prolong the drift considerably by walking downstream as you reel, if conditions allow). Or you can use a side planer (see illustration on page 35). But most anglers fish Spin-N-Glos from a skiff, drifting or trolling with 25 to 75 feet of line, depending on water depth. Since the drift bobber is buoyant, it's nearly impossible to foul on bottom, and it is effective fished slow or fast. The important thing is to have enough lead rigged to keep it on bottom. You'll see the rod tip twitch with each bounce if it is properly weighted. You also need razor-sharp hooks, as chinooks have a super-hard mouth. Anglers generally wait on the strike until the fish takes the rod down hard, especially when fishing with bait.

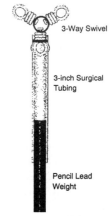

3-Way Swivel

3-inch Surgical Tubing

Pencil Lead Weight

Next to drift bobbers, plugs are the most commonly used trolling lures on Alaska's king rivers, and you'll see great boxes crammed full of them in guides' boats along the Kenai, Naknek, Gulkana and other popular big rivers. Big diving plugs like Magnum Tadpollys, Wiggle Warts and Hot Shots, or the Flatfish (T-55) or Kwikfish

Alternate way of rigging dropper weight

(K14-16) in blue/silver, fire red-orange, metallic red or green and chartreuse seem to be the most used.

Back trolling is a very efficient and frequently used technique. For this, you point your skiff upriver. Use the motor to slow the drift considerably, so that the lure is essentially working in the current with little or no actual upstream movement. The idea is to probe the bottom slowly and intercept kings holding around underwater structure or moving up deep channels. Spin-N-Glos, plugs and spinners are the

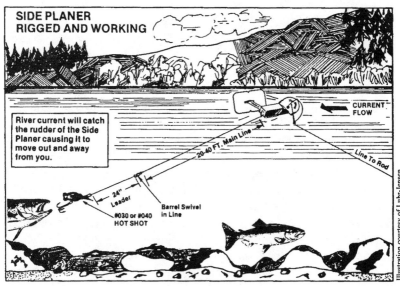

SIDE PLANER RIGGED AND WORKING

River current will catch the rudder of the Side Planer causing it to move out and away from you.

CURRENT FLOW

20-40 FT. Main Line

Line To Rod

24" Leader

#030 or #040 HOT SHOT

Barrel Swivel in Line

Illustration courtesy of Luhr-Jensen

lures most commonly used. They are usually rigged off a diving planer, which is a fan-shaped, flat plastic device that planes downward in the current when pulled behind the boat (see illustration below). Plugs with deep diving lips, like the Model 25 and 35 Hot Shots, Magnum Wiggle Warts and Tadpollys, can usually be fished alone. For rigging, use three to four feet of heavy mono line, 15- to 25- pound test, run off the back of the planer with a swivel for the terminal end and a swivel and clip for attaching to the main line. Then let out the whole thing gradually at speed until it's about 30 to 75 feet behind the boat, depending on the depth of the river. You can sit and wait for the fish or drift slowly backwards and probe bottom; depending on how many kings are in the river, either method will produce strikes. Note that most anglers wait for the fish to bury the rod tip before setting the hook. Planers will pull a lure or bait down to about 20 feet, and can even be rigged alone as lures, as they are available in a variety of bright colors.

Diving Planer

Drift Bobber

Bead

Eggs

40° of 15-pound Test Leader

To Rod

Jet Diver™

Illustration courtesy of Luhr-Jensen

If you back troll with plugs, always check the action of your rig in shallow water before using it to ensure that your lure is swimming upright in a straight line. You may have to "tune" the action with a pair of pliers, especially if you are using a plug and bait combination. To do this, bend the eye on the nose of the plug to compensate for the direction of lean so that the lure swims upright. Adjustments can also be made on the belly eye or eyes, holding the hook, if the plug is really out of balance. It's important to check the lure's action at fast speed, too.

Back Bouncing

Back bouncing is an intensive technique similar to back trolling that can be very effective in deep holes or eddies. The boat is faced upstream and motored or anchored against the current. The lures are fished off the back, but by hand, like jigging—raising and lowering off bottom and playing more line out as the lure is worked farther and farther downstream from the skiff. The rigging is virtually the same as used for drifting, although you may want to shorten the leader somewhat, with a sliding sinker setup being slightly more efficient than swivel rigging; you should usually use more weight (up to six ounces). The boat can be slipped backwards in a strong current to help keep the lure on bottom. Spin-N-Glos, plugs and eggs are most commonly used.

Like jigging, most fish taken by back bouncing will be hooked on the upstroke, so a quick and powerful motion is required and hooks must be kept razor-sharp by frequent honing.

Spinfishing & Spinners

Spin fishermen have traditionally relied on large, "flasher type" spinners like the Jensen Tee-spoon (size #5 and #6) or Skagit Special (size #6 to #8) in hammered nickel, brass, fire red, chartreuse or rainbow blades as their standard Alaska chinook drift lure, rigged like a drift bobber with a lead dropper and 24-inch leader off a three-way swivel. The spinner can be used alone or with bait like salmon roe. Dragging it behind a boat requires more attention than with a Spin-N-Glo, however, as the big spinner will hang on bottom if worked too slow. For casting, these big spinners are too clumsy and unbalanced, especially in heavy wind. Spincasters instead should opt for the 1.25-ounce Mepps Giant Killers (in silver, gold, prism or fluorescent red or orange blades, dressed in bright bucktail) or the superbly balanced, $7/8$-ounce #6 Super Vibrax Series spinners (silver or gold blades with a fluorescent orange, yellow or green bell, or the new "Firetiger" finish). Big spoons like the $7/8$-ounce Pixee (green or pink insert) are also extremely effective. The trick is to fish slow and deep, allowing the spinner to sink properly after the cast, and using a retrieve just fast enough to keep it off the bottom. Depending on the current and depth, additional weight may be required—use a half-ounce rubbercore sinker attached above the lure or rig a dropper and swivel as you would for drifting. For more efficient and enjoyable casting, if conditions allow (such as in bigger, slower water), you might want to try dropping down a notch in tackle, say to 12- to 15-pound test and a medium-weight salmon rod. You'll be making obvious sacrifices in your ability to handle big fish, but you will be able to cast the big spinners farther without adding extra weight.

Bait Fishing

In glacial, extremely deep or turbid waters where the use of bait is still allowed, its effectiveness on kings is unmatchable, either alone or as an attractant on lures. Most anglers use salmon roe, herring, sardines and even shrimp. Spin-N-Glos and cured salmon roe have perhaps taken more Alaska kings than any other lure and bait combination, but big spinners and even plugs benefit immensely from the addition of a "natural sweetener." A short strip of herring or sardine, wound flesh-side-out with fine thread to the bottom of a plug, is a standard enticement used by many Southcentral river guides. Remember that you'll definitely need to "tune" the plug before fishing it in this manner. Some fishermen even add fish oils and other scents to their baits or lures, claiming increased success.

Gearing Up for Freshwater King Salmon

Most anglers with little or no experience on Northwest rivers have difficulty imagining just how strong a big chinook can be. Your pet "beefstick," no matter how well it handles lunkers back home, can snap like a twig and your biggest reel can become a smoldering piece of useless scrap metal under the awesome strain of an Alaska king salmon in strong current. To give yourself half a chance with these giants, start with a heavy-weight, medium-action, spinning or backbounce casting rod; match it with a tournament-quality, heavy freshwater or light saltwater reel (such as Ambassadeur 6500 to 7000 series, Shimano AX or Spheros) capable of holding 200 yards of 20-pound test mono. Use only the highest quality line (17- to 30-pound test mono or braided) and terminal tackle (swivels, snaps, hooks, etc.), and check frequently for wear.

Flyfishing Kings

There comes a time in your evolution as a sport angler when you should forsake the fancy, high-tech ease of modern gear and boats and stalk the king of salmon on more even terms: in waders, armed with no more than a long limber rod, braided line and some bright feather- and tinsel-adorned hooks. Ideally, you should seek a productive salmon river with clear water, not too deep or far from the sea, where you can sight fish, as it usually takes fairly precise presentation (within a few feet, depending on conditions) to prompt chinooks to strike a fly. The closer to saltwater, the brighter and more aggressive they'll be. The best areas will be river channels, mouths, confluences, tailouts, edges of sloughs, ledge pools and behind boulders and islands. Keep in mind that kings usually don't have any problem moving up through the main channel, so don't overlook any possible mainstem lies. Fish deep, with a light strip, always working the fly directly in front of holding or moving salmon. If you must fish blind, look for signs of fish before you commit to extensive casting, lest your efforts be wasted on empty water. The take of a king in freshwater is usually not vigorous, although they can certainly hit hard at times, especially when on the move. For this reason, keep your hooks razor-sharp, your line taut and your rod ready for the slightest response. Fishing late and early hours, overcast or windy days and after high tides will be the most productive times in lower river areas.

Shallow, moderately fast holding water is ideal for flyfishing king salmon in lower rivers.

•*Gear and Flies:* You'll need stout, high quality gear: a stout ten- or eleven-weight, slow-action fly rod, with a matching, high performance, heavy freshwater or light saltwater reel (capable of holding 150 yards of backing), and a variety of lines for the conditions you'll encounter. This includes saltwater or steelhead taper floating, five- and ten-foot sink tip, full sink, and even high-density sink or shooting tapers. Super-long, two-handed Spey rods to 13 feet (or more) are used on some of the big rivers, for efficient long casting of the big flies in the all-too-frequent winds, but they are difficult and tiring to use. Some of the new generation light and powerful, moderately long rods (to 11 feet) might prove a better alternative (other than fishing from a boat or from locations where you can cast downwind).

King salmon flies should be big, gaudy creations of mylar, tinsel, maribou, bunny hair or bucktail, tied on sharp, forged hooks (size #2 to #5/0) like the Mustad AC3406 or AC36890, Tiemco TMC 800S or Gamakatsu Aberdeen, in colors of silver, red, orange, pink, purple, yellow or chartreuse. Some of the more popular commercially tied patterns for kings are the Alaskabou, Outrageous, Wiggletail and Fat Freddie. Oversized versions of popular Alaska salmon/trout patterns like the Polar Shrimp, Bunny Bug, Woolly Bugger, Maraflash and Egg-Sucking Leech are also very effective, as are saltwater patterns—Clouser Minnow, Deceiver, Tarpon Fly, Herring Fly and Shrimp—and big tube flies. Leaders and tippets should be short, no more than three or four feet, of 15- to 20-pound test.

Guides' Tips for Freshwater King Salmon

•*Fish 'em early, fish 'em late:* Kings are more active in freshwater during the low-light, quiet hours. Plan your serious fishing for 9 p.m. to 1 a.m. and 5 a.m. to 8 a.m. (remember there is no real darkness this time of year).

•*Watch the tides:* If you're within 15 miles of the sea, you'll do better if you consult a tide book and fish intervals after the high tides, or during incoming tides at or near river mouths.

•*Bad weather, good fishing:* Cloudy, rainy days may be miserable, but fishing is always better then than on bright, sunny days.

•*Hot colors:* Bring an assortment of the most vibrant, fluorescent colors you can find in flies, plugs, spoons, spinners and drift bobbers, and change frequently until you find what's hot. Don't get stuck in a rut with what worked on yesterday's river or yesterday's conditions. Experiment!

•*Single and sharp:* If you haven't already done so, replace all treble hooks with super-sharp, single siwash or bait hooks (#1/0 to #5/0). Check and sharpen your hooks frequently out in the field.

•*Get 'em while they're fresh:* Try to fish kings no more than 50 miles from saltwater if possible; they'll be brighter and more aggressive, and they'll give a totally undiminished account of themselves on the end of a line.

•*Keep it short:* Use shorter leader/tippet lengths of three to four feet for all your sinking presentations on a fly rod.

SALTWATER METHODS & GEAR

In the salt, king salmon can be taken year-round in the form of immature fish called "feeders," which spend part, if not all, of their adult lives in inshore waters. Along with the larger, mature, prespawning chinook available in late spring, these fish are taken throughout Southeast and parts of Southcentral with rigging and methods similar to those used further south. The strategies used to take them exploit the chinooks' powerful feeding drives; trolling and "mooching" bait and lures from boats are far and away the most popular ways of working the water. A very limited amount of shore fishing takes place in certain locations, and flycasting is even more rare. Area and seasonal variations exist in the methods and gear used, so it's certainly wise to get some local input before you gear up for any serious Alaska saltwater king salmon pursuits. However, an understanding of the basic techniques and rigging will serve you well, no matter where, when and how you decide to challenge the king of salmon in the ocean environment.

Trolling

As the most efficient method of taking kings over a wide range of conditions, saltwater sport trolling borrows considerably from decades of experience hard-won by commercial salmon trollers throughout Southeast and elsewhere, who have refined the art of attracting and hooking salmon to a high level of efficiency.

Dodgers & Flashers

Trolling Rig

Main Line

Small Swivel

Swivel Bead chain tied to leader to prevent line twisting

Leader should be 1-1/2 to 2 times the length of the chain

Leader

Distance should be 3 to 4 feet

Dodger or Flasher

#5/0 Hook

#4/0 Hook

A diving/trolling sinker such as the Pink Lady or Deep Six (both by Luhr-Jensen) is most often substituted for the keel sinker weight. When using downriggers, run the main line directly to the dodger/flasher.

The use of metal fish attractors has been a standard practice for saltwater salmon fishing for years. The most commonly used types are "flashers" and "dodgers"—long, thin rectangular blades that spin or sway when trolled, adding considerable, strike-inducing stimuli (flash, sound and erratic action) to trailed baits or lures. Dodgers are usually four to 10 inches long, with a slightly concave shape to develop a side-to-side motion best suited to complement the action of spoons, plugs and live bait at a slow to medium trolling speed. Flashers are generally larger (up to 14 inches or more) and spin completely around in full 360-degree rotations. They are generally used with lures like hoochies and flies that have no action of their own, and in deep water trolling situations where maximum attractor stimuli is desired. Both kinds come in a variety of sizes, colors and finishes; chrome, chrome/silver scale, green, pearl pink, white and orange are some of the most popular used in Alaska.

For sport trolling kings, usually two to (rarely) six lines are employed off the back and sides of the boat, using downriggers, diving sinkers (i.e. Pink Lady) or keel weights to pull the terminal rigging down to the desired depth. In Alaska, dodgers or flashers in combination with herring (whole, plug-cut or

Pink Lady diving/trolling sinker

strips), hoochies, plugs, spoons or streamer flies are most often used. For best action, the attractor is generally rigged a minimum of three to four feet behind the sinker or diver, and at least six feet (or more) from a downrigger. A stout leader (30-pound test) about twice as long as the flasher or dodger connects to the terminal end. Trolling depth and speed vary, but kings generally are found deeper than coho (60 to 120 feet for feeders, generally less for prespawners) and take a slower trolled lure or bait.

Bait Fishing

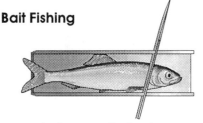 

A plug cutter for herring   *Rigged, "plug-cut" herring*

Most serious Alaska saltwater king salmon anglers prefer bait over all other enticements, as a properly handled and rigged herring will generally outfish anything else over a broad range of conditions. A four- to seven-inch, fresh or flash-frozen, whole, "plug cut" or harness-rigged herring (using a "Herring Aid") is generally preferred by most experienced sport trollers. The idea, similar to when fishing coho, is to rig the bait to impart the lifelike spin of a stunned or maimed baitfish when pulled through the water. "Hoochies," plastic-skirted squid imitations (in colors of pink, green, blue), are frequently added above the herring for more appeal.

Mooching

Mooching is a popular and very effective saltwater technique for fishing bait in the sheltered, tidally influenced waters of bays, estuaries and river mouths, anywhere fish tend to be deeper or concentrated by currents or structure. You'll see it done much more frequently by recreational fishermen than by high-powered charter boat operators, since it's a more laid-back and personal technique that puts the action in the hands of the individual fisherman, not the man at the throttle. Because the bait can move through the water column, it is also a more efficient and intensive way of working water when fish are not actively feeding near the surface.

For mooching, the herring is generally rigged the same as for trolling: either cut or whole, to spin when pulled through the water. Attractors are not used, with the leader running straight off the banana

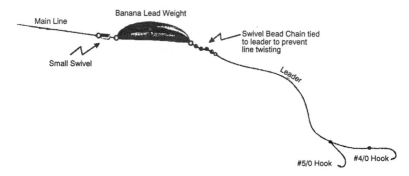

Main Line

Banana Lead Weight

Small Swivel

Swivel Bead Chain tied to leader to prevent line twisting

Leader

#5/0 Hook   #4/0 Hook

lead (one to six ounces) four to five feet to the bait. Fishing with the tides, line is stripped or slowly free-spooled from the reel until the rig hits the desired depth (usually above bottom). The bait is then worked by the action of the drift, by retrieving line, or with a slight troll (motor mooching). The most efficient way is determined by the tides, concentration of fish, prevailing winds and/or personal preference. A certain amount of finesse and skill is required. For instance, setting the hook is delayed on fish that hit the bait on the upswing until the rod loads, while salmon that pick up the bait while its descent will create slack line, which should be reeled in quickly to set the hook.

Jigging

An intensive technique related to mooching, jigging employs long, weighted metal baitfish imitations (jigs) fished vertically from a drifting or anchored boat. It can be extremely effective under the right conditions—sometimes more effective than any other technique—and has caught on with many serious salmon anglers throughout Southeast. Line is free-spooled out to the desired depth, then the jigs are raised and lowered quickly, giving them a tantalizing, fluttering action through the water column. Jigging works best in tight fish concentrations, such as around bait balls, and is usually done with a fish finder.

Finding the Fish

Saltwater king salmon fishing in Alaska, as elsewhere, targets "feeder" or prespawning kings, each with their own behavior, movements and locations that at times will demand separate strategies. Some of the best locations for mature, prespawning chinook are the well-known commercial trolling drags (such as the Breadline out of Juneau, Biorka Island out of Sitka, the west side of Gravina Island out of Ketchikan and others) where anglers traditionally intercept returning salmon at shallow depths. Feeder chinook will be found in areas of greatest food concentration, generally, but not always, deeper than pre-

---

KING SALMON

spawners. Locating bait patches or conditions favorable to feeding is the name of the game. Other than obvious visual signs like seabird flocks or other boats, the most common way to do this is with fish-finders, depth sounders and nautical charts, concentrating on areas like channels, points, straits, bays, rip zones and reefs. Fishing the tides (especially the period from two hours before to two hours after the change), or during the low-light times of day will usually be much more important when fishing chinook, as they are less energetic and more light-sensitive than coho.

These are just some of the basics involved in Alaska saltwater king salmon angling. A more complete knowledge of the habits and prefer-ences of the chinook and how tides, currents, time of day, and other factors affect fishing conditions is of course best acquired firsthand, in the company of others more experienced, like charter boat skippers, commercial trollers or seasoned saltwater sport anglers.

For beginners, the best advice is to go out a few times with people in the know, observe carefully and ask plenty of questions (for a list of recommended saltwater guides in Southcentral and Southeast, see the regional hot spots sections beginning on pages 371 and 477).

Gearing Up for Saltwater King Salmon

For general saltwater trolling, most Alaska anglers use a stiff, heavy-weight trolling or downrigger rod, usually seven- to eight-and-a-half feet long, with medium-fast action, to handle the increased resistance from weights, flashers, planers, etc. A high quality, levelwind inshore reel (Shimano TLD, Daiwa Sealine, Ambassadeur 7000 series, etc.) capable of holding at least 250 yards of 25-pound test is used. Lighter gear can be employed when fishing from downriggers.

Mooching rods are generally longer (to 11 feet), more limber, and with faster action, and are usually mated with sturdy baitcasters capable of holding 200 yards of 20-pound test. Jigging rods are generally short (six to seven feet) and stout, with a fast, cuestick taper for working lures vertically and producing a strong hookset. Reels are generally the same size as those used for trolling or mooching, with strong drags and spooled with 25- to 40-pound braided line.

TOP TEN TROPHY KING SALMON

97 pounds, 4 ounces, Kenai River (Southcentral), 1985,
    Les Anderson (state and world record)
95 pounds, 10 ounces, Kenai River (Southcentral), 1990
93 pounds, 0 ounces, Kelp Bay (Southeast), 1977
92 pounds, 4 ounces, Kenai River (Southcentral), 1985

91 pounds, 10 ounces, Kenai River (Southcentral), 1988
91 pounds, 4 ounces, Kenai River (Southcentral), 1987
89 pounds, 3 ounces, Kenai River (Southcentral), 1989
89 pounds, 0 ounces, Kenai River (Southcentral), 1994
88 pounds, 11 ounces, Kenai River (Southcentral), 1980
88 pounds, 0 ounces, Kenai River (Southcentral), 1979

ALASKA'S MAJOR KING SALMON LOCATIONS

Southeast

Sportfishing effort here is mostly a saltwater intercept fishery. Feeder kings are available year-round in most locations, with mature, streambound fish taken from mid-April to mid-July. A few, scattered shoreline fisheries exist, mostly for returning hatchery fish. Among the many straits, sounds and bays of the region, each can have a number of concentration points for feeding and migrating king salmon. Southeast's only significant freshwater king fishery is in the Situk River, near Yakutat, with more limited activity at Akwe River.

•*Yakutat:* Yakutat Bay; Situk and Akwe rivers

•*Haines:* Chilkat and Chilkoot inlets

•*Skagway:* Taiya Inlet

•*Juneau:* Lynn Canal, Favorite and Saginaw channels, Stephens Passage, Cross Sound, Icy and Chatham straits

•*Sitka:* Sitka and Salisbury sounds; Whale Bay

•*Petersburg:* Frederick Sound, Wrangell Narrows, Duncan Canal

•*Wrangell:* Eastern Passage; Stikine, Zimovia and Sumner straits; Ernest Sound

•*Ketchikan:* Behm Canal, Gravina Island, Clarence Strait, Revillagigedo Channel

•*Klawock (Prince of Wales):* Bucareli Bay, Gulf of Esquibel

Southcentral

Fishing for chinook in Southcentral is predominantly freshwater fishing, and includes the state's most heavily targeted, world-famous trophy fisheries of Kenai River and surrounding Cook Inlet. Ninety-nine percent of all Alaska trophy fish over 70 pounds come from these waters. Feeder kings are available year-round in lower Cook Inlet, Kachemak Bay, Outer Resurrection Bay, Prince William Sound, and along most of the Gulf Coast (Kodiak to Cordova). Mature streambound fish are available late April to late July. Some shoreline opportunities exist, primarily for hatchery fish. The run timing for freshwater king salmon fisheries is usually late May to early August.

•*Wrangell:* Klutina, Gulkana, Tonsina and Tazlina river systems

•*Kenai:* Lower Cook Inlet saltwater (Whiskey Gulch, Deep Creek, etc.); Kachemak Bay (Homer Spit, Halibut Cove, etc.); Kenai and Moose rivers; Anchor, Ninilchik, Kasilof and Deep creeks

•*Lower Cook Inlet:* Chakachatna and McArthur river systems

•*Susitna:* Deshka, Talachulitna and Talkeetna rivers; Lake, Montana, Willow, Little Willow, Sheep, Peters and Alexander creeks; clearwater sloughs and stream mouths along mainstem Susitna

•*Upper Cook Inlet:* Little Susitna, Chuitna, Lewis, Ivan and Theodore rivers; Beluga River tributaries

•*Kodiak:* Karluk and Red (Ayakulik) rivers; Chiniak Bay saltwater

•*Chugach:* Resurrection Bay, Passage Canal, Valdez Arm, Orca Inlet

Southwest

Southwest has no saltwater fishing for chinook, but it does have the state's most abundant, highest quality stream fishing, with unexcelled opportunities for flyfishing. The run timing is from the beginning of June through July; the peaks are mid-June to early July.

•*Bristol Bay:* Alagnak, Naknek, Wood, Togiak and Nushagak river systems

•*Alaska Peninsula:* King Salmon (Ugashik), Chignik, Meshik and Sandy rivers; Nelson Lagoon system

•*Kuskokwim:* Goodnews, Arolik, Kanektok, Aniak and Holitna river systems

•*Lower Yukon:* Andreafsky and Anvik rivers

Northwest

Most drainages from Yukon to Kotzebue Sound support some spawning populations; only a few (in Norton Sound) are noteworthy. The run timing is mid-June to mid-July.

•*Norton Sound:* Unalakleet, Shaktoolik, Inglutalik, Tubutulik and Kwiniuk rivers

Interior

Most fish have travelled extensively in freshwater to reach locations in Interior and are in less than prime condition, but good fishing can be found in and below nearly every clearwater confluence and slough of the Yukon River (for fish migrating to spawning sites on the upper Yukon and in Canada). The run timing is late June to early August.

•*Tanana:* Salcha, Chena and Chatanika rivers; Nenana River clearwater tributaries

King salmon

2
SILVERS:
THE AUGUST SALMON

It is the height of the short northern summer, and fireweed stands tall as corn next to old Charlie Wassilie's gear shed. From this vantage point high above the Kuskokwim, he scans a landscape little changed since his ancestor's arrival eons ago, then offers me a chunk of smoked salmon and some of his thoughts.

"Fishing should pick up, soon—Freddie's caught some out in the Bay already—but with the river so low, I don't know. I remember when I was a boy, one summer we didn't get any until September."

Charlie's been busy these last few weeks, using this special lull time—when the rivers ebb with the last of the runoff and the big runs of king and chum subside—to fix gear, smoke fish and work on boats. He has faith that soon enough, Alaska's late summer rains will flood the rivers, and on the crest will come frantic hordes of salmon, pumping new life into the land. For Charlie and his people, the arrival of these last salmon of summer means the completion of crucial food stores necessary to carry them through the long winter. But for "gussocks," or white men like me, these fish have a significance that goes far beyond their food value. Silvers or coho salmon are the punchiest fighters of the entire Pacific salmon clan. Nothing gets the adrenaline flowing like the thought of bright, rambunctious coho, and the sweet torture they can inflict on a fly and an eight-weight rod. The show of these August salmon marks the end of Alaska's glorious summer—a bittersweet but exhilarating time for Alaska anglers—and a call to embrace some of the best and last fishing of the season.

INTRODUCTION

The aggressive and acrobatic silver or coho salmon *(Oncorhynchus kisutch)* gets high marks from Pacific anglers, who pursue them with a passion perhaps second only to that shown for the mighty chinook. Found in great numbers along the coast of Alaska from Southeast to Norton Sound, the silver has traditionally been an important commercial and subsistence species, as well as the cornerstone of Alaska's fabulous late summer sportfishery. The arrival of these fish along the coast in late July kicks off a wave of excitement, as dozens of fish derbies get underway and countless sport anglers prepare for what many consider the high point of Alaska's fishing season.

A reckless and voracious predatory nature—important to his success as a species—is what sets the silver apart as a world-class gamefish. No other salmon takes a lure as vigorously or predictably, even long after it has stopped feeding in freshwater. And once hooked, the August salmon fights spectacularly, with long, hard runs and vigorous leaping. With big fish of 12 to 15 pounds or more on a fly rod or light- to medium-weight spinning tackle, the battle can be one of freshwater angling's most challenging.

DESCRIPTION

The Alaska silver is a powerful, medium-sized salmon. When fresh from the sea, it has a steel blue or green back, chrome sides and whitish belly, with moderate-sized, irregular black markings along the topsides. It can easily be mistaken for a small chinook, although a silver's tail is usually less forked, smaller and spotted only on the upper lobe, and the silver does not have the dark gumline of a king salmon. Like other Pacific salmon, spawning silvers undergo dramatic changes in appearance—particularly males. A deepening of the body, with dark red hues developing along the sides, greenish-black shading on the back and head, and enlarged jaws and teeth are some of the more recognizable transformations that occur after the silver enters freshwater.

The third largest of the Pacific salmon, Alaska's silvers can attain weights of up to 20 pounds or more, although generally they average six to nine pounds (more in certain areas of the state). For many years, the world's largest silver salmon came from Southeast Alaska and the coast of British Columbia (up to 30 pounds), but recently, transplanted stocks in the Great Lakes have surpassed the largest specimens caught from the species' natural range. The current IGFA world record is a whopping 33-pounder caught in Pulaski, New York, in 1989, while the biggest sportfish caught in Alaska's waters was a 26-pound silver taken from Icy Strait in 1976.

Besides providing some of the greatest sport to be had on rod and reel, silver salmon also make for some of the finest eating of any fish in the North Pacific. Their flesh is orange-red, firm and flavorful, not as rich or as prized as that of the sockeye or chinook, but in many ways more suited for grilling, frying, smoking or canning.

RANGE, ABUNDANCE & STATUS

Silver salmon have a potential range that encompasses most of the North Pacific basin, from Hokkaido, Japan (and scattered points further south) north to the Anadyr River, across the Bering Sea and south along the North American coast to Monterey Bay, California. Comprising only a small portion of the total Pacific salmon population—less than 10 percent—they are much more abundant along our coast than in Asia, and have had their range extended considerably through extensive propagation efforts.

In Alaska, silvers are found continuously from Dixon Entrance below Ketchikan to Norton Sound, then sporadically to Point Hope (68 degrees north latitude), with their greatest numbers concentrated from Kuskokwim Bay south. The Kuskokwim River is the state's largest producer, with runs reaching up to a million fish in peak years.

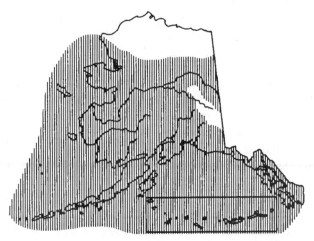

Shaded area shows range of silver salmon in Alaska.

This mid-sized salmon has a noted preference for short, coastal streams, and you'll find him at his best in the steep, well-watered terrain of Kodiak Island, the North Gulf Coast and Southeast Alaska. (There are over 2,000 known silver salmon streams there alone.) Silvers in these waters routinely reach weights of 12 pounds or more, with 20-pounders not uncommon. Via the immense Yukon and Kuskokwim Rivers, the silver salmon is able to penetrate the state's vast interior and utilize the abundant glacial gravels of the Alaska Range, spawning inland as far as tributaries of the upper Tanana River. Through intensive stocking and propagation efforts by the Alaska Department of Fish and Game, numerous landlocked, enhanced and "terminal" (non-breeding) populations of silver salmon currently exist, providing increased opportunities, particularly for urban anglers.

Many areas of Alaska, like Southeast, are currently enjoying record harvest levels, and even though enhanced runs comprise a significant part of the total catch, overall the status of Alaska's silver salmon is as good as it's ever been, which means that anglers can expect to encounter some of the most world's most productive fishing for the species for years to come, on thousands of rivers, lakes and bays.

LIFE HISTORY & HABITS

Silvers, like the rest of the salmon, have interesting life histories and habits. After emigrating from the sea in late summer (from mid-July to September in most of Alaska, later in Southeast), they seek out river headwaters and side channels to spawn, mating and depositing fertilized eggs in a manner similar to the other salmon species. As in all Pacific salmon, the breeding act is terminal.

Hatching sometime in mid-winter, young coho quickly move into stream margins, side channels, and small pools to feed on small insects and plankton. Territorial and voracious, they display the same aggressive tendencies that will distinguish them as great sportfish later in life. (The small fry that congregate under cutbanks and chase and nip passing objects are usually coho.) Minnows, smolt and even their own kind are subject to their depredations, and they can inflict serious damage on other important species like sockeye salmon and rainbow trout.

From the data available, it seems that Alaska's silvers spend a year or two (rarely three) in freshwater, before "smolting" and heading to the ocean in spring or early summer (May to July). While at sea, they feed heavily and grow rapidly on steady diets of fish (herring, sandlance, smelt and other small salmon) and invertebrates (crab larvae and shrimp), generally preferring the top of the water column to 100 feet down.

Spending their entire ocean existence near shore or in circular wanderings far out into the Gulf of Alaska, Alaska's silver salmon mostly return to spawn at the end of their second summer at sea, at three or four years of age. A significant percentage of oddball age classes—precocious, two-year-old fish called "jacks," or five- or even six-year-old fish—can occur at times in some systems. Timing and duration of runs varies, as the fish seek optimum stream flow and water temperatures before entering freshwater, but silvers can usually be found in the mouths of rivers anywhere from late July and early August in the north to September and October in Southeast.

Generally more social than the chinook, but not as gregarious as the sockeye or pink salmon, prespawning silvers will congregate extensively in bays, river mouths, lake outlets, pools and sloughs, and show themselves frequently, making easy targets for sport anglers. But it is their temperament and feeding behavior more than anything that is their undoing in encounters with the sport angler. Born bullies, young coho in small, enclosed areas will kill each other in their drive for food and territory (unlike chinook and other salmon). Their legendary gluttony inflicts serious depredation on young sockeye salmon, trout and charr in rivers. Out at sea, silvers will commonly drive schools of frantic baitfish up to the surface in tightly packed balls, and with chomping jaws gorge to the bursting point.

FRESHWATER METHODS & GEAR
Spin Casting and Baitcasting

The vast majority of coho caught in the state's rivers and tidewaters are taken on spinning gear and hardware. A light- to medium-weight, medium-action salmon rod (seven to eight-and-a-half feet long), matched with a high quality open-faced reel and 8- to 12-pound test, along with an assortment of popular spinners, plugs, and spoons is the preferred armament, from northern Southeast to Norton Sound.

More than any other salmon, silvers are suckers for flash, which explains why the Super Vibrax spinner and Pixee spoon (both made by Blue Fox of Cambridge, Minnesota) are the most popular salmon lures in Alaska. Silver and gold, with orange, pink, yellow or chartreuse attractors, seem to be the most productive color combinations, in sizes #4 to #6 for the spinners and $1/2$-ounce and $7/8$-ounce for the spoons. Other popular silver salmon lures for spin casting are the larger-sized Mepps Aglia, Panther Martin and Rooster Tail spinners, and the Krocodile, Hot Rod and Kastmaster spoons ($1/2$-ounce or larger) in nickel/chrome, brass, fire red, red prism, yellow or chartreuse combinations.

Because of their innate aggressiveness, silvers will quite often pursue lures through the water, even rising to the surface on occasion, especially in tidal water or in the lower sections of rivers. Once in freshwater for any time, however, they tend to avoid extravagant expenditures of energy, so careful casts and slower retrieves generally produce the most strikes. Fish mainstem lies like you would for kings, but give special attention to sloughs, cutbanks, eddies, tailouts of pools and feeder confluences, as silvers will group in these areas to rest and engage in prespawning behavior, making for concentrated fishing opportunities. In clear streams, locating and targeting silvers in these holding zones is greatly simplified, but in turbid or very deep water, the angler must look for showing fish or choose the most likely holding locations.

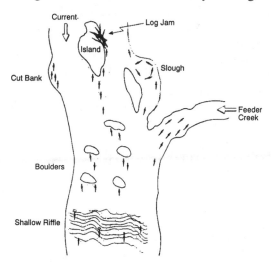

Typical silver salmon river lies.

From an upstream position, cast ahead of the lie. In very clear or shallow water, use caution when approaching silvers, as they can be spooky. With a steady but slow retrieve, work the lure so that it passes through at fish eye level. Work the lie several times, varying the placement, retrieve speed and depth; then move on (no matter how good the water looks), for there are almost always plenty of eager silvers to be had elsewhere. If you are sight-fishing a salmon group, work the lure deep along the upstream or downstream edge of the school, watching carefully for a response of any kind. Quite often, a "taker" (usually an aggressive male), will burst from the ranks and nab or pursue the lure. If you don't hook him immediately, you can usually get him on subsequent casts.

There may be times when silvers will refuse to bite the normal enticements, such as in bright and sunny conditions, in extremely turbid or clear water, or when the silvers have been in freshwater too long. You may see them cruising sloughs, holding in tailouts, showing themselves and generally doing the same things they normally do, but refusing to hit the standard spinners, spoons or plugs. This is normal and to be expected every now and then, but you can sometimes force these non-biters to hit with different tactics. For one, if you're sight-fishing, tighten up your casts and retrieves to work the lure right in front of their noses, repeatedly, until you anger them into striking. Another trick is to change lure size and color. Go oversize and brighter (orange, red, yellow) for turbid waters, and smaller and more subdued (black, purple, brown) for bright, clear waters. If that doesn't work, try a different action or retrieve. Some anglers are able to induce strikes with erratic, jerky retrieves of their spinners and spoons, while others have done the same by switching to plugs and crankbaits. The idea here is to incite a response with stimuli that go beyond what the silver normally encounters under these conditions.

•*Bait Fishing:* One traditional, surefire way of loosening the jaws of even the most finicky August salmon is to drift some salmon roe through their lies. This is still an immensely popular technique on many silver streams (only where it's legal, though). Under most conditions, a ball of roe on a single egg hook drifted along bottom will outfish any other method ten to one, especially when fishing glacial or runoff water. Most egg fishermen use the conventional "egg loop" snell on a #1/0 egg or steelhead hook, fished with a lead dropper or rubber core sinker. You can dress things up with a piece of colored yarn, or even more deadly, a drift bobber, like a #4 Spin-N-Glo. The bait is fished on a drift, keeping a taut line as the rig bounces along bottom. Generally silvers will pick up roe gently and mouth it a bit before either spitting it out or running with it, so you need to be ready and watchful of the slightest hesitation or disturbance in your line.

•*Drift/Troll Fishing:* On larger rivers like the Kenai, Naknek and Alagnak, trolling and drifting plugs, drift bobbers and spinners from boats is standard practice for silver salmon. Spin-N-Glos, Tee-spoons, Hot Shots and Okie Drifters are the lures of choice, usually sweetened with bait (salmon roe). Rigging and techniques are almost identical to those used for king salmon (drifting, trolling, back trolling, back-bouncing, etc.—see the chinook chapter on page 28 for details), except that the gear is lighter and smaller. A medium-weight, fast-action, steelhead or salmon casting rod (seven- to eight-and-a-half feet) works fine, mated to a high quality casting reel loaded with 200 yards of 10- to 15-pound line.

Flyfishing

In many ways, the silver salmon is the Pacific Coast's perfect game-fish for flyfishing. More abundant and widespread than either the chinook or steelhead, they are quick on the take, very sporting and great jumpers. In the quality and variety of angling they can provide over a wide range of conditions, they are certainly without peer.

You don't need expensive, sophisticated gear or techniques to enjoy Alaska's matchless fishing for the species. An eight-weight rod, matching reel, some floating or sink tip line, 1X to 3X (8- to 12-pound) tippet and some basic patterns, will work fine for most conditions in Alaska. For big fish in heavy current you may want to bump up to a nine-weight rod. The basic streamer and wet fly presentations used for trout and the other salmon will be equally effective on Alaska's silvers most of the time, with long casts, long leaders and fancy presentations being neither necessary nor desirable.

As with the other salmon, the closer to saltwater you can intercept the Alaska silver, the better. Bays and estuaries, river mouths, and lower stream sections right above tidewater are ideal. Further up into freshwater, the silvers' behavior, appearance and gaminess begins to change. The basic approach will be similar to that used for chinooks: deep drift presentations and "short strip" streamer swings through mainstem lies and holding water—channels, sloughs, pools, confluences, eddies and current seams—anywhere silvers might be resting or moving through. (Keep in mind that silvers usually move less through main channels than kings do.) Sight-fishing in clear water, with the more precise casting it allows, certainly is ideal. The take of a silver is usually much more noticeable and abrupt than that of a chinook, and quite often they'll hook themselves and begin running and jumping immediately. During the peak of the runs in average streams, they can congregate by the dozens in good holding water, so you can easily have all the action your arms can handle once you find a good location.

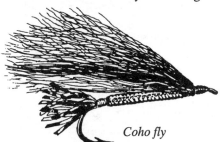

Coho fly

A whole genre of Alaska salmon flies has evolved to capitalize on the silver's fondness for bright, gaudy patterns (not to mention the average flyfisherman's fetish for colorful, artsy creations). Flash Flies, Sparklers, Maraflash Flies, Krystal Bullets, Flashabous, Silver Comets and the like vie for your attention and dollars at the local fly shop. They're all very effective on Alaska's August salmon, as are the more traditional Northwest patterns like the Skykomish Sunrise, Polar Shrimp, Leech and Woolly Bugger (all in sizes #2 to #6). What's more, these flies are all easy to make on your own, with a vise, some thread, hooks, and an assortment of colored tinsel, feathers and yarn. With very little imagination and some practice, you can come up with your own creations that are just as effective, more durable and inexpensive, not to mention the satisfaction you'll receive from hooking fish on your own hand-tieds.

Under certain conditions, silver salmon can even be lured up to the surface with dry flies, a fact anglers quite often discover by accident when skating streamers at the beginning of a backcast or the end of a drift. Generally, it works best to have shallow, clear water (four feet or less), with good floaters like the Irresistible, Bomber, Wulff, Elk Hair Caddis or Double Humpy in sizes #4 to #10. Some anglers even do well with shrew or mouse imitations. Unlike flyfishing for trout, for silvers you'll want to use short, fast strips across the current, to make surface commotion and noise. (Remember, these fish are not feeding.) Techniques and patterns used for summer steelheading (such as skating flies, riffle hitches, etc.) would certainly work for raising Alaska silver salmon.

•*Top Ten Flies for Alaska Silver Salmon:* Flash Fly, Coho Fly, Polar Shrimp, Egg-Sucking Leech, Purple Woolly Bugger, Maraflash Fly, Krystal Bullet, Alaskabou, Comet and Everglow.

SALTWATER METHODS & GEAR

Like any salmon, silvers are at their fighting best in saltwater, and a good number of the state's sport anglers wouldn't have them any other way. From Kodiak to Ketchikan, an almost unlimited amount of inshore opportunity beckons, with the excitement of abundant fishing and the incomparable beauty of Alaska's magnificent coast. The basics of saltwater silver fishing are within easy grasp of most anglers and involve more or less the following:

Bait Fishing

Despite all the advances in gear and lures, trolling or "mooching" herring remains far and away the most productive method for taking saltwater silver salmon, if you believe the fishing derby records and salty old boat captains. Using fresh if possible (or frozen if not), small-to medium-sized fish (three to five inches), whole or "plug cut" according to preference, you rig the bait to impart a tantalizing spin when dragged or drifted behind the boat (see the saltwater section in the chinook salmon chapter on page 40 for more details on trolling and mooching). The bait is usually rigged behind an attractor (flasher or dodger), with downriggers, weight or diving planers used to reach proper depth. The addition of bait harnesses ("Herring Aid" or "Salmon Killer"), plastic jig skirts (hoochies) and fish oils are popular ways of enhancing the action and appeal of the bait.

Regardless of how you cut (or don't cut) the bait, the trick is to imitate the action of a stunned or wounded minnow, with the bait rolling in tight, fast circles or big lazy spirals. The action should be determined by the speed of the troll, drift or retrieve and the way the fish are rigged (or cut). The two different types of movement are both very effective for salmon under a wide range of conditions, but the tighter, faster action is preferred by most coho anglers. Fishing 25 to 75 feet behind the boat, most fishermen will work the herring along the edge of bait patches and in other areas likely to hold salmon, varying their speed and course to work the water most efficiently.

Lures

Spoons, spinners, plugs and jigs can also be very effective, at times even more so than bait. Commercial trollers have caught countless tons of salmon over the years fishing only simple spoons and plastic squid-like jig skirts called "hoochies." And some of the best saltwater sport anglers in Southeast can catch more fish on hardware, if the conditions are right, than an army of bait anglers could. When coho are concentrated and actively feeding, trolling, casting or jigging lures is certainly the most exciting and enjoyable way to fish. Some of the more popular lures used for silvers in salt are medium-sized ($^1/_2$-ounce to one-ounce) Krocodile, Pixee, Reflecto, HotRod and Crippled Herring spoons; medium to large ($^3/_8$-ounce to $^5/_8$-ounce) Super Vibrax, Mepps Aglia, Bolo, Skagit and Shyster spinners; small to medium ($^1/_8$-ounce to $^5/_{16}$-ounce)

Pierce lead hook through side of mouth (do so with mouth closed), pushing shank completely through. Then the point of the hook should be pushed completely back through the side of the fish, just forward of the edge of the gill cover, as shown in illustration. The trailing hook can either be buried

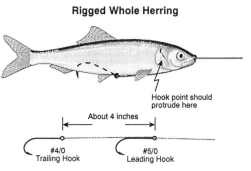

Rigged Whole Herring

Hook point should protrude here

About 4 inches

#4/0
Trailing Hook

#5/0
Leading Hook

into the herring (as shown) or left trailing freely behind. This arrangement will give the head of the herring a slight bend that will force the fish to spin and roll as it is drawn through the water.

J-Plugs, Flatfish, Hot Shot, Rapalas and Kwikfish; and small (two-and-a-half-inch) jigs like the Buzz Bomb, Dart, Teezer and Stinger. The most effective colors seem to be combinations of green, white, silver and blue (sometimes spiced with attractor red, orange or yellow). Small keel sinkers (one to three ounces) can be used to get the lure down if needed. The best areas for fishing lures are usually along beaches, small bays, tide rips, jetties, kelp beds and anywhere baitfish concentrations or showing salmon are spotted. There are shorefishing opportunities around nearly every community along Alaska's southern coasts; check with locals for the best spots.

Sea bird activity is a sure sign to look for when searching for feeding silvers.

Finding the Fish

To freshwater anglers accustomed to stalking their quarry within the confines of river banks, the challenge of locating salmon in the wide open marine environment can be daunting. But since silvers are predominantly top water feeders (usually within the top 40 feet or so) finding fish in inshore waters can be as simple as spotting surface activity or locating bait patches. Flocking seabirds, jumping or rolling salmon, milling baitfish, even the presence of other boats are dead giveaways. Always bring binoculars for scouting water! If nothing obvious is present, examine kelp beds, shorelines, tide rips, the back eddies of points and islands, the heads of bays with salmon streams, and around any kind of underwater structure (such as dropoffs, shoals or reefs). You can expect to encounter silvers at anywhere from 60 feet to the surface in these likely locations. Depending on how hungry they are, the availability and concentration of baitfish, their prespawning condition, the tides and many other factors, you can expect to do well with trolling, mooching, casting or jigging lures and bait.

Fish locators and depth sounders, marine charts, downriggers and what-have-you, in addition to a knowledge of the waters, go a long way toward ensuring success in the challenging marine environment. The services of a licensed charter boat operator or friend with a boat, gear and local experience are highly recommended for someone new to saltwater silver salmon angling.

Gearing Up for Saltwater Silver Salmon

For trolling with diving planers and weights, you'll need a medium-action, heavy salmon trolling rod, seven to eight-and-a-half feet long, mated with a high quality levelwind reel capable of holding several hundred yards of 20- to 30-pound test mono or braided line. For fishing downriggers, lighter gear is often used: 10- to 20-pound line on a medium-weight salmon rod and matching reel. Mooching usually involves a longer, more limber rod (up to 10 feet) than that used for trolling, and a good levelwind reel loaded with at least several hundred yards of 12- to 20-pound test line. Jigging outfits are usually comprised of short, stout, fast-taper rods mated to a levelwind with a good drag and loaded with 15- to 25-pound test braided line. For spincasting, a medium-weight, fast-action salmon or steelhead rod, seven-and-a-half to eight-and-a-half feet long, with a matching spinning reel loaded with 200 yards of 8- to 12-pound test mono, is recommended.

Saltwater Flyfishing

Herring fly

Flyfishing silvers in Alaska's inshore waters isn't anywhere near as prevalent or popular as you might think. Most of it is done in the sheltered inside waters of Southeast, where conditions are more conducive to flycasting. The basic challenge is locating salmon near the surface. Anglers work bait patches, kelp beds, creek mouths, shorelines and the like with long, fishair or bucktail baitfish imitation streamers (three to five inches long), tube flies, or standard saltwater patterns like the Tarpon Fly, Deceiver and Clouser Minnow (size #2 to #3/0). The most productive colors seem to be combinations of white, yellow, green, pink, blue, purple and orange. A long, seven-, eight- or even nine-weight rod is preferred, with matching reel, a long sink tip or full sink line, and short leader/tippet of 8- to 12-pound test.

Trolling flies with downriggers or "bucktailing" along the surface, a common practice in British Columbia and waters further south, is done only infrequently in Alaska. To do this requires a big fly reel spooled with mono (15- to 20-pound test); large, bushy, single or tandem hook streamer flies; and weights up to three ounces if fishing without downriggers. Anglers usually fish more than one rod, with different weights and lengths of line, to work the flies at various depths and increase the chances of a strike.

Alaska's Top Trophy Silver Salmon Locations
•Yakutat—Situk, Italio and Lost rivers (Southeast)
•Juneau—Shelter Island, Handtrollers Cove, Stephens Passage (Southeast)
•Kodiak—Pasagshak, Karluk, Uganik and Saltery Rivers (Southcentral)
•Kenai River (Southcentral)

ALASKA'S TOP TEN TROPHY SILVERS
26 pounds, 0 ounces, Icy Strait, Juneau (Southeast), 1976 (state record)
25 pounds, 4 ounces, St. Nicholas Creek, Prince of Wales Island (Southeast), 1991
24 pounds, 0 ounces, Grant Cove-Ketchikan (Southeast), 1986
23 pounds, 8 ounces, Yakutat (Southeast), 1981
23 pounds, 2 ounces, North Shelter Island-Juneau (Southeast), 1974
23 pounds, 0 ounces, Italio River (Southeast), 1981
23 pounds, 0 ounces, Handtrollers Cove-Juneau (Southeast), 1982
22 pounds, 14 ounces, Pasagshak River, Kodiak (Southcentral), 1993
22 pounds, 11 ounces, North Pass, Juneau (Southeast), 1987
22 pounds, 9 ounces, Lynn Canal, Juneau (Southeast), 1976

ALASKA'S MAJOR SILVER SALMON LOCATIONS
Alaska anglers catch over one-half million silver salmon each year, predominantly by saltwater trolling and freshwater spincasting, with most effort concentrated in Southeast (Ketchikan, Juneau and Yakutat) and Southcentral (Kenai Peninsula and Susitna River). A smaller but significant amount of silver fishing occurs on clear-flowing drainages of the North Gulf Coast (east of Cordova) and the more remote rivers of Southwest (northern Alaska Peninsula to the lower Kuskokwim) and Norton Sound. Popular stocked, landlocked coho fisheries also exist in and around the Anchorage area, the Kenai Peninsula and Interior.

Southeast
Angling for silvers here is predominantly marine trolling. The Haines/Skagway, Prince of Wales and Yakutat areas receive most of the freshwater sport effort. Runs peak in September and October.

•*Yakutat:* Yakutat Bay; Situk, Italio, Lost, East Alsek, Akwe, Doame, Kiklukh, Tsiu, Kaliakh and Tawah rivers

•*Haines/Skagway:* Chilkoot and Chilkat rivers, Lutak Inlet

•*Juneau:* Upper Lynn Canal, Favorite/Saginaw channels, Northern Stephens Passage, Chatham and Icy Strait, Cross Sound; Montana and

Cowee creeks; Surge, Klag Bay, Mitchell Bay, Youngs (Admiralty Creek) and Sweetwater lake systems

•*Sitka/Petersburg:* Ernest, Sitka and Frederick sounds; Wrangell Narrows/Duncan Canal, Lower Stephens Passage, Eastern Passage; Stikine, Zimovia, Upper Clarence and Sumner Straits; Duncan Saltchuck and Blind Slough; Petersburg, Kadake, Thoms, Ohmer, Anan, Aaron and Sitkoh creeks; Salmon Bay, Eva, Redoubt, Petersburg and Red lake systems; Kah Sheets, Harding, Kadashan, Plotnikof and Castle rivers; Stikine River system; Port Banks, Katlian River and Bay, Starrigavan Creek and Bay

•*Ketchikan:* Gulf of Esquibel, Bucareli Bay, Clarence Strait, Behm Canal (Yes Bay, Bell Island, Clover Pass, etc.), Revillagigedo Channel, Gravina Island; Staney, Wolverine, Ward and Ketchikan creeks; Sarkar, McDonald, Salmon Bay and Saltchuck lakes; Klawock, Thorne, Karta, Wilson, Blossom, Naha and Kegan river systems

Southcentral

Southcentral has Alaska's most fished silver salmon streams, many offering outstanding fishing. The run timing is from late July into October, with a peak in August and early September.

•*Chugach:* Katalla and Bering river systems; Alaganik Slough and Martin River systems, Thirtynine Mile, Ibek and Clear creeks; Controller Bay Stream; Eyak, Johnson Bay, Nellie Martin-Patton, Beach, Robe and San Juan rivers; Valdez Arm, Wells Passage, Knight Island/Passage, Montague Strait, Hinchinbrook Entrance, Orca Bay, Resurrection Bay, Passage Canal

•*Wrangell:* Tonsina River system. (Landlocked: Strelna and Lou's lakes)

•*Kenai Peninsula:* Kenai, Moose, Russian, Anchor, Swanson, Kasilof and Ninilchik rivers, Deep and Crooked creeks; Kachemak Bay, English Bay and Rocky River. (Landlocked: Engineer, Upper Jean, Portage, Scout, Union, Island, Stormy, Arc, Centennial and Encelewski lakes)

•*Upper Cook Inlet:* Little Susitna River; Cottonwood, Wasilla, Fish and Jim creeks; Lewis and Theodore rivers

•*Lower Cook Inlet:* Kamishak, Chakachatna-McArthur, Crescent, Kustatan, Beluga, Chuitna and Amakdedori rivers; Polly and Silver Salmon creeks

---

•*Mat-Su Valley:* (Landlocked: Matanuska, Echo, Victor, Wolf, Finger, Lucille, Memory, Loon and Christiansen lakes)

•*Susitna River:* Chulitna, Deshka, Talachulitna, Talkeetna and Upper Susitna (tributaries) rivers; Alexander, Lake, Willow, Montana, Sunshine, Peters, Caswell, Greys and Sheep creeks

•*Anchorage/Turnagain:* Ship, Campbell and Bird creeks; Twentymile and Placer river systems

•*Kodiak/Afognak/Shuyak Islands:* Shuyak, Chiniak, Ugak, Big and Neketa bays; Carry Inlet; Portage, Danger, Deadman, Akalura, Roslyn and Salonie creek systems; Pauls Creek system and Bay, Karluk, Afognak, Red (Ayakulik), Saltery, Uganik, Dog Salmon, Terror, Zachar, Pasagshak and Spiridon rivers; Chiniak Bay streams (Buskin, Sid, Olds and American rivers, etc.); Olga, Malina, Miam and Little River lake systems

•*Shelikof Strait (West):* Swuishak and Big rivers

Southwest

Southwest has some of Alaska's finest freshwater silver salmon opportunities in terms of quality and abundance, with flyfishing possibilities almost limitless. Many streams with strong runs (especially on Alaska Peninsula) receive little or no pressure. The run timing is late July into early September, with the peak in August.

•*Bristol Bay:* Nushagak-Mulchatna, Wood, Togiak, Alagnak and Naknek river systems

•*North Alaska Peninsula:* Egegik and Ugashik river systems (including King Salmon Rivers); Nelson Lagoon system; Port Heiden; Cinder, Chignik, Meshik and Ilnik rivers; Swanson Lagoon

•*South Alaska Peninsula:* Russel Creek, Mortensen Lagoon, Thin Point Cove (Cold Bay), Lefthand Bay, Beaver River, Volcano River, Belkofski Bay

•*Kuskokwim:* Goodnews, Arolik, Kanektok, Kisaralik, Kwethluk, Kasigluk, Aniak and Holitna rivers

•*Lower Yukon:* Andreafsky and Anvik rivers

Northwest

Northwest's high quality fishing opportunity is limited to eastern Norton Sound and a few Seward Peninsula drainages. The run timing is from August to mid-September, with a peak in August.

SILVER SALMON

•*Norton Sound:* Unalakleet, Shaktoolik, Ungalik, Inglutalik, Kwiniuk and Tubutulik rivers

•*Seward Peninsula:* Fish-Niukluk, Nome and Sinuk rivers

Interior

There are a few outstanding opportunities for late fall-running silver salmon in Interior (late August into October).

•*Upper Tanana:* Delta Clearwater River; Nenana—Clear Creek and Seventeenmile Slough

Silver salmon

3
SOCKEYE:
THE SHY SALMON

It is early July, and an amazing spectacle is visible on the rivers of southwest Alaska. For days and weeks on end, waters that lie fallow most of the year seethe with hundreds of thousands of bright salmon, fresh from a journey across the open sea. En route to spawning areas miles upriver, these energetic hordes choke side channels and crowd the banks in numbers that must be seen to be believed, at times forming a shimmering blue wave of tails and fins that stretches for miles through these crystal waters.

The guide beaches the raft at the head of a set of rapids and you hop ashore, hastily assembled rod in trembling hands. A familiar lure flipped into the current tumbles through the surging ranks with no takers. Surprised, you cast again, this time with careful presentation and retrieve. Nothing. Still another cast brings not the slightest response, although these waters literally boil with salmon. How can this be? You try different lures and tactics, flailing the river with increasing frustration, as fish jump everywhere in mockery of your efforts. After 20 minutes of nary a nibble, you're about to give up and swear off fishing for good, when your guide steps in with a knowing smile.

Wielding a long, limber rod and a strange fly you've never seen before, he wades out and lays his line in a short arc upriver. It moves quickly downstream, then stops, as a chrome torpedo crashes through the foam and flips furiously along the surface. Like a skyrocket on a tether, the fish careens wildly. It reenters the river, rips out into the main channel at the speed of light, then somersaults into the boil of a big rapid. Levering its body against strong current, the enraged salmon strips into the backing. This is a fish out of control, and no one knows it more than your guide, who wisely lowers the rod, tightens up and parts ways with this freedom-crazed fighter. Wasting no regret, your trusted companion quickly busies himself with raising another, while you scramble to do the same—if you can get a hold of one of those flies!

INTRODUCTION

The sockeye or red salmon *(Oncorhynchus nerka)* is in many ways the most challenging and enigmatic of Alaska's five salmon for sportsmen. Prolific almost beyond measure in some parts of the state and extremely coveted for its flesh—the richest of all the salmon—the sockeye has long been the state's most valuable commercial species, contributing millions to Alaska's economy (up to $200 million a year for Bristol Bay alone). But because of its steadfast reluctance to take a lure, for the longest time it was not even considered a sportfish.

Since they spend most their lives grazing plankton, sockeyes are more predisposed to passive behavior than fly-shredding bouts of predatory aggression. But beneath that meek exterior and generic appearance lies an intensity and physical prowess that is truly astounding. Endowed with amazing energy—they are the strongest swimmers of the salmon and can easily leap 15-foot waterfalls—sockeyes move up from the sea into the far reaches of rivers with remarkable speed. More than any other salmon, they are creatures of single-minded purpose, possessing a supreme will to let nothing short of instant death keep them from their destiny upriver.

Anglers who succeed in tempting this normally tight-lipped salmon are in for one of the world's wildest battles on light tackle. With explosive leaps, mad, reel-smoking dashes up and down river and incredible stamina, they are, for their size, the strongest and most demanding of all gamefish in Alaska, an assessment unanimously confirmed by all who have come away from their first sockeye encounter with bruises, broken gear and battered nerves.

DESCRIPTION

Sockeyes display a remarkable uniformity of appearance throughout their range in Alaska. Millions of fish come in from the sea averaging around six pounds in weight (8 to 12 pounds or more in large specimens; the state and world record sportfish is a 16-pounder from the Kenai River). They average 24 inches in length, with streamlined bodies of metallic blue/grey/green on the back, silver sides and silver-white bellies. Prominent markings on the topsides and tailfins of sockeyes are

---

almost always absent, and this, along with the presence of 30 to 40 fine, closely spaced and serrated rakers on the first gill arch identifies the species. Sea-bright sockeye can closely resemble chum salmon. As the sockeye is predominantly a plankton feeder, teeth on prespawning fish are usually less developed than those on other salmon.

Spawning sockeye salmon present one of Nature's most striking images. The males develop vivid red bodies, green heads, black, thick humps and pronounced hooked jaws, while females are generally more subdued in appearance. Color can vary in intensity and hue in different populations. Juvenile sockeye have short, dark oval parr marks usually terminating at or shortly below the lateral line. Kokanee, the land-locked form of the sockeye, are very similar in appearance, but much smaller, reaching about 10 inches average length and rarely exceeding a pound and a half in weight in Alaska.

Sockeye are the most prized of Alaska salmon for eating, with rich, red flesh of unparalleled flavor, whether grilled, smoked, or canned. Their value as a food fish, uniformity in size, and relative abundance has made them the most desirable and economically significant component of Alaska's commercial, subsistence and personal use fisheries.

Range, Abundance & Status

Sockeye salmon were originally found coastally from northern California and Oregon to Point Hope, Alaska (with scattered sightings in the Arctic Ocean) and in Asia from Hokkaido, Japan to the Anadyr River in northeastern Siberia. The third most abundant of the Pacific

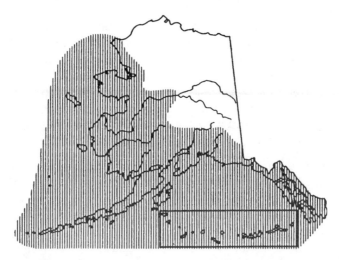

Shaded area shows range of sockeye salmon in Alaska.

SOCKEYE SALMON

salmon, they are found now in greatest numbers from the Fraser River in British Columbia to Alaska's Bristol Bay (and in Asia, in the rivers of Kamchatka). In the immense, lake-river habitat of the Alaska Peninsula and Bristol Bay, sockeye runs can number in the millions, supporting valuable fisheries and rich, diverse food chains (see the chapters on charr and rainbow trout on pages 100 and 128).

Alaska's sockeye populations have fluctuated over the years, rebounding from depressed levels in the 1960s and 1970s to current record levels. (Commercial fishermen caught 65 million and sport anglers caught well over a half million fish in 1993.) Overall, in terms of habitat, current runs and changes in the world salmon market, things look very good for the future of this amazing resource and the almost unlimited potential it holds for world class sportfishing.

LIFE HISTORY & HABITS

The remarkable success of sockeye salmon as a species stems from their ability to directly exploit the astounding productivity of the North Pacific, using its rich blooms of plankton as their main food source and the countless lakes found along the coast as their nurseries. Because of the economic importance of this fabulous fishery, Alaska's sockeyes have been the most extensively studied of the state's salmon, and quite a bit is known of their life history and movement patterns.

Mature prespawning sockeye salmon begin appearing in rivers across the state in early summer—usually from late May on—with peak migration periods occurring mid-June through early August (even later in Southeast). Their local abundance can be staggering, choking the larger river systems in the most productive parts of their range with numbers in the millions. As a general rule, sockeyes are found in rivers that are connected in some way with lakes, but some sockeye are adapted to breeding entirely in rivers, or rarely, in estuaries (these fish will tend to go to sea the first summer after hatching). Residuals—sea-run fish that for some reason spend their entire lives in freshwater—and true landlocked populations such as the kokanee exist in numerous lakes throughout Southeast and a few in Southcentral. Favored sockeye spawning locations are in stream outlets directly below lakes, in feeder creeks, and along gravelly lakeshores, with peak activity taking place in late summer and fall (August through October).

Like the rest of the Pacific salmon, the female sockeye digs the gravel nest, then mates in several bouts of egg-laying that may involve the digging of more than one redd and fertilization by several males. Up to 4,000 or more eggs are deposited and incubate in anywhere from six weeks to five months, depending on water temperature. Breeding is terminal, though fish may linger for weeks after spawning, despite pronounced physical deterioration. Young sockeye fry emerge in early spring (April to May) and usually migrate to the nursery lake by summer. There in the shallows, they feed primarily on insects and crustaceans before moving in schools to deeper waters to consume plankton in the upper water column. Some fry migrate downriver to the sea after their first summer, but most Alaska sockeye will spend two, and in some cases even three years in freshwater before "smolting up." Smolt out-migration occurs in the spring, usually May to June.

Once in the ocean, young sockeye grow rapidly on diets of crustaceans, squid, zooplankton, and on rare occasion even small fish such as sandlance, eulachon, herring and rockfish. Their deep ocean existence takes them considerable distances out into the North Pacific, where they usually complete two or three immense, counterclockwise circuits before returning to inshore areas to begin preparing for spawning. In open water, they generally prefer to be near the surface (less than 15 meters deep) a large percentage of the time. Ocean stay of Alaska sockeyes varies, but it is usually two or three years (rarely four), making the predominant returning age classes four-, five- and six-year-old fish. Principal predators of sockeye in the ocean are whales, seals and man. In rivers and lakes they are preyed on by charr, rainbow trout, coho salmon, sea birds, eagles, bears and man.

Sockeyes have some unique and interesting habits that can be exploited by anglers. Along with pinks, they are the most gregarious of salmon, grouping by the thousands for their upstream migrations, where they mill in estuaries, river mouths, lake outlets, sloughs and pools, to rest from their strenuous journey. They also have a tendency to hug shorelines and utilize side channels and sloughs. Both of these habits make them especially vulnerable to predation (by bears and anglers).

Like the other salmon, sockeyes will show themselves quite frequently in freshwater—breaching and jumping as they engage in prespawning behavior. This is easily mistaken for aggression, and has led many an unknowing angler into futile bouts of casting. Their legendary aloofness is perhaps the most mysterious and exasperating aspect of their nature for anglers to comprehend. Standard hardware and conventional salmon/trout patterns, along with traditional techniques, can be, under most conditions, totally ineffective. Until someone comes up with the magic "plankton fly" that somehow sparks a strike response from deep within the primitive sockeye brain, sport angling for the shyest of salmon will continue to be Alaska's most iffy enterprise, involving a special set of conditions, techniques and fly patterns.

FISHING ALASKA'S SOCKEYE SALMON

Almost all of the state's sport angling for sockeye salmon occurs in streams and rivers, concentrated in areas of greatest abundance, from Southeast to Kuskokwim Bay, but especially Prince William Sound, Kenai Peninsula and Bristol Bay. A limited number are taken in saltwater by salmon trollers, incidentally or with special lures, flies and techniques developed further south in the coastal waters of British Columbia and the Pacific Northwest states. Saltwater flyfishing effort at present is rare or nonexistent. Nearly all the consistent freshwater methods involve specialized techniques with streamer flies, with the exception of fishing for the landlocked, kokanee populations, where certain lures are used.

FRESHWATER METHODS & GEAR

Despite their general non-aggressive nature, sockeye salmon can, under certain conditions, be coaxed to strike. Saltwater commercial trollers, especially in waters down south, have known for years that specially rigged spoons, hoochies (plastic-skirted jig streamers), streamers, and even bare, colored hooks, will draw strikes from red salmon, albeit usually not in great numbers. In some areas of British Columbia and further south, a thriving saltwater sport fishery has developed using streamers of certain pattern and color. In Alaska, however, sockeyes are taken mostly in freshwater, on a variety of enticements. On most rivers, sparsely tied flies of bucktail or yarn in certain colors produce the most results, although in a few areas, spoons, spinners, bait and even colored sponge balls seem to work at times. Though no one seems to have any rational explanation as to why sockeyes will hit certain things in some areas and not in others, there seems to be a consensus, at least for freshwater, of the conditions that are most favorable for eliciting a strike response of some kind.

Conditions

•*Concentration:* Dense fish concentration is perhaps the one factor common to all situations, both in salt and freshwater, where sockeyes routinely hit sport gear. For reasons obvious and obscure, sockeyes are more prone to strike when they're jammed up in great numbers, even though they lack a strong predator response. Since your lure passes in front of many mouths in these conditions, your chances of a take are obviously much greater. There's an undeniable stress factor at work that may prompt a sockeye strike response, whether it be feeding reflex, aggravation or territoriality. Timing your efforts to coincide with the height of the run, the tides or commercial fishing closures, or selecting more prolific locations, are all ways to maximize your chances.

So too is an ability to read water and hone in on better areas. Shallow waters tend to concentrate fish, as do lake outlets and inlets, river mouths, confluences, and structures like waterfalls, channels, rapids and islands.

•*Movement:* Another important aspect common to most good Alaska sockeye water is current of some kind. Despite what you may be inclined to believe, your chances of enticing sockeyes in dead calm water are very slim under most conditions. (Sockeyes will hit at rare times on the edge of sloughs, in lake outlets and river mouths.) Moving fish seem more apt to respond to strike stimuli, for various reasons (aggravation, oxygen stress, reflexive feeding behavior, etc.); they mouth the fly more frequently in swift current, especially when in great concentrations.

•*Water Depth and Clarity:* Because of the effect water depth has on fish concentration, visibility and fly presentation, shallow waters of three feet or less are considered ideal for fishing sockeyes. Water clarity is also important. Clear streams and rivers are preferred, as they allow for sight-fishing and precise casting. Deep, turbid waters should be shunned by the sockeye angler, for obvious reasons.

•*Presentation:* Direct observation of countless sockeyes during river migrations will reveal that under most conditions, it is a rare fish (usually one in a thousand, or less) that breaks rank even slightly for a lure moving above or below it in the water column. Any lure worked at eye level has the most chance of a take, but only for the brief second it passes in front of the fish's mouth, for sockeyes will rarely if ever pursue a lure in freshwater. Unless you have no other options, blind casting for sockeyes should be avoided. Clear water and sight-fishing with tight presentations is the name of the game for the most success.

Flyfishing for Sockeyes

The Comet

Flyfishing for sockeyes in Alaska began in earnest during the 1960s and early 1970s on streams in Katmai and the Kenai Peninsula. The success of trollers working southern waters prompted river anglers to search for sporting ways of catching the feisty reds, which up to that point had been caught almost exclusively by snagging, a practice the

Alaska Department of Fish and Game was soon to ban in freshwater. Experimenting anglers had initial luck in certain rivers using sparsely tied streamer flies of select color and pattern, fished with a modified, tight wet fly swing. Over a period of time, some of these patterns—the Coho (Russian River) Fly, Comet, Sportsman Special, Kenai Fly and others—developed reputations as surefire sockeye slammers, and a new, exciting sportfishery was well on its way.

The question of what patterns and colors work best for sockeye salmon (and why) is something no two Alaska anglers can seem to agree on, but if you observe the action on some of the state's more noted sockeye locales, you'll have to conclude that there are indeed certain patterns that still seem to take a good share of the fish landed. A lot of this, no doubt, comes from familiarity and reputation—what the local shops and "experts" are pushing and/or what happens to be "hot" at the moment. The important thing to remember is the basic principles that seem to work: simply tied, sparse hackle, yarn or buck-tail wing flies in color combinations of yellow, red, chartreuse, orange, pink and white (mostly in sizes #2 to #6). With a little experimenting, it's easy to create your own sockeye standards that outperform the old "tried and trues."

Technique

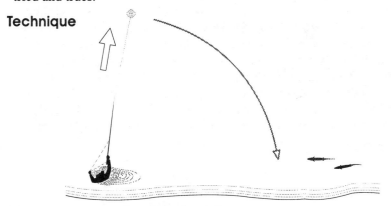

Modified, wet fly swing for sockeye salmon.

Let us imagine the ideal freshwater sockeye salmon fishing location: a stream of gin-clear water, two to three feet deep, with moderately fast current. Thick schools of advancing sockeye salmon pass not far from shore. Here, spin fishermen should rig up with a soft-core sinker, split shot, or pencil lead dropper with a short 18-inch leader, experimenting to find the correct amount of weight to keep the fly at the proper depth (eye level of the sockeyes) for its drift above bottom. Flyfishermen, depending on conditions, should use a sink-tip or floating line, as short a leader/tippet as possible (two to three feet is fine for sinking line), and possibly a split shot or even short section of lead core line for proper depth. Both types of fishermen should cast and retrieve in typical wet fly fashion (as shown in illustration on page 71), quartering upstream so that the fly swings by the noses of sockeyes directly in front or slightly downstream of position.

Once you've determined the right weight to get the fly to fish level and have the basic cast and retrieve down, concentrate on presentation. Keep a taught line at all times (flyfishers use a slight strip) with the fly always swinging past the salmon at eye level. Sockeyes usually aren't too spooky, and you should be able to wade fairly close to them. Make your casts short—15 feet is fine—and work only the stretch of water that lies in the arc 45 degrees above and 45 degrees below your position. A "flipping" technique (borrowed from trout fishing) can be very effective: Use a short length of line and a circular whip of the rod (aided by a sharp downward pull of line through the guides as you begin lifting upward) to lob out for another drift in a fraction of the time it takes for an overhead or side cast. Practice this until it becomes automatic; it's much more efficient and less tiring than regular casting and reeling.

One of the hardest things for beginners to learn is the subtle nature of the sockeye take; it can be very similar to that of a finicky winter steelhead—barely perceptible. Keep a tight line at all times! Any variation in the drift that might signal a connection with a sockeye should be treated as such, with an instant snap of the rod (and downward pull of the line if you've got it in your other hand) to set the hook instantly. Keep your hooks "sticky sharp," using the new, chemically sharpened, forged hooks (Gamakatsu Octopus, Mustad Accu-Point or Tiemco saltwater stainless) for best results.

When you hang a sockeye, you'll know it, as they usually become airborne as soon as they feel the slightest resistance. Drive the steel home and hang on, keeping the rod up at all times to slow the fish down. After some initial spectacular leaps, sockeyes will generally try a rod-ripping run into the main channel. Try to keep the fish out of the strongest currents if possible, and don't hesitate to break one off if it is foul-hooked or hopelessly downriver, as a prolonged battle that exhausts the fish (and your wrist) isn't sensible or desirable, with all the sockeyes available this time of year.

SOCKEYE SALMON

Other Tactics

If you don't have any luck getting them to hit using the technique just outlined, check your depth and presentation carefully. Try different patterns or colors, smaller flies (to size #10), a faster retrieve—even some hardware if everything else fails. Sockeyes will mysteriously go on and off the bite or change preferences for no apparent reason, so you must be flexible and prepared to try different things, even changing locations if necessary. By the way, there are instances where bait, if legal, can be used with good results when all else fails. In the slower, lower sections of some rivers, sockeyes will sometimes pick up balls of roe bounced along the bottom. A split shot about 18 inches in front of a super-sharp, #1/0 egg or steelhead hook, and fresh roe if you can get it, works best. Be warned, however, that this is also a deadly method for hooking king and chum salmon, which run at the same time, so be prepared for *big* surprises!

SALTWATER METHODS & GEAR

Saltwater sport angling for sockeyes has been done only minimally in Alaska, mostly in Southeast by trollers. Using flashers or dodgers rigged in front of small hoochies, spoons, plugs, streamers and even bare, colored hooks, trollers are able to interest sockeyes into striking in some areas, although not with the consistency seen in waters off southern British Columbia. The most productive colors seem to be pink, fluorescent red/orange, blue, green, white and purple. Downriggers, diving planers (Pink Lady), or salmon sinkers (four to eight ounces) are used to reach proper depth, which can vary considerably and is usually determined by trial or with fish locators. The best trolling speed is generally very slow, but varies. Inlets, bays and straits that are associated with abundant sockeye streams are obviously the best areas to concentrate effort on.

For saltwater flycasting, sparse bucktail or bunny hair streamer flies, tied in sizes #2 to #2/0, in colors of pink, orange, green or red, seem to work best. You'll need to locate schools of returning salmon holding in bays and estuaries, then work a streamer through with a light strip, using a saltwater taper, 15-foot sink tip line and short leader. As in freshwater sockeye fishing, you'll have the most success with heavy concentrations of fish and precise presentations of your fly. The most productive areas are Kachemak Bay, Kodiak, Prince William Sound and southern Southeast.

FISHING KOKANEE

To fish Alaska's diminutive, lake-dwelling kokanee, you'll most certainly need a boat, as most kokanee lakes are deep and fish populations are scattered during open water season. In Southeast, home to most all the state's good kokanee water, these fish are taken on a variety of flies, small spoons and spinners, jigs, and even bait. Kokanee rarely reach a pound in weight, so an ultra-light spinning or lightweight fly rod works best. Most are caught incidentally, while angling for more desirable species like cutthroat trout.

As feeders on small aquatic organisms, kokanee will school at various depths and locations through the season. Shorelines, bays, inlets and outlets, drop-offs, and islands are common areas to locate this concentrated activity, with the subdued light of early morning and late evening, or cloudy, breezy days most conducive to surface feeding. Once you locate schools of kokanee, try working a small spoon or spinner (like the Luhr-Jensen #0 Kokanee Special Needlefish, #1 Kokanee King or $1/32$-ounce Panther Martin) in their vicinity, fished right below the surface with an erratic retrieve. Experiment with different color combinations, lures and retrieves until you connect with a fish (keep in mind that kokanee, unlike their saltwater brethren, have soft mouths, so set the hook gently). Flyfishermen should similarly fish small (size #12 to #16) nymph, midge, shrimp or scud patterns, in orange, pink or brown.

If no obvious signs of feeding are present, the best strategy is to troll a spoon or spinner at various depths through likely areas (mentioned above) until fish are located. Begin deep right above bottom and work your way up through the water column until you connect with a feeding kokanee, then stay with that depth and location as long as possible. A fish locator is obviously the way to go for these blind fishing situations. Like saltwater sockeye, kokanee can be extremely finicky and capricious, going off and on the bite without any warning or reason. (They'll sometimes hit only tiny bait-shrimp, maggots, grubs, scuds, etc.) Patience and experimentation are the keys to success.

Equipment

•*Spinning/Casting:* Fishermen who want to use spin or baitcasting gear for sockeyes should equip themselves with a medium-weight, seven- to eight-and-a-half-foot, medium-action salmon or steelhead rod and matching high quality reel. Line used should be a minimum of 150 yards of tough, tournament-quality monofilament, such as Trilene Big Game, Trilene XT, or Maxima, in 12- to 15-pound test.

•*Flyfishing:* Flyfishermen should use a stout seven- or eight-weight graphite rod (nine to ten feet long), a matching, heavy-duty reel with strong drag and sufficient capacity for at least 100 yards of backing, and floating or five-foot sink-tip line. Use a short leader/tippet two to three feet long, of size 2X to 0X (with 10- to 14-pound test).

•*Top Ten Flies for Alaska Sockeyes:* Coho (Russian River) Fly, Comet (orange, pink or chartreuse), Brassie, Sockeye Willie, Kenai Fly (red, pink or chartreuse), San Juan Worm (red or chartreuse), Alaska Mary Ann, Green Butt Skunk, Sportsman Special, Egg-Sucking Leech (all size #2 to #8 hooks).

Alaska's Top Trophy Sockeye Salmon Locations
•Brooks River (Southwest)
•Mulchatna River system (Southwest)
•Lake Iliamna-Kvichak River system (Southwest)
•Agulukpak River (Southwest)
•Kenai River system (Southcentral)

ALASKA'S TOP TEN TROPHY SOCKEYES
16 pounds, 0 ounces, Kenai River (Southcentral), 1974
  (state record)
15 pounds, 11 ounces, Kenai River (Southcentral), 1989
15 pounds, 3 ounces, Kenai River (Southcentral), 1987
  (world record)*
15 pounds, 2 ounces, Brooks River (Southwest), 1993
15 pounds, 0 ounces, Kijik Lake (Southwest), 1980
14 pounds, 12 ounces, Kenai River (Southcentral), 1979
14 pounds, 12 ounces, Koktuli River (Southwest), 1993
14 pounds, 8 ounces, Kenai River (Southcentral), 1973
14 pounds, 8 ounces, Lynn Canal (Southeast), 1974
14 pounds, 8 ounces, Stuyahok River (Southwest), 1978

ALASKA'S MAJOR SOCKEYE SALMON LOCATIONS
Although sockeyes can be taken on sport gear nearly everywhere within their range under the right conditions, the most consistent fishing can be had on clear-flowing streams that receive great concentrations, from Southeast to Kuskokwim Bay. Far and away the best of these are the crystal waters of Bristol Bay and the Alaska Peninsula, where individual runs can number in the millions, and conditions are perfect for flyfishing. The Kenai Peninsula, Kodiak Island and, to a lesser extent, a few other areas in Southcentral are the state's most productive and popular areas for freshwater sport angling.

First and second largest sockeye caught in Alaska were not properly registered with the IGFA to qualify for world record status.

Southeast

Southeast has scattered opportunities that exist mostly in southern Southeast (Petersburg, Prince of Wales, Ketchikan), with quite a few kokanee lakes. The run timing is from June to September, with a peak in July.

•*Yakutat:* Situk, East Alsek and Doame rivers

•*Haines:* Chilkoot and Chilkat river systems

•*Juneau:* Auke and Taku rivers. (Kokanee: Hasselborg, Turner and Florence lakes)

•*Sitka/Petersburg:* Petersburg, Thoms, Sitkoh and Anan creeks; Kah Sheets, Stikine and Sarkar river systems; Sweetwater and Red lake systems; Salmon, Mitchell and Klag bay systems; Virginia Lake and Creek; Lake Eva. (Kokanee: Marten Lake)

•*Ketchikan/Prince of Wales:* Kegan, Karta, Thorne and Naha river systems; Hatchery, Smuggler's, Salmon Bay and Ward creeks; McDonald and Hugh Smith lake systems; Yes Bay. (Kokanee: Orchard, Manzanita, Wilson and Reflection lakes)

Southcentral

Alaska's most heavily utilized fisheries occur here on the Kenai River and tributaries and clearwater tributaries of Susitna and Copper Rivers. The run timing is from June to August, peaking in July.

•*Kenai Peninsula:* Kenai, Russian, Moose, Kasilof rivers. (Kokanee: Hidden Lake)

•*Kachemak Bay:* China Poot Lagoon

•*Cook Inlet:* Susitna River (clearwater tributaries)—Lake Creek, Talachulitna River and Talkeetna River (clear-flowing tributaries); Fish Creek (Big Lake), Jim Creek, Little Susitna River, Big River Lakes, Crescent and Little Kamishak rivers

•*Copper River:* Gulkana River system, Klutina, Tonsina, Tazlina rivers

•*Copper River Delta and Eastern Prince William Sound:* Eyak River, Alaganik Slough, McKinley Lake, Martin River, Clear Creek System (including Tokun Lake), Bering River system (clearwater tributaries)

•*Western Prince William Sound:* Eshamy Lagoon/Lake, Coghill River

•*Kodiak:* Dozens of good sockeye streams, with Southcentral's best flyfishing: Karluk, Buskin, Pasagshak, Saltery, Uganik, Fraser, Upper Station, Afognak, Kaflia, Litnik, Dog Salmon and Red rivers; Portage, Pauls and Malina creeks; Olga Lake system

Southwest

Southwest has the world's most abundant sockeye salmon runs, along with the most perfect conditions for flyfishing, with dozens of great locations. The run timing is from late June to early August, with a peak in July.

•*Bristol Bay:* Lake Iliamna-Kvichak (including Lake Clark and tributaries), Nushagak-Mulchatna (including lower Tikchik Lakes), Togiak, Igushik, Wood (including Wood River Lakes and tributaries) and Alagnak river systems

•*Alaska Peninsula:* Many outstanding possibilities, most seldom fished due to remoteness and weather: Naknek (including all locations in Katmai), Egegik (including Becharof and tributaries), Ugashik, Meshik, Chignik, Nelson Lagoon, Sandy and Bear river systems

•*Kuskokwim:* Goodnews, Arolik and Kanektok river systems

Northwest

The Northwest's fishing opportunities for sockeye are extremely limited, with only scattered occurrences in Norton Sound, and even rarer sightings in Kotzebue Sound. The run timing is from late June to early August, with a peak in July.

•*Norton Sound:* Sinuk, Snake and Pilgrim river systems

•*Kotzebue Sound:* Kelly River (Kelly Lake) of lower Noatak River

Interior

The Interior has no known spawning populations of sockeyes occurring in the Yukon drainage. Kokanee are found in Harding Lake.

4
CHUM SALMON:
BULLDOG BATTLERS

Late June on the lower Kanektok River in Southwest Alaska's Kuskokwim Bay is as good a place as any to sample some of the state's finest stream fishing for salmon. Here, in crystal waters perfect for the fly, you can witness an amazing procession of Pacific salmon in numbers that few rivers this size can match.

Most folks who travel to this world-famous destination this time of year aren't expecting to have their big rods yanked, tweaked or even snapped by a species that some barely consider a sportfish: the chum salmon. But in Alaska, land of surprises, where the obscure, medium-sized salmon is regarded as mere dog food in many places, these coastal waters hold bright, aggressive chums so full of energy and stamina that they frequently outperform the mighty king of salmon, the chinook, much to the amazement of all. Schooled in sloughs along the lower river, these silvery, husky brutes frequently slam flies meant for the big salmon monarchs, and provide fast-paced, incredibly exciting fishing action that has changed more than one fisherman's attitude toward the "lowly" chum. Indeed, after witnessing firsthand the workout a rampaging chum salmon can put a nine- or even a ten-weight through, anglers are apt to forget the great king and concentrate their efforts on the more numerous and sporting "bulldog battler."

INTRODUCTION

Many anglers get to know the humble ocean-fresh chum, *Oncorhynchus keta,* by mistake, and never suspect its true identity, thinking it instead to be a sockeye or silver salmon. The most under-rated of all salmon species, chums are not highly regarded within the angling community for various reasons, none of which are based on truth. When hooked, a bright chum is capable of matching ounce for ounce any battle antics its near relative, the silver salmon, can dish out. They are strong, and when encountered in large numbers, tend to be very aggressive. Rarely performing the aerial ballet of a sockeye salmon, the chum instead will employ tactics more in line with that of a bulldog holding on to a bone—a tug-of-war equalled by none.

DESCRIPTION

Ocean-bright chum salmon are at times difficult to distinguish from fresh red salmon, since both species have dark greenish-blue metallic backs, silvery sides and the same general body shape. However, the chum's belly, in addition to being white, often has an iridescent silvery shine. Also, some of the fins have whitish tips, and the pupil of the eye may appear larger. The wrist of the tail is typically narrower, propor-tionally, than on other salmon. Faint, black specks may be present on the dorsal and adipose fins and back of some specimens.

Spawning chum salmon are calico in color; vertical stripes in flam-ing red, yellow and black are present on the sides, while the head is greenish brown with a touch of golden yellow on the cheeks. Males de-velop a hooked jaw with a series of large, protruding teeth which par-tially accounts for their nickname, "dog" salmon. Females have a dark horizontal band along the lateral line and are generally not as colorful. The pectoral, anal and pelvic fins all have whitish tips.

Chum salmon fresh from the sea have a flesh color of light orange, which in some populations may be closer to red. Like pink salmon, chums are not prized table fare, due to the rapid deterioration of the flesh as the fish close in on spawning grounds. However, they are ex-tremely important both as a commercial and subsistence species, and they are becoming increasingly popular as sportfish. The flesh is excel-lent eating on bright fish fresh from the sea.

Second largest of the Pacific salmon, chums have been known to at-tain weights of 30 to 40 pounds and lengths to three feet in certain lo-cations. Averaging 5 to 10 pounds, occasionally more, any fish over 15 pounds is considered very large in most areas of Alaska, with South-east consistently producing the heaviest specimens (20-plus pounds). Fish of exceptional size are also reported from parts of Northwest.

RANGE, ABUNDANCE & STATUS

Of all species of Pacific salmon, the chum has the widest natural geographic distribution. It is found from South Korea and the island of Kyushu in the Sea of Japan up along the coast of Siberia and over into Alaska, and from there south along the coast to Monterey, California. In the Arctic Ocean, chum salmon are present from the Lena River in Russia to at least the Mackenzie River in the Northwest Territories. Chums have also been planted in arctic Russia's White Sea, with reports of strays in the North Atlantic of northern Europe. Throughout its range in North America, chum salmon are rarely encountered in any abundance south of the Columbia River and are most plentiful in Alaska.

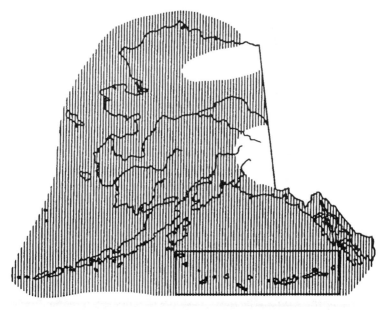

Shaded area shows range of chum salmon in Alaska.

Within Alaska, the chum salmon is known to appear along the entire coastline, being especially abundant from Dixon Entrance below Ketchikan north to Point Hope above Kotzebue. Major populations occur in every region of the state except the Arctic. Even Interior has large runs—the Yukon River produces numbers fluctuating between two and nine million, possibly more in some years. Major commercial and subsistence fisheries exist in areas of Southeast, Prince William Sound, Kodiak Island, Cook Inlet, Bristol Bay, Kuskokwim and Yukon Rivers and Kotzebue Sound.

Usually found within 50 miles of saltwater, some populations commit extensive migrations: Chum salmon swim up the Yukon River through the entire state of Alaska into Canada to reach their spawning grounds near the Yukon-British Columbia border—an incredible distance of over 2,000 miles.

Of all the Pacific salmon in Alaska, chums have been the least utilized, except in specific areas of Northwest and Interior where they are an important and traditional source of food. Though often viewed as nothing more than potential dog food by many users, chums are rapidly gaining recognition for their value as a commercial and sport species. Stocking programs have become quite widespread in certain areas of Southcentral and Southeast to benefit commercial fishing fleets.

LIFE HISTORY & HABITS

Starting in spring and continuing through summer into fall, mature chum salmon begin migrating through the clear, blue waters of the Pacific Ocean and Gulf of Alaska towards their riverine places of origin. Age of the returning fish varies between two and five years (the average is three), with some northern populations as old as six or seven years. Nearing inshore waters, the fish begin to congregate in schools or runs, according to which river they are bound for. The exact time of arrival is influenced by many factors, but is usually from midsummer to early fall, with older fish appearing earlier than younger fish.

Once in close vicinity of freshwater, chums begin a period of milling that may last from a few days (if spawning areas are far up inland rivers) to several weeks (when spawning occurs in intertidal stretches of streams or vicinity). The period of milling becomes shorter as the spawning season progresses. Entrance up chosen drainages concurs with high tides and often with rising water levels, such as after a heavy rain.

Runs peak from early July to early September in most of Alaska. The time of entrance, however, extends from early May to mid-December, depending greatly on geographic location (runs generally occur earlier to the north and progressively later to the south). Runs called "early" and "late" locally are usually the "summer" and "fall" runs described by biologists.

Reluctant to ford barriers of any significance, chums are predominantly found in shallow rivers and creeks, one to three feet deep, with clean gravel bottoms and moderate current flow. As a rule, glacial or heavily silted waters are not preferred for reproduction but commonly serve as migration corridors for fish bound for clearwater tributaries. There are exceptions to this rule, however. In Southeast, Southcentral and Interior, a few populations of fall-run chums spawn in mainstem glacial rivers late in the season as cooling temperatures halt the flow of silt from meltwater.

Early-run spawners are known to utilize mainstems of deep, fast flowing rivers and streams where the colder temperatures require longer time for egg incubations and juvenile growth, while late-run chums commonly spawn in shallower, slower-flowing spring water that has more favorable temperatures through the winter and thus allows shorter incubation time and higher growth rates among offspring. There are also more subtle differences between the two races of fish, both physiological and behavioral.

Spawning peaks during periods of falling temperatures from August to October throughout most of the range, but may proceed as early as July or as late as February in some locations. Similar to pink salmon, intertidal spawning of chums is widespread in many areas (mostly Southcentral and Southeast). Chum eggs are comparatively larger than those of the other salmon, and an average female can carry between 2,000 and 4,000. Eggs hatch sometime in winter and early spring; soon after (April to June), the young fry migrate directly to sea, much like pink salmon. Feeding on a variety of small organisms like plankton, crustaceans and crab larvae, young chums eventually switch to a mixed diet that includes small fish. Size increase is greatest during the first three years of ocean life, slowing after age four. Due to the genetic variability among stocks and habitat, chums from different areas differ in growth rate, age at maturity and ultimate size.

FRESHWATER METHODS & GEAR

It is important to dispel the myth that chum salmon will seldom strike in freshwater. Not only will these fish strike lures and flies, but they will do so as readily as a king or silver under the right conditions. The trick is to find the right water.

The Right Water

The best water to consistently hook chum salmon is two to three feet deep, with moderate to fast current, and clear with perhaps just a slight tint of glacial green or turbidity. Lures and flies should be fished near or along bottom, and allowed to tumble or drift through pools, runs, sloughs, under cutbanks, etc.—any prime holding areas for migrating chum salmon. Although there are times when chums will strike under nearly any conditions, the situations to avoid are extremely shallow and clear waters, or deeply turbid or glacial streams (except for situations described that follow).

Many an angler who has fished for silver or red salmon during late summer and early fall is familiar with the chum in its splendid glory of calico colors. These spawners are usually quite aggressive, and can even be a nuisance when encountered in large numbers—especially when other, more desirable species are around (like coho or rainbows). But few anglers who have fished around Alaska will argue that the chum, when fresh in on the tide, chrome-flanked and full of sea lice, isn't every bit the equal in sport of his cousins that get all the attention. Surprisingly, many anglers claim never to have encountered a chum in this condition in freshwater. The fact is, they are fairly common in lower rivers, but are almost always misidentified as silver or red salmon.

The brightest fish and best action for the species occurs in early summer in the major coastal drainages, the closer to salt the better. As chums like the intertidal zone and lower reaches of rivers, you'll encounter aggressive hordes in holding areas there during the peak of immigration (usually late June through early August). Kodiak Island, Southcentral's Susitna drainage, the Alaska Peninsula, Bristol and Kuskokwim bays and countless areas throughout Southeast all offer some of the best conditions possible for these feisty, early-run river chums. Changing into spawning colors quickly, these chums will lose a little of their zip and aggressiveness further up into freshwater, but they still can provide some abundant and exciting fishing in holding water, often in company with sockeye and king salmon.

Large, glacial watersheds can provide prime locations to intercept chums destined for clear headwater tributaries. Dime-bright fish can be taken out of the mouths of streams up to 40 or 50 miles or more from the sea, with a few populations staying reasonably fresh even after several hundred miles. These fish are genetically programmed to stay brighter longer than stocks spawning lower in the river!

The Right Lure

The best lures for river chums are large ($\frac{1}{2}$-ounce or bigger) spoons like Pixees, Hot Rods and Krocodiles in silver, brass or gold with orange, green or red highlights; large Vibrax or Mepps spinners (#4 to #6) in silver, gold, "firetiger," red or orange blades (and/or bells); and medium large (#2) Spin-N-Glos in orange, red, yellow or silver. A wide range of flies can be used under most conditions to successfully stimulate a strike response—flash flies, attractors, egg patterns, leeches and specialty patterns like the Alaskabou and Outrageous, in sizes #1/0 to #6. Fish them deep, with short, erratic strips, for best results. Quite often in glacial or turbid waters, the use of roe is common practice for fishing chums, either alone or as a sweetener on lures like Spin-N-Glos. Drifted along bottom, these scent-emitting enticements are deadly when all else fails.

Whereas kings and silvers and to some degree also pinks will attack hardware out of a basic feeding and aggravation response, chums seem to hit more out of aggravation alone, and will frequently pursue lures for short distances, nabbing as they go. Spot casting can usually be both exciting and very rewarding, as fish can be prompted to strike with repeat casts. Chums rarely hit with the authority of a hungry trout or charr; usually the take is more of a bump than anything. Anglers must be on the alert and ready to respond with a powerful hook set, as these fish, like all salmon, have very hard jaws. Super-sharp hooks are a necessity. Once hooked, chums will react instantly with powerful bulldog runs and frequent leaps in a remarkable display of strength and will. Fish of full nuptial maturity, as mentioned earlier, are very prone to strike lures out of territorial aggression, and should be avoided for obvious reasons.

GEARING UP FOR FRESHWATER CHUMS
Spinning
A six- to seven-foot, medium-action, light- to medium-weight salmon rod, with a matching, high quality reel loaded with tournament-grade 8- to 12-pound test line is preferred for Alaska's chum salmon. Heavier gear is used for difficult stream conditions or saltwater (use 15- to 20-pound test). Because of the prominent, razor-sharp teeth that chums develop once in freshwater, a shock leader of at least 20-pound test is recommended, which should be inspected frequently for wear. Needlenose pliers or vice grips are definitely recommended for hook releases.

The best lures are medium-sized ($^1/_2$-ounce to $^7/_8$-ounce) spoons or spinners in green, blue and silver with bright orange, red and yellow highlights: Pixee, Krocodile, Little Cleo, Dardevle, Hot Rod, Syclops, Mepps, Vibrax, Bang Tail and Rooster Tail. Drift bobbers and plugs in colors of orange, red, yellow and silver are also used.

Flyfishing
A stout seven- or eight-weight rod, nine- to ten-and-a-half feet long, with complementary reel, and matching floating sink tip and high-density sink lines, along with 8- to 12-pound test tippet is recommended. Heavier setups (nine-weight rod and 15-pound tippet) are required for strong current. Tippet/leader length should be short, about four feet or less.

•*Top Fly Patterns for Freshwater:* Comet, Boss, Polar Shrimp, Flash Fly, Mickey Finn, Orange/White Wiggletail, Coho, Alaskabou, Outrageous, Egg-Sucking Leech, Alaska Mary Ann, Woolly Bugger, Teeny Nymph.

•*Top Fly Patterns for Saltwater:* Herring Fly, Clouser Minnow, Deceiver, Candlefish, Sandlance.

Saltwater Fishing for Chums

Chum and red salmon seem to have a common trait whenever encountered at sea—they both are reluctant to strike anglers' offerings. In much of the popular literature, the finicky nature of the "salty dog" is described, with little or no explanation why and even less offered as to what can be done to remedy the situation. In some accounts, "snagging" is given as the only legitimate harvest method! But for an angler wishing to square off with these brutes in an honest, sporting way, there certainly are other options to consider.

Anglers trolling or mooching for salmon every now and then hook into chums incidentally—that much is true. However, these anglers are targeting kings, silvers and pinks with the appropriate lures and methods for those particular species. What must be realized is that chum (and red) salmon are not primary fish predators (the major part of their diet consists of various forms of plankton, although small fish and squid are preyed upon to a certain extent). Were they rapacious fish gluttons like the coho, they obviously would swallow a plug-cut herring without hesitation and assault large, rotating spoons or spinners with a vengeance.

The key to successful saltwater chum fishing is concentration and natural presentation. Do not look for hot angling in wide open, offshore areas. Chums out at sea have generally not schooled up yet, and, given their feeding habits, are extremely hard to fish, unlike silvers or even feeder kings that can sometimes be found in tight concentrations working bait patches. Usually, greatest success with the species will be inshore, around estuaries, off beaches, and in bays associated with major spawning streams. When fish are stacked up in dense masses, with some rolling or even jumping on the surface, conditions are ideal. All that is needed is the appropriate "jawbreaker."

Large, flashy spoons and spinners can trigger a response in these tidewater chums, particularly the large males. Best colors seem to be silver/blue prism, silver/green prism, gold/orange and yellow/green. As some anglers have already discovered, these fish can also be worked with exciting results using flies resembling plankton or small baitfish, stripped through schools of fish in short, erratic bursts. Herring, candlefish and smolt patterns in blue/green/silver/white have proven highly effective. A touch of attractor orange, pink or red seems to liven the response.

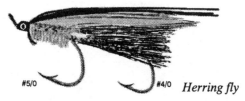

Herring fly

Still in its infancy, saltwater fishing for chums is wide open for exploration and discovery. Kodiak and Southeast have almost infinite possibilities for inshore angling of chums, which are neglected for the pursuit of more glamorous fish like the coho or king. Prospective anglers should strive to know the chum's habits and responses in its natural environment—and go from there with experimentation and intuition.

ALASKA'S TOP TEN TROPHY CHUM SALMON

32 pounds, 0 ounces, Caamano Point (Southeast), 1985
   (state and world record)
28 pounds, 2 ounces, Caamano Point (Southeast), 1985
28 pounds, 0 ounces, Boca de Quadra (Southeast), 1991
27 pounds, 9 ounces, Jackpot Bay Creek (Southeast), 1989
27 pounds, 8 ounces, Behm Canal (Southeast), 1990
27 pounds, 3 ounces, Behm Narrows (Southeast), 1977
25 pounds, 6 ounces, Island Point (Southeast), 1985
25 pounds, 0 ounces, Behm Narrows (Southeast), 1983
25 pounds, 0 ounces, Herring Cove (Southeast), 1982
25 pounds, 0 ounces, Caamano Point (Southeast), 1991

ALASKA'S MAJOR CHUM SALMON LOCATIONS

Southeast

Southeast has outstanding fishing for both salt and freshwater, with some of Alaska's largest chums taken from select areas. The run timing is from July to October, peaking from late July to early August.

•*Yakutat:* East Alsek River

•*Juneau:* Cross Sound, Icy Strait, Stephens Passage; Chilkat River; Fish and Cowee creeks

•*Sitka:* Sitka Sound, Mitchell Bay system, Katlian River

•*Petersburg/Wrangell:* Stephens Passage; Castle, Kah Sheets, Eagle and Harding rivers; Kadake, Petersburg, Ohmer, Red Lake, Falls, Irish,

North Arm and Thoms creeks

•*Ketchikan:* Behm Canal and Gravina Island/Tongass Narrows; Sarkar, Unuk, Klawock and Karta rivers; Fish Creek

Southcentral

Southcentral has some outstanding fishing, mostly on Kodiak, Prince William Sound, Susitna tributaries and upper Cook Inlet. The run timing is from July through early August, with a peak in mid-July through early August.

•*Susitna:* Little Susitna, Deshka, Talachulitna and Talkeetna rivers; Alexander, Willow, Little Willow, Goose, Sheep, Caswell, Montana, Lake and Jim creeks

•*Kenai:* Kachemak Bay; Chuitna River; Silver Salmon Creek

•*Kodiak:* American and Dog Salmon rivers; Roslyn, Salonie and Russian creeks

•*Chugach:* Resurrection Bay, Valdez Arm, Knight Island, Wells Passages

Southwest

Southwest has some of Alaska's most abundant stream fishing, with perfect conditions for sight fishing and flyfishing. There are dozens of outstanding locations here, often with great concurrent action for king and sockeye salmon. The run timing is from late June through July, with a peak in the first two weeks of July.

•*Bristol Bay:* Nushagak (includes Mulchatna and Nuyakuk), Wood, Igushik, Togiak and Kvichak rivers

•*Alaska Peninsula:* Ugashik Lake system; Egegik, Naknek and Alagnak rivers; Izembek-Moffet Bay streams; Russel Creek, Belkofski Bay River, Canoe Bay River, Stepovak Bay streams

•*Kuskokwim:* Goodnews, Kanektok, Aniak and Holitna rivers

•*Lower Yukon:* Andreafsky and Anvik rivers

Northwest

Northwest has some outstanding but little-fished opportunities throughout the region, primarily in eastern Norton and Kotzebue Sounds. The run timing is July and August, with a peak in the first part of July.

•*Eastern Norton Sound:* Unalakleet, Shaktoolik, Ungalik, Inglutalik, Tubutulik rivers

•*Seward Peninsula:* Fish-Niukluk, Fox and Kwiniuk rivers

•*Kotzebue Sound:* Kobuk, Noatak and Wulik rivers

Interior

Interior has abundant fish runs, but the fish are in less than prime condition because of their great distance from the sea. The Yukon River is North America's prime producer. Many areas are possible for sportfishing, including all river mouths along the Yukon and Tanana rivers. The run timing is from July through mid-September and into October.

•*Yukon River:* Nulato, Nowitna and Chandalar rivers

•*Tanana River:* Salcha, Chatanika and Delta Clearwater rivers

•*Nenana River:* Julius and Clear creeks

•*Koyukuk River:* Gisasa, Hogatza, South Fork, Dakli and Jim rivers

•*Porcupine:* Sheenjek, Coleen and Black rivers

Chum salmon

5
PINKS:
THE HUMPBACK SALMON

If you visit any of Alaska's major coastal rivers in late summer for silver salmon and trout, you must be prepared to encounter another fish that can quite literally steal the show: a diminutive brawler that floods estuaries and lower rivers with his kind in some years and pounces without hesitation on nearly every offering flung into the water—the pink, or humpback, salmon.

Rather than curse him, as some anglers do, for his unceasing interference and often strange looks—a gnarlish caricature of a salmon with a grotesque hump and pinched jaws—you may wisely decide to enjoy the abundant sport this spunky little fellow has to offer. Partial to bright flies, small spoons and spinners, these smallest of salmon can provide endless hours of diversion and additional highlights to Alaska's mixed bag of late-summer fishing excitement.

INTRODUCTION

One of the most delightful light-tackle gamefish found in Alaska's coastal waters is the pink salmon (*Oncorhynchus gorbuscha*). Although hampered by persistent rumors concerning their sporting abilities as well as edibility (or lack thereof), pinks have nonetheless stood the test of time and today enjoy a growing interest among anglers who have learned to recognize the fine qualities of these feisty little salmon.

Catch them in the prime of their life, at sea or intertidal areas of clearwater streams, and prepare to witness firsthand a fishery of magnitude and intensity never before imagined. A very prolific member of the Pacific salmon clan, pinks quite often outnumber their larger brethren. When encountered by the tens of thousands, the water seemingly boils with activity, in an experience that can trigger mixed emotions—awe and humility. Surrounded by countless dime-bright, three- to five-pound fish swarming in a seething mass of heads, tails and fins, one can only begin to comprehend the importance of this species within the ecosystems of coastal Alaska. Angling for these playful fish and the nonstop action they provide touches close to the essence of Alaska.

DESCRIPTION

When encountered fresh from the sea, the pink salmon is a sleek and slender fish displaying a dark blue or green back, silvery sides and white belly. Faint oval-shaped spots cover the back and both lobes of the tail fin. Due to their size, bright pinks are sometimes misidentified as jack king salmon.

Spawning fish appear dirty brown with sides of mottled, yellowish green. Males develop a distinctive humped back (hence its popular name, "humpback") and an elongated hooked snout. Females generally retain their seagoing shape. Large, black oval markings are scattered about on the back and are especially prominent on both tail lobes. The belly and lower jaw is creamy white to yellowish white.

The flesh of bright, sea-run pink salmon is an orange to a slight pink hue and of moderately soft texture. It is not much sought-after by most anglers, since pinks have a tendency to change from the ocean phase to spawning phase during a short period of time, often even before entering freshwater. But when caught fresh and bright from the sea, the pink makes good table fare. Pink salmon are an important species within the commercial fishing industry and comprise the bulk of Alaska's canned salmon.

The smallest members of the Pacific salmon family, the pinks' size range is rather uniform and varies little from one watershed to another. Typically averaging only three to five pounds in weight (20 to 25 inches in length), the pink salmon seldom exceeds seven or eight pounds throughout its range. However, a few rivers and streams produce larger specimens that may approach 10 or 12 pounds or more. Throughout the state, it is interesting to observe that odd-year pinks tend to be slightly heavier than even-year fish, except for Alaska Peninsula. Trophy pinks are usually taken from certain areas of Southeast and Southcentral.

PINK SALMON

RANGE, ABUNDANCE & STATUS

The pink salmon is without a doubt the most abundant of all salmon species (comprising 60 percent in numbers and 40 percent in weight of the commercial catch in the North Pacific) and ranges from Sacramento, California north to the Bering Strait and along the coast of Siberia as far south as northern Japan and North Korea. Transplant projects involving pink salmon have put the species in such remote locations as northern Europe and Russia, parts of South America, and the east coast of the United States and Canada.

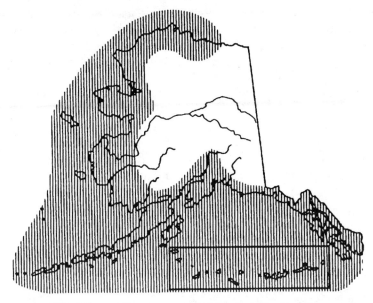

Shaded area shows range of pink salmon in Alaska.

In Alaska, pink salmon are considered abundant from Dixon Entrance below Ketchikan north to Point Hope above Kotzebue, with sporadic occurrences around Point Barrow in the Arctic Ocean to the Mackenzie River delta in the Northwest Territories.

Major pink salmon populations are found in the multitude of island streams in Southeast and Prince William Sound, coastal Blying Sound, Kodiak Island, Cook Inlet, Bristol Bay, the lower Yukon and Kuskokwim rivers and Norton Sound. Seldom do pinks move far upriver, and they usually spawn within 50 miles of the coast. However, they are occasionally found as far inland as Ruby on the Yukon River (about 350 miles from the sea), with unconfirmed reports of fish in Fairbanks area streams.

Intense stocking efforts by various private hatcheries have created "terminal" fisheries in many parts of the state, mostly to benefit commercial interests.

LIFE HISTORY & HABITS

Coastal offshore areas begin to see pinks returning from Gulf of Alaska feeding grounds in late spring. Runs are typically strong by midsummer in inshore waters and continue to arrive until early fall, concentrating in huge schools according to which spawning stream they belong. During the final homeward migration, the fish feed heavily and significantly increase in growth and distance travelled.

Unlike other Pacific salmon, pinks have a fixed lifespan of about two years (18 months, to be exact). One- or three-year-olds are rarely found. Fish planted in lakes as landlocked stocks have demonstrated higher deviance in age variation than sea-run populations. Thus, even-year and odd-year fish do not mix and are considered two quite distinct genetic stocks.

Nearing freshwater, a period of "milling" commences which may last up to several weeks until full maturity, in some instances, if spawning beds are situated in intertidal areas or near saltwater. However, this milling period may be no longer than a few days if the fish are committed to an extensive migration through a major river to reach headwater streams where they will reproduce. There is no milling after pinks have attained full maturity. Sharp increases or decreases in stream volume or temperature regulate migration into freshwater.

Pink salmon runs typically appear in midsummer to late summer to spawn in fast-flowing coastal rivers and streams. Runs tend to peak during July and August throughout most of the range, but bright pinks may be present in freshwater anytime between early June and late October, depending on location, area and region. Similar to other salmon species, runs with varying peaks are distributed by geographic zones associated with different temperature regimes. Males tend to appear earlier than females, and when pinks are large, run timing is earlier.

Many regions of the state have stronger runs of pinks on even-numbered years, with smaller returns on odd-numbered years. However, the trend may be reversed in some areas or even nonexistent in others. In addition, the resilience of pink populations can be demonstrated by weak runs rebounding to strong runs in only one or two generations.

Not adept at leaping waterfalls or negotiating even short stretches of high-velocity current flow, these small salmon are much more prone to spawn in lower areas of rivers and creeks. During abnormally strong runs with high spawner density, pinks tend to migrate further upstream than in normal years. "Straying" is particularly common among artificial runs of pink salmon, but is otherwise relatively low to almost nonexistent in natural populations.

Spawning typically peaks in August and September throughout Alaska, with a few populations beginning as early as July or as late as November. One of the reasons why these salmon are so abundant almost everywhere they are found is that they can spawn in almost any conditions, from mere trickles of water up to large rivers. However, their general preference is for shallow (five inches to three feet deep), moderate-flowing, clearwater streams with clean gravel substrate. Waters with mud-covered bottoms, slow or no current, and deep, quiet pools are avoided. The low-light hours see the most active spawning, with size of males and females defining an assortative mating hierarchy. Up to five males may spawn with one female and males with more than one female.

Utilization of intertidal areas for reproduction purposes is a very common feature with pinks, especially in parts of Southcentral and Southeast, since pink eggs can withstand a high degree of salinity. In some coastal streams, as much as 75 percent or more of spawning takes place in tidal areas, with spawners returning to their redds after the tide recedes and current resumes.

A female pink may deposit anywhere between 1,100 and 2,300 eggs in several nests, guarding the area from ten days up to three weeks. About 50 percent of the eggs are lost during spawning due to predators or, as is the case when spawning density is very high, suffocation. The eggs hatch in late winter and, after a brief stay in freshwater, the juvenile salmon move out into the sea in spring (April to May). For the first couple of months, the pink fry remain within a few miles of the stream mouth and are preyed upon heavily by other fishes, including silver salmon smolts. The growing pinks feed on a variety of small organisms, such as larval fishes, plankton and occasionally insects, eventually switching to a diet of small fishes as size increases. High seas pinks are suspended at a depth between 30 and 120 feet, may travel vast expanses during their stay (3,000 to 4,000 miles), and suffer a marine mortality of nearly 97 percent, most of which occur during the first few months of life.

FISHING ALASKA'S PINK SALMON
Saltwater Fishing for Pinks

There are times when it seems pink salmon will hit anything that moves through the water. There are also those times when they appear to be shy and very reluctant to strike at any lure. One might say that such is the way of the salmon, but it is always interesting (and often very rewarding) to study in more detail the habits of these fish and what will work under certain conditions.

It is fairly common to hook pink salmon during the summer and fall months while trolling or mooching for other species like silvers. These small salmon, when encountered in heavy concentrations, can sometimes be a nuisance because of their aggressiveness; yet there are moments when the bite is off and every lure in the tacklebox won't get as much as a single strike. The type of water sometimes plays a huge role in saltwater pink fishing, and knowing exactly what kind of lure to use under various conditions is the trick. And, of course, concentration is another very important factor.

The typical diet of an adult, sea-run pink usually consists of small baitfish and plankton. A medium-sized, flashy spoon is without a doubt an all-time favorite lure among anglers in coastal regions. Needless to say, they do not always work, but then again, what does? Quite recently, a few anglers began experimenting with alternative lures, imitating the food of pink salmon. They came up with great results, proving that herring, sculpin and smolt pattern flies (Black-Nosed Dace and Blue Smolt) in green or blue are effective in clear or semi-clear waters wherever large concentrations of pinks can be found.

Due to their often staggering numbers, it is possible to experience good action for pinks in most coastal areas; but the most consistent pink fishing is to be had in bays and coves with clearwater spawning streams in the immediate vicinity. These fish have a habit of "milling" around in big schools near freshwater outlets and are commonly spotted porpoising not far from shore. Incoming and high tides are generally the best times to try surfcasting, as the movement of ocean currents puts the fish in a migrational mode and forces them closer to shore. At low tide, look for pinks further offshore where they are primarily reached by boat.

In crystal-clear waters, salmon sometimes have a tendency to spook, and with pinks it is no different. Small spoons, spinners and flies in silver with a touch of dark, neutral colors such as blue and green work well under such conditions. Avoid very large, flashy lures in fluorescent orange, chartreuse and red. Although such spectacular high-visibility lures may produce fish at times, they are much more useful in glacially influenced waters. A cut piece of herring suspended beneath a bobber is a trick many anglers enjoy and fishes well in clear and semi-clear coastal waters.

Freshwater Fishing for Pinks

The world of angling does not have much to equal the fast and frenzied light tackle action possible when fishing freshwater pinks. In many parts of the range, their abundance can be truly awesome; a fish on every cast is not at all unusual. Coastal streams in particular receive heavy runs of beautiful pinks, and should definitely be the focus of attention for the highest quality fishing.

Like chum salmon, pinks or "humpies" are very underrated among the majority of anglers. It certainly is not because of a lack of fish or their finicky feeding habits. At times they are so plentiful and aggressive one would be hard put not to catch them. The main impediment to their acceptance is probably the grotesque appearance they develop when in full spawning phase, especially males with their snarly jaws and humped backs. Few anglers would recognize a sleek and slender dime-bright pink full of spunk straight out of the blue Pacific Ocean. They are frequently mistaken for jack kings, small silvers and even Dolly Varden.

Another myth is that pinks are poor sportfish and do not give anglers the exhilarating fight commonly associated with other salmon species. Well, the majority of anglers with these opinions have not had the chance to hook into a sea-run pink on ultra-light gear with four-pound test line. Since these little salmon only average three to four pounds, who would expect them to perform like great sportfish on tackle intended for much larger reds or silvers? Gear down appropriately and get ready for a showdown not soon forgotten.

The best places to find chrome-bright pink salmon are in coastal rivers and streams. Since pinks commonly spawn in lower reaches of most drainages and within a week to ten days turn into full nuptial maturity, it is vital that anglers serious about catching quality fish head straight to intertidal areas and deep holes and runs immediately above. Large glacial systems that force pinks to migrate extensive distances to reach spawning beds can yield silvery specimens at the mouth of tributaries some 40 or 50 miles from saltwater. In contrast, small and shallow creeks may never see anything other than full-fledged spawners, as the fish usually mill around off the stream mouth until ripe and ready. So, in other words, pick a location with at least a fair amount of volume in addition to a few feet of depth, with water preferably clear or semi-clear, and a moderate current flow.

Another thing to strive for is finding fresh pinks in the early stages of a run. With few exceptions, when a typical drainage peaks in terms of numbers of fish present, it usually means that the best is already over. As discussed above, these salmon change into spawning mode quickly, often while still in saltwater, and many, if not most, will arrive ripe during what would otherwise be the high point of the season. The general period of availability for pinks is relatively short compared with kings, silvers and reds. It lasts a total of about four to six weeks, with the second or third week producing the freshest fish.

Try to avoid using oversized lures for pinks. Although they may be very aggressive towards these lures at times when conditions are right, truly outstanding action can be expected using small spoons and spinners in neutral colors (green, blue, silver, bronze) in waters with high visibility, and bright, fluorescent colors (red, orange, chartreuse) in semi-glacial or low-visibility locations. The larger sizes tend to do better under difficult conditions, such as when fishing streams high with brown runoff from heavy rains, during twilight hours, or in greenish-grey meltwater as in glacially-influenced drainages. Medium-sized chartreuse and silver combination lures work well in glacial waters. Much the same goes for flies as for hardware.

Pinks seem to be "on the bite" more often in rivers and creeks that have a fairly rapid flow and at least two to three feet of water. As with most salmon, all lures, including flies, should be fished near or right above bottom for best results. Holding areas such as deep holes, runs and pools are great for finding schools of waiting pinks. Although one may spot a lot of fish in spawning condition in shallower areas, it is a fact that the brighter (and larger) specimens are usually caught from the deeper sections of a stream.

In very slow and still waters, pink salmon can be considerably more difficult to catch, especially under bright, clear conditions. Anglers trying small, dark lures and flies do best. A slow, erratic retrieve is warranted. Flyfishers should strip their flies in short bursts. However, if the water is a bit on the greenish glacial side, slightly larger lures may be necessary and the colors less neutral with more accent towards visibility. Fish tend to respond more readily to anglers' offerings in such drainages.

Spin Gear/Tackle

Ultra-light six- to seven-and-a-half-foot rods, fast-action, with matching reels and four- to six-pound test line are the preferred setups for the best sport with pink salmon, but heavier tackle is used in areas with strong current or when surfcasting.

For lures, use small, flashy spoons and spinners in color combinations of silver, gold, green, blue, black, red, orange and chartreuse (Pixee, Krocodile, Little Cleo, Syclops, Dardevle, Vibrax, Mepps, Rooster Tail and Bang Tail).

Fly Gear/Tackle

Flyfishermen prefer a five- to six-weight rod (eight-and-a-half to nine-and-a-half feet) for pinks, matched with a suitable reel and either floating or sink tip line. Tippets are generally four- to eight-pound test, no more than four feet long for sinking presentations.

Fly Patterns for Pinks

The most effective flies have a bit of flash and/or attractor color: Comet, Boss, Polar Shrimp, Flash Fly, Kispioux Special, Thor, Alaska-bou, Blue Smolt, Coho, Egg-Sucking Leech and Black-Nosed Dace.

ALASKA'S TOP TEN TROPHY PINK SALMON

12 pounds, 9 ounces, Moose River (Southcentral), 1974
(state record)
12 pounds, 4 ounces, Kenai River (Southcentral), 1974
11 pounds, 14 ounces, Shelter Island (Southeast), 1980
11 pounds, 8 ounces, Montana Creek (Southeast), 1973
11 pounds, 7 ounces, Chilkoot River (Southeast), 1983
11 pounds, 6 ounces, Coghill Lake (Southcentral), 1977
11 pounds, 6 ounces, Biorka Island (Southeast), 1969
11 pounds, 4 ounces, Chilkoot River (Southeast), 1981
11 pounds, 0 ounces, Kenai River (Southcentral), 1984
10 pounds, 8 ounces, Tongass Narrows (Southeast), 1977

ALASKA'S MAJOR PINK SALMON LOCATIONS

It would be difficult indeed to find a coastal stream that does not have a population of pink salmon, since this species has a habit of invading just about any type of water more than two or three feet wide and four or five inches deep. However, to experience the best fishing possible for the brightest fish, look for rivers and streams of at least moderate width and depth, near saltwater.

Southeast

Southeast has tremendous opportunities for pinks, given the multitude of coastal clearwater streams. The saltwater action is almost unparalleled. The run timing is from mid-July through mid-August.

•*Yakutat:* Situk River

•*Juneau:* Cross Sound, Icy Strait, Lynn Canal, Stephens Passage, Favorite/Saginaw channels; Chilkat and Chilkoot rivers; Montana, Turner, Auke and Cowee creeks

•*Sitka:* Sitka Sound and Chatham and Peril straits; Nakwasina and Katlian rivers; Lake Eva and Sitkoh creeks; Mitchell Bay system

•*Petersburg/Wrangell:* Wrangell Narrows/Duncan Canal, Stephens and Eastern passages, Ernest and Frederick sounds; Clarence, Sumner and Zimovia straits; Kah Sheets, Eagle and Castle rivers; Hamilton, Gunnuck, Bear (Big), Irish, Andrew, Aaron, Anan, Red Lake, Thoms, Petersburg, Ohmer, Falls, Pat, Fools, Ketili, Government, St. John, Oerns, Marten, North Arm, Snake, Kunk, Porcupine and Kadake creeks

•*Ketchikan:* Behm Canal, Revillagigedo Channel, Gulf of Esquibel, Bucareli Bay, Gravina Island, Clarence Strait; Sarkar, Klawock, Harris, Thorne, Karta, Naha, Unuk, Kegan, Wilson and Blossom rivers; Ward, Wolverine, Ketchikan and Whipple creeks

Southcentral

Southcentral's Cook Inlet and Kodiak offer top freshwater angling for bright, sea-run pinks, while Prince William Sound enjoys some of the best ocean fisheries for the species statewide. The run timing is from July into early August.

•*Susitna:* Talkeetna, Deshka, Talachulitna, Little Susitna and Theodore rivers; Willow, Little Willow, Sheep, Montana, Alexander, Goose, Caswell and Lake creeks

•*Kenai-Cook Inlet:* Lower Cook Inlet and Kachemak Bay; Kenai, Anchor, Ninilchik, Chuitna, Seldovia, Windy Left, Windy Right, Bruin Bay, Kamishak, Amakdedori, Little Kamishak and Rocky rivers; Deep, Stariski, Brown's Peak, Humpy, Port Dick, Bird, Sunday and Resurrection creeks

•*Kodiak:* Shuyak Island; Uyak, Ugak, and Chiniak bays; Karluk, Ayakulik, Pasagshak, Saltery, Afognak, Buskin, Uganik, Olds, American and Dog Salmon rivers; Pauls, Portage, Salonie, Roslyn, Akalura, Malina, Olga and Russian creeks

•*Chugach:* Resurrection Bay, Valdez Arm, Wells Passage area and Orca Bay; Coghill River; Cow Pen Creek

Southwest

Southwest has abundant opportunities, many little-utilized because of remoteness or the presence of other more prized species. The run timing is July and August, peaking in the first half of August.

•*Bristol Bay:* Nushagak River system (includes Mulchatna, Nuyakuk and lower Tikchik lakes); Wood, Kvichak and Togiak rivers

•*Northern Alaska Peninsula:* Naknek, Alagnak, Ugashik and Egegik river systems; Herendeen-Port Moller Bay streams

PINK SALMON

•*Southern Alaska Peninsula:* Abundant throughout, including Aleutian and Shumagin Island streams

•*Kuskokwim Bay:* Goodnews, Eek, Arolik and Kanektok rivers

•*Lower Yukon:* Andreafsky and Nulato rivers

Northwest

The pink salmon is one of the primary species (along with chum) in Norton Sound, with lots of fishing opportunities that are seldom utilized because of the area's remoteness. Run strength fluctuates greatly from year to year, with general timing from July to August, and a peak in mid-July to early August.

•*Norton Sound:* Golsovia, Unalakleet, Shaktoolik, Inglutalik, Ungalik and Tubutulik rivers

•*Seward Peninsula:* Kwiniuk, Eldorado, Nome, Snake, Fox, Sinuk, Niukluk, Pilgrim, Solomon and Kuzitrin rivers; Safety Lagoon

Pink salmon

6
CHARR:
FISH OF THE RAINBOW

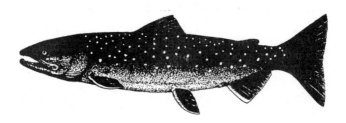

Mike Spisak and his Supercub fishing buddies have taken the concept of reading water to new, unheard-of heights in remote northwest Alaska. As pilots based out of Kotzebue, they survey the fishing potential of hundreds of miles of crystal streams from a thousand feet up, and then, with small, maneuverable planes that can set down on gravel bars no bigger than your driveway, they are able to tap an untouched treasure of trophy angling on those big, braided Arctic streams.

As you can well imagine, Mike's got quite a reputation for making fish dreams come true, especially for giant charr, a fish he takes special interest in (judging by the number of trophies that cover his office walls). If you're persistent enough, like I was a few years back, he might even take you to some of his choice spots, like the upper Kelly River, a dazzling clear tributary of the Noatak that has produced a string of record fish in recent years, including the largest charr ever taken on rod and reel in Alaska, a whopper of nearly 20 pounds. I was lucky enough to go on charr safari with Mike scant weeks after this record fish was taken, during an exceptionally mild and beautiful fall for that part of the world. Because of the dry weather, the Kelly was flowing low and very clear, with crystal blue pools strung out like beads into the horizon. Even more tantalizing were the unmistakable forms of fish—hundreds of them crowding the larger pools and runs.

"Are they really charr?" I shouted, astounded by the sight of so many salmon-sized fish holding position in water that seemed more appropriate for small grayling.

"Yeah, they're charr, all right. But wait till you see the big ones!" teased Mike, like a true bush pilot. We continued up the valley and then I saw he wasn't kidding: In a set of deep pools hemmed in by steep rock walls were some of the largest charr I'd set eyes on. Either I was dreaming, or some of these fish would go 20 pounds or more. Mike assured me there were no king salmon in the Kelly, so this was the real thing—a trophy charr bonanza!

The next four days were a magical blend of sun-kissed afternoons, frosty, aurora-filled nights and some of the most incredible fishing I've ever experienced. I caught scores of charr, many of them big enough to grace the walls of a man's castle, and a few that might have even placed in the record book, easily pushing the 16-pound mark. But for someone who had spent the best part of his youth getting cranked up over bright, ten-inch brookies from beaver ponds, the excitement of stalking these big brutes in the full lusty bloom of their spawning colors was almost more than I could handle.

It would be difficult, indeed, to imagine a creature of more exquisite beauty than a fall charr. *Akalukpik* to the Eskimo, they are the "fish of the rainbow." Said to have descended from the sky ages ago, they retain all the colors of the Heavens, in an artistry so sublime it can inspire visions of taxidermy in the most confirmed catch-and-release angler. (A 13-pound buck with scarlet spots the size of silver dollars and a belly as fiery as the most awesome northern sunset prompted me, a longtime devotee of "no-kill fishing," to take a trophy for my den wall.)

On my last evening on the Kelly, I finally hooked one of the monsters we'd seen from the air. He had a tail as big as a shovel, and though I didn't see too much of him before he snapped my nine-weight in a mad dash downriver, I know he was probably the biggest charr I'll ever lose in my allotted days roaming and fishing this great world of ours. When Mike came to get me the next morning, he laughed when I showed him the rod and told me he'd seen a couple of 30-pounders on his way upriver.

INTRODUCTION

Perhaps more than any other fish, the charr is associated with the mystique of our wildest places and most pristine waters. Its delicate beauty has inspired poetic admiration from generations of anglers. Part of a worldwide northern fish group (genus *Salvelinus*), charrs in North America include some of our most well-known and widespread sport species—the brook trout of eastern streams, the Dolly Varden and bull trout of the west, and lake trout and Arctic charr of the north.

In Alaska, they are found in a variety of forms, from the creeks and sheltered tidewaters of Southeast to the vast, naked rivers of the Arctic, in numbers, at times, that are truly astounding. In preliminary investigations done in Alaska during the late 1800s, the U.S. Fish Commission encountered thick hordes of the feisty "salmon trout" in nearly every stream and bay surveyed. Later, intense efforts by the salmon industry to control their numbers during the 1920s and 1930s barely affected their abundance, despite the eradication of millions annually. This remarkable fishery, for the most part, remains undiminished to this day—which is a good thing, as the Alaska charr is a fine, underrated gamefish, certainly the equal of the more glamorous species it shares waters with. It is capable of providing exciting fishing action 12 months of the year, in nearly every fishable body of water from Ketchikan to Kotzebue (and beyond).

The different varieties of charr found in the state may be an endless delight to anglers, but they are a perpetual headache for biologists, who are still struggling to make sense of their complex life histories and develop a universal classification for the species. Major problems arise in differentiating the various forms of Dolly Varden *(Salvelinus malma)*, the western brook charr, from the arctic charr *(Salvelinus alpinus)*, as their ranges overlap in western and Arctic Alaska, and outward appearance can be almost identical at times. It would certainly simplify matters greatly for sportsmen, guides and outdoor writers (perhaps scientists as well), if we could begin to think of the various forms of this species complex as simply "charr." With this in mind, we'll try to use "charr" throughout this book to mean Dolly Varden and/or arctic charr, although we may be more specific when dealing with areas like Southeast or Southcentral, where almost all the fish are Dolly Varden. Lake charr, or lake trout as we have come to know them, have long been recognized as a distinct, stable species *(Salvelinus namaycush)*, so we'll treat them separately (see page 116).

DESCRIPTION

The charrs are built along the same classic lines as the trouts, with powerful, streamlined bodies, slightly forked tails, large mouths, small scales and attractive coloration. What distinguishes them from the true trouts is their more minute scales (100 to 150 along the lateral line), lack of teeth on the upper middle jaw shaft, and different marking scheme (lighter spots on a dark background, as opposed to the trouts' darker spots on a light background).

Coloration and markings on Alaska's Dolly Varden/arctic charr vary considerably, according to location, age, life history and sexual ripeness. Back and upper sides on sea-run fish are generally steel blue to silver or grey, varying to brown or green in river and lake resident charr. Sides are usually silver-blue or grey in sea-runs, or brown, orange-brown, dusky green and even gold in lake and river forms; bellies are usually whitish. Markings consist of small to medium-sized concentric red, pink, cream or orange spots across the back and sides, not always distinct in bright sea-run fish. Lower fins are dusky yellow, orange or carmine, with prominent white leading edges; tails are slightly forked. Worm-like markings on the back and dorsal fins, found on the eastern brook charr *(S. fontinalis)*, are usually absent on Alaska fish.

Sexually mature charr are among Nature's most striking creations, developing intense coloration and physical changes. Beginning in late summer, the bellies and lower sides of fish preparing to spawn are imbued with flaming red-orange (the word "charr" itself has Gaelic or French roots for blood or blood-red colored), backs turn emerald green or brown, and spotting becomes a brilliant scarlet. Males develop hooked jaws tinged with black and orange, and ridged backs.

Charr are also one of the finest eating fish in the world, with firm, pink or orange flesh more delicately flavored than the salmon. Its fat content is perfect for all methods of cooking, whether deep fried, baked, sautéed, broiled or smoked. Lightly seasoned, grilled steaks of charr or tender fillets, dipped in spicy batter and deep fried, certainly rank as some of the finest treats from Nature's kitchen.

RANGE, ABUNDANCE & STATUS

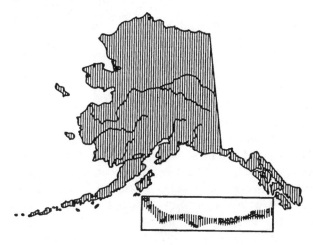

Shaded area shows range of charr in Alaska.

Alaska's charr are part of a northern species complex that dominates the waters of northern Europe, Siberia, Alaska, Canada and some of our northern states. They are found in nearly all Alaska's coastal drainages, in a continuous band from the Beaufort Sea down to the tip of the Southeast Panhandle (including the Aleutian Islands), occurring mostly as resident and sea-run river forms, with isolated populations of lake dwelling and even dwarf stream charr found throughout Arctic Alaska, the Interior, Kodiak Island and the Kenai Peninsula.

As the state's most widespread and abundant sport species, Dolly Varden/arctic charr have shown no measurable decline in numbers or distribution, despite a long history of exploitation. Now recognized as a legitimate and desirable gamefish, the future of charr in Alaska has never looked so good; hopefully the state will continue to offer what is undoubtedly some of the world's most prolific and varied angling for the species.

LIFE HISTORY & HABITS

Alaska's charr have interesting and, in many ways, little-understood life histories. Sea-run forms begin their lives in much the same way as salmon, spending their initial development in freshwater lakes and streams, feeding on minute aquatic life. At anywhere from one to seven years of age (usually four to six) they "smolt," heading seaward in the spring of the year. Unlike salmon, however, they usually remain close to shore for the duration of their ocean stay (generally less than 120 days), wandering in nearby bays or, in some instances traveling as far as several hundred miles along the coast. Almost all charr overwinter in freshwater. Sea-run fish begin their in-migration sometime in late summer or fall (late July through September), though not necessarily to their natal streams. Charr have been found wintering in rivers hundreds of miles from home—recently several tagged fish from Northwestern Alaska were found in a river along the coast of Siberia.

Resident or freshwater charr in Alaska can have complicated and varied movement patterns, with some fish spending their entire lives in streams (stream-resident charr); some overwintering in lakes and moving into streams to feed and spawn (lake-resident charr); and others, like the dwarf charr (the "old man fish" of the Inuit), living out their entire existence in small creeks, springs or headwaters. The presence of different forms of resident and anadromous charr in the same system may be exasperating to biologists, but anglers need only concern themselves with the general habits of the species, which are similar for all forms.

Charr are opportunistic and voracious predators, utilizing any available food sources—insects, leeches, snails, small fish, salmon spawn (and flesh), even rodents and small birds. Growth rate and potential size are variable, but generally Alaska's Dolly Varden/arctic charr are slow-growing and long-lived (up to 20 years), with the most northerly occurring fish reaching maximum size and age for the species. Canada's Northwest Territories has produced some of the largest charr in the world (25 pounds or more, with the current IGFA world record of 32 pounds, nine ounces from the Tree River in 1981), and there are reports of even bigger fish from eastern Siberia. But in Alaska, the largest charr (up to 15 pounds or more) come from the Kotzebue Sound area, in the northwest corner of the state. The current state record, a 19-pound, $12\frac{1}{2}$-ounce fish, was caught there from a tributary of the Noatak River in 1991. Stream-resident forms are generally much smaller and slower-growing than lake-resident or ocean-going fish, and in some systems, residual or dwarf forms might only reach 10 to 12 inches in length.

Alaska's charr reach sexual maturity at anywhere from four to seven years of age (up to nine in the extreme Arctic) and spawn in late summer and fall (July through November), with most systems receiving major spawning activity in September and October (some rivers have a separate summer and fall run). Their spawning behavior closely mimics that of the Pacific salmon, except that they do not necessarily die after breeding and can return to repeat the mating ritual two or even three times in rare cases. In some areas, overwintering sea-run charr will remain in freshwater during their spawning years, feeding and competing with resident fish before heading upriver in late summer (late July to August) to breed.

The northern charr's gluttony and lack of feeding sophistication is legend; stories of monster 20- and 30-pound fish hanging around shoreside canneries feeding on fish waste or of anglers limiting out on bare hooks are not hard to believe if you've fished around the state much. One of my own early encounters with the delicate feeding habits of the species involved a 12-pound Dolly Varden that tried to swim away with a stringer of rainbows I had tied to a riverbank. Similar stories abound. The charrs' well-known fondness for salmon smolt and spawn led at one time to a territorial bounty for their eradication, though later studies proved their appetite no more destructive than that of the rapacious rainbow trout or coho they share waters with.

FISHING ALASKA'S CHARR

Anglers in Alaska catch almost one-half million charr each year, close to ten percent of the state's total sportfish catch. Most of these fish come from northern Southeast, the Kenai Peninsula, Kodiak and Bristol Bay, with smaller but significant numbers from the Kuskokwim, Northwest Alaska, the Arctic and Prince William Sound. A good portion of Alaska's charr are taken incidentally, while trolling for king and coho salmon, flyfishing for rainbows, and the like; but a significant, growing number of anglers target charr specifically, particularly during spring and fall, or in areas such as Northwest, Arctic or Southwest that are known for outstanding trophy potential.

Spring

Although Alaska's charr can be caught any time of year, they are best fished in spring and late summer through fall, when the great seasonal changes and movements of salmon bring concentrated feeding patterns. After ice-out, all charr become extremely active, leaving overwintering areas and feeding heavily on emerging food sources (such as fish, insect larvae and crustaceans). They'll gather in river mouths, estuaries, confluences, inlets and outlets of lakes and along shorelines, as these are the first waters to stir with life as winter loosens its grip. Studies have shown charr to feed extensively and at times exclusively on salmon fry, smolt and alevins when available, and it is the presence and movement of great numbers of these young salmon, more than anything else, that makes Alaska's spring charr fishing so extraordinary.

On any of the hundreds of salmon-rich streams and lakes across Alaska (particularly those of Bristol Bay, Kodiak, the Alaska Peninsula and Southeast), during peak periods of young salmon emergence in the spring, waters can actually churn with the frenzy of feeding charr as they slash through schools of fry, smolt or alevins. If you time it right, you can get in on some of the most exciting, fast-paced fishing action imaginable, using spinners, spoons, flies, jigs or what-have-you to easily provoke these ravenous hordes.

The trick is to locate feeding fish or concentrations of young salmon, not always a simple task in Alaska's immense waters and vagary conditions. Timing and location are of the essence. May and June are the peak months for spring juvenile salmon movement across most of Alaska, with the most prolific waters—Katmai, Kodiak, Iliamna, etc.— the obvious choices for best fishing. Target lake outlets and inlets, bays, shorelines with deep drop-offs, river mouths and confluences, pool eddies and cutbanks—anywhere that young salmon might be concentrated and/or provide efficient ambush sites for charr. Studies have shown the

CHARR

low-light, extreme late evening and early morning hours (10 p.m. to 2 a.m.) to be most conducive to juvenile salmon movement, so time your efforts to fish as close to those hours as humanly possible (cloudy, windy and rainy days are also best). Look for obvious signs of feeding or shoaling activity—surface disturbances, "shimmering" in the water, or flocks of wheeling and diving seabirds (gulls and terns).

Many guides and lodges nowadays spot charr from the air, hopping from one locale to the next until they locate a sizable group worth fishing. But if you don't own a plane, you'll have to rely on the whims of Nature and your own fish sense to connect with these hungry spring feeders. You may have to fish "blind," casting to likely holding water or trolling from a boat, using spoons and plugs as the best first choices (try $1/4$- to $1/2$-ounce Krocodiles, Pixees, Crippled Herrings, or HotRod spoons in nickel, chrome/neon blue, chrome/silver prism, chrome/fire stripe or gold/orange; or $1/8$- to $1/2$-ounce Wiggle Warts, Hot Shots, Tad Pollys and Shad Raps, in silver, blue-silver and gold scale finish). Vary your retrieve, depth and location until you locate feeding fish, much as you would for lake trout this time of year. Spinners are also excellent choices for spring charr, especially in inlet/outlet waters or streams. Try #0 to #3 Mepps silver or gold, long-bladed Aglias, or the Super Vibrax #1 to #3 in nickel and gold blades.

The outlet/inlet waters and associated tributaries of Alaska's salmon-rich lakes are prime areas for exciting spring charr action.

If you are flyfishing, start with a generic smolt or fry imitation streamer—say a #2 to #4 Coronation or Supervisor—as a "searching" pattern, fishing a light strip (inches, not feet) through likely holding areas. A floating line or sink tip works best, depending on the strength of the current and depth of the water. On flowing water, make cross-current, downstream sweeps, just as you would for spring trout down south. Use the line drag and a little rod tip action, if necessary, to imitate the nervous pulses of movement these little fish display as they dart through the water. Some other patterns to include in your spring charr arsenal are Marabou and Silver Muddlers, Matukas, Woolly Buggers, Leeches and an assortment of smolt/fry variations (even alevin patterns) and attractor patterns (Polar Shrimp, Skykomish Sunrise, Mickey Finn, etc.), in sizes #2 to #8 (the larger hooks sink better). Don't be afraid to experiment; some of the biggest charr you'll ever see are taken on the most unlikely fly creations.

SEA-RUN CHARR

Surprisingly, most overwintering sea-run charr do not linger long in freshwater during the spring dispersal, but instead move quickly down into river mouths. Studies done in western and Arctic Alaska show a great proportion (50 percent or more) of fish captured during outmigration to have empty stomachs. Once they reach the mouths and estuaries, however, they begin feeding heavily like their freshwater counterparts, with diets that consist almost exclusively of fish and crustaceans. They are caught quite freely at these times (usually late March, April or early May, depending on location) by fishermen casting from shore or boats—working tide rips, saltchucks, spits, jetties, beaches, bays and river mouths. Southcentral (Kodiak, Homer, Seward, Prince William Sound) and northern Southeast are traditionally the most popular areas for this spring saltwater charr fishing.

Long, silver, "Norwegian-style" casting spoons and jigs ($^3/_8$- to $^3/_4$-ounce) are deadly on these sea-roving spring charr, as they imitate very closely the sandlance, herring and young salmon they feed on. Spinners, diving minnow plugs, crankbaits, flutter spoons, etc., in silver, gold, green, white and blue combinations can be worked effectively as well, depending on conditions. If conditions are right, you can even find success flyfishing—working river mouths, spits, beaches and other likely areas with baitfish imitation streamers (smolt, candlefish, sandlance and herring patterns).

Look for signs of surface activity just as you would in freshwater, but be aware that saltwater charr will quite often be feeding deep or off bottom. If you're fishing from a boat, a fish locator/depth sounder can certainly save a lot of time putting you where the action is. Most anglers working the salt this time of year have the best luck fishing the tides (two hours before and after high tide), although you can find good charr fishing around the clock in the more productive zones.

Early Summer

From June on, Alaska's coastal waters jam up with mind-boggling numbers of salmon. In the major systems, thousands, even millions of fish, swim up from the sea into rivers, lakes and streams, creating an absolute manna of abundant angling, not just for salmon but also for the countless charr and trout (rainbow trout and cutthroat) that gather in anticipation of the feast to come. Most of these egg pirates are primed and anxious, and can be easily provoked into striking.

These fish are keyed in to slightly different stimuli than during their spring smolt bash, with attractor colors the spice that really turns them on. Spinners, spoons and plugs in silver or gold with fluorescent red, orange, pink or chartreuse seem to work best. For flyfishermen, best results will be with patterns like the Polar Shrimp, Egg-Sucking Leech, Mickey Finn, Alaska Mary Ann and Purple Woolly Bugger, along with proven standby forage imitations like the Silver Muddler Minnow, Matukka, Smolt, etc. Fish with a sink-tip line, short leader and short strip, for best results.

The trick now will be to fish deep and not too fast, as charr become less inclined to energetically pursue prey once the salmon arrive. Work river mouths, confluences, pools and inlet/outlet waters, giving special attention to any areas where you locate salmon (cast around and behind them). Generally that is where the quick, agile charr (and rainbow and cutthroat) hold, as they "shadow" their larger cousins' movements. If you're working deep lake or river water from a boat or raft, you might want to try a drift rig (pencil lead or walking sinker off a three-way swivel) with a plug ($^3/_8$- to $^5/_8$-ounce) or fluorescent Spin-N-Glo (size #4 to #10). I've witnessed outstanding results with these in the big waters of Southwest in conditions where spinners or spoons weren't really efficient.

Late Summer

Just when you think Alaska's fishing can't get any better, August rolls around and the action peaks. By now, most charr and trout will be concentrated in the gravelly middle and upper mainstems of rivers and in feeders, where considerable salmon spawning is underway. First king salmon, then sockeye and chum, and finally silvers and pinks glut these areas with their profuse spawn and carcasses—and spur hosts of resident species like charr, rainbow trout, cutthroat trout, grayling and even whitefish into a frantic free-for-all.

In late summer (usually mid-July to early August) in most coastal systems, the great influx of sea-run charr peaks. They form mass congregations in river mouths and lower holding areas before moving upriver to join their egg-pirating cohorts on the spawning gravels. These sea-run charr are in peak condition—firm, fat and full of energy—and with their great abundance and voracious hunger can provide some of the best sport Alaska has to offer.

This late in summer, Alaska's river scene is a high-energy, mixed bag of fishing excitement. Gangs of charr, along with squads of zippy rainbows (or cutthroat trout in Southeast) and even bold grayling compete for a piece of the action, while waves of fresh salmon arrive daily. Different species can be taken on consecutive casts and amazing numbers of fish hauled from the better holes. This is the premier time for egg patterns, flesh flies and bright attractors—the familiar Alaska standards like the Glo Bug, Two Egg Maribou, Polar Shrimp, Bunny Bug and Egg-Sucking Leech. Depending on how much these fish have had to eat and other factors, you can expect good to excellent results drifting any of the above through holding water—pools, riffles, cutbanks, sloughs or confluences—anywhere salmon might congregate or spawn. Cast to the periphery of any holding salmon you can locate (avoid disturbing or provoking them when on their redds) and fish a dead drift or light strip above bottom. Just as you would for spring charr, don't use a leader longer than four feet, as these fish are not the least bit leader-shy under most conditions.

Spinners can be deadly this time of year. Thousands of August charr have succumbed to the potent appeal of a #1 to #5 Mepps—Black Furies, fluorescent Aglias and Comets; or pink, red or chartreuse Rooster Tails ($^3/_8$-ounce to $^3/_4$-ounce); or the eminently popular Blue Fox Super Vibrax series spinners (#2 to #6) with gold, brass, silver or "firetiger" blades and fluorescent orange, red or yellow bells. Fish them deep and with slow retrieve for best results.

There are certain conditions that can arise during late summer—high, turbid flows from heavy rains, an overabundance of salmon spawn during peak run years (especially for sockeyes or pinks) and other conditions, when the standby patterns and techniques may not produce as they should. This is when some extra "oomph" on the end of your line is needed. For flyfishers, an assortment of specialty Alaska patterns has evolved for these situations—gaudy, flashy, overstated streamers like the Outrageous, Pink Sparkler, Baker Buster, Orange Wiggletail, Alaskabou, etc., that clobber a fish with maximum doses of color and flash. They're a little bit much to cast, but these flies can produce when nothing else seems to, so be sure to include some in your late summer charr arsenal. Adding bright yarn, "dropper flies," spinner-fly combinations, super-bright or oversize lures, erratic retrieves, and even fish oils (where legal) are some other tactics fishermen use for added punch under these difficult conditions.

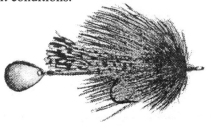

"The Almighty One," a.k.a. "The Gay Blade," a specialty spinner-fly tied by Matt Potter, is deadly on late summer charr and rainbow trout.

Fall

Beginning in August and continuing into October across much of coastal Alaska, vast numbers of charr crowd rivers and streams to spawn and/or overwinter, providing some unique fishing opportunities. Some of the year's best trophy angling can be had in the fall, with an abundance of fish in prime condition, many in striking spawning colors. Charr at this time are overly aggressive, and will readily hit spoons, spinners, plugs and flies in bright attractor colors (spawners may become picky as they begin breeding, but they should be left alone anyway). The big waters of Bristol Bay and the Alaska Peninsula, Southcentral's Kenai River, the lower Kuskokwim tributaries and the fabulous fisheries of Northwest and Arctic Alaska are some of the more outstanding areas for fall charr fishing, particularly for magnificent trophy specimens (to 10 pounds or even more). Late August through September is the preferred time for fall charr safaris, as the weather then is still generally not too extreme. (The Arctic is the exception, as winter can set in from early September on.)

Charr have been harvested in great numbers by native people during these fall migrations. At traditional sites along the Arctic coast, before the advent of white man and his nets, charr were herded into stone weirs and speared by the thousands. Quite a bit of fall subsistence harvesting still occurs along the northwest coast, where villagers net fat charr by the thousands in river mouths and estuaries.

Winter

Because charr are one of the few fish that can be taken readily and in abundance through the ice all winter long, they sustain an important fishery through Alaska's long dark, cold season. The Inuit used carved ivory jigs, spears and fur-adorned bone hooks in the old days, but now most charr are taken through the ice with small jigs, spoons and bait. Certain lakes in Southcentral's Kenai Peninsula and Mat-Su Valley, parts of Bristol Bay, a few lakes in Interior (for stocked fish) and waters along Kotzebue Sound are where most of the ice fishing effort occurs for charr.

Gearing Up for Charr

Ultra-light or light-weight, medium-action, five- to seven-foot graphite rods, with matching reels and four- to eight-pound test line are the most popular spinning outfit sizes for fishing Alaska's charr. On bigger water or for trophy fishing, anglers will usually upgrade to a light- to medium-weight, slightly longer (to eight feet), stiffer rod and 8- to 12-pound line, or they will use a light to light/medium, fast-action casting rod (six to seven-and-a-half feet) with 8- to 12-pound line.

For flyfishing, a six- to eight-weight, eight- to nine-foot, fast-action graphite rod with matching reel and floating sink-tip line is the preferred setup. Keep your leaders short on the sinking line presentations, three to four feet being plenty. Larger hooks (to size #1/0), high-density sinking lines and weights can be used to help achieve proper depth in extreme water conditions.

Where to Go

There are so many areas in Alaska that can offer outstanding fishing for charr, it is difficult to rate any above the others. You can definitely narrow the choices, however, depending on what you're after. For saltwater angling, the waters around Kodiak Island, Prince William Sound and northern Southeast are probably the most popular. For spring charr, I would certainly rate the big lakes and rivers of Iliamna, Katmai, the Tikchik Lakes area and the Alaska Peninsula as tops, while for late summer charr action, I would have to add the streams of the lower Kuskokwim, the Togiak, Nushagak and Wood river systems to the above. Where to go for the best trophy charr angling? The big lakes of the northern Alaska Peninsula (Becharof, Ugashik, Naknek), Iliamna, the Kenai River, the North Slope and the incredible drainages of Kotzebue Sound would all provide world class opportunities.

Alaska's Top Trophy Charr Locations
•Wulik River (Northwest)
•Noatak River (Northwest)
•Iliamna Lake and River (Southwest)
•Ugashik Lake (Southwest)
•Naknek Lake (Southwest)
•Kenai River (Southcentral)

ALASKA'S TOP TEN TROPHY CHARR

19 pounds, 12.5 ounces, Noatak River (Northwest), Ken Ubbin, 1991 (state record)
18 pounds, 15 ounces, Wulik River (Northwest), 1994
17 pounds, 8 ounces, Wulik River (Northwest), 1968
16 pounds, 14 ounces, Lake Iliamna (Southwest), 1973
16 pounds, 8 ounces, Wulik River (Northwest), 1988
16 pounds, 4 ounces, Noatak River (Northwest), 1994
16 pounds, 0 ounces, Wulik River (Northwest), 1967
15 pounds, 6 ounces, Wulik River (Northwest), 1992
15 pounds, 3 ounces, Noatak River (Northwest), 1992
15 pounds, 1 ounce, Deer Creek (Northwest), 1985

ALASKA'S MAJOR CHARR LOCATIONS
Southeast

Southeast has some of the state's most abundant Dolly Varden charr, found here in nearly every stream that supports fish. Saltwater angling opportunities abound. Nearly three-fourths of the fish taken are from northern Southeast (Yakutat, Haines and Juneau areas).

•*Yakutat:* Situk, Italio, Akwe, Lost, Tsiu, Kaliakh and Alsek river systems

•*Juneau:* Chilkat, Chilkoot and Lutak inlets, Northern Stephens Passage, Icy Strait, Cross Sound, Gastineau Channel; Auke, Goulding, Kathleen, Turner, Dewey and Windfall lakes; Cowee, Montana, Admiralty and Peterson creeks; Taiya, Chilkat, Chilkoot rivers and Mitchell Bay system

•*Sitka/Petersburg:* Lower Stephens Passage; Salisbury, Ernest, Frederick, Nakawasina and Sitka sounds; Peril, Upper Clarence, Zimovia and Chatham straits; Wrangell Narrows/Duncan Canal, Bradfield Canal; Blind Slough, Wilson Beach; Falls, Bear, Exchange, Aaron, Thoms, Anan, Kadake, Andrew, Pat, Sweetwater, Hamilton, Petersburg, Ohmer, Starrigavan and Saltchuck creeks; Castle, Eagle, Harding, Indian, Nakawasina and Kah Sheets rivers; Salmon, Eva, Surge and Klag Bay lake systems

•*Ketchikan:* Clarence Strait, Behm Canal, Gravina Island, Revillagigedo Channel, San Alberto Bay; Carroll and Whipple Creeks; Wilson, Blossom and Harris rivers; Thorne, Kegan, Karta and Naha river systems; Humpback, Hugh Smith, Essowah, McDonald, Ward Cove and Orchard lakes

Southcentral

Almost 70 percent of the state's sport-caught charr are taken here, mostly from the Kenai Peninsula.

•*Kenai Peninsula:* Kenai, Kasilof, Anchor, Russian, Ninilchik Rivers; Deep, Stariski creeks; Grouse, Summit, Jerome and Swanson river lakes; Rocky River; Kachemak and Resurrection bays

•*Copper River and Eastern Prince William Sound:* Cordova and Valdez Arm; Eyak, Klutina, Bering, Katalla and Tonsina river systems; Power and Clear creeks; Alaganik Slough; Martin, Tsaina and McKinley lake and river systems

•*Prince William Sound:* Jackpot Bay, Eshamy Lagoon; Coghill, Beach, Nellie-Martin Patton and San Juan rivers; Boswell and Markarka creeks

•*Knik Arm:* Big Lake, Little Susitna River, Wasilla Creek, Nancy lakes

•*Susitna River:* Talkeetna River system; Willow, Lake and Alexander creeks

•*Upper Cook Inlet:* Chuitna and Theodore rivers; Crescent Lake system

•*Lower Cook Inlet:* Kamishak River

•*Kodiak:* All bays in vicinity of salmon streams, especially Uyak, Ugak, Chiniak, Mill, Monashka, Perenosa and Seal bays; Shuyak Island. All salmon-producing streams, especially: Karluk, Buskin, Pasagshak, Saltery, Olds, Thumb, Uganik, Ayakulik, American, Spiridon, Dog Salmon, Zachar and Little rivers; Portage, Pauls, Akalura, Roslyn, Salonie and Malina creeks; Barabara Lakes

Southwest

Southwest has some of Alaska's finest freshwater charr angling in terms of abundance and size (to 10 pounds). Saltwater fishing occurs only on Kodiak Island.

•*Alaska Peninsula:* Nearly all streams and lakes, down to and including the Aleutian Islands; those with heavy salmon runs generally offer the most outstanding fishing: Naknek Lake and River system (including Brooks Rivers, American Creek, Idavain Creek and Lake and other associated streams and lakes); Becharof Lake and Egegik River system; Ugashik Lakes and River system; Chignik River system; Aniakchak, Meshik and Bear rivers; Nelson Lagoon system, etc.

•*Bristol Bay:* All major salmon systems also have prolific charr populations, especially: Iliamna-Kvichak system (mostly Iliamna, Kvichak and Newhalen rivers and Lake Iliamna), Nushagak system (mostly Mulchatna, Nuyakuk, upper Nushagak mainstem), Wood River-Tikchik Lakes (mostly outlet and inlet streams—Agulukpak, Agulowak, Wood River, Peace River, Lynx Creek, Little Togiak, etc.); Togiak River system, Igushik River, Kulukak River

•*Kuskokwim:* Outstanding fishing for sea-run and resident charr from Kuskokwim Bay to Holitna: Goodnews, Arolik, Kanektok, Eek, Kwethluk, Tuluksak, Kisaralik, Kasigluk, Aniak and Holitna river systems

•*Nunivak Island:* Some huge, trophy sea-run specimens have been taken from streams here.

•*Lower Yukon:* Andreafsky and Anvik rivers

Northwest

Thirty percent of the state's largest trophy charr have been taken from this region.

•*Eastern Norton Sound:* Unalakleet, Shaktoolik, Inglutalik, Ungalik, Tubutulik and Kwiniuk rivers

•*Seward Peninsula:* All salmon streams, especially Fish-Niukluk, Nome and Pilgrim rivers; Salmon Lake; Snake, Sinuk, Solomon, Kuzitrin, Agiapuk, Bonanza, Eldorado and Buckland rivers

•*Kotzebue Sound:* All trophy potential: Lower Noatak River and tributaries (Kelly, Kugururok, Nimiuktuk rivers, etc.), Kobuk River drainage (including Walker and Selby lakes), Wulik and Kivalina rivers

Arctic

Arctic has outstanding, barely explored fishing possibilities for big charr.

•Colville River system (especially Anaktuvuk, Chandler and Killik rivers); Sagavanirktok, Canning, Kongakut and Hulahula rivers; also Chandler, Karupa-Cascade, Galbraith, Elusive, Schrader-Peters lakes

Interior

Only small, stream resident charr occur naturally in streams here, but some stocked fishing is available in lakes near Fairbanks.

•Tanana and Nenana rivers (clearwater tributaries); Quartz, Harding, Coal Mine Road and Chena lakes

7

LAKE TROUT:
OLD MAN OF THE LAKES

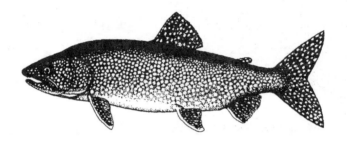

Among the Inupiat of Northwest Alaska, there is an age-old legend of a giant fish they call *Idluk*, found in the deepest, most remote lakes of the Brooks Range. Said to be as old as the hills, this finny will-o'-the-wisp is reputed to reach sizes large enough to swallow a man whole, should he stray too near the water. Fabulous tales like this are easy to dismiss as nothing more than silly folklore, having no basis in the reality that surrounds most of our lives. But perhaps they are more than legend.

Some years back, two men were fishing the headwaters of the Kobuk River at Walker Lake in the central Brooks Range. It was early summer, and they were putzing around in a small raft, enjoying the exquisite weather and 24-hour daylight that time of year brings to Northern Alaska. The hour was late, but they had a notion to troll some big plugs before they headed in to camp and called it a night. Fishing with heavy lines and stout baitcasters, they were awestruck when one of the beefy rods doubled and its reel screamed, only seconds after they had let their lures out. Now these fellows were experienced Alaska anglers and men of the wilderness, with years of time in some of Alaska's most remote backcountry. But to this day, they swear that whatever it was on the end of their line that night was no ordinary fish. Clamping down on the drag and pumping the big rod for all he was worth, one of them barely brought the beast under control. As it gyrated and spun the light boat around and around, they realized they didn't have a ghost of a chance with the thing. But what really got them was that when the behemoth headed for the lake's far shore, some 15 miles away, it was only slightly fazed by the raft it was dragging behind. They way they tell it, after 20 minutes in tow, with no indication of the fish tiring and a strong offshore breeze kicking up, they had a very brief discussion and agreed it was best to cut loose, and so they parted ways with this lake monster.

INTRODUCTION

The lake trout, *Salvelinus namaycush*, is certainly one of our better-known northern fish denizens. Originally found in deep, clear, cold waters from New England to the Arctic, the big, native trout of the northern lakes is actually a charr, closely allied with the familiar eastern brook trout and Dolly Varden of the West. It has the distinction of being our continent's largest and longest-lived freshwater salmonid, reaching potential weights of 100 pounds or more and lifespans of over 50 years.

In Alaska, the lake trout is widely distributed and thriving, with fishing potential in many waters comparable to some of the better fisheries in Northern Canada. But because anglers in Alaska have a variety of world-class fisheries at hand, few areas in the state receive the intense, systematic effort seen in lake trout waters elsewhere. For that reason, much of the state's good lake trout water remains underutilized, a bonanza of exciting angling yet to be discovered.

Not a spectacular gamefish by any stretch of the imagination, the laker's reputation is nonetheless secure. He is the fish of the primitive northern wilderness, inhabiting the crystal depths of the loneliest watersheds, even where no other species will thrive. Draw out a map of Alaska, pick out any lake of size, depth and elevation who-knows-where, and it's a safe bet you'll find some testy, spotted, gray charr waiting to pick a fight with you there, should you travel and fish those far-flung waters.

DESCRIPTION

Built like a true trout, with a large mouth and protruding belly, the lake trout looks every bit the predator that he is. His basic color scheme involves a darker background of silver gray to brown (sometimes greenish) with a profusion of white, yellow or gold oval spots and vermiculations across the back and sides. Bellies are usually cream-colored, with lower fins of trademark charr coloration: clear, milky, yellow or orangish, with narrow white borders. Tail fins on lake trout are usually deeply forked, with red or pink spots absent from the sides—two distinctive character differences that distinguish them from the other charrs.

The average size of Alaska's lake trout varies, but is generally from three to five pounds in most waters that are not overfished. The state's largest lake trout generally come from deep, large lakes with abundant food sources, with fish of 20 pounds or more considered trophy specimens for Alaska (the state record is a 47-pound fish from a lake in the central Alaska Range). The predominance of smaller fish seen in many of the more popular lakes in recent years is a direct result of overfishing. New, stringent harvest regulations and more active management policies (a departure from the liberal days of early statehood) should hopefully restore and maintain the high quality of some of Alaska's more accessible waters.

The lake trout's appeal is certainly enhanced by its excellent eating qualities. Its firm, white, pink or orange flesh has a delicate flavor and is superb fried, baked or smoked. Don't count your outdoor career complete until you've sat on some gravelly shore and indulged your hearty appetite with succulent lake trout fillets, lightly seasoned and grilled over a smoky fire.

RANGE, ABUNDANCE & STATUS

Lake trout, interestingly enough, occur only in North America, originally in a wide swath of lakes stretching from New England to the Great Lakes, across most of Canada, down into the Rockies and up into

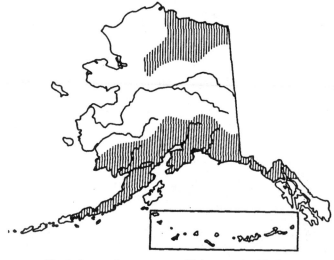

Shaded area shows range of lake trout in Alaska.

LAKE TROUT

Alaska (a range that coincides with the limits of the last major period of glaciation).

In Alaska, lake trout are common in the alpine lakes of the Alaska Range, Bristol Bay, the Kenai and Alaska peninsulas, the Brooks Range and the central and eastern Arctic coastal plain. They are absent from Kodiak, the Seward Peninsula, low-lying lakes of the Yukon and Kuskokwim basins, the northwest Arctic coast and most of the Alaska Peninsula. Though they are almost always associated with lake systems, some stream-dwelling populations may possibly occur in the Sagavanirktok, Colville and Canning rivers of the Arctic.

Very little has been done to adequately assess the status of any but the most accessible of the state's lake trout stocks. All indications, however, point to a healthy fishery overall, although many of the state's more heavily fished locations are showing the effects of over-harvesting, with a decline in average size and number of trophy specimens. More conservative management and a growing trend toward catch-and-release hopefully mean a brighter future for the high quality of angling currently available.

LIFE HISTORY & HABITS

Much of what has been learned about the general life history and habits of lake charr comes from extensive studies done throughout Canada. Lake trout research in Alaska has been very limited, focused mostly on the more accessible lakes of the Alaska Range. We know that, like all charr, lake trout are voracious, opportunistic predators that spawn in the fall (not necessarily every year), and have movement and feeding patterns that change with the season. There are some key differences, however, between lake trout and their charr cousins that are of prime importance to anglers.

The most obvious characteristic unique to the species is their preference for lake habitat for rearing, feeding and spawning. Almost all of the lake trout you'll encounter in Alaska will be associated with some lake body (except the distinct river-dwelling populations mentioned above). The need for cold, highly oxygenated water determines to a great extent their movements and feeding patterns. With the arrival of spring breakup, lakers move into shallows to feed, consuming small fish, molluscs, crustaceans, insect larvae and even rodents. When available, fish are the preferred prey of larger lake trout. As water temperatures rise, lake trout will go deep, preferring to remain within the thermally stratified sections of water closest to 50 degrees. Studies have shown that even in lakes with abundant food supplies, many lake trout will forgo a meal for an empty stomach if it means they have to leave their preferred band of cooler water for any length of time.

With the arrival of fall and cooler temperatures in Alaska in late August and September in most of the state, lake trout begin to congregate for spawning in offshore areas of shallow to moderate depth (less than 40 feet), with gravel or rocky bottoms free of sand or mud. Ideal spawning areas are far enough from shore to escape the pounding of wind-induced wave action, but shallow enough to resist sedimentation. Spawning at night, lake trout, unlike salmon, do not use a nest. Instead, they scatter their eggs to settle into the cracks and crevices of the substrate, where they slowly develop and hatch in late winter.

Alaska's lake trout are slow-growing, late-maturing and long-lived; fish older than 25 years are not uncommon, with some specimens from the Arctic exceeding 50 years. (Arctic populations generally mature later and live longer.) Because of their slow growth rates, long lives and rather low fecundity, trophy lake trout populations are surprisingly easy to overfish, a fact that many fish managers (and lodge owners) are just coming to realize, hopefully in time to save the trophy potential of the more hard-hit locales that have already had most of the worthy specimens gleaned by overharvesting. Many of the better trophy lake trout fisheries in northern Canada nowadays have strict catch-and-release policies, a trend that may soon catch on in some of the more urban-accessible waters of Alaska.

FISHING ALASKA'S LAKE TROUT

Because of the similarities in life cycle and feeding habits across their range at high latitudes, many appropriate fishing strategies for Alaska's lakers will be similar to those used in lakes of northern Canada, with some key differences. We'll begin our discussion and comparison with a look at conditions in the spring, the most productive and exciting time for fishing lake trout everywhere.

Spring

Across the North, as the returning sun frees fish from their icy prisons and winter stupor, all charr become very active and begin feeding extensively. Lake trout will cruise shallows and feed near the surface. They'll aggressively pursue anything that remotely resembles a food item, but especially small fish, crustaceans and molluscs. In Alaska waters, their spring recklessness may be heightened by the presence of competitor species or a richer, more varied forage (such as juvenile salmon or charr).

Rambunctious feeding and spring conditions make for some of the easiest fishing of the year. Almost any properly presented lure or fly will have an even chance with spring lakers, and in shallow crystal lake waters, there's no trick to locating them either. Timing, weather and location will be the most significant factors in your success this time of year. Though many of these lakes don't get fished until they're open enough to allow for floatplane or boat access, if you can

The Dardevle, a classic lure for Alaska lake trout.

somehow get to them just as the leads are opening up—especially around outlet waters—you can have some amazing action. Some fish-crazed pilots even land ski planes on the rotten ice of remote lakes in late spring and toss spoons or jigs into the slush water surrounding the edges, with awesome results.

No matter how soon after ice-out you get to fish these trout lakes, the idea is still the same: work the open water as it becomes available, which generally occurs sooner around outlet and inlet streams, bays and shorelines that lie on the windward side. Sunny weather can really bring the lakers out into these open areas, much the same as it does for people emerging from a long winter's confinement. Bright spoons, jigs or spinners (Krocodile, Dardevle, Super Vibrax, Mr. Twister, etc.) tossed into these pocket waters will usually do the trick.

Spring is one of the few times you can do well with flies, as lakers tend to scatter and go deeper later in the season. Smolt, leech, sculpin and attractor patterns, size #1/0 to #6, work exceedingly well for Alaska spring lakers, with nymphs and even dry flies eliciting strikes under the right conditions. Look for signs of fish in the shallows of small bays, outlet and inlet waters and beaches with drop-offs, in the early morning or late evening hours, when they are prone to prowl. One of the greatest thrills of fishing wild lake trout waters is to be gently stirred from sleep by the slurping of big fish in the shallows, only yards from your lakeside camp.

After the ice completely disappears and lakes start to warm, fish may not be so easy to find. Work any obvious shallow feeding locations, just as you would for charr this time of year (in many of Alaska's lake systems the two will freely mingle with each other during spring feeding). If you don't have any luck, you'll need to probe deeper water, from shore or from a boat or raft. A big, heavy, bright spoon (such as the Krocodile, Dardevle or Pixee) is a time-tested, favorite choice for this kind of fishing, as is a diving plug (Wiggle Wort, Tadpolly, Rapala or Flatfish). Both should be worked deep and with a slow retrieve or troll. Quite often during the period between late spring and early summer, lakers will be found moderately deep, to 15 feet or so, in offshore areas like shoals or bays that have concentrations of baitfish. A small boat and fish locator/depth sounder are certainly advantageous for these conditions, especially on the big water lakes.

Summer

Much has been said and written about the lake trout's preference for cooler, oxygen-rich waters and bottom structure. As northern waters warm from the advancing sun and nonstop daylight, lakes will stratify into more or less defined layers of temperature and oxygen saturation. This is especially true in big deep lakes of southern Canada, but may not always be the case in Alaska's high latitude waters, where the thermocline may not be so pronounced because of cooler yearly temperatures, size and depth.

As summer advances, lake trout will tend to scatter from their spring haunts to deeper water, but not necessarily to the deepest parts of the lake. Depending on factors like the availability of food, bottom structure, weather and time of day, you can expect to encounter them in water 10 to 40 feet deep in most Alaska lakes during summer (July and August). Many smaller lakers (two to eight pounds) will stay fairly close to shore near lake outlets and inlets, islands, bays with cover and beaches with fast drop-offs, even during the hottest part of summer; they can provide some of the more consistent and enjoyable fishing this time of year. The low-light hours and cloudy or windy days are the best times to encounter these shallow holding summer lakers, with spinners, small spoons or baitfish and attractor patterns the most popular and effective enticements.

No matter what kind of stratification or structure a lake has, summer feeding habits and movements of Alaska's lake charr can be greatly influenced by the wide range of food sources available. This is particularly true in the salmon-rich Southwest lake systems of Katmai, Iliamna, the Tikchiks and Kuskokwim Bay—and to a lesser extent, certain locations on the Arctic slope, where it is not uncommon to encounter lakers feeding heavily in streams, miles from lake sources. Though these fish rarely push the ten-pound mark, they are quite often abundant, fat and feisty—a welcome surprise when angling the standard river fare.

For trophy fishing the big water lakes, the summer months of July and August are the prime times for deepwater trolling. This usually means stout rods, downriggers, fish locators, thermistors (temperature reading devices), flashers and what-have-you, if you're a serious fishermen or guide on the more popular big water fisheries. Large (four-inch plus) trolling spoons like the Canadian Wonder, Diamond King,

Tom Mack and Apex along with long plugs (up to nine inches) like the Kwikfish, Flatfish, Magnum Rapala and Jensen Minnow, in colors of silver, gold, silver/blue, silver/green, green/yellow, or white pearl are the most commonly used lures, producing excellent results. Slow but varied trolling speeds at depths of 15 to 60 feet through areas of structure (shoals, reefs, islands, shelves, etc.), seem to produce the most fish. A good knowledge of the lake's bottom structure, thermocline, forage and areas of fish concentration (along with fish locators/depth sounders) certainly can make a difference in success with trophy lakers in these waters. For this reason, it certainly makes good sense to seek the services of a reputable guide, especially if you're new to an area or have limited experience with lake trout.

Fall

Fall is another favored time for lake trout fishing, though the season in Alaska can be quite short. From late August well into September, lake trout begin their prespawning movements. During this phase, they are more concentrated near gravelly or rocky beaches, shoals or small bays and other areas conducive to spawning, in water anywhere from a few to fifteen feet deep. If you time it right and know where to go, you can get into some of the year's best fishing. The company of a knowledgeable guide or local fisherman can save a lot of guesswork and wasted time in searching out these areas. Bright spinners, spoons, jigs and baitfish/attractor pattern streamers (Yellow Maribou, Mickey Finn, Smolt, Gray Ghost, Maribou Muddler and Leech) all work well on these excitable, concentrated fall lakers. Since many Alaska fishermen are busy with hunting activities this time of year, some truly outstanding and accessible fall fishing opportunities go underutilized (see Where to Go on page 124).

Winter

Lake trout are one of the few Alaska sport species that can provide consistent angling through the long winter season. Most ice fishing for lake trout occurs in the more urban-accessible waters of the upper Susitna, Tanana and Copper Rivers and the Kenai Peninsula, where fisherman generally take lakers along with other winter species—burbot, charr, whitefish, pike, etc. Jigs, spoons and bait are the most commonly used enticements.

GEARING UP FOR ALASKA'S LAKE TROUT

Spin & Casting Gear

For spinfishing Alaska's lake trout under most conditions, you'll want to rig up with a light/medium or medium-weight, six- to eight-and-a-half-foot, medium-action, freshwater spinning rod, matched with a high quality open-faced reel capable of holding at least 175 yards of 8- to 12-pound test nylon monofilament line. Casting gear fishermen will probably want a medium-weight, fast-action seven- to eight-and-a-half-foot rod, with a matching reel that holds 200 yards of 12-pound test.

For deepwater trolling, a medium-weight, downrigger or backbounce rod, seven-and-a-half to eight feet, is recommended, matched with a sturdy reel (Ambassadeur 6500 or 7000 series, Penn 9M, or Daiwa Sealine LD30) and at least 200 yards of 15- to 30-pound test (depending on whether you are fishing downriggers) mono or braided line.

Flyfishing Gear

Depending on water depth, length of casts, wind and other factors, you'll probably want to rig up with something like a long (nine to ten foot) seven- or eight-weight rod for most of your fishing, matched with an appropriate reel and assortment of lines—floating, short and long sink tips and full sinks—to handle the variety of conditions. Keep leaders short (four feet or less) for all but the rare surface presentations, and use a tippet of around (2X) 10-pound test for best results.

Fishing Bait

The use of live bait, a deadly effective and time-honored tradition elsewhere, is restricted in Alaska by a statewide ban to prevent introduction of non-native species. Though you can't rig a squirming, six-inch grayling to tantalize the big ones like they do in Canada, you can do quite well at certain times trolling a rigged whitefish or a spoon with a four- to five-inch whitefish, grayling or herring strip added for extra pizazz. Some fishermen have even had good results at certain times drifting chunks of whitefish, shrimp, even salmon eggs through weedy bays, channels and outlet and inlet waters. Keep this in mind if conditions aren't favorable to the more standard approaches.

WHERE TO GO

With all the attention lavished on Alaska's world-famous salmon and rainbow fisheries, the state's outstanding lake trout potential is easily overlooked. Well-known and perennially favorite locations like Lake Louise-Susitna, Paxson-Summit, Crosswind, Hidden and Harding continue to produce some amazing trophy fishing (20- to 30-pound-plus fish) year after year, despite mounting pressure. More remote, higher-quality fishing experiences can be had with short hikes in to the mountain lakes off the Denali Highway (Landmark Gap, Glacier, Sevenmile, Butte lakes) or the more out-of-the-way Dalton, Alaska's only road to the Arctic (see descriptions on page 217 in the Arctic chapter).

The best lake trout fishing in the Last Frontier can't be reached by car or foot, of course. You'll need to climb in a small plane and fly beyond the fringes of civilization to the state's more isolated waters. Some of these are not too far or expensive to access. The majestic Wrangell and Talkeetna Mountain Ranges, north and east of Anchorage, all contain numerous lakes with great fishing that can be reached with relatively short, inexpensive flights from the nearby hub towns of Palmer, Talkeetna and Glennallen. Fabulous southwest Alaska likewise contains many headwater lakes that are seldom sampled, but have some of the state's best wild lake trout angling. And for those lucky souls blessed with time and resources to explore Alaska's ultimate wilderness watersheds, there are the remote lakes of the Brooks Range and Arctic North Slope, where one can encounter the "old man of the lakes" in his most primeval surroundings.

Alaska's Top Trophy Lake Trout Waters
•Lake Louise (Southcentral)
•Lake Clark (Southwest)
•Harding Lake (Interior)
•Paxson Lake (Southcentral)
•Crosswind Lake (Southcentral)

ALASKA'S TOP TEN TROPHY LAKE TROUT
47 pounds, 0 ounces, Clarence Lake (Southcentral), 1970 (state record)
33 pounds, 8 ounces, Lake Clark (Southwest), 1980
33 pounds, 4 ounces, Harding Lake (Interior), 1993
32 pounds, 4 ounces, Lake Clark (Southwest), 1983
30 pounds, 15 ounces, Lake Louise (Southcentral), 1973
29 pounds, 8 ounces, Skilak Lake (Southcentral), 1985
29 pounds, 2 ounces, Old John Lake (Interior), 1981
28 pounds, 6 ounces, Lake Clark (Southwest), 1982
28 pounds, 5 ounces, Harding Lake (Interior), 1994
28 pounds, 4 ounces, Lake Clark (Southwest), 1983

ALASKA'S MAJOR LAKE TROUT LOCATIONS

Southcentral

Southcentral holds some of Alaska's most heavily fished but productive lake trout waters, including some outstanding trophy locations.

•*Susitna Drainage:* Susitna, Tyone, Louise, Clarence, Watana, Crater, Big, Deadman, Chelatna, Stephan, Shell and Butte lakes

•*Copper Drainage:* Paxson, Summit, Crosswind, Fish, Deep, Shell, Fielding, Tangle (Upper and Landlocked), Klutina, Tonsina, Tazlina, Tanada, Tebay and Hanagita lakes

•*White River Drainage:* Rock, Ptarmigan and Beaver lakes

•*Kenai Peninsula:* Hidden Lake; Kenai River system (including Skilak and Kenai lakes); Swan, Juneau and Trail lakes; Trail River, Tustumena Lake-Kasilof River

•*Cook Inlet:* Beluga, Chakachamna and Crescent lakes

•*Prince William Sound:* Tokun Lake

Southwest

Southwest has some of the state's best lake trout waters in terms of abundance, though few trophy (20-pound-plus) fish are taken, perhaps because these lakes receive so little focused fishing effort.

•*Kvichak Drainage:* Lakes Clark and Iliamna; Kokhanok Lakes, Gibraltar, Lachbuna, Kontrashibuna and Kijik lakes

•*Katmai:* Lakes Naknek, Brooks, Kulik, Nonvianuk, Kukaklek and Coville-Grosvenor

•*Alaska Peninsula:* Ugashik and Becharof lakes

•*Nushagak Drainage:* Tikchik Lakes (all); Twin, Fishtrap, Snipe and Turquoise lakes

•*Togiak Drainage:* Nenevok Lake

•*Upper Kuskokwim River:* Whitefish (Hoholitna), Telaquana and Two lakes

•*Lower Kuskokwim River:* Aniak, Kisaralik, Heart and Kanektok river lakes (Kagati-Pegati, Kanuktik, Klak, Ohnlik, etc.), Goodnews River Lakes (Goodnews, North and South Middle Fork, Kukatlim, Canyon, etc.) and Arolik Lakes

Interior
Interior includes some of the state's most popular fisheries in the Tanana drainage and some excellent remote lakes.

•*Eastern Brooks Range:* Upper Chandalar River—Ackerman, Squaw and Chandalar lakes; Upper Koyukuk River— Big and Twin lakes; Sheenjek River drainage and Old John Lake

•*Tanana:* Tangle Lakes; Fielding, Boulder, Glacier, 16.8 Mile, Sevenmile, Harding, Landmark Gap, Monte, Tetlin and Two-Bit lakes

Northwest
The Northwest has many outstanding possibilities in numerous, remote Brooks Range mountain lakes. A few of the more well-known ones are listed below:

•*Kobuk River Valley:* Walker, Minakokosa, Selby-Narvak and Norutak lakes

•*Noatak River Valley:* Feniak, Matcharak and Desperation lakes; Kiingyak, Kikitaliorak and other Howard Pass lakes

•*Koyukuk River:* Wild, Iniakuk, Helpmejack and Agiak lakes

Arctic
Arctic has the state's wildest lake trout waters, many receiving little, if any fishing pressure. Their potential for high-quality fishing is tops.

•*Colville River:* Etivluk River Lakes (Betty, Etivluk, Nigu, Tukuto, etc.); Karupa and Cascade lakes; Chandler and Amiloyak lakes; Anaktuvuk River Lakes (Irgnyivik, Shainin, Tulugak, Lower Anayak, etc.); Itkillik Lake

•*Central Plain Lakes:* Teshekpuk and other lakes east of the Ikpikpuk River

•*Dalton Highway Lakes:* Galbraith, Elusive, Toolik, Itagaknit, Kuparuk and Campsite lakes

•*Eastern Slope:* Porcupine, Schrader and Peters lakes

8
RAINBOW TROUT:
FISH WITH A HEART

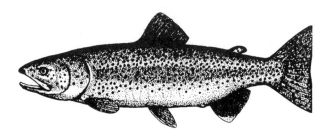

An Alaska guide's job might seem a dreamy, fun-filled adventure to some folks. The reality, however, is one of long hours of difficult, demanding work dealing with the vagaries of Alaska's weather, wild rivers and unpredictable fishing. But it does have its special moments.

Billie, a young wrangler from Montana up for a summer of guiding, isn't quite sure he likes this game. It's been a most trying trip so far—nasty weather, very poor fishing conditions and some difficult guests who are relentless in hounding the new guide for his lack of experience. At one of our stops to make lunch and a much-needed fire, he grabs one of the spinning outfits off the back of the boat, and in his only attempt at fishing the entire trip, sends a #6 Vibrax spinner hurtling across river with an angry heave. I watch it make an enormous arc and plunk down behind an island, and then it happens: As if on cue, a bright, muscular missile as long as my arm launches from the same spot, straight up, clearing the water by an easy four feet. It's a rainbow trout, by God, with a spinner dangling from its mouth!

There's only one problem—Billie's got a quarter-mile of line billowing in the wind, and from the looks of things, this wild 30-incher will have him stripped before he's even got his bail flipped. The berserk rainbow jumps six or seven times, furious at an easy meal gone bad. By now, every eye on shore is riveted to this spectacle. The husky mossback reenters his watery realm and holds in the strong current, allowing Billie precious seconds to regain line—but only for an instant, for the fish shoots off in a blinding run that cruelly strips all the hard-won gains from the reel. I can see there isn't a prayer of holding this fish, but that doesn't really matter. In these brief, crazy moments, the whole trip is turning around.

The giant rainbow—by now beyond all hope of landing—launches into a frenzy of cartwheels that seems to defy gravity. The inevitable is close at hand, and I sense a shared feeling of relief when the line finally parts with a loud "twang" and the incredible fish goes free. In the strange hush that follows, Billie, acting like he does this sort of thing all the time, calmly walks back to the boat, puts the rod down and hiding a grin that says it all, mutters, "Yeah, I guess they're out there." (The next day, I can't help but notice, guests are thronging him for fishing advice.)

INTRODUCTION

The rainbow trout *(Oncorhynchus mykiss)* certainly needs no intro-duction to American anglers. Perhaps the most prized of all our coldwater game fishes, the colorful, native trout of the Pacific Coast has been dazzling us for decades with its high-spirited antics. And few will argue that this glamorous fighter reaches its finest expression in the icy, vast waters of Alaska, where an age-long struggle in a chal-lenging but rich environment has honed him to a robustness seldom seen elsewhere. Alaska rainbows are indeed big! And in the deep, strong currents you'll find them in, they certainly rank as one of the premier challenges in the world of light tackle angling.

The state's immense, wild rainbow territory—from Southeast to Kuskokwim Bay—encompasses hundreds of rivers and lakes, in what is undoubtedly the last significant stronghold for the species. For seri-ous trout anglers the world over, visiting this ultimate rainbow mecca is the dream of a lifetime. In terms of dollars and effort anglers put forth to pursue good fishing, no other Alaska species, except perhaps the great king salmon, elicits the same kind of fanatical esteem from anglers of all persuasions.

DESCRIPTION

More streamlined and graceful in form than any salmon, Alaska's rainbow trout presents an unmistakable but varied appearance. The back is generally an olive green or gray, the sides are silver (silver-gray) and the belly whitish. A broad pink, lilac or scarlet stripe along the midline is the salient identifying feature, from which the fish also derives it name. It also has a liberal sprinkling of small- to moderate-sized black spots over the upper body and entire tail fin, which is usually less forked than in the salmon or charrs. Belly fins are generally pinkish to pearly white. Appearance can vary with time of year, diet, maturity and location. Each watershed seems to produce its own color variation. Fish from the big lakes, like Iliamna, Naknek and Kenai, are bright silver and sparsely marked, like steelhead, while rainbows from small tributary systems can be exquisitely hued (lilac, rose or crimson) with pronounced markings (the leopard rainbows of Bristol Bay, for instance). Spawning in spring brings coloration and physical changes, but not as dramatic as in salmon.

Size is similarly varied, with the largest rainbows coming from the state's big lake and river systems (Naknek, Iliamna, Wood-Tikchik and Kenai). Fish of four to seven pounds or more are caught there with predictable regularity, with rainbows of more than ten pounds not uncommon. On most Alaska rainbow streams, however, you can expect to catch fish averaging somewhere around two to three pounds, with the occasional five-pounder or bigger. (The largest sport-caught rainbow ever taken in Alaska was an IGFA world record steelhead, a few ounces over 42 pounds, but freshwater resident fish of more than 20 pounds are rare these days. See the steelhead chapter beginning on page 143 for more details on Alaska's sea-run rainbows.) The isolation of most of the state's waters, the short fishing season, and the growing predominance of catch-and-release no doubt contribute to the hefty average size of most of Alaska's wild rainbows.

RANGE, ABUNDANCE & STATUS

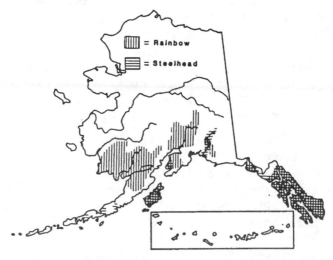

Shaded area shows range of rainbow trout and steelhead in Alaska.

RAINBOW TROUT

Rainbow trout were historically distributed along most of the Pacific slope, from northern Mexico to Kamchatka. In Alaska, they occur naturally from streams and lakes in Southeast to tributaries of the lower Kuskokwim River in Southwest, but not continuously along this range, as they are conspicuously absent from areas such as the Northern Gulf Coast, Prince William Sound and most of the Alaska Peninsula. Steelhead, the sea-run form of the rainbow trout, have a more extensive but sporadic Alaska distribution. Through propagation and transplanting, numerous new lake fisheries for rainbows now exist in parts of Alaska, such as Southcentral and Interior.

The status of the wild rainbow in Alaska seems remarkably secure, bolstered by the new ethics in sport angling, and its call for catch-and-release, single, barbless hooks, the phasing out of bait and more conservative management. Though many an old-timer may wistfully recall the bygone days of really stupendous rainbow fishing, Alaska still has far and away the world's best fishing for the species, in terms of abundance, variety and trophy potential.

LIFE HISTORY & HABITS

The key to success in stalking the wild, big and beautiful Alaska rainbow lies in a thorough understanding of its life cycle and feeding habits and associated movement patterns. Rainbow trout begin their lives in much the same manner as their larger cousins the salmon, hatching from eggs laid and fertilized in a gravel stream bed (spawning usually occurs in late April, May or June in Alaska). Young fry develop quickly, feeding on insect and crustacean life almost exclusively in their first year of life, but opportunistically utilizing any food source that becomes available, especially as they grow older.

Larger rainbows will feed extensively—and at times exclusively—on minnows (sticklebacks, sculpins and juvenile salmon) and when available, they will also prey heavily on leeches, freshwater shrimp, snails and even small rodents (voles, mice and shrews). Insect life (nymphs and emerging) is also utilized to a varying extent. During summer and fall, practically every rainbow trout in Alaska becomes associated at some time or another with spawning salmon for a chance at their abundant, rich roe, a choice food source for achieving the prime condition necessary to survive Alaska's long, lean winters. At times, they may even pick flesh off dead salmon. In major systems that see annual returns of millions of salmon, the significance of this roe (and flesh) to resident populations of rainbow, charr and other fish species is both substantial and crucial, for it allows large populations of these species to survive in waters that are otherwise quite unproductive.

The Alaska rainbow usually reaches sexual maturity in three to five years, and can live to well over ten, with habitat and available food resources playing a big part in life span and ultimate size. Generally, growth is slow, and occurs mostly during the four to five warm months of the year, when food is most plentiful. A 10-pound rainbow may well be 12 years old. Despite the apparent abundance of large fish, most of Alaska's waters are deceptively low in productivity: All the more reason to practice a strict catch-and-release policy when fishing these beauties in their last wild strongholds.

Knowing what the main food sources are for Alaska's rainbows (and how to imitate and present them) can be the easy part of the angling equation. The real trick is locating fish, for like Alaska's charr, rainbows can have immense and complicated movement patterns, shifting locations and feed throughout the season to exploit all food sources as they become available. In smaller lakes and other closed systems, the Alaska rainbow will have movements more local and predictable. An understanding of these important feeding movements—when, where and how they occur, and the appropriate angling strategies—is essential for success.

FISHING ALASKA'S RAINBOW TROUT
Spring

As the ice leaves Alaska's lakes and rivers in April and May, rainbow trout become more active, feeding heavily and (mature fish) preparing for spawning. Like the charr, they'll opportunistically seize any available insects, crustaceans or small fish, especially young salmon. In most of the large lake and river systems that contain rainbows (Kenai, Iliamna, Naknek, Wood-Tikchiks, etc.), alevins, fry and out-migrating smolt will be a primary food source for rainbow trout and charr, making fishing strategies similar for both (see charr chapter beginning on page 100 for additional details on fishing techniques this time of year). The best fishing locations at this time will be the lake outlets and inlets, river mouths, confluences and pools of these major salmon systems, with the most effective lures usually those that mimic young salmon or other forage species—small spinners and spoons, plugs, smolt- and fry-patterned streamers, sculpin and leech patterns, etc. Cloudy days and the darker hours of early morning and late evening will generally offer the most productive fishing.

The potent appeal and ease of fishing spinners makes them hard to beat for Alaska spring rainbows, with the most popular being the Super Vibrax, Mepps Aglia (long), Rooster Tail and Panther Martin, in silver, gold or copper, sizes #0 to #3 or $^1/_{32}$ to $^1/_6$ ounce. In deep water near lake outlets or in big rivers, spoons can be more effective, and many Alaska fishermen use the smaller ($^1/_8$ to $^3/_8$ ounce) Pixees, Krocodiles, Kastmasters and Hot Rods with good results. Under most spring conditions, you'll do best fishing with a steady, not-too-fast retrieve, working areas of likely fish concentration or any water where you see feeding activity.

Super Vibrax spinner

In smaller lakes and rivers, rainbows will rely more on insect larvae, crustaceans, leeches and fish like sculpins or sticklebacks. Nymph patterns and Muddler, Leech and Woolly Bugger streamers, along with small spoons, spinners and jigs, can all be equally effective under these conditions. In deep lakes with no outlet, good locations to target for fishing effort are shorelines and around prominent structure (islands, reefs and drop-offs), if no signs of feeding are present. Early morning and late evenings will generally be the most active times. Here, a boat and an electronic fish finder can improve your chances of success tenfold, but don't underestimate the effectiveness of skillful shore angling on these usually hungry and plentiful lake rainbows. Some of the better locales for this kind of spring fishing are the dozens of small lakes scattered throughout the Kenai Peninsula, Mat-Su Valley, Kodiak, Interior and Southeast.

Summer

As spring shifts into summer, Alaska's incredible salmon runs pump life into most of the state's waters, and rainbow trout, like charr and other resident species, will shift their activities to key into the movements of their larger spawning cousins. In river mouths, lake outlets, sloughs, confluences and deep pools—anywhere salmon congregate—you can expect attendant hordes of excitable rainbows "shadowing" the salmon that will later provide vital sustenance through their rich roe and flesh.

The outlets and inlets of the big lakes in Southwest, when the huge sockeye migrations hit in early July, come to mind as the best of Alaska's early summer rainbow fishing. If you time it right in these waters, you can have some incredible action with the big, excitable fish that gather there. Egg-pattern flies, bright attractors, and silver, gold or fluorescent spinners, spoons, plugs and even drift bobbers all seem to work well on these easily provoked trout. The techniques used for charr this time of year are equally effective on rainbows: fishing the periphery of salmon lies, using deeper presentations and attractor colors, etc. (See the charr chapter beginning on page 100 for details.)

When spinner-fishing these early summer rainbows, colors like fluorescent red, orange, pink and chartreuse are most effective, especially when used in combination with the standard silver or gold. Stick-on reflective tape or a piece of colored yarn works well to dress up unadorned lures, and allows for creative experimentation with a variety of colors and combinations. The most popular and effective spinners for early summer are the same as used earlier in the spring—Vibrax, Mepps, Rooster Tail, Panther Martin, etc.—with sizes up to #5 or $^7/_{16}$-ounce used. Locate groups of salmon if possible, and cast directly behind or to either side of them, fishing deep with a steady retrieve. In turbid flows or other situations where salmon can't be located, work deep pools, sloughs, confluences, cutbanks, river mouths and lake outlets—anywhere salmon might hold.

Floating down headwaters in rafts can be the best way to access and fish late summer rainbow trout hot spots.

Once the salmon reach their home gravels and begin their passion play, Alaska's rainbow fishing kicks in high gear. A favorite time of year for many anglers is late August and September, as the bugs generally have diminished and the sporting silver salmon arrive to spice up the action. In just about every lesser tributary stream or gravelly middle to upper mainstem of the hundreds of salmon systems spread along the coast, thousands of salmon will be busily engaged in the mating ritual, some of them already occupying their shallow, scooped-out nests on bottom. These are the areas where late summer rainbows (and charr) can be found in greatest concentration.

The big salmon get so caught up in their ardor, they can seem almost oblivious to the egg-stealing onslaughts of trout, charr and grayling. Anything that comes drifting through these areas remotely resembling salmon roe (of pink, red, orange or white color)—be it egg-pattern fly, fluorescent-bladed spinner, drift bobber, or even a yarn-wrapped hook—will usually draw immediate response from the hungry hordes that get quite rambunctious under these competitive conditions. In many ways, this is Alaska rainbow fishing at its best, as you can do things that would astound most conventional trout fishermen and still catch dozens of fish.

Some of the more popular spinning lures for late summer rainbow fishing are #2 to #5 Super Vibrax ("firetiger" finish or silver or gold blade with fluorescent orange bell), #2 to #5 Mepps Black Fury or Aglia (fluorescent red, orange or yellow blade), $^{1}/_{4}$- to $^{1}/_{2}$-ounce Rooster Tail (fluorescent red, pink or chartreuse), $^{1}/_{2}$-ounce Pixee with red or pink insert, and the $^{3}/_{8}$- and $^{1}/_{2}$-ounce Hot Rod (in nickel or brass with fire stripe).

Fall

From September until freeze-up, cooling temperatures, diminishing daylight, and tightening food supplies spark a desperate hunger and wanton recklessness among Alaska's rainbow population. With the wane of the salmon runs, they will leave the upper sections of rivers and tributaries and move down into the mainstems, feeding heavily all the while. In the large lake and river systems, big rainbows will move into the shallows of tributary streams and rivers, scouring the bottom for lingering salmon roe, even stripping the flesh off carcasses to bolster reserves against the long, dark siege ahead. It is a premier time for the trophy angler. Bristol Bay's Lake Iliamna-Kvichak River system, Naknek Lake and River system of Katmai, Southcentral's Kenai River, and other locations are world-famous for their late fall, big rainbow trout fisheries. If you haven't already done so, you owe it to yourself to make at least one fall outing to fish these waters. With any luck, you can have the kind of trout fishing most folks only dream about. (See the location descriptions on pages 310, 324, 404 and 406 for more details on fishing these areas.) Egg patterns, flesh flies, attractors, plugs, spoons and bright drift bobbers fished deep are most effective. Late September and October are the traditional peak periods for this special trophy season.

Winter

Once hard winter starts in Alaska (usually sometime in November), rainbows will seek the sanctuary of deep pools, river mainstems and lakes, slowing down to conserve energy with the cold and diminished light. Feeding is limited and consists of the occasional minnow, crustacean or larvae. Not as exciting to catch this time of year, these winter trout will still put up a tussle, and provide a significant amount of angling opportunity through the ice in areas like Southcentral's Mat-Su Valley and Kenai Peninsula, and around Fairbanks, Delta and Glennallen.

FLYFISHING

There is something about a big trout on a fly that no other fishing experience can match, especially when it's a wild, husky Alaska rainbow. Seasoned anglers who've fished around are often disappointed, however, when they discover that these Alaska fish are not wily, selective trout requiring fancy casts and artful presentations. For the most part, Alaska's trout ask little in the way of technique or finesse from fly anglers. The challenge instead is one of determining those "here today, gone tomorrow" rainbow whereabouts and dealing with the varied and often demanding conditions encountered on most of the state's waters. Here's a rundown of the basics:

Spring

Spring conditions on most Alaska waters are similar to those encountered in many western rivers at this time—high, turbid flows, marginal weather, and feeding activity concentrated on forage fish, crustaceans and nymphs. The challenge for the flyfisherman remains the same: to locate feeding fish, then determine and present the proper prey imitation in a manner most like the real thing. You'll use most of the same techniques here as you would stateside for streamer fishing this time of year—floating lines or sink tips, quarter casts, and downstream, cross-current swings of the fly. Since minnows are the predominant prey, you'll be fishing mostly smolt, fry, leech and sculpin patterns (sizes #2 to #6), in addition to perennial rainbow favorites (in the same sizes) like purple, black or brown Matukas, Woolly Buggers, Muddler Minnows, and attractors like Polar Shrimp, Mickey Finn and Skykomish Sunrise. Small alevin and nymph patterns (size #8 to #12) can also be quite effective early in the season. Short, fast strips and "jigging" rod twitches to impart lifelike, strike-provoking action seem the most productive retrieve tactics for these heavily feeding spring rainbows.

River mouths, lake outlets and inlets, confluences, pools and tailouts—anywhere rainbows might advantageously locate themselves to ambush prey—are the areas where you should concentrate your efforts. In smaller, closed lakes with no signs of surface feeding, you may have better success with nymphs, shrimp or scud patterns (#6 to #10), so experiment a little if you don't have any luck with streamers. And since Alaska rainbows are not leader-shy, all your subsurface presentations will be much easier and more effective with tippets shortened to three to four feet.

Summer

Summer brings the great influx of salmon and rainbows that are keyed almost exclusively into feeding on roe. This means egg-pattern flies and drift presentations for most waters. The simplest, most popular Alaska egg fly is, of course, the Glo Bug—a puff of orange, pink or red chenille on a size #2 to #12 egg hook. It's extremely effective fished on a dead drift, right above bottom, especially in the vicinity of holding or spawning salmon. Other popular egg patterns include the Babine Special, Two-Egg Maribou, Egg-Sucking Leech and Spawn Sac. Polarized sunglasses, sink tip lines and strike indicators are all very useful in these summer conditions.

Situations and conditions arise during summer when a simple egg or attractor pattern might not bring the results you expect. Here, you may need more precise casting and presentation (if you can sight-fish), or some oversized, gaudy attractor and egg flies like the Pink Sparkler, Wiggle Tail, Outrageous, Alaskabou or other specialty patterns developed to tantalize rainbows with maximum color and flash. Purists may shudder at the thought of even considering such creations for flyfishing, but no one will argue their effectiveness.

Fall

Fall flyfishing for Alaska's rainbows is usually the most exciting and productive of the year, as fish are in prime condition and actively feeding on all available food sources. Egg, Flesh Fly, Attractor, and to a limited extent, bait imitations like Leeches, Muddlers and Sculpins will all take fish this time of year. If you are lucky enough to make your way to the big waters of Katmai, Kenai or Iliamna for the fabulous late fall fishery there, you'll definitely want to bring some heavy trout or steelhead gear along: long, stout eight- or even nine-weight rods, beefy steelhead lines (floating, 5- and 10-foot sink tips; full-sink, high-density, even shooting tapers) and some of your biggest flies— Bunny Bugs, Woolly Buggers, Matukkas, Two-Egg Maribous, Spawn Sacs, Polar Shrimp, etc. Quite often, you'll be fishing deep, fast water, and the stout gear will give you a fighting chance with the steelhead-sized rainbows you'll encounter.

Dry Fly Fishing & Patterns

The Mouse—Alaska's most famous "dry fly."

Not too much is said about dry flies for Alaska's rainbows, for the simple reason that wet presentations produce so fabulously well in most waters throughout the year. Great opportunities for exciting surface fishing go underutilized during late spring and summer all across Alaska's rainbow country, but you can get in on some of this abundant action if you know what to look for and come prepared with the proper gear and fly selection.

Emerging insect activity in Alaska's waters occurs mostly during the warmest days of June and July, although skillful anglers can raise fish any month of the year under the right conditions. The Alaska rainbow doesn't seem very discriminating in its surface feeding behavior, with numerous patterns producing good results: Elk Hair Caddis, Humpy, Wulff, Adams, Cahill, even the Gnats or Mosquito, in sizes #8 through #14. Standard floating line presentations seem to work fine for these northern trout, and you can probably shorten your leaders somewhat under most conditions without any noticeable effect. Your best chances for hooking a trout on a dry fly this time of year will be during warm, sunny spells, in water that is less than six feet deep, of moderate to fast current—in tail-outs, riffles, lake outlets and shallow runs.

•*Alaska's Ten Deadliest Rainbow Patterns:* Polar Shrimp, Woolly Bugger, Glo Bug Smolt, Egg-Sucking Leech, Marabou Muddler, Babine Special, Mouse, Flesh Fly, Elk Hair Caddis.

Gearing Up for Rainbow Trout

Hardcore Alaska flyfishers can amass an amazing arsenal of gear for the wide range of situations they fish rainbows in, but one can get by quite nicely with just the basics. For most of Alaska, we're talking about a six- to eight-weight, eight- to nine-and-a-half-foot, medium-action graphite rod, matching reel and an assortment of lines (floating, sink-tips, full-sink, high-density, etc.). Hook sizes most commonly used vary from #2 to #12, while tippets for Alaska's rainbows are usually in the 4- to 12-pound range. You must either have gear to match the water or find the water to match the gear, as the saying goes. Nowhere will this be more true than in Alaska's rainbow country, where you'll find an amazing range of conditions from mile to mile, making for difficult, if not impossible fishing at times. The trick is to have a system that is versatile and easy to use. Many folks bring along two or three or even more complete outfits to handle the changing water conditions normally encountered during the course of a trip (for instance, a six- or seven-weight and floating line for dry flies and shallow pocket water, and a seven- or eight-weight with sinking tip line for fishing the deeper pools and runs). "Shooting heads" (short, 30-foot, looped sections of fly line) are a versatile, less-expensive alternative to bringing a boatload of spare spools and lines, and are now available in a variety of weights and tapers.

Spinning

The majority of Alaska's spin anglers gear up for rainbows with ultra-light or light- to medium-weight graphite rods (six- to seven-and-a-half feet), medium- to fast-action, matched with monofilament line of four- to ten-pound test, on high-quality, open-faced reels. For big water trophy fishing, a light to medium steelhead or heavy trout rod (seven- to eight-and-a-half feet) with fast action, and a matching high-quality reel with line weights of 8- to 15-pound test is most popular.

Bait Casting

For driftfishing and trolling the big lakes and rivers (Kenai, Naknek, Kvichak, Wood-Tikchiks and others), baitcasters are the equipment of choice. You'll generally be working these waters by boat, pulling plugs, spoons or specially-rigged drift bobbers (Spin-N-Glos, Tee-Spoons, Okie Drifters, Hot Shots or Tadpollys) right above bottom, through deep, swirling blue pools for giant, silvery rainbows. For these conditions, eight- to nine-foot, medium- to fast-action steelhead rods are hard to beat, matched to 10- to 15-pound mono on high quality reels (200-yard line capacity) like the Ambassadeur series.

Alaska's Top Trophy Rainbow Trout Waters
•Naknek River and Lake (Southwest)
•Kenai River (Southcentral)
•Lake Iliamna-Kvichak River system (Southwest)
•Nushagak River System (Southwest)

ALASKA'S TOP TEN TROPHY RAINBOWS

23 pounds, 0 ounces, Naknek Lake (Southwest), 1991
22 pounds, 7 ounces, Kenai River (Southcentral), 1982
20 pounds, 1 ounce, Kenai River (Southcentral), 1985
20 pounds, 0 ounces, Kenai River (Southcentral), 1992
19 pounds, 12 ounces, Kvichak River (Southwest), 1981
19 pounds, 8 ounces, Naknek Lake (Southwest), 1981
19 pounds, 6 ounces, Naknek Lake (Southwest), 1979
18 pounds, 8 ounces, Naknek River (Southwest), 1969
18 pounds, 8 ounces, Kvichak River (Southwest), 1980
18 pounds, 4 ounces, Kenai River (Southcentral), 1987

ALASKA'S MAJOR RAINBOW TROUT LOCATIONS

Anglers in Alaska catch well over one-half million rainbow trout a year. Most of this angling effort takes place in populous Southcentral, and concentrates on the Kenai and Susitna River systems and lakes in and around Anchorage. A considerable amount of rainbow fishing also takes place in the immense, clear river and lake systems of Bristol Bay, which offer the state's finest trout fishing experiences. Some promising but presently underutilized rainbow fishing exists in scattered lakes and streams throughout Southeast, the Kenai Peninsula, Susitna and Copper River valleys and Kodiak Island.

Southeast

Most of Southeast's waters have steelhead, which in their younger forms are commonly mistaken for resident rainbows, but there are dozens of lakes containing stocked and native, non-anadromous rainbow populations.

•*Yakutat:* Situk Lake

•*Juneau/Skagway:* Dewey, Hoktaheen, Surge and Peterson lakes

•*Sitka/Petersburg/Wrangell:* Hugh Smith, Sarkar, Red, Thoms, Anan, Boulder, Reflection, Avoss, Rezanof, Plotnikof, Davidof, Salmon, Politofsky, Sukoi, Grebe, Swan, Goat, Eagle, Khvostof, Gar, Betty, Jetty, Marten, Petersburg, Blue, Sitkoh and Sweetwater lakes

•*Ketchikan:* Naha River and Lake system; Karta and Thorne rivers; Harriet Hunt, Connell, Ketchikan, Nakat, Filmore, McDonald, Rainbow and Kegan lakes

Southcentral

•*Kenai:* Kenai River, Russian River, upper Deep Creek and Anchor rivers, upper Moose River and associated lakes; Swanson, Longmere,

Dolly Varden, Vagt, Grant, Upper and Lower Russian, Upper and Lower Ohmer, Jean, Kelly, Peterson, Egumen, Watson, Mosquito, Forest, Rainbow, Paddle, Longmere, Douglas, Cabin, Chugach Estates, Wik, Daniels, Barbara, Cecille, Stormy, Johnson, Quintin and Encelewski lakes

•*Anchorage:* Campbell Creek, Otter Lake

•*Mat-Su Valley:* Matanuska, Echo, Kepler/Bradley, Irene, Long, Ravine, Knik, Reed, Kalmbach, Seymour, Dawn, Marion, Nancy, Lynne, Honeybee, Crystal and Florence lakes

•*Susitna:* Deshka, Talachulitna, Upper Talkeetna, East Fork Chulitna, and upper Susitna (Indian River, Portage and Prairie creeks) river systems; Upper Kashwitna, Montana, Little Willow, Peters (Kahiltna River), Lake, Sheep and Byers creeks

•*Cook Inlet:* Chuitna, Theodore and Beluga rivers

•*Wrangell:* Upper Gulkana and Tebay river systems; Crater, Tex Smith, Tolsona, Van, Silver and Sculpin lakes

•*Chugach:* Blueberry and Worthington lakes

•*Kodiak:* Reports of rainbow trout populations in lakes and rivers quite often turn out to be immature steelhead trout. Some natural, though small, populations of true rainbow trout occur in the following drainages: Saltery, Buskin, Uganik and Olga lakes and Ayakulik River. Stocked rainbow trout are found in a few lakes along the Kodiak road system, like Woody and Long lakes.

Southwest

Southwest is Alaska's ultimate region for abundant, wild rainbows. Hundreds of rivers, streams and lakes offer some of the world's best fly-in fishing, with many trophy opportunities.

•*Bristol Bay:* Lake Iliamna-Kvichak River system (Kvichak, Newhalen, Copper, Gibraltar and Tazimina rivers; Talarik, Dream and Belinda creeks); Nushagak/Mulchatna River system (Chilikadrotna, Mulchatna, Little Mulchatna, Koktuli, Stuyahok, Nuyakuk and upper Nushagak rivers); Wood River lakes and associated tributaries (Wood, Agulowak, Agulukpak and Peace rivers; Lynx, Grant and Little Togiak lakes, etc.); Tikchik and Nuyakuk lakes, lower Tikchik River; Togiak Lake and River system

•*Alaska Peninsula:* Naknek Lake and River system (Brooks River, Grosvenor and Coville lakes, American and Idavain creeks, etc.); Alagnak River system (Nonvianuk-Kukakluk, Kulik and Battle lakes;

Funnel and Moraine creeks, etc.); Egegik River system (King Salmon River—clear tributaries)

•*Lower Kuskokwim River:* Goodnews, Kanektok, Arolik, Kwethluk, Kasigluk, Kisaralik and Aniak rivers

Interior

Interior does not have naturally occurring populations of rainbows, but it has numerous stocked lakes with good fishing: Quartz, Birch, Harding, Little Harding, Johnson, Robertson, Donna, Little Donna, Koole, Rainbow, Dune, Jan, Lisa, Lost, Craig, Coal Mine Road and Fort Greely lakes; Piledriver Slough

Rainbow trout

9
STEELHEAD:
PRINCE OF SPORTFISH

by Gary Souza

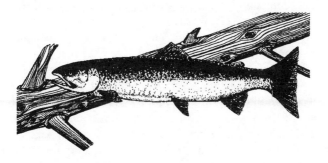

The early morning fog hangs like a heavy curtain at water's edge and the mercury hasn't yet crested the magic 40-degree mark, but it's time to don waders and leave the warm security of the 48-footer anchored in the inlet and head into shore on the ebb tide.

Once ashore, a mile-and-a-half hike takes us through alder, spruce, hemlock, cedar and a despised thorny shrub that grows everywhere along these coasts and lives up to its name—Devil's Club. We arrive near several promising-looking runs below a 12-foot falls. The tannin-stained water here is the color of weak tea, but looks fishy nonetheless. We waste no time breaking the rods out and getting our lines in the water.

"Fish on!" yells Larry. I turn and see a dark fish of about 12 pounds tear downstream, jumping all the while. After 30 seconds his line suddenly slacks. Fish off, Larry. Our little group fishes out the remainder of the day and manages to hook 16 steelhead and several Dollies, cutthroats and rainbows. Not bad numbers for a day's fishing, although the majority are dark fall fish.

The weather on the second day is similar to the first—drizzly and cold. The fishing is about the same. Thirteen hooked, but most of them dark fish. The troller rocks and rolls all that night, as the southeast wind gusts to 60 miles per hour. Forced to "lay on the hook" instead of attempting the trip back across Clarence Strait, the skipper fights a grin as he informs his guests: "Oh well, I guess we'll just have to stay here and make the best of the situation."

A late start the next morning puts us on the river at 11 a.m. It's risen a foot and a half, yet still appears very fishable. I begin at one of my favorite holes about a mile up from saltwater and quickly hook a hot, bright hen. They're unmistakable when hooked, as half their fight is in the air. Bright males are great, too, but they usually jump less and fight more in bulldog fashion, shouldering down in a prolonged tug of war. I admire her gunmetal blue back and silvery flanks, noticing several sea lice above her anal fin. "New fish!" I slide her back to her freedom.

After hooking three more bright steelhead, I move upstream to join my companions. We are the only ones on the river that day and are thankful for it. Another bright hen leaps for the sky four times and runs off 50 feet of line in a single burst. When the fish is brought in, she turns and streaks like a lightning bolt downstream 75 yards into a log-jam, where the line parts with a twang and the steelhead goes free.

Rain and the southeast wind have given us a special bonus day of fishing. We paddle back to the *Julie Ann,* our floating hotel, having hooked 19 steelhead.

INTRODUCTION

The steelhead trout *(Oncorhynchus mykiss),* the sea-roving form of the rainbow, is perhaps the most sought-after and prized of the North Pacific's many fine gamefish. An elite band of anglers the world over diligently pursues them with a passion that borders on the fanatical, braving all manner of stream conditions, weather, and logistics—not to mention expense—to enjoy some high-quality fishing.

And while the mystique of "steelheading" may be hard to grasp for some, its appeal is infectious and easily understood with only a single bout with the supercharged saltwater rainbow. They fight spectacularly, with the same high energy and astounding leaps of their river-bound brothers—only more so, because of their size and the vigor imparted by their life in the sea. As iron is to steel, the rainbow trout's noble qualities of spirit, beauty and grace are refined and tempered in rare form to produce the steelhead, prince of sportfish.

Steelheading in Alaska has been described in many ways. Of all that has been written and said, however, perhaps the most significant and attractive feature is the opportunity to angle for wild fish in wild environs—a luxury in these days of put-and-take fisheries. Alaska, too, is changing, and unfortunately some places are not as wild as they once were and some runs have been depleted. Yet overall, the state still offers some of the world's best remaining opportunities to experience a little of "how it used to be" everywhere for this magnificent species.

"Explosive fish are the steelhead and salmon that stalk our memories and dreams," wrote Ernest Schwiebert. We stalk steelhead in Alaska not because of their size or numbers, but because of the experience afforded. Through these experiences, one welcomes the stalkers of our memories and dreams.

DESCRIPTION

The steelhead can be identified from the various salmon species by having eight to twelve rays in the anal fin (most salmon will have 12 to 17). Usually more streamlined and slender than resident rainbow trout, the steelhead in its ocean phase exhibits a bright silvery sheen that is essential to survival. The topsides are generally a shiny gunmetal blue, contrasted with silver-white below the lateral line. There are black, regularly spaced spots on the back and sides, as well as on both lobes of the tail.

In preparation for spawning, the steelhead's colors become more similar to resident rainbow trout. The gunmetal blue dorsum changes to an olive black. A distinct reddish color develops on the flanks above and below the lateral line, and the shiny white undersides become a dusky gray. Upon completion of spawning, the steelhead's colors gradually revert to their ocean phase.

Steelhead in Alaska are not noted for their size relative to races elsewhere, such as the outsized fish of the Skeena River drainage in northern British Columbia. Steelhead in Southeast and Yakutat generally average eight to nine pounds. The fish of the other regions are slightly smaller, usually averaging eight pounds (the steelhead from Kodiak's famous Karluk River fall into this size class). Stories of 20-pound-plus fish run rampant, but most of these accounts are just that—good fish stories. Of all the hooked steelhead logged in my fishing diary, the largest remains a 38-inch buck which was probably slightly less than 20 pounds. I have personally witnessed two fish over 20 pounds landed and released. Will Jones, owner of Prince of Wales Lodge, for the past 14 seasons has seen only five hooked steelhead that have reached or exceeded 20 pounds. Note: The world record sport-caught fish, a steelhead of 42 pound, 3 ounces, was taken from Southeast's Behm Canal in 1970.

RANGE, ABUNDANCE & STATUS

The native range of the steelhead closely follows that of the resident river rainbow along the north Pacific rim—from the mountains of northwest Mexico to the rocky coast of the Kamchatka Peninsula. In

Alaska they are distributed from Dixon Entrance to the vicinity of Cold
Bay on the Alaska Peninsula. They are found most continuously from
southern Southeast to the North Gulf Coast, with sporadic distribution
west into Cook Inlet, Kodiak and the Alaska Peninsula (both sides).
Though numerous isolated occurrences suggest otherwise, no documented spawning populations exist north of Chignik on the Alaska
Peninsula, or in Bristol Bay or upper Cook Inlet. The state's most isolated northern run occurs in the Upper Copper River north of Cordova.

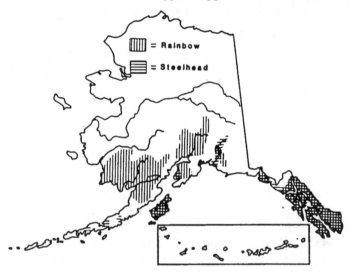

Shaded area shows range of rainbow trout and steelhead in Alaska.

There are 331 streams in Southeast now known to receive steelhead.
The majority of these, totaling 276, occur from south of Frederick
Sound to Dixon Entrance. Comprehensive data on the great majority of
Alaska steelhead systems is, unfortunately, not available at present.
There is a great need for further research.

Runs of steelhead in Southeast are relatively small compared to
steelhead streams in many other places. The largest runs total only 500
or more fish annually. There are far more streams receiving 200 to 300
annually, and the greatest number of streams are estimated to receive
runs of 100 fish or slightly more. These numbers are obviously quite
low relative to the size of salmon runs in Alaska, and to many steelhead runs elsewhere. The largest estimated run in southern Southeast
returns to the Karta River on Prince of Wales Island and exceeds 1,000
fish annually. The Anchor River on the Kenai Peninsula and the Karluk
River on Kodiak Island are systems that historically receive larger

numbers than average. The fabulous Situk River near Yakutat in its heyday had runs of more than 5,000, although in recent years, it has dwindled along with many others.

With regard to Southeast streams, one can only guess why run numbers are less in comparison to streams elsewhere. The Alaska Department of Fish and Game's Southeast sportfish biologists surmise that it may be due in part to low insect diversity and lower nutrient recruitment. That is, the streams of Southeast tend to exhibit a shortage of minerals and other factors critical to a productive stream's ecology. Most, if not all, Alaska steelhead streams are strongly influenced by the presence of salmon, and without the addition of these spent fish to the nutrient cycle, would most likely be almost sterile.

LIFE HISTORY & HABITS

Steelhead are large anadromous rainbow trout that rear in freshwater streams. Most Alaska fish spend three years in fresh water before they journey to the ocean as six- to seven-inch smolts. It is during this time that they attain such large size relative to most resident rainbow trout.

They return to fresh water as sexually mature adults after two or three years. Most runs of spring steelhead are comprised of a significant portion of repeat spawners (research has shown that repeat spawners can account for as high as 45 percent of a given run, although the average percentage is usually lower). These repeat spawners usually account for the fish that exceed 30 inches.

Steelhead return to streams in Southwest, Kenai Peninsula, and Kodiak Island primarily in the fall. Southeast receives runs in three seasons. There are only a few known runs of summer steelhead (Baranof Island). Fall-run fish begin returning to Southeast in September and October and continue through December and early January, depending upon the system's timing and weather conditions. Fall-run fish are limited in their habitat requirements compared to spring run fish. The majority of fall runs return to river systems with lakes. The exceptions are large streams with enough deep pools to allow overwintering survival (in lieu of lakes). Most fall-run fish exhibit habits similar to spring run steelhead. Generally, they hold in the same water, and can be found in the same type of spawning habitat. All races spawn in the spring regardless of when they enter fresh water.

There are some key exceptions to the many common traits among fall- and spring-run fish: Fall fish return sexually immature. Fall fish also tend at times to be more aggressive toward the fisherman's offering than spring fish. This is due in part to warmer water temperatures and to true feeding tendencies. I have personally landed many early fall fish that were gorged with pink salmon spawn—with small, pale pink eggs dropping from their jaws while I was releasing them. Some of these fish will hold in the upper reaches of holes and runs in order to opportunistically pick off drifting eggs. Fish under these conditions are easy prey to egg imitations drifted through their lie.

Spring-run steelhead are by far the most widespread race in Southeast. Many streams with low flows are host to spawning steelhead during the spring months. These fish begin returning in March, with April and May being the peak arrival periods. Spring fish are therefore generally available to the angler for a shorter period of time. Some research has determined that female spring fish also spend less time in fresh water than males. On occasion I have landed chrome-bright hen fish with sea lice, which had already spawned just a short distance from tidewater. These short appearances in fresh water are especially common in smaller streams during low water periods, and can present a frustrating challenge to the angler.

My fishing log (and similar records of other Southeast steelhead fanatics) reveals steelhead hooked in 10 calendar months, a relatively long season for Alaska. However, the peak and best fishing times can be relatively short.

FISHING ALASKA'S STEELHEAD
Drift Fishing

Drift fishing is the most effective way of hooking steelhead in all seasons and under most water conditions and situations. Steelhead can usually be hooked in deep water with drift fishing, when all other methods fail. In Alaska, as elsewhere in the Pacific Northwest, most (but not all) drift fishing is done with an eight- to nine-foot graphite, medium-action rod, in tandem with a level wind baitcasting reel. The rod should have a sensitive tip for detection of fish "mouthing" bait, and a stout butt section for solid hook-setting and fighting capabilities. Most accomplished drift fishermen agree that the bait caster affords advantages for drift fishing that the spinning reel does not. The bait caster, mounted on top, allows "more feel," as the angler has greater contact with the stream bottom through the line and because his thumb is on the spool. Hook-setting is done quickly, with the thumb firmly on the spool while briskly lifting the rod. In so doing there is no slippage of the reel drag system during the hook set (most spinning reels lack some sort of drag overriding feature and often slip during the hook set). Also, the level wind reel, because of its design, is inherently stronger and has a superior drag. Lamiglass and G. Loomis make several fine graphite drift rods. Several manufacturers—Daiwa, Shimano and Ambassadeur among them—make high-quality reels with different models to choose from.

The single most important element to drift fishing is the dynamics of the terminal end of the line during the drift. (This ought to be obvious, but surprisingly, is not.) Regardless of what type, color, or size of attractor the angler is using, its correct action during the drift is paramount to the angler's success. (Here, "attractor" is used in a much broader sense than elsewhere in this book.) Simply stated, the attractor must drift with a natural appearance. It must not hang on the bottom, and should not even "skip" with the weight as some have proposed. It should, rather, drift with as near a neutral buoyancy as possible. The closer you can come to attaining a natural drift, the better your chances are of getting steelhead to pick up the "bait." When attempting to choose the amount of weight to attach above the attractor, you should remember that too little weight is always better than too much, as a general rule. Numerous attractor lures are used effectively for drift fishing, the most effective for Alaska being Li'l Corkies, Spin-N-Glos, Glo Glos and other "egg-simulating" attractors.

The angler who has become accomplished at drift fishing prior to graduating to flyfishing will usually become a more effective flyfisher with a greater experience base upon which to draw. These anglers have greater insight into the steelhead's habits of holding in various lies, and how they "take" or "mouth" the attractor.

Spinner Fishing

Spinners can be very effective for steelhead. However, the angler must remember that steelhead in very cold water will generally not move well to take spinners, but would more readily mouth an attractor drifted directly to them. Many anglers work around this by using ultra-light gear and smaller spinners for coldwater conditions, working the blade ever so slightly as the lure tumbles through steelhead lies and into close striking range of lethargic fish. With the smaller, more sensitive gear, the often subtle take is more easily felt. These setups can also be very effective in extreme shallow or bright conditions, when steelhead get spooky. Some of the more popular spinners used for steelhead are the Mepps Aglia, Vibrax and Rooster Tail, in sizes #1 to #5 ($^{1}/_{8}$- to $^{3}/_{4}$-ounce for the Rooster Tails) and colors of silver, gold, fluorescent red, black, chartreuse/yellow, pink and green. Many of the techniques used in fishing spinners for Alaska steelhead are similar to those used for rainbow. (See the chapter on rainbow trout that begins on page 128.)

FLYFISHING ALASKA'S STEELHEAD

Green Butt Skunk

The experience of stalking and hooking a steelhead in its wild environs using fly gear arguably is the most sporting and satisfying in all of angling, and certainly among the most exciting to be had in Alaska. Under most conditions, the flyfisher knowingly sacrifices a percentage of potential hook-ups when choosing fly equipment over drift gear. The exceptions are during low water conditions or in extremely shallow parts of a stream, like riffles, tailouts and some pocket water.

Although most hardcore steelheaders have amassed a large arsenal of tackle, a modest amount of main tackle will suffice. A nine- to nine-and-a-half-foot, eight-weight rod is the main stick used. Some choose seven-weights followed by the lesser used nine-weight for extreme conditions. In choosing main tackle it is more practical to invest money in good rods, rather than reels with expensive disc drag systems. The majority of streams are small relative to the large streams of the Pacific Northwest. Thus, quality rods are always a necessity for casting, line mending and fighting. For much of Alaska, expensive disc drag reels are often overkill, as fish do not make the long runs they would in big water down south. In terms of brands of rods, Sage, Loomis and Lamiglass all make very popular, high-quality rods known for their casting and mending performance. They are also, most importantly, aesthetically pleasing and easy to fish with. The choice of reels should be made based upon one's own fishing needs and personal finances, as there exists a myriad selection of high-quality models to choose from.

In selecting fly lines for Alaska, several lines should be carried astream. Generally the same rules apply as when fishing the state's rainbow water—a full-floating line, a sink-tip or two and a full-sink, with maybe a high-density sink or shooting taper thrown in for extreme conditions. Some anglers carry short sections of these super high-density lines instead, to attach when conditions warrant. (For more applicable information on fly lines for steelhead, see the chapter on rainbow trout that begins on page 128.)

Of all folklore circulated among the steelheading fraternity, none is so great as that which surrounds fly patterns. Far too much is said and has been written about the subtle nuances of fly patterns for steelhead. This tendency likely stems from the real need for hundreds of trout patterns to meet the many great variables involved in fishing the variety of species and conditions encountered elsewhere. Though one may greatly respect the rich tradition and background behind the evolution of many local patterns and beliefs, the angler should keep some general principles in mind.

Lani Waller simplified the discussion, describing it accurately in his 3M videos when he classed flies as bright, drab and dark patterns. The bright patterns would include flies of loud color, such as orange, pink and chartreuse. These are generally most effective on bright fish under normal and high water conditions. Flies such as the burlap and muddler are examples of drab patterns, which are especially effective during low-water periods and for fish that have been worked over by other anglers. Dark patterns describe such well known standbys as the Skunk, Silver Hilton and Black Bunny Leech. These patterns are effective in a broad range of conditions and situations; on some systems in the Skeena drainage in British Columbia, they are the main patterns used. As a general rule, they can be more effective on long river systems where fish have already journeyed quite a distance from salt water.

When a flyfisher exclaims "this is *the* fly for this system," one can only presume that there are special conditions on that stream causing that to be so or, more often, he is trying to apply trout fly pattern methodology to steelheading. I will never forget the horrified looks of guides on New Brunswick's Miramichi as they watched my fishing partner and me release Atlantic salmon that were hooked on traditional steelhead and Alaska coho patterns. The fish struck the given pattern because it was right for the situation with regard to size, general color, silhouette and drifting dynamics—not because it contained or lacked a small tuft of some obscure feather or material. Unfortunately, with far too many fly patterns, it seems that a certain amount of ego can be wrapped in with the feathers, fur and tinsel, making it impossible for some to assess their true worth.

Anglers determined to represent something found naturally in streams with their fly might try using Glo Bugs. As the accomplished fly tier and teacher André Puyans has often commented, "Why be a snob about it? After all, it is matching the hatch." It is ironic that the pattern that does "match the hatch" is scorned by some as not being a real fly pattern. However you feel about them, Glo Bugs are highly effective and can out-produce all others in some situations. A wide variety of colors and sizes should be carried in one's vest.

Techniques

The methods employed in terms of technique can be classified in two ways. The first is the traditional across- and down-current technique referred to simply as the "wet fly swing." This involves a cast across or quartered upstream, followed by a series of line mends (repositioning the trailing line with a flip of the rod, which alters the amount of drag on the fly) to slow down, speed up, or sink the fly. The second, less-popular method used in creeks and smaller systems is to use strike indicators. This method is not new at all to accomplished trout nymph fishermen. The indicator, made of a Li'l Corkie, a piece of styrofoam, or a tuft of synthetic fabric, is placed at a point between the floating fly line and the fly. After casting upstream, the angler makes a series of mends in order to sink the fly en route to attaining a true drag-free, dead drift. The fly may be weighted, or the angler may elect to add a microshot a short distance above the fly. It seems ironic that this latter method has been sneered at as not being "true flyfishing" by some well-known voices in the steelheading community, while the same method has been accepted for years among trout anglers. There certainly is a lot to be said for keeping an open mind.

Reading the Water

Steelhead are usually found in holding water that has a depth of four feet or more. They usually opt for moderate current, instead of slack water where some Pacific salmon will hold, or fast white water. They prefer currents moving at a rate of a few miles per hour. They are especially fond of secondary currents or seams on the edge of the main current. Anglers should look for these flow characteristics and any obstructions that may cause them, such as boulders and logs. As in steelheading elsewhere, if a fish is hooked in a given spot, chances are good fish will be there again under similar conditions, provided there are no major changes in the stream bed composition.

Most steelhead streams in Alaska are fairly short, small and brushy, in comparison to the huge and wide mainland streams of the Pacific Northwest states and British Columbia. The structure of the stream beds remains more constant in these smaller Alaskan streams, and they also hardly ever "go out" in the sense of being too muddy to fish, though they may be occasionally too high and of less than ideal clarity. The large mainland streams usually experience a great disparity in flow range due to the large areas they drain.

ETHICS FOR ALASKA STEELHEADERS

Preserve Wild Steelhead

Any discussion of ethics has to begin with the importance of preserving wild steelhead stocks. Only a handful of Alaska's streams have been enhanced by a hatchery smolts. The mixing of gene pools that results from these "mixed stock" fisheries is detrimental in the long run to the sustained health of the wild stock. It also is expensive and unrealistic in that it sustains the angling public's false hope of fixing serious problems caused by overfishing, habitat destruction and poor management with the quick fix of hatchery enhancement. Alaska's greatest resources is the health and integrity of her wild fisheries. Educate yourself to truly know why it is important to keep the wild fish runs as they are, and join the cause.

Practice Catch-and-Release

When a wild stock is lost or mixed, it is lost permanently, never to be restored again. If this is so obvious, why aren't more folks practicing catch-and-release in Alaska? Perhaps it is because of misconceptions and a lack of knowledge about the fragility of the resource. If most of Southeast's runs are comprised of 100 fish or thereabouts, can there be any harvesting without damage? Probably not on quite a few of these small systems. Numerous runs have already shown signs of depletion. Learn the correct techniques for playing and releasing a fish with minimal impact. These include using barbless hooks and gearing up with the proper line and rod weight so as not to overstress the fish. (See the appendix on pages 637 and 638 for more information on catch-and-release.)

Don't Use Bait

The use of bait is generally a poor practice for this day and age. Bright steelhead—indeed all trout and salmon—are suckers for good-looking roe. Even very inexperienced anglers soon learn this. Unfortunately, few anglers respond with a hook-set in a timely enough manner when the fish mouths the bait, resulting in a deeply hooked fish, with the inevitable serious harm or death. Most streams in Alaska restrict the use of bait while fishing for steelhead.

Leave Spawning Fish Alone

Steelhead that are observed holding for any length of time in tailouts, small riffles or other shallow stream locations in April and May are probably nearing spawning. Many of these fish can be spotted digging out redds, swimming in mating rituals, guarding nests and the like, acting in ways that normal fish do not. To try for these fish, especially when there are other steelhead in normal holding water, is unsporting. Why harass fish that are doing the very thing that sportfishers should want them to be doing—producing more wild steelhead?

Respect the Privacy of Others

With the exception of several streams accessible by roads and near towns, most Alaska steelhead streams are still uncrowded. When other anglers are encountered working a run or hole, one should proceed on to another unfished area. One should only join another angler on a given hole after receiving permission. This differs from the practice in many Northern British Columbia rivers where flyfishers follow fellow anglers through fish-holding runs.

Get Involved

Join your local chapter of Trout Unlimited and get involved with issues of conservation, no matter how small or insignificant they may seem. The skills and knowledge you gain will be helpful in understanding some of the broader more complex issues that are affecting the health of the entire North Pacific fishery. Educate yourself, inform others and set the example with your personal responsibility, on and off the river.

ALASKA'S TOP TEN TROPHY STEELHEAD

42 pounds, 3 ounces, Bell Island, Behm Canal (Southeast), 1970 (state and world record)
26 pounds, 0 ounces, Douglas Island (Southeast), 1980
26 pounds, 0 ounces, Situk River, Yakutat (Southeast), 1988
24 pounds, 8 ounces, Waterfall Resort, Prince of Wales (Southeast), 1990
23 pounds, 9 ounces, Situk River, Yakutat (Southeast), 1987
23 pounds, 8 ounces, Situk River, Yakutat (Southeast), 1982
23 pounds, 0 ounces, Situk River, Yakutat (Southeast), 1985
22 pounds, 0 ounces, Situk River, Yakutat (Southeast), 1987
21 pounds, 14 ounces, Situk River, Yakutat (Southeast), 1974
21 pounds, 8 ounces, Yakutat (Southeast), 1986

ALASKA'S MAJOR STEELHEAD LOCATIONS

Southeast

Most of Alaska's steelhead streams are located in Southeast. There are several hundred documented systems, with small runs (200 fish or less) the general rule. Spring steelhead dominate, with peaks in May, but some significant late winter and late fall fishing can be had also.

•*Ketchikan:* Fish, Ketchikan, Kah Sheets and Ward creeks; Naha River; McDonald Lake system

•*Prince of Wales:* Harris, Karta, Klawock, Kegan and Thorne rivers; Staney and Salmon Bay creeks

•*Wrangell:* Anan, Aaron, Eagle and Thoms creeks

•*Petersburg:* Petersburg, Hamilton, Kadake, Ohmer, Falls and Duncan Saltchuck creeks; Castle River

•*Sitka:* Sitkoh, Hasselborg and Eva creeks; Plotnikof and Port Banks rivers

•*Juneau:* Peterson Creek, Taku River

•*Yakutat and Gulf Coast:* Situk, Italio and Tsiu rivers

Southcentral

Southcentral has some of the state's most heavily fished steelhead streams on the Kenai Peninsula, with considerable high-quality opportunities on Kodiak Island (17 known steelhead systems). These are mostly all fall and winter run fish, with peaks in late September through October.

•*Kenai:* Anchor, Ninilchik and Kasilof rivers; Deep and Stariski creeks

•*Chugach:* Copper River tributaries—Tebay (including Hanagita River), Tazlina and Upper Middle Fork Gulkana rivers (Dickey, Twelvemile and Hungry Hollow creeks)

•*Kodiak:* Karluk, Ayakulik, Afognak and Uganik rivers; Pauls, Akalura, Malina and Saltery creeks

Southwest

Southwest has a handful of documented spawning streams that are scattered along the Alaska Peninsula to Cold Bay, with rumors of many more. All indications are that these are fall run fish, September through October being their peak run. This is definitely the unexplored frontier of steelheading in North America.

•*Port Moller:* Bear and Sandy rivers

•*Nelson Lagoon:* Sapsuk and Nelson rivers

•*Cold Bay:* Russel and Trout creeks

10
Cutthroat:
Noble Trout

by Thomas Cappiello

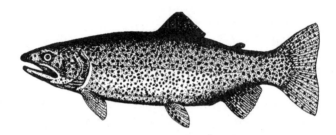

It was the end of my junior year in college, and my '62 VW van was packed for a summer of flyfishing the West, when I received a fateful call from the U.S. Forest Service. They were looking for help on a remote project in Prince William Sound, Alaska, and I listened intently to details of the job offer, over piles of maps, insect hatch charts and astounding estimates of Montana's 2,000 fish per mile. The lure of blue ribbon western trout streams was certainly hard to resist, but Alaska—land of salmon, ultimate wilderness and scenery—was the chance of a lifetime.

Six weeks later I was in Cordova, loading my gear into a 1955 DeHavilland Beaver. An awesome, hour-long flight through a forested maze of bays and islands, and a 45-minute hike straight up a mountain, brought me to base camp (and a realization of what "remote" in Alaska means). My supervisor and campmates, a seasoned bunch, lost no time briefing me, a total greenhorn, on the finer points of Alaska fishing. They spoke of run timing, spinning gear, barndoor halibut, salmon by the thousands and Pixee lures. But I had my designs at the moment on some slightly different rewards—casting a fly into some of those delectable ponds and streams I had passed earlier on the trail.

A light breeze from the ocean spilled over a hill and rippled the surface of the most perfect little lake you could imagine. Lily pads covered the edges, and near the small outlet, a rise and some tiny grayish bugs swarming above water hinted of action to come. Nervously, I tied a #16 Mosquito on and promptly hung my first two casts in the bushes nearby. A good-sized fish swirled not six feet in front of me—I was such a wreck I could barely tie a knot! I finally rolled a fly out, letting it drift in the weak current and twitching it ever so slightly. It vanished in a vortex of carnivorousness as a bright little package of muscle took off for the sky. Not more than a foot long, this feisty little warrior was everywhere at once in his valiant struggle for freedom, and threw me off guard when I saw blood streaming from under his gills. Horrified, I drew him in and realized I'd been had, by a fish that was no stranger to me. This beautiful trout, heavily spotted, with a luster like a newly minted gold coin, had two brilliant scarlet slash marks on his throat— the definitive brand of a cutthroat trout, a fish I knew well from my youth on the coastal streams and rivers of northern California.

As if looks weren't enough, these fish were abundant and eager, and I was soon hooking them on practically every cast. I stayed until sunset, then stumbled back to camp, where the guys were finishing a came of cards in the kitchen tent. It was midnight, and I'd been fishing for six hours—this Alaska scene was definitely going to take some getting used to! As I lay collapsed on my bunk, drifting off to sleep to the haunting lullabies of loons in the distance, thoughts of new and wonderful fishing experiences filled my head. I pondered on how many lovely cutthroats had never seen a fly in the countless ponds and streams of this coastal paradise. The Madison River would have to wait.

INTRODUCTION

The cutthroat trout, *Oncorhyncus clarkii,* was the first true trout to be documented in the United States of America. Described in early accounts of exploration as far back as the 1500s, specimens sent to England in 1833 from a river in Washington were officially recorded and the species named in honor of Captain William Clark of the famed Lewis and Clark expedition.

Cutthroats are the native trout of the Rocky Mountains—the abundant and at times gullible fish found in small foothill creeks, rivers and mountain lakes from New Mexico to Alberta. They occur in a coastal form as well; as "harvest trout" or "bluebacks" they are well known and sought after in the tidal waters of the Pacific Northwest states and British Columbia. In Alaska, these fish are the jewels of the coastal wilderness; small brightly colored trout that liven the fishing and enhance the overall ecology of countless small streams, bogs and lakes from Prince William Sound to Ketchikan. And though they take a back seat to the state's other sport species when it comes to prestige and glamour, cutthroats have a definite mystique and noble character, that, like the small brook trout of the East, endears them to a dedicated following of anglers.

DESCRIPTION

The cutthroat trout of the Pacific Northwest are most easily recognized by the two red slash marks under the lower jaw from which they derive their name. An upper jaw line that extends well beyond the eye, heavy spotting on the body and fins and the presence of small teeth behind the tongue are other recognizable features to look for, although they may not always be present, making the fish sometimes difficult to distinguish from the rainbow trout (rainbows and cutthroats can hybridize, which can further complicate identification). Markings are often indistinct or nonexistent on sea-run fish. Color can vary from a dark olive-green back, gold or bronze sides and pale-white belly to a deep metallic blue back and bright silver sides.

Most of the cutthroats caught in Alaska are four and five years old and average eight to ten inches long. The larger, trophy size (three-pounds-plus) resident fish are at least nine and up to 15 years old. Moving between salt- and freshwater places additional stress on sea-run fish and they rarely live longer than eight years and grow more than 20 inches.

RANGE, ABUNDANCE & STATUS

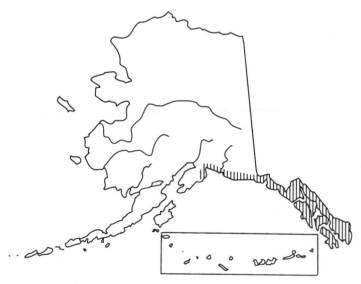

Shaded area shows range of cutthroat trout in Alaska.

CUTTHROAT TROUT

Coastal cutthroat trout range from Eel River in northern California to Prince William Sound, Alaska, and thrive in many watersheds within the coastal temperate rain forests. Both resident and sea-run (anadromous) forms occur in Alaska. Sea-run cutthroat normally do not travel more than 20 to 50 miles from the mouth of their home stream. Populations of resident forms rarely exceed 4,000 fish, and most anadromous populations are several hundred to a thousand (2,000 is large). Resident fish are typically small and stunted, although in some Southeast lakes they grow as large as eight pounds. Despite being few in number within a single drainage, over 50,000 cutthroats are caught yearly by anglers from hundreds of lakes and streams in Alaska. Populations are fragile and highly susceptible to over-fishing and habitat destruction. Even the enhancement of other desirable species such as coho salmon can have a negative impact on cutthroat abundance. In the past 10 years, sport harvests in Alaska have declined while effort has increased dramatically. This has prompted the Department of Fish and Game and other agencies to take a much more aggressive management approach to expand knowledge of cutthroat ecology and enact more conservative regulations in many areas.

LIFE HISTORY & HABITS

There are two main forms of coastal cutthroat found in Alaska: anadromous and resident. Anadromous or sea-run cutthroats in Alaska have a life history similar to that of sea-run Dolly Varden. They usually go to sea in the spring (late April to early June) at two or three years of age, but as early as age one or as late as age six. Little is known of their lives in the ocean, but tagging studies have shown most fish venture no more than 20 miles from their home stream, many staying within estuaries or the mouths of rivers. They return to freshwater in late summer through fall, and by October, most of Alaska's "cuts" are in their overwintering streams and lakes. After overwintering, mature fish will move into spawning tributaries, immature fish will head out to sea and juveniles remain in freshwater. This will usually occur during April or May. Cutthroats can display the same complexity of movement as charr, spawning in different streams than they overwinter in, even traveling through salt water from overwintering lakes to reach spawning areas. After spawning, adults begin seaward migrations, sometimes lingering in freshwater or estuaries to feed on smolts. Time at sea is usually short, anywhere from six weeks to three months.

Resident Alaska cutthroats spend their entire lives in the freshwater of lakes, streams, sloughs and small bog ponds. With the exception of seaward migrations, their life history closely parallels the sea-run forms'. They mature at four to six years of age and spawn primarily in tributaries of small to moderate size, with gentle gradients. The number of eggs per female depends on size and condition of fish and can be as few as 200 to as many as 4,000, but the average is between 1,100 and 1,700. Eggs are buried in redds, similar to other members of the salmon-trout-charr family. Preferred gravel is pea-sized or slightly larger and fairly clean of sand and fines. Spawning usually takes place in the spring from late March to early June, depending on latitude and local climate. Hatching occurs in six to seven weeks and fry emerge one to two weeks later (usually during June). Fry grow quickly, usually to three to four inches long by the first fall and five to six inches long by the end of their second growing season.

Whether resident and anadromous forms are genetically different is not clear, but the two forms can occur in the same system. Little research has focused on why certain stocks are anadromous and others are not, beyond situations where a physical barriers, such as waterfalls, prevent migration.

Diet

Knowing what cutthroats feed on is certainly important to anglers. Small trout will heavily utilize terrestrial and aquatic insects, especially midge and mosquito larvae. As opportunists, however, their diet will vary with location and time of year. As they get older, "cuts" will still pursue midges, mosquitoes, caddis flies, mayflies and stone flies, but will prey more heavily on fish, such as sticklebacks, kokanee, juvenile salmon and sculpins. Leeches also make up a small portion of the cutthroat's diet. In saltwater, "cuts" will feed on small shrimp (euphausiids), juvenile herring, capelin and salmon smolts. Salmon spawn is an extremely important food source to all cutthroat trout, as it allows for the rapid weight gain that is essential for winter survival. Availability of salmon eggs may be one of the primary motivations for sea-run cutthroats to return to freshwater. Resident cutthroats often do not have the luxurious and diverse food sources the sea-runs enjoy, yet the largest cutthroats taken in Alaska (over five pounds) have been from lakes without anadromous salmon. The key to the potential size of these landlocked forms is the availability of kokanee or landlocked sockeye for forage in many Southeast lakes.

FISHING ALASKA'S CUTTHROAT TROUT

Since cutthroat trout are notoriously voracious and will respond to just about any enticement—such as bait, flies, spinners, spoons and jigs—locating fish is the key challenge for the Alaska cutthroat angler.

First page: For abundance and sport, the silver salmon is tops among Alaska's five species of Pacific salmon.

Opposite, top: The male sockeye (or red) salmon shows extreme changes in physical appearance during spawning.

Opposite, bottom: Alaska's coastal cutthroat trout, generally not large, quite often have exquisite hue and markings.

This page, top: Alaska's rainbow trout vary in appearance from drainage to drainage; this fish is from a lower Kuskokwim stream.

This page, right: Alaska's abundant halibut are easily taken in nearly all inshore areas along the southern coast.

Above: The sheefish, world's largest whitefish species, achieves record size in the Northwest.
Below: The arctic grayling can be found in nearly every headwater stream on the mainland.

Opposite: The rainbow trout reaches hefty size in Alaska's large lake and river systems—
Kenai, Naknek and Iliamna.

Opposite, top: A male silver salmon ascends a small waterfall en route to spawning upriver.

Opposite, bottom: Spring steelhead provide angling excitement from March through May.

This page, top: The average king salmon in Alaska weighs under 20 pounds, with weights to 60 pounds or more possible.

This page, bottom: The toothy northern pike is abundant in western and interior Alaska.

Next page: The charr (shown in fall spawning colors) is Alaska's most widespread sport species.

Throughout most of their range in the 49th state, they are few in number and have dynamic and at times elusive behavior, so understanding their life history and migratory patterns is essential. Generally cuts prefer slow to moderate water velocity and will often hunker near bottom or around structures. In streams, they will be found in pools, under cutbanks, in confluences and tailouts and behind logs and boulders. In lakes, they usually linger near outlet and inlet streams, shorelines with lily pads, islands and drop-offs. Southeast lakes can stratify dramatically in the summer—especially tea-colored bog waters that act as solar energy collectors and attain unbearable surface water temperatures—so fish may avoid the shallower feeding locations, seeking deeper, cooler waters.

Spring

Access to cutthroats in the early spring (April and May) can be difficult with rotting snow and ice conditions, and some areas are closed to protect spawning populations. But the opportunities for exciting early spring fishing are many and worth going for. Best areas for spring "cuts" are the mouths of inlet and outlet streams in lakes, river mouths, estuaries, and the main stems and confluences of rivers with spawning populations. After ice-out, anglers can fly in to some of the better Southeast lakes (see locations at end of this chapter on pages 166 and 167) and enjoy some of Alaska's best fishing—Humpback, Turner, Jims, Wilson and other lakes have all produced trophy cutthroat during the month of May.

After spawning, cutthroat in or near salmon systems will congregate in strategic locations for intercepting out-migrating smolt—at lake outlets, stream pools, river mouths, estuaries, etc. Salmon smolt out-migrations occur sporadically throughout the day but peak between 10 p.m. and 2 a.m., so fishing during evening hours can be extremely productive. When fishing lower rivers, I like to fish around a moderate high tide, the best time being about two to three hours before and after flood. I look for smolts scattering and fleeing, seabird activity or surface disturbances of any kind that might signal concentrations of cutthroat. This can be exciting fishing for short periods of times and the angler must be ready to make quick, accurate casts when a feeding binge is in progress. Because Dolly Varden charr are more numerous in Alaska's coastal systems, you'll probably catch much more of them than cutthroat, as well as other surprises (I've caught greenling, juvenile Pacific cod and starry flounder while fishing these tidal zones for cutthroats).

Imitating forage fish with lure and fly is, of course, "most killing" at this time. Small, bright spinners like the matchless Super Vibrax series in sizes #0 to #2, or ¹/₈- to ¹/₄-ounce Rooster Tail, are hard to beat, as are ¹/₈-ounce Pixee, Kastmaster or Crippled Herring spoons. Streamer fishing with smolt and other baitfish patterns (Coho fly, Muddler, etc.) and bright attractors can be equally effective, using the standard "wet fly swing" through likely holding water.

Summer

•*Anadromous:* Sea-run cutthroat can be extremely difficult to locate once out in the ocean, and few anglers have consistent success catching them after the smolt runs are over and they move seaward. (Cutthroats that spend the entire summer in estuaries are the exception.) These fish will begin reentering freshwater along with salmon in some systems during early to mid-July. This inward migration can take place rapidly within a week or be spread out through the summer, depending on location. Generally, however, cutthroat runs occur with either the first pink salmon runs in July or the later coho runs of August and September. The first places to try are estuaries, river mouths, tidal pools and any holding water in lower rivers and streams, fishing the incoming tides for best results.

If you've done your research and picked a stream with a healthy run of sea-run "cuts," you can expect an exciting, mixed bag of fishing in and around tidewater, especially during the height of the salmon invasions. Pink or silver salmon will be jumping and surfacing everywhere, difficult to avoid in their prespawning testiness. Dollies, too, will most likely be thick, providing additional encounters. Interspersed among this rowdy bunch should be some incredibly aggressive cutthroat trout. A deep, slow retrieve of a small spinner or streamer in bright, attractor colors is usually all it takes to bring them in, too.

•*Resident:* Resident cutthroats spend considerable time surface feeding during the warm summer months, and usually can be easily targeted for some excellent dry fly fishing. Look for them along lake shorelines, in outlets and inlets, pools and riffles, much the same as you would in streams and mountain lakes further south this time of year. A small boat or float tube will allow you greater access to prime areas. Lily pads can offer some challenging fishing (use heavier tippets of 8- to 10-pound test line to minimize breakoffs in these snag-filled waters). They attract damselfly nymphs and adults, amphipods (freshwater shrimp), snails and other prey. Cutthroats will cruise the borders and employ the "ambush predator" strategy of pike on unsuspecting prey. My favorite flies for these conditions are a Hare's Ear Nymph (size #10, #12), olive or brown Leech (size #8 to #10) and a #12 Haystack. (A deerhair wing, no hackle, with muskrat-dubbed body is highly visible to the angler, floats well and holds up to numerous takes, especially if the dubbed body is reinforced with gold or copper wire.) In the evenings in some of the lakes, a small (#12 to #14) Black Caddis danced along the shoreline works well to antagonize cutthroats (and juvenile coho). I've experimented and also had some success with adult damselfly imitations.

Hardware tends to target larger, more aggressive fish this time of year. I like to use $1/12$- to $1/8$-ounce red and yellow Roostertail spinners, $1/8$-ounce Pixee and $1/12$- to $3/16$-ounce silver or gold Kastmaster spoons. Lead head (bright yellow, pink or black) jigs work well, too, and are less susceptible to snags. Fish the same holding areas you would target for spring fishing, along with any spots that show signs of feeding activity, below or on the surface, and vary the depth and speed of the retrieve until you connect with a fish. Spinning gear allows fast coverage of water and often quick results.

In systems with sticklebacks, gold lures or flies tend to work very well. In lakes where kokanee are the dominant forage species, silver smolt imitations can be very effective. Solid black leech patterns do not seem to work quite as well as olive or brown. I've also had good success with a small Woolly Bugger-type pattern tied with peacock herl body, marabou or ostrich tail, and palmered with dark brown or black hackle. During salmon runs, Glo Bugs, other egg patterns and flesh flies are the ticket to "match the hatch." During heavy pink salmon invasions, when fish tend to be glutted with spawn, I've had good luck fishing Egg-Sucking Leeches and weighted white Marabou Muddlers (both #8), perhaps because they imitate other prey species making off with something good.

•Fishing streams, bogs and sloughs: The islands in Prince William Sound and Southeast are full of small, unnamed lakes and muskeg bog ponds, many receiving little, if any, angling pressure. From waters as small as a quarter acre, with little more than a trench connecting to a lower-order stream, I've yanked dozens of colorful, feisty "cuts." The presence of juvenile coho is a good sign to look for when prospecting for cutthroat trout in likely areas, as the two occur together most frequently. Taking a minute or two to search for surface activity of any kind is another way to answer the big question. Exploring Alaska's abundant coastal waters for trout can be one of the most satisfying aspects of fishing this species, with rich rewards of abundant, wild fishing and quiet contemplation in the most inspiring of settings.

Fall

Fall is a popular time to fish for cutthroat trout, both resident and sea-run, because fish are in prime condition and extremely voracious. Some of the best fishing for sea-run cutthroats can be had in small lakes with overwintering populations or the inlet and outlet waters of larger lakes. The cooling temperatures and shortening days prompt fish into reckless feeding binges that can make for some electrifying fishing action. My most memorable experiences with cutthroat have taken place in September and October, when coho are busying streams and lake tributaries with spawning activity. In some places I've seen hundreds of fat sea-run "cuts" concentrated near outlets, in deep pools or river mouths, ravenous for anything that comes their way. Attractor patterns, egg and flesh flies, forage imitation streamers (Sculpins, Muddlers, Leeches), bright spinners, spoons and even jigs all work well for these hungry fall "cuts."

Winter

It's common knowledge that cutthroats can be caught through the ice, but because of fluctuating winter conditions, few anglers are willing to risk the potentially dangerous ice conditions on Southeast lakes during most winters, regardless of how good fishing could be. Unlike streams in Washington and Oregon, no migrations of cutthroats have been documented in Alaska in the winter, although there are persistent rumors of bright sea-runs being caught in estuaries in February and March.

GEARING UP FOR CUTTHROAT

Tackle

Use an ultra-light spinning rod, five- to six-feet, medium-action, with 150 yards four- to eight-pound test mono on a high-quality, ultra-light spinning reel. Or use a five- to six-weight, seven- to nine-foot flyrod with matching, floating or sinktip line and 2X to 4X tippet. Use leader of seven to nine feet. For deepwater trophy fishing, use a light- to medium-weight spinning or steelhead casting rod, seven- to eight-and-a-half feet, medium-action, with 150 yards of 10- to 15-pound line on a high-quality spinning or casting reel.

Lures

Many lures work well for cutthroat. The list includes: Vibrax spinners size #0, #1 and #2 in silver or gold blades/body and fluorescent orange bell; Roostertail spinners size #0, #1 and #2 in red and yellow; $1/8$-ounce Pixees with red or pink inserts; Kastmasters in $1/12$-, $1/8$- and $1/4$-

ounce sizes in silver or gold (or with blue or red); and lead head jigs (Foxee Jigs) in ¹/₃₂-, ¹/₁₆- and ¹/₈-ounce and natural colors such as amber, black and chartreuse.

Also effective are Wet Flies (size #6 to #12) including Glo Bug, Polar Shrimp, Spruce and Scud (in orange, pink or brown), Hare's ear Nymph (size #10 and #12) and Fall Favorite; Dry Flies (size #10 to #14) including Haystack, Dark Blue Damsel, Mosquito, Black Gnat, Irresistible and Elk Hair Caddis; Streamers (size #6 to #8) including Muddler Minnow, Woolly Bugger, Sculpin, Bunny Bug, Smolt, Olive Leech, Brown Leech, Black Leech, Egg-Sucking Leech and White Maribou Muddler.

CATCHING TROPHY CUTTHROAT

If catching a trophy in one of the Southeast Panhandle's premier lakes is your goal, specific strategies should be employed. A boat is almost a necessity to fish the better water. The U.S. Forest Service is kind enough to provide small boats for the fortunate souls able to obtain cabin reservations at some of the more popular locations (check beforehand for availability and condition of craft). If you're not so lucky, a canoe or inflatable raft might be the way to go. A portable fishfinder and bathymetric lake map, if available, will greatly improve your chances of locating fish.

Trophy resident cutthroat trout can be taken shallow during spring near inlet waters, but generally will disperse and go deep during the summer. The most effective way of catching them is by trolling. Conventional trolling gear—lead weights or planer on 10- to 15-pound test, with a small flasher or "cowbell" attractor and medium-sized spoons (Luhr Jensen Crippled Herring, Nordic and Diamond King or Blue Fox Trixee) trolled slowly, moderately deep (15 to 30 feet), works best. Also try deep diving plugs like Normark's Rapala and the Jensen Power Dive Minnow. Downriggers can also be employed, but remember that one line per person is all that's allowed in Alaska's cutthroat lakes. Keep in mind that the immensely popular and effective method of trolling bait such as herring or shrimp is now illegal in these lakes.

If you're fishing without electronic aids, concentrate your trolling effort along shorelines with steep drop-offs, in deep waters surrounding islands or rocks, bays with inlets and any other areas that might appeal to larger, lazier trout in search of a fish dinner. The lower-light periods of the day have proven most productive for catching the big ones, so time your efforts accordingly.

ALASKA'S TOP TEN TROPHY CUTTHROATS

8 pounds, 6 ounces, Wilson Lake (Southeast), Robert Denison, 1977 (state record)
7 pounds, 8 ounces, Wilson Lake (Southeast), 1981
6 pounds, 5 ounces, Wilson Lake (Southeast), 1973
7 pounds, 6.5 ounces, Turner Lake (Southeast), 1991
6 pounds, 7 ounces, Turner Lake (Southeast), 1980
6 pounds, 14 ounces, Reflection Lake (Southeast), 1977
6 pounds, 12 ounces, Orchard Lake (Southeast), 1973
6 pounds, 3 ounces, Ella Lake (Southeast), 1982
6 pounds, 2 ounces, Humpback Lake (Southeast), 1969
6 pounds, 0 ounces, Patching Lake (Southeast), 1980

ALASKA'S MAJOR CUTTHROAT LOCATIONS

There are so many water systems known to contain cutthroat in Alaska (and many more yet to be cataloged) that it is impossible to list all the best areas. Some locations, like Hasselborg and Turner Lakes, are so noteworthy and popular that they barely need mentioning, while others may be local hot spots known to only a few anglers. Local Fish and Game or Forest Service offices, guides, air taxis and regional publications can provide invaluable help in identifying the better cutthroat trout locations. Most lakes have resident fish, but some also support sea-run cutthroats as well, while certain lakes and stream have only sea-run fish. Remember that timing is crucial for anadromous fishing, but not a critical consideration for resident populations. Some notes and a brief list of the better known areas follows.

Southeast Panhandle

•*Ketchikan:* More cutthroat are caught in this region than in any other. This area includes Revillagigedo (locals call it simply "Revilla") Island and the mainland, which includes Misty Fjords National Monument. The U.S Forest Service has cabins and shelters located on some of the prime cutthroat locations. Lakes and streams on the road system such as Ward Creek and Ketchikan Creek also provide good fishing for cutthroat and other species, including steelhead. Small rowboats that can handle two- to nine-horsepower motors are available at some of the cabin locations, but check with the Forest Service on the latest conditions before finalizing your plans.

For trophy fish, try Humpback, Ella, Wilson, Reflection, Manzanita, Orchard and Patching lakes, For good sea-run cutthroat, try Ward Cove Creek, Naha River and Manzanita Bay.

•*Juneau:* This area encompasses Admiralty Island, but includes part of the mainland. Not much is available along the road system in Juneau, except Twin Lakes, which is popular. Anglers caught over 2,000 cutthroats there in 1992. The most popular cutthroat trout lakes are accessed by plane.

For roadside fishing, try Twin Lakes and Auke Lake.

For trophy fish, try Hasselborg and surrounding lakes, Turner Lake and Jims Lake.

Other good spots include: Florence Lake (excellent fishing, but logging in the area detracts from the experience); Young and Salmon lakes, Sitkoh Lake and Stream, Baranof Lake and Stream (no other species are available here) and Eva Lake and Stream.

•*Petersburg/Wrangell:* Eagle, Kah Sheets, Pats and Virginia lakes; Castle River, Thomas Creek and Lake, Petersburg Creek and Lake, Blind Slough

•*Haines/Skagway:* Chilkat Lake and River, Mosquito Lake and Chilkoot Lake

•*North Gulf Coast:* This is an unexplored paradise of streams and small lakes, including: Bering River tributaries, Katalla, Akwe, Situk and Kiklukh rivers; and the Kaliakh River system.

•*Prince William Sound:* Here many named and unnamed ponds and lakes have feisty populations of small resident cutthroats. Many rewards await the angler with the interest and enthusiasm to explore unfished or unknown areas. Try Stump Lake (Montague Island), Green Island Lake (Green Island), Eshamy Lake and Cowpen Lake

•*Cordova and vicinity:* For roadside fishing, try Alaganik Slough, McKinley Lake, Eyak Lake and River, Southern Orca Inlet; also Hawkins Island Cutoff (this is saltwater fishing—a boat is needed).

For remote fishing in the Cordova area, try Junction\Hidden Lake (Canoe Passage, Hawkins Island) and Marten Lake and River (East Copper River Delta)

11
ARCTIC GRAYLING: THE SAILFIN

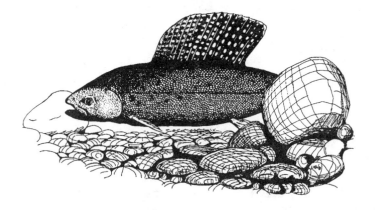

Midsummer in Alaska, the fishing wanes as the great salmon runs subside, and some anglers have a hard time drumming up action that can compare in any way with the electrifying excitement of June. Things might slow to a complete crawl were it not for an amazing fishery that comes into its own this time of year. In headwaters, lake outlets and countless swift, rocky streams across this immense state, abundant insect hatches brought on by the warmest, sunniest days of the year spark a frenzy of feeding activity among resident populations of one of the Northland's most charming fighters—the arctic grayling. In some of the more prolific areas, such as the lakes of the northern Alaska Peninsula, the headwaters of Bristol Bay and the rambling, clear streams of Northwest, vast armies of these "sailfins" can be encountered, dimpling the surface of rivers and lakes like raindrops as they feed continuously on emerging insect life.

It can be a simple matter of laying a dry fly on these waters to produce some nonstop fishing fun, reminiscent of youthful days and plucky panfish. These grayling, usually not the least bit shy, will rise to the occasion instantly and fight vigorously, running in tight circles and using their broad shape to great advantage. This is Alaska's best and only real dry fly fishing of the season, and folks here wouldn't consider the summer complete if they didn't at least once break out light, whippy rods and enjoy some of this delightful diversion.

INTRODUCTION

The arctic grayling, *Thymallus arcticus,* is a most interesting and exotic resident of northern waters. Found in the clear, swift stretches of nearly every river and stream throughout the Northland, including Alaska, the grayling is a valued sport species, abundant and eager to the fly as no other fish is in these high latitudes.

With his unfurling banner decorated in royal colors of purple, crimson and gold, the grayling has a striking, aristocratic appearance that distinguishes him from all other fishes he shares waters with. A valiant and spirited fighter, he'll surprise you with his topwater antics and sub-surface rolls, outmaneuvering other species many times his size. Pursued by a dedicated following of anglers, the grayling is an essential part of the Alaska fishing experience, not to be missed in the rush to sample the state's other fabulous species.

DESCRIPTION

The general appearance of the grayling is of a sleek and slender dark whitefish, with a characteristically large dorsal fin that may extend as far as the adipose fin on some mature males, but is slightly smaller and rounder in females. The mouth is small, and numerous fine teeth are present on both jaws. Coloration varies considerably between watersheds and range, from silvery grey to dirty brown to almost black; spawning individuals generally are darker. Black vermiculations decorate forward sides and scales are large. The dorsal and pelvic fins are especially noteworthy for their unusual color variety—pink to blue dots and stripes, their leading edges being white to pink, increasing in brilliance during spawning. The belly is yellowish white but may appear grey in some populations.

The flesh is white and flaky and of delicate taste when eaten fresh. Due to its fragile nature, grayling meat has no commercial value. However, the fish is regarded with high esteem for its food value within the angling community and often seen as a significant supplement for subsistence users in remote areas.

Not particularly known for size, Alaska grayling average about 8 to 12 inches in length, with some populations producing good numbers of fish in the 15- to 18-inch range. Maximum weight is four to five pounds and 22 to 23 inches, given the right growing conditions, but rarely exceeding three pounds and 20 inches. Most trophy-sized grayling are taken from parts of Southwest and Northwest, but a few specimens from isolated stocks in Southcentral and Interior can also reach significant proportions.

RANGE, ABUNDANCE & STATUS

The arctic grayling is a widespread species found in varying degrees of abundance from Hudson Bay in Canada westward to the Ob River in Russia and south along the Asian continent to the Yalu River. It is present from central Alberta and the headwaters of the Missouri River in Montana north to Alaska, being most abundant in northern Canada and Alaska. A near relative of the arctic grayling is present in northern Scandinavia, Finland and western Russia. Introductions of the species have extended its range into mountainous regions of Colorado, Utah and Vermont.

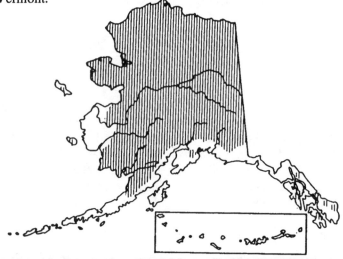

Shaded area shows range of arctic grayling in Alaska.

In Alaska, grayling are most numerous in cold, clear waters of the subarctic from the Alaska Peninsula north to the Seward Peninsula in inland rivers, streams and lakes, and east through the vast Yukon River watershed into Interior and in clearwater drainages of the Copper River. The grayling is considered abundant in all remote waters of Alaska—particularly Southwest, Northwest, Interior and Southcentral—with minor populations in large, glacial mainland rivers in Southeast. Successful stockings of this prolific sportfish have been made into several lakes on the Kenai Peninsula, the Anchorage area, Kodiak Island and parts of Southeast.

LIFE HISTORY & HABITS

Starting in March or April in lowland areas and populations to the south, but not until June in mountainous regions to the north, arctic grayling congregate at the mouths of spawning streams. As soon as the ice breaks, the fish move on up, usually in numbers that may range in the hundreds to thousands or more depending on drainage size. The urge to spawn is so intense at times that some fish proceed upstream through channels cut in the ice by overflow. Chosen waters for spawning are generally fairly small bog or marshland streams with sandy gravel substrate, although this is not a strict preference. Spring-fed creeks, however, are avoided.

Grayling commit quite extensive migrations, up to 100 miles or more in some areas and regions. This is particularly true for populations overwintering in deep channels of large, glacial watersheds with spawning streams at the headwaters. It is a journey that may last from a few days to one or two weeks. The fish usually mill around the immediate area for some time, waiting for rising temperatures which trigger a major upstream movement.

Peak reproductive activity takes place anytime between mid-May and mid-June. There is no redd constructed, but a slight depression is often created during the mating rituals. Females deposit from 3,000 to 9,000 eggs, which are adhesive, attaching to bottom structure. The eggs hatch in 11 to 30 days, depending on water temperature.

The young, which some describe as "two eyeballs on a thread," begin feeding on minute aquatic organisms on the third or fourth day, and do so vigorously after the eight day. Growth accelerates each year from birth up to age five, at which time it slows down, the length of the fish being about 8 to 15 inches. After age 10, growth is minimal if any. As is common in many resident fish populations, growth rates are higher in regions to the south due to longer open water season and optimal feeding conditions. In the southern part of the range in Alaska, maturity is reached as early as age two or three, but mostly not until age four or five. Maturity is later in the Arctic and colder mountainous regions, usually commencing at age five but sometimes not until age eight. (Seward Peninsula fish have been aged at up to 20 years, which accounts for their larger-than-average size.)

After spawning has been completed, the adult grayling, depending on stream habitat, either moves to upstream areas within the same drainage or leaves it altogether for another watershed more suitable for feeding. It is very common for grayling to utilize streams full of spring meltwater for spawning purposes and, after the water levels recede in early summer and become too shallow, to move back into lakes or larger rivers and creeks until freeze-up.

Typical summer feeding grounds are often located at the headwaters of large river systems in small, clearwater streams or springs with plenty of riffles and deep pools and undercut banks. In landlocked lakes, the fish are distributed throughout specific areas with cooler temperature regimes, but tend to avoid deep water, seeking cool, up-welling springs instead. Showing a low tolerance towards warm water, these fish thrive best in cold drainages (35 to 50 degrees Fahrenheit) where they actively feed on insects, both aquatic and terrestrial, in addition to small numbers of fish. Night feeding is common.

As temperatures drop in autumn, arctic grayling begin to prepare for winter by going into a feeding frenzy. Night feeding halts, shifting to midday, and insects are no longer the staple diet. In areas with heavy runs of spawning salmon, grayling will prey heavily on salmon eggs and scavenge along the bottom on intercept free-floating eggs. Towards the end of September into October, just prior to freeze-up, the fish begin a rapid downstream movement to overwintering areas. By November there are very few grayling left in upstream areas, with most spending the winter in the lower stream sections where the water is deep enough to survive.

During the cold winter months, grayling are suspended in lakes and deep holes and pools of large rivers until the following spring. They are lethargic at this period of time, moving about relatively little, and feeding is minimal.

FISHING ALASKA'S GRAYLING

The arctic grayling is indeed one of the more pleasant sportfish species to angle in Alaska. Despite its somewhat diminutive size compared to most salmon, trout and charr, it is a delight on ultra-light tackle or a light fly rod, attacking flies as well as hardware with abandon. Not too picky about anything, grayling can be caught throughout the open water season, unlike salmon and other species. Excellent fishing can be had on any day from spring through fall, given proper knowledge of the habits of this fine gamester.

Spring

One of the very best times of the year to get in on nonstop action for grayling is during the spring spawning runs (April to May). Even before the ice breaks up on tributary streams draining into large lakes and glacial rivers, these sporty fish gather in masses at the mouths waiting for the right moment. Anglers lucky enough to find such a school can expect literally a fish on every cast using small spinners and flies. Salmon smolt and parr streamers in sizes #8 and #10 are particularly effective, as are smaller dry flies (Humpy, Elk Hair Caddis, Black Gnat, etc.) in sizes #12 to #18. However, care should be exercised on small creeks not to deplete the population by overharvesting, as they can be easily "caught out" by a few anglers in a very short period of time. Catch-and-release is a good idea. As the spawning streams break up, the fish swarm up by the thousands in many areas and provide a near nirvana of opportunities for two to three weeks before dropping back into mainstem rivers or moving on to other streams for the rest of the summer to feed.

Summer

Although some locations may see a lull in activity during the short summer months (June to August), superb angling can still be found in many areas. Avoid lowland waters in the southern range and concentrate efforts on clear mountain lakes and streams or inland areas to the north. Grayling do not take the summer heat well. They get sluggish in warm water and migrate in large numbers to cooler locations to feed. That is exactly where anglers must go. Seek out cold and shallow creeks for best results. In true grayling country it is hard to find a trickle of water deeper than a few inches that does not at least have a few fish present. Lakes can be very productive, especially in the early mornings or late evenings along the shorelines, but also at the inlets, outlets and springs where cooler water temperatures are prevalent. A good, steady rainfall is often great for fish-on-every-cast action, and makes larger specimens a possibility. Summer means dry fly fishing at its best, with spinners also producing exceptional results.

Fall

From September to October is probably the best time of year to tangle with grayling. After the long summer days and abundant feed, the fish are now in prime shape, strong and chunky and full of fight, and, with falling temperatures, very aggressive towards most anything that moves through the water. Nymph and wet flies tend to yield fast-paced action, and egg imitations work like a charm in waters where spawning salmon are present. Traditionally, the week or so before freeze-up is tops for large grayling; the lower sections of clearwater streams are best bets. Sculpin pattern flies and spinners buzzed through deep holes and runs are deadly, and have tricked many a trophy-sized fish. Dry flies, although they may work at times, are not always very effective.

Winter

This is without a doubt the most challenging time of year to catch grayling. From November to March, most all streams are frozen over, and icefishing on lakes has never been truly consistent. The fish are less active, quite deep, and do not show much interest in the way of artificial lures. Occasionally a few specimens may be taken incidentally when fishing for other species such as rainbow trout and landlocked salmon; they then seem to prefer small baits above anything else. Cocktail shrimp, worms and maggots do make connections, but action is best described as "fair." In other parts of the grayling's range (northern Europe), anglers have experienced good results using tiny jigs called "Mormyshka," but as of yet these have not been tried to any extent in Alaskan waters.

TECHNIQUES FOR MORE AND BIGGER GRAYLING

Arctic grayling are primarily visual feeders, and anglers must do their utmost to present their offerings in a way that seem both natural and favorable to the fish. Learning how to read the water is important, as is a complete and thorough understanding of the fish's habits and behavior under various climatic conditions.

During the warmer summer months when insect activity is peaking, feeding primarily occurs at or near the surface and mid-depth. It is during this period of time that flies, both wet and dry, will produce outstanding fishing. The ones that most closely resemble insects are preferred, particularly light, neutral and dark patters in sizes #10 to #20. For waters with fast current, use the larger sizes; use smaller ones for quiet or flat waters such as lakes. Roostertail-type spinners are also highly productive in sizes #0 to #3.

In many areas, fish is an important dietary supplement, and sculpin and salmon smolt patterns in size #2 or smaller are good for vicious strikes. Larger grayling are often fooled by the larger sizes. If salmon are present, salmon egg imitations can be unbeatable. But perhaps most of all, spinners are the best fish imitators since they have the correct combination of flash, vibration and motion. Sizes #0 to #3 are most popular; many a trophy grayling has fallen for the irresistible buzzing.

Anybody can catch a grayling out of a hole, but to consistently hook larger fish is a trick. A curious fact is that these arctic gamesters almost always display a form of hierarchy whenever present in pools and deep holes and runs. The largest and most dominant fish are found at the head of the flock, so to speak, with fish size decreasing throughout the holding area until only the smallest are left. The "leaders" are in an ideal position to have the first choice of food, intercepting particles as they drift by. Knowing this, anglers should place casts in the riffles just above the holding area and allow their offerings to tumble or drift downstream precisely on line to where the lineup begins and the big fish lurk. Remember, the larger-sized grayling tend to hug the bottom while the youngsters are found in the middle water column—so fish at the right depth. In fall, however, the hierarchical order begins to break down as the grayling hastily leave smaller streams bound for overwintering areas in lakes or larger rivers.

During the summer months when arctic grayling are actively feeding, avoid still or quiet water in stream areas and prospect for pools or runs with moderate to strong current flow, since calm stretches lack the amounts of forage drifting by. In faster water the fish are in a much better position to partake of, with a constant flow of nutrients important to sustaining energy and growth. And unlike other resident freshwater sportfish, grayling are much more pliable in their habits and commonly chase dragging flies several yards. They will move upward in the water column more frequently to intercept items floating on the surface.

In lakes, look for concentrations of fish at the inlets and outlets and areas that have a mud- and sand-covered bottom. Bottom structure is important because only certain types attract forage that grayling are dependent on. Rock and gravel structures are less ideal and will probably not hold many fish. On sunny days it pays to fish the deeper water columns around vegetation mats using shiny spinners and flies with some flash, but darker lures are more effective in the shallows at the mouth of tributary streams or along the shoreline in early morning and late evening.

Crystal-clear drainages are where grayling feel right at home, but significant populations also exist in lakes, ponds and streams with murky, muskeg-type water. The same standard fishing techniques apply, but lures and flies should be a bit more on the colorful or flashy side since grayling are very visible feeders. This is particularly true in flooding streams, tinted brown due to heavy rainshower activity. During periods of turbid water, grayling seek out areas with less current and will often hold near the bottom. Under such conditions, larger spoons and spinners outfish flies due to their mass, sonic vibrations and flash.

A most curious behavior tied into the feeding pattern of grayling is excitement and agitation. Anglers that have fished quite extensively for these fish know that there are times when a large school of grayling holding in a pool will show no interest in any type of lure presented to them. However, at a certain point, perhaps one fish will dash out and mouth an offering out of irritation. Oddly enough, this commotion will stir up the school considerably, triggering an aggressive response, and more fish will follow the plight of the first.

Spin Tackle and Gear

Ultra-light gear (six- to seven-and-a-half-foot, fast-action rod) with two- to four-pound test line is preferred, but a slightly heavier outfit may be advisable in waters where larger species such as salmon, trout and charr are present.

For lures, use small spoons and spinners, and plugs. Dark, natural colors are best, such as black, brown, blue, green and copper, but silver and gold with a touch of red and yellow works very well also. Popular brand-name spinners include Mepps, Vibrax, Panther Martin and Rooster Tail.

Fly Tackle and Gear

For flyfishing the Alaska grayling, a four-, five- or six-weight rod (eight to nine feet in length) is most commonly used, but under the right conditions anglers may want to gear down and use a six- to seven-foot, two- or three-weight rod. Single action reels are fine as long as they match the rod. Floating line and a short sink tip are all that's usually needed in the way of flylines. When floating dries for grayling, leaders and tippets should be shorter (four to six feet) than those used for dry fly presentations for trout as grayling are not leader-shy. Shorten up to four feet for sinking presentations. Tippets most commonly used are two- to four-pound test.

•*Fly Patterns:* Most any pattern dry fly will work: Black Gnat, Mosquito, Light Cahill, Elk Hair Caddis, Humpy, Wulff and Adam, in size #10 or smaller. Egg imitation or attractor patterns are also very effective, with Orange Woolly Buggers, Two-Egg Marabou, Glo Bugs, Iliamna Pinkie and Polar Shrimp among the top producers. Forage imitations like the Woolly Worm, Black Ant, Muddler Minnow, Hare's Ear Alevin, and Nymph and Stonefly patterns are also good.

ALASKA'S TOP TROPHY GRAYLING LOCATIONS

•Becharof Lake (Southwest)
•Sinuk River (Northwest)
•Pilgrim River (Northwest)
•Goodnews River (Southwest)
•Boston Creek (Northwest)

ALASKA'S TOP TEN TROPHY GRAYLING

4 pounds, 13 ounces, Ugashik Narrows (Southwest), 1981
4 pounds, 4 ounces, Ugashik River (Southwest), 1975
4 pounds, 3 ounces, Ugashik Lake (Southwest), 1973
4 pounds, 3 ounces, Ugashik River (Southwest), 1976
4 pounds, 2 ounces, Ugashik Lake (Southwest), 1972
4 pounds, 2 ounces, Sundial Lake (Southwest), 1977
4 pounds, 0 ounces, Ugashik Lake (Southwest), 1972
4 pounds, 0 ounces, Ugashik Lake (Southwest), 1978
4 pounds, 0 ounces, Ugashik Narrows (Southwest), 1979
4 pounds, 0 ounces, Sinuk River (Northwest), 1984

ALASKA'S MAJOR GRAYLING LOCATIONS

Arctic grayling are not tolerant of polluted environments, and thrive best in clean, clear lakes and streams in remote areas.

Southeast

Scattered opportunities exist from stockings done years ago.

•*Sitka:* Beaver Lake

•*Juneau:* Antler Lake

•*Petersburg/Wrangell:* Tyee Lake

•*Ketchikan:* Naha River system; Big Goat, Manzoni, Shinaku, Marge and Summit lakes; Big Goat and Shinaku creeks

Southcentral

Southcentral has some fairly good fishing, but much of the more accessible locations have been well worked over for larger fish; the best bet is to hike or fly in to remote headwater tributaries.

•*Matanuska/Susitna:* Bonnie, Harriet, Long and Seventeenmile lakes; Clear, Lake, Coal and Alexander creeks; Deshka, Talachulitna, Talkeetna and Upper Susitna rivers

•*Kenai:* Crescent, Grayling, Fuller, Twin, Bench and Paradise lakes; Crescent Creek

•*Kodiak:* Abercombie, Aurel, Cascade, Cicely and Long lakes

•*Chugach:* Long Island lakes

•*Wrangell:* Gulkana, Little Tonsina and Tyone rivers; Mendeltna, Cache, Tolsona, Moose, Gunn, Sourdough, Haggard and Poplar Grove creeks; Mae West, George, Little Junction, Louise, Connor, Susitna, Gillespie, Tyone, Dick, Kay, Tolsona, Arizona, Twin, Paxson, Summit and Tanada lakes

Southwest

Southwest has some of Alaska's best fishing in terms of abundance and average size, with trophy potential possible in many watersheds, particularly those with headwater lakes. Flyfishing conditions are the best in Alaska.

•*Bristol Bay:* Kvichak River/Lake Iliamna/Lake Clark system; Wood-Tikchik Lakes; Nushagak, Igushik and Togiak river systems

•*Alaska Peninsula:* Alagnak, Naknek, Becharof Lake systems

•*Lower Kuskokwim:* Goodnews, Arolik, Kanektok, Kwethluk, Kisaralik, Aniak and Holitna rivers

•*Lower Yukon:* Andreafsky and Anvik rivers

Northwest

Some of the largest trophy grayling come from this area (Seward Peninsula streams).

•*Norton Sound:* Unalakleet, Shaktoolik and Ungalik rivers

•*Seward Peninsula:* Fish-Niukluk, Sinuk, Snake, Nome, Kuzitrin, Tubutulik, American-Agiapuk and Pilgrim river systems

•*Kotzebue Sound:* Noatak, Kobuk and Wulik rivers

•*Arctic:* Kuparuk, Sagavanirktok, Kongakut and Canning rivers

Interior

•*Tanana:* Goodpaster, Salcha, Chatanika, Chena, Chitanana, Cosna, Zitziana and Tangle rivers; Kantishna and Nenana river systems; Clearwater, Rock, Fish and Crooked creeks; Big Swede, Landmark Gap, Glacier, Boulder and Tangle lakes

•*Yukon:* Nowitna, Ray, Dall, Hadweenzic, Melozitna, Tozitna, Charley, Black, Kandik, Nation, Seventymile and Hodzana rivers; Birch and Beaver creeks

•*Brooks Range:* Jim River

12
NORTHERN PIKE:
THE WATER WOLF

A small floatplane skims with diminishing speed along the surface of a giant lake in the heart of Bristol Bay. It slows and drifts into a quiet lagoon near a major inlet stream. A group of East Coast anglers, looking like they stepped from the pages of a catalog, clamber ashore, loudly proclaiming to the pilot and no one else in particular of their intention to catch every big rainbow trout occupying these vast waters, by day's end and their scheduled return. The pilot smiles—he's heard this kind of talk before. He shoves his plane off and taxis to the far side of the lake, then quickly lifts off into the wind and the stretching horizon.

The members of our group busy themselves with the matter at hand. There are dozens of trout lurking here, surely, and giant grayling and charr as well, for these are Bristol Bay's prime waters—nirvana for the elite of coldwater's finest fighters. None of this bunch is quite prepared, however, for the surprise that Nature has in store for them this August morning. As one East Coast gentleman strips a big fly through the deep crystal waters, an ominous, crocodile form emerges from the shallows. Hesitating at first, then with lightning speed, it streaks in a greenish blur toward the center of the lake, in a line that intersects the angler's retrieve. With little warning, the man has his rod wrenched violently from his grasp. The limber stick offers little resistance and quickly vanishes in the lake's waters, with an astonished angler in vain pursuit.

INTRODUCTION

The northern pike, *Esox lucius,* a.k.a. the water wolf, jackfish, snake or devilfish, is the familiar and notorious toothy glutton of northern waters, known for its supreme savagery when feeding. Lean and mean, with a giant maw and rakish jaws like the barracuda, the pike is the ultimate, "lie-in-wait" ambush predator, with body plan and demeanor designed to wreak havoc on a variety of prey—fish, rodents, even waterfowl—with lightning-swift speed. No other fish attacks a lure with the resolve and vigor of a hungry northern pike!

The pike's wantonness lends well to fantastic legends among Alaska's indigenous people. The Athapaskans speak of giant pike that dwell in large lakes and sloughs along the great waterways of Interior, where, should a man be foolish enough to stray by these "devil waters," they can consume him in a single gulp. The Eskimo similarly has tales of forbidden waters, wherein lurk evil spirits incarnate in the form of monster northerns the size of trees. White folks too speak of the northern's incredible boldness. One old trapper I knew swore a six-footer had gone after him one spring when he fell into a slough in a remote part of the Kuskokwim country.

Legends and spirits aside, the northern pike, in Alaska at least, is a tremendously underrated and underutilized sport species. Perhaps due to the presence of so many other more notable gamefish, and the prejudice many folks feel toward this maligned fighter, little focused effort occurs for pike in many areas that offer outstanding fishing. But the fact remains—Alaska's better pike potential is every bit the equal of anything that Canada has to offer, with the added appeal of almost no angling competition on most waters.

DESCRIPTION

An adult northern pike is not easily confused with other fish. Its body is elongated and somewhat compressed, the dorsal fin riding far back towards the tail. The head is large and dark green above, and light or pale below; the snout is flattened, and some 700 very sharp teeth decorate the pike's powerful jaws. The back and sides are dark green or brown or grayish green, with the sides also displaying numerous yellowish spots arranged in irregular longitudinal rows. The scales are moderately small and may have a touch of gold to the edges. The belly and lower jaw is creamy white. Dorsal, anal and caudal fins are typically greenish yellow, in some populations even appearing almost orange or red with dark blotches. A color variant known as silver pike is also found in Alaska, as well as in the Lower 48.

Pike meat is white and flaky and considered quite flavorful, but it is also very bony, which may contribute to its false reputation of not being a good food fish. However, after mastering how to cut boneless filets, most folks agree that pike are no less than scrumptious.

Northern pike in Alaska are not officially known to achieve the same dimensions as fish in central and northern Europe (65 to 90 pounds), but specimens up to 50 pounds or more are speculated to thrive in many vast, remote watersheds of the state. Typically averaging between three and 10 pounds, depending more or less on location and amount of angling effort, many areas yield trophy pike up to 20 pounds. A fish of "about 45 pounds" is reputed to have been taken from a drainage near Circle on the Yukon River, and stories of much larger catches abound in rural villages.

RANGE, ABUNDANCE & STATUS

Northern pike enjoy a circumpolar distribution ranging from northern Italy and Spain in the south to the Scandinavian countries, and from the British Isles to the Pacific coast of Siberia. In North America, pike are found from New England, Missouri and Nebraska to the Arctic coast of Alaska. They are particularly abundant in Alaska, northern Canada and Russia and on the Scandinavian peninsula.

Within Alaska, pike are most numerous in sloughs and slow-flowing clearwater drainages of Interior and Southwest, particularly the Yukon and Tanana River systems, but are also very common in lakes and streams of Northwest and Southcentral. Southeast is the only region in

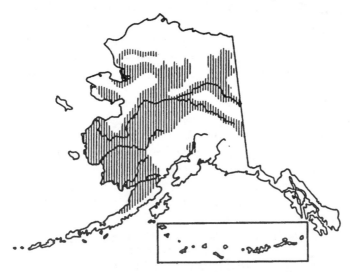

Shaded area shows range of northern pike in Alaska.

Alaska that does not have populations of northern pike, aside from a small remnant stock from the last Ice Age present in the Ahrnklin River system in the Yakutat area. Illegal transplants of this species have extended its range to include the Susitna River drainage, waters in and around Anchorage, and lakes connected to the Kenai River in Southcentral.

Although the pike's popularity as a sportfish is beginning to spread from Interior to other parts of the state, there are still untold numbers of ideal waters yet to be discovered and fully recognized. Few locations have been tapped to their maximum potential, and many more outstanding pike waters are discovered each year.

LIFE HISTORY & HABITS

Each and every spring, mature northern pike leave the cold depths of overwintering areas to seek out shallow, marshy areas to spawn. This significant movement commences right after break-up, usually sometime in May or even June, depending largely on geographic allocation. Lake populations commonly utilize shoreline areas, channels and sloughs with suitable bottom structure, but may at times leave the lake environment and migrate to slow-moving streams. River populations commit similar migrations, preferring sloughs and lower reaches of tributary rivers and creeks for reproduction. However, spawning migrations are seldom extensive and generally no more than a few miles.

The most important factors in choice of spawning habitat are shallow and quiet water with emergent vegetation and mud bottoms with vegetation mats. Actual spawning occurs only during daylight in areas no deeper than one or two feet, and ceases at night or during periods of heavy cloud cover, rain, and, in some instances, cold air temperatures. Like other sportfish species, pike may return to spawn in the same exact location every year.

Northern pike are neither very territorial nor monogamous and frequently spawn with several members of the opposite gender. The spawning act is repeated often (every few minutes for up to several hours), as only relatively few eggs are released at a time. Depending on the size and age of the mature female, eggs number anywhere between 2,000 and 600,000. A ready-to-spawn female contains both large, ripe eggs as well as immature eggs that will ripen the following year.

After expulsion, the eggs settle anywhere along bottom, where they remain until hatched—a period of time that may range from four or five days up to a month, depending largely on water temperature. After hatching, the young feed off the yolk sacks until they are old enough to consume zooplankton, later switching to a diet consisting of insect larvae and nymphs. Mortality from egg to fry is very high (99.9%), primarily caused by predation from fish species and birds, competition for food and even cannibalism by larger pike. Before long, juvenile pike begin to forage on small fishes, at which time growth increases dramatically. Rate of growth is fast the first few years, then slows. Also, the growth rate appears to be more rapid in the southern range, progressively slower to the north and largely tied in with water temperature. However, pike in more northern latitudes live to a greater age. Maturity is attained as early as age two, but for the most part not until age three or four.

After spawning, the spent adult pikes stay on or near the spawning beds anywhere from one-and-a-half months up to four months. At this time, they are engaged in a feeding frenzy and particularly vulnerable to anglers. Fish makes up the greater part of big northerns' diet and in some areas may be their exclusive food. They are not picky at all about what kinds of fish are consumed, either, devouring whatever is available. Burbot, grayling, whitefish, suckers and even smaller pike are among the favored species, but juvenile and adult salmon are preyed upon as well. Pike consume frogs, mice, shrews and large insects without hesitation, and are also thought to be serious predators of young waterfowl in some areas. To sum things up: Northern pike will eat whatever they can catch and swallow.

Northern pike have long been both despised and admired for their uncanny ability to infiltrate new drainages, utilizing rivers as well as tiny trickles of water to spread their range. Their hardiness is of prehistoric proportion. Reports of pike in brackish water have been confirmed, with one such specimen caught in a set net in upper Cook Inlet. The fish was purple in color due to its reaction to salt water; more than likely, it was scouting for new watersheds to inhabit. But usually, pike are strictly freshwater residents.

FISHING ALASKA'S NORTHERN PIKE

For many years, the pike had a reputation as a trash fish and nuisance with no purpose whatsoever except to prey upon valuable young salmon and trout. However, after decades of disregard (including massive extermination attempts), the northern pike has finally received the respect it deserves and is today regarded as a legitimate sport species throughout the northern hemisphere. They are aggressive towards artificial lures, plentiful and popular as a food item. To successfully engage in combat with these duck-billed eating machines, read on.

Some of the fastest and most rewarding action of the year for large trophy pike occurs in the spring. Starting in mid-May and continuing through June, big spawners take up their positions in the shallows around weedbeds near shore in lakes, ponds, sloughs and streams. Just prior to and after reproduction, fishing can be excellent. Approach weed beds carefully as not to spook any fish. In many locations, it is possible to spot the pike suspended right beneath the surface, still and motionless, looking like driftwood or logs—until a lure is thrown out.

The Dardevle: the classic lure for northern pike.

Flashy spoons and plugs retrieved with an erratic action through promising water almost always produce smashing strikes, but few things can match the excitement of watching a topwater lure or fly get assaulted from below by a 20-pound-plus toothy monster. It is a thrill not soon forgotten. However, anglers should be selective at this time about the number and gender of the fish they retain. Since the majority of large pike are female and crucial to the well-being of the local stock, and the total number of fish present on the spawning beds represent a good portion of the adult population, catch-and-release is encouraged. If flyfishing, do not use a dead-drift—it will most likely be ignored. Instead, use short, fast strips—enough to leave a good wake on surface presentations. If there are pike nearby, the fly will not make it back unassaulted.

Come summer, topwater lures cease to be the most effective and many anglers switch to traditional hardware such as spoons and plugs; they also use spinners. At this time, most of the fish have left the shallows for slightly deeper water, but the action is still good. Pike do not generally migrate far from the spawning grounds, and seem to be found on edges of deep water and heavily vegetated areas until freeze-up. Boaters fare the best on lakes, although angling from shore is productive in some rivers and streams. On lakes with minimal vegetation growth, pike tend to migrate more in search of food and rely more on smell than any other sense to catch a prey. Oily baits are very effective here, with herring, hooligan and whitefish making excellent attractors when rigged up with two single or two treble hooks.

Some of the better locations to find pike in summer and fall are in backwater sloughs and the mouths of slow-flowing streams where they empty into silty rivers. The glacial-green mix is a favorite hangout for big northerns, and many of these succumb to properly presented spoons and plugs and even bait. But, as always, avoid totally open water and concentrate efforts near vegetation structure.

In winter, icefishing for pike can be both exciting and fascinating. Towards the early part of the season (November to January), pike are found in relatively deep water between 15 and 30 feet but can certainly be encountered throughout all layers at times. Ice houses come in handy on lakes as they provide anglers with shelter, and the darkness inside accents the little light illuminating from the water. Decoys have been used for decades to bring fish in close enough to be speared, but spoons jigged a few feet below the ice are equally deadly. Be prepared for big fish and drill a hole at least one foot in diameter.

Spin Tackle and Gear

For spinning, a six- to eight-foot medium- to heavy-weight, medium-action rod with matching high-quality reel and 8- to 20-pound test line is the preferred setup. Wire or super heavy mono shock leaders are prerequisite for preventing break-offs from the northern's abundant, sharp teeth. Larger trophy fish and bigger waters require heavier gear.

Effective pike lures include spoons and plugs in an assortment of colors as long as they have full bodies and an attractive wobbling action. Blue, yellow, brown, black, silver and gold all work; it is up to the individual angler to find which color combination works best under current conditions. Ideally, lures should match the type of local forage found in the specific watershed as closely as possible. Popular varieties include Pixee, Krocodile, Dardevle, Red Eye and Wigglerspoons; Rapala, Flatfish and Tadpolly plugs; #6 Super Vibrax and Mepps Giant Killer Spinners; and Moss Boss and Jaw Breaker topwater lures.

Fly Tackle and Gear

Flyfishers wanting to do battle with pike need at least an eight-weight rod (nine-and-a-half feet to ten-and-a-half feet) with good backbone and matching reel with a good drag. Lines used are generally floating or, rarely, sink tip, mated to a 12- to 20-pound tippet with the last 12 inches a wire leader.

•*Fly Patterns:* Large attractors and forage imitations—Flash Fly, Alaska Mary Ann, Outrageous, Alaskabou, Gray Ghost, Sculpin, Bunny Bug, etc.—are excellent, as are tubeflies and saltwater patterns like the Clouser Minnow, Deceiver and Tarpon. Topwater flies like poppers, frogs, lemming and mouse imitations are exciting to fish (and expensive), but seldom survive more than four or five vicious strikes before disintegrating. Keep it simple and cheap. Aim for flies with a certain amount of bulk since they help grip pike's teeth. Super sharp, size #3/0 to #4 hooks are recommended.

ALASKA'S TOP TROPHY PIKE WATERS
•Innoko River (Southwest)
•Alexander Lake (Southcentral)
•East Twin Lake (Interior)
•Nowitna River (Interior)
•Trapper Lake (Southcentral)

TOP TEN TROPHY NORTHERN PIKE
Interior has long represented Alaska as the leading producer of trophy and record northern pike, but angling interest is shifting to little-fished drainages of Southwest and Southcentral, which are developing reputations for large pike that may exceed 30 pounds and perhaps nudge the 40-pound mark.

38 pounds, 8 ounces, Innoko River (Southwest), 1991 (state record)
38 pounds, 0 ounces, Fish Creek (Interior), 1978
31 pounds, 2 ounces, Donkey Lake (Southcentral), 1992
29 pounds, 11 ounces, East Twin Lake (Interior), 1988
29 pounds, 0 ounces, Innoko River (Southwest), 1990
28 pounds, 6 ounces, Innoko River (Southwest), 1991
28 pounds, 2 ounces, Wilson Lake (Interior), 1971
28 pounds, 0 ounces, Lake Clark (Southwest), 1982
27 pounds, 8 ounces, Alexander Lake (Southcentral), 1992
27 pounds, 8 ounces, Tolovana River (Interior), 1969

ALASKA'S MAJOR PIKE LOCATIONS
The most abundant northern pike populations are found in parts of Interior, Southwest, Southcentral and Northwest, with the best fishing found in low-lying river, slough and lake habitat (such as the Yukon, Tanana and Kanuti flats, and lower Innoko, Selawik, Noatak rivers, among others). The larger fish are primarily present in Southwest, Northwest and Interior, but respectable specimens are now being caught in certain locations in Southcentral.

Southeast
•*Yakutat:* Antlen River Lakes

Southcentral
•*Susitna:* Chelatna, Bulchitna, Red Shirt, Lynx, Vern, Flathorn, Sucker, Alexander, Hewitt, Whiskey and Trapper lakes

•*Kenai:* Cisca Lake

Southwest
•*Bristol Bay:* Nushagak River system; Wood Tikchik, Clark, Telaquana, Chulitna, Long, Whitefish and Pike lakes

•*Alaska Peninsula:* Naknek Lake system (portions)

•*Kuskokwim:* Lower Aniak and Holitna rivers

•*Lower Yukon:* Lower Andreafsky, Anvik and Innoko rivers

Northwest
•*Norton Sound:* Unalakleet, Shaktoolik, Ungalik and Kwiniuk rivers

•*Seward Peninsula:* Fish, Kuzitrin and Pilgrim rivers; Imuruk Basin, Buckland River

•*Kotzebue Sound:* Lower Kobuk, Selawik and Noatak rivers

•*Lower Koyukuk River:* Mainstem and tributaries—Gisasa, Dulbi, Huslia, Dakli, Hogatza and Kateel rivers

Interior
•*Tanana:* Chisana and Nabesna river systems; Chatanika, Tolovana, lower Tatalina, Cosna, Chitanana, Chena and Zitziana rivers; Swan Neck Slough; Fish, Gardiner, Moose and lower Goldstream creeks; Jatahmund, Wellesley, Dog, Island, Wien, Wolf, East Twin, West Twin, Deadman, Mucha, Volkmar, Tetlin, Minchumina, Mansfield, George and Bear lakes

•*Middle Yukon:* Melozitna, Tozitna, Nowitna, Hodzana, Hadweenzic, Chandalar, Christian, Sheenjek, Porcupine and Black rivers; lower Hess, Birch and Beaver creeks

•*Brooks Range:* Upper Chandalar and Sheenjek River system lakes

13
SHEEFISH:
TARPON OF THE NORTH

by Kenneth T. Alt

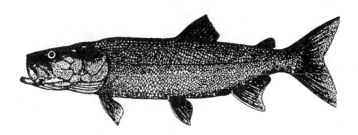

I'd heard the Eskimos many times tell of the early summer spawning run of smelt in the lower Kobuk and of the ravenously hungry sheefish that congregated there. But I fished the river for many years before I had the good fortune of being at the right place and time to actually witness this amazing spectacle. It was during the second week of June one year, when I was stirred from sleep by a commotion in the river, scant yards from my tent door. Just as my native friends had said, the water churned with untold thousands of silvery smelt, driven into a mad frenzy by the savage onslaught of big sheefish that seemed everywhere. A lure tossed into the fray was instantly pounced on by fish weighing anywhere from three to 30 pounds, supercharged with an energy and jumping ability like I'd never seen before. My fishing partner brought out his flyrod and, with a white streamer, hung one big shee after another in exhilarating battles that were every bit as spectacular as fishing for tarpon. The action continued as the smolt made their way upriver, but after an hour or two of nonstop arm-yanking excitement, we were too bushed to pursue them any further.

INTRODUCTION

The sheefish, *Stenodus leucichthys,* also called "inconnu" and "Eskimo tarpon," is a large, predatory whitefish related to the salmon and trout. Its long, slender body shape, extended lower jaw (similar to the pike), silvery color and size distinguish it from the more common whitefish species. The world's largest and only whitefish consistently caught on hook and line, the sheefish is generally freshwater river dwelling, although in the Kuskokwim, lower Yukon and Selawik-Kobuk rivers, certain populations may spend part of their life cycle in the estuarine portions of river mouths. They spawn in the upper reaches of clearwater rivers and are highly migratory, with some sea-run populations travelling a total of 2,000 miles to and from spawning sites. Fish of the more local populations may only undertake migrations of 200 miles or less. They do not die after spawning, as do salmon, and may return to spawn repeatedly.

The major significance of sheefish in Alaska and elsewhere has been as a subsistence food for rural residents and their dogs. A few small, highly regulated commercial fisheries exist on the more abundant populations. Called "inconnu" for "unknown fish" by early French-Canadian fur traders, the Alaska shee today still remains obscure as a sportfish, mostly because of its remote and limited distribution, seasonal availability and the presence of more glamorous and desirable sportfish species. Indeed, only in recent years has the International Game Fish Association recognized it as a trophy fish for record-keeping purposes. Many are taken incidentally by anglers fishing for pike, who are surprised by a long, silvery torpedo of a fish exploding from the water.

Despite its lack of notoriety, the sheefish has tremendous sportfish potential, as it readily takes a variety of lures and flies, reaches respectable size and has outstanding fighting and eating qualities. Its tail-walking, topwater acrobatics have earned it the respectful name of "Eskimo tarpon" or "Tarpon of the North," for it indeed compares favorably with the silvery, leaping giant of tropical waters.

DESCRIPTION

Sheefish from all stocks show little variation in shape and color throughout life. They have narrow, tapered bodies, with long heads and pike-like mouths that can open wide like a tarpon. Their color is silvery, with backs of light blue or pale brown and whitish bellies. Markings are usually absent. Sheefish inhabiting darker-colored waters in interior Alaska are slightly darker than fish coming up from the sea. The sheefish body is deepest behind the pectoral fins, with a fleshy adipose fin in front of the tail. Eyes are large; scales are silvery and come off easily. During spawning, males maintain their torpedo-like body shape, while the belly of a female becomes flaccid and the vent area enlarges.

Juveniles as small as six inches have the same recognizable pike-like mouth and head as adults. Occasionally they are found with a metallic green sheen on the upper body, which turns to blue or brown as the fish grows. In all populations in Alaska, a sheefish-whitefish hybrid can be encountered. This fish is a bit browner in color than a sheefish and has a terminal (trout-like) mouth rather than the extended lower jaw of sheefish. The hybrid fights more like a whitefish, rapidly wiggling its head during capture. It seldom exceeds five pounds in weight.

Sheefish from most Alaska populations obtain a weight of five pounds at 26 inches and 10 pounds at 30 inches. At 30 pounds, a sheefish might be 34 to 38 inches. There is much variation in potential size, with sheefish of local populations in the Minto Flats, Nowitna, Porcupine and upper Yukon River areas seldom exceeding 12 pounds and 32 inches in length while Kuskokwim and Yukon River anadromous populations reach 25 pounds and 39 inches. Only in the Kobuk-Selawik drainages are fish of 50 pounds or more found (the current Alaska and world record sport-caught fish is a 53-pounder from this area). Females generally grow larger than males.

Sheefish flesh is white in all cases. The small-sized fish are quite bland in taste, while larger-sized fish contain more fat and are very tasty. Sheefish are excellent baked, fried, barbecued or smoked. Raw frozen sheefish, eaten with seal oil, is an Eskimo delicacy. As with other fish, sheefish lose body fat during the spawning process and eating value diminishes.

RANGE, ABUNDANCE & STATUS

In Alaska sheefish have a limited distribution from the Kuskokwim River to the Kobuk-Selawik drainages in Northwest. Except for feeding and overwintering fish that appear in Selawik Lake and Hotham Inlet, sheefish are not normally found in lakes. (Small numbers have been stocked in landlocked lakes in Interior, however.) In the Kuskokwim River they are found from tidewater upstream to the vicinity of Telida. In the Yukon River, they reside throughout the entire drainage, from the mouth upstream to the Laird and Bell rivers (Porcupine drainage) in Canada. Sheefish are not found in smaller rivers that empty directly into the ocean, with the possible exception of a small population in the Koyuk River. They are not found on the Seward Peninsula or on Alaska's North Slope. Worldwide, they are found in all the great north-flowing rivers of central and eastern Siberia, including the Ob, Irtysh, Lena, Yenesei and Kolyma. They are absent on North Slope Alaska rivers but are encountered east in Canada's Mackenzie River system as well as in the Anderson River.

Sheefish reach their greatest abundance in the larger, slower-moving waters of Alaska. They do enter first-order tributaries of the Kuskok-wim and Yukon rivers, but on the Kobuk and Selawik rivers they are confined to the mainstem and associated sloughs in the lower reaches. In general, anadromous populations are larger both in numbers and in individual size; the lower Yukon River or Kobuk-Selawik populations might contain 10,000 spawners, while the non-anadromous local populations in the Minto Flats, and the Nowitna, Porcupine, Black and upper Yukon rivers may contain only a few hundred fish each at most.

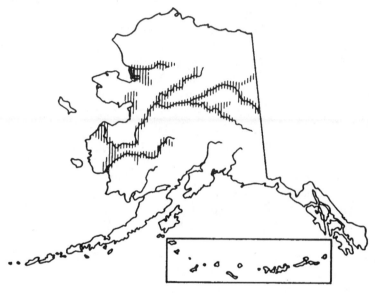

Shaded area shows range of sheefish in Alaska.

Sheefish stocks in Alaska are not as closely monitored as salmon, but all indications show stable, healthy populations, with some natural fluctuations due to climatic conditions and other variables. Since sea-run populations do not venture far out into the ocean, they are safe from most marine predators and gill nets. Presently there is little development threatening overwintering, spawning and rearing habitat, and in Alaska at least, their migrations are not impeded by dams as is the case elsewhere in some parts of their range. The small, non-anadromous populations are most easily affected by overfishing and habitat alteration. Because of scant biological data available, sheefish management has always been rather conservative. Subsistence fishing harvests declined during the 1970s and 1980s as snow machines replaced dog teams, while commercial harvests have remained stable and sport-take only slightly increased. As more anglers become familiar with the fabulous "Eskimo Tarpon," fishing pressure can only rise; hopefully, this will be offset by the growing catch-and-release ethic taking hold among anglers everywhere.

LIFE HISTORY & HABITS

A most important aspect of sheefish behavior in terms of sport-fishing is their migratory nature. Since sheefish do not die after spawning, they undertake both upstream and downstream migrations to prime areas for feeding and overwintering. In the major rivers the upstream spawning movements begin at ice break-up, generally preceding the salmon in-migration. These migrations slow considerably as fish linger at mouths of tributary streams to feed. For instance, in the Kuskokwim River, sheefish reach Aniak by early June, Sleetmute by late June and the McGrath area by late July. In the Yukon River, the spawning run is spread throughout the lower and middle river in June and July, but the peak of the run reaches the Tanana area by mid-August and the Rampart area by early September. In the Kobuk and Selawik rivers, the run hits the lower rivers in late spring, then proceeds upriver as summer progresses; it reaches the Kiana and Selawik areas in late June, the Ambler area in mid-July and the upper Kobuk River area in August and early September. A portion of the lower Yukon River stock continues up the Koyukuk River to spawn near Hughes and Allakaket, while the majority of the population spawn in the main Yukon River between Beaver and Fort Yukon.

Total distance travelled can be quite impressive. Fish tagged on the Alatna River and in the mainstem Yukon near Fort Yukon have been recovered at the mouth of the Yukon River three to four months after spawning, for a round-trip migration of 2,000 miles. Migrations of freshwater local populations may range from less than 100 miles for fish in the Koyuk River to over 400 miles for Porcupine River sheefish. Sheefish are quite old before their first spawning, with females from the Kobuk-Selawik population spawning at age 12 to 14. Males spawn three to four years earlier. Fish of the faster growing Minto Flats population spawn at younger ages and have a shorter life span.

The sheefish is an Arctic spawner, evidenced by major populations on the Kobuk, Selawik, Koyukuk, Alatna, Porcupine and Black rivers breeding within a few miles of the Arctic Circle. For egg laying, they require a combination of six to eight feet of water, moderate to fast current and a bottom of small to medium gravel—a condition found only in upper sections of certain rivers within their range, usually quite remote. Spawning occurs in late September and early October, with fish in the mainstem Yukon spawning as late as October 18, when water temperatures are near freezing and the river runs with ice. Sheefish cease feeding for three to four months before spawning (their large reserves of body fat sustain them during migration, spawning and overwintering), but can still be enticed to take a lure or fly. The spawning act takes place only during late afternoon and early evening, and frequently occurs on or near the surface, with eggs often shot into the air. Fertilized eggs sink to the bottom where they slowly develop in the near-freezing water and young hatch out in April or May. Fry are carried downstream by spring floods to suitable slow moving habitats for rearing.

Sheefish in the rearing and feeding portions of their life history are found in association with pike, burbot, suckers, lampreys and five species of whitefish. They grow rapidly and will usually weigh three to four pounds at five years of age, feeding on plankton and insects initially but turning to fish predation by age one. Suckers, lampreys, small pike and whitefish are the most important forage species. Sheefish must swallow their prey whole since they have no teeth for gripping; consequently food items tend to be less than eight inches in length. Concentrations of sheefish in Selawik Lake and Hotham Inlet feed actively throughout the winter, as it is believed all sheefish in Alaska do.

Sheefish continue to grow throughout life. The impressive size of the Kobuk and Selawik River fish is due to the fact that they live so much longer than other Alaska sheefish. (A 40-pound trophy there might be 19 to 21 years old, whereas age 13 for Yukon River and 11 for Minto Flats sheefish is about tops.) They have no significant predators other than man, although adult pike, burbot and even their own kind prey on the young.

The incredible abundance of sheefish one day and their total absence in the same area the next can be extremely frustrating for anglers. Being a schooling species, they are prone to move en masse from areas, for reasons related to food availability, water clarity, depth and temperature. They exhibit these same schooling tendencies under the ice, while feeding and during migrations. Except for the later stages of the spawning migration, when they no longer feed (but can be enticed with attractor flies and lures), sheefish of all sizes are found in these schooling aggregations.

Shees are not considered strong swimmers. They often utilize large eddies, sloughs and stream mouths for resting, hugging the shore and staying close to bottom in strong current. In these situations they are vulnerable to a well-placed lure or fly and subsistence gill nets. Their upstream migrations are easily blocked by falls or other impasses that pose no problem for salmon or trout.

Sheefish feeding habits vary. Quite often they will feed deep or off bottom (on lampreys for instance), but under certain conditions (when baitfish are present) they will be active near or on the surface. The frenzy of sheefish smashing bait on top of the water presents, of course, classic conditions for the most exciting angling, as this is when they are at their most reckless and prone to wild leaping.

Unfortunately not all sheefish fight like the tarpon they resemble and, like any other species, at times they may be as challenging as the proverbial log—especially prespawners or fish in the warm water habitats of interior Alaska. Fish taken off bottom generally do not fight as spectacularly as those from the upper water column. Unlike salmon or trout, shees generally do not make long runs and tend to be more acrobatic the larger they get.

FISHING ALASKA'S SHEEFISH

Sheefish sport angling in Alaska is still in its infancy; recreational fishing pressure has increased only slightly over the past 10 years, unlike the phenomenal growth seen in other sport fisheries in Interior and Arctic Alaska. The estimated 1993 catch was 6,666 fish (1,619 harvested). The majority (almost two-thirds) comes from Northwest Alaska's Kobuk and Selawik Rivers, while the Kuskokwim River, Yukon River and Tanana River drainage follow. A sizable number of sheefish harvested in Northwest Alaska are taken through the ice in the slightly brackish waters of Hotham Inlet and Selawik Lake.

Methods

For successful sheefish angling, locating your migratory quarry is the primary goal. Once you've found the general area containing fish, you'll need to determine the depth they are holding or feeding in. Surface-feeding shees will be easy to spot. They'll often jump completely out of the water pursuing their prey, or drive "boils" of baitfish to the surface—which often draws gulls and terns to the melee, making it even more obvious. In these situations, a fly or lure fished in the upper three feet of the water column will usually produce bone-jarring strikes. The annual out-migration of chum, king and silver salmon smolt in northern Alaska rivers during June and early July provides a short but rich feeding bonanza for sheefish and excellent opportunities for the sport angler. That's if he can locate feeding concentrations, especially those at the mouths of clear tributary streams.

Occasionally sheefish in a spawning aggregation can be observed rolling on the surface, especially in early evening. These fish are not feeding but may be trying to break the eggs loose in the egg skein prior to spawning. These fish can be enticed to strike a slowly retrieved lure or fly in the upper water column.

Special consideration by anglers should be given to sheefish which spend the entire summer feeding at the mouths of virtually all clearwater streams and sloughs of Interior and northern Alaska rivers. A lure or fly cast into the interface of the muddy and clear water usually gets results, as sheefish often feed or rest throughout the entire water column in this zone. The fish in these groups generally are smaller, but quite often they bite more readily than spawners. In the Yukon River, there are anadromous sheefish which do not migrate annually to sea, in addition to a number of freshwater local populations; these fish can provide steady angling from break-up to freeze-up.

When sheefish are feeding or holding on bottom, it is imperative to get your lure or fly down deep, as close to the fish as possible. Quarter casts with heavy lures, slow retrieves, high-density fly lines and sinkers are the ticket in these conditions, but keep in mind that the strike from these fish is much more subtle than from surface feeders. Most of the fishing for sheefish in Alaska is done from a boat, anchoring near feeding or holding areas, then using short casts with lure or fly. Bait fishing is generally not employed to catch the species.

While sheefish and pike often coexist in the same general area of a river, their specific habitat requirements are different. Sheefish are hardly ever found in shallow water, close to willows and brush or in grassy sloughs. Instead, they prefer the open water of deep holes and sloughs or tributary mouths. If the angler is catching more pike than sheefish, the water he is fishing is probably too shallow. If he is catching charr, salmon or grayling, he is probably in the wrong habitat. Sheefish have a hard mouth, and the angler must strike with sufficient force to drive the hook home. Those fish that jump will become airborne as soon as they feel the hook and, as with tarpon, present a special challenge to hold, especially with energetic fish in the 20- to 40-pound range.

In ice fishing, locating the school of sheefish is 90 percent of the battle. In rivers, deep holes located during open water are the best locations to try, but on Selawik Lake, Hotham Inlet and certain other locations, random testing of a large number of holes by groups of anglers on snow machines is the preferred technique. Once a school is located, a large number of holes are drilled in the vicinity and excellent fishing is usually enjoyed, sometimes for days before the school leaves in their search for food. Most anglers use a stout jigging stick with 15 to 25 feet of 75- to 100-pound dacron line. A three- to four-inch lure is tied directly to the line and jigged two to four feet under the surface with an erratic, slow motion. As you can imagine, hauling a big, 30- or 40-pound fighting shee up through the ice can be quite a job, not unlike trying to contain a bucking horse on a short rope.

Gear

Medium- or medium/heavyweight freshwater spinning or casting rods, matched to high-quality reels with good drags and 200 yards of 10- to 15-pound line are the accoutrements of most successful sheefish outings in Alaska. When fishing for smaller shees in Interior and the upper Yukon River, lighter tackle (down to six- to eight-pound line) is sufficient and can provide better action. Best lures include Dardevles, Krocodiles, Hot Rods and Pixees in weights from three-eighths to one ounce. Traditional red and white, bright orange and silver seem the best colors. (There are situations, like on the upper Kobuk River, when only bronze-colored lures work.) Fish the heavier sizes to get down in deeper, swifter water. Diving plugs and rattling crankbaits (Wiggle Warts, Shad Raps, Hot Shots, Rat-L-Traps, etc.) can also be worked effectively. For ice fishing, large (three-inch) Doktor lures in silver and bronze are dynamite, but other bright spoons and jigs can be used, with good results at times.

Fly rods should be seven- to nine-weight with plenty of backbone to coax large fish from the currents. In slower water or for smaller fish, you can get by with lighter gear, down to a five-weight in some instances. Flies used for feeding sheefish should resemble prey items— white Woolly Buggers, Smolt patterns, Leeches (including Egg-Sucking Leech), etc., in sizes #4 to #1/0. Large (up to size #3/0), attractor streamer flies work well for fish that aren't feeding, with colorful patterns utilizing some of the newer materials such as Krystal Flash and Flashabou most popular.

It is most essential to get the fly close to the fish for best results. Use short leaders and tippets of 8 to 12 pounds, depending on conditions and the size of fish pursued. Flies should be weighted even when sheefish are feeding on the surface. Floating and sinking tip lines are adequate for feeding fish, but for fish holding in deep water or non-feeding prespawners, a weighted line such as the Teeny Nymph is better. A shock leader or wire leader is not really necessary because sheefish do not have teeth, but sharp hooks are a definite plus for penetrating their hard bony mouths.

ALASKA'S TOP TEN TROPHY SHEEFISH

53 pounds, 0 ounces, Pah River (Northwest), 1986
(state and world record)
52 pounds, 8 ounces, Kobuk River (Northwest), 1968
43 pounds, 0 ounces, Kobuk River (Northwest), 1993
42 pounds, 4 ounces, Kobuk River (Northwest), 1994
39 pounds, 8 ounces, Kobuk River (Northwest), 1967
38 pounds, 12 ounces, Kobuk River (Northwest), 1987
38 pounds, 0 ounces, Kobuk River (Northwest), 1979
37 pounds, 11 ounces, George River (Northwest), 1971
37 pounds, 4 ounces, Kobuk River (Northwest), 1978
32 pounds, 2 ounces, Pah River (Northwest), 1992

ALASKA'S MAJOR SHEEFISH LOCATIONS

•*Kuskokwim River:* Most sheefish taken in the Kuskokwim River are fish feeding during the summer upstream migration. Since the Kuskokwim is muddy, prime angling locations are always at the mouths and lower reaches of clearwater tributaries. Sheefish are found in early June in streams between Bethel and Aniak, while in July, they appear in the Holitna, Tatlawiksuk and clearwater streams between Sleetmute and McGrath. Upstream of McGrath, the spawning migration spreads out and fish are found in the Takotna River, Middle Fork, Big River, North Fork and in the Telida area. A few non-spawning fish are present all summer in Kuskokwim streams. Since most sheefish in the Kuskokwim overwinter below Bethel, little ice fishing for them occurs.

•*Yukon River:* In the lower Yukon River, sheefish stop at the mouths of tributary rivers to feed while migrating upstream during early summer. Often the water is too muddy early on, but as tributaries clear, sheefish can be taken. The lower Innoko River in the Shageluk and Holikachuk areas is a major feeding zone. In the Ruby area, sheefish are present in the Yuki, Melozitna and Nowitna rivers from late June to mid-July. During July and August they can be found in the lower reaches of Ray, Dall, Hodzana and Chandalar rivers, and Hess, Birch and Beaver creeks. They are present in the streams between Circle and Eagle such as the Charley, Kandik, Nation, Seventymile and Tatonduk rivers and Eagle Creek. The huge migration of spawners reaching the vicinity of the Dalton Highway bridge in early September remain in the muddy water and thus are inaccessible to anglers.

After these sheefish have migrated back to the lower Yukon River area for overwintering, there is an active ice fishery during November, March and April in the villages from Holy Cross downstream to the mouth of the Yukon. The Koyukuk River has its own spawning migration and although fish are passing through lower Koyukuk River villages during August, little sportfishing occurs until the run reaches Hughes in late August and September. The main Koyukuk River from Hughes to Allakaket and the lower 40 miles of the Alatna River provide good sportfishing during September and early October. The Porcupine contains two populations of sheefish, but their small numbers and small size has little appeal to anglers. Sheefish are found in the Porcupine during summer in all sloughs and rivers that enter the Porcupine from the mouth at Fort Yukon to the Canadian border. They are found up the Black River beyond Chalkytsik area and up the Sheenjek River to the mouth of the Koness River.

•*Tanana River:* In the Tanana River, most sheefish are found in the Minto Flats, although they can be taken in clearwater streams from the mouth at Tanana upstream to Fairbanks. The Tolovana, Tatalina and Chatanika rivers and Goldstream Creek in the Minto Flats contain sheefish in the deeper holes from break-up to early August. They are found throughout most of the Chatanika River to milepost 30 on the Steese Highway and in the Tolovana River upstream of Minto village. Other locations where sheefish are found in the lower Tanana River include Fish and Baker Creek and the Chitanana, Zitziana and Kantishna river systems, while closer to Fairbanks a few are taken at the mouths of clearwater streams such as Rosie and Nelson Clearwater creeks and the Chena River. Most of the Chena River fish are taken soon after break-up near the mouth, while smaller numbers are taken throughout summer in the lower 20 miles of the Chena.

•*Kobuk and Selawik Rivers:* Major sheefish fishing areas include the entire Kobuk River upstream to the Reed River, the Selawik River upstream for about 125 miles and the extensive lake, stream and slough system of Hotham Inlet and Selawik Lake. In the Selawik area, sheefish are found in the Tuklomarak and Fox rivers, Inland Lake and its tributaries as well as the man-made channel connecting Inland Lake to the Selawik River. Once sheefish begin moving up the Kobuk and Selawik rivers, they remain in the main river except for resting stops at mouths of sloughs and tributary streams. Don't expect to find sheefish very far up the tributaries of these two rivers.

As summer progresses, good fishing locations in the Selawik River are the deep holes upstream of Selawik village. In the Kobuk River, prime early summer (June) fishing grounds include all the channels making up the mouth of the Kobuk River, Hotham Inlet and deep holes and sloughs upstream to Kiana. This run reaches the Ambler area by mid-July. During mid- to late summer the run spreads out, but prime fishing spots include deep holes in the main river, sloughs and tributary mouths from Ambler upstream to Kobuk village. The spawning run of fish can be intercepted at various points from Kobuk upstream to Reed River up until the last week of September, when the fish complete spawning and migrate rapidly downstream to feeding and overwintering areas.

Winter ice fishing locations are essentially all of Hotham Inlet and Selawik Lake, as the fish form huge schools and migrate throughout both bodies of water during winter.

Sheefish

ALASKA FISHING BY REGION: ARCTIC

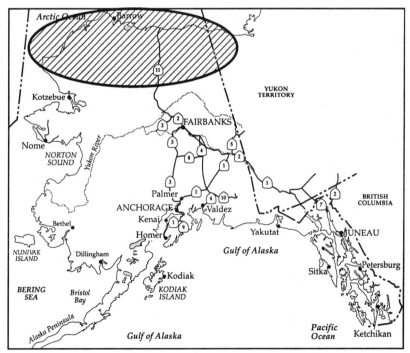

Shaded area shows Arctic region

MAP 1—ARCTIC HOTSPOTS

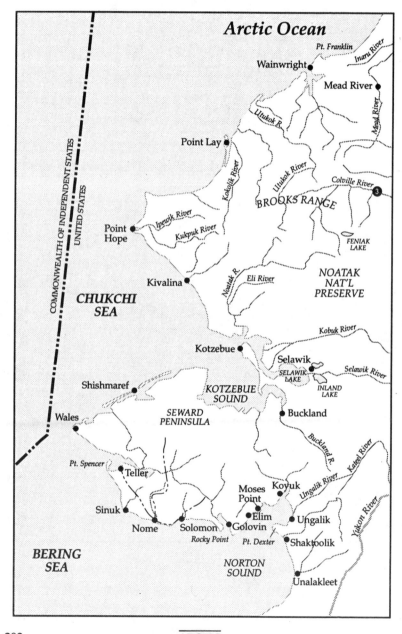

MAP 2—ARCTIC HOTSPOTS

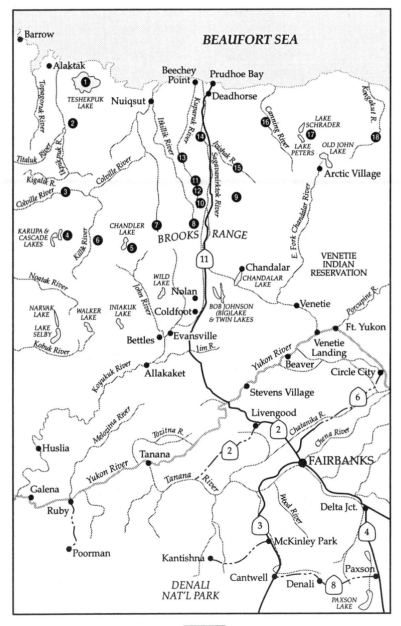

Arctic Hot Spots

ARCTIC

Like a great wall, the 720-mile arc of the Brooks Range divides waters flowing west and south to the Yukon and Kotzebue Sound from those flowing north to the Arctic Ocean. The Brooks Range also seals off the northernmost part of the state from the climate, vegetation and human development to the south. This area, from the crest of the Brooks Range north to the Beaufort and Chukchi seas, is called the Arctic or North Slope or simply "the Slope." It is Alaska's true Arctic, the state's most remote, inhospitable and least-visited region. Offering limited fishing variety and a short open-water season, and with expensive access and notoriously difficult weather, the Slope certainly can't compete solely as an angling destination with Alaska's gentler and more endowed regions. But it does have some unique fishing opportunities, in addition to some of the last true wilderness—the Arctic National Wildlife Refuge—and most pristine rivers in North America. For those adventurers willing to take on the Slope, there are rich rewards to be had on the rivers, lakes, tundra and mountains of Alaska's Arctic.

COUNTRY, CLIMATE & CONDITIONS

The broad, flat, treeless coastal plain is the major feature that most people associate with the Slope. Underlain by permanently frozen ground, with poor drainage, much of this area is covered with small, shallow, similarly oriented "thaw" lakes, most of which are barren of fish populations (Teshekpuk and the central coastal plain lakes are the exceptions—see their descriptions on pages 208 and 209 for details). The rivers, almost all north-flowing, rapid-runoff streams, originate in the foothills and mountains of the Brooks Range to the south. The more outstanding ones, clear flowing and spring-fed, along with a handful of scattered, deep mountain lakes, provide most of the region's better fishing opportunities.

The extreme climate is the major factor limiting the area's fishing potential. For much of the year, the Arctic Slope suffers a cruel regime of darkness, bitter cold (temperatures running minus 30 to minus 50 degrees Fahrenheit), and near constant winds, alleviated only by the return of the spring sun in April. Ice can reach thicknesses of seven feet and persist into July in some areas, with many rivers and shallow lakes freezing solid by winter's end. The surprisingly scant precipitation—

eight inches or less for most of the region—creates rapidly fluctuating and turbid water conditions in most of the streams, many of which can practically dry up after the spring thaw. All this doesn't sound very appealing to fish, and species like the salmon are at their very limits of environmental tolerance here. Chum and pinks are found only sporadically, while other types of salmon are practically nonexistent. The charrs—arctic, Dolly Varden and lake trout—and grayling are the only sportfish that really thrive here, providing most of the Slope's fishing opportunities. A few northern pike, along with whitefish and some burbot, round out the Slope's species variety.

Beyond curtailing fishing options, the climate is also a major impediment to exploring and enjoying this area. Ice break-up generally comes in late May or early June, but can be delayed into July in the high-elevation lakes and in certain areas along the coast, while freeze-up can begin as early as mid-September. From late May through August, you can expect sunny and reasonably temperate weather here, with temperatures in the 40s to 70s (degrees Fahrenheit), even climbing to the 80s in the foothills. You should come prepared for damp, cold winds, extended foggy periods and even snow at any time during summer. This is true especially along the coast, where the advancing and retreating ice pack greatly affects the weather. Swarms of mosquitoes and other biting insects infest the inland tundra during the warmer months of June and July, making head nets, bug jackets and repellent mandatory.

If all this has put you off from even considering this region, be assured that it's not as bad as it sounds, but you must come well prepared. Few places on Earth can be so unforgiving, and nowhere in Alaska will you be so isolated. Only highly experienced wilderness trekkers, with the finest quality gear and a meticulously planned expedition, should attempt this region without the assistance of a veteran guide.

ARCTIC FISHING HIGHLIGHTS

While the Arctic's sportfishing certainly won't win any awards for diversity, most of its streams and lakes get little or no pressure—only from occasional hunters or native subsistence users—so they offer potentially very high quality wild fishing, particularly for lake trout, big sea-run charr and grayling. Countless lakes and streams beckon with the promise of virgin angling, but the price of getting in and out is high, and the window of opportunity for good weather and open water very narrow.

ACCESS, SERVICES & COSTS

Except for a few scattered villages and some oil industry facilities, the Arctic Slope is totally uninhabited. Access is almost exclusively by plane (from Bettles or Fairbanks), except along the North Slope Haul Road (also known as the Dalton Highway), which bisects the region from Prudhoe Bay to Atigun Pass (see the descriptions of the Dalton Highway locations on pages 217). Distances are great; services and facilities are extremely limited and expensive. Air taxi from the major hubs (Deadhorse, Umiat, Kaktovik and Barrow) to and from area fishing locations typically can cost up to $1,000 or more for a party of two.

ARCTIC RUN TIMING

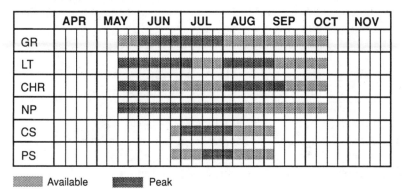

	APR	MAY	JUN	JUL	AUG	SEP	OCT	NOV
GR								
LT								
CHR								
NP								
CS								
PS								

▓ Available ▓ Peak

GR=Grayling, LT=Lake Trout, CHR=Charr, NP=Northern Pike, CS=Chum Salmon, PS=Pink Salmon

Note: Time periods shown are for bright fish, in the case of salmon entering rivers, or for general availability for resident species. Salmon are present in many systems long after the periods shown, but are usually in spawning/post spawning condition. Peak sportfishing periods for each species are highlighted. Be aware that run timing can vary somewhat from drainage to drainage and generally follows a later trend in waters to the west and north in Alaska. Check with local contacts listed for area run-timing specifics before confirming plans.

REGION 1
WESTERN CENTRAL SLOPE

The barren coastal plain predominates (to 115 miles inland) in the western and central Arctic Slope regions, with expansive wet tundra, winding rivers and thousands of shallow lakes. Significant sportfishing possibilities are limited to the giant Colville River system and certain lakes (many unnamed) near the coast, between the Colville and Ikpikpuk rivers. Because of the isolation and difficulty of access, these waters see little visitation at present, but have noteworthy potential for high-quality wild fishing (lake trout, grayling and some salmon). Access is from Umiat, Prudhoe Bay or Barrow.

1. TESHEKPUK LAKE

Location: Central Arctic coastal plain, 75 miles southeast of Barrow, 430 miles northwest of Fairbanks.

Reference: Teshekpuk B-1, B-2, C-1, C-2; Harrison Bay C-5.

Access: By floatplane or helicopter from Barrow, Umiat or Deadhorse (via scheduled or chartered flights from Fairbanks).

Highlights: One of the Arctic's least visited but most promising lake trout fisheries.

Species: Grayling, lake trout.

Regulations: Open year-round, all species.

Facilities: No developed public facilities.

Contact: For an air taxi, contact Umiat Air Service, P.O. Box 60569, Fairbanks, AK 99706; (907) 452-9158.

Description: Teshekpuk Lake is the largest body of water on Alaska's North Slope—running 25 miles across and covering 315 square miles. Located on the coast 12 miles west of Harrison Bay, it is an anomaly (along with other nearby lakes east of the lower Ikpikpuk River) among the thousands of shallow, coastal plain thaw lakes. Teshekpuk Lake's abundant fish populations include substantial numbers of grayling and hefty lake trout (which are larger than average sized, judging from samples taken by the Alaska Department of Fish and Game and locals). For anyone seeking largely untouched, concentrated lake trout opportunities, with the potential for large fish, Teshekpuk Lake, and the neighboring Ikpikpuk Lakes, are worth a visit.

2. CENTRAL COASTAL PLAIN LAKES

Location: Central Arctic coastal plain, 75 miles southeast of Barrow, 415 miles northwest of Fairbanks.

Reference: Teshekpuk A-1, A-2, A-3, B-1, B-2, B-3; Harrison Bay A-4, A-5, B-4, B-5; Umiat C-5, D-5.

Access: By floatplane or helicopter from Barrow, Umiat or Deadhorse (all serviced by regularly scheduled flights from Fairbanks).

Highlights: An unexplored frontier of wild lake trout fishing.

Species: Grayling, lake trout.

Regulations: Open year-round, all species.

Facilities: No developed public facilities.

Contact: For an air taxi, contact Umiat Air Service, P.O. Box 60569, Fairbanks, AK 99706; (907) 452-9158.

Description: The Ikpikpuk River flows from the foothills of the Brooks Range onto the coastal plain and into Smith Bay, west of Teshekpuk Lake. It is sluggish and shallow, with tea-colored water, and only an occasional grayling or northern pike to tempt anglers. Of greater interest here are the dozens of small, unnamed lakes lying east of the river in the central coastal plain, south of Teshekpuk and west of the Colville River (see below). All of the lakes are relatively shallow, but the deeper ones (depths greater than 20 feet) support fish populations. Like Teshekpuk, many of these lakes contain abundant grayling and good-sized lake trout. These are remote and expensive waters to access, but they are also virtually unexplored and offer exciting fishing possibilities.

3. COLVILLE RIVER

Location: Western Arctic coastal plain, 335 miles northwest of Fairbanks.

Reference: Misheguk Mountain C-2, C-3, D-2, D-3; Utukok River A-1, A-2; Lookout Ridge A-4, A-5; Howard Pass D-1, D-2, D-3, D-4; Killik River D-5; Ikpikpuk River A-1, A-2, A-3, A-4, A-5; Umiat A-5, B-3, B-4, B-5, C-3, D-3; Harrison Bay A-2, A-3, B-1, B-2.

Access: By floatplane or wheelplane from Umiat, Kaktovik, Fairbanks, Bettles or Deadhorse to points along the river, or by boat access from Umiat to the lower river and tributaries.

Highlights: The Arctic Slope's major river system, with good fishing potential for big sea-run charr, grayling, lake trout and some salmon (chum and pink) in its mainstem and tributaries.

Species: Charr, (chum salmon), grayling, (lake trout, pink salmon).

Regulations: Open year-round, all species.

Facilities: The town of Umiat, located along the lower river, has limited services and facilities; otherwise, there are no developed public facilities.

Contact: For guided or unguided float trips down Colville headwaters, contact Sourdough Outfitters, P.O. Box 90, Bettles, AK 99726, (907) 692-5252; or ABEC's Alaska Adventures, 1550 Alpine Vista Court, Fairbanks, AK 99712, (907) 457-8907. For an air taxi, contact Umiat Air Service, P.O. Box 60569, Fairbanks, AK 99706; (907) 452-9158.

Description: The Colville River is the largest river on the Arctic Slope, running over 420 miles (the seventh largest river in Alaska) with numerous, meandering tributaries. It supports a remarkable diversity and abundance of fish for a river this far north (16 species total), with charr, chum and pink salmon, grayling, lake trout, whitefish and others found in its vast reaches. Fish are most abundant in the mainstem (Itkillik River to Umiat), and mouths and lower sections of the tributaries. Killik, Anaktuvuk, Chandler and Itkillik rivers contain the best stream fishing.

Not much real sportfishing occurs on the Colville, except by locals or occasional forays by hunters and kayakers. It's a big river with deep, long pools—not easy to fish unless you know your way around. The best solution is to contact Umiat Air Service, which can provide boat or plane transportation to the local hot spots. Because of its length, the river is seldom floated in its entirety from its headwaters, but a few of the tributaries can be run by kayak or raft, usually in early summer when the water is high. (For details on floating the Colville, contact ABEC's Alaska Adventures or Sourdough Outfitters.)

REGION 2
NORTH SLOPE FOOTHILL & MOUNTAIN LAKES

Considering the major ice-scouring the Brooks Range received during the last periods of glaciation, surprisingly few glacial lakes of any size exist in the mountains and foothills north of the divide. Most of the North Slope foothill and mountain lakes that support fish populations are small, deep-catch basins, lying at the headwaters of tributary streams of large rivers, like the vast Colville River System. Almost all of these basins have abundant lake trout, grayling and charr and can provide some outstanding fishing adventures, especially when combined with raft or kayak floats down the rivers they are associated with. The open-water season is short, however; the elevation and latitude of most of these lakes generally results in ice cover from early October (if not before) until late June.

4. KARUPA & CASCADE LAKES

Location: Central North Slope, 515 miles northwest of Anchorage.

Reference: Killik River B-3.

Access: By plane to Bettles or Umiat via Fairbanks, then by floatplane to the lakes.

Highlights: Two of the North Slope's prettiest mountain lakes, with excellent fishing for lake trout, landlocked charr and grayling.

Species: Charr, grayling, lake trout.

Regulations: Open year-round, all species.

Facilities: No developed public facilities.

Contact: For an air taxi, contact Bettles Air Service, 2453 Homestead, North Pole, AK 99705; (800) 770-5111.

Description: Lovely Karupa and Cascade lakes, twin headwaters for the Karupa River, lie in the high mountains of Gates of the Arctic National Park, about 15 miles west of the upper Killik River. They are small but very deep—more than 120 feet, making them two of the deepest lakes in the Brooks Range. The lakes' milky turquoise waters provide good to excellent fishing for lake trout and landlocked charr, with abundant grayling in the inlet and outlet streams.

Traditional sites for Eskimo hunters intercepting migrating caribou, these lakes aren't visited much by anglers because of their isolation and elevation (3,000 feet), but they are certainly among the more outstanding small mountain lakes on the North Slope.

Cascade Lake lies on the other side of a high ridge, about a mile northeast of Karupa, and is connected to it by a short gorge at its southern end. Cascade is smaller (about two miles long), but higher in elevation by 500 feet than its twin, Karupa. Cascade usually has more abundant fishing and clearer water than Karupa. The outlet stream is noted for its fine grayling fishing. With nice beaches for camping, Cascade is certainly worth the hike over from Karupa if you're planning a trip there.

5. CHANDLER LAKES

Location: Central North Slope, 274 miles northwest of Fairbanks.

Reference: Chandler Lake A-5, B-5.

Access: By plane to Bettles or Umiat via Fairbanks, then by floatplane to the lakes.

Highlights: A more popular North Slope fly-in lake with good to excellent fishing for landlocked charr, lake trout and grayling.

Species: Charr, grayling, lake trout.

Regulations: Open year-round, all species.

Facilities: No developed public facilities.

Contact: For information, contact Gates of the Arctic National Park and Preserve, P.O. Box 74680, Fairbanks, AK 99707; (907) 456-0281. For an air taxi, contact Bettles Air Service, 2453 Homestead, North Pole, AK 99705; (800) 770-5111.

Description: On the edge of Gates of the Arctic National Park, 26 miles west of Anaktuvuk Pass, lies lovely Chandler Lake. In a beautiful setting at nearly 3,000 feet elevation, it is the largest mountain lake on the North Slope (five miles long). Along with several other good fishing lakes (Little Chandler, White and Amiloyak lakes), it forms the headwaters of the Chandler River. Chandler Lake is known for its lake trout and landlocked charr fishing, with larger fish (including lakers up to 30 pounds) more common than in most other mountain lakes of the region. Grayling are also abundant in the inlet and outlet streams.

Amiloyak is the uppermost lake in the Chandler chain, situated in a valley near the Continental Divide, about seven miles southwest of Chandler Lake. It is small, less than two miles long, but has excellent fishing for lake trout (up to 20 pounds) and landlocked charr (up to six pounds), with some grayling in several tributary creeks. You can also hike to fish nearby Agiak Lake, two miles on the other side of the divide. Little Chandler lies to the north, adjacent to and a tributary of the big lake, connected by a short outlet. It has good fishing, too. White Lake lies in a bowl off the river, a few miles northwest of Big Chandler. It also has good lake trout and charr populations. However, being situated at a 3,000-foot elevation this far north, these waters have a very limited amount of ice-free time.

6. KILLIK RIVER LAKES

Location: Central North Slope, 490 miles northwest of Anchorage.

Reference: Killik River A-2, A-3, B-2, C-2, D-1; Ikpikpuk River A-2.

Access: By plane to Bettles or Umiat via Fairbanks, then by wheel-plane or floatplane to the lakes or gravel bars along the upper river. It is possible to float by kayak or raft to the Colville River and the outpost of Umiat, or to plane-accessible points downriver.

Highlights: One of more popular North Slope drainages for recreation, with good fishing potential for grayling, charr, lake trout and rare northern pike in its many headwater lakes.

Species: Charr, (chum salmon, pink salmon), grayling, lake trout, northern pike.

Regulations: Open year-round, all species.

Facilities: No developed public facilities.

Contact: For guide services, contact Sourdough Outfitters, P.O. Box 90, Bettles, AK 99726; (907) 692-5252. For an air taxi, contact Umiat Air Service, P.O. Box 60569, Fairbanks, AK 99706; (907) 452-9158.

Description: The Killik is one of the better-known North Slope rivers, with a reputation for its outstanding float trip possibilities. The river begins in the Brooks Range in Gates of the Arctic National Park, then flows 105 miles north to the Colville River. As it emerges from the mountains, the upper river area encompasses quite a few small, clustered lakes (Udrivik, Imiaknikpak, Kaniksrak and Tululik) that are moderately deep and hold lake trout and charr, along with some of the Slope's few opportunities for northern pike. Wildlife viewing and hiking along the river are quite outstanding. Below the lakes, the Killik picks up steam, with canyons, rapids (some rated Class II and Class III), and heavily braided sections, so continuing down to the Colville by raft or kayak is certainly an exciting option.

7. ANAKTUVUK RIVER LAKES

Location: Central Brooks Range, 260 miles northwest of Fairbanks.

Reference: Chandler Lake A-3, B-3, C-2, C-3, D-2, D-3.

Access: By plane to Bettles via Fairbanks, then by floatplane or wheelplane to the headwaters. Raft or kayak trips are possible on the river to points below the headwaters, with wheelplane pickup.

Highlights: An important North Slope river, with good fishing potential for grayling, lake trout and big charr.

Species: Charr, grayling, lake trout.

Regulations: Open year-round, all species.

Facilities: No developed public facilities.

Contact: For guide services, contact Sourdough Outfitters, P.O. Box 90, Bettles, AK 99726; (907) 692-5252. For an air taxi, contact Umiat Air Service, P.O. Box 60569, Fairbanks, AK 99706, (907) 452-9158; or Bettles Air Service, 2453 Homestead, North Pole, AK 99705, (800) 770-5111.

Description: The Anaktuvuk is one of the more significant North Slope rivers, not only for its good fish populations (sea-run charr, grayling and lake trout), but also because of its association with the central Brooks Range Eskimo culture (Nunamuit), which has utilized the fish and caribou of the upper river valley for thousands of years. The river rises in the Endicott Mountains (on the edge of Gates of the Arctic National Preserve), and flows 135 miles to the Colville. Numerous small and moderately deep lakes (such as Tulugak, Irgnyivik and Natvakruak), nearly all with good lake trout and grayling fishing, lie along the upper river. The swift and braided Anaktuvuk River, known for abundant, big grayling and charr, can be floated during higher water (which occurs in July generally, but check with air taxis for the latest conditions) down to the Colville. It's a rewarding trip.

Shainin or Willow Lake is located 22 miles northeast of Anaktuvuk Pass, at the head of the Kanayut River, a major tributary of the Anaktuvuk River. It is a small but pretty alpine lake (elevation 2,700 feet), with milky blue, deep water and abundant grayling and lake trout, even some charr. It doesn't get fished much, except by a few Eskimo hunters, but it's worth considering if you're planning a trip to the Anaktuvuk area. Folks who have fished it report outstanding catches from August through early September.

8. ITKILLIK LAKE

Location: Central Brooks Range, 270 miles northwest of Fairbanks.
Reference: Philip Smith Mountains B-5.
Access: By plane to Bettles or Umiat via Fairbanks, then by floatplane to the lake. There is also winter trail access from the Dalton Highway at Galbraith Lake.
Highlights: A well-known Brooks Range lake with good fishing for lake trout and grayling.
Species: Charr, grayling, lake trout.
Regulations: Open year-round, all species.
Facilities: No developed public facilities.
Contact: For an air taxi, contact Bettles Air Service, 2453 Homestead, North Pole, AK 99705; (800) 770-5111.
Description: Itkillik Lake has been one of the more popular foothill lakes, owing to its proximity to the Dalton Highway (just 15 miles west of Pump Station #4) and good fishing. Slightly smaller than Shainin Lake (see listing on page 214), Itkillik is located within Gates of the Arctic National Preserve, where it heads a river by the same name that drains into the Colville River, 220 miles south. Fishing has always been good for lake trout and grayling, but it has been hit more in recent years by folks who access the highway lakes north of Atigun Pass.

9. ELUSIVE LAKE

Location: Central Brooks Range, 12 miles east of the Dalton Highway, 260 miles north of Fairbanks.
Reference: Philip Smith Mountains C-3.
Access: By small wheelplane or floatplane from Arctic Village, Bettles or Umiat. There is also winter trail access by snowmachine from the Dalton Highway.
Highlights: Good lake trout fishing with relatively easy access.
Species: Grayling, lake trout.
Regulations: Open year-round, all species.
Facilities: No developed public facilities.
Contact: For an air taxi, contact Umiat Air Service, P.O. Box 60569, Fairbanks, AK 99706, (907) 452-9158; or Bettles Air Service, 2453 Homestead, North Pole, AK 99705, (800) 770-5111.
Description: Elusive Lake is located in the Ribdon River Valley, 12 miles east of the Dalton Highway, accessible by wheelplane (there's a gravel strip on the east end of the lake) and floatplane, or by a

snowmachine trail during the winter from a highway maintenance camp on the Dalton. Elusive Lake is one of the more popular foothill lakes for ice fishing (lake trout), especially in late winter and early spring.

Adventure, solitude and some outstanding fishing can be had on Alaska's remote Arctic lakes and rivers.

REGION 3
DALTON HIGHWAY

The 414-mile Dalton Highway, or North Slope Haul Road, was built in 1974 by Alyeska Pipeline Service Company to facilitate construction and maintenance of the Trans-Alaska Pipeline. Originally reserved for support services and oil field personnel, the Dalton south of Disaster Creek (Dietrich Camp, milepost 211) was opened to the general public in June of 1981. Sportfishing for all species, except salmon, is now allowed along the road corridor (five miles on each side). Public use along the highway in recent years has not been monitored. There are plans to lift road-use restrictions in 1995.

The Dalton north of Atigun Pass provides limited access to a number of North Slope lakes and rivers, including the Toolik, Galbraith and Campsite Lake areas and the Kuparuk, Toolik and Sagavanirktok rivers. Fishing opportunities for lake trout, charr and grayling are plentiful in most of these waters, especially for folks who take the initiative to explore beyond the immediate reaches of the road. For instance, there are dozens of small, fish-filled lakes that lie within hiking distance of the highway between Pump Stations #3 and #4. The Sagavanirktok River, a prime drainage for large sea-run charr, can be reached from certain points north of Pump Station #3. With an inflatable raft or canoe, the possibilities are almost limitless. Adventuresome anglers planning on travelling this primitive road should come prepared, however, for a shortage of services (there are none north of Coldfoot), hazardous driving with dust, flying rocks and barreling 18-wheelers, with few pullouts to stop at along the way. The most popular time to travel the Dalton for fishing is from July through mid-September, with late spring (April) ice-fishing safaris by snowmachine a tantalizing option.

10. GALBRAITH LAKES

Location: Central Brooks Range, 250 miles north of Fairbanks, adjacent to the Dalton Highway (mileposts 270 and 276) near Pump Station #4.

Reference: Philip Smith Mountains B-5.

Access: By wheelplane to an airstrip 1.5 miles west of the Galbraith lakes, or by hiking from the Dalton Highway.

Highlights: Easily accessible lakes with good seasonal fishing for lake trout, charr and grayling
Species: Charr, grayling, lake trout.
Regulations: Open year-round, all species except salmon.
Facilities: No developed public facilities.
Contact: For an air taxi, contact Umiat Air Service, P.O. Box 60569, Fairbanks, AK 99706, (907) 452-9158; or Bettles Air Service, 2453 Homestead, North Pole, AK 99705, (800) 770-5111. For the latest road conditions, contact the Department of Transportation at (907) 456-7623.
Description: Galbraith, Tee and Atigun lakes lie in the lower Atigun River Valley, adjacent to the west side of the Dalton Highway near Pump Station #4. Situated at a 2,600-foot elevation, these are mountain lakes, with beautiful scenery and fairly abundant fishing, but with a limited season of open water. Galbraith has always been the most productive and popular of these waters, with good seasonal catches of lake trout and landlocked charr. The other two lakes, the largest of a group of lakes along the upper Atigun River, contain good fishing as well, and may be reached from milepost 270, near the access road to Pump Station #4. The best time to fish these waters is from late June through early July and August.

11. TOOLIK & ITAGAKNIT LAKES

Location: Approximately 257 miles north of Fairbanks in the upper Kuparuk River drainage, adjacent to the Dalton Highway (milepost 284).
Reference: Philip Smith Mountains C-5.
Access: By plane or car. There is a marked access road leading one mile west to Toolik Lake.
Highlights: A very popular Dalton Highway lake area, with good seasonal fishing for lake trout and grayling.
Species: Charr, grayling, lake trout.
Regulations: Open year-round, all species except salmon. For details, consult the current Alaska Department of Fish and Game regulations or the ADF&G Fairbanks office, (907) 456-4359.
Facilities: No developed public facilities.
Contact: For an air taxi, contact Umiat Air Service, P.O. Box 60569, Fairbanks, AK 99706, (907) 452-9158; or Bettles Air Service, 2453 Homestead, North Pole, AK 99705, (800) 770-5111. For the latest road conditions, contact the Department of Transportation at (907) 456-7623.

Description: Toolik and Itagaknit are the largest of a group of clustered lakes along the upper Kuparuk River drainage, just a short distance west of the Dalton Highway (the nearest lake can be reached by access road or by a nearby airstrip). Small but deep (up to 100 feet), the lakes and their numerous connecting streams have good populations of grayling, and small- to medium-sized lake trout and charr. With a little hiking and exploring in the spring or fall, you can find some less fished, more productive waters.

12. Campsite Lakes

Location: Five miles south of the Dalton Highway, 12 miles east of Toolik Lake.

Reference: Philip Smith Mountains C-4.

Access: By hike-in trail.

Highlights: Easy hike-in lakes off the Dalton Highway, with fairly abundant lake trout and charr fishing.

Species: Charr, grayling, lake trout.

Regulations: Open year-round, all species.

Facilities: No developed public facilities.

Contact: For an air taxi, contact Umiat Air Service, P.O. Box 60569, Fairbanks, AK 99706, (907) 452-9158; or Bettles Air Service, 2453 Homestead, North Pole, AK 99705, (800) 770-5111. For the latest road conditions, contact the Department of Transportation at (907) 456-7623.

Description: The Campsite Lakes area includes about a dozen or more small, fairly deep lakes clustered along upper Oksrukuyik Creek, a tributary of the Sagavanirktok. Nearly all have fish in them—abundant lake trout, landlocked charr, even burbot. Campsite Lake is the largest and most popular of the group. They all can be reached by trail from the Dalton Highway (milepost 295), and along with Toolik and Galbraith lakes, offer the area's best chances for some really fine, road-accessible lake trout and charr fishing.

13. Kuparuk River

Location: West of the Sagavanirktok River, flowing north, crossed by the Dalton Highway (milepost 290) approximately five miles east of Toolik Lake.

Reference: Philip Smith Mountains C-4.

Access: By foot trail from the Dalton Highway.

Highlights: One of the North Slope's best grayling rivers, with excellent flyfishing.

Species: Grayling, lake trout.

Regulations: Open year-round, all species.

Facilities: No developed public facilities.

Contact: For an air taxi, contact Umiat Air Service, P.O. Box 60569, Fairbanks, AK 99706, (907) 452-9158; or Bettles Air Service, 2453 Homestead, North Pole, AK 99705, (800) 770-5111. For the latest road conditions, contact the Department of Transportation at (907) 456-7623.

Description: The Kuparuk River, which is the most popular grayling fishery on the North Slope, flows west of the Sagavanirktok River and is easily accessed along its upper east fork from the Dalton Highway, about six miles beyond Toolik Lake Road, at milepost 290. Kuparuk has great flyfishing along its upper reaches, and by North Slope standards, the grayling are plentiful and big. Further upstream lies a small headwater lake of the same name, which is known to have abundant lake trout.

---

14. SAGAVANIRKTOK RIVER

Location: Central Arctic Slope, 300 miles north of Fairbanks.

Reference: Philip Smith Mountains A-4, B-4, B-5, C-3, C-4, D-3, D-4; Sagavanirktok A-3, A-4, B-3, C-3, D-3; Beechey Point A-2, A-3, B-2, B-3.

Access: By small plane to the upper river (Atigun River or upper mainstem) from Umiat, Deadhorse, Fairbanks or Bettles. It is possible to float by kayak or raft with takeout along the lower river (Franklin Bluffs or Deadhorse). Access is also possible from the Dalton Highway at several points.

Highlights: An accessible North Slope river with outstanding fishing potential for large charr; also good grayling fishing.

Species: Charr, (chum salmon), grayling, (lake trout, pink trout).

Regulations: Open year-round, all species except salmon. For details, consult the current Alaska Department of Fish and Game regulations or the ADF&G Fairbanks office, (907) 456-4359.

Facilities: No developed public facilities.

Contact: For guide services, contact Sourdough Outfitters, P.O. Box 90, Bettles, AK 99726; (907) 692-5252. For an air taxi, contact Umiat Air Service, P.O. Box 60569, Fairbanks, AK 99706, (907) 452-9158; or Wright Air Service, P.O. Box 60142, Fairbanks, AK 99706, (907) 474-0502.

Description: The Sagavanirktok, or "Sag," is one North Slope river that most folks have heard of, since it's closely associated with the Dalton Highway—the highway parallels the river for 100 miles—and Prudhoe Bay. In addition, the Sag has a reputation as an exciting whitewater float. As the North Slope's most significant drainage for sea-run charr, with major habitat in its deep pools and miles of spring-fed tributaries, the Sag has great potential as a trophy fishery (with average size three to five pounds, and fish up to 10 pounds or more not uncommon), especially given its relatively easy access.

The Sag is wide and swift (Class I mostly, with some Class II and Class III stretches), with extensive braids for most of its length. It heads into the Philip Smith Mountains of the Arctic National Wildlife Refuge, flowing south for 175 miles before emptying into the Beaufort Sea east of Prudhoe. It has 20 tributaries, some like the Ivishak River, with exceptional qualities, including substantial sportfishing potential. The best thing about the Sag is its access. You can fly into the headwaters, float down and be picked up by plane, or access the river from the Dalton Highway at several locations where the road passes nearby (north of Pump Station #3, milepost 325 and in Happy Valley). Oil field workers commonly fish channels and sloughs on the lower river, with excellent results. The charr begin their fall spawning migrations sometime in early August; the best time to fish the river is probably from mid-August into the first part of September. The Sagavanirktok also offers some fine grayling and occasional lake trout catches.

REGION 4
EASTERN ARCTIC SLOPE

From the Canning River east to the Canadian border, the land becomes significantly more varied in form and character than the rest of the Arctic Slope. The highest peaks of the Brooks Range, running north to east, crowd out the coastal plain to a narrow strip of rolling tundra (to less than 10 miles wide near the border) and give rise to some of Arctic's most significant rivers. This area, perhaps best known for its wilderness (the 19-million-acre Arctic National Wildlife Refuge, including eight million acres of designated wilderness) and wildlife (caribou, musk-ox, polar bear and wolves), also has quite a few outstanding sportfishing possibilities for trophy-sized charr, grayling and lake trout. Access is from Arctic Village, Kaktovik and Prudhoe Bay.

15. IVISHAK RIVER

Location: Central Arctic coastal plain, 320 miles north of Fairbanks.

Reference: Arctic C-5, D-5; Sagavanirktok A-1, A-2, B-2, B-3; Philip Smith Mountains C-1, D-1.

Access: Small floatplane to Porcupine Lake or wheelplane to gravel bars along upper river; you can float from headwaters to takeout points below or continue down to Sagavanirktok River.

Highlights: A National Wild and Scenic River and outstanding North Slope float trip, with excellent fishing for trophy-sized charr; also good grayling fishing.

Species: Charr, (chum salmon), grayling, (lake trout, pink salmon).

Regulations: Open year-round, all species.

Facilities: No developed public facilities.

Contact: For guide services, contact Sourdough Outfitters, P.O. Box 90, Bettles, AK 99726, (907) 692-5252; or ABEC's Alaska Adventures, 1550 Alpine Vista Court, Fairbanks, AK 99712, (907) 457-8907. For an air taxi, contact Umiat Air Service, P.O. Box 60569, Fairbanks, AK 99706, (907) 452-9158; or Wright Air Service, P.O. Box 60142, Fairbanks, AK 99706, (907) 474-0502.

Description: The Ivishak Wild and Scenic River is one of the North Slope's premier float rivers, making for an outstanding wilderness trip that can be finished on the Sagavanirktok River. The Ivishak is also the Sagavanirktok's most significant tributary for big sea-run charr, with abundant spawning and wintering populations and excellent sportfishing potential.

You can fly into Porcupine Lake at the headwaters and enjoy some good lake trout fishing, then float down through a beautiful canyon to the foothills and the flat coastal plain. (Some dragging of the boats will be necessary right below the lake in low water conditions.) There's a strip near the confluence of the Echooka River where you can take-out, or you can continue down to the Sagavanirktok (approximately 92 miles below the lake) for a five- to seven-day trip. Scenery, hiking and wildlife viewing opportunities are excellent on the upper river, as is the fishing, making this one of the best all-around trips on the North Slope. The best time to fish the Ivishak for big charr is in August, but like all Slope rivers, you should check with local air taxis for conditions before making final arrangements.

16. CANNING RIVER

Location: Eastern Arctic coastal plain, 350 miles north of Fairbanks.
Reference: Arctic C-4, C-5, D-3, D-4; Mt. Michelson A-3, A-4, B-4, C-4, D-4; Flaxman Island A-4, A-5.
Access: By wheelplane from Kaktovik, Deadhorse, Fairbanks or Arctic Village to numerous gravel bar locations along headwaters, then floating down by raft or kayak (five to seven days), with wheelplane pickup on the lower river anywhere above the delta.
Highlights: Along with the Sagavanirktok River, one of the North Slope's most significant sea-run charr rivers, with exciting float possibilities; also good grayling fishing.
Species: Charr, (chum salmon), grayling, (lake trout, pink salmon).
Regulations: Open year-round, all species.
Facilities: No developed public facilities.
Contact: For guided float trips, contact ABEC's Alaska Adventures, 1550 Alpine Vista Court, Fairbanks, AK 99712; (907) 457-8907. For an air taxi, contact Wright Air Service, P.O. Box 60142, Fairbanks, AK 99706, (907) 474-0502; or Alaska Flyers, 398 Eagle Ridge, Fairbanks, AK 99712, (907) 479-7750.
Description: The Canning River certainly deserves mention among the North Slope's better options for sportfishing, as it supports an abundant sea-run charr population with numerous headwater springs for overwintering survival. It begins in the steep recesses of the Philip

Smith Mountains of the Arctic National Wildlife Refuge (ANWR), flowing north 120 miles to Camden Bay, west of Kaktovik. It's a whitewater river, nothing major (Class I and Class II), but heavily braided and silty along most of its mainstem below the mountains. Your best bet would be to put in somewhere along the upper Marsh Fork where the water is clear, then float, fish and camp down to the confluence, with your pickup somewhere below in the river's middle or lower section.

Fishing is good for big charr and grayling all along the upper river in late summer, and it's a pretty float with awesome mountain scenery and lots of wildlife, well worth the time and expense of getting in and out. This trip is a great way to combine the wonders of the Arctic National Wildlife Refuge with some superb fishing.

17. LAKES SCHRADER & PETERS

Location: Arctic National Wildlife Refuge, Sadlerochit River drainage, 325 miles northeast of Fairbanks.

Reference: Mount Michelson B-2.

Access: By small plane from Kaktovik, Deadhorse, Fairbanks or Arctic Village.

Highlights: The Arctic National Wildlife Refuge's only major lake system, with excellent fishing possibilities for lake trout and land-locked charr.

Species: Charr, grayling, lake trout.

Regulations: Open year-round, all species.

Facilities: No developed public facilities.

Contact: For an air taxi, contact Alaska Flyers, 398 Eagle Ridge, Fairbanks, AK 99712; (907) 479-7750.

Description: Schrader and Peters lakes are well off the beaten path, even for the remote Arctic Slope. Seldom visited except by locals (mostly from Kaktovik), these deep and lovely twin lakes at the headwaters of the Sadlerochit River in the Arctic National Wildlife Refuge are reputed to have some of the best trophy lake trout and landlocked charr fishing on the Slope. Fish in the 20- to 30-pound range are possible, especially in the spring.

Access is expensive, with a small plane fly-in usually from Umiat, Deadhorse or Kaktovik, landing at a small gravel strip or on the lakes (with floats). Kaktovik residents visit the lakes mostly in late spring, by snowmachine. The ice doesn't melt until late June, so the open-water season is quite short.

18. KONGAKUT RIVER

Location: Eastern Arctic coastal plain, 335 miles northeast of Fairbanks.

Reference: Table Mountain D-2, D-3, D-4; Demarcation Point A-1, A-2, B-1, B-2, C-2, D-2.

Access: By wheelplane (from Kaktovik, Fairbanks or Deadhorse) to gravel bars along the headwaters. It is possible to float down by raft or kayak (8 to 10 days), with wheelplane pickup on the lower river.

Highlights: The Arctic National Wildlife Refuge's most popular river, with outstanding sea-run charr and grayling fishing.

Species: Charr, (chum salmon), grayling, (lake trout, pink salmon).

Regulations: Open year-round, all species.

Facilities: No developed public facilities.

Contact: For guided float trips, contact ABEC's Alaska Adventures, 1550 Alpine Vista Court, Fairbanks, AK 99712; (907) 457-8907. For more information, contact Arctic National Wildlife Refuge (ANWR), P.O. Box 20, 101 12th Street, Fairbanks, AK 99701; (907) 456-0250. For an air taxi, contact Alaska Flyers, 398 Eagle Ridge, Fairbanks, AK 99712, (907) 479-7750; or Wright Air Service, P.O. Box 60142, Fairbanks, AK 99706, (907) 474-0502.

Description: It would be remiss not to list the Kongakut among the North Slope's better fishing rivers, even though this drainage certainly needs no more attention of late. Hidden in Alaska's most remote northeast corner, the "Kong" was somehow unofficially chosen as the showcase river for all the wild, delicate values of the Arctic coastal plain threatened by the oil exploration proposals of the late 1980s. It has perhaps seen more visitation in the last few years than in all the time since the Ice Age.

The Kong is, without a doubt, an extraordinary river. It flows strong and clear through the rugged heart of some of Alaska's most remote and exemplary wildernesses, where, with any luck, you can catch glimpses of caribou, wolves, even musk-ox, while you float through "a pristine mountain setting of great aesthetic value" (according to the U.S. Fish and Wildlife Service). The fishing is very good; everyone who floats this river is impressed, rating the charr and grayling fishery of exceptional quality (the average Kongakut charr is larger in size than those encountered in any other North Slope river). Sounds exciting, right? But remember, this is an expensive, serious trip, certainly not for casual or unassisted wilderness trekkers. The time to float for the best fishing, weather and stream conditions is from early July through early August.

Caribou in the southern Arctic.

ALASKA FISHING BY REGION: NORTHWEST

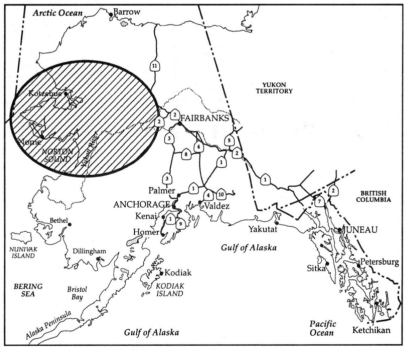

Shaded area shows Northwest region

Map 1—Northwest Hotspots

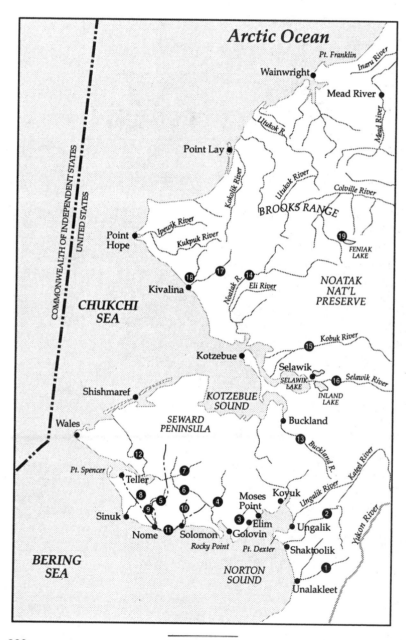

MAP 2—NORTHWEST HOTSPOTS

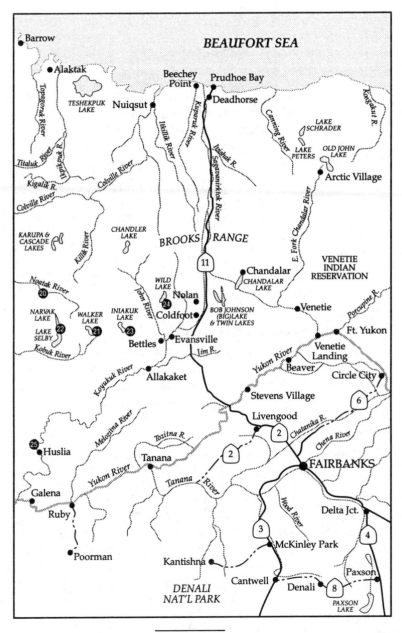

NORTHWEST HOT SPOTS

NORTHWEST

Mike Spisak is a dangerous man. Give him five minutes on the phone and he'll have you tossing aside all worldly concerns and hopping the next plane to Kotzebue. You see, Mike is a pilot with his own air taxi service, and he gets to do what most of us mortals can only dream about—he spends his working hours flying around in some of God's most awesome country, with long lunch breaks sampling some of the greatest fishing this side of Heaven. Of all the lies you'll hear in Alaska, his fish stories are among the best. A conversation with Spisak in early April is all that's needed to get the juices flowing after a long Alaska winter. It goes something like this:

"Yep, just 20 miles across the Sound—Kobuk Lake. They're taking the big shees through the ice."

"How big?"

"Thirty, forty pounds all the time. You're not gonna believe this, but I saw an old guy draggin' what I thought was a seal behind his four-wheeler, and when I got closer, it was a sheefish. Must have been 70 pounds!"

"Mike, the world record is only 53."

"You're kidding me!"

"No. Was the fish certified anywhere?"

"Hell no, he chopped it up and fed his family and dogs with it!"

I should have ended the conversation right there. Instead, I let him go on about four-foot lake trout, pike as big as logs, 30-pound charr and sheefish so big it takes three grown men to pull them in. Not that I'm a sucker for a story. It's just that, having been on Supercub safari with him and seen some of those tall tales come alive in the most amazing ways, I'm not so quick to debunk any of his fantastic yarns any more. I know now, from all I've heard and seen, that the area Mike calls home, Northwest Alaska, is, without a doubt, one of the last true frontiers of fishing adventure. It is one of the world's few places where charr, sheefish, grayling and pike reach giant sizes and succumb to old age or native stew pots long before their first encounter with a sport angler's lure. Land of the Inupiat Eskimo, big caribou herds and Nanook the polar bear, this wilderness, with its amazing sportfish potential, promises to be the next area to open up to the inevitable wave of anglers pushing north and west for new thrills.

COUNTRY, CLIMATE & CONDITIONS

Alaska's Northwest is the region above the lower Yukon which includes Norton Sound, the Seward Peninsula, Kotzebue Sound and the western Brooks Range. (For our purposes here, we're including all north-flowing Arctic Ocean drainages in the Arctic chapter—see pages 201-229.) Northwest encompasses a diverse and vast terrain, from the marshy Yukon flatlands and slight uplands along the coast to the expansive valleys and massive peaks of the Brooks Range, with the general character of the land showing the transition from the more moderate taiga to the extreme tundra regime of the Arctic. Here, you'll find weird, frost-heaved polygonal sections of tundra, hundreds of shallow thaw lakes and scraggly stands of trees strung along river valleys, as the land and vegetation give way to the cold.

Northwest fishing is a mixed bag. Pacific salmon extend into the limits of their natural range here, with king and coho thinning out as you move up the coast (fishable runs are found only as far as Norton Sound) and sockeye occurring only sporadically north of the Yukon, leaving chum and pink salmon as the predominant species for most drainages of the region. Too far north to support rainbow trout, Northwest Alaska's waters still support surprising numbers of sea-run charr, grayling, lake trout, northern pike and sheefish as resident species.

Fortunately the strong maritime influence of the nearby Bering and Chukchi seas moderates the extreme harshness of the subarctic climate somewhat, especially along the coast. Summer days are usually cool, often overcast or foggy, with temperatures averaging in the low 50s (degrees Fahrenheit), though they can be much warmer—into the 80s—and drier further inland. Winters are long and cold, frequently with terrifying windchills, but generally without the absolute extremes of temperature seen in the interior regions. Annual precipitation is surprisingly sparse, 15 inches or less for much of the region, with most of it falling during the warm months. Ice break-up usually occurs in late May or early June, with freeze-up sometime in October.

NORTHWEST FISHING HIGHLIGHTS

Of the many outstanding attractions awaiting sportfishermen here, perhaps the best known are the trophy grayling and charr fishing opportunities on the Seward Peninsula and rivers of Kotzebue Sound, where the two species generally run larger on average than anywhere else in the state. Trophy sheefish are another unique possibility, with waters of the Kobuk-Selawik area routinely yielding fish that far outclass specimens from other Alaska locations. Similarly, the remote and pristine lakes of the upper Noatak, Kobuk and Koyukuk valleys can offer quality wild lake trout fishing that is hard to match anywhere else.

ACCESS, SERVICES & COSTS

Beyond a few short roads linking Nome to surrounding towns on the Seward Peninsula, travel in Alaska's Northwest region is totally restricted to airplanes and boats. There is regular commercial airline service from Anchorage to Nome, Kotzebue and Unalakleet, from which numerous air taxi services provide connections to the more remote areas.

Anglers will find a more limited variety of services and facilities than in other, more accessible parts of the state. There are few full-service lodges or outfitters (see listings on the Seward Peninsula and other areas below). Some lodging and guiding is available in scattered villages along the coast and rivers. Air taxis are expensive, with typical fly-in costs (from the major hubs) to the better locations ranging from $600 to well over $1,000 dollars per person.

NORTHWEST RUN TIMING

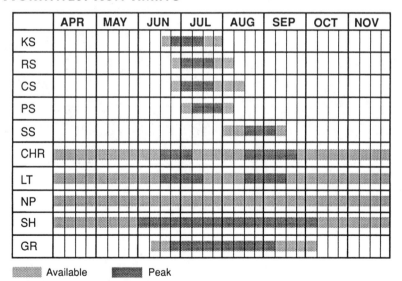

Available   Peak

KS=King Salmon, RS=Red Salmon, CS=Chum Salmon, PS=Pink Salmon, SS=Silver Salmon, CHR=Charr, LT=Lake Trout, NP=Northern Pike, SH=Sheefish, GR=Grayling

Note: Time periods shown are for bright fish, in the case of salmon entering rivers, or for general availability for resident species. Salmon are present in many systems long after the periods shown, but are usually in spawning/post spawning condition. Peak sportfishing periods for each species are highlighted. Be aware that run timing can vary somewhat from drainage to drainage and generally follows a later trend in waters to the west and north in Alaska. Check with local contacts listed for area run-timing specifics before confirming plans.

A floatplane lands on Walker Lake.

REGION 1
EASTERN NORTON SOUND

The arc of eastern Norton Sound, from Stebbins to Cape Darby, includes several rivers of significant sportfishing potential and the last major runs of silver and king salmon along the coast. These are all runoff streams draining the highlands west of the lower Yukon, with water conditions that vary considerably through the season. Access is the limiting factor, as most of them can be reached safely only by boat or (sometimes) by small plane, and facilities and services are scarce to nonexistent.

1. UNALAKLEET RIVER

Location: Eastern Norton Sound, 375 miles northwest of Anchorage.

Reference: Norton Sound A-1, A-2; Unalakleet D-2, D-3, D-4.

Access: By plane from Anchorage to Unalakleet, then by boat transportation to numerous sites along river.

Highlights: One of western Alaska's most promising rivers for fishing king salmon (from late June through mid-July) and silver salmon (from late July through mid-September).

Species: Charr, chum salmon, grayling, king salmon, northern pike, pink salmon, (red salmon), silver salmon.

Regulations: Open year-round, all species.

Facilities: There is a private lodge on the lower river and several outfitter tent camps. Otherwise, there are no developed public facilities.

Contact: For lodge-based guided fishing, contact the Unalakleet Native Corporation, P.O. Box 100, Unalakleet, AK 99684; (907) 624-3032. For outpost camp fishing (guided and unguided), contact Vance Grishkowsky, P.O. Box 38, Unalakleet, AK 99684; (907) 624-3352.

Description: The Unalakleet is the most significant river in Norton Sound, supporting substantial commercial and subsistence fisheries with its consistent, strong runs of salmon (all species except sockeye). It is recognized as potentially one of the finest streams in all of western Alaska for sportfishing, although it receives only minimal angling attention at present due to its remoteness.

A Wild and Scenic River, the Unalakleet rises in the Nulato Hills and flows southwest approximately 105 miles through uplands and rolling tundra before emptying into Norton Sound below the village of Unalakleet. Access to the upper river is almost impossible by any means other than boat. Most anglers enlist the services of local guides or outfitters to fish the river's most productive water (the lower 15 miles of the main river and five miles of the North River). You can raft the river down from the confluence of Old Woman River or Ten Mile Creek to the village in about five to seven days, with no major hazards except sweepers.

The clear-flowing Unalakleet has always been noted for its outstanding king and silver salmon fishing, but it also has staggering runs of chum and pink salmon, as well as numerous charr and grayling. There are plenty of deep pools and clear, not-too-fast runs, so it's easy water to fish. Wildlife—moose, bear, occasional caribou and numerous waterfowl—are commonly seen throughout the little-visited surrounding valley. All who have visited this remote drainage speak very highly of the experience. It's a prime trip to consider for a real out-of-the-way Alaska fishing adventure.

2. SHAKTOOLIK RIVER

Location: Eastern Norton Sound, 410 miles northwest of Anchorage.

Reference: Norton Bay B-4, B-5, C-2, C-3.

Access: By scheduled or chartered wheelplane from Nome or Unalakleet to Shaktoolik Village, then by boat transportation upriver. Limited small wheelplane access is also possible along gravel bars upriver, with float by raft or kayak down to the mouth.

Highlights: A remote Norton Sound drainage with high sportfish potential for salmon, charr and grayling.

Species: Charr, chum salmon, grayling, king salmon, northern pike, pink salmon, silver salmon.

Regulations: Open year-round, all species.

Facilities: No developed public facilities.

Contact: For air taxi service to the village or river, contact Haagland Air, P.O. Box 207, Unalakleet, AK 99684; (907) 624-3595. For boat transportation upriver and guided fishing, contact Shaktoolik Native Corporation, P.O. Box 46, Shaktoolik, AK 99771; (907) 955-2341 or (907) 955-3241.

Description: The Shaktoolik River, along with the Unalakleet, is one of Norton Sound's most significant fish producers. With solid runs of salmon (all species except sockeye), plentiful charr and grayling, and excellent stream conditions, it has quite a bit of sportfishing potential that, up to now, has been underutilized because of its remoteness and difficult access.

Like other promising rivers of the area, the Shaktoolik is a medium-sized, clear, runoff stream that flows 100 miles or so to the coast from the uplands surrounding Norton Sound. Gravel-bottomed, moderately fast (two to five feet per second, some rapids to Class II), with abundant pools, long runs and shallow riffles, the river forks about 60 miles up from the mouth, at Kingmetolik Creek. Most of the fishing for salmon, grayling and charr occurs in the stretch of river from this confluence down to the coastal flats 40 miles below.

Access is the trick. For starters, it's perhaps best to hop a flight from Unalakleet or Nome to Shaktoolik, run upriver by boat with someone from the village, then camp and fish (with a guide if you want). It's also possible at times to land a small wheelplane on gravel bars in the foothills halfway up the river (check with the air taxi folks in Unalakleet first), then float down to the village in rafts (about three to four days). The fishing is good. In fact, there are some who rate the Shaktoolik among Western Alaska's finest "undiscovered" streams for flyfishing, with excellent stream conditions for flyfishing, along with abundant, sea-run salmon (king and silver especially), charr and big grayling. (Fish up to 20 inches are common.) It's definitely a river to add to the "dream list" of promising, unexplored Alaska fishing possibilities. The first part of July or the second half of August are the best times for a safari to these far-flung waters.

3. KWINIUK RIVER

Location: Norton Bay, Seward Peninsula, 445 miles northwest of Anchorage.

Reference: Solomon C-1, C-2, D-1.

Access: By scheduled/chartered wheelplane from Nome or Unalakleet to Moses Point or Elim. There is road access to the upper river or boat access to the mouth. It can be floated down to the mouth by raft or kayak, from a put-in at the hot springs 25 miles upriver.

Highlights: A very promising "out of the way" Norton Sound drainage with abundant salmon, charr and grayling.

Species: Charr, chum salmon, grayling, king salmon, pink salmon, silver salmon.

Regulations: Open year-round, all species.

Facilities: Limited services, supplies and trip assistance are available in the villages of Moses Point and Elim.

Contact: For air taxi service to the village and river, contact Olsen Air Service, P.O. Box 142, Nome, AK 99762, (907) 443-2229; Bering Air, P.O. Box 1650, Nome, AK 99762, (907) 443-5464; or Haagland Air, P.O. Box 207, Unalakleet, AK 99684, (907) 624-3595. For boat transportation, access to upper river and guided fishing on the Kwiniuk and nearby Tubutulik River, contact John Jemewuk, P.O. Box 39046, Elim, AK 99739; (907) 890-3071.

Description: The Kwiniuk River is a short coastal stream that runs along upper Norton Bay, near the villages of Elim and Moses Point. Clear-flowing and moderately fast, it is quite productive for its size, producing some of the last really strong runs of silver and king salmon this far north and west along the coast. According to locals and other sources, it has very promising sportfishing potential, with near-perfect stream conditions and relatively easy access.

The lower Kwiniuk can be reached by boat from Moses Point, while the upper river can be reached via a primitive road leading out from the village of Elim to a hot spring on the river, which is about 25 miles up from the mouth. From here, it is possible to float down by raft/canoe/kayak, to a take-out at the mouth and village of Moses Point. The Elim-White Mountain area is perhaps the prettiest in all of Seward Peninsula, and nearby Tubutulik River is reputed to have impressive fishing as well (not to mention hot springs and some exciting whitewater canyons). An exploratory trip to sample the country and some of its promising fishing possibilities is highly recommended to adventuresome anglers.

REGION 2
SEWARD PENINSULA

The Seward Peninsula almost touches Siberia, nearly separating the icy Bering Sea from the even colder Chukchi. What it lacks in scenic grandeur, wildlife or forests, it makes up for with a fabulous history and some unique fishing opportunities. Remnants of its Gold Rush glory days are found everywhere. Even the names of some of its better rivers—spread along the southern half from Teller to Koyuk—speak of a colorful past: the Bonanza, Eldorado, Pilgrim, Snake, Fish, Solomon and Nome. These streams still hold a treasure of fine angling for salmon, pike, charr and trophy grayling. (A good portion of Alaska's record grayling have come from Seward Peninsula streams.) What's more, road access via three gravel highways links many of these great waters with Nome, making it possible to sample some of the area's best fishing by car. Check with the Department of Transportation in Nome, (907) 443-3444, for latest road conditions before making arrangements.

4. FISH-NIUKLUK RIVERS

Location: Seward Peninsula, 475 miles northwest of Anchorage, 60 miles east of Nome.

Reference: Solomon C-3, D-3, D-4; Bendeleben A-5.

Access: By commercial flight from Anchorage to Nome, wheelplane to Golovin or White Mountain, or 67-mile road access to the upper river at Council.

Highlights: The Seward Peninsula's premier fishing location, with excellent fishing for salmon, charr and grayling.

Species: Charr, chum salmon, grayling, (king salmon), northern pike, pink salmon, silver salmon.

Regulations: Open year-round, all species.

Facilities: Private lodges are located in the towns of Council and White Mountain.

Contact: For guided or unguided lodge and tent camp fishing, contact John Elmore, Camp Bendeleben, P.O. Box 1045, Nome, AK 99762, (907) 443-2880; or White Mountain Native Corporation, General Delivery, White Mountain, AK 99784, (907) 638-3511. For an air taxi to the river, contact Olsen Air Service, P.O. Box 142, Nome,

AK 99762, (907) 443-2229; or Bering Air, P.O. Box 1650, Nome, AK 99762, (907) 443-5464. For car rentals, contact Stampede Rent a Car, P.O. Box 633, Nome, AK 99762, (907) 443-3838; or Checker Cab, (907) 443-5136.

Description: The Fish-Niukluk River system of the Seward Peninsula is one of the most popular and productive fisheries in Northwest Alaska. It is widely used by villagers from three communities along the river, as well as by residents of Nome, who travel the 67-mile Nome-Council Road to make use of these waters for recreational, commercial and subsistence fishing. A few local lodges and outfitters service the growing number of visiting anglers drawn by the river's outstanding reputation.

Heading in the Darby and Bendeleben Mountains, the Fish and Niukluk rivers (and tributaries) flow south toward Golovin Lagoon on Norton Sound. The rivers' character and fishing change from clear, gravelly upper stretches (both Fish and Niukluk), which harbor grayling, salmon and charr, to slow, braided, dark water in the lower river (from Steamboat Slough down to the mouth–about 20 miles), where pike lurk.

The Fish-Niukluk system is noted for its fast-growing, big grayling (up to three pounds or more) and good silver salmon and charr fishing (also pink and chum salmon). It is also one of the few Seward Peninsula streams with a consistent spawning population of king salmon, and the lower river also has fairly abundant pike. Access is primarily via the 67-mile Nome-Council Road or by boat travel from the three riverside villages. Popular fishing areas include: the upper Fish River and its tributaries—Boston Creek (salmon, including king and charr), the Rathlatulik River (big grayling) and the Etchepuk River (salmon, including king, and grayling); Steamboat Slough (pike); the Fox River (salmon and grayling—access from the adjacent Nome-Council Road); Ophir Creek (grayling); and the mouth of the Niukluk (all species in the river). Roads from Council provide access to many tributary creeks, and there are gravel bars and a few scattered airstrips for small plane landings, allowing for many different ways of exploring this drainage, including float trips.

5. NOME RIVER

Location: Seward Peninsula, 515 miles northwest of Anchorage.
Reference: Nome B-1, C-1, D-1.
Access: By commercial flight to Nome via Anchorage, then four miles

east on Main Street to the river mouth. Follow the Nome-Taylor Road to upriver access points.

Highlights: The Seward Peninsula's most popular, easily accessed river with good salmon and charr fishing.

Species: Charr, chum salmon, grayling, king salmon, pink salmon, silver salmon.

Regulations: Open year-round, all species except grayling and chum salmon. For the latest updates on closures or restrictions, consult the Alaska Department of Fish and Game's Nome office, (907) 443-5796.

Facilities: No developed public facilities.

Contact: For guided fishing, contact Nome Custom Adventures, P.O. Box 480, Nome, AK 99672; (907) 443-5134. For transportation, contact Stampede Rent a Car, P.O. Box 633, Nome, AK 99762, (907) 443-3838; or Checker Cab, (907) 443-5136.

Description: The Nome River's close proximity to the Seward Peninsula's main hub has always made it an extremely popular and heavily fished drainage, especially since all 44 miles of its length can be easily accessed by road. Fished for years by locals for its salmon (pink, chum and silver), grayling and charr, it is worth considering if you are planning a trip to Nome, even though the fishing in recent years is not what it used to be.

With headwaters in the Kigluaik Mountains, the river flows swiftly south through tundra and empties into Norton Sound about 3.5 miles east of Nome. It has numerous tributaries, all of them swift and clear runoff streams like the Nome itself. The most popular areas to fish are the mouth and the section between Mile 8 and the bridge at Mile 13 of the Nome-Taylor Road. The river is usually fished for charr in late May and June down at the mouth and in August and September, from the Mile 13 bridge down. Pink and chum have been the Nome's main salmon highlights (usually from July through September), though in recent years, depressed runs have forced closures on chum salmon fishing. Some silvers are also taken (from late August through September). Grayling, not as abundant in the Nome as in other prime Seward Peninsula streams, have been overfished in recent years; in 1992, the river was closed to grayling fishing.

Since the Nome lies just a stone's throw from town, you can inquire with the Nome office of the Alaska Department of Fish and Game at (907) 443-5796 for the latest sportfish updates. If conditions warrant, hit the river on the way to the Seward Peninsula's more glamorous fishing locales.

6. PILGRIM RIVER

Location: Seward Peninsula, 540 miles northwest of Anchorage.

Reference: Nome D-1; Solomon D-6; Bendeleben A-6; Teller A-1.

Access: By commercial flight to Nome via Anchorage, then north on the Nome-Taylor Road to Salmon Lake or river points above. It can also be reached by boat from Teller via the Imuruk Basin.

Highlights: A very famous Seward Peninsula drainage, well known for its trophy grayling and pike fishing.

Species: Charr, chum salmon, grayling, (king salmon), northern pike, pink salmon, (red salmon), silver salmon.

Regulations: Salmon Lake and tributaries (including 300 feet of outlet) are closed to salmon fishing. For the latest updates on closures or restrictions, consult the Alaska Department of Fish and Game's Nome office, (907) 443-5796.

Facilities: A public Bureau of Land Management campground is available at the Salmon Lake outlet. There is no fee. Camping is first come, first served.

Contact: For guided fishing, contact Nome Custom Adventures, P.O. Box 480, Nome, AK 99672, (907) 443-5134; or Kify Expedition Services, P.O. Box 181, Nome, AK 99762, (907) 443-2996. For camping information, contact the Bureau of Land Management, Nome Field Station, P.O. Box 952, Nome, AK 99672; (907) 443-2177. For transportation, contact Stampede Rent a Car, P.O. Box 633, Nome, AK 99762; (907) 443-3838.

Description: The Pilgrim River is perhaps the best known of the Seward Peninsula's famous trophy grayling fisheries, with a reputation for large sailfins (two to three pounds) that few rivers its size can match. Originating at the outlet of Salmon Lake north of Nome, it flows northeast then northwest for some 71 miles before joining the Kuzitrin River at New Igloo above Imuruk Basin.

Nineteen miles down from the lake, the bridge for the Nome-Taylor Road (Mile 65) provides the most popular put-in for boats to fish the productive middle and lower stretches of river. Anglers target big grayling, salmon and charr in the next 15-mile stretch down to Historic Pilgrim Hot Springs, and from there to the mouth—30 miles of slower-moving, slough-filled water—most of the river's pike (up to 20 pounds) are taken. Salmon Lake and its main tributary, the Grand Central River are important spawning areas for a rare run of sockeye salmon, but you can't fish them or any other salmon there. Instead, anglers target the lake's grayling and charr. Chums and pinks are the Pilgrim's main salmon species, with a few coho taken. The most popular areas to fish on the Pilgrim system are the lake outlet, the section of river below the bridge, and Iron Creek. The best time to fish is in July and August.

7. KUZITRIN-KOUGAROK RIVERS

Location: Seward Peninsula, 525 miles northwest of Anchorage.
Reference: Teller A-1; Bendeleben A-6, B-3, B-4, B-5, B-6, C-6.
Access: By plane to Nome via Anchorage, then north on the Nome-Taylor Road to the Kuzitrin bridge crossing at Mile 68. The road parallels the Kougarok River beyond bridge; boat travel is possible along both rivers.
Highlights: A fine, abundant grayling fishery, also with significant pike opportunities.
Species: Charr, chum salmon, grayling, (king salmon), northern pike, pink salmon, silver salmon.
Regulations: For closures or restrictions, consult the Alaska Department of Fish and Game's Nome office, (907) 443-5796.
Facilities: No developed public facilities.
Contact: For guided fishing, contact Nome Custom Adventures, P.O. Box 480, Nome, AK 99672, (907) 443-5134; or Kify Expedition Services, P.O. Box 181, Nome, AK 99762, (907) 443-2996. For transportation, contact Stampede Rent a Car, P.O. Box 633, Nome, AK 99762; (907) 443-3838.
Description: The Kuzitrin River, adjacent to the Pilgrim is the largest drainage on the Nome-Taylor Road. It has outstanding fishing potential. Grayling, in particular, are super abundant, but generally run smaller than those on other area streams. Northern pike, chum, pink and some coho salmon are also taken.

The Kougarok is a major tributary that joins the Kuzitrin about 25 miles up from the mouth. It is reached by a rough four-wheel-drive road leading past the Kuzutrin bridge at Mile 68. It is fished mostly for grayling and charr. Both of these rivers are best worked from a boat.

8. SINUK RIVER

Location: Seward Peninsula, 30 miles west of Nome, 560 miles northwest of Anchorage.
Reference: Nome C-2, C-3, D-2.
Access: By plane to Nome via Anchorage, then west on Teller Road 26 miles to the lower river.

Highlights: One of the Seward Peninsula's best road-accessible fishing streams, with outstanding trophy grayling potential.

Species: Charr, chum salmon, grayling, (king salmon), pink salmon, (red salmon), silver salmon.

Regulations: Closed to chum salmon fishing. For additional closures or restrictions, consult the Alaska Department of Fish and Game's Nome office, (907) 443-5796.

Facilities: No developed public facilities.

Contact: For guided fishing, contact Nome Custom Adventures, P.O. Box 480, Nome, AK 99672, (907) 443-5134; or Kify Expedition Services, P.O. Box 181, Nome, AK 99762, (907) 443-2996. For transportation, contact Stampede Rent a Car, P.O. Box 633, Nome, AK 99762, (907) 443-3838; or Checker Cab, (907) 443-5136.

Description: The Sinuk is the largest and best fishing river along the Nome-Teller Road, with outstanding potential for large grayling. (More than half of all record Seward Peninsula grayling were taken on the Sinuk.) Its headwaters lie in the Kigluaik Mountains and Glacial Lake, northwest of Nome. The river can be reached by a short drive west from town to a bridge crossing at Mile 26.7. From there, it can be further accessed by foot trails or jet boat. The Sinuk also has good fishing for charr and pink and silver salmon, as well as one of the Seward Peninsula's only significant spawning populations of red salmon, though few anglers have figured how to get them to bite.

9. SNAKE RIVER

Location: Seward Peninsula, eight miles west of Nome, 550 miles northwest of Anchorage.

Reference: Nome C-1, C-2, D-1.

Access: By commercial flight to Nome via Anchorage, then west on Teller Road eight miles to bridge. The upper river is accessible from Glacier Creek Road, and boat travel possible upriver from the bridge or the mouth.

Highlights: One of the Seward Peninsula's more popular and productive fishing streams, noted for good grayling, silver salmon and charr.

Species: Charr, chum salmon, grayling, (king salmon), pink salmon, silver salmon.

Regulations: Closed to chum salmon fishing. For additional closures or restrictions, consult the Alaska Department of Fish and Game's Nome office, (907) 443-5796.

Facilities: No developed public facilities.

Contact: For guided fishing, contact Nome Custom Adventures, P.O. Box 480, Nome, AK 99672; (907) 443-5134. For transportation, contact Stampede Rent a Car, P.O. Box 633, Nome, AK 99762, (907) 443-3838; or Checker Cab, (907) 443-5136.

Description: The Snake is a popular road fishery located only eight miles west of Nome via the Nome-Teller Road. Best known for its good grayling fishing, the river also provides considerable opportunities for salmon (silvers and pink mostly) and charr in season.

Most people fish the Snake by foot, working the river from trails that lead from the bridge or Glacier Creek Road. Boat access is also possible along the lower river via the launch at the Nome Port. Fish it in July and August for salmon and grayling, or in June or late August through September for charr.

10. SOLOMON RIVER

Location: Seward Peninsula, 30 miles east of Nome, 500 miles northwest of Anchorage.

Reference: Solomon C-5.

Access: By commercial flight to Nome via Anchorage, then east on Nome-Council Road to miles 40 to 50, where the road parallels the east fork of the river.

Highlights: A popular fishing stream for charr and salmon, with plenty of access from the road to the Fish-Niukluk River.

Species: Charr, chum salmon, grayling, (king salmon), pink salmon, silver salmon.

Regulations: Closed to grayling and chum salmon fishing. For additional closures or restrictions, consult the Alaska Department of Fish and Game's Nome office, (907) 443-5796.

Facilities: No developed public facilities.

Contact: For guided fishing, contact Nome Custom Adventures, P.O. Box 480, Nome, AK 99672; (907) 443-5134. For transportation, contact Stampede Rent a Car, P.O. Box 633, Nome, AK 99762, (907) 443-3838; or Checker Cab, (907) 443-5136.

Description: Thirty-two miles east of Nome, the Solomon River enters Norton Sound near the old mining town of the same name. Accessed by the Nome-Council Road, which parallels the river for about 10 miles (between Mile 40 and 50), the Solomon is one of the more popular Seward Peninsula road streams. It is fished mostly for charr and salmon. There are many good spots along the upper river where you can pull off the road and fish (or try the mouth), so it's certainly worth a stop or two on the way out to the more productive Fish-Niukluk River (see listing on page 239 in this chapter).

11. SAFETY SOUND

Location: Seward Peninsula, 30 miles east of Nome, 500 miles northwest of Anchorage.

Reference: Solomon B-6, C-5, C-6.

Access: By commercial flight to Nome via Anchorage, then east on Nome-Council Road to Mile 22, where the road crosses the lagoon outlet, then continues 11 miles along spit. Boat access is possible.

Highlights: Some potentially good, road-accessible beach fishing.

Species: Charr, chum salmon, (king salmon), pink salmon, silver salmon.

Regulations: Closed to chum salmon fishing. For additional closures or restrictions, consult the Alaska Department of Fish and Game's Nome office, (907) 443-5796.

Facilities: No developed public facilities.

Contact: For transportation, contact Checker Cab, (907) 443-5136.

Description: Safety Sound, traversed completely by the Nome-Council Road, beginning at about Mile 17, is another location worth trying on the way out to Council. Salmon (mostly pinks) and charr are fished with some success at the lagoon outlet and along the inshore side of the spit. However, the action is much better on several notable fishing streams emptying into the other side (the Bonanza, Eldorado and Flambeau rivers). Access to these is by boat (or helicopter) only, and negotiating the tides and mudflats can be tricky. June and August are the best times to fish here.

12. AMERICAN-AGIAPUK RIVERS

Location: Seward Peninsula, Imuruk Basin drainage, 65 miles northwest of Nome, 560 miles northwest of Anchorage.

Reference: Teller A-2, B-2, B-3, C-2, D-2.

Access: By small plane or boat. There is boat access from Teller (serviced by flights from Kotzebue or accessed via the Nome-Teller Road) or Kuzitrin River (accessed from Kougarok Road); small plane access is possible to strips or gravel bars on the Agiapuk or American.

Highlights: A more inaccessible Seward Peninsula location with outstanding sportfishing potential.

Species: Charr, chum salmon, grayling, (king salmon), northern pike, pink salmon, silver salmon.

Regulations: For the latest updates on closures or restrictions, consult the Alaska Department of Fish and Game's Nome office, (907) 443-5796.

Facilities: No developed public facilities.

Contact: For guided fishing, contact Kify Expedition Services, P.O. Box 181, Nome, AK 99762; (907) 443-2996. For an air taxi, contact Olsen Air Service, P.O. Box 142, Nome, AK 99762; (907) 443-2229.

Description: The Agiapuk is one of the more outstanding prospects for anyone looking for an "out of the way," high-quality Seward Peninsula fishing experience. The river is visited, along with its tributary, the American, only by small numbers of Nome and Teller folk who hunt, fish and camp along its remote stretches. It has abundant grayling and charr, and is a major spawning stream for chum, pink and silver salmon.

Access is from either Teller, the Kuzitrin River or Nome. Many people put in by small wheelplane on gravel strips along the upper American and spend their entire vacations here; some even float down. The Agiapuk is most frequently accessed by jet boat from Teller or from the Kuzitrin via the Kougarok Road. According to locals, this is a very pretty area, and the fishing is totally unexploited.

13. BUCKLAND RIVER

Location: Seward Peninsula, 160 miles northeast of Nome, 485 miles northwest of Anchorage.

Reference: Selawik A-2, A-5; Candle B-2, B-3, B-4, C-1, C-2, C-3, C-4, D-2, D-3, D-4, D-5.

Access: By boat or small plane. There is scheduled air service to Buckland from Kotzebue, then boat travel upriver. Small planes can land on gravel strips or river bars along the upper river. The river can be floated.

Highlights: A significant, untapped river of lower Kotzebue Sound, with a variety of adventure fishing possibilities.

Species: Charr, chum salmon, grayling, (king salmon), northern pike, pink salmon, sheefish, silver salmon.

Regulations: For the latest updates on closures or restrictions, consult the Alaska Department of Fish and Game's Nome office, (907) 443-5796.

Facilities: Boat rentals, sporting goods, groceries, licenses and fuel are available in Buckland.

Contact: For information on guided fishing, contact Buckland's mayor, Lester Hadley, P.O. Box 24, Buckland, AK 99727; (907) 494-2107. For an air taxi to Buckland or the upper river, contact Olsen Air Service, P.O. Box 142, Nome, AK 99762, (907) 443-2229; or Bering Air, P.O. Box 1650, Nome, AK 99762, (907) 443-5464.

Description: The Buckland is a pristine, multi-forked river that drains the Selawik and Nulato Hills at the base of the Seward Peninsula. Little-known and seldom visited by any other than locals, it nonetheless has potential for some high-quality fishing adventure, as it has significant salmon runs (all species except sockeye) and grayling, charr, pike and even sheefish populations.

There are two major forks on the 125-mile Buckland, the South and West forks, which merge about 44 miles up from the mouth. Most of the fishing is done from this point down to the village, but there are some outstanding possibilities (for salmon, grayling and charr) on the clear-flowing West and North forks and the Fish River. Numerous oxbow lakes and sloughs along the lower river provide outstanding pike fishing (also sheefish).

Locals access the Buckland almost exclusively by jet boat, travelling upriver to camp, fish, hunt or pick berries. The upper river can also be accessed in spots by small wheelplane, landing on gravel strips or suitable river bars, making headwater float trips a possibility. According to locals, this area is "very pretty, with nice hills for hiking, plenty of animals, no people and lots of fish." The folks in the village are friendly and eager to show visitors just how special their river is, with boats and guides available. (Buckland's mayor, Lester Hadley, is the contact for local services, and even guides trips himself.) Before you go, contact the Northeast Arctic Native Association, Regional Corporation, P.O. Box 49, Kotzebue, AK 99752, (907) 442-3301, for information on camping on native lands along the Buckland.

Region 3
Kotzebue Sound

Within a space of 150 miles, some of the most significant sportfishing drainages in all of western Alaska empty their waters into Kotzebue Sound, north of the Arctic Circle. These include the Kobuk, Selawik, Noatak, Wulik and Kivalina rivers, which are known the world over for their abundant trophy charr and sheefish. Very pristine and highly regarded recreational waters, the largest and most fish-endowed of these drainages—the Noatak and Kobuk—are considered Alaska's premier rivers for wilderness adventure. Area angling highlights also include excellent grayling fishing and some fabulous, but virtually unexploited, northern pike opportunities.

14. Noatak River

Location: Kotzebue Sound, 550 miles northwest of Anchorage.

Reference: Survey Pass C-5, C-6; Ambler River C-1, D-1, D-2, D-3, D-4, D-5, D-6; Howard Pass A-5; Misheguk Mountain A-1, A-2; Baird Mountains D-3, D-4, D-5, D-6; Noatak A-1, A-2, B-2, B-3, C-2, C-3, D-1, D-2.

Access: By small plane from Bettles or Kotzebue to headwater lakes (Matcharak and Pingo) or gravel bars along river. It is possible to float fish in a raft/kayak, taking out at the village of Noatak (one- to three-week duration, depending on put-in) or gravel bars along way. Boat travel is possible along the lower river.

Highlights: Alaska's premier wild river, world famous for its trophy charr fishing.

Species: Charr, chum salmon, grayling, (king salmon), lake trout, northern pike, pink salmon, (red salmon, silver salmon).

Regulations: Open year-round, all species.

Facilities: No developed public facilities.

Contact: For guided/unguided fishing, contact Sourdough Outfitters, c/o Gary Bensen, P.O. Box 90, Bettles, AK 99726; (907) 692-5252. For general information, contact the Noatak National Preserve, P.O. Box 1029, Kotzebue, AK 99752; (907) 442-3890. For an air taxi, contact Mike Spisak, Ram Aviation, P.O. Box 1167, Kotzebue, AK 99752; (907) 442-3205.

Description: By anyone's estimation, the 425-mile giant Noatak is Alaska's most superlative backcountry river. (It was designated a UNESCO World Heritage Site in 1976, and later incorporated into Noatak National Preserve as a Wild River in 1978.) Along with several other Kotzebue Sound drainages (such as Wulik, Kobuk and Kivalina rivers), it has a world reputation for abundant, trophy searun charr (up to 15 pounds and more), as thousands of these robust fish traditionally jam the mainstem and tributaries in late summer through fall (from August through September), to prepare for spawning and overwintering.

Lying totally above the Arctic Circle, the Noatak rises on the slopes of the Schwatka Mountains in the western Brooks Range and flows southwest to Kotzebue Sound. Clear and fast for most of its length, with only minor rapids (Class I and Class II at most), the Noatak presents no major technical obstacles for floating, other than its size and remoteness (a trip down its entire length is a major, three-week undertaking that should not be taken lightly by anyone). Since the best angling is on the lower and middle sections of the river, a far better option for anglers is to put in on gravel bars or small tributary lakes at mid-river (the Aniuk or Cutler rivers are popular put-in areas). This cuts travel time considerably and allows more enjoyment of the lower river's abundant fishing. (Most of the Noatak's big, chunky charr are intercepted at the mouths of the Kelly, Kugururok, Kugrak, Kaluktavik and Nimiuktuk rivers, though they do occur throughout most of the drainage.) The current Alaska state-record charr came from the Kelly River in 1991. See page 100 for the charr chapter, "Fish of the Rainbow."

A popular option for fishermen is to fly from Kotzebue in a small wheelplane, land on gravel bars on the lower Noatak or tributaries mentioned above, then camp and fish, even float downriver (to the village of Noatak or pick-up points along the river). In addition to the river's great charr fishing, grayling and big chum salmon are very abundant. Fishing the Noatak for ravenous spring charr and grayling right after break-up (June) is also an exciting possibility, and there are countless unnamed lakes and sloughs in the Noatak Flats (between the Eli and Agashashok rivers) that are reputed to have pike of legendary proportions.

15. KOBUK RIVER

Location: Kotzebue Sound, 475 miles northwest of Anchorage.

Reference: Survey Pass A-3; Hughes D-3, D-4, D-5, D-6; Shungnak D-1, D-2, D-3, D-4; Ambler River A-4, A-5, A-6; Baird Mountains A-1, A-2; Selawik C-5, C-6, D-3, D-4, D-5, D-6.

Access: By floatplane to headwater lakes via Bettles. Float fishing is a popular option by raft or kayak down to the villages of Kobuk, Ambler or Kiana, with wheelplane pickup and return to Kotzebue. Boat travel is possible to points along the lower river from villages.

Highlights: A giant among Alaska's wild rivers, with superb fishing for trophy sheefish; also charr, pike, lake trout and grayling.

Species: Charr, chum salmon, grayling, lake trout, northern pike, pink salmon, sheefish.

Regulations: Open year-round, all species.

Facilities: No developed public facilities.

Contact: For guided/unguided fishing trips, contact Sourdough Outfitters, c/o Gary Bensen, P.O. Box 90, Bettles, AK 99726, (907) 692-5252, or Peace of Selby, 90 Polar Road, P.O. Box 86, Manley Hot Springs, AK 99756, (907) 672-3206. For an air taxi, contact Bettles Air Service, 2453 Homestead, North Pole, AK 99705, (907) 770-5111; or Ram Aviation, P.O. Box 1167, Kotzebue, AK 99752, (907) 442-3205.

Description: The Kobuk River, like the Noatak, flows west to Kotzebue Sound, through the heart of some of the finest wild country in Alaska. Almost 350 miles long—one of Alaska's largest clear rivers—the Kobuk's size and features make it suited for a variety of high-quality, wilderness fishing adventures, particularly float trips. This area has so much to offer that, like the Noatak, it's impossible to see it all in one trip. Many folks begin with an exploration of the upper river, flying in to one of several, beautiful headwater lakes (such as Walker, Selby and Nutuvukti), camping and fishing (for lake trout, charr, pike and grayling) for a few days, then continuing downriver by raft or kayak. There are two stretches of major rapids (Class III and Class IV) in the canyons of the upper river below Walker Lake. Other than that, the Kobuk is fairly wide and serene as it winds its way through immense, scenic valleys, where caribou, bear, wolves, moose and countless birds can be seen.

The trip downriver to the village of Kobuk takes at least eight days (more or less), and will take you through some astounding grayling and salmon holes, especially the mouths of the countless tributary creeks that empty into this 125-mile stretch of river. If you're interested in some of the Kobuk's world-famous, giant sheefish, you'll need to float down sometime in August or early September, when the big shees make their way upriver to spawn. The best fishing for these silvery brutes seems to be in the vicinity of the notorious Pah River, where fish of 30 pounds or more can be taken.

Most people pull out at Kobuk, but there are some unique attractions downriver that make continuing worthwhile. Some of the river's best salmon and charr fishing can be had during late summer in the north adjoining tributaries, from Ambler down to Kiana, while the biggest northern pike cruise the lower river's slow-moving pools and sloughs. There are some amazing sights as well, like the incredible Kobuk Sand Dunes, or Onion Portage—the timeless caribou crossing halfway down the river and the site of numerous archeological digs. The float to Kiana will add an additional six days minimum to the overall trip time; kayaks or motor-assisted rafts are highly recommended, as the wide lower sections of river can slow to a crawl in headwinds. It's certainly possible to put in at Kobuk and float down, if you don't have two weeks to burn.

There are many other options, of course. The Kobuk has several tributaries that make outstanding float trips on their own, sparkling clear, pristine mountain streams like the Salmon, Ambler or Squirrel rivers, with superb fishing for grayling, charr and chum salmon. The numerous lakes in the upper Kobuk Valley are among the loveliest in all of the Brooks Range, nearly all holding lake trout, grayling and pike. Arrangements can be made with outfitters for a variety of experiences–tent camps, canoe trips and hiking expeditions—that will allow for some adventuresome exploration and fishing.

16. SELAWIK RIVER

Location: Kotzebue Sound, 475 miles northwest of Anchorage.

Reference: Shungnak B-2, B-3, B-4, B-5, B-6, C-3, C-5; Selawik B-2, B-3, B-4, B-5, C-1, C-2, C-3, C-4, C-5.

Access: By small plane to headwater lakes (in the Shiniliaok Creek vicinity) or gravel bars, with float options down to the village; or wheelplane to Selawik village, with foot or boat access to points along the river.

Highlights: One of Northwest Alaska's most potentially significant trophy sheefish rivers, which also holds outstanding northern pike fishing possibilities.

Species: Charr, chum salmon, grayling, northern pike, pink salmon, sheefish.

Regulations: Open year-round, all species.

Facilities: No developed public facilities. Limited supplies and services are available in Selawik village.

Contact: For guide services, contact Ralph Ramos, P.O. Box 12, Selawik, AK 99770; (907) 484-2102.

Description: In early spring, some of Northwest Alaska's most exciting fishing action takes place on the ice of the large, freshwater estuary formed at the mouths of the Kobuk and Selawik rivers, southeast of Kotzebue. Here locals, using bright jigs and spoons, stir the giant sheefish of Kotzebue Sound from their winter lethargy, with electrifying results. These semi-anadromous stocks attain the largest size of any sheefish in Alaska, and catches of 20- to 30-pound fish are not uncommon at this time. As break-up proceeds in May, the action shifts inland, following the sheefish as they gorge on whitefish and spring smolt. Later on in summer, many of these same fish will be found upriver, feeding heavily and preparing for their fall spawning.

The Selawik takes it name, most aptly, from the Inupiat for "place of sheefish." Along with the Kobuk River, it shares the reputation for Alaska's finest trophy angling for the species. The majority of visiting anglers come in summer and fall. Most fish upriver from Selawik village, targeting the mouths of the tributary creeks and mainstem river up to about 20 miles beyond Ingruksukruk Creek. The countless sloughs and lakes in the immense flatlands surrounding the lower Selawik also make perfect habitat for monster northern pike, so don't miss the opportunity for some outstanding trophy fishing for "Mr.Gator Jaws" if you plan on visiting this drainage.

17. WULIK RIVER

Location: Seward Peninsula, 600 miles northwest of Anchorage.

Reference: Noatak C-5, D-3, D-4, D-5; De Long Mountains A-2, A-3, B-2.

Access: By small wheelplane from Kotzebue to gravel bars along river. Raft or kayak travel is possible to locations downriver, with wheelplane pick up. Boat travel is possible along the lower river from the village of Kivalina.

Highlights: Alaska's most famous location for trophy charr.

Species: Charr, chum salmon, grayling, (king salmon), pink salmon, (silver salmon).

Regulations: Open year-round, all species.
Facilities: No developed public facilities. A private lodge is located on the river.
Contact: For guided/unguided fishing, contact Midnight Sun Adventures, 1306 East 26th Avenue, Anchorage, AK 99508; (907) 277-8829. For an air taxi, contact Ram Aviation, P.O. Box 1167, Kotzebue, AK 99752; (907) 442-3205.
Description: The Wulik River for many years has had the reputation as "the place" for trophy charr in Alaska. It is accessible from Kotzebue and easy to fish. In an average year, the Wulik receives tens of thousands of robust (on average five to seven pounds and up to 15 pounds or more), sea-run Dolly Varden that enter the river in late summer through fall to spawn and overwinter. A good portion of all of Alaska's record fish for the species have come from the Wulik.

Draining the westernmost slopes of the Brooks Range (the De Long Mountains) and emptying into the Chukchi Sea, for much of its length the 89-mile Wulik is perfect for wade-and-cast fishing: clear, gravel-bottomed, with pools, runs and braided sections interspersed with plenty of bars for camping. Most of the fishing on the Wulik takes place from above Kivalina Lagoon to where the river branches into East and West forks (42 miles above the mouth), with the greatest concentration of fall charr located above and below Ikalukrok Creek. Other popular areas for fishing are the channels above Kivalina Lagoon (chum salmon), the West Fork below the falls and 16 miles up from the East-West confluence (charr), Sheep Creek (big charr), Ikalukrok Creek (charr and salmon) and upper Tutak Creek (big grayling and charr).

For a fall trophy charr safari (from mid-August through mid-September), the Wulik is hard to beat. There's also exciting fishing during the spring out-migration in June and in late July for an early run of spawners. Besides charr, the Wulik also has abundant grayling and chum salmon, along with some rare coho. Animal encounters—bears, caribou, wolves and moose—are possible, and extreme weather, especially in September, is highly likely.

18. KIVALINA RIVER

Location: Chukchi Sea coast, 90 miles north of Kotzebue, 600 miles northwest of Anchorage.
Reference: Noatak D-5, D-6; De Long Mountains A-3, A-4, B-3.
Access: By small wheelplane from Kotzebue to gravel bars along the

river, or scheduled wheelplane to Kivalina village, then boat transport upriver. It can be floated by raft or kayak.

Highlights: One of Alaska's best trophy charr fisheries.

Species: Charr, chum salmon, grayling, (king salmon), northern pike, pink salmon, (silver salmon).

Regulations: Open year-round, all species.

Facilities: No developed public facilities. Some limited supplies and possibly rental boats are available in Kivalina village.

Contact: For an air taxi to the Kivalina River, contact Mike Spisak, Ram Aviation, P.O. Box 1167, Kotzebue, AK 99752, (907) 442-3205; or Cape Smythe Air, P.O. Box 810, Kotzebue, AK 99752, (907) 442-3020. For boat rentals and guide services, contact Caleb Wesley, P.O. Box 48, Kivalina, AK 99750; (907) 645-2150.

Description: The Kivalina is the less-known sister river of the fabulous Wulik, Northwest Alaska's best trophy charr stream. Of similar origins, size and character, the clear-flowing, 64-mile Kivalina is also blessed with abundant runs of big sea-run charr that overwinter and spawn in its spring-fed tributaries and mainstem. Slightly more remote and difficult to fish than the Wulik, the Kivalina doesn't quite receive the attention it deserves, considering the quality of fishing it offers.

The river has three main forks that converge about 27 miles above the mouth. Most of the sportfishing for fall charr and salmon takes place from there down to the lagoon. The lower sections of Grayling Creek (east fork) and the middle fork of the Kivalina are important upper river spawning areas. The best time to fish here is mid-August through early September. Spring charr are fished heavily by natives in the lower river and lagoon in early June.

You can access the Kivalina from Kotzebue by wheelplane, putting down on gravel bars upriver or at the strip in the village near the mouth. (Rental boats and a guide can be had there, too.) The river can be floated by raft or kayak to its mouth at Kivalina Lagoon, with a return via scheduled or chartered wheelplane to Kotzebue. See the charr chapter on page 100 for details on fishing techniques and equipment.

Region 4
Northwest
Mountain Lakes

In the upper Kobuk, Noatak and Koyukuk valleys lie scattered dozens of small, deep glacial lakes, many unnamed and seldom visited. Some of the more outstanding, listed below, are among Alaska's most pristine mountain lakes, offering solitude, impressive scenery and fine fishing for lake trout, grayling, pike and even landlocked charr. Access is from Kotzebue or Bettles, with early summer (from June through early July) or fall (from mid-August through early September) the best times for fishing. Check with local air taxi services for latest conditions.

19. Feniak Lake (Noatak Drainage)

Location: Upper Noatak Valley, 550 miles northwest of Anchorage.
Reference: Howard Pass A-4, B-4.
Access: By commercial flight to Kotzebue or Bettles, then floatplane or wheelplane to the lake.
Highlights: One of the prettiest lakes in the western Brooks Range, with excellent fishing for lake trout and grayling.
Species: Grayling, lake trout.
Regulations: Open year-round, all species.
Facilities: No developed public facilities.
Contact: For an air taxi, contact Mike Spisak, Ram Aviation, P.O. Box 1167, Kotzebue, AK 99752; (907) 442-3205.
Description: Feniak Lake is perhaps the finest of the many glacial lakes in the upper Noatak Valley. Set in beautiful mountain country, its deep (75 feet) blue waters hold some superb lake trout fishing, with abundant catches and large fish (15 pounds or more) not uncommon. There is a major inlet stream on the north side, while the outlet, Makpik Creek, exits from the south. Fishing is good in both streams for grayling. Access is by float or wheelplane (there is a gravel strip nearby). Try Feniak in the spring or early summer (from June through July) for the most exciting fishing.

20. Matcharak & Isiak Lakes (Noatak Drainage)

Location: Upper Noatak Valley, 475 miles northwest of Anchorage.
Reference: Ambler River C-1, D-1.
Access: By small plane from Kotzebue or Bettles.
Highlights: Beautiful, remote mountain lakes, with good fishing for lake trout and grayling.
Species: Charr, grayling, lake trout, northern pike.
Regulations: Open year-round, all species.
Facilities: No developed public facilities.
Contact: For an air taxi, contact Mike Spisak, Ram Aviation, P.O. Box 1167, Kotzebue, AK 99752; (907) 442-3205.
Description: Matcharak is one of many small but fairly deep lakes situated along the upper Noatak River. It is commonly used as a floatplane put-in for float trips on the Noatak (with a small portage). It is very scenic, and known for its good lake trout and grayling fishing, with a few pike thrown in. Still, it can be inconsistent. Late spring and early summer are probably the best times to try.

Isiak Lake lies less than two miles from Matcharak, on a small plateau above the Noatak. A gravel strip next to the lake provides access. A lovely little lake, it, too, has lake trout, grayling and pike. Isiak makes for a nice lake fishing side trip when you put in at Matcharak to float the Noatak.

21. Walker Lake (Kobuk Drainage)

Location: Upper Kobuk Valley, 425 miles northwest of Anchorage.
Reference: Survey Pass A-3, A-4.
Access: By floatplane from Bettles.
Highlights: The most significant lake in the Kobuk Valley and one of the most outstanding western Brooks Range lakes, with excellent lake trout, grayling, pike and landlocked charr fishing.
Species: Charr, grayling, lake trout, northern pike.
Regulations: Open year-round, all species.
Facilities: No developed public facilities.
Contact: For an air taxi, contact Bettles Air Service, 2453 Homestead, North Pole, AK 99705; (907) 770-5111.
Description: Walker Lake is one of the most well-known and popular fly-in destinations in the entire Brooks Range. Located about 45 minutes by small plane west of Bettles at the head of the Kobuk River (in Gates of the Arctic National Park), this scenic, narrow

14-mile body of water is a popular put-in spot for floaters setting out for the long haul down the Kobuk River headwaters to the village of Kobuk. It has outstanding fishing for lake trout (up to 30 pounds) and landlocked charr (up to 15 pounds), with good grayling fishing in the outlet and mouths of tributary creeks and even some pike to be had. Late spring and early summer (from June through early July) is probably the best time to fish it, but it does offer fairly consistent opportunities throughout the season, especially to boat anglers.

22. SELBY-NARVAK & MINAKOKOSA LAKES (KOBUK DRAINAGE)

Location: Upper Kobuk Valley, 435 miles northwest of Anchorage.
Reference: Hughes D-5, D-6.
Access: By floatplane from Bettles.
Highlights: Good lake trout, grayling, pike and landlocked charr fishing in a pristine and highly scenic setting.
Species: Charr, grayling, lake trout, northern pike.
Regulations: Open year-round, all species.
Facilities: A private lodge, cabins and camps are available.
Contact: For lodge, cabin or tent camp-based fishing, contact Peace of Selby, 90 Polar Road, P.O. Box 86, Manley Hot Springs, AK 99756; (907) 672-3206. For an air taxi, contact Bettles Air Service, 2453 Homestead, North Pole, AK 99705; (907) 770-5111.
Description: Located only about 40 miles southwest of Walker Lake, these two beautiful, connected lakes are worth a visit by themselves, but especially so if you're making a trip to the Kobuk or Pah rivers, as the Selby-Narvak lakes lie but a short distance off the river, midway down. (You can fish the lakes for a few days, then float down the outlet stream to join with the Kobuk right above the Pah.) Fishing is very good for lake trout, pike and grayling, in a lovely, most secluded setting.

Minakokosa lies in between Selby and Walker lakes. It's small, but very pretty and private, with decent lake trout fishing. Like the Selby-Narvak lakes, it connects to the Kobuk, so it can be included in an itinerary for an extended float trip. Peace of Selby keeps a tent camp there, as well as cabins and camps on Selby-Narvak and other nearby lakes. They can provide everything needed—such as lodging, canoes, provisions and guides—for outpost-based fishing adventures of the highest order. Give them a call.

23. INIAKUK LAKE (KOYUKUK DRAINAGE)

Location: Upper Koyukuk Valley, central Brooks Range, 45 miles west of Bettles, 425 miles northwest of Anchorage.

Reference: Survey Pass A-1.

Access: By floatplane from Bettles.

Highlights: An easily accessed Brooks Range lake, with good northern pike, grayling and lake trout fishing

Species: Grayling, lake trout, northern pike.

Regulations: Open year-round, all species.

Facilities: No developed public facilities. A private lodge is located on the lake.

Contact: For lodge-based fishing, contact Iniakuk Lake Lodge, P.O. Box 80424, Fairbanks, AK 99708, (907) 479-6354; or contact Sourdough Outfitters, c/o Gary Bensen, P.O. Box 90, Bettles, Alaska 99726, (907) 692-5252. For an air taxi to the lake, contact Bettles Air Service, 2453 Homestead, North Pole, AK 99705; (907) 770-5111.

Description: A short flight northwest from Bettles takes you to lovely Iniakuk Lake in the Alatna drainage. Small (five miles long and only one mile wide), clear and very deep (200 feet), Iniakuk is in a spectacular setting, with abrupt, tall mountains on its west and east sides. Fishing is good for lake trout, grayling and pike, especially in the spring after ice-out. There's a lodge on the north end of the lake. A short stay there, with a float down the outlet (Malemute Fork) to the Alatna, a Wild and Scenic River, is highly recommended. (Note: Water levels vary through the summer. Check with the folks at the lodge or Bettles Air Service for latest river conditions before attempting a float down to the Alatna drainage.)

24. WILD LAKE (KOYUKUK DRAINAGE)

Location: Central Brooks Range, 40 miles north of Bettles, 435 miles northwest of Anchorage.

Reference: Wiseman B-4, C-4.

Access: By floatplane from Bettles.

Highlights: An easily-accessed, popular Brooks Range lake destination, with outstanding scenery and good fishing for lake trout, pike and grayling.

Species: Grayling, lake trout, northern pike.

Regulations: Open year-round, all species.

Facilities: No developed public facilities.

Contact: For guided/unguided fishing and outfitting, contact Sourdough Outfitters, c/o Gary Bensen, P.O. Box 90, Bettles, AK 99726; (907) 692-5252. For an air taxi, contact Bettles Air Service, 2453 Homestead, North Pole, AK 99705; (907) 770-5111.

Description: Wild Lake is located at the head of its namesake river, a short distance north of Bettles. One of the deepest lakes of its size (up to 250 feet) in the Brooks Range, the five-mile-long Wild offers good seasonal fishing for lake trout, pike and grayling, especially around the inlet and outlet waters. It's best right after break-up in early June or in the fall (from late August through early September). A raft or other inflatable craft will greatly improve your chances of success on these deep waters. You can combine a stay at the lake with a short, four-day float down the Wild River, ending your trip at Bettles, a fairly inexpensive, but outstanding, Brooks Range experience. Because of its easy accessibility and some private land development, however, at times this fly-in lake may be tamer than its name suggests.

25. LOWER KOYUKUK RIVER

Location: Middle Yukon River tributary, 370 miles northwest of Anchorage.

Reference: Kateel River Quadrangle; Nulato D-4, D-6; Melozitna D-3; Hughes A-3, B-1, B-2, B-3; Bettles B-6, C-5, C-6, D-5, D-6.

Access: By floatplane or boat. The main boat access points are from Galena, Huslia and Hughes.

Highlights: An unexplored fishing frontier, with high potential for trophy pike; also sheefish and grayling.

Species: (Charr), chum salmon, grayling, (king salmon), northern pike, sheefish.

Regulations: Open year-round, all species.

Facilities: Limited services, supplies and lodging are available in nearby villages of Hughes and Huslia.

Contact: For lodging, guided fishing and boat rentals, contact Athabasca Cultural Journeys, P.O. Box 10, Huslia, AK 99746; (800) 423-0094.

Description: The 320-mile Koyukuk River, one the Yukon's largest tributaries, dominates north central Alaska with its vast network of sprawling streams, which provide major habitat for a wide variety of fish species. In the extensive flatlands downstream of Hughes, the Koyukuk usually runs turbid from sediment and tannic water, but still has considerable sportfish potential for large pike (up to 48 inches) and sheefish in its countless, meandering sloughs, tributary lakes and adjoining streams. Grayling (some of trophy size) and some salmon (chums mostly, and a few, rare kings) can be taken from the clearer waters of the Gisasa, Kateel, Dakli and Alatna rivers and Hensaw Creek. Some Dolly Varden charr are even reported in the Gisasa. Aside from locals, these areas receive very little fishing pressure. They are definitely worth investigating by the angler with time, resources and a yen for truly wild fishing adventure.

Fishing for charr under a midnight sun in Alaska's Northwest.

Alaska Fishing by Region: Interior

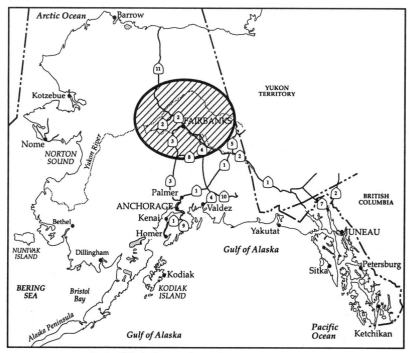

Shaded area shows Interior region

MAP 2—INTERIOR HOTSPOTS

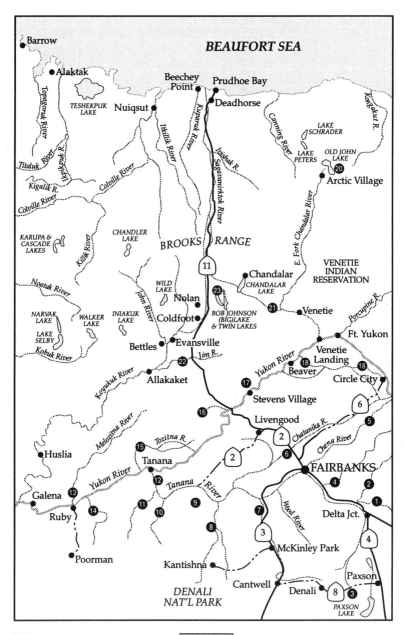

Barrow

Alaktak

BEAUFORT SEA

Beechey Point

Prudhoe Bay

Deadhorse

Nuiqsut

TESHEKPUK LAKE

Topagoruk River

Ikpikpuk R.

Titaluk River

Kigalik R.

Colville River

Colville River

Ikilik River

Kuparuk River

Sagavanirktok River

Ivishak R.

Canning River

LAKE SCHRADER

LAKE PETERS

OLD JOHN LAKE

Kongakut R.

(20)

Arctic Village

KARUPA & CASCADE LAKES

CHANDLER LAKE

BROOKS RANGE

Noatak River

Killik River

John River

WILD LAKE

Nolan

Coldfoot

INIAKUK LAKE

(11)

(23)

Chandalar

CHANDALAR LAKE

(21)

Venetie

E. Fork Chandalar River

VENETIE INDIAN RESERVATION

Porcupine R.

NARVAK LAKE

WALKER LAKE

LAKE SELBY

Kobuk River

Bettles

Evansville

BOB JOHNSON (BIG) LAKE & TWIN LAKES

Jim R.

Ft. Yukon

Venetie Landing

(18)

Beaver

(18)

Circle City

(22)

Allakaket

Koyukuk River

(17)

Stevens Village

Yukon River

(16)

Livengood

(2)

Chatanika R.

(6)

(5)

Huslia

Melozitna River

(15)

Tozitna R.

Tanana

(2)

(6)

Chena River

FAIRBANKS

Yukon River

(12)

Tanana

(11)

(10)

(9)

River

(7)

Wood River

(4)

(2)

Galena

(13)

Ruby

(14)

(8)

(3)

Delta Jct.

(1)

(4)

Poorman

Kantishna

(8)

McKinley Park

Cantwell

Denali

Paxson

DENALI NAT'L PARK

(8)

(3)

PAXSON LAKE

MAP 3—INTERIOR HOTSPOTS

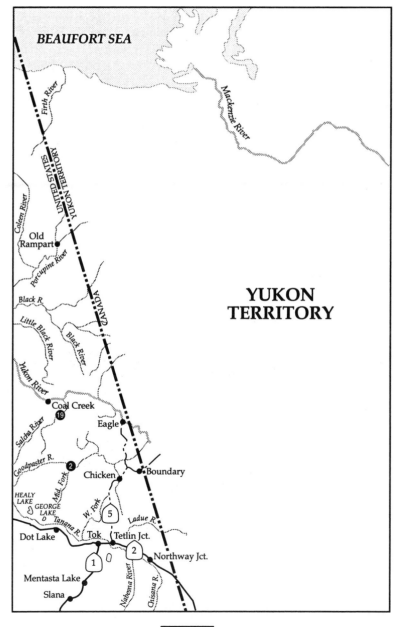

INTERIOR HOT SPOTS

Region 1: Tanana River Valley—p. 270
1. Delta Clearwater River—map page 264
2. Goodpaster River System—map pages 264 and 265
3. Tangle Lakes System—map page 264
4. Salcha River—map page 264
5. Chena River System—map page 264
6. Chatanika River System—map page 264
7. Nenana River System—map page 264
8. Kantishna River System—map page 264
9. Zitziana River System—map page 264
10. Cosna River System—map page 264
11. Chitanana River System—map page 264
12. Fish Creek System—map page 264

Region 2: Middle Yukon River—p. 287
13. Melozitna River System—map page 264
14. Nowitna River System—map page 264
15. Tozitna River System—map page 264
16. Ray River—map page 264
17. Dall River System—map page 264
18. Birch-Beaver Creek Systems—map page 264
19. Charley River—map page 265

Region 3: Eastern Brooks Range—p. 297
20. Old John Lake—map page 264
21. Upper Chandalar River—map page 264
22. Jim River-Prospect Creek—map page 264
23. Bob Johnson (Big) & Twin Lakes—map page 264

INTERIOR

Alaska's vast heartland, the Interior region, encompasses one-third of the state, in a gigantic area bound on the north and south by formidable mountains—the Alaska and Brooks ranges—and on the east by the Canadian border. (For our purposes, the Middle Fork of the Koyukuk River is the western boundary.) The immense Yukon River system, the fifth largest on the continent, is the dominant feature of this region, shaping the character of the land and its people. Along the great waterways here—the Yukon, Koyukuk, Porcupine, Tanana and others—you can still catch a rare glimpse of the "real Alaska," with its native villages and fish wheels, old trapper's cabins, birch forests and country that, for the most part, is still the sparsely settled wilderness it always was.

Although it can't match the southern coastal regions' diversity of sportfishing, Interior still has quite a bit to offer anglers, with thousands of miles of scenic, winding rivers, clear headwater streams and countless lakes, ponds and sloughs, where some of Alaska's most abundant fishing opportunities for pike, sheefish and grayling are found.

COUNTRY, CLIMATE & CONDITIONS

Interior's varied terrain consists of extensive plateaus and moderate mountains, rolling hills and immense lowland valleys created by the state's largest sprawling rivers. Great stands of paper birch, aspen and spruce cover most of the lower elevations, with timberline at 2,300 to 3,000 feet in elevation. To the north and west, expanses of tundra take over, in country which resembles that along the coast.

Interior's climate is strongly continental, with harsh seasonal extremes. Summer temperatures frequently climb into the 80s or even 90s (degrees Fahrenheit), while winter lows routinely plummet to minus 20 or minus 30 degrees, reaching minus 50 or less during intense cold snaps. Fort Yukon, in the center of the region, has recorded temperatures from 100 degrees to minus 75. Precipitation is scant (12 inches or so annually), with the area having considerably more sunny, dry weather than coastal Alaska. Freeze-up generally occurs in October, earlier in elevated locations in the Brooks Range; break-up is usually from late April to early May. Because of the size of most of the rivers here, extreme and rapid changes in water conditions can occur during spring and summer, with heavy flooding always possible. As such, care should be taken when selecting campsites and planning trip itineraries.

INTERIOR FISHING HIGHLIGHTS

The abundance of large mainstem, lowland river terrain, with its preponderance of sloughs, lakes and marshy ponds, is the perfect habitat for a variety of still-water baitfish like whitefish, cisco and suckers, which in turn provide ample forage for predatory game species like northern pike and sheefish. The Interior is well known for its outstanding fisheries for these two fighters (such as in the Tanana and Yukon Flats).

Because of the great distances from the coast, salmon here are fewer in number and species—mostly chum, with some kings and coho. High-quality fishing for these species is limited, occurring mostly in the mouths and lower sections of clearwater rivers, particularly those in the Tanana River drainage. (Alaska's most significant fall runs of chum salmon occur all along the middle Yukon River and its tributaries, but are used primarily for subsistence.) Grayling opportunities abound, however, in nearly every clear stream and headwater, with even some Dolly Varden found in scattered, swift streams (Tanana, Nenana and Koyukuk river tributaries mostly). Some outstanding opportunities for lake trout in the upper Tanana River drainage and Brooks Range round out the fishing highlights of the Interior region.

ACCESS, SERVICES & COSTS

Access to Interior fishing locations is available by road, rail, plane and boat. Fairbanks, the major hub, is serviced daily by jetliners from the outside world, with air taxi services providing access to numerous fly-in locations from there or to smaller hubs like Bettles and Fort Yukon. A highway network crisscrosses the region, linking the major communities to the rest of the state and Canada (via the Alaska Highway) and providing anglers with road access to quite a few good fishing areas. On the big waterways like the Tanana, Yukon and Porcupine rivers, boats are the best (and sometimes only) travel option to reach prime waters.

There are a variety of local services to choose from in planning an Interior fishing excursion. Everything from half-day guided fishing tours to full-service wilderness lodges, at prices that range from fees comparable to those in Southcentral or Southeast Alaska, to considerably more for remote areas of the Brooks Range or upper Yukon (anywhere from $125 to $450 per day per person).

INTERIOR RUN TIMING

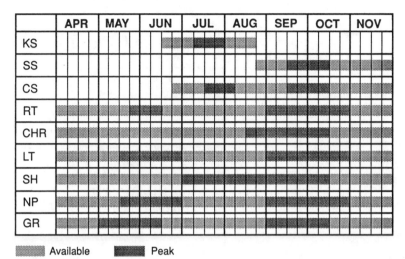

	APR	MAY	JUN	JUL	AUG	SEP	OCT	NOV
KS								
SS								
CS								
RT								
CHR								
LT								
SH								
NP								
GR								

▓ Available   █ Peak

KS=King Salmon, SS=Silver Salmon, CS=Chum Salmon, RT=Rainbow Trout, CHR=Charr, LT=Lake Trout, SH=Sheefish, NP=Northern Pike, GR=Grayling

Note: Time periods shown are for bright fish, in the case of salmon entering rivers, or for general availability for resident species. Salmon are present in many systems long after the periods shown, but are usually in spawning/post spawning condition. Peak sportfishing periods for each species are highlighted. Be aware that run timing can vary somewhat from drainage to drainage and generally follows a later trend in waters to the west and north in Alaska. Check with local contacts listed for area run-timing specifics before confirming plans.

REGION 1
TANANA RIVER VALLEY

The Tanana is a major tributary of the Yukon that originates primarily from meltwater draining off the immense Nabesna and Chisana glaciers high in the Wrangell Mountains. The Tanana flows northwest more than 500 miles before joining the mighty Yukon just west of the town of Manley. The most accessible and popular Interior watershed for recreation, the Tanana River drainage offers a wide variety of water and fishing, with abundant grayling, northern pike, lake trout, some sheefish and the best of Interior's limited fishing for chinook and coho salmon. Since the Tanana is a braided, glacial river system, sportfishing potential is concentrated in clear, upland tributaries—the Salcha, Chena, Chatanika and Delta Clearwater rivers—and in sloughs, lakes and slower streams along the Tanana Flats (the Minto, Tolvana and Kantishna rivers and Fish Creek).

---

1. DELTA CLEARWATER RIVER

Location: Upper Tanana River drainage, Delta Junction area, 85 miles southeast of Fairbanks, 245 miles northeast of Anchorage.

Reference: Mount Hayes D-3; Big Delta A-3, A-4.

Access: By car from Alaska Highway via Clearwater and Remington roads or from Richardson Highway via Jack Warren and Remington roads. To access the river mouth, most anglers use power boats or canoes launched at the campground near Clearwater Ranch. From there, it is a 10-mile run. However, some opt to launch at Clearwater Lake off Jack Warren Road, into the outlet stream, then continue up the Tanana River a few miles to the mouth of the Delta Clearwater.

Highlights: One of the best salmon streams in all of Interior Alaska. Excellent fishing for silver salmon (from late September through mid-October); good fishing for grayling (from July through September).

Species: Chum salmon, grayling, northern pike, silver salmon.

Regulations: For restrictions on salmon, consult the current Alaska Department of Fish and Game regulations or the ADF&G Delta Junction office, (907) 895-4632.

Facilities: A campground, a boat launch and lodging are available in the Clearwater Ranch area.

Contact: For camping and lodging information, contact the Public Land Information Center, 250 Cushman Street, Suite 1A, Fairbanks, AK 99701, (907) 451-7352; or the Delta Junction Visitor Information Center, P.O. Box 987, Delta Junction, AK 99737, (907) 895-9941 or (907) 895-5068.

Description: The Delta Clearwater has its origins on the slopes of Granite Mountain as well as from upwellings and seepages in the Tanana Valley just east of the Gerstle River. Its crystal-clear waters are lined with dense vegetation as the stream meanders west to join the glacial Tanana River. With constant flow from its spring sources and abundant spawning habitat, it supports the Interior's largest runs of silver salmon, with outstanding sportfishing possible.

The mainstem Delta Clearwater River is known to have as many as 20,000 coho or more invade its waters in some years. Nearly all the fishing is catch-and-release, as the salmon are generally too far advanced in prespawning to eat. Still, the fishery is extremely popular with boat and shore anglers seeking a taste of some of the finest salmon action available in the Interior.

Usually beginning in early September, the run here is extended, lasting through the fall until the snow flies in November. Although fish are present in great numbers throughout the river, the lower section and confluence area is recommended for catching brighter, scrappier coho.

Another popular sport species you'll find here is the arctic grayling. These plucky, lightweight fighters are present in force from early summer through fall and will attack a variety of dry and wet flies and small spinners. Anglers targeting grayling usually do best in the upper sections of the Delta Clearwater around the forks where tributary streams join, but fishing can be productive in all parts of the river during certain times of the year, like the fall out-migration. Around the confluence with the Tanana, you can expect some northern pike encounters during the summer months and fair numbers of late-running chum salmon in September and October.

Even with temperatures down to minus 40-degrees Fahrenheit, the Delta Clearwater remains partially ice-free, though few anglers have the moxie to challenge the conditions beyond the normal season (from June through November).

2. GOODPASTER RIVER SYSTEM

Location: Upper Tanana River drainage, Delta Junction area, 75 miles southeast of Fairbanks, 250 miles northeast of Anchorage.

Reference: Eagle B-6, C-6; Big Delta A-1, A-2, A-3, A-4, B-1, B-2, B-3, C-1, C-2.

Access: By boat, floatplane and snowmachine. The river itself has traditionally been accessed by boat from Big Delta, launching at the Richardson Highway bridge where it crosses the Tanana River and running upstream to the confluence with the Goodpaster. Float planes are limited to Volkmar Lake, a tributary of the Goodpaster, which is a few miles southeast of the main river. In winter, snowmachines access Volkmar Lake by running up the frozen Tanana River, crossing over a wooded area to the lake.

Highlights: A traditional local hot spot with excellent fishing for northern pike (from June through September) and grayling (from May through September).

Species: Grayling, (king salmon), northern pike.

Regulations: Closed to salmon fishing; pike season runs from June 1 through March 31. For additional restrictions, consult the current Alaska Department of Fish and Game regulations or the ADF&G Fairbanks office, (907) 456-4359.

Facilities: No developed public facilities.

Contact: For fishing information, contact the Alaska Department of Fish and Game, Sportfish Division, 1300 College Road, Fairbanks, AK 99701; (907) 456-8819. For an air taxi, contact Wright Air Service, P.O. Box 60142, Fairbanks, AK 99706, (907) 474-0502.

Description: Originating from Shawnee Peak and the Black Mountain area just north of Tanana Valley State Forest, the clear-flowing Goodpaster meanders through mountainous terrain and flatlands before reaching the glacial Tanana River. The drainage has a long history as one of the better sportfishing waters of the upper Tanana, with a fair amount of angling for pike and grayling from late spring into fall.

The lower river, around Goodpaster Flats, has plenty of slow-moving water with oxbow lakes and sloughs, creating a perfect habitat for large, hungry northerns. These toothy, aggressive fighters are abundant from the mouth upstream into the foothills beyond South Fork. In addition, Volkmar Lake, which connects to the river via a very small creek, also offers some consistent pike action, with the best occurring in early summer and fall. Generally not very large (ranging from 3 to 10 pounds), there are a few oldsters there that may weigh as much as 25 pounds or even more.

The Goodpaster is also known for its superb flyfishing for fat arctic grayling. These fine light-tackle scrappers are available throughout the system, from the mouth upstream to the headwaters, and are at their best from early summer into fall.

For a remote river experience within a reasonable distance from the road but far enough to escape the crowds, the Goodpaster River is highly recommended.

3. TANGLE LAKES SYSTEM

Location: Upper Tanana River drainage, 125 miles southeast of Fairbanks, 195 miles northeast of Anchorage.

Reference: Gulkana D-5; Mount Hayes A-4, A-5.

Access: By car from Anchorage or Fairbanks. The Denali Highway provides easy access to the entire lake system. Canoes or kayaks can be launched from areas near the road crossing and Tangle River to reach the most remote parts of the drainage. Some lakes annexed by the system, such as Landmark Gap and Glacier Lakes, are accessed by trails from the Denali Highway.

Highlights: Outstanding angling opportunities for lake trout and Interior's best road fishing for grayling (from June through September), in an area of undisturbed scenic beauty.

Species: Grayling, lake trout.

Regulations: Open year-round, all species.

Facilities: Lodging, campgrounds and canoe rentals are available.

Contact: For fishing information, contact the Alaska Department of Fish and Game, Sportfish Division, P.O. Box 605, Delta Junction, AK 99737; (907) 895-4632. For camping information, contact the Public Land Information Center, 250 Cushman Street, Suite 1A, Fairbanks, AK 99701, (907) 451-7352; or Paxson Lodge, P.O. Box 3001, Paxson, AK 99737, (907) 822-3330.

Description: Situated in the Ampitheater Mountains on the south slope of the Alaska Range, near milepost 22.5 of the Denali Highway, the Tangle Lakes system consists of eight lakes and interconnecting streams that head the Delta River. The surrounding landscape is breathtaking—rugged peaks to 6,000 feet and abundant wildlife (including grizzly bear) are present throughout this nationally designated Wild and Scenic River system. Even more appealing is the fact that this watershed has the very best road-accessible grayling fishing in Interior Alaska, if not the entire state.

The system includes all waters upstream of the "Falls" on the upper Delta River. Generally crystal-clear, this extensive drainage has major fish-producing lakes and streams that receive little angling pressure, except for those parts near the highway.

Starting in early summer and continuing through most of the fall, anglers have outstanding success fishing abundant sailfins with dry and wet flies and small spinners. They average 8 to 15 inches, with occasional lunkers approaching the magic 20-inch mark. Though the action can be very good in lakes and streams near the Denali Highway, the best of it certainly is found in locations only reached by trail or canoe. Inlet and outlet streams in the lakes and the shallow runs of the connecting streams and rivers are the hot spots to look for. The Delta River, from the outlet down to Eureka Creek, has excellent fishing and makes a great float trip from the lakes down to a take-out point adjacent to the Richardson Highway at milepost 212. (There are a series of falls and rapids two miles below the lake, however.)

Lake trout are fairly abundant in the deep-water lakes of the system and are best sought during late spring through early summer and in fall. Most of the fish taken are not very large as lakers go (averaging three to four pounds), but occasionally some reach trophy size (20 pounds). Landlocked Tangle, about four miles south of the highway, is probably the best to try. An inflatable craft of some kind is recommended for fishing the big ones.

The following are some of the better areas within the Tangle Lakes system for grayling, as well as lake trout where noted: Upper Tangle, Middle Tangle, Round Tangle (also lake trout), Landlocked Tangle (also lake trout), Long Tangle (also lake trout), Landmark Gap (also lake trout) and Glacier Lakes (also lake trout); Rock Creek, Upper Delta, Upper Tangle and Tangle rivers.

4. SALCHA RIVER

Location: Middle Tanana River drainage, 40 miles southeast of Fairbanks, 250 miles northeast of Anchorage.

Reference: Circle A-1, A-2; Big Delta B-5, B-6, C-2, C-3, C-4, C-5, C-6.

Access: By car from Fairbanks. The Richardson Highway crosses the lower river. To reach the mouth of the Salcha and its confluence with the Tanana River, a well-developed trail is present beginning at Munson Slough heading west a half mile to the area. Boats are frequently launched from the highway bridge to access upper sections of the river or the mouth.

Highlights: A unique, road-accessible catch-and-release fishery for king salmon (in mid-July); also good grayling fishing (from June through September).

Species: Chum salmon, grayling, king salmon, northern pike, silver salmon.

Regulations: Unbaited, artificial lures only, with hooks with 3/4-inch gap or less; salmon fishing is prohibited upstream of marker 2.5 miles above the Richardson Highway bridge. For additional restrictions, consult the current Alaska Department of Fish and Game regulations or the ADF&G Fairbanks office, (907) 456-4359.

Facilities: A boat launch and a campground are available near the highway crossing.

Contact: For camping information, contact the Public Land Information Center, 250 Cushman Street, Suite 1A, Fairbanks, AK 99701; (907) 451-7352.

Description: The Salcha River is one of the larger clearwater drainages of the Tanana accessible from the road system. It is wide and very deep in places, with a slow, steady current. Originating from the mountains near Fort Wainwright Military Reservation, the Salcha meanders west about 120 miles to join the glacial Tanana River near Aurora Lodge on the Richardson Highway. It is a very popular river for recreation among Interior residents and receives a good amount of angling pressure during the midsummer salmon runs.

The Salcha River has one of the largest runs of king salmon in the Tanana Valley and offers good opportunities for catch-and-release fishing for chinook averaging 20 to 25 pounds, with lunkers to 45 pounds possible. The mouth of the river has the best fishing, with heavy concentrations of kings staging in the area in July, but deep holes and runs upstream may also yield good results. Fair numbers of summer-run chums are present in July as well, and come fall, some acrobatic coho show up. The silvers are destined for the Delta Clearwater River further up the Tanana and are intercepted at the mouth of the Salcha in September and October, along with a few fall-run chums.

Although retention of salmon is legal, it is not recommended since the majority of fish will be very close to spawning and certainly not prime table fare. Occasionally, however, a few semi-bright fish are taken in the early part of the run.

Arctic grayling are also available throughout summer and fall, with the best action on the middle and upper river, which can be accessed by boat only. Flies are the favored lure, but spinners work well here, too. Northern pike are not abundant, but a few are landed now and then in sloughs or quiet stretches of the lower and middle river or at the mouth.

For anyone planning to cruise the road system of Interior Alaska during the middle of summer, the Salcha River is worth checking out for its opportunities for salmon and other sportfish species.

5. CHENA RIVER SYSTEM

Location: Middle Tanana River drainage, Fairbanks area, 265 miles north of Anchorage.

Reference: Circle A-1, A-2, A-3, A-4, A-5, A-6; Livengood A-1; Big Delta C-4, C-5, C-6, D-4, D-5, D-6; Fairbanks D-1, D-2.

Access: By car from a series of city roads within Fairbanks (please see a detailed city map). Upper areas are easily reached via Chena Hot Springs Road from the Steese Expressway.

Highlights: Easy access and great variety make up one of Interior's most popular fishing locations. Good fishing for king (in late July) and landlocked silver salmon (from November through April), rainbow trout (in June and from September through October), arctic charr (from August through October) and grayling (from June through September).

Species: Arctic charr, chum salmon, grayling, king salmon, northern pike, rainbow trout, sheefish, silver salmon.

Regulations: Closed to salmon upstream of the dam; other restrictions apply. For details, consult the current Alaska Department of Fish and Game regulations or the ADF&G Fairbanks office, (907) 456-4359.

Facilities: Hotel, commercial lodging, boat launching, sporting goods, groceries, water, gas and fuel and guide services are available in Fairbanks.

Contact: For fishing information, contact the Alaska Department of Fish and Game, Sportfish Division, 1300 College Road, Fairbanks, AK 99701; (907) 456-8819. For hotel and lodging information, contact Fairbanks Convention and Visitor's Bureau, 550 First Avenue, Fairbanks, AK 99701; (907) 456-5774 or (800) 327-5774.

Description: The Chena River originates from the mountains south of the Steese National Conservation Area. A multitude of small tributaries enter the river along its course with at least one sizeable lake annexed to the drainage. While the upper sections are fairly narrow and fast-flowing, the lower Chena is wide and smooth with little current. Because of its proximity to Fairbanks, local angling interest is high, with a great deal of other recreational opportunities available.

Once a most productive arctic grayling fishery, the Chena River today is only beginning to recover from depressed populations caused by overharvesting. After a brief period of total closure, the fishing is rebounding with catch rates increasing substantially the last few seasons. The upper river sections are delightful to fish as they have classic stream conditions—deep holes, pools, cutbanks and shallow riffles and runs, perfect for enticing grayling with flies and small spinners. Badger Slough on the lower river also yields fish.

The lower Chena is a productive location for salmon, with sporadic catches of sheefish and northern pike also reported. Summer runs of king and chum are present, with good catch-and-release fishing for kings possible in various holding areas throughout the lower river (such as below the Flood Control Dam). A few tarpon of the north sheefish are caught occasionally during the summer months when they come in to feed. Pike, however, are slightly more common and there are fair chances of hooking one in sloughs and side channels (Badger Slough among others).

Chena Lake, located on Eielson Air Force Base and connected to the system via a small creek, is stocked with species that are not native to the area, such as landlocked silver salmon, rainbow trout and arctic charr. It is a very popular and well-known Interior fishing location that provides locals with fair to good action 12 months a year.

If a visit to Fairbanks is on the itinerary, plan a few hours of pleasant diversion checking out the Chena. Though the lower river is quite urban, the upper sections along Chena Hot Springs Road will surprise you with their solitude.

6. CHATANIKA RIVER SYSTEM

Location: Lower Tanana River drainage, 20 miles northwest of Fairbanks, 265 miles north of Anchorage.

Reference: Circle A-6, B-4, B-5, B-6; Livengood A-1, A-2, A-3, A-4, A-5, B-2, B-3; Fairbanks D-2, D-3, D-4.

Access: By car from Fairbanks. The Elliott Highway crosses the middle section of the river, while the Steese Highway crosses and parallels the upper sections with trails or side roads providing additional access. Small rafts or inflatables may be floated between the road access points. Canoes can be used on calmer sections of the middle and lower river.

Highlights: One of Interior's most popular rivers, offering good fishing for northern pike (from June through September), king salmon (in late July) and grayling (from June through September).

Species: Chum salmon, grayling, king salmon, northern pike, sheefish, (silver salmon).

Regulations: Closed above the Elliot Highway bridge for king salmon fishing; other restrictions apply. For details, consult the current Alaska Department of Fish and Game regulations or the ADF&G Fairbanks office, (907) 456-4359.

Facilities: Campgrounds and boat launches are available at road crossings.

Contact: For camping information, contact the Public Land Information Center, 250 Cushman Street, Suite 1A, Fairbanks, AK 99701; (907) 451-7352. For an air taxi, contact Wright Air Service, P.O. Box 60142, Fairbanks, AK 99706, (907) 474-0502.

Description: The clear Chatanika River flows through a very scenic valley—surrounded by the Tanana Hills to the south and the White Mountains to the north and west—joining the Tolovana River near Minto Flats State Game Refuge. The lower river meanders considerably, with deep holes and quiet sloughs, while the upper Chatanika is shallower and faster, with many riffles and runs. Situated so close to Fairbanks, the river serves as a recreational hub for many outdoor activities, including some varied and abundant fishing.

Starting in late spring or early summer, a number of fine sportfish can be taken on the Chatanika. Arctic grayling invade the river, bound for summer feeding areas near headwaters, and voracious northern pike settle into slower sections on the middle and lower drainage. Later on, summer runs of king and chum salmon arrive and draw a fair amount of angling interest around the road crossings. (By the time they have gotten this far, they are usually well advanced into prespawning, so catch-and-release fishing is the general rule.) Towards fall, anglers can intercept migrating grayling and even some small spawning runs of sheefish (from September through October).

Major tributaries of the Chatanika, like the Tatalina, Washington and Goldstream creeks, are all good for grayling during the summer months, while pike fishing is usually hot in the deeper holes and pools around confluence areas. Lower Goldstream Creek and Minto Lakes have both been long known as top pike locations in the Interior, with trophy specimens up to 20 pounds or more present. Other areas to try for big pike are the mainstem Chatanika and the sloughs and holes of the nearby Tolovana River.

The middle and upper portions of the Chatanika River also offer some unique opportunities for spearing whitefish in the fall, as large schools of these fish move through the shallows in September and October during spawning migrations. "Fishing" is usually done at night using lanterns, and some folks even take whitefish with bow and arrow. Despite fairly high use over the years, the Chatanika River still holds up as a very productive drainage, with a variety of good fishing opportunities. It's well worth the time if you're planning a trip to the Fairbanks area.

7. NENANA RIVER SYSTEM

Location: Middle Tanana River drainage, 50 miles southwest of Fairbanks, 160 miles north of Anchorage.

Reference: Healy A-2, A-3, A-4, B-2, B-3, B-4, B-5, B-6, C-2, C-3, C-4, C-5, C-6, D-3, D-4, D-5, D-6; Fairbanks A-4, A-5, A-6, B-4, B-5, B-6, C-5.

Access: By car from Fairbanks or Anchorage. The George Parks Highway crosses the river and some of its tributaries on several occasions and parallels the system for many miles. To reach the better fishing, however, a boat is necessary. The Denali Highway from Cantwell provides access to the upper drainage streams.

Highlights: A road-accessible Interior fishery with good fishing opportunities for silver salmon (in late September), grayling (from June through August); also king salmon (in late July), chum salmon (from mid-July through mid-September) and lake trout (from June through September).

Species: Chum salmon, Dolly Varden, grayling, king salmon, lake trout, (northern pike, sheefish), silver salmon.

Regulations: Open year-round, all species.

Facilities: Campgrounds are available in several places along the highway. A boat launch is available in Nenana. Lodging and limited services and supplies are available in Nenana and McKinley Village.

Contact: For fishing information, contact the Alaska Department of Fish and Game, Sportfish Division, P.O. Box 605, Delta Junction, AK 99737; (907) 895-4632. For guide services, contact Arctic Grayling Adventures, P.O. Box 83707, Fairbanks, AK 99708; (907) 479-0479. For camping and lodging information, contact the Public Land Information Center, 250 Cushman Street, Suite 1A, Fairbanks, AK 99701, (907) 451-7352; or Fairbanks Convention and Visitor's Bureau, 550 First Avenue, Fairbanks, AK 99701, (907) 456-5774 or (800) 327-5774.

Description: The silty Nenana River originates from Nenana Glacier high in the Alaska Range east of Denali and flows north to its confluence with the larger Tanana River near the town of Nenana. It is a fairly large system encompassing small lakes, numerous clearwater streams and even glacial rivers like the Teklanika of Denali National Park. The roadside fishing spots can produce action that ranges from poor to very good, but some of the best fishing takes some legwork or a boat ride to reach.

Arctic grayling are the most abundant sport species in the Nenana. They are available anytime between March and October, but are at a peak during the warmer months. Nearly all the clear tributary streams, from the headwaters above Cantwell down, offer some measure of fishing for them, but the more accessible locations have been worked over, with predictable effects on size and abundance. Some of the more out-of-the-way locations to try for bigger and better grayling are: streams along the Denali Highway (Upper Jack River, Monahan and Brushkana creeks); streams off the Stampede Trail north of Healy (Fish Creek, Eightmile Lake, Upper Savage and Teklanika rivers); clear tributaries of the Yanert (Moose and Revine creeks); eastside tributary streams (Moose and Walker creeks); and the less-accessible sections of streams along the highway (Panguingue, Clear and Julius creeks). Spring and fall are the best times to fish, but the mainstem has some exciting fishing as well in late winter, when the water clears. Open leads by the mouths of tributary streams and beaver ponds are good places to try with flies and small spinners, and you might even run into a few small Dolly Varden. (Some of the more remote clearwater creeks are also good places to encounter this increasingly rare Nenana species.) Use extreme caution on the river ice, however.

Broad Pass Lakes along the Parks Highway have populations of lake trout as well as grayling. Summit and Edes lakes produced fish in the 10- to 15-pound range during their heyday, but now only a few small lakers are all one can expect. Small lake trout are rumored to be in Slate Lake and other small lakes at the head of tributary streams.

In midsummer, small runs of king and chum salmon make their way up the Nenana, followed by a much heavier showing of silvers in fall. Since most of these salmon are well into their prespawning changes, catch-and-release fishing is the only way to go. Several streams receive salmon, but the more outstanding ones are Seventeenmile Slough, the lower sections of Julius and Clear creeks, June

Creek and an unnamed creek that used to be an old channel of the Nenana near Anderson. The best times for silvers are August and September.

8. KANTISHNA RIVER SYSTEM

Location: Lower Tanana River drainage, 65 miles southwest of Fairbanks, 165 miles north of Anchorage.

Reference: Mount McKinley A-2, A-3, A-4, A-5, B-1, B-2, B-3, B-4, B-5, C-1, C-2, C-3, C-4, C-5, C-6, D-1, D-2, D-3, D-4, D-5; Healy B-6, C-6, D-6; Fairbanks A-6, B-6, C-6, D-6; Kantishna River A-1, A-2, A-3, A-4, B-1, B-2, B-3, C-1, C-2, D-1.

Access: By small plane from Fairbanks. There are several lakes adjoining the system that are used as landing sites for floatplanes and some skilled pilots may also try oxbow lakes or quiet sloughs and straight stretches of the main river. Wheelplanes have access to a landing strip at Lake Minchumina.

Highlights: A very remote and scenic system with excellent fishing opportunities for northern pike (from June through September) and grayling (from May through September).

Species: Chum salmon, grayling, king salmon, northern pike, (sheefish), silver salmon.

Regulations: Seasonal closures on portions of the drainage for chum salmon. For details and further restrictions, consult the current Alaska Department of Fish and Game regulations or the ADF&G Fairbanks office, (907) 456-4359.

Facilities: Commercial lodging is available at Lake Minchumina.

Contact: For an air taxi, contact Wright Air Service, P.O. Box 60142, Fairbanks, AK 99706; (907) 474-0502. For lodging information, contact Denali West Lodge, P.O. Box 40, Lake Minchumina, AK 99757; (907) 674-3112.

Description: With headwaters in the Alaska Range, the Kantishna River system is extensive and remote, with an amazing number of tributary streams, lakes and sloughs, many of which are within Denali National Park. Some truly great fishing on this system is largely ignored, save for a few main lakes and other locations.

Northern pike and arctic grayling are the two main species of interest around the Kantishna drainage, with some of the finest pike opportunities in the state available here, particularly for trophy specimens. Lakes and sloughs of the Lake Minchumina area are particularly noteworthy, as are drainages further down along the mainstem. Mucha, Wein, West and East Twin lakes are relatively well-known hot spot locations for large northerns up to 30 pounds, with many smaller lakes, such as Alma, John Hansen, Sandless and dozens of others with no names in the Bearpaw River area, offering abundant fishing. (These lakes are great ice fishing spots, too, and can be accessed by snowmachine via a trail from the Parks Highway.)

Arctic grayling are abundant in all clearwater streams, with the more alpine, faster and clear-flowing sections being especially productive. Look for suitable locations near the headwaters of the Kantishna or clear tributaries of the glacial Toklat River.

The Kantishna River system also receives a number of salmon, including king, silver and chum, during the summer and fall months. Although found throughout the drainage, some of the more concentrated areas are the mouths of clearwater streams and creeks that drain into the Toklat River. (A portion of the mainstem Toklat is also home to a major run of fall chum salmon.)

The lower river has two small lakes, Geskakmina and Triangle, that have been stocked with fish. Geskakmina contains landlocked silvers and rainbow trout, while Triangle has some lake trout and grayling.

9. ZITZIANA RIVER SYSTEM

Location: Lower Tanana River drainage, 85 miles west of Fairbanks, 250 miles north of Anchorage.

Reference: Kantishna River B-3, C-2, C-3, D-1, D-2.

Access: By boat from Manley Hot Springs. Visitors can use the launch at the bridge crossing Hot Springs Slough to access the mainstem Tanana River and the mouth of the Zitziana on the south side several miles upstream.

Highlights: A small, remote Interior river receiving little angling attention, but with good potential for sheefish (from June through August), northern pike (from June through September) and grayling (in May and September).

Species: Grayling, northern pike, sheefish.

Regulations: Open year-round, all species.

Facilities: No developed public facilities.

Contact: For fishing information, contact the Alaska Department of Fish and Game, Sportfish Division, 1300 College Road, Fairbanks, AK 99701; (907) 456-8819.

Description: The Zitziana is a small, meandering system that issues from the southwest Kuskokwim Mountains about 75 miles west of Fairbanks. A fair amount of swamp and bog water contribute greatly to its brown, tannic-stained color. Its lower reaches however, are ideal habitat for northern pike. Because of its remoteness, it receives very little angling pressure.

A local favorite among residents of Manley Hot Springs, the "Zit" has a history of producing good angling for at least three important sportfish species. Northern pike, the obvious favorite, are taken at the Tanana confluence and upstream for several miles. Typically weighing six to eight pounds, they are aggressive and plentiful, and best fished during summer and early fall. Sheefish are also present on the lower Zitziana and yield good catches where the off-colored water of the drainage mixes with silty Tanana River. Generally not very large (four to six pounds average, up to about 12 pounds) the Zitziana shees are quite numerous. Arctic grayling are also encountered in spring and fall during the annual migrations to and from summer feeding grounds in the headwaters.

The surrounding country is totally wild, enhancing the experience for anyone wanting to partake of some serious pike fishing, with additional opportunities for sheefish and grayling.

10. COSNA RIVER SYSTEM

Location: Lower Tanana River drainage, 110 miles west of Fairbanks, 250 miles north of Anchorage.

Reference: Kantishna B-4, B-5, C-4, C-5, D-3, D-4.

Access: By floatplane from Fairbanks or boat from Manley Hot Springs. Boaters can launch from Hot Springs Slough and access the mouth of the Cosna via the Tanana River. Experienced floatplane pilots can attempt to land on the mainstem Tanana near the confluence.

Highlights: A remote Interior river with great angling potential for northern pike (from June through September).

Species: Grayling, northern pike, sheefish.

Regulations: Open year-round, all species.

Facilities: No developed public facilities.

Contact: For fishing information, contact the Alaska Department of Fish and Game, Sportfish Division, 1300 College Road, Fairbanks, AK 99701; (907) 456-8819. For an air taxi, contact Wright Air Service, P.O. Box 60142, Fairbanks, AK 99706; (907) 474-0502.

Description: Like the Zitziana River to the east, the Cosna originates from a highland region of the Kuskokwim Mountains in central Alaska. Meandering considerably during its northward course to a confluence with the glacial Tanana, The Cosna is a true wilderness drainage, with a reputation for good northern pike fishing.

Receiving very little angling effort, mostly at the mouth where its slightly tannic waters hit the silty Tanana, the Cosna drainage has miles of highly productive water, as it is an active feeding ground for hungry northerns and even a few sheefish. The summer and early fall months are without a doubt the best times to hit its waters. Try the slow, deep stretches where pike between 4 and 10 pounds (even larger) have a habit of lurking for prey. Sheefish are less common and, for the most part, are only caught incidentally. Fair numbers of arctic grayling are also available in spring and fall.

11. CHITANANA RIVER SYSTEM

Location: Lower Tanana River drainage, 115 miles west of Fairbanks, 265 miles north of Anchorage.

Reference: Kantishna River C-5, C-6, D-4, D-5.

Access: By plane from Fairbanks. Experienced floatplane pilots may land near the mouth of Chitanana on the mainstem Tanana. Wheelplanes can land on the large gravel bar southeast of the confluence.

Highlights: A very remote, little-fished drainage with outstanding potential for northern pike (from June through September).

Species: Grayling, northern pike, sheefish.

Regulations: Open year-round, all species.

Facilities: No developed public facilities.

Contact: For fishing information, contact the Alaska Department of Fish and Game, Sportfish Division, 1300 College Road, Fairbanks, AK 99701; (907) 456-8819. For an air taxi, contact Wright Air Service, P.O. Box 60142, Fairbanks, AK 99706; (907) 474-0502.

Description: Also known as Redlands Creek, the Chitanana River originates from the northwest slopes of Chitanatala Mountains west of the Kantishna drainage, where it flows north and east towards the glacial Tanana. Not a particularly broad river, it is nonetheless quite vast with considerable meandering, slow-moving water—perfect conditions for large numbers of toothy pike. Rarely fished, the Chitanana seldom disappoints the few anglers who make the effort to try its waters during the peak of pike season.

This tannic-stained river with its classic northern pike water has an abundance of fish in the 4- to 10-pound range, and ample numbers much larger. (This area of the Tanana is known for its monster pike up to 30 pounds and more.) Casting flashy spoons for these greedy fish devourers can result in an occasional sheefish as well, especially when fishing near the confluence where the clear waters of the Chitanana mix with the silty Tanana. You can also expect fair numbers of arctic grayling during the spring and fall months.

Along with the Cosna River, the Chitanana has yet to be "discovered" and can still offer some fabulous fishing before the masses work it over.

12. FISH CREEK SYSTEM

Location: Lower Tanana River drainage, 115 miles northwest of Fairbanks, 275 miles northwest of Anchorage.

Reference: Tanana A-3, A-4.

Access: By plane from Fairbanks. Experienced floatplane pilots can land on the mainstem Tanana near the mouth of Fish Creek. Wheelplanes can use Fish Creek Island as a landing site, then anglers can canoe over to the fishing area.

Highlights: A small but famous stream known for its healthy pike population, with outstanding fishing possible (from June through September).

Species: (Grayling), northern pike.

Regulations: Open year-round, all species.

Facilities: No developed public facilities.

Contact: For fishing information, contact the Alaska Department of Fish and Game, Sportfish Division, 1300 College Road, Fairbanks, AK 99701; (907) 456-8819. For an air taxi, contact Tundra Air, P.O. Box 87, Manley Hot Springs, AK 99756, (907) 672-3692; or Wright Air Service, P.O. Box 60142, Fairbanks, AK 99706, (907) 474-0502.

Description: Fish Creek is a small, meandering stream draining out of Fish Lake, a fair-sized body of water about 20 miles southeast of the town of Tanana. Known for its high productivity, Fish Creek receives a fair amount of angling pressure for northern pike, with a reputation for trophy specimens. The old state record fish of 38 pounds was taken from the mouth back in 1978. Fishing in this drainage continues true to its reputation, with many fine pike still reported.

Considerably smaller in size and length than many other rivers along the Tanana, Fish Creek manages to hold its own because it has all the necessary ingredients for a healthy population of large northerns—plenty of sloughs, braided channels, ponds and still backwaters, and abundant forage in the form of whitefish and suckers. The water is tannic-stained from heavy bog and tundra infiltration. Most anglers concentrate their attention on the lower stream area and do very well there all through summer into fall, for pike in the 4- to 10-pound class, with occasional catches up to 20 pounds or more. Spoons, top water plugs and big, bushy flies are the ticket, according to locals, who insist the new state record is lurking somewhere within the area's deep, dark waters.

Immense, meandering rivers and countless sloughs and lakes in Alaska's vast Interior make ideal habitat for northern pike, sheefish and other slow-water species.

REGION 2
MIDDLE YUKON RIVER

With its many sprawling tributaries and extensive, lake-dotted lowlands, the winding, wide Middle Yukon dominates the Interior region and provides major habitat for a variety of important sport species, including chum and king salmon, northern pike, sheefish and grayling.

Silty in its mainstem all the way up to the headwaters, the river's sportfish potential is concentrated in clearer tributary lakes, sloughs and streams, with some well known for outstanding fishing—the Nowitna Flats, Tozitna, Ray, Dall, Hodzana and Melozitna rivers and others. Access is usually by riverboat from Fairbanks or major communities along the Yukon (Galena, Ruby, Tanana and Manley).

The Yukon Flats, a vast wetland between Circle and Stevens Village, below the confluence of the Porcupine, is particularly noteworthy for its tens of thousands of lakes, marshy backwaters and slow-moving streams—a paradise for big toothy pike and sheefish, as all reports seem to verify. Though this area, like the others, lies well off the beaten path, its potential shouldn't be overlooked. Access is by boat or small plane from Fort Yukon or Circle. Some of the better fishing locations within the Yukon Flats are the lower Hadweenzic, Christian, Chandalar, Sheenjek, Porcupine and Black rivers.

13. MELOZITNA RIVER SYSTEM

Location: Central Yukon River drainage, 230 miles west of Fairbanks, 305 miles northwest of Anchorage.

Reference: Melozitna A-4, A-5, B-4, C-1, C-2, C-3; Ruby D-5, D-6.

Access: By boat from Ruby to the mouth of the Melozitna and the lower river. Floatplanes arriving from Galena or Fairbanks can land on the mainstem Yukon River near the confluence or on the middle river in straight sections of water. It is possible to raft/kayak from the middle of the river downstream to the mouth with three sets of rapids in Melozitna Canyon.

Highlights: A vast, remote drainage with good fishing potential for northern pike and grayling (from June through September).

Species: Arctic charr, chum salmon, grayling, (king salmon), northern pike, sheefish.

Regulations: Open year-round, all species.
Facilities: No developed public facilities.
Contact: For fishing information, contact the Alaska Department of Fish and Game, Sportfish Division, 1300 College Road, Fairbanks, AK 99701; (907) 456-8819. For an air taxi, contact Wright Air Service, P.O. Box 60142, Fairbanks, AK 99706; (907) 474-0502.
Description: The Melozitna originates in the Slokhenjikh Hills of the Ray Mountains in central Alaska and flows southwest to join the Yukon River near Ruby. It is a slow-moving river in the upper reaches, draining a significant area with many small ponds and muskeg swamps which greatly influence the color of the water. The river picks up speed as it moves through Melozitna Canyon (Class II and Class III) until the last few miles, where it slows down just prior to reaching the Yukon. Fairly remote but productive, the Melozitna offers good angling opportunities throughout for several popular sportfish species.

Northern pike are abundant in the middle section of the Melozitna as this area is ideal habitat–slow, deep water with numerous sloughs. While the action can be fast and furious for anglers in spots, the fish are seldom very large. (A typical Melozitna pike weighs 4 to 10 pounds, but larger specimens are frequently taken.) The lower river section is generally too swift for pike, though a few fish may be taken at the confluence.

During the summer months, anglers whipping flies and tossing small spinners may connect with feisty arctic grayling up to 18 inches or more in any of the many clear tributaries from the headwaters to the mouth. Selecting swift, clear streams to feed in through the warmer months, the grayling move back into the mainstem in fall when temperatures cool. Hot Springs Creek is one popular hot spot for great flyfishing for this species.

Salmon are also present in the Melozitna. Chums are the most abundant, but a few kings may be encountered spawning in some of the tributaries. In July, large numbers of summer-run chum ascend the river destined for suitable clearwater spawning areas, yet they do not support any extensive fishery and are only caught incidentally.

In midsummer, it is possible to hook sheefish in the 4- to 12-pound range at the mouth, with fair action to be expected. These fish will be feeding and are intercepted here on their way upstream to fall spawning grounds. Charr are also taken now and then from the mainstem river and a few tributaries.

The Melozitna River does not receive a great amount of angling effort and is mostly fished by folks from nearby Ruby and Galena, and occasionally Fairbanks. Given the size and productivity of the system, however, there is still much to be discovered by anglers. Any likely parties looking to explore a little-known river with great fishing possibilities—this is it.

14. NOWITNA RIVER SYSTEM

Location: Central Yukon River drainage, 190 miles west of Fairbanks, 250 miles northwest of Anchorage.

Reference: Ruby A-1, A-2, A-3, A-4, B-1, B-2, B-3, C-2, C-3, C-4, D-3; Kantishna River A-6, B-6; Medfra B-6, C-4, C-5, C-6, D-4, D-5.

Access: By boat from the nearby town of Ruby to the mouth; by plane from Fairbanks or Galena, landing on the mainstem Nowitna, sloughs, lakes or the larger Yukon River. Rafting parties can put in near the headwaters and float to the mouth.

Highlights: A huge, remote clearwater Interior drainage with excellent fishing potential for northern pike (from June through September); also good fishing possibilities for sheefish (from June through October) and grayling (from June through September).

Species: Chum salmon, grayling, northern pike, sheefish, (silver salmon).

Regulations: Open year-round, all species.

Facilities: No developed public facilities.

Contact: For fishing information, contact the Alaska Department of Fish and Game, Sportfish Division, 1300 College Road, Fairbanks, AK 99701; (907) 456-8819. For an air taxi, contact Wright Air Service, P.O. Box 60142, Fairbanks, AK 99706; (907) 474-0502. For more information, contact the Nowitna National Wildlife Refuge, P.O. Box 287, Galena, AK 99741; (907) 656-1231.

Description: Nowitna, designated a Wild and Scenic River, originates from the northwest slopes of the Kuskokwim Mountains and flows 283 miles to its confluence with the Yukon. The entire drainage covers over 7,000 square miles and is one of the larger, more productive clearwater systems in the Interior. There are over 14,000 lakes and ponds within the Nowitna National Wildlife Refuge, a vast area that encompasses the lower and middle portions of Nowitna River, along with surrounding wetlands. This makes some remarkable sportfishing possible for slow-water species like pike and sheefish, which, up to now, have received very little attention from anglers.

Over the past few years, more and more interest has been directed toward the Nowitna's abundant and potentially large northern pike.

These greedy water wolves are found throughout much of the river and reach weights of up to 32 pounds (sometimes larger), with specimens larger than 20 pounds not uncommon. Due to prime habitat, particularly on the middle and lower mainstem and adjoining lakes, the fish are year-round residents, with phenomenal catch rates reported among anglers fishing there during the summer months. The lower portions of major tributaries also yield good numbers of pike, including the Sulatna, Little Mud, Lost and Big Mud rivers and Grand Creek.

Resident sheefish are found throughout most of the system with the greatest concentrations occurring in the middle and lower mainstem Nowitna, sloughs and lower portions of major tributaries. Lakes in this area only contain small numbers of sheefish. Good action can be expected along the Nowitna River in summer and fall, and Sulatna River in September and October for large spawners typically weighing between 6 and 15 pounds. Arctic grayling are also found in fishable numbers in the mainstem during spring and fall, while fairly swift, headwater tributaries are generally better in summer.

Other species like salmon and charr are available, but in lesser numbers. Both "summer" and "fall" runs of chum salmon ascend Nowitna, spawning in various locations throughout the drainage. Silver salmon have also been reported but are far less numerous, while a small population of stunted, resident Dolly Varden are present in a few tributaries, such as California Creek and the Sulukna River.

The Nowitna is becoming increasingly popular for floating, which is a great way for anglers to discover the superb fishing and wildlife on one of the more remote rivers of Alaska's great Interior. Put-in is via small plane at Meadow Creek confluence, with take-out at the Yukon River, after about 250 miles of mostly Class I water.

15. TOZITNA RIVER

Location: Central Yukon River drainage, 140 miles west of Fairbanks, 290 miles north of Anchorage.

Reference: Tanana A-5, A-6, B-5, B-6, C-2, C-3, C-4, C-5, C-6, D-5.

Access: By boat and floatplane. From the community of Tanana, boaters can access the river mouth and upstream stretches for many miles. Visitors arriving by floatplane from Fairbanks, Galena or other population centers usually land on the mainstem Yukon River near the confluence with the Tozitna River.

Highlights: A largely remote and unexplored river system providing good fishing for sheefish (from June through August) and northern pike (from June through September).

Species: (Chum salmon), grayling, (king salmon), northern pike, sheefish.

Regulations: Open year-round, all species.

Facilities: No developed public facilities.

Contact: For fishing information, contact the Alaska Department of Fish and Game, Sportfish Division, 1300 College Road, Fairbanks, AK 99701; (907) 456-8819. For an air taxi, contact Wright Air Service, P.O. Box 60142, Fairbanks, AK 99706; (907) 474-0502.

Description: Draining the south slopes of Ray Mountains, the tannic-stained Tozitna meanders southward to Yukon River. Not quite equivalent in size to the nearby Melozitna and Nowitna rivers, it is nonetheless a significant system consisting of numerous small lakes, ponds and clearwater streams offering good sportfishing opportunities for anyone willing to take the time to explore this remote drainage.

Except for some of the creeks at the headwaters, the mainstem Tozitna is slow-flowing with many sloughs and oxbow lakes, particularly on the lower section near the mouth. The little angling pressure that does take place here occurs where the Tozitna empties into the silty waters of the Yukon. Fishing is good overall with sheefish and northern pike being the more sought-after gamefish species. During the summer months, look for feeding sheefish to be found right in the mouth where the two drainages mix. Flashy spoons tossed into the glacial Yukon and retrieved into the clear Tozitna often produce vicious strikes. Northern pike are spread throughout the lower and middle river. The best action occurs in areas with characteristic pike habitat, such as sloughs, oxbow lakes and outlets of tributaries, including the mouth of the Tozitna. There is plenty of prey in the river as evidenced by the huge numbers of whitefish in the system. Arctic grayling are sometimes taken in spring and fall during their migrations between the summer feeding grounds at the headwaters and the overwintering areas in the Yukon River.

Salmon are present in midsummer and may be caught accidently when fishing for other species. Kings and chums both spawn in the river, but are usually quite dark when entering the fishery. However, an occasional semi-bright specimen may be hooked at the mouth of the Tozitna.

Generally only subsistence fished by residents of Tanana, a small community located near the confluence of the Yukon and Tanana rivers a few miles upstream from Tozitna, there is some sport angling taking place during the summer months. It is worth a visit whenever in the area.

16. RAY RIVER

Location: Central Yukon River drainage, 90 miles northwest of Fairbanks, 335 miles north of Anchorage.

Reference: Livengood D-6; Tanana C-2, D-1, D-2; Bettles A-1.

Access: By boat from the Dalton Highway bridge where it crosses Yukon River. It is a short ride, about 3.5 miles, to the mouth of the river. Another option is to use a floatplane from Fairbanks, landing on the mainstem Yukon near the confluence.

Highlights: One of the more popular locations among boaters due to easy access and good fishing for northern pike (from June through September).

Species: Grayling, northern pike, sheefish.

Regulations: Open year-round, all species.

Facilities: There are no developed public facilities at the river, but there is a boat launch located at the Dalton Highway bridge.

Contact: For fishing information, contact the Alaska Department of Fish and Game, Sportfish Division, 1300 College Road, Fairbanks, AK 99701; (907) 456-8819. For an air taxi, contact Wright Air Service, P.O. Box 60142, Fairbanks, AK 99706; (907) 474-0502.

Description: Smaller than many other drainages frequented by anglers on the Yukon, the Ray still holds some good angling opportunities. Originating from the north slope of the Ray Mountains, the river meanders southward to silty Yukon. It is fairly wide from the mouth on upstream for perhaps a little less than a mile, but is navigable to boaters for at least six to eight miles up the mainstem. For many years, the Ray River has been a local hot spot and continues to produce great pike fishing even today.

Although a few incidental sheefish may be taken from the mouth of the Ray in summer, the main fishery here is for northern pike. Generally not known to produce very large fish (3 to 10 pounds), the river does hold some good, consistent action for these scrappy fighters, with occasional catches into the teens. The last mile or so of the river is sometimes a hot spot, but pike may be encountered in numbers throughout much of the drainage, except around the headwaters.

Deep, slow holes and pools often yield a few fish as do sloughs and still-water areas. Arctic grayling are present in fair numbers in spring and fall during their annual migrations to and from summer feeding grounds further upstream. They may be effectively taken using flies and small spinners.

For easy access and a pretty descent shot at pike action on a semi-remote river, the Ray River is hard to beat.

17. DALL RIVER SYSTEM

Location: Upper Yukon River drainage, 95 miles northwest of Fairbanks, 340 miles north of Anchorage.

Reference: Beaver A-5, A-6, B-6.

Access: By boat from the Dalton Highway bridge on the Yukon River via a launch by the bridge and a 20-mile ride up the Yukon to the mouth of the Dall River. Floatplanes can land on the mainstem Yukon River near the confluence area.

Highlights: A noted, local fishery with trophy potential for northern pike (from June through September); also good grayling fishing.

Species: Grayling, northern pike, sheefish.

Regulations: Open year-round, all species.

Facilities: No developed public facilities.

Contact: For fishing information, contact the Alaska Department of Fish and Game, Sportfish Division, 1300 College Road, Fairbanks, AK 99701; (907) 456-8819. For an air taxi, contact Wright Air Service, P.O. Box 60142, Fairbanks, AK 99706; (907) 474-0502.

Description: The mainstem Dall originates just south of Dall Mountain near the Arctic Circle, while the West and East forks flow out of the Yukon Flats within the Yukon Flats National Wildlife Refuge. It is a very extensive drainage, comprising numerous clearwater streams, lakes of various proportions, and stillwater sloughs—the ideal habitat for pike, sheefish and other "slow-water" species. The Dall is especially known for its hefty northerns. (A typical fish weighs anywhere between 4 and 12 pounds, with larger pike not uncommon—some old northerns up to 25 and 30 pounds have been taken.)

Most angling activity in this system occurs at or near the confluence of the Dall and Yukon rivers, but fishing is noteworthy in the lower sections of many adjoining streams and lakes, such as the area around East Fork. Although infrequently caught, sheefish there sometimes attack flashy spoons meant for pike. These silvery, aerial fighters are usually hooked where the clear waters of the Dall mix with the silty Yukon. Sometimes arctic grayling are encountered in good numbers on the lower river, especially in spring and fall, with the better action found during the brief summer months near the headwaters in small streams, lakes and ponds. This river is one of the better bets for a do-it-yourself trip as access is fairly easy and the fish abundant and aggressive.

18. BIRCH-BEAVER CREEK SYSTEMS

Location: Upper Yukon River drainage, 50 to 125 miles north of Fairbanks, 300 to 375 miles north of Anchorage.

Reference: Livengood B-1, B-2, C-1, C-2, D-1, D-2; Circle B-1, B-2, B-3, B-4, C-1, C-2, C-3, C-4, C-5, C-6, D-1, D-2, D-3, D-4, D-5, D-6; Fort Yukon A-2, A-3, A-4, A-5, A-6, B-3, B-4, B-5, B-6, C-5; Beaver A-1, A-2, B-1.

Access: By car and floatplane. The upper portions of Birch and Beaver creeks are accessed by the Steese Highway from Fairbanks and often serve as starting points for extensive float trips, while the mouth of these two drainages and surrounding lakes are more commonly reached by floatplane from Fairbanks or other towns and communities in the region.

Highlights: A vast watershed with optimum angling opportunities; good fishing for northern pike and grayling (from June through September).

Species: (Chum salmon), grayling, (king salmon), northern pike, (sheefish).

Regulations: Open year-round, all species.

Facilities: No developed public facilities.

Contact: For fishing information, contact the Alaska Department of Fish and Game, Sportfish Division, 1300 College Road, Fairbanks, AK 99701; (907) 456-8819. For an air taxi, contact Wright Air Service, P.O. Box 60142, Fairbanks, AK 99706; (907) 474-0502.

Description: Birch Creek originates from within the Steese National Conservation Area on the east side of the White Mountains. It predominantly flows through areas with upland plateaus, forested valleys and heavy marshland northward to the Yukon River. Beaver Creek, on the other hand, begins in the midst of the White Mountains National Recreation Area and runs through an area with rolling hills, jagged mountain peaks and, finally, Yukon Flats marshes to the glacial Yukon River. Both systems are designated as Wild and Scenic Rivers and are popular with floaters wanting to experience a remote yet accessible part of Alaska.

Birch and Beaver creeks are connected through a long channel towards the lower end of the drainages, but in reality they are two separate systems. The fishing in both can be outstanding with northern pike and grayling being the dominant species. Pike are most abundant in the lower areas of the systems where ideal habitat can be found, such as sloughs, ponds, oxbow lakes and a lot of deep, slow-flowing water. Although smaller pike may be found up near the headwaters, larger fish are generally found on the lower end. The drainages are not heavily fished due to their remoteness, but anglers who do fish here are able to find trophy northerns that may weigh as much as 20 pounds or more.

Grayling thrive up around the higher elevations near the headwaters where the current is swifter and deep pools and riffles are present. Action can be very good at times using flies and spinners during the summer months. Feeding sheefish are taken incidentally while pike fishing at the mouths of Birch and Beaver creeks and seldom ascend the systems for more than a few miles.

To thoroughly enjoy the very scenic upper sections around White Mountains, prospecting floaters have two options: Beaver Creek or Birch Creek. If taking the Beaver Creek route, put-in is off the Steese Highway on Nome Creek with a 127-mile Class I float down to the confluence with Victoria Creek. Take-out here with a prearranged pickup by plane. For the Birch Creek route, access is also off Steese Highway at the headwaters of the stream. Put in there and float 126 miles to the Steese Highway bridge near the town of Circle. For the most part, Birch Creek has Class I water, except for a few Class III rapids that must be negotiated. Keep in mind that after long dry spell periods the water can be very low, making for difficult floating conditions. Kayaks and canoes are best suited for these trips.

19. CHARLEY RIVER

Location: Upper Yukon River drainage, 125 miles east of Fairbanks, 330 miles northeast of Anchorage.

Reference: Charley River A-4, A-5, B-4; Eagle C-6, D-4, D-5, D-6.

Access: By plane and helicopter from Fairbanks, Tanacross or other towns and communities in the area. Wheelplanes and helicopters can use a primitive landing strip just above Copper Creek, while floatplanes access the river mouth by landing on the Yukon River near the confluence.

Highlights: A National Wild and Scenic River with good to excellent fishing for grayling (from June through September).

Species: (Chum salmon), grayling, (king salmon), northern pike, (sheefish, silver salmon).

Regulations: Open year-round, all species.

Facilities: No developed public facilities.

Contact: For fishing information, contact the Alaska Department of Fish and Game, Sportfish Division, 1300 College Road, Fairbanks, AK 99701; (907) 456-8819. For an air taxi, contact Wright Air Service, P.O. Box 60142, Fairbanks, AK 99706; (907) 474-0502. For more information, contact the Public Lands Information Center, 250 Cushman Street, Suite 1A, Fairbanks, AK 99701; (907) 451-7352.

Description: Originating at the 4,000-foot level of the Mertie Mountains within the Yukon-Charley Rivers National Preserve, this beautiful, meandering river has some great floating possibilities as well as good fishing opportunities.

The lower 16 miles or so of the drainage hold northern pike with the best chances for angling located near the confluence with the Yukon River. Expect fair action using flashy spoons and wobblers in sloughs and deep holes with slow-flowing current. Arctic grayling are considerably more abundant and usually encountered in the more mountainous regions of Charley and in clearwater tributaries near the headwaters. Anglers opting to float the Charley are in for some magnificent scenery, as well as a chance to match wits with both pike and grayling.

If you are spending some time at the mouth of the Charley where it meets the silty Yukon, sheefish are occasionally hooked in June and July and do not be surprised to find a salmon on the end of the line. Small runs of king, silver and chum salmon ascend the Charley River, starting in midsummer and continuing through fall.

Charley River is rated Class II with some stretches of Class III rapids. Usually running low and clear in summer, the river has a habit of rising several feet in mere hours after rainstorms, which may create a hazard for floaters. Put-in is at Copper Creek with take-out at the river mouth–about a four-day trip. It is possible to extend the float an additional two days by continuing down the Yukon to the town of Circle, which can be accessed by the Steese Highway from Fairbanks.

REGION 3
EASTERN BROOKS RANGE

This large area, from the Middle Fork of the Koyukuk River to the Canadian border, contains some very significant waters, like the Chandalar River, the north tributaries of the vast Porcupine, and the South Fork of the Koyukuk. Principal highlights in this remote and seldom-visited area include untold miles of pristine grayling streams, virgin pike populations (especially the Chandalar River drainage), a few deep-water lakes with trophy lake trout potential, occasional sheefish and even some rare opportunities for salmon (the lower Porcupine and Koyukuk drainages). Aside from locations reached from the Dalton Highway, access can be expensive, and services scarce—mostly locals operating from Bettles, Fort Yukon, Arctic Village or Fairbanks. But the potential for high-quality, wilderness adventure angling is certainly there.

20. OLD JOHN LAKE

Location: Central Brooks Range (south side), Sheenjek drainage, 230 miles north of Fairbanks.

Reference: Arctic A-2.

Access: By floatplane from Fairbanks or Fort Yukon. The lake can also be reached by four-wheeler trail from Arctic Village.

Highlights: A trophy lake trout water in the Brooks Range.

Species: Grayling, lake trout, northern pike.

Regulations: Open year-round, all species.

Facilities: Lodging, a guide service and limited supplies are available in Arctic Village.

Contact: For an air taxi, contact Wright Air Service, P.O. Box 60142, Fairbanks, AK 99706, (907) 474-0502; or Bob Elliott, 4582 Elliott Lane, Fairbanks, AK 99709, (907) 479-6323. For lodging and guided fishing information, contact Arctic Village Tours, P.O. Box 82896, Fairbanks, AK 99708; (907) 479-4648.

Description: Old John Lake lies in the central Brooks Range about 10 miles southeast of Arctic Village. A deep, mountain-basin lake of fairly good size (five miles long) draining into the upper Sheenjek River, Old John is one of the most well-known and beautifully situated of Alaska's Brooks Range lakes, significant as a centuries-old native hunting site for caribou and a consistent trophy lake trout water. (Two of the largest 10 lake trout caught in Alaska were from Old John.)

The lake is fished year-round by natives from Arctic Village who access it by snowmachine or four-wheeler trail. Most visiting anglers fly in from Fairbanks or Fort Yukon in spring at break-up (late May) or in fall (September), and enjoy outstanding fishing. The lake and outlet stream also have an abundant grayling population, and some big northerns have come out of Old John and nearby lakes of the upper Sheenjek and East Fork Chandalar as well. The best bet would be to give the locals a call and arrange for a guided outing, as they have a lodge in town and are developing a tent camp facility on the lake for a variety of trip options. Rental boats are also available.

21. UPPER CHANDALAR RIVER

Location: North-central Brooks Range, Yukon drainage, 170 miles north of Fairbanks.

Reference: Chandalar A-1, A-2, A-3, A-4, A-5, B-1, B-2, B-3, B-4, C-1, C-2, C-3, C-4, D-1, D-2, D-3, D-4, D-5; Christian A-6, B-5, B-6, C-5, C-6, D-4, D-5, D-6; Fort Yukon C-4, C-5, D-5; Philip Smith Mountains A-2, A-3, A-4.

Access: By small plane from Fairbanks, Bettles or Fort Yukon to head-water lakes, river bars or gravel strips along river.

Highlights: A remote river system with high wilderness recreation potential and good fishing possibilities for lake trout, northern pike and grayling.

Species: Chum salmon, grayling, lake trout, northern pike, sheefish.

Regulations: Open year-round, all species.

Facilities: No developed public facilities.

Contact: For an air taxi, contact Wright Air Service, P.O. Box 60142, Fairbanks, AK 99706, (907) 474-0502; or Bettles Air Service, 2453 Homestead, North Pole, AK 99705, (800) 770-5111.

Description: The Chandalar River system drains a major portion of the central Brooks Range in its journey from mountain headwaters to the Yukon. (It joins the big river near the village of Venetie Landing.) An extensive, multi-forked wilderness river known for exciting float adventures, the Chandalar also has some notable angling possibilities.

There are northern pike, sheefish and even some salmon in its lower reaches above Yukon Flats, but it is the upper river, with its many swift and pristine headwaters and numerous associated lakes that has the most exciting fishing possibilities. The larger headwater lakes of the Middle and North forks—Chandalar, Squaw and Ackerman—are scenic, deep mountain lakes that have good lake trout populations. Chandalar probably has the best fishing, with definite trophy potential and the bonus of some good pike as well. All the lakes have abundant grayling in their outlet and inlet streams. Late spring and fall are the best times—Chandalar and Squaw lakes can get turbid from runoff and are best right at break up and in the fall. The three main forks (especially the East Fork) of the Chandalar all have a proliferation of foothill lakes in their upper reaches–many with untouched pike and grayling populations–and are very scenic and wild.

Though fly-ins to Chandalar, Ackerman or Squaw Lakes in spring or fall (combined with hunting) are the most common way of fishing the system, a raft/kayak trip down from the headwaters is a tantalizing option that combines some exciting sportfish exploration with pristine whitewater, making an ideal wilderness float adventure.

22. JIM RIVER-PROSPECT CREEK

Location: Central Brooks Range south side, 165 miles north Fairbanks.
Reference: Bettles D-1, D-2, D-3; Beaver D-6.
Access: By car via the Dalton Highway. There are several bridge crossings (mileposts 135, 140, 141 and 144) over Prospect Creek and different branches of the Jim River, the last being the most commonly used by anglers fishing the river. A winter road from Bettles provides additional access.
Highlights: A Haul Road location providing access to good fishing for grayling (from May through September) and other species.
Species: Chum salmon, grayling, (king salmon), northern pike.
Regulations: Open year-round, all species.
Facilities: No developed public facilities. Undeveloped campsites are available at several spots along Bettles Winter Road.
Contact: For fishing information, contact the Alaska Department of Fish and Game, Sportfish Division, 1300 College Road, Fairbanks, AK 99701; (907) 456-8819.
Description: Prospect Creek and the Jim River are known as two of the better fishing locations along the Dalton Highway. Tributaries of the South Fork Koyukuk, these clear, shallow streams, in their reaches

beyond the immediate area of the highway, can provide some decent grayling fishing, with some northern pike and a few salmon as added bonuses.

Most folks access and fish them at one of several bridge crossings, but it's best to float them by canoe or raft from the highway put-ins, then take out at the Bettles Winter Road that crosses at several points below (either 10 miles down on the Jim River or a few miles further on the Koyukuk). The idea is to get beyond the frequently fished stretches of river to more virgin water. Spring and early fall are the best times for grayling, while midsummer brings opportunities for catch-and-release salmon fishing. If you're fishing the Haul Road, you'll probably want to stop at one of the Jim River or Prospect Creek crossings. They just look too good to pass by.

---

23. BOB JOHNSON (BIG) AND TWIN LAKES

Location: Central Brooks Range, 195 miles north of Fairbanks.
Reference: Chandalar B-5, C-5.
Access: By small plane from Fairbanks, Bettles or Fort Yukon. They can also be reached by trail from the Dalton Highway.
Highlights: Well-known, scenic lake destinations in the central Brooks Range, with good fishing for lake trout and grayling.
Species: Grayling, lake trout, northern pike.
Regulations: Open year-round, all species.
Facilities: No developed public facilities.
Contact: For an air taxi, contact Wright Air Service, P.O. Box 60142, Fairbanks, AK 99706, (907) 474-0502; or Bettles Air Service, 2453 Homestead, North Pole, AK 99705; (800) 770-5111.
Description: No discussion of central Brooks Range fishing locations would be complete without mention of these two well-known, neighboring mountain lakes—Bob Johnson (Big) and Twin. Very scenic, deep-basin lakes that lie in the upper Koyukuk drainage east of Wiseman and just west of Chandalar Lake, Bob Johnson and Twin have been traditional sites for hunting camps as well as popular Brooks Range recreation spots for vacationers out of Fairbanks. Scattered cabins exist along the lakes and in the vicinity.

These clear lakes have good fishing for lake trout and grayling, with pike present in Bob Johnson. Twin is deeper and generally has bigger lake trout on average, although both lakes have seen a decline in larger fish over the years due to increasing angling pressure. The outlet and inlet streams (and connecting stream on Twin) right at break-up (late May usually) are probably the best bet for fishing these two.

ALASKA FISHING BY REGION: SOUTHWEST

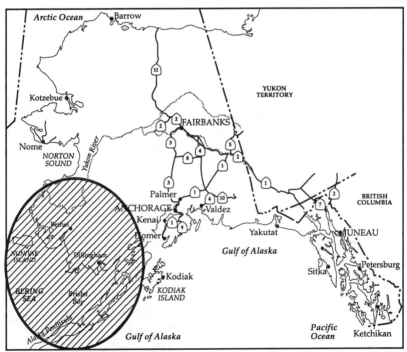

Shaded area shows Southwest region

MAP 4—SOUTHWEST HOTSPOTS

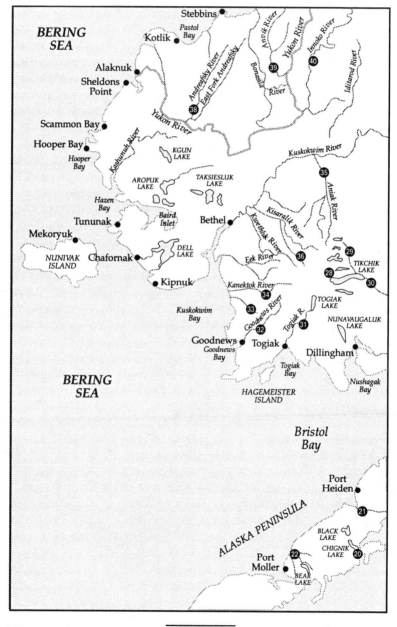

MAP 5—SOUTHWEST HOTSPOTS

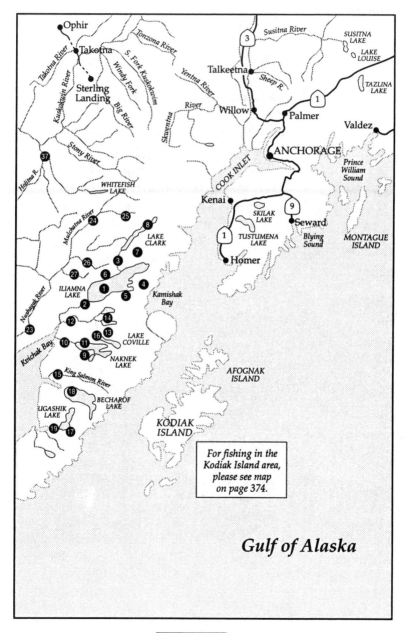

Ophir

Takotna

Sterling Landing

Takotna River

Kuskokwim River

Tonzona River

S. Fork Kuskokwim

Windy Fork

Big River

Yentna River

Skwentna

River

Talkeetna

Willow

Sheep R.

Susitna River

SUSITNA LAKE

LAKE LOUISE

3

Palmer

1

TAZLINA LAKE

Valdez

ANCHORAGE

Stony River

37

Holitna R.

WHITEFISH LAKE

Mulchatna River

24

25

26

27

Nushagak River

23

ILIAMNA LAKE

1

2

5

6

3

8

7

4

LAKE CLARK

Kvichak Bay

12

14

16

13

10

11

9

LAKE COVILLE

NAKNEK LAKE

15

King Salmon River

18

BECHAROF LAKE

UGASHIK LAKE

19

17

Kamishak Bay

Kenai

SKILAK LAKE

1

TUSTUMENA LAKE

Homer

COOK INLET

9

Seward

Blying Sound

Prince William Sound

MONTAGUE ISLAND

AFOGNAK ISLAND

KODIAK ISLAND

For fishing in the Kodiak Island area, please see map on page 374.

Gulf of Alaska

SOUTHWEST HOT SPOTS

SOUTHWEST

From the Alaska Peninsula west and north to the shores of Norton Sound lies an area that is almost the size of Montana. This is a region so rich and varied in resources and unspoiled beauty that it truly defies adequate description. Here are found the world's largest runs of Pacific salmon and the fabulous sportfishing locations of Bristol Bay, as well as the stark and scenic landscapes of Katmai (with its famous fishing brown bears) and the timeless Yupik Eskimo culture. A haven for wildlife, it has special marine mammal sanctuaries and one of the world's largest expanses of waterfowl habitat, which, along with other important wildlands in the area, have been set aside in some of the largest parks, refuges and preserves in America.

Sportfishermen will find special attraction in the thousands of miles of rivers and immense lakes found here. Unlike the glacial drainages that predominate elsewhere in Alaska, most of these waters run sparkling clear from abundant runoff sources and springs, providing perfect habitat for a profusion of salmon and an unrivalled variety of resident sport species—charr, grayling, rainbow trout, pike, lake trout and even sheefish in some waters. There is no area more representative of Alaska's extraordinary fishing opportunities than Southwest.

Devoid of any real roads, this is Alaska's definitive fly-in fishing country, with a world-famous coterie of lodges, guides and outfitters offering a range of exciting options for that ultimate fishing vacation. Fly in to remote headwaters and spend days rafting a lonely river where fish have seldom seen a fly and brown bears stalk the shallows, or stay at a deluxe lodge and be pampered with gourmet meals and plush accommodations while you enjoy daily excursions to world-class fishing locales. If your tastes run somewhere in between, you can even visit rustic "spike camps" on far-flung rivers with unpronounceable names, where you'll get a cot in a wall tent, three square meals a day and all the fishing action your arms can handle. No matter how you decide to go, Southwest Alaska can consistently deliver a quality of angling that few areas in the world can match, a place where the truly serious can put their fishing passion to the ultimate test.

COUNTRY, CLIMATE & CONDITIONS

Southwest Alaska is awesome country—wild and primitive, with unique and distinct features. There are over 50 active volcanoes, remnant glaciers, ice-sculpted highlands and valleys and immense rolling expanses of tundra, forests and flat coastal plain. The intense glaciation during the last Ice Age created many deep bedrock basins that are of special significance. They cradle enormous lakes that have become the rearing grounds for the largest concentrations of salmon, trout and charr in the world. Iliamna, Becharof, Ugashik, Naknek, Nonvianuk and, to a lesser extent, the interconnected Wood-Tikchiks all support phenomenal fisheries and provide in their outlets and associated river systems some of the greatest angling to be had anywhere. Unlike the fishing, Southwest's climate is nothing to get excited about. It's definitely maritime and a bit on the raw side. The 1,600-mile arc of the Alaska Peninsula and Aleutian Islands effectively isolates the region from the moderating influences of the Gulf of Alaska; here the stormy Bering Sea and icy Bristol Bay are the dominant forces shaping the weather. Summers are typically cool, cloudy and breezy, with brief sunny interludes (April through June is generally the sunniest part of the year) and temperatures ranging from the upper 40s to mid-70s (average 50s). Yearly rainfall is from 20 to 40 inches, with August through October the wettest months. Winters are long and cold, although not as extreme as those in Interior, with freeze-up occurring sometime in late October and break-up occurring usually in early May (later in some of the mountain lakes). At any time, intense cyclonic activity can bring sudden, prolonged periods of high winds (up to 100 miles per hour) and precipitation. For this reason, travellers who venture into any part of this country during summer must come equipped with expedition-quality raingear, tents, sleeping bags, undergarments and footwear.

SOUTHWEST FISHING HIGHLIGHTS

A list of the area's outstanding angling locations reads more like a roster of North America's dream waters, so blessed is this region with extraordinary fishing. In fact, there is so much good water that it makes for difficult, if not impossible, vacation choices for anglers (especially newcomers), as the fishing on any of these streams and lakes will easily eclipse the best angling most folks have experienced back home. If you've never been to Alaska and want a mind-blowing introduction to the smorgasbord of wild angling possible here, you can hardly lose in choosing any of the dozens of great Southwest locations. On the other hand, if you are a seasoned Alaska angler with a yen for something different than what you have experienced elsewhere in the state, you'll find major areas and locations with features that set them apart from other waters in Alaska (and the rest of the world).

Some of the region's more notable angling highlights are the fantastic streamfishing opportunities for salmon, particularly king, silver and sockeye, as most of Alaska's major producing rivers for these species are located here (the Kvichak, Naknek, Egegik, Nushagak, Togiak and Kuskokwim rivers). Flyfishing possibilities in the countless clear streams and lakes are almost infinite. So too are the numbers of feisty, fat charr and grayling you'll encounter in nearly every body of water, with trophy potential in some waters exceeded only by a few locations in Alaska's remote Northwest. And, of course, there are those fabulous rainbows. Can enough can be said of the peerless Southwest rivers and their armies of hungry, husky, wild Alaska rainbow trout? Nearly every drainage from Katmai to the Kuskokwim is amply endowed with them, with many waters holding trout of mythical proportions. The flyfishing conditions couldn't be better, especially in spring and fall.

ACCESS, SERVICES & COSTS

With no connecting surface transportation, access to Southwest is generally by plane, through these main hubs: Dillingham, King Salmon, Bethel and Iliamna. All these towns are serviced by regular scheduled commercial flights from Anchorage and have local air charters and connections available to make access possible to just about every village and fishing location within the region.

SOUTHWEST RUN TIMING

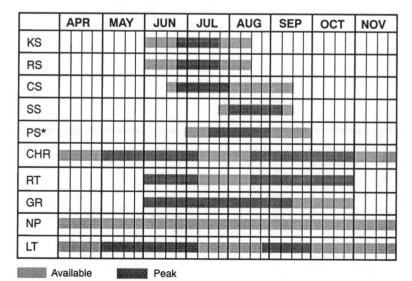

	APR	MAY	JUN	JUL	AUG	SEP	OCT	NOV
KS								
RS								
CS								
SS								
PS*								
CHR								
RT								
GR								
NP								
LT								

▓ Available   ■ Peak

KS=King Salmon, RS=Red Salmon, CS=Chum Salmon, SS=Silver Salmon, PS=Pink Salmon, CHR=Charr, RT=Rainbow Trout, GR=Grayling, NP=Northern Pike, LT=Lake Trout

*Available in even years

Note: Time periods shown are for bright fish, in the case of salmon entering rivers, or for general availability for resident species. Salmon are present in many systems long after the periods shown, but are usually in spawning/post spawning condition. Peak sportfishing periods for each species are highlighted. Be aware that run timing can vary somewhat from drainage to drainage and generally follows a later trend in waters to the west and north in Alaska. Check with local contacts listed for area run-timing specifics before confirming plans.

Southwest Alaska—land of abundant bears and salmon.

REGION 1
LAKE ILIAMNA &
KVICHAK RIVER SYSTEM

Ocean-sized Iliamna, the largest lake in Alaska (over 1,000 square miles), is the world's most productive sockeye salmon system. Along with the associated Lake Clark drainages, it supports runs of millions of returning fish. (In 1965, a staggering 42 million sockeyes returned to spawn.) The vast, rich Lake Iliamna environs also produce bumper yields of some of the largest rainbow trout in the state. Studies done over the last 30 years show these fish to be a late-maturing, larger growing strain, with an average size around 20 inches. Trout up to 15 pounds are not uncommon in these waters. Along with the fabulous locations of Katmai, Iliamna's immense, productive fisheries have long been synonymous with the finest trophy trout angling in Alaska, if not the world.

1. LAKE ILIAMNA

Location: Eastern Bristol Bay, 175 miles southwest of Anchorage.
Reference: Iliamna B-5, B-6, B-7, B-8, C-3, C-4, C-5, C-6, C-7, C-8, D-3, D-4, D-5.
Access: By plane via scheduled commercial flights from Anchorage, and floatplane or boat to various points along the lake.
Highlights: Alaska's most productive lake system, world famous for trophy rainbow trout and abundant sockeye salmon.
Species: Charr, (chum salmon), grayling, lake trout, (northern pike), pink salmon, rainbow trout, red salmon, (silver salmon).
Regulations: Spring closures (April 10 through June 7) for rainbow trout; single-hook, artificial lures only. Certain lake drainages are flyfishing only and seasonal catch-and-release. For details and additional restrictions, consult the current Alaska Department of Fish and Game regulations or the ADF&G Dillingham office, (907) 842-2427.
Facilities: The lake area is serviced by a score of reputable lodges, guides, outfitters and air taxis.
Contacts: For flights from Anchorage to Iliamna, contact ERA

Aviation Inc., 6160 South Airport Drive, Anchorage, AK 99502; (800) 426-0333. For air taxi service within the Lake Iliamna area, contact Iliamna Air Taxi, P.O. Box 109, Iliamna, AK 99606; (907) 571-1248. For full-service lodges for the entire Iliamna area, contact Chris Goll, Rainbow River Lodge, 4127 Raspberry Road, Anchorage, AK 99502, (907) 243-7894; or Iliaska Lodge, P.O. Box 30, Homer, AK 99603, (907) 235-6188. For daily lodging, boat rentals and guide services, contact Airport Hotel, P.O. Box 157, Iliamna, AK 99606; (907) 571-1501.

Description: With its mesmerizing blue vastness and infinite bays, islands and gravel beaches, Lake Iliamna has a mystique all its own. One of the deepest lakes ever surveyed in Alaska (1,000 feet or more in spots), it has some rather unique fauna, such as freshwater seals, sturgeon and even a mysterious giant creature that longtime residents swear is Alaska's equivalent to Scotland's famous serpent of Loch Ness.

The steelhead-sized rainbows are, of course, the main attraction. Very little fishing is done in the lake itself, however; anglers instead target the numerous creeks and rivers emptying into this freshwater behemoth. Some of the more popular drainages have become legends on their own, places like the Talarik Creeks or the Copper, Gibraltar, Tazimina or Kvichak rivers, all with a history of remarkable fishing over the years. Generally, these streams are best hit in late spring (right after the opening in June) or fall (September and October) when the big trout cruise out of the lake for spawning or feeding activities. Most of the smaller water is flyfished, with the larger, deeper rivers worked most efficiently by boat, drifting lures steelhead-style along the bottom. In early summer, some of Alaska's best opportunities for sockeye salmon also occur in the larger lake tributaries, including the Newhalen, Kvichak, Tazimina and Iliamna rivers.

Special note: Much of the land surrounding Lake Iliamna is privately owned by native corporations. There are no developed public facilities along the lake or tributaries. Before you attempt any unguided ventures in this watershed, check with the agencies listed below for information on the locations of public easements, restrictions and fees: Iliamna Natives Ltd., P.O. Box 245, Iliamna, AK 99606, (907) 571-1256; or Bureau of Land Management, Alaska State Office, 222 West Seventh Avenue, P.O. Box 13, Anchorage, AK 99513, (907) 271-5960.

2. KVICHAK RIVER

Location: Iliamna Lake outlet, Bristol Bay, 250 miles southwest of Anchorage.

Reference: Iliamna B-8; Dillingham A-1, A-2, A-3, B-1; Naknek D-3.

Access: By plane. Access is from Anchorage to Iliamna via commercial flight, wheelplane flight to Igiugik at the mouth of the river, or floatplane directly to the river or outlet. Transport up and downriver by boat is also possible.

Highlights: Perhaps Alaska's finest rainbow trout fishery; also known for its phenomenal sockeye salmon.

Species: Charr, chum salmon, grayling, (king salmon), lake trout, northern pike, pink salmon , rainbow trout, red salmon, silver salmon.

Regulations: Spring closures (April 10 through June 7) to protect spawning trout; unbaited, single-hook, artificial lures only. For additional restrictions, consult the current Alaska Department of Fish and Game regulations or the ADF&G Dillingham office, (907) 842-2427.

Facilities: Lodge-based fishing, guide services and boat rental are available.

Contact: For guide services, boat rentals and lodging, contact Airport Hotel, P.O. Box 157, Iliamna, AK 99606; (907) 571-1501. For lodged-based fishing, contact Ole Creek Lodge, 506 Ketchikan Street, Fairbanks, AK 99701; (907) 452-2421.

Description: As the primary outlet for giant Lake Iliamna, the state's largest, most productive body of fresh water, the Kvichak is arguably Alaska's foremost locale for jumbo rainbows (up to 15 pounds). In spring and fall, hordes of the big, lake-resident trout converge on the river to spawn and feed, providing some of Alaska's most exciting trophy fishing possibilities.

From its outlet at Igiugik, the Kvichak winds through flat, coastal tundra for 60 miles before spilling its jewel-like waters into muddy Kvichak Bay. It's a big river—wide, deep and fast, not easy to fish from shore, except at the outlet and mouths of the tributary creeks (such as Peck's, Kaskanak and Ole). Most fishermen drift it from boats, from the outlet down through the extensive braided section (Kaskanak Flats) that begins five miles below the lake, using Spin-N-Glos, plugs, spoons and Okie Drifters fished right above bottom. Flyfishing is difficult and best done at the lake outlet, from the cutbanks of Kaskanak Flats, or in the mouths and lower sections of the tributaries. (Bright attractors, egg patterns, sculpins or smolt imitations work best.)

Weather and timing are crucial to your success in these big waters. Fall, which is the best time for trophy fish, also has some notoriously foul weather that can quickly turn a fishing trip into a survival ordeal. Most of the big, lake resident rainbows are usually gone by the time the sockeyes return in late June, making the spring fishing period very short (these waters don't open for fishing until June 8). When it all comes together, though, the Kvichak shines as one of the world's finest big rainbow fisheries, with more large trout encounters possible in a day's fishing here than in a lifetime of effort most anywhere else.

Note: With its predictable runs of millions of sockeye salmon, the Kvichak also offers some of Alaska's best sportfishing for the species. Since there's lots of water to fish, it's best to enlist the services of a local guide if you're new to fishing the area.

3. NEWHALEN RIVER

Location: North shore Lake Iliamna, 200 miles southwest of Anchorage.

Reference: Iliamna C-6, D-5, D-6.

Access: By plane from Anchorage to Iliamna via commercial flight, then by car or foot to the river; boat transportation is available from the village of Newhalen.

Highlights: Some of the Alaska's best, most easily accessed sockeye salmon and rainbow trout fishing.

Species: Rainbow trout, charr, red salmon, grayling, lake trout.

Regulations: Spring closures (April 10 through June 7) to protect spawning rainbow trout; single-hook, unbaited, artificial lures only. For additional restrictions, consult the current Alaska Department of Fish and Game regulations or the ADF&G Dillingham office, (907) 842-2427.

Facilities: Lodging, guide services and boat rentals are available.

Contact: For flight information, lodging, guide services and boat rentals, contact Airport Hotel, P.O. Box 157, Iliamna, AK 99606; (907) 571-1501.

Description: A short flight west from Anchorage to the village of Iliamna and a half-mile hike from the end of the airstrip takes you to one of Alaska's best fishing holes, the "Falls" on the Newhalen River. In early July, you'll find bright, frantic sockeye salmon stacked thick as cordwood here, and in the pools and rapids below the Falls (especially in spring and fall), maybe some of those famous jumbo, Iliamna rainbow trout. You might have to share these waters with some other folks, but it won't be anything like the mad scenes on the Kenai Peninsula and it's a whole 'nother class of fishing besides.

A big, transparent-blue, whitewater river, the 25-mile Newhalen connects Six Mile Lake and adjoining Lake Clark with immense Lake Iliamna. It is the major pathway for a mind-boggling migration of sockeye salmon that make their way up into the far reaches of this drainage in early summer. Most of the fishing effort for these salmon occurs right below a series of impenetrable rapids (Class IV and Class V)—the Falls—on the lower river a couple of miles up from the mouth, but some productive water upriver can be accessed by road at a place called Upper Landing.

Below the Falls, you can fish for salmon until your arms go numb, then rent a boat (and a guide's services, if you want) and drift the stretch of river down to the lake for big rainbows (up to 12 pounds). However, the trout fishing doesn't really heat up until later on in the season—try September and October for the biggest fish. Drifting egg and attractor patterns, or Spin-N-Glos and Li'l Corkies seems to be the ticket. (You can do quite well fishing from shore in spots, too.) The Newhalen is highly recommended for those who seek an inexpensive alternative to the overrated and overcrowded fishing on most of the popular streams of Southcentral Alaska.

During the first three weeks in July, the Newhalen's famous run of sockeyes peaks, making easy targets for the skilled angler. Consult the chapter on sockeye salmon on page 64 for the best flies and techniques to use.

Special note: If you plan on a do-it yourself excursion along the Newhalen, be aware that much of the land along the river is owned and managed by native corporations. For details on public easements and land ownership, contact the Bureau of Land Management, Alaska State Office, 222 West Seventh Avenue, P.O. Box 13, Anchorage, AK 99513 (907) 271-5960.

4. COPPER RIVER

Location: Eastern Lake Iliamna drainage, 190 miles southwest of Anchorage.

Reference: Iliamna C-4, C-5.

Access: By plane from Anchorage to Iliamna via commercial flight. There is floatplane access to several headwater lakes (such as Copper, Meadows and Pike) or the lower river. A one- to three-day (depending on the put-in location) float trip by raft or kayak is possible from the upper river.

Highlights: One of Lake Iliamna's most famous flyfishing streams. Excellent angling for rainbow trout, sockeye salmon and grayling.

Species: Charr, grayling, northern pike, rainbow trout, red salmon.

Regulations: Spring closures (April 10 through June 7) for spawning trout. Seasonal flyfishing only and catch-and-release for rainbows (June 8 through October 31). For additional restrictions, consult the current Alaska Department of Fish and Game regulations or the ADF&G Dillingham office, (907) 842-2427.

Facilities: Lodging, lodge-based fishing and guide services are available.

Contact: For air taxi service to the Copper River, contact Iliamna Air Taxi, P.O. Box 109, Iliamna, AK 99606; (907) 571-1248. For guided fishing on the Copper, contact Airport Hotel, P.O. Box 157, Iliamna, AK 99606; (907) 571-1501. For a private, custom lodge experience on the river, contact Chris Goll, Rainbow River Lodge, 4127 Raspberry Road, Anchorage, AK 99502; (907) 243-7894.

Description: The Copper River, along with Talarik Creek, is perhaps the best known of Lake Iliamna's fabulous trout streams, and is particularly renowned for its superb flyfishing. In its glory days, it was visited routinely by just about every fly-out lodge in the area; for years, it was one of the lake's most floated streams.

The clear Copper originates in a series of lakes in the Chigmit Mountains east of Iliamna, flowing swiftly for some 15 miles before emptying into Intricate Bay. A 36-foot waterfall below Lower Copper Lake, 12 miles up from the mouth, serves as an effective barrier for most fish and fishermen; several lakes adjoining the river below the falls are the best points of access. (The river can be run from up above, as long as you take great care not to miss the short portage on the left side.)

The Copper's reputation comes from its near perfect flyfishing conditions and ample supply of husky rainbows, which migrate in from the lake in spring and fall. Though the fish here generally don't average as large as those taken in the big water of the Kvichak or Katmai's Naknek River, the Copper's much more suited for the wade-and-cast stream angler. It's also a great river to fish dry flies for rainbows, perhaps one of Alaska's best in early season (June and July). The preferred method of fishing the Copper is to float down from below the falls in a raft (put-in on Upper Pike Lake), fishing as you go, with a pick up at Lower Pike Lake (a one-day trip) or down below in the bay. There is also a fancy lodge on the river (Rainbow River Lodge), for those who want to go in style. June, July and September are the best times for rainbows on the Copper.

5. GIBRALTAR RIVER

Location: Southeast shore Lake Iliamna drainage, 215 miles southwest of Anchorage.

Reference: Iliamna B-5, B-6.

Access: By plane from Anchorage to Iliamna via commercial flight, then floatplane to Gibraltar Lake or (sometimes) the river mouth area. Floating down from the lake by raft is possible, with pick-up by floatplane.

Highlights: A popular Lake Iliamna rainbow trout location.

Species: Charr, grayling, lake trout, rainbow trout, red salmon.

Regulations: Spring closures (April 10 through June 7) for spawning trout. Seasonal flyfishing only and catch-and-release for rainbows (June 8 through October 31). For additional restrictions, consult the current Alaska Department of Fish and Game regulations or the ADF&G Dillingham office, (907) 842-2427.

Facilities: No developed public facilities. Guide services are available.

Contact: For an air taxi, contact Iliamna Air Taxi, P.O. Box 109, Iliamna, AK 99606; (907) 571-1248. For guide services, contact Airport Hotel, P.O. Box 157, Iliamna, AK 99606; (907) 571-1501.

Description: The Gibraltar River is one of the better known Iliamna flyfishing streams, offering its own lake access and fairly abundant fishing for rainbow trout and red salmon in season. Only about six miles long, the river drains Gibraltar Lake flowing north into Iliamna near Kakhonak Bay.

Most of the fishing on Gibraltar occurs near the lake outlet and on tributary streams like Dream and Southeast creeks, both of which are outstanding trout locales on their own. The entire river offers good fishing, however, and is best worked by floating down from the lake in rafts (a one-day trip). A two-mile section of swift water in the middle section of the river is the only possible hazard. Floatplanes may not be able to land by the mouth for a pick-up if it's too windy; you may have to hike about three miles to the nearby village of Kakhonak for a plane ride back to Iliamna. Best times for rainbows are June and September, with the bigger fish more abundant in the fall.

6. TALARIK CREEK

Location: Northwest shore Lake Iliamna drainage, 220 miles southwest of Anchorage.

Reference: Iliamna C-7.

Access: By plane from Anchorage to Iliamna via commercial flight, then a short floatplane flight west to the lagoon at the mouth of the river.

Highlights: The most famous Lake Iliamna flyfishing stream; hard hit, but still worth a visit for its great rainbows.

Species: Charr, grayling, rainbow trout, red salmon.

Regulations: Spring closures (April 10 through June 7) for spawning trout. Seasonal flyfishing only and catch-and-release for rainbows (June 8 through October 31). For additional restrictions, consult the current Alaska Department of Fish and Game regulations or the ADF&G Dillingham office, (907) 842-2427.

Facilities: No developed public facilities. Guide services are available.

Contact: For an air taxi, contact Iliamna Air Taxi, P.O. Box 109, Iliamna, AK 99606; (907) 571-1248. For guide services, contact Airport Hotel, P.O. Box 157, Iliamna, AK 99606; (907) 571-1501.

Description: Lower Talarik Creek enters Lake Iliamna from the north about 25 miles west of the Newhalen River. Most people are amazed, even disappointed, when they see it for the first time. The giant reputation this place carries is beyond all measure of its physical size, as it is truly just a creek, dwarfed by most of the other drainages that empty into Lake Iliamna. Still, this short dribble of a stream is amazingly productive, due to its location and perfect habitat for trout and salmon spawning. Since the '50s, Talarik's abundant, big rainbows and easy access have drawn anglers from all over to sample its waters.

Talarik's also one of the most studied trout streams in Alaska. The Alaska Department of Fish and Game has done sampling and tagging of the creek's rainbows for the last 30 years or so, with some interesting findings. The majority of the rainbows here live the first few years of their life in the creek, then migrate to the lake, where they grow rapidly, most reaching 18 inches or better by five years of age. They return to the creek (or other streams) yearly to spawn and/or feed on the abundant roe, smolt and flesh of the sockeye salmon. The best time to fish Talarik is during these periods of in-migration—June through early July and September through October. For a river this small, the average size of Talarik's rainbows compares favorably with the best Lake Iliamna locations (the

Kvichak and Newhalen rivers), especially during late fall (October), when a large percentage of trophy fish are taken.

Most fishermen land on the lagoon at the mouth, then hike upriver, fishing either fork for good results. You can also put in at one of the headwater lakes, then fish and wade down to Iliamna—a good tactic in the fall. Upper Talarik Creek nearby has some good fishing at times also, but it lacks the lower creek's convenient access and is quite shallow in spots.

7. TAZIMINA RIVER

Location: Six Mile Lake drainage, Lake Iliamna, 180 miles southwest of Anchorage.

Reference: Lake Clark A-2, A- 3, A-4; Iliamna D-5.

Access: By plane from Anchorage to Iliamna or Port Allsworth via commercial flight, then floatplane to the lakes or the lower river. Jet boat access is also possible to the mouth and lower river .

Highlights: One of the more popular Iliamna-Lake Clark area stream locations, with excellent rainbow trout, sockeye salmon and grayling fishing; also a great short float trip.

Species: Charr, grayling, rainbow trout, red salmon.

Regulations: Spring closures (April 10 through June 7) for spawning trout; unbaited, single-hook artificial lure fishing only. Catch-and-release only for rainbows in the lower river (one mile up from the mouth to the falls) during summer and fall. For additional restrictions, consult the current Alaska Department of Fish and Game regulations or the ADF&G Dillingham office, (907) 842-2427.

Facilities: No developed public facilities. Guide services are available.

Contact: For an air taxi, contact Iliamna Air Taxi, P.O. Box 109, Iliamna, AK 99606; (907) 571-1248. For guide services, contact Airport Hotel, P.O. Box 157, Iliamna, AK 99606, (907) 571-1501; or Marchant's, 6414 Tolhurst Court, Anchorage, AK 99504, (907) 337-0215 or (907) 781-2299.

Description: The Tazimina River has been a popular fishing location of the Lake Iliamna-Lake Clark lodge crowd for years, visited regularly for its consistently superb rainbow trout, sockeye salmon, and grayling fishing. It also has one of the few area fishing rivers, along with the Gibraltar and Copper, that can be floated (for one- to four-day trips).

Located within Lake Clark National Park, the 54-mile, clear Tazimina drains a series of lakes of the same name before emptying into Six Mile Lake and the Newhalen River. Because of some waterfalls and portages (the most serious located nine miles from the mouth), most fishermen usually access only the lower river (from the mouth to Alexcy Lake) via jet boat or floatplane. Rafters put in at either Lower Tazimina, Alexcy or Hudson lakes (with short portages) and vary the length of their float. Flyfishing conditions on the Tazimina are excellent.

8. LAKE CLARK

Location: Lake Clark National Park, 180 miles southwest of Anchorage.

Reference: Lake Clark A-4, A-5, B-2, B-3, B-4.

Access: By wheelplane to Point Allsworth from Anchorage or Iliamna, then boat or floatplane to various points around the lake or associated tributaries. There is also direct floatplane access from Anchorage or Kenai.

Highlights: Alaska's most scenic lake area with good fishing for lake trout, grayling, pike and sockeye salmon.

Species: Charr, grayling, lake trout, northern pike, red salmon.

Regulations: Open year-round for waters above Six Mile Lake; only unbaited, single-hook, artificial lures in Six Mile and tributaries. For additional restrictions, consult the current Alaska Department of Fish and Game regulations or the ADF&G Dillingham office, (907) 842-2427.

Facilities: Several private lodges are located on the lake, some offering daily guide service and boat rentals.

Contacts: For information on the park, contact Lake Clark National Park and Preserve, 4230 University Drive #311, Anchorage, AK 99508; (907) 271-3751. For air taxi service, guide services and tent camps, contact Air Adventures, P.O. Box 22, Kenai, AK 99611-0022; (907) 776-5444. For full-service lodges, contact Alaska's Wilderness Lodge, P.O. Box 700, Sumner, WA 98390, (800) 835-8032 or (907) 781-2223; or Northward Bound, 13830 Jarvi Drive, Anchorage, AK 99515, (907) 345-2891. For lodging and unguided fishing on Lake Clark drainage, contact Marchant's, 6414 Tolhurst Court, Anchorage, AK 99504; (907) 337-0215 or (907) 781-2299.

Description: Beautiful, turquoise Lake Clark is the gateway attraction for a 3.6-million-acre national park and preserve, located west of the Chigmit Mountains, a short hop from Anchorage. Said by many to contain Alaska's most spectacular lakes and alpine scenery, this area also has some noteworthy fishing opportunities, though the predominantly glacial waters and isolation from the coast considerably limit its potential.

The outstanding mountain lakes—including Clark, Twin, Telaquana, Tazimina and Kijik—are the prime attraction here. These waters are perhaps best known for their superb lake trout (up to 30 pounds), charr and sockeye salmon fishing, with some good grayling opportunities in the clearer tributary streams and northern pike in some of the shallower lakes, ponds and sloughs. Rainbow trout are generally not found above the Six Mile Lake drainage. Because of its relative proximity to Anchorage and outstanding mountain scenery, the Lake Clark area is seeing more use every year, with a developing variety of visitor services available. There are plush lodges that offer weekly stays with daily fly-outs, or more modest, family-style lodges and inns that can provide boat excursions and guides to fish the lake and nearby streams. You can even contract the use of remote tent camps and cabins on the area's best fishing lakes and rivers.

For the true adventure fisherman, the park has two Wild and Scenic Rivers—the Mulchatna and Chilikadrotna—that can provide unforgettable float angling experiences. (See the listing on the Nushagak River on page 341 for detailed descriptions.) All in all, the Lake Clark area has great angling possibilities that should not be overlooked by anyone seeking a nearby, affordable alternative to the more humdrum fishing along Alaska's road system.

Region 2
Katmai

Few places in the world offer the visitor such diverse and superlative wonders as magnificent Katmai National Park and Preserve. Located on the neck of the Alaska Peninsula, 300 miles southwest of Anchorage, Katmai has fascinating landscapes shaped by intense volcanic action, with unique wildlife (the famous fishing brown bears), glaciers and scenic lakes and streams holding some of Alaska's best trout and salmon fishing.

It was Katmai's jumbo rainbow trout—some of Alaska's largest—that established the region as a world-class fishing destination back in the 1950s. Although the Park has been in existence since 1918, it wasn't until after World War II, when military personnel from the newly established Naknek Air Base at nearby King Salmon "discovered" the amazing trout fishing nearby, that word got out about the area's fabulous sportfish potential. Ray Peterson, a Bristol Bay bush pilot and entrepreneur, established some of the first sportfish camps to cater to the growing public demand for facilities in this fishing nirvana. These rustic camps—Brooks, Kulik and Grosvenor—have changed little over the years, offering folks a chance to savor some of the world's best fishing and surroundings in the relaxed atmosphere and comfort of "family-style" lodging.

9. Brooks River

Location: Katmai National Park, 275 miles southwest of Anchorage.
Reference: Mount Katmai C-6.
Access: By plane from Anchorage to King Salmon via commercial flight, then floatplane to Brooks camp on Naknek Lake or Brooks Lake. Boating is also possible from King Salmon.
Highlights: Katmai's most famous location, still producing great fishing for rainbow trout and sockeye salmon, with more bears than ever.
Species: Charr, chum salmon, grayling, lake trout, pink salmon, rainbow trout, red salmon.
Regulations: Fishing open from June 8 through April 9; single-hook, unbaited artificial lures. Flyfishing only from the bridge upriver

(June 8 through October 31). For additional restrictions, consult the current Alaska Department of Fish and Game regulations or the ADF&G Dillingham office, (907) 842-2427.

Facilities: A National Park Service campground, concessionaire-run lodge and rental cabins are available.

Contact: For campground and general information, contact Superintendent, Katmai National Park and Preserve, P.O. Box 7, King Salmon, AK 99613; (907) 246-3305. For lodging, cabin and boat rentals and guided fishing, contact Katmailand, Inc., 4700 Aircraft Drive #2, Anchorage, AK 99502; (800) 544-0551 or (907) 243-5448. For an air taxi, contact Branch River Air Service, 4540 Edinburgh Drive, Anchorage, AK 99515; (907) 248-3539 (in winter) or (907) 246-3437 (in summer).

Description: For over 40 years, Brooks Camp has been one of Alaska's most unique and alluring locations. As the quintessential Katmai attraction, Brooks has arm-long rainbow trout, nearby smoldering volcanic valleys, 1,000-pound bears that fish for salmon and a rustic "real Alaska" lodge in one of the world's prettiest lake and mountain settings.

The river itself is barely more than a mile long, connecting Naknek Lake with Lake Brooks. One of the major migration and spawning areas for the incredible, salmon-rich Naknek Lake system, it is amazingly productive for its size. Originally known solely for its outstanding rainbow trout fishing (in the early days, 30 inchers were quite common), Brooks has also achieved notoriety as one of the few places where anglers routinely coax strikes from the normally tight-lipped sockeye salmon.

This area is also well known for it brown bears, with some of Alaska's highest densities during the salmon season. On a typical day in July, a dozen or more of Katmai's famous cinnamon grizzlies can be seen from the observation platform at Brooks Falls, as they try their fishing skills on the milling, leaping salmon. It's quite a show, with scenes hilariously reminiscent of human streamside follies—don't dare forget your camera if you go!

You can rent one of the lodge cabins or stay in the National Park Service campground, then get supplies, meals, canoes and even daily guide service through the concessionaire. Although Brooks is showing strains of burgeoning visitor use and the fishing might not be all it used to be, the overall experience remains quite worthwhile—a glimpse of one of the more charming and rustic outpost camps that were once found throughout the Last Frontier.

Guides' tip: Brooks is a great river for dry fly fishing, especially in early summer—try a Cahill, Adams, Caddis, Irresistible or Wulff. The lagoon and lower river are the traditional angling locations, but some excellent flyfishing water can also be found from the Brooks Lake outlet down to the falls. Be cautious and aware of your profile when working these crystal waters, as the rainbows are easily spooked.

Other popular flies for Brooks Camp include: Sockeye John (rainbows, charr); Green Marvel (sockeye salmon); Montana Brassy (sockeye salmon); Orange and Chartreuse Comets (sockeye salmon); Muddler Minnow (rainbows, charr); and Katmai Smolt (rainbows, charr).

---

10. NAKNEK RIVER

Location: Eastern Bristol Bay, 300 miles southwest of Anchorage.

Reference: Naknek C-2, C-3.

Access: By plane from Anchorage to King Salmon via commercial flight, then boat and car to locations along the river.

Highlights: Southwest Alaska's most popular fishing location, with outstanding rainbow trout, king and silver salmon opportunities.

Species: Charr, chum salmon, grayling, king salmon, lake trout, pink salmon, rainbow trout, red salmon, silver salmon.

Regulations: Fishing opens June 8 through April 9 on most of the upper river; king salmon fishing open June 8 through July 31. Unbaited, single-hook, artificial lures only; size restriction for rainbows. For details and additional restrictions, consult the current Alaska Department of Fish and Game regulations or the ADF&G Dillingham office, (907) 842-2427.

Facilities: No developed public facilities. Lodges, hotels, guide services and boat rentals are available in King Salmon.

Contact: For lodging, guide services and boat rentals on the Naknek River, contact King Ko Inn, 301 West Northern Lights #403, Anchorage, AK 99503; (907) 258-0648 (in winter), (907) 246-3377 (in summer) or (907) 279-7973 (fax). For guided fishing, contact Mark Emory, Wet Waders, P.O. Box 516, Ocklawaha, FL 32179; (904) 288-3341.

Description: The Naknek River drains the immense lake system of the same name in Katmai National Park, emptying into Kvichak Bay some 30 miles or so to the west. Since the 1950s, it has been popular as one of Alaska's premier locales for big rainbows (up to 10 pounds or more). The lakes' abundant food sources support a trout population that rivals that of famed Iliamna for numbers and average size, and provides lively fishing in the river during spring and fall. The Naknek's easy access and availability of species other than trout—abundant king, silver and sockeye salmon, as well as charr and grayling—have made it the most popular river in Southwest Alaska. (Up to a fifth of the region's total angling effort takes place here.)

The lake outlet and river down to the Rapids Camp (about nine miles) are the most popular areas to fish rainbow, grayling and sockeye. (Flyfishing opportunities abound in the crystal blue waters.) King and coho salmon are mostly drift fished from boats on the lower river, from the mouth of Big Creek to Pauls Creek. The river and surrounding area are serviced by many reputable lodges and guides. The most productive times for jumbo trout and charr are spring (as early as April in portions of the river) and fall (September and October), but don't pass up the opportunity to visit this top-rated fishery for salmon either (kings in late June and early July, silvers in August). A short junket here combined with a trip to nearby Katmai and the Brooks River is easily arranged and highly recommended.

For flyfishing Naknek River rainbow and charr, use smolt and egg patterns, Sculpins, Woolly Buggers, Leeches and attractors. Also try dry flies (on warm, sunny days) and deer hair mice.

11. NAKNEK LAKE

Location: Katmai National Park, 300 miles southwest of Anchorage.
Reference: Naknek C-1, C-2; Mount Katmai C-5, C-6.
Access: By plane from Anchorage to King Salmon via commercial flights, then floatplane to Brooks Camp or various spots along lake. Boat access is possible from the Naknek River (King Salmon).
Highlights: One of Alaska's top lake fisheries for giant rainbows and charr; also good fishing for lake trout.
Species: Charr, chum salmon, grayling, lake trout, pink salmon, rainbow trout, red salmon, silver salmon.
Regulations: From March 1 through November 14, unbaited, artificial lures only; size restriction for rainbows. For additional restrictions, consult the current Alaska Department of Fish and Game regulations or the ADF&G Dillingham office, (907) 842-2427.
Facilities: A National Park Service campground and a concessionaire-operated lodge and cabins are available on the lake at the Brooks River; lodging, gas, groceries and boat rentals are available in King Salmon.

Contact: For campground and general information, contact Superintendent, Katmai National Park and Preserve, P.O. Box 7, King Salmon,
AK 99613; (907) 246-3305. For guide services, lodging and boat
rentals on Naknek Lake, contact King Ko Inn, 301 West Northern
Lights #403, Anchorage, AK 99503, (907) 258-0648 (in winter),
(907) 246-3377 (in summer) or (907) 279-7973 (fax); or Katmailand, Inc., 4700 Aircraft Drive #2, Anchorage, AK 99502, (800)
544-0551 or (907) 243-5448. For an air taxi, contact Branch River
Air Service, 4540 Edinburgh Drive, Anchorage, AK 99515; (907)
248-3539 (in winter), (907) 246-3437 (in summer).

Description: The Naknek Lake system is one of Alaska's most productive fisheries for rainbow trout, charr and sockeye salmon. Thousands of folks fish the numerous streams and lakes of this system
each summer, yet few take the opportunity to see what Naknek Lake
itself has to offer. Over the years, its deep emerald waters have provided some remarkable and consistent trophy fishing—big rainbows
to 10 pounds or more, giant charr to 20 pounds and lake trout to 30
pounds.

Not an easy lake to fish, Naknek is immense, deep and subject to
wild weather; the services of a seasoned area guide are prerequisite
for first-time anglers. The most popular areas to fish are the Naknek
River outlet, the Bay of Islands in the North Arm and the coves and
bays along the northwest shore. Anglers jet into King Salmon, then
usually rent boats and/or guides there or fly over to Brooks Camp
for some reasonably priced daily guided fishing in the nearby Bay
of Islands (see the listing on page 321). If you're planning a vacation
in Katmai, leave a day open to fish the lake; Naknek has been
known to yield exciting treasure when the fishing in the streams has
cooled down.

Guides' tip: Naknek Lake rainbows are the state's largest on average—
over 24 inches. (A 23-pounder was taken from the Bay of Islands in
1991.) Trolling with big spoons and plugs, or drift jigging is the
ticket. Use big Krocodiles (chrome, silver prism, blue prism), Hot
Shots (silver, silver-blue, fluorescent red) or Crippled Herrings
(chrome, nickel/neon blue, fluorescent red/yellow).

12. ALAGNAK RIVER

Location: Eastern Bristol Bay, 250 miles southwest of Anchorage.
Reference: Iliamna A-7, A-8; Dillingham A-1, A-2, A-3.
Access: By plane from Anchorage to King Salmon via commercial

flight, then floatplane to either headwater lake (Nonvianuk or Kukaklek) or points along the river. Floating by raft or kayak is possible to take-outs on the middle and lower river, with return to King Salmon via floatplane.

Highlights: One of Southwest Alaska's best trout and salmon rivers and most popular for floatfishing. Outstanding flyfishing opportunities.

Species: Charr, chum salmon, grayling, king salmon, lake trout, pink salmon, rainbow trout, red salmon, silver salmon.

Regulations: Spring closures (April 10 through June 7) for rainbows; single-hook, unbaited, artificial lures only. Catch-and-release fishing only (June 8 through October 31) for rainbows at the Kukaklek outlet. For additional restrictions, consult the current Alaska Department of Fish and Game regulations or the ADF&G Dillingham office, (907) 842-2427.

Facilities: There are concessionaire cabins at Nonvianuk Lake and several private lodges along the lower river.

Contact: For lodge-based fishing, contact Alagnak Lodge, 4117 Hillcrest Way, Suite 1102, Sacramento, CA 95821; (800) 877, 9903. For cabin rentals and guided fishing on the Alagnak, contact Katmailand, Inc., 4700 Aircraft Drive #2, Anchorage, AK 99502; (800) 544-0551 or (907) 243-5448. For guided floatfishing, contact Ouzel Expeditions, P.O. Box 935, Girdwood, AK 99587, (800) 825-8196. For an air taxi, contact Branch River Air Service, 4540 Edinburgh Drive, Anchorage, AK 99515; (907) 248-3539 (in winter) or (907) 246-3437 (in summer).

Description: For a long time, the Alagnak Wild and Scenic River has provided sportsmen some of Southwest Alaska's more easily accessed, world-class fishing for trout and salmon, along with abundant wildlife and pleasant scenery. With twin lake sources (Nonvianuk and Kukaklek) in fabulous Katmai country, the Alagnak (sometimes called the Branch River) flows spiritedly some 70 miles or so before emptying into Kvichak Bay. Crystal clear, rocky and swift, the upper sections (both branches) offer perfect conditions for flyfishing, and are particularly noted for big and abundant rainbows, grayling and prolific sockeye salmon in season. (The lake outlets, particularly Kukaklek's, have been famous trophy rainbow locales since the late 1940s.) King and silver salmon fishing, usually quite good in most years, is best done in the slower, deeper lower river.

The best way to fish the Alagnak is by raft, putting in at either lake from King Salmon via floatplane, then floating, fishing and camping along the river (for four to six days) to pick-up points below. The best times are July for sockeyes and kings, and late August through September for silvers and rainbows. The Alagnak is also known for its abundant bear population (the famous bruins of Katmai National Park), which are especially prominent during the height of the sockeye run in July. Anglers are advised to use caution and common sense along the river corridor during this time of year. Caribou, moose and wolves are also commonly seen.

There are sections of whitewater (mostly Class I, some Class II and one Class III rapid 12 miles below Kukaklek), but overall the Alagnak presents no great technical challenge to floaters. It is a highly recommended trip for first-time fishermen new to the wonders of Southwest Alaska.

Guides' tip: The upper Alagnak in early July has some of Alaska's finest flyfishing for sockeye salmon. Consult the sockeye salmon chapter on page 64 beforehand for details on technique. Bring plenty of these along if you go: Sockeye Willies, Orange Comets and Coho flies (orange/red/white and purple/yellow/white).

13. AMERICAN CREEK

Location: Katmai National Park, North Alaska Peninsula, 250 miles southwest of Anchorage.

Reference: Mount Katmai D-4, D-5, D-6.

Access: By plane from Anchorage to King Salmon via commercial flight, then floatplane to the headwaters at Hammersly Lake or the mouth at Coville Lake. Jet boat access is possible along the lower creek.

Highlights: One of Katmai's more famous and productive rainbow trout and charr locations, particularly in spring and fall.

Species: Charr, grayling, lake trout, (northern pike), rainbow trout, red salmon.

Regulations: Open year-round. Single-hook, unbaited, artificial lures only (March 1 through November 14); catch-and-release only for rainbows (June 8 through October 31). For additional restrictions, consult the current Alaska Department of Fish and Game regulations or the ADF&G Dillingham office, (907) 842-2427.

Facilities: No developed public facilities. Guide services and private lodging are available nearby at Grosvenor Camp or King Salmon.

Contact: For campground and general information, contact Superintendent, Katmai National Park and Preserve, P.O. Box 7, King Salmon, AK 99613; (907) 246-3305. For guide services and lodging for fishing American Creek, contact Katmailand, Inc., 4700 Aircraft Drive #2, Anchorage, AK 99502; (800) 544-0551 or (907) 243-5448. For guided floatfishing, contact Ouzel Expeditions, P.O. Box 935, Girdwood, AK 99587, (800) 825-8196. For an air taxi, contact Branch River Air Service, 4540 Edinburgh Drive, Anchorage, AK 99515; (907) 248-3539 (in winter) or (907) 246-3437 (in summer).

Description: American Creek, along with Brooks and Kulik, has some of Katmai's better streamfishing for rainbows and charr. It is a short (40 miles long), relatively small stream (about 15 yards wide) that flows swiftly from Hammersly and Murray lakes down into Coville Lake, about 45 miles east of King Salmon. Because of its rocky rapids and size, access to most of American Creek is restricted to the outlet and lower few miles of river at Coville Lake. It can be floated by raft or kayak, but it has demanding whitewater. (The average gradient is 30 to 60 feet per mile, with two canyons and continuous rapids over much of the river—certainly not recommended for anyone who is not an expert wilderness boater.)

Flyfishing conditions are excellent—some of Katmai's best—particularly in early spring and fall when abundant lake resident charr and rainbows feed heavily on the young and eggs of salmon. (Smolt-and-egg patterns and small spinners are deadly.) The creek is especially noted for its dry fly fishing opportunities (in June and July) and heavy sockeye salmon runs (in August). Be prepared to share the river with an abundant bear population, however, particularly in mid- to late summer.

You can fly-in from King Salmon to Hammersly Lake, camp and fish the outlet and few miles of stream below (for rainbows, charr and lake trout), or obtain a boat and guide from the park concessionaire and fish the lower creek (for rainbows and charr). The upper creek can also be accessed via a small pothole lake and trail about five miles down from Hammersly. If you're planning a trip to fish Katmai, American Creek is certainly a location you'll want to include in your itinerary. The best times to plan a trip are in late June and from late August through early September.

14. NONVIANUK & KUKAKLEK LAKES

Location: Katmai National Preserve, 250 miles southwest of Anchorage.
Reference: Iliamna A-6, A-7; Mt. Katmai D-3, D-4, D-5.
Access: By plane from Anchorage to King Salmon via commercial flight, then floatplane to lake locations.
Highlights: Very famous Katmai destinations for rainbow trout.
Species: Charr, grayling, lake trout, (northern pike), rainbow trout, red salmon, silver salmon.
Regulations: Spring closures (April 10 through June 7) for seasonal spawning trout. Unbaited, single-hook artificial lures only; catch-and-release for rainbows in portions of both lake drainages. For details and additional restrictions, consult the current Alaska Department of Fish and Game regulations or the ADF&G Dillingham office, (907) 842-2427.
Facilities: A concessionaire cabin camp (at Nonvianuk Lake) and lodge (at Kulik Lake) are available.
Contact: For campground and general information, contact Katmai National Park and Preserve, P.O. Box 7, King Salmon, AK 99613; (907) 246-3305. For guides, cabins and lodge information, contact Katmailand, Inc., 4700 Aircraft Drive #2, Anchorage, AK 99502; (800) 544-0551 or (907) 243-5448. For an air taxi, contact Branch River Air Service, 4540 Edinburgh Drive, Anchorage, AK 99515; (907) 248-3539 (in winter) or (907) 246-3437 (in summer).
Description: No list of the great fishing locations of Southeast Alaska would be complete without mentioning the famous Nonvianuk and Kukaklek lakes. At the very edge of the chain of lakes that makes up the heart of Katmai, these two have been the focus of serious angling effort for decades, thanks to their relative proximity to Anchorage and abundant supply of big rainbows (routinely to 10 pounds, sometimes even more). As headwaters of the renowned Alagnak, they have also seen quite a bit of use by rafters who begin their trips here.

The most popular spots for fishing the lakes' rainbows are, of course, the outlets and the mouths of the tributary streams, with Kukaklek and Kulik rivers and Moraine, Funnel and Nanuktuk creeks being especially noteworthy. Early June (right after season opening) and September through October are the prime times to encounter the big, bright, lake-dwelling trout. (The lakes and associated tributaries also offer excellent lake trout, grayling and charr fishing.)

As some of Katmai's most perfectly suited waters for wade-and-cast fishing are located here, quite a few lodges serve the area. Angler's Paradise Lodge on Kulik Lake (run by Katmailand) is perhaps the most famous of these. Their reputation has been built by the unmatchable quality of flyfishing available right out their door. Nonvianuk Camp, also run by Katmailand, offers a more rustic and affordable option for folks wanting a modicum of comfort while enjoying some of Alaska's best trout fishing.

15. KING SALMON RIVER

Location: North Alaska Peninsula, 350 southwest of Anchorage.

Reference: Mount Katmai A-6; Naknek A-1, A-2, A-4, A-5, B-2, B-3, B-4.

Access: By plane from Anchorage to King Salmon via commercial flight, then floatplane to upper Gertrude Creek or wheelplane to gravel bars on upper Contact Creek. Camp, hike and fish the surrounding area or raft/kayak down to Egegik River (five-day trip) and village, with scheduled wheelplane flights to King Salmon and connecting flights to Anchorage.

Highlights: An out-of-the-way Katmai river featuring rainbow trout in its clear tributaries with good charr, grayling and seasonal salmon fishing.

Species: Charr, chum salmon, grayling, king salmon, pink salmon, rainbow trout, red salmon.

Regulations: Open year-round, all species. Consult the current Alaska Department of Fish and Game regulations or the ADF&G Dillingham office, (907) 842-2427.

Facilities: No developed public facilities.

Contact: For information on the lower river area, contact the Alaska Peninsula/Becharof National Wildlife Refuge, P.O. Box 277, King Salmon, AK 99613; (907) 246-3339. For an air taxi, contact Branch River Air Service, 4540 Edinburgh Drive, Anchorage, AK 99515; (907) 248-3539 (in winter) or (907) 246-3437 (in summer). For guided floatfishing, contact Eruk's Wilderness Tours, 12720 Lupine Road, Anchorage, AK 99516; (907) 345-7678.

Description: The King Salmon River of the Egegik River system (draining Becharof Lake) offers some seldom sampled fishing and country to explore as an out-of-the-way alternative to the better, more accessible—and sometimes slightly crowded—rainbow locales of Katmai. The extreme southern occurrences for rainbow trout on the Alaska Peninsula are in its headwaters, along with some pretty decent charr, grayling and fair to good fishing for salmon in season. Usually accessed by floatplane at the headwaters of Gertrude Creek, the 60-mile King Salmon for the most part is a silty, tundra river with good fishing only in its headwaters and some of the clear south side tributaries. It can be floated, but the weather is real iffy and navigation along the flat lower sections are complicated by strong headwinds and tidal action. Wildlife, especially bears, is abundant, so precautions must be taken. It is an interesting area, with some promising rainbow fishing possibilities, so it's worth checking out.

16. COVILLE-GROSVENOR LAKES

Location: Katmai National Park, North Alaska Peninsula, 250 miles Southwest Anchorage.

Reference: Mount Katmai C-4, C-5, D-5, D-6.

Access: By floatplane from King Salmon.

Highlights: One of Katmai's best lake fishing locations, noted for lake trout, rainbows and charr.

Species: Charr, grayling, lake trout, rainbow trout, red salmon.

Facilities: Grosvenor Lodge, a concessionaire-run lodge, is on the lake narrows.

Regulations: Unbaited, artificial lures only, March through November 14. For additional restrictions, consult the current Alaska Department of Fish and Game regulations or the ADF&G Dillingham office, (907) 842-2427.

Contact: For campground and general information, contact Katmai National Park and Preserve, P.O. Box 7, King Salmon, AK 99613; (907) 246-3305. For lodge-based fishing on Coville-Grosvenor, contact Katmailand, Inc., 4700 Aircraft Drive #2, Anchorage, AK 99502; (800) 544-0551 or (907) 243-5448.

Description: Coville-Grosvenor is one of the more noteworthy lake locations within Katmai (along with Kulik, Naknek and Nonvianuk-Kukaklek) and the site of one of the original Peterson fish camps, Grosvenor. Part of a major migration corridor for the substantial Naknek sockeyes, the two lakes are well known for their productive rainbow trout, charr, grayling and lake trout fishing.

Rustic Grosvenor Lodge is situated at the narrows between the two lakes, which is a most advantageous fishing spot. Rainbows, charr and lake trout are taken there frequently, especially in the spring. Coville and Grosvenor both have a reputation for the best of

Katmai's lake trout fishing, with trophy fish (20 pounds plus) taken almost every season, and this is one of the few Katmai areas where serious effort for this species occurs. Nearby American Creek and the outlet to Savonoski provide additional opportunities for rainbows and charr. The Bay of Islands (Naknek Lake) can also be accessed by a one-mile trail from the southwest shore of Grosvenor.

In many ways, Grosvenor is the best of the three Katmai camps, as it is ignored by the crowds that flock to Brooks and is more laid back than Kulik. (It also has more fishing variety.) If you're planning a Katmai trip, you might want to consider it over the others. The best times for fishing are in the spring (June) and late summer through early fall (mid-August through mid-September).

Heading off for another day of fishing adventure.

REGION 3
ALASKA PENINSULA

South of Katmai lies the Alaska Peninsula—a narrow strip of barren tundra, volcanic peaks, glaciers and rugged coasts sprawling hundreds of miles out into the stormy North Pacific. A true No Man's Land, this area has some of the most remote and inhospitable terrain on the continent, which is routinely lashed by some of the world's worst weather. It's not a particularly attractive area to humans, of course, but its myriad clear streams, lakes and abundant runoff are perfectly suited for fish. Salmon and charr throng in nearly every drainage, including those in the Aleutians, and there are even steelhead trout in a handful of streams.

For years, the peninsula has been the almost exclusive domain of commercial anglers and hunters. But more and more, this area is opening up to sportfishing, with new lodges and outpost camps making it possible to sample waters that not too long ago were just points on the map of fishing dreams.

17. UGASHIK LAKE & RIVER

Location: North Alaska Peninsula, 350 southwest of Anchorage.
Reference: Ugashik B-3, B-4, B-5, C-2, C-3, C-4, C-5, D-2.
Access: By plane from Anchorage to King Salmon via commercial flight, then floatplane to the lake or wheelplane to Pilot Point or Ugashik, with boat access to river.
Highlights: A legendary Southwest Alaska hot spot for charr; also receives strong runs of silver and sockeye salmon.
Species: Charr, chum salmon, grayling, lake trout, pink salmon, red salmon, silver salmon.
Regulations: Closed to grayling fishing, but open year-round for other species. For additional regulations, consult the current Alaska Department of Fish and Game regulations or the ADF&G Dillingham office, (907) 842-2427.
Facilities: Two private lodges are located in area.
Contact: For public lands information, contact Alaska Peninsula/ Becharof National Wildlife Refuge, P.O. Box 277, King Salmon, AK 99613, (907) 246-3339; or Aniakchak National Preserve, P.O.

Box 7, King Salmon, AK 99613, (907) 246-3305. For lodge-based guided fishing, contact Gus Lamoureux, Ugashik Lakes Lodge, P.O. Box 90-444, Anchorage, AK 99502, (907) 248-3012; or Butch King, 202 East Northern Lights Boulevard, Anchorage, AK 99502, (800) 777-7055. For an air taxi, contact Peninsula Airways, Inc., 4851 Aircraft Drive, Anchorage, AK 99502; (907) 243-2485 (in Alaska), (800) 448-4226 (outside Alaska) or (907) 243-6848 (fax).

Description: For the longest time, the Ugashik Lakes were Alaska's top trophy grayling fishery. (The former IGFA world record, a four-pound, 13-ounce fish, was caught there in 1981.) In the glory days of the '60s and '70s, countless anglers from the world over made the long trip to the windblown, barren "narrows" between the lakes for an almost certain chance at a wall-hanging (19-inch or more) sailfin.

The heavy fishing pressure and other factors brought a noticeable decline in the quality of angling, so much so that drastic regulatory measures were enacted by the Alaska Department of Fish and Game to save the fishery—in 1990, all Ugashik drainages were closed to the taking of grayling. Charr fishing, according to local sources, still remains outstanding.

Most of the fishing effort has targeted the short, but extremely productive, water connecting the lower and upper lakes (the narrows), but the mouths of the numerous creeks that flow into both lakes and the Ugashik River outlet are other favored locations for encountering the system's abundant charr. Salmon are also plentiful, with notable silver and sockeye runs. The best times for Ugashik are early summer (June through mid-July) and fall (late August through early September).

18. BECHAROF LAKE

Location: North Alaska Peninsula, 325 miles southwest of Anchorage.
Reference: Naknek A-2, A-3; Karluk C-6, D-6; Ugashik C-1, D-1, D-3.
Access: By plane from Anchorage to King Salmon via commercial flight, then a floatplane charter to various points on the lake.
Highlights: An underutilized giant fishery, with abundant sockeye salmon and giant grayling and charr; also good fishing for silver salmon and untapped possibilities for lake trout.
Species: Charr, chum salmon, grayling, lake trout, pink salmon, (rainbow trout), red salmon, silver salmon.
Regulations: Open year-round, all species.
Facilities: No developed public facilities.

Contact: For public lands information, contact Alaska Peninsula/
Becharof National Wildlife Refuge, P.O. Box 277, King Salmon,
AK 99613, (907) 246-3339; or Aniakchak National Preserve, P.O.
Box 7, King Salmon, AK 99613, (907) 246-3305. For guided fishing
services, contact Gus Lamoureux, Ugashik Lakes Lodge, P.O. Box
90-444, Anchorage, AK 99502, (907) 248-3012; or Butch King, 202
East Northern Lights Boulevard, Anchorage, AK 99502, (800) 777-
7055. For an air taxi, contact Peninsula Airways, Inc., 4851 Aircraft
Drive, Anchorage, AK 99502; (907) 243-2485 (in Alaska), (800)
448-4226 (outside Alaska) or (907) 243-6848 (fax).

Description: Becharof Lake on the north Alaska Peninsula is an isolated, monstrous body of water—the second largest in Alaska—best
known for its abundant sockeye salmon runs, wildlife (including
brown bears, caribou and waterfowl) and unforgiving weather. It is a
sleeping giant as far as fishing goes and nearly all who have sunk
line in its vast waters have come away impressed with its awesome
potential. This lake and river system receives one of the most significant sockeye salmon runs in Alaska, with smaller numbers of silver, pink, chum and even a few king salmon. Stories of monstrous
charr and giant grayling and lake trout are substantiated now and
then by some remarkable catches from the few anglers intrepid
enough to challenge these waters. (Some of the state's largest specimens for these species have been caught here.) When you consider
the size, remoteness and productivity of this drainage, there's no
telling what this lake might hold.

But there's a catch: This part of Alaska is known for its wind tun-
nel weather—and on a lake of this size with no cover, that can make
for some scary conditions. But if you can duck in on a nice day, all
the guides, fishermen and biologists familiar with Becharof say the
outlet waters and numerous creek mouths around the lake offer
some truly remarkable fishing. Some of these drainages are even
rumored to have rainbows, though you'll have a hard time prying
any details from the folks who would know these things. For the
adventuresome angler with time and money to burn, Becharof Lake
is definitely on the list of Alaska's most promising untapped waters.

19. UGASHIK BAY STREAMS

Location: Ugashik Bay, Alaska Peninsula, 375 southwest of Anchorage.

Reference: Ugashik A-3, A-4, A-5, A-6, B-3, B-4, B-5, B-6; Bristol Bay B-1.

Access: By plane from Anchorage to King Salmon via commercial flight, then scheduled or chartered wheelplane to Pilot Point and boat or small plane (floats or wheels) to the streams.

Highlights: Ugashik Lake area drainages with good angling potential for all five species of salmon and charr.

Species: Charr, chum salmon, grayling, king salmon, northern pike, pink salmon, red salmon, silver salmon.

Regulations: Open year-round, all species.

Facilities: No developed public facilities. A few private hunting and fishing lodges serve the area, including one in Pilot Point.

Contact: For public lands information, contact Alaska Peninsula/ Becharof National Wildlife Refuge, P.O. Box 277, King Salmon, AK 99613; (907) 246-3339. For lodging, contact Painter Creek Lodge, 7111 Spruce Street, Anchorage, AK 99507; (907) 344-5181. For lodge-based guided fishing, contact Butch King, 202 East Northern Lights Boulevard, Anchorage, AK 99502; (800) 777-7055. For guided fishing, contact Tracy's Great Alaskan Outfitters, P.O. Box 433, Pilot Point, AK 99649; (907) 797-2246. For an air taxi, contact Peninsula Airways, Inc., 4851 Aircraft Drive, Anchorage, AK 99502; (907) 243-2485 (in Alaska), (800) 448-4226 (outside Alaska) or (907) 243-6848 (fax).

Description: There are several notable streams in the Ugashik Lakes vicinity that are visited regularly by area guides and lodges for their fine runs of all five species of salmon, abundant charr and even grayling and northern pike. They are accessed by small plane or boat from Pilot Point on lower Ugashik Bay.

The King Salmon River emptying into lower Ugashik Bay is perhaps the most popular of these, as it is easily accessed by floatplane at Mother Goose Lake and offers good fishing for (what else?) chinook salmon, as well as sockeye, coho and charr in the river below the lake and in adjoining tributaries. (The well-known, private Painter Creek Lodge is in the area, along the creek of the same name.) Dog Salmon River, a few miles away, is turbid, with fishing limited to its clear feeders. (Both streams have glacial sources, but the King Salmon benefits from the settling effect of Mother Goose Lake.) Like its neighbor, it has all five species of salmon, plus northern pike and grayling—in fact, it is one of the southernmost spots to fish grayling on the peninsula.

The Cinder River, 12 miles south, is a small runoff stream originating from the cinder beds of nearby Aniakchak. Braided and clear, this black sand drainage is fished only infrequently for its abundant silver salmon. A small hunting camp is located there, with access limited to small wheelplane landings on the beach or on cinder beds along the upper river.

20. CHIGNIK RIVER

Location: Southern Alaska Peninsula, Pacific side, 175 miles southwest of Kodiak, 475 miles southwest of Anchorage.

Reference: Chignik A-3, B-3.

Access: By plane from Anchorage to King Salmon via commercial flight, charter or scheduled plane service to the town of Chignik Lagoon or Chignik Lake, then river access by boat or raft. Access from Kodiak by the state ferry system or a plane charter is also possible.

Highlights: A remote, highly productive river system with untapped sportfishing potential for salmon (kings, reds and silvers) and charr.

Species: Charr, chum salmon, king salmon, pink salmon, red salmon, silver salmon.

Regulations: Open year-round, all species.

Facilities: No developed public facilities. Bed-and-breakfast-style lodging and guide services are available at the town of Chignik Lake.

Contact: For public lands information, contact Alaska Peninsula/ Becharof National Wildlife Refuge, P.O. Box 277, King Salmon, AK 99613, (907) 246-3339; or Aniakchak National Preserve, P.O. Box 7, King Salmon, AK 99613, (907) 246-3305. For lodging and guide service on the Chignik River, contact Johnny Lind, P.O. Box 4, Chignik Lake, AK 99548; (907) 845-2228. For an air taxi, contact Peninsula Airways, Inc., 4851 Aircraft Drive, Anchorage, AK 99502; (907) 243-2485 (in Alaska), (800) 448-4226 (outside Alaska) or (907) 243-6848 (fax).

Description: Chignik River, 175 miles southwest of Kodiak, is one of the most important salmon systems of the entire Alaska Peninsula, supporting extensive runs of sockeye, coho, pink and chum salmon and the south side peninsula's only significant population of chinook. Because of its remoteness, it receives virtually no outside angling pressure. Keep it in mind for future angling adventures, as more and more of the state's accessible waters become well visited.

This short river system connects two very productive sockeye salmon nurseries, Black and Chignik lakes, to the Pacific coast. Most of the present sportfishing effort occurs from Chignik Lake to the lagoon, where boat anglers target the river's chinook, silver salmon and abundant charr populations. The Chignik's substantial sockeye salmon runs (from early June through late July) receive almost no sportfishing pressure and there are even some rumors of steelhead spawning there. Access is by two gravel airstrips or by floatplane at the lake or lagoon. At present, visitor facilities are minimal, but there are definite plans for the construction of a lodge by the village native corporation. If you're looking for something different and have the time and resources to explore this unique fishery, give Johnny Lind a call at Chignik Lake.

21. MESHIK RIVER

Location: Central Alaska Peninsula, 400 miles southwest of Anchorage.
Reference: Sutwik Island D-6; Chignik C-1, C-2, D-1, D-2.
Access: By floatplane from King Salmon or Port Heiden (both are serviced by scheduled flights) to Meshik Lake or the lower river. Floating by raft or kayak is possible, with floatplane pick-up at the mouth. The lower river also may be reached by boat from Port Heiden.
Highlights: One of the more out-of-the-way Alaska Peninsula drainages, with untapped potential for salmon and charr fishing.
Species: Charr, chum salmon, king salmon, red salmon, silver salmon.
Regulations: Open year-round, all species.
Facilities: No developed public facilities. Lodge-based guided fishing is available from area lodges.
Contact: For public lands information, contact Alaska Peninsula/ Becharof National Wildlife Refuge, P.O. Box 277, King Salmon, AK 99613, (907) 246-3339; or Aniakchak National Preserve, P.O. Box 7, King Salmon, AK 99613, (907) 246-3305. For lodge-based guided fishing, contact Butch King, 202 East Northern Lights Boulevard, Anchorage, AK 99502; (800) 777-7055. For guided float-fishing, contact Eruk's Wilderness Tours, 12720 Lupine Road, Anchorage, AK 99516; (907) 345-7678. For an air taxi, contact Peninsula Airways, Inc., 4851 Aircraft Drive, Anchorage, AK 99502; (907) 243-2485 (in Alaska), (800) 448-4226 (outside Alaska) or (907) 243-6848 (fax).
Description: Very little serious sportfishing effort occurs south of the Ugashik Lakes area, because of the expense of transportation, lack

of services, weather and other factors. Most of the better streams (there are quite a few having outstanding salmon and charr runs) receive only light pressure from locals or the occasional hunter. The Meshik River of the Port Heiden area is worth mentioning because of its high potential, relatively easy access and location (the upper river) within Aniakchak National Preserve. With more and more folks discovering the outstanding adventure recreation potential of this area, it's only a matter of time before the Meshik becomes well known and utilized for its exciting fishing and floating possibilities.

Originating on steep mountain slopes southeast of Aniakchak Peak, the Meshik flows west for about 50 miles before emptying into Port Heiden. It's known for strong runs of chinook and coho salmon, along with sockeyes, chums and abundant charr. A headwater lake 40 miles up from the mouth, and numerous smaller lakes along the lower river, provide access possibilities for floatplanes. The best way to fish the Meshik is to float down from the upper river by raft or kayak, or to access the lower river and tributaries (where the best silver, king and charr fishing is) by boat or floatplane from Port Heiden.

With its many clear, shallow tributaries and wadable runs, the Meshik has considerable flyfishing opportunities. Aside from the abundant bear population and unpredictable weather, there is nothing here to preclude some very productive and enjoyable fishing explorations along this remote and utterly pristine drainage.

22. PENINSULA STEELHEAD STREAMS

Location: Lower Alaska Peninsula, Cape Seniavin to Cold Bay.
Reference: Chignik A-5, A-6, A-7, A-8; Port Moller C-4, C-5, C-6, D-4, D-5, D-6; Cold Bay A-2, A-3, B-2, B-3.
Access: By small wheelplane from Port Heiden or points north. Some primitive airstrips are available; floatplane landings are also possible in some areas.
Highlights: North America's last frontier for wild steelhead.
Species: Charr, chum salmon, king salmon, pink salmon, red salmon, silver salmon, steelhead.
Regulations: Open year-round, all species.
Facilities: Scattered outpost hunting camps, guided fishing and lodging are available in the area.
Contact: For public lands information, contact Alaska Peninsula/ Becharof National Wildlife Refuge, P.O. Box 277, King Salmon,

AK 99613, (907) 246-3339; or Aniakchak National Preserve, P.O. Box 7, King Salmon, AK 99613, (907) 246-3305. For guided fishing, contact Mel Gillis, Alaska Trophy Hunting and Fishing, P.O. Box 220247, Anchorage AK 99522, (907) 344-8589; or Wildman Lake Lodge, 3646 North Point Drive, Anchorage, AK 99515; (907) 243-5807. For an air taxi, contact Peninsula Airways, Inc., 4851 Aircraft Drive, Anchorage, AK 99502; (907) 243-2485 (in Alaska), (800) 448-4226 (outside Alaska) or (907) 243-6848 (fax).

Description: On the lower arc of the westward extending Alaska Peninsula lie the continent's last unexplored wild steelhead streams. At least a dozen small drainages from Chignik to Cold Bay are known to have spawning populations of the coveted sea-run rainbows, with the best occurring along Cape Seniavin, the Nelson Lagoon area and Cold Bay. They are undoubtedly more widespread than this, judging from accounts of locals, hunters, commercial fishermen and others who have had the rare opportunity to sample the far-flung waters of Unimak and the rugged Pacific side of the lower peninsula.

These peninsula steelhead runs are all very small, most numbering in the hundreds. As with Kodiak Island, they occur predominantly during fall, with peaks from late September through October. (Some bright spring fish have been reported in certain areas during April and May, however.) The average size of the fish is about the same or slightly more than those on Kodiak, with fish in the low teens reported on some streams.

The streams are very remote, brushy and difficult to access and fish. Most of them have only been worked a little by hunting guides during the fall season, with some focused effort recently on a few of the better ones. All reports indicate some outstanding possibilities for virgin fishing. Drawbacks are the notorious peninsula weather and the expense of getting in, factors that shouldn't stop hard-core adventure anglers from exploring this promising Last Frontier of wild steelhead fishing.

REGION 4
NUSHAGAK RIVER SYSTEM

West of Lake Iliamna, the heart of Bristol Bay is dominated by a river of immense size and importance—the Nushagak. Southwest Alaska's largest clear river system, it is a veritable giant of adventure fishing opportunity. With vast headwaters that stretch from the scenic Tikchik Lakes to the rugged highlands of Lake Clark country, the Nushagak and its hundreds of miles of pristine tributaries encompass a remarkable variety of terrain, enhanced by the presence of major runs of all five species of salmon and abundant populations of rainbow trout, charr (including lake trout), grayling and northern pike (10 sport species in all). A river of rare character and uncommonly high potential, the Nushagak offers a diversity of fishing experiences that few rivers anywhere can match—alpine float trips, spike camps, custom lodges and even big water trolling.

Some of the angling highlights of the mainstem and several of the more outstanding tributaries are detailed in the descriptions that follow (the Nuyakuk and Tikchik rivers are covered in the region section beginning on page 348). Access to the Nushagak system is generally from Dillingham and Lake Iliamna.

23. NUSHAGAK RIVER

Location: Central Bristol Bay, 275 miles southwest of Anchorage.

Reference: For the mainstem river: Dillingham A-5, B-4, B-5, C-3, C-4, D-4; Taylor Mountains A-4, B-2, B-3, B-4, C-1, C-2, C-4, C-5. See additional listings for tributary map coordinates.

Access: By floatplane from Dillingham or Iliamna. Boat access is possible from Dillingham.

Highlights: Southwest Alaska's most significant river system, with unlimited fishing possibilities.

Species: Charr, chum salmon, grayling, king salmon, lake trout, northern pike, pink salmon, rainbow trout, red salmon, silver salmon.

Regulations: Most of the river closed to king salmon from July 25 through December 31; otherwise open year-round, all species. Much of the upper river unbaited, single-hook, artificial lures only, with portions catch-and-release for rainbows. For details and additional restrictions, consult the Alaska Department of Fish and Game regulations or the ADF&G Dillingham office, (907) 842-2427.

Facilities: No developed public facilities. Guide services and lodge-based fishing are available.

Contacts: For spike camp fishing on the Nushagak, contact: (lower river—king and sockeye salmon) Ultimate Rivers, 5140 East 104th Avenue, Anchorage, AK 99516, (907) 346-2193; (upper river—rainbow, charr, grayling, salmon) Western Alaska Sportfishing, S.R. Box 2131, Hardin, MT 59034; (406) 665-3489 (in winter); (Mulchatna River and tributaries) Dennis Harms, P.O. Box 670071, Chugiak, AK 99567, (907) 696-2484. For lodge-based fishing on Nushagak and tributaries, contact Bill Martin Fish Alaska, Inc., P.O. Box 1887, Anchorage, AK 99510; (907) 346-2595 (in winter) or (907) 842-2725 (in summer). For guided Nushagak float trips, contact Ultimate Rivers; address and phone listed above. For an air taxi to all points along the Nushagak, contact Freshwater Adventures, Inc., P.O. Box 62, Dillingham, AK 99576; (907) 243-7676 (in winter) or (907) 842-5060 (in summer).

Description: For those who like their fishing on the wild side, the Nushagak River has got it all. If you're hot on kings (and who isn't?), you can fly out to the lower river (the Portage Creek area) in early summer (late June and early July), stay at a spike camp and experience some of Alaska's best streamfishing for the species, as tens of thousands of chrome-bright chinooks herd in fresh from the sea. (The Nushagak has Alaska's third largest king run, with 75,000 to 100,000 fish returning in an average year. Its ample gravel bars, beaches, sloughs and clear waters make it a natural for flyfishing.)

Later on in summer, the action shifts upriver for silver salmon, charr and abundant rainbows and grayling, with spike camp fishing on the upper mainstem above Koliganek or at the mouths of the major tributaries (Koktuli, Stuyahok or Mulchatna). If river rafting is more your style, the Nushagak has world-famous tributaries—two of them Wild and Scenic Rivers—that can provide some of Bristol Bay's best floatfishing. With nearly every lodge in Southwest Alaska visiting the river at some time during the season and dozens of area guides and outfitters providing a wide range of services, finding a Nushagak fishing adventure to suit your tastes and budget should be no problem.

Special note: Most of the land along the middle and lower Nushagak is owned by native corporations. For the location of public easements and current land status, check with the Bureau of Land Management, 222 West Seventh Avenue, Suite 13, Anchorage, AK 99513, (907) 271-5960; or the Alaska Department of Natural Resources, Public Information Center, 3601 C Street, Suite 200, Anchorage, AK 99503; (907) 762-2261.

24. MULCHATNA RIVER

Location: Northeast Bristol Bay, Nushagak drainage, 175 miles southwest of Anchorage.

Reference: Lake Clark B-7, B-8, C-6, C-7, C- 8, D-3, D-4, D-5, D-6; Taylor Mountains A-1, A-2, B-1; Dillingham C-3, D-1, D-2, D-3.

Access: By floatplane to the upper river via Lake Clark or Lake Iliamna. Camp and fish or raft/kayak to points downriver, with floatplane pick-up or take-out in villages along the Nushagak (with return to Dillingham via scheduled or chartered small plane flights). The lower and middle river are also accessible by boat from the Nushagak River.

Highlights: A Wild and Scenic River, and the largest and most heavily utilized tributary of the famed Nushagak, with good to excellent fishing for salmon, rainbow trout, grayling and charr.

Species: Charr, chum salmon, grayling, king salmon, lake trout, northern pike, pink salmon, rainbow trout, red salmon, silver salmon.

Regulations: Open year-round, all species; portions of the Mulchatna, unbaited, single-hook, artificial lures only. For details and additional restrictions, consult the Alaska Department of Fish and Game regulations or the ADF&G Dillingham office, (907) 842-2427.

Facilities: No developed public facilities.

Contact: For public lands information on Turquoise Lake and the upper river, contact Lake Clark National Park and Preserve, 4230 University Drive #311, Anchorage, AK 99508; (907) 271-3751. For guided spike camp fishing, contact Dennis Harms, P.O. Box 670071, Chugiak, AK 99567; (907) 696-2484. For guided float-fishing, contact Ultimate Rivers, 5140 East 104th Avenue, Anchorage, AK 99516, (907) 346-2193. For an air taxi to the upper river, contact Iliamna Air Taxi, P.O. Box 109, Iliamna, AK 99606, (907) 571-1248; or Air Adventures, P.O. Box 22, Kenai, AK 99611-0022, (907) 776-5444.

Description: The Mulchatna River, as the main, first-order tributary of the immense, fish-rich Nushagak, is one of Bristol Bay's most popular fly-in fishing destinations. A Wild and Scenic River with headwaters in the majestic Lake Clark country, the Mulchatna (and its main tributary, the Chilikadrotna) is also one of Southwest Alaska's most popular rivers for floating.

In its 250 miles, the Mulchatna changes character considerably, from a small, rocky alpine stream to a broad, braided river coursing through lowland forest. Along the way, it is joined by numerous tributaries, some of them well known and popular fishing streams on their own, such as the Chilikadrotna, Stuyahok and Koktuli. Access to the upper river is usually by floatplane from Lakes Clark or Iliamna, putting in at the Half Cabin Lakes area about 30 miles down from Turquoise Lake. (The headwaters at the lake are not commonly floated because of rocky, shallow conditions.) From there, it's an easy float, with fast water, some minor rapids (all Class I, one short Class II), but no major challenge to anyone possessing basic boating skills and a high-quality raft or kayak. (Be forewarned, however: There are abundant sweepers, especially below the Chilikadrotna confluence.) Most floaters end their trip somewhere below the Mulchatna-Chilchitna confluence (a five- to seven-day float), but longer trips are certainly possible.

Fishing on the Mulchatna is generally good to excellent, depending on water conditions and the time of year. (The river tends to muddy easily during heavy rains.) The mouths of the larger tributaries and mainstem up to the Koktuli have traditionally been some of Bristol Bay's most productive and popular fly-in areas for king and silver salmon, rainbow, grayling and charr. Also, the river's abundant wildlife, particularly caribou and moose, attracts quite a bit of use from hunters each fall, who float in rafts or stay in commercial outpost camps and enjoy good fishing as a bonus. For folks wanting to sample some of Alaska's better outpost tent camp fishing or an outstanding floatfishing trip, the Mulchatna is pretty hard to beat.

25. CHILIKADROTNA RIVER

Location: Northeast Bristol Bay, Nushagak drainage, 100 miles southwest of Anchorage.

Reference: Lake Clark C-2, C-3, C-4, C-5, C-6, C-7.

Access: By floatplane to the river headwaters via Clark or Iliamna lakes. A raft or kayak trip is possible down to Mulchatna River, with floatplane pick-up below the Mulchatna-Chilchitna confluence.

Highlights: A Wild and Scenic River, one of western Alaska's prettiest, and an exciting floatfishing trip, with good opportunities for grayling, rainbows, charr and salmon.

Species: Charr, chum salmon, grayling, king salmon, lake trout, northern pike, pink salmon, rainbow trout, red salmon, silver salmon.

Regulations: Open year-round, all species.

Facilities: No developed public facilities.

Contact: For public lands information on upper river area, contact Lake Clark National Park and Preserve, 4230 University Drive #311, Anchorage, AK 99508; (907) 271-3751. For air taxi service, contact Iliamna Air Taxi, P.O. Box 109, Iliamna, AK 99606, (907) 571-1248; or Air Adventures, P.O. Box 22, Kenai, AK 99611-0022, (907) 776-5444. For guided floatfishing, contact Ultimate Rivers, 5140 East 104th Avenue, Anchorage, AK 99516; (907) 346-2193.

Description: The Chilikadrotna Wild and Scenic River is one of Southwest Alaska's premier float trips, with outstanding wilderness values and good fishing. It begins in the rugged alpine reaches of the Alaska Range in Lake Clark National Park, 100 miles southwest of Anchorage. A whitewater river, the 62-mile Chili is wide (100 to 200 feet), with swift, rocky flows, rapids (Class I to Class III), logjams and plenty of sweepers—definitely not a river for inexperienced or lazy boaters.

Fishing is good from late June into September for charr, grayling, rainbows and some salmon (mostly chum, silvers and a few kings), with excellent conditions for flyfishing along much of the river. The beautiful Twin Lakes at the headwaters have some very good lake trout populations, and there are even some pike to be had in the sloughs along the river. Magnificent scenery, wildlife and numerous hiking opportunities are a definite bonus along the way.

Most rafters put in at Twin Lakes or at several small lakes down below and generally take a seven-day journey down to the Mulchatna, putting out on long, flat stretches of river 12 to 13 miles below the confluence. Longer voyages continuing down the Mulchatna can be easily done—check with the air service for details.

26. KOKTULI RIVER

Location: Northeast Bristol Bay, Nushagak drainage, 220 miles southwest of Anchorage.

Reference: Iliamna D-7, D-8; Dillingham D-1, D-2.

Access: By plane from Anchorage to Iliamna via commercial flight, then floatplane to lakes (along the upper river or in the Swan River-Koktuli area) or to the Koktuli-Mulchatna confluence. Raft or kayak trips are possible from the headwaters down to the Mulchatna confluence (four to six days), with floatplane pick-up from Iliamna.

Highlights: One of the more popular upper Nushagak tributaries for sportfishing and an excellent float trip, known for its rainbow, grayling, king, silver and sockeye salmon angling.

Species: Charr, chum salmon, grayling, king salmon, lake trout, northern pike, pink salmon, rainbow trout, red salmon, silver salmon.

Regulations: Open year-round; unbaited, single-hook, artificial lures only. For additional restrictions, consult the Alaska Department of Fish and Game regulations or the ADF&G Dillingham office, (907) 842-2427.

Facilities: No developed public facilities.

Contact: For air taxi to the Koktuli River, contact Iliamna Air Taxi, P.O. Box 109, Iliamna, AK 99606; (907) 571-1248. For guided floatfishing, contact Ultimate Rivers, 5140 East 104th Avenue, Anchorage, AK 99516; (907) 346-2193.

Description: The Koktuli River, which is similar in size and character to the Stuyahok (see next listing), has been one of the more popular upper Nushagak tributaries for some time, and is easily accessible by floatplane from nearby Lake Iliamna or Lake Clark. It is noted for its consistent salmon, grayling and rainbow trout angling, with good flyfishing opportunities in its clear waters. The majority of users are fly-in fishermen working the mouth and lower river, but quite a few folks float it regularly.

Floatplanes can put in at the mouth or on lakes along the upper river or vicinity of the Swan River confluence. (Short portages are sometimes necessary.) From there, the river is an easy float (one to two days from the Swan River, four to six days from upper river), with no major hazards except sweepers and logjams. Floaters can take-out at the mouth or continue down the Mulchatna. Wildlife is abundant and includes bear, caribou, wolf, moose and waterfowl.

27. STUYAHOK RIVER

Location: Northeast Bristol Bay, Nushagak drainage, 250 miles southwest of Anchorage.

Reference: Iliamna C-8, D-8; Dillingham C-1.

Access: By plane from Anchorage to Iliamna via commercial flight, then floatplane to lakes along the upper river or the Mulchatna confluence. Camp and fish, or raft and fish, to points downriver for floatplane pick-up and return to Iliamna or Dillingham.

Highlights: A delightful headwater of the Nushagak and a well-known float trip, with good fishing for grayling, charr, rainbow trout and king and silver salmon in season.

Species: Charr, chum salmon, grayling, king salmon, northern pike, pink salmon, rainbow trout, silver salmon.

Regulations: Open year-round, all species; unbaited, single-hook, artificial lures only. For additional restrictions, consult the Alaska Department of Fish and Game regulations or the ADF&G Dillingham office, (907) 842-2427.

Facilities: No developed public facilities.

Contact: For air taxi service to the Stuyahok, contact Iliamna Air Taxi, P.O. Box 109, Iliamna, AK 99606; (907) 571-1248. For guided floatfishing down the Stuyahok, contact Ultimate Rivers, 5140 East 104th Avenue, Anchorage, AK 99516; (907) 346-2193.

Description: The Stuyahok is one of several small Nushagak tributaries that drain the highlands west of Lake Iliamna. It is short, only about 50 miles in length, and is fished mostly from rafts or from camps at its confluence with the Mulchatna. With no real whitewater, it is an easy, enjoyable float (a three- to five-day trip) for people of average wilderness boating skills. It offers pleasant scenery and good to excellent fishing for rainbow trout, charr, grayling and king and silver salmon.

The upper river is usually accessed from Lake Iliamna by floatplane, using one of several pothole lakes for a put-in. (Some may require short portages to reach the river.) Below this area, there is no floatplane access until the confluence. The upper "Stu" winds through pretty alpine foothills before entering the forested lowlands surrounding the Mulchatna. While it has no rapids to speak of, sweepers are abundant. There is plenty of good flyfishing water. The lower five miles or so of river, including the mouth, have the Stuyahok's best salmon fishing (and its most concentrated angling effort, too). All in all, the Stu makes for a sweet little fishing trip, highly recommended for newcomers as a great introduction to the fabulous streams of Bristol Bay.

REGION 5
WOOD-TIKCHIK LAKES

Legend has it that a giant bear flattened the western end of the Alaska Range and carved the Tikchik Lakes with swoops of his great paws. Like long, deep gouges from colossal claws, the 12 lakes that make up the Wood River-Tikchik chain at the head of Bristol Bay run more or less parallel, varying in length from 15 to 45 miles and to depths of up to 900 feet. Hemmed in by steep, pinnacled slopes, they bear a striking resemblance to the deep blue fjords of northern Europe. Even more alluring is the fishing in the lakes and numerous streams and outlets; the abundant, pristine habitat supports major runs of salmon and a diverse assemblage of resident fighters—rainbow trout, charr, grayling, lake trout and even big northern pike. With so much to offer, this area is one of the most coveted recreation destinations in all of Alaska.

To preserve the scenic wonder and diverse resources of this amazing area, the state of Alaska in 1978 designated 1.6 million acres of this region as Wood-Tikchik State Park. At 2,500 square miles, it is the largest state park in the nation, and is managed as a total wilderness.

28. WOOD-TIKCHIK LAKES

Location: Head of Bristol Bay, 325 miles southwest of Anchorage.

Reference: Bethel A-1, B-1; Dillingham A-8, B-7, B-8, C-7, C-8, D-6, D-7, D-8; Goodnews Bay B-1, C-1, D-1; Taylor Mountains A-7, A-8, B-8.

Access: By plane from Anchorage to Dillingham via commercial flight, then floatplane to the lake system. Kayak, canoe, raft or sportboat travel is possible throughout the area, as is road access from Dillingham to the bottom lake (Aleknagik).

Highlights: America's largest state park—a wonderland of 12 scenic glacial lakes, with superlative possibilities for fishing adventure.

Species: Charr, chum salmon, grayling, king salmon, lake trout, northern pike, pink salmon, rainbow trout, red salmon, silver salmon.

Regulations: Open year-round, all species. On portions of the Agulo-wak River, single-hook, unbaited, artificial lures only; on the Agulukpak River, flyfishing only during summer and catch-and release rainbow trout from June 8 through October 31. For details and additional restrictions, consult the Alaska Department of Fish and Game regulations or the ADF&G Dillingham office, (907) 842-2427.

Facilities: No developed public facilities. Lodge-based fishing, guide services and gear rental are available.

Contact: For park information, contact Wood-Tikchik State Park, P.O. Box 107001, Dillingham, AK 99576; (907) 842-2375 (in summer) or (907) 345-5014 (in winter). For a premier lodge experience, contact Bristol Bay Lodge, P.O. Box 580, Ellensburg, WA 98926; (509) 964-2094 (in winter) or (907) 842-2500 (in summer). For guide services, contact Ultimate Rivers, 5140 East 104th Avenue, Anchorage, AK 99516; (907) 346-2193. For an air taxi, contact Freshwater Adventures, Inc., P.O. Box 62, Dillingham, AK 99576; (907) 243-7676 (in winter) or (907) 842-5060 (in summer).

Description: The possibilities for the adventure angler are almost without peer in Bristol Bay's fabulous lake country. Fly in to any one of the lakes and camp, fish and explore—on foot or boat—for days, even weeks if you desire. (Interconnected by short rivers, the lakes can be traversed almost entirely with a few short portages.) Or take a raft or kayak down one of the swift outlet rivers (such as Tikchik or Nuyakuk) and enjoy superb fishing as you drift through magnificent wild country. On the tamer end of things, there are several world-class fishing lodges nestled here that will pamper you with all the comforts of home (and more) while you enjoy great fishing action out the front door. If your tastes run somewhere in between, the score of reputable guides and outfitters who service the area can accommodate just about any adventure whim.

Guides' tip: Bristol Bay's "lake country" has some of Alaska's most abundant and exciting spring and late season fishing for rainbow trout and charr (including lake trout), which is concentrated in the major connecting streams and outlets. If you can make it to some of these waters at the right time (from June to early July and August to late September) with egg, attractor or smolt patterns or flashy spoons and spinners, you'll find out what "wild" fishing is really all about.

Some of the better Wood-Tikchik hot spots for this kind of fishing are: the Wood River outlet and the Agulowak River (Aleknagik Lake); Agulukpak River (Lakes Beverley-Nerka); the outlet of Little Togiak Lake (Lake Nerka); Goldenhorn and Peace rivers (Lake Beverley); the narrows connecting Tikchik and Nuakuk lakes; and the mouth of the Tikchik River and the outlet of the Nuyakuk River (Tikchik Lake).

29. Tikchik River

Location: North-central Bristol Bay, 330 miles southwest of Anchorage.

Reference: Dillingham D-7; Taylor Mountains A-7, A-8, B-7, B-8.

Access: By plane from Anchorage to Dillingham via commercial flight, then floatplane to Nishlik and Tikchik lakes. A raft or kayak trip is possible down from Nishlik Lake (six to eight days), with floatplane pick-up at Tikchik and return to Dillingham.

Highlights: Outstanding wilderness float river with good fishing for grayling, charr, pike, rainbow trout and some salmon (sockeye, chum and pink).

Species: Charr, chum salmon, grayling, lake trout, northern pike, pink salmon, rainbow trout, red salmon.

Regulations: Open year-round, all species.

Facilities: Lodge-based fishing, guide services and gear rental are available in the area.

Contact: For guide services for the Tikchik River, contact Ultimate Rivers, 5140 East 104th Avenue, Anchorage, AK 99516; (907) 346-2193. For lodge-based fishing, contact Bill Martin Fish Alaska, Inc., P.O. Box 1887, Anchorage, AK 99510; (907) 346-2595. For an air taxi, contact Freshwater Adventures, Inc., P.O. Box 62, Dillingham, AK 99576; (907) 243-7676 (in winter) or (907) 842-5060 (in summer).

Description: The Tikchik is one of Southwest Alaska's most outstanding wild rivers, with superb scenery, swift but not too challenging water, abundant wildlife and good fishing. It drains the uppermost lake of the Wood-Tikchik chain, emptying into Tikchik Lake some 65 miles or so below. Clear, fast and gravelly, it makes an exciting wilderness float through some of Bristol Bay's more remote back-country, with some good fishing (for grayling, charr, salmon and some rainbows) along the way.

The trip begins with an exciting plane ride through the heart of the Tikchik Lakes (an experience some say is worth the price of admission alone) to remote Nishlik Lake, where most folks put in. From there, it's a serene cruise (fast water, with some Class I) through a broad, mountain-ringed tundra valley, where you can expect to see caribou, wolf, moose, ptarmigan and waterfowl and enjoy outstanding flyfishing for grayling and charr. Further down, the river gets braided and wider as it takes on more tributaries and enters lowland forest. (Watch the sweepers!) The fishing gets more interesting, too—some rainbows, brighter salmon and more charr in the sections above Tikchik Lake. But be mindful of the bears, as

there will be plenty along the river during salmon season.
Figure on at least a six- to seven-day trip to allow for leisurely
floating and fishing. Allow plenty of time to enjoy Tikchik Lake. It
makes a superb trip finale, with its scenic views and great fishing for
charr, lake trout, rainbows and even monster pike in the backwater
sloughs. If you want, you can continue down the Nuyakuk River for
an additional four to five days of exciting rafting and great fishing,
ending your trip at the village of Koliganek on the Nushagak River.
(See the Nuyakuk listing below.) With or without continuing on the
Nuyakuk, the Tikchik River is one of the most highly recommended
and enjoyable floatfishing trips in all of Southwest Alaska.

Guides' tip: August and early September are the best times to float the
Tikchik for fishing (rainbows, charr, salmon). You can even combine a moose/caribou hunt with your float fishing at that time if you
are so inclined. Don't forget some big spoons or big, flashy flies for
the lake trout and pike in Tikchik Lake.

30. NUYAKUK RIVER

Location: North-central Bristol Bay, 300 miles southwest of Anchorage.
Reference: Dillingham D-4, D-5, D-6.
Access: By plane from Anchorage to Dillingham via commercial
flight, then floatplane to Tikchik Lake, the upper river (below the
falls) or other points. Raft or kayak trips are possible downriver to
the town of Koliganek on Nushagak River, with wheelplane pick-up
for a return to Dillingham. Boat access from Koliganek to the lower
river is also possible.
Highlights: One of the Nushagak River's most outstanding tributaries,
with excellent rainbow, grayling, charr and silver and sockeye
salmon fishing.
Species: Charr, chum salmon, grayling, king salmon, lake trout, northern pike, pink salmon, rainbow trout, red salmon, silver salmon.
Regulations: Open year-round, all species; on the upper river, single-
hook, unbaited, artificial lures only. For additional restrictions, consult the Alaska Department of Fish and Game regulations or the
ADF&G Dillingham office, (907) 842-2427.
Facilities: A private lodge is available on the upper river. An undeveloped campground is available near Nuyakuk Falls.
Contact: For guided floatfishing, contact Ultimate Rivers, 5140 East
104th Avenue, Anchorage, AK 99516; (907) 346-2193. For an air
taxi, contact Freshwater Adventures, Inc., P.O. Box 62, Dillingham,

AK 99576; (907) 243-7676 (in winter) or (907) 842-5060 (in summer).

Description: In many ways, the Nuyakuk River is the most exceptional tributary of the renowned Nushagak River system. Issuing crystal blue from Tikchik Lake north of Dillingham, it flows wide, swift and deep for 45 miles to its juncture with the mainstem above the town of Koliganek. As the sole connection and fish pathway linking the Tikchik lakes with the Nushagak, it receives a sizeable influx of migrating salmon and supports abundant populations of rainbow trout, charr and grayling. Sportfishing, especially along the upper river, is certainly among the best in all of Bristol Bay.

The Nuyakuk can be accessed by plane and boat along much of its length, but is best fished by raft, floating down from the lake (a trip of four to six days). Surprisingly few folks have done this outstanding trip, considering the quality of the fishing and relatively uncomplicated logistics. It might be the river's serious whitewater (two stretches of rapids, Class II to Class III, and one set of Class IV on the upper river) scares them off, but it shouldn't. With good gear, intermediate boat skills and common sense, just about anyone can safely negotiate the upper Nuyakuk.

You should begin the trip at Tikchik Lake, as the fishing around the outlet and in the first few miles of river below is really too good to miss, especially if you're keen on big rainbows, lake trout and charr. The rapids right below the lake, however, are substantial and should be scouted beforehand from the ridge along the right side of the river. (The pilot who flies you in will generally know the current conditions and can advise you.) Don't miss fishing the deep holes right below the rapids, though; some of the biggest rainbows to come out of the Nushagak system are taken there.

If you're not up to a white knuckle challenge (or if your pilot advises that the river conditions are too hairy), you can put in five miles downriver, below Nuyakuk Falls, at one of the prettiest undeveloped campsites in all of Bristol Bay. For those running down from the lake, an unmistakable landing and portage trail on the right side of the river will allow safe passage. The fishing and camping at the falls is so good that you might not want to leave, but when you do, you'll find mostly smooth sailing (fast water and one stretch of Class I rapids) all the way down to the Nushagak, where you can end your trip at the town of Koliganek. You'll also find good fishing for silver and sockeye salmon, which are best fished in the section of river below the falls.

The whitewater, scarcity of gravel bars for camping, and deep, fast flows are challenges that should only enhance your appreciation for the fine fishing and other exquisite qualities found on this premier Southwest river.

Fishing for sockeye salmon in the Katmai region.

REGION 6
TOGIAK RIVER SYSTEM

Between the drainages of Kuskokwim Bay and the Tikchik Lakes lies some noteworthy adventure fishing potential, mostly concentrated in the Togiak River system, in the national wildlife refuge of the same name. Though the main river from Togiak Lake down to the mouth gets fished consistently, most of the remote headwaters to the west and north get almost no pressure and offer tantalizing possibilities for totally wild stream and lake fishing in awesome surroundings.

31. TOGIAK RIVER

Location: Western Bristol Bay, 350 miles southwest of Anchorage.
Reference: Goodnews A-4, B-3, B-4, C-2, C-3, D-2.
Access: By plane from Anchorage to Dillingham via commercial flight, then floatplane to a headwater lake (usually Togiak or Upper Togiak) or points downriver. Four- to five-day float trips by raft or kayak are possible down to lower river, with floatplane pick-up from Dillingham.
Highlights: A very scenic Southwest Alaska river with a history of good silver and king salmon runs and outstanding charr fishing.
Species: Charr, chum salmon, grayling, king salmon, pink salmon, rainbow trout, red salmon, silver salmon.
Regulations: Open year-round, all species.
Facilities: Lodge-based fishing and guide services are available in the area.
Contact: For public lands information on the Upper Togiak River, contact Togiak National Wildlife Refuge, P.O. Box 270, Dillingham, AK 99576; 907-842-1063. For guide services for the Tikchik River, contact Ultimate Rivers, 5140 East 104th Avenue, Anchorage, AK 99516; (907) 346-2193. For lodge-based fishing, contact Bill Martin Fish Alaska, Inc., P.O. Box 1887, Anchorage, AK 99510; (907) 346-2595. For an air taxi, contact Freshwater Adventures, Inc., P.O. Box 62, Dillingham, AK 99576; (907) 243-7676 (in winter) or (907) 842-5060 (in summer).
Description: The Togiak River is a 60-mile, crystal-clear waterway connecting the Togiak Lakes with Bristol Bay, west of the Nush-

agak. A tundra river, it has been fished for years, at times offering outstanding silver and king salmon angling, in addition to superb charr and fair to good rainbow trout and grayling. It flows through some of the most scenic country in all of Southwest Alaska.

Fair-sized, deep and wide, with considerable current but virtually no whitewater, the Togiak is an easy float, but it's difficult to fish with anything but spin and casting gear. Flyfishing is essentially limited to the lakes, mouths of tributary streams and occasional shallow riffle sections and sloughs. Most folks fly in to Togiak Lake and float down to the lower river (four to six days) by raft, putting out right below the Togiak Wilderness boundary at the mouth of Pungokepuk Creek. The headwater tributaries (including Gechiak, Kashiak and Pungokepuk) and lakes are seldom visited, but known to have outstanding possibilities for salmon, charr and big rainbows.

Guides' tip: If you have the time, a put-in on Upper Togiak Lake is highly recommended for its scenery and fishing. If you're planning a float trip, figure on adding three days to your trip time. Take a small "kicker" outboard along to make the lake crossing more enjoyable (it's 18 miles), if you plan on using a river raft.

REGION 7
KUSKOKWIM RIVER

The 800-mile Kuskokwim is the second largest river in Alaska. Like many others in the state, its headwaters are primarily glacial (located in the west Alaska Range), so sportfishing is limited to its clear-flowing tributaries. The best of these empty into the lower river and Kuskokwim Bay, from runoff sources in the Bristol Bay highlands. These swift mountain streams are all very similar in size and character, issuing from crystal headwater lakes over beds of rock and gravel. All support abundant runs of salmon and substantial populations of charr, grayling and the state's westernmost rainbow trout. Some of these drainages are quite exceptional and are considered among the finest floatfishing rivers in Alaska, if not the world.

For public lands information on the lower Kuskokwim rivers, contact the Bureau of Land Management, Alaska State Office, 222 West Seventh Avenue, Suite 13, Anchorage, AK 99513, (907) 271-5960; Togiak National Wildlife Refuge, P.O. Box 270, Dillingham, AK 99576, (907) 842-1063; or Yukon Delta National Wildlife Refuge, P.O. Box 346, Bethel, AK 99559, (907) 543-3151.

32. GOODNEWS RIVER

Location: Lower Kuskokwim Bay, 375 miles southwest of Anchorage.
Reference: Goodnews Bay A-6, A-7, B-4, B-5, B-6, B-7, C-4, C-5.
Access: By floatplane from Dillingham or Bethel to headwater lakes or the lower river. Four- to seven-day raft or kayak trips are possible from area lakes, with floatplane or boat pick-up on the lower river or wheelplane pick-up from the strip in the Goodnews Bay village.
Highlights: One of Alaska's premier floatfishing rivers, excellent for king and silver salmon, rainbow trout, grayling and sea-run charr, with outstanding flyfishing possibilities.
Species: Charr, chum salmon, grayling, king salmon, lake trout, pink salmon, rainbow trout, red salmon, silver salmon.
Regulations: Open year-round. On river sections within the Togiak National Wildlife Refuge, unbaited, single-hook, artificial lures only.
Facilities: No developed public facilities. A private outpost tent camp is located on the lower river.

Contact: For spike camp fishing, contact Alaska River Safaris, 4909 Rollins Drive, Anchorage, AK 99508; (907) 333-2860. For guided floatfishing, contact Ultimate Rivers, 5140 East 104th Avenue, Anchorage, AK 99516, (907) 346-2193. For floatplane charters to and from the river, contact Freshwater Adventures, Inc., P.O. Box 62, Dillingham, AK 99576; (907) 243-7676 (in winter) or (907) 842-5060 (in summer). For wheelplane flights to and from the village of Goodnews, contact Kuskokwim Aviation, Box 1425 Airport, Bethel, AK 99559, (907) 556-8811.

Special note: Portions of the lower river are owned by the Goodnews Village Corporation; for information, contact Kuitsarak Inc., General Delivery, Goodnews Bay, AK 99589; (907) 967-8520. For public lands information, contact the Bureau of Land Management, Alaska State Office, 222 West Seventh Avenue, Suite 13, Anchorage, AK 99513, (907) 271-5960; or Togiak National Wildlife Refuge, P.O. Box 270, Dillingham, AK 99576, (907) 842-1063.

Description: The Goodnews River system is one of the best known of the fabulously productive fishing streams of Kuskokwim Bay. Like its sister drainage, the Kanektok, it has some of Southwest Alaska's finest streamfishing for salmon, trout, grayling and sea-run charr. It is also a world-renowned float trip destination.

Like other neighboring drainages, the Goodnews is a tundra river. Short (only 60 miles) and sparkling clear, it is comprised of three forks that drain the most southerly valley in Kuskokwim Bay. The Middle Fork and mainstem are the most commonly fished sections. Floatplane access is possible on numerous headwater lakes (including Goodnews, Canyon, Awayak, Nimgun, Middle Fork and Kukatlim) and the lower river, which can also be accessed by boat. None of the forks contain any major hazards to boaters, except for swift water and some minor rapids between Canyon and Arayak creeks in the upper mainstem. (Low-water conditions can be a real "drag" in the shallow sections below the lakes, especially on the Middle Fork.) They can be floated in anywhere from four to seven days.

With its different forks, miles of tributaries and numerous headwater lakes, the Goodnews certainly has a wealth of good fishing possibilities. It is noted for its abundant, beautifully marked rainbow trout (the famous leopard rainbows, to 10 pounds), big grayling (to three pounds), sea-run charr (to eight pounds) and outstanding fly-fishing opportunities, particularly for king and silver salmon. Nearly all of the deep, bedrock basin headwater lakes contain abundant, underfished lake trout and charr, in addition to supporting good runs of sockeye salmon.

Raft fishing is certainly the most exciting way of experiencing rivers like the Goodnews, but there are drawbacks, one being the weather, which in Kuskokwim Bay can be notoriously bum. The river and surrounding terrain afford little cover, so come prepared with the finest quality raingear, tents and extra warm clothes. Also, bears are a real hazard with the brush and abundant salmon. If all this sounds too serious, you might want to consider the benefits of a stay in an outpost camp. (The Goodnews has one major spike camp operator; see listing above.) However you decide to go, the Goodnews is about good as it gets in Alaska, especially if you fish it during the months of July and August.

33. AROLIK RIVER

Location: Kuskokwim Bay, 400 miles southwest of Anchorage.

Reference: Goodnews Bay B-6, C-7, C-8.

Access: By plane from Anchorage to Bethel via commercial flight, then floatplane to Arolik Lake or wheelplane to the airstrip at Snow Gulch. From there, raft or kayak down to the lower river, with boat pick-up from Quinhagak village. The lower river can also be accessed and fished by jet boat. Return to Bethel via scheduled or chartered wheelplane, then commercial flight back to Anchorage.

Highlights: Another outstanding Kuskokwim Bay river for fishing; not as heavily fished as the Goodnews or Kanektok, but with the same abundant rainbow, sea-run charr, grayling and salmon.

Species: Charr, chum salmon, grayling, king salmon, lake trout, pink salmon, rainbow trout, red salmon, silver salmon.

Regulations: Open year-round, all species.

Facilities: No developed public facilities. Guide services are available.

Contact: For guided fishing, contact Kanektok River Safaris, P.O. Box 9, Quinhagak, AK 99655, (907) 556-8211. For an air taxi to the Arolik, contact Kuskokwim Aviation, Box 1425 Airport, Bethel, AK 99559, (907) 556-8811; or Freshwater Adventures, Inc., P.O. Box 62, Dillingham, AK 99576, (907) 243-7676 (in winter) or (907) 842-5060 (in summer).

Description: While the Arolik is among the outstanding waters of Kuskokwim Bay, it receives just a fraction of the attention lavished on the more glamorous rivers it is situated between, the Kanektok and Goodnews. It flows northwest for about 70 miles from headwaters in the ridge of mountains above the Goodnews, with two main forks and numerous tributaries. The lower mainstem braids heavily and then splits into separate mouths that empty into Kuskokwim Bay just south of the village of Quinhagak.

With abundant rainbows, charr, grayling and salmon, fishing on the Arolik is every bit as good as that on the Kanektok or Goodnews; in fact, the trout fishing may even be better because the river doesn't get hit as hard as the other two. Arolik Lake is noted for having some of the best lake trout fishing in the region. The catch to it all is that the Arolik is not a cake walk river float like the others. The upper river is rocky and shallow in spots, especially at the headwaters, and during low-water times, floating may be difficult, if not impossible. You can float early in the season and take your chances, using a lightly equipped raft, inflatable canoe or kayak. Or you can put in by wheelplane at the old mining strip on Snow Gulch about 10 miles below the junction of the East and South forks and skip those shallow stretches altogether. (Most of the better fishing is below there anyway.)

Ending your float trip on the Arolik won't be easy either. It would be ideal to have someone from Quinhagak run up in a skiff and meet you on the lower river, as the tidal influence makes rafting down into the mouth tricky and dangerous, not to mention trying a floatplane pick-up there. The native village corporation, Quanirtuuq, Inc., owns lands along the lower river and is hoping to develop a rather exclusive sportfish operation there, with tent camps and guided/unguided fishing from jet boats. Give them a call at (907) 555-8211 (ask for Joshua Cleveland) to make arrangements for a boat pick-up or a short stay at their tent camp (not a bad way to end your float trip). They have regular week-long guided fishing packages, too, if you're not keen on rafting the river.

34. KANEKTOK RIVER

Location: Kuskokwim Bay, 350 miles southwest of Anchorage.
Reference: Goodnews Bay C-4, C-5, C-6, D-3, D-4, D-5, D-6, D-7, D-8.
Access: By plane from Anchorage to Dillingham or Bethel via commercial flight, then floatplane to Kagati Lake (or other headwater lakes) or wheelplane to Quinhagak village, with boat access to the lower river. A raft or kayak trip is possible from the lake to Quinhagak (five to seven days), with wheelplane pickup and return to Bethel, then Anchorage.

Highlights: One of Alaska's most celebrated floatfishing rivers. Beautiful scenery and outstanding rainbow trout, sea-run charr, grayling, king and silver salmon fishing. Perfect flyfishing water.

Species: Charr, chum salmon, grayling, king salmon, lake trout, pink salmon, rainbow trout, red salmon, silver salmon.

Regulations: Open year-round. On portions within the Togiak National Wildlife Refuge, single-hook, unbaited, artificial lures only. For additional restrictions, consult the current Alaska Department of Fish and Game regulations or the ADF&G Dillingham office, (907) 842-2427.

Facilities: No developed public facilities. Guide and air taxi services are available.

Contact: For guided float trips, contact Ultimate Rivers, 5140 East 104th Avenue, Anchorage, AK 99516; (907) 346-2193. For guided/unguided spike camp fishing, contact Kanektok River Safaris, P.O. Box 9, Quinhagak, AK 99655, (907) 556-8211; or Bill Martin Fish Alaska, Inc., P.O. Box 1887, Anchorage, 99510, (907) 346-2595. For air taxi service, contact Freshwater Adventures, Inc., P.O. Box 62, Dillingham, AK 99576, (907) 243-7676 (in winter) or (907) 842-5060 (in summer); or Kuskokwim Aviation, Box 1425 Airport, Bethel, AK 99559, (907) 556-8811.

Special Note: The lower 17 miles of the river are owned by Quinhagak Village Corporation; for information, contact Quanirtuuq Inc., P.O. Box 69, Quinhagak, AK 99655; (907) 556-8211. For information on public lands along the upper river, contact the Togiak National Wildlife Refuge, P.O. Box 270, Dillingham, AK 99576; (907) 842-1063.

Description: The Kanektok is one of several, sparkling blue tundra rivers that drain the fringe of mountains in the state's extreme southwest corner. Since the early 1980s, it has enjoyed worldwide notoriety for its exquisite streamfishing qualities. An abundance and variety of species—rainbow trout, sea-run charr, grayling and king, red and silver salmon—along with perfect conditions make it one of Alaska's finest rivers for floatfishing.

The river rambles for 90 miles from mountain sources at Kagati Lake to the flat coastal plain and silty waters of Kuskokwim Bay. Gravel bottomed, moderately swift (three to four miles per hour), with lots of shallow braids and pools containing amazing fish populations, the Kanektok is a flyfisher's dream. (At one time, it had some of the highest concentrations of catchable-size rainbow trout of any river studied by the U.S. Fish and Wildlife Service.)

The best way to fish it is, without a doubt, from rafts, floating down from Kagati. There are no serious rapids, mostly just fast water (occasional Class I stretches). The only hazards to speak of are the abundant sweepers, which can be dangerous in the numerous switchbacks and fast current. On the upper river, you'll find great scenic views and good grayling and charr fishing, while the best rainbow trout habitat seems to be the heavily braided middle and lower sections (from Klak Creek down). The lower 10 miles of river is the preferred location for intercepting the Kanektok's abundant runs of sea-bright silver and king salmon (some of the state's largest in average size), as well as sea-run charr.

One of the prettiest rivers you'll ever see, the Kanektok is blessed with some truly amazing fishing. The rainbows are certainly not the potential trophies you'll find in some of the big lake and river systems further east, but they're abundant and very pretty, with deep crimson stripes and big, black spots (the "leopard rainbow" you may have heard of in the tourist hype). This river also has some of the best, late summer sea-run charr fishing south of Kotzebue, with lots of feisty, bright fish in the three to six pound range and an occasional eight-pounder. (The best time to catch them is from late July on.) You can stay at an outpost tent camp, if you're not into rafting, and several area lodges maintain spike camps on the middle and lower sections of the river, using jet boats for accessing the better holes. Ask anyone who has fished Alaska about the Kanektok, and you'll get a unanimous appraisal for its rank among Alaska's top 10 exceptional fishing waters.

Guides' tip: The Kanektok is one of the rivers where the Alaska "deer hair mouse" got its notorious reputation. In certain years, they can be very effective, so bring some along. Fish 'em under cutbanks and in shallows for explosive surface strikes from rainbow trout and charr.

35. ANIAK RIVER

Location: Lower Kuskokwim drainage, 300 miles west of Anchorage.
Reference: Bethel B-1, C-1, C-2, D-1, D-2; Russian Mission A-1, A-2, B-1, C-2.
Access: By plane from Anchorage to Aniak village via commercial flight, then wheelplane or floatplane to several headwater or mid-river access points. It can be floated by raft or kayak from the headwaters (seven days or more to the lower river). Access to the lower river by boat is possible from the village of Aniak.
Highlights: One of Southwest Alaska's better mountain rivers for all-

around fishing and high-quality wilderness float trips. Good to excellent rainbow trout, charr, grayling and salmon (especially king, chum and silver), with nice scenery and wildlife along the upper river and relatively light angling pressure.

Species: Charr, chum salmon, grayling, king salmon, lake trout, northern pike, pink salmon, rainbow trout, red salmon, silver salmon, sheefish.

Regulations: Open year-round; upstream of Doestock Creek, only unbaited, single-hook, artificial lures and catch-and-release on rainbows. For additional restrictions, consult the current Alaska Department of Fish and Game regulations or the ADF&G Dillingham office, (907) 842-2427.

Facilities: Several lodges and outpost camps operate along the lower river.

Contact: For lodge-based fishing, contact Alaska Dream Lodge, Route 1, Kuna, ID 83634; (208) 922-5648. For floatfishing trips, contact Ouzel Expeditions, P.O. Box 935, Girdwood, AK 99587, (907) 783-3220 or (907) 783-3220 (fax); or Eruk's Wilderness Tours, 12720 Lupine Road, Anchorage, AK 99516, (907) 345-7678. For an air taxi, contact Haagland Air, P.O. Box 211, Aniak, AK 99577, (907) 675-4272; or Yukon Aviation, P.O. Box 976, Bethel, AK 99559, (907) 543-3280.

Description: The Aniak is a wild and remote, three-pronged mountain river of the lower Kuskokwim. In terms of its fishery, size and recreation potential, it is perhaps the most significant river of the entire Kuskokwim drainage, and has only recently been "discovered" by sportsmen for its abundant salmon, charr, rainbow trout and grayling possibilities.

Except for the lower section above the Kuskokwim, the Aniak flows clear and fast (with some whitewater in the upper tributaries) as it comes off the western edge of the Kuskokwim Mountains in three main headwaters—Aniak Lake (and river) and the Kipchuk and Salmon rivers. These three all begin as swift, rocky alpine streams having outstanding grayling and charr fishing (including lake trout in Aniak Lake), superb scenery and quite a bit of wildlife (bears, moose and caribou). Their lower sections and the main river below the fork confluence (60 miles down from Aniak Lake) become a maze of channels, sweepers and logjams that are a nightmare to boaters (especially in high water), but make great cover for pot-bellied rainbows and throngs of charr and salmon. Fishing for these species is best from the Kipchuk-Aniak-Salmon River confluence down to about nine miles above the mouth at Doestock Creek, where the river becomes silty and meandering. The lower Aniak does have good pike fishing, and sheefish are even taken from the river's mouth in spring.

There are several lodges and outpost camps scattered along the lower river, which are accessible from the village of Aniak. For float trips, most folks put in on either the upper Salmon or Kipchuk rivers by wheelplane (primitive airstrip access) via Aniak or Bethel. The trip down from Aniak Lake (floatplane access) is extremely arduous and dangerous, best done by kayak, inflatable canoe or small, light raft, as heavy logjams, snags, sweepers and vegetation make for difficult passage and frequent portages. Abundant salmon spawning and healthy bear populations (both brown and black) make for frequent animal confrontations all along this drainage, so take necessary precautions. The river can be floated in anywhere from a week to 12 days depending on where you put in.

The Aniak certainly has much to offer; its rainbow and charr fishing in late summer can be quite superb, among the best available anywhere in the region. The trick seems to be catching good weather, as the river easily silts and spills out of its channel with disastrous results on the fishing and navigation. This is definitely not the river to try fishing unassisted, unless you are an experienced wilderness voyager.

Guides' tip: Much of the Aniak is not easy to fish or float. Fast currents, logjams and snag-infested, deep pools characterize most of the middle river. Bring plenty of terminal tackle and use heavier line or tippets to avoid excessive break-offs. Also, a large brush saw, ax or small chainsaw is highly recommended for safe, enjoyable passage downriver.

36. KASIGLUK RIVER

Location: Lower Kuskokwim River, 360 miles southwest of Anchorage.
Reference: Bethel A-3, A-4, B-3, B-4, B-5, B-6, C-5, C-6, D-5.
Access: By plane from Anchorage to Bethel via commercial flight, then jet boat to the lower river.
Highlights: A popular local fishing spot, known for good salmon, charr and rainbow trout fishing.
Species: Charr, chum salmon, grayling, king salmon, (northern pike), pink salmon, rainbow trout, (red salmon), silver salmon.
Regulations: Open year-round, all species.

Facilities: No developed public facilities. Guide services are available.

Contact: For guided/unguided fishing on the Kasigluk River, contact KORV, Inc., P.O. Box 215, Akiak, AK 99552; (907) 765-7228. For boat transportation to and from the Kasigluk, contact Alaska River Runners, P.O. Box 7055, Bethel, AK 99559; (907) 543-3633.

Description: If you spend any time in the villages along the lower Kuskokwim River, you'll probably get an invitation to fish the Kasigluk. One of the best of the area's rivers that rise from the scenic Kilbuck Mountains, the Kasigluk flows north and west, clear and fast, before degenerating into maze of muddy braids and sloughs in the flats along the big Kuskokwim.

Fishing is very good for king, silver and chum salmon, as well as rainbow trout and charr, once you get above the silty, meandering lower section (usually the first 30 miles). The river is accessed by boat from Bethel or one of the nearby villages (Kwethluk, Akiak or Akiachak) and can be run quite a ways with a jet unit. There are rumors of people even floating down from the headwaters, although access would be difficult and navigation hindered by the extensive braids and logjams. A few local guides and outfitters currently work the river with outpost camps; they're the best bet for anyone wanting to sample this outstanding, off-the-beaten-path fishery.

---

37. HOLITNA RIVER

Location: Middle Kuskokwim River, 225 miles southwest of Anchorage.

Reference: Taylor Mountains B-7, C-5, C-6, C-7, C-8, D-1, D-2, D-5, D-6, D-7; Sleetmute A-2, A-4, A-5, B-2, B-3, B-4, C-3, C-4; Lake Clark D-6, D-7, D-8.

Access: By floatplane (or in places small wheelplane) from Iliamna, Bethel, Aniak or Lake Clark to the headwaters or the lower and middle river sections. Raft or kayak trips are possible down from headwaters (trips of one week to 12 days), with take-out on the lower river by floatplane or boat from the village of Sleetmute.

Highlights: A remote, seldom-visited wilderness river system with good fishing possibilities for salmon, grayling, charr and pike; also good seasonal fishing for sheefish.

Species: Charr, chum salmon, grayling, king salmon, lake trout, northern pike, pink salmon, (rainbow trout) silver salmon, sheefish.

Regulations: Open year-round, all species.

Facilities: No developed public facilities. Lodge-based fishing and guide services are available.

Contact: For guided/unguided floats, contact Alaska Bush Adventures, P.O. Box 243861, Anchorage, AK 99524; (907) 522-1712. For lodge-based, fly-out fishing, contact Stony River Lodge, 13830 Jarvi Drive, Anchorage, AK 99708; (907) 345-2891. For an air taxi, contact Haagland Air, P.O. Box 211, Aniak, AK 99577, (907) 675-4272; Yukon Aviation, P.O. Box 976, Bethel, AK 99559, (907) 543-3280; or Iliamna Air Taxi, P.O. Box 109, Iliamna, AK 99606, (907) 571-1248.

Description: The Holitna River system is comprised of some fairly significant middle Kuskokwim tributaries that drain parts of the Taylor Mountains and west Alaska Range before joining near the village of Sleetmute. These include the mainstem Holitna, Hoholitna, Kogrukluk and Chukowan rivers. Although they receive limited attention from sport anglers (mostly locals), collectively they support one of the most productive fisheries in the entire region, known for fair to good king, silver, chum, grayling, pike and charr fishing. Sheefish are also taken in early summer on the lower river.

Access to the headwaters is limited; most folks put in either by floatplane or small wheelplane on the upper Holitna (from Kashegelok up) or at Whitefish Lake on the Hoholitna (for float trips). Fishing in the clearer, faster upper sections is generally quite good for grayling, charr and salmon, with abundant sheefish and pike taken seasonally in the sloughs and backwaters along the lower river. There are persistent rumors of rainbow trout being found in certain clear tributary streams. (Some are caught now and then from the river's mouth at Sleetmute.) The scenery and wild animal populations in the primitive backcountry of this system are outstanding, which explains the Holitna's popularity with hunters, who have traditionally been the river's only major users.

A few guides work the river, most of them locals, and some air taxis and lodges occasionally fly groups in to fish salmon, pike or sheefish, but for the most part this system doesn't get anywhere near the attention it deserves, considering what it has to offer. Like other similar drainages, the Holitna is greatly affected by runoff, with periods of even moderate rain raising river levels quickly and clouding the water, so fishing is very weather dependent. Other than that and the logistics involved in getting here, there is nothing major to prevent this drainage from becoming the "next big thing" for Southwest anglers in search of new, uncrowded waters.

REGION 8
LOWER YUKON

Alaska's two greatest rivers—the Yukon and Kuskokwim—spill their waters within 200 miles of each other in a broad, fan-shaped delta that is one of the world's great wetland habitats. Ideally suited for waterfowl, this area is too flat and marshy to support any high-quality sportfishing. However, the surrounding uplands give rise to a few notable drainages that presently receive little attention, though they contain some abundant, even world-class angling opportunities. (See the listing for the Innoko River on page 368.) Access, difficult logistics and lack of visitor services are the main obstacles for anyone looking to explore these more remote, but promising, rivers of the Southwest region.

38. ANDREAFSKY RIVER

Location: Lower Yukon River, 400 miles northwest of Anchorage.
Reference: Kwiguk A-2, A-3, B-1, B-2, C-1, C-2, D-1; St. Michael A-1; Unalakleet A-6; Holy Cross C-6, D-6.
Access: By plane from Anchorage to St. Marys via commercial flight, boat transport upriver or small wheelplane to gravel bars at the headwaters; raft or kayak trips are possible down to the mouth and the village of St. Marys.
Highlights: A seldom-visited western Alaska Wild and Scenic River, with good fishing for king, silver and chum salmon and charr; outstanding float trip possibilities.
Species: Charr, chum salmon, grayling, king salmon, northern pike, pink salmon, silver salmon.
Regulations: Open year-round, all species.
Facilities: No developed public facilities. Guide services are available.
Contact: For air taxi service and information on river conditions, contact Haagland Air, P.O. Box 195, St. Marys, AK 99658; (907) 438-2246. For guided float trips, contact Ultimate Rivers, 5140 East 104th Avenue, Anchorage, AK 99516; (907) 346-2193.
Description: The Andreafsky Wild and Scenic River of the lower Yukon has two parallel forks that flow southwest out of the Nulato Hills for 100 miles or so before joining on the coastal flatlands five miles north of the village of St. Marys. Although remote and diffi-

cult to access, this crystal-clear mountain stream has great potential
for high-quality wilderness fishing excursions, with good salmon
runs (kings, silvers and chums), abundant pike, charr and grayling,
pleasant scenery and wildlife.

Getting up into the headwaters is difficult. You can contract
through Haagland Air in St. Marys to run you a ways upriver by
boat (they also have guide service and tent camps available). It's
also possible to land on gravel bars (mostly on the upper North
Fork) with small wheelplanes, depending on water levels. The river
can be rafted in about a week; other than fast water, sweepers and
grizzly bears, there are no real major hazards. Due to the cost and
difficult logistics in getting here, not too many folks get to visit this
lovely, pristine drainage, but everyone who has considers the experience well worth the extra effort and expense.

39. ANVIK RIVER

Location: Lower Yukon River, 375 miles northwest of Anchorage.

Reference: Holy Cross C-3, C-4, D-4; Unalakleet A-4.

Access: By plane from Anchorage or Aniak to Anvik via scheduled
commercial flight, then boat to points upriver. Wheel and floatplane
access is also possible to points along the river via St. Marys, Aniak
or Bethel.

Highlights: One of the Yukon River's major fish producers, with underutilized sportfishing potential for salmon, charr and other species.

Species: Charr, chum salmon, grayling, king salmon, northern pike,
pink salmon, silver salmon, sheefish.

Regulations: Open year-round, all species.

Facilities: No developed public facilities. A private lodge is located on
the river, 60 miles above the mouth. Guide services are available.

Contact: For an air taxi to Anvik River, contact Haagland Air, P.O.
Box 207, St. Marys, AK 99684; (907) 438-2246. For guided/un-
guided lodge-based fishing, contact Andy and Kim Cook, Anvik
River Lodge, General Delivery, Anvik, AK 99558, (907) 663-6324
(in summer) or R.R. 1 Box 196C, Milo, ME 04463, (207) 943-7401
(in winter).

Description: Not too many folks know of the Anvik River of western
Alaska; fewer yet have fished it. But it is one of the most important
fish producing tributaries of the entire Yukon—a million or more
chum salmon spawn there in certain years. The Anvik can offer
high-quality angling adventure for a variety of species with virtually

no fishing pressure.

The Anvik heads in the Nulato Hills and flows south 120 miles or so before joining the Yukon at Anvik village, 318 miles up from the mouth. Like many Yukon and Kuskokwim drainages, it has a slow, wide, meandering lower section (with good pike and sheefish fishing), with the best fishing conditions for salmon, charr and grayling available in the clearer, swifter upper sections (above the Yellow River confluence, 60 miles from the mouth).

Most people fish the Anvik by boat, but it can be floated down from the headwaters, although access is difficult and generally limited to gravel bar landings with a small wheelplane. Anvik River Lodge, the area's only visitor establishment, offers an interesting variety of fishing options. They access most of the river by jet boat, but also have handmade cedar canoes for quiet, self-powered fishing. They do fly-outs to neighboring drainages like the Andreafsky and Innoko rivers for salmon, sheefish and monster pike (30 pounds plus) and can even provide raft, gear and transport for floatfishing trips. For anyone unfamiliar with the territory but wanting to explore its off-the-beaten-path angling adventure, the lodge and local flying service are probably the best contacts to show you the way.

40. INNOKO RIVER

Location: Lower Yukon River tributary, 330 miles northwest of Anchorage.

Reference: Ophir A-4, A-5, A-6, B-5, C-1, C-2, C-3, C-4, C-5, A-1, A-2, B-2; Unalakleet A-1; Holy Cross A-2, B-2, C-2, D-1, D-2; Iditarod D-3.

Access: By scheduled or chartered wheelplane service (via McGrath, Bethel or Aniak) to Holy Cross, Shageluk, Ophir, Cripple or Takotna, then boat (or raft) along the river. Floatplane access is possible to numerous points.

Highlights: An enormous, remote, meandering tributary of the lower Yukon, with tremendous potential for world-class trophy northern pike and abundant sheefish.

Species: Charr, chum salmon, grayling, king salmon, northern pike, silver salmon, sheefish.

Regulations: Open year-round, all species.

Facilities: No developed public facilities. Lodge-based fishing is available.

Contact: For wheelplane flights to villages and strips along river, contact Haagland Air, P.O. Box 211, Aniak, AK 99577; (907) 675-4272. For lodge-based fly-outs, contact Andy and Kim Cook, Anvik River Lodge, General Delivery, Anvik, AK 99558, (907) 663-6324 (in summer) or R.R. 1 Box 196C, Milo, ME 04463; (207) 943-7401 (in winter).

Description: Like a sleeping giant, the Innoko River sprawls lazily across the Yukon flatlands west of McGrath, its vast potential unknown to most of the fishing world. Not the kind of river to excite trout and salmon fishermen, much of it is big, slow water better suited for Alaska's "other" sport species—the wolfish northern pike and leaping sheefish. Fishing for these unsung fighters in the Innoko's abundant backwater is so good that word is spreading fast beyond the small circle of residents and local guides. This may soon become one of the hottest fishing spots in western Alaska.

This is an immense river system—the mainstem flows over 500 miles before emptying into the Yukon at Red Wind Slough, near the village of Holy Cross. (The Innoko's major tributary, the Iditarod, is over 350 miles long.) For most of this length, it is a slow, wide, lowland river, with meandering and interconnected sloughs and lakes, especially in the lower section (downstream of the abandoned village of Holikachuk, about 90 miles). The water quality is turbid from the mud and swamp water. It is only in the extreme upper reaches (above the North Fork) that the Innoko's character changes noticeably toward that of a mountain stream, with swifter flows, gravel bottom and clear water. This is really the only part of the river suited for salmon (coho, chum and some king), grayling and (occasionally) charr fishing, with several, adjoining swift and clear mountain creeks (such as Beaver and Folger) offering some of the better angling options.

Access is by floatplane to points all along the river, or by wheelplane to airstrips at Holy Cross, Shageluk, Cripple or Ophir. The upper river can be floated by raft, with a put-in at Ophir (or further upriver, from a trail accessed from Takotna) and take-out at Cripple or at points below by floatplane.

The lower Innoko is an important feeding area for the migratory Yukon River sheefish population. (See the sheefish chapter on page 188.) In spring, it can offer some of Alaska's finest fishing for the species. Pike are especially plentiful, with the lower river's perfect habitat and abundant food sources (whitefish and cisco) producing some really big fish. Recent efforts by local lodges and guides on the lower Innoko have produced dozens of northerns over 20, even

30, pounds (including the state record, a 38.5-pounder, in 1991), capturing worldwide attention and catapulting this sluggish behemoth of a river into notoriety. The secret's out on Alaska's top water for monster pike and abundant sheefish.

Fishing for grayling in Southwest.

ALASKA FISHING BY REGION: SOUTHCENTRAL

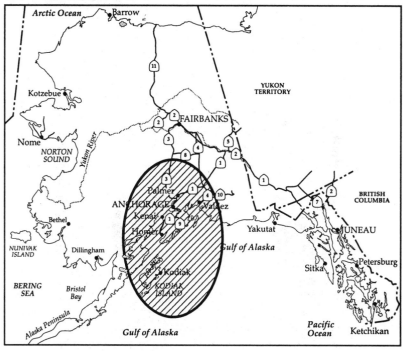

Shaded area shows Southcentral region

MAP 5—SOUTHCENTRAL HOTSPOTS

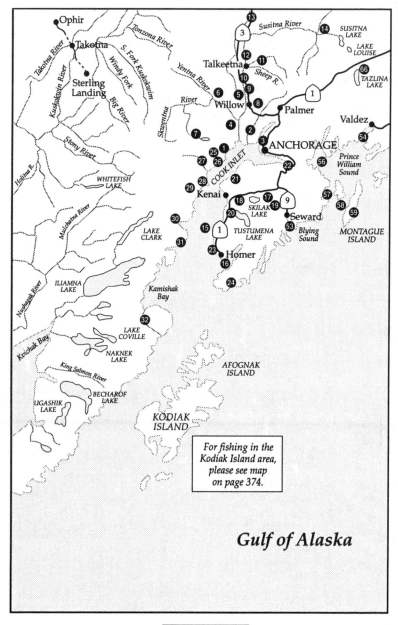

MAP 6—SOUTHCENTRAL HOTSPOTS

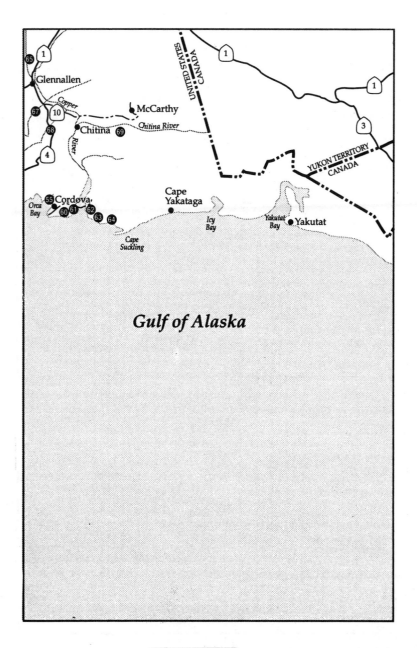

KODIAK ISLAND—SOUTHCENTRAL HOTSPOTS

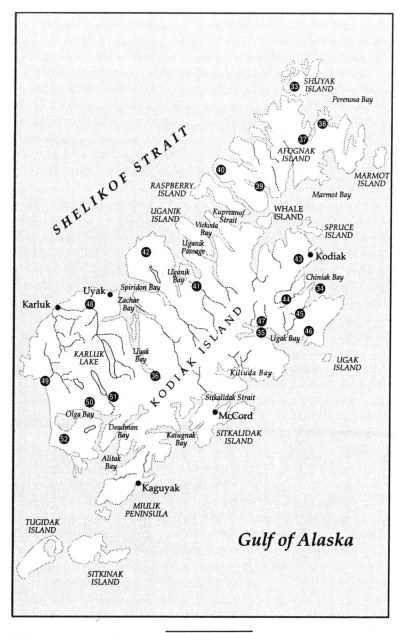

SOUTHCENTRAL HOT SPOTS

SOUTHCENTRAL

On a clear bedrock creek above the silty tidewaters of Turnagain Arm, an interesting assemblage of anglers shares a stretch of water and some warm August sunshine. Some retired folks, a young couple with two small children, a woman who looks like a school teacher, a few business types and others crowd a piece of riverbank no bigger than your driveway, flipping lines and lures nonstop in all directions. The intensity and anticipation grow unbearable. Then, suddenly, a commotion erupts downstream as one of a group of foreigners connects with a big, bright fish that catapults instantly toward the Pacific Ocean. Seconds later, a lad in a designer sweatshirt screams as another salmon bursts through the rapids and threatens to pull his rod from his hands. The silvers are in! Pandemonium ensues. Like a chain reaction, the surge of salmon spreads up the creek and wreaks havoc on rods and limbs everywhere. For the next hour, a wild melee of leaping salmon and screaming reels, mad downriver dashes and muddy smiles, takes over, as every man, woman and child gets a taste of salmon fishing the way it was meant to be.

This scene would be remarkable enough just for its level of fishing excitement, but when you consider that these folks are only a 20-minute drive from Alaska's largest city, Anchorage, in the heart of the state's most populous region, it's no less than astounding. Most states can't match this kind of angling in their wildest backcountry, yet Alaska's most "developed" region, Southcentral, can provide an abundance of similar opportunities no more than a short ride by car, plane or boat from any of its major (and modern) towns and cities. And while it's true that some of the more popular and accessible of these locations are becoming quite crowded by Alaska standards, Southcentral still has plenty of quality fishing that is light years beyond anything available in the Lower 48.

COUNTRY, CLIMATE & CONDITIONS

In many ways, Southcentral Alaska is the most well endowed of the state's geographic regions. Blessed with benign weather, majestic scenery and abundant resources, the mainland area south and east of the Alaska Range understandably attracts the most folks to live and play. Dominated by a massive arc of mountains, its diverse and impressive geography includes Alaska's tallest peaks and largest glaciers (some the size of states), immense, sprawling rivers, tundra uplands, dense coastal forests and some of the world's richest marine environments.

Shielded from arctic blasts by the high and wide Alaska Range, Southcentral's weather is surprisingly mild, greatly influenced by the Gulf of Alaska and warm, moist air from the Pacific—some of the rainiest and snowiest places in the world are found here. Summers are very pleasant with ample sunshine. Temperatures usually range in the 60s to low 70s, with low 50s to high 80s possible. Winters vary with location, but are generally mild, with moderate snow loads (5 to 10 feet total on average). Highs reach 40 degrees or more, while lows dip to 10 below, rarely less. Break-up comes in mid- to late April, later at elevation, while the rivers and lakes usually freeze by late October or early November. The sunniest, driest time of year is from April through July; the wettest time is from August through October.

SOUTHCENTRAL FISHING HIGHLIGHTS

The region's fishing is as varied and impressive as its geography. Abundant runs of all five salmon species occur in countless coastal streams and lakes as well as in immense glacial systems like the Susitna and Copper. These are major producers, even though their fishing potential is confined to clearwater tributaries. World-class trophy king salmon and halibut are found in the fabulous fisheries of the lower Cook Inlet, along with some of Alaska's best rainbow trout, steelhead and silver salmon fishing on the Kenai Peninsula and Kodiak Island. Cutthroat trout, grayling, trophy lake trout and even some fine northern pike fishing round out the delightful variety of angling possible in the Southcentral region.

ACCESS, SERVICES & COSTS

Perhaps Southcentral's most attractive feature is the well-developed network of access, services and facilities that allows visitors of any age, physical condition or economic status to enjoy a measure of the unbeatable fishing. There are four major highway systems, a state ferry, millions of acres of national forests and scores of parks, campgrounds and public use cabins, not to mention the hundreds of private lodges, guides and outfitters eager to help make that dream vacation come true. From lonely lakes tucked high and far in some of North America's most rugged mountain country to hatchery-enhanced creeks and ponds in the middle of Alaska's largest city, there is an angling adventure for everyone in Southcentral Alaska. Nowhere else in the world will you find the splendors of wilderness so seamlessly matched with the easy comfort and conveniences of civilization.

Four major highways—the Glenn, Parks, Seward and Sterling—connect the major communities of Southcentral with each other and the outside world. A state-run railroad and ferry system provide additional access to parts of the region. Commercial airlines service the major hubs of Anchorage, Kenai, Cordova and Kodiak with daily flights (some connecting) from the West Coast and points beyond, while numerous air taxis provide regular connections to the more remote areas. Access to the best Southcentral fly-in fishing locations generally involves floatplanes. Costs vary with the distance and size of party, but typically run from $125 to $350 per person.

SOUTHCENTRAL RUN TIMING

Freshwater

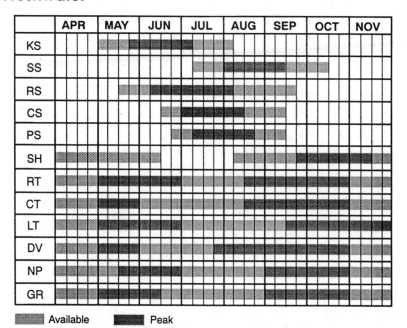

	APR	MAY	JUN	JUL	AUG	SEP	OCT	NOV
KS								
SS								
RS								
CS								
PS								
SH								
RT								
CT								
LT								
DV								
NP								
GR								

▓ Available ■ Peak

KS=King Salmon, SS=Silver Salmon, RS=Red Salmon, CS=Chum Salmon, PS=Pink Salmon, SH=Sheefish, RT=Rainbow Trout, CT=Cutthroat Trout, LT=Lake Trout, DV=Dolly Varden, NP=Northern Pike, GR=Grayling

Saltwater

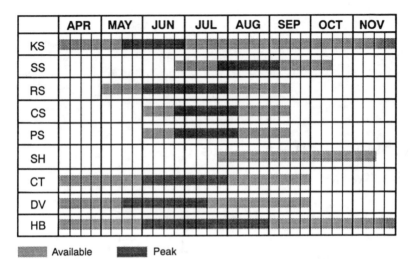

	APR	MAY	JUN	JUL	AUG	SEP	OCT	NOV
KS								
SS								
RS								
CS								
PS								
SH								
CT								
DV								
HB								

▨ Available   ■ Peak

KS=King Salmon, SS=Silver Salmon, RS=Red Salmon, CS=Chum Salmon, PS=Pink Salmon, SH=Sheefish, CT=Cutthroat Trout, DV=Dolly Varden, HB=Halibut

Note: Time periods shown are for bright fish, in the case of salmon entering rivers, or for general availability for resident species. Salmon are present in many systems long after the periods shown, but are usually in spawning/post spawning condition. Peak sportfishing periods for each species are highlighted. Be aware that run timing can vary somewhat from drainage to drainage and generally follows a later trend in waters to the west and north in Alaska. Check with local contacts listed for area run-timing specifics before confirming plans.

REGION 1
MATANUSKA-SUSITNA VALLEYS

The glacial Susitna is Southcentral Alaska's most significant river in terms of size and recreational use, offering a world of extremely popular, quality sportfishing opportunities for salmon, trout and grayling in its many outstanding clearwater tributaries. Important adjacent drainages along the Upper Cook Inlet enhance the area's great sportfish potential. Access is almost entirely by boat, floatplane or car via the George Parks Highway.

1. THEODORE RIVER

Location: West Upper Cook Inlet drainage, 30 miles west of Anchorage.
Reference: Tyonek A-3, B-3, B-4.
Access: By floatplane, landing on small ponds next to the lower river, or by wheelplane to two small runways west of the lower river. A road running parallel to the river upstream from one of the runways provides additional access.
Highlights: A great fly-in fishing spot, only 20 minutes from Anchorage. Good fishing for king salmon (in June), silver salmon (in early August) and rainbow trout (from June through September).
Species: (Chum salmon), Dolly Varden, (grayling), king salmon, pink salmon, rainbow trout, (red salmon), silver salmon.
Regulations: King salmon fishing is closed from July 1 through December 31. For additional restrictions, consult the current Alaska Department of Fish and Game sportfishing regulations or the ADF&G Palmer office, (907) 745-5016.
Facilities: No developed public facilities.
Contact: For an air taxi, contact Ketchum Air Service, Pouch O, P.O. Box 190588, Anchorage, AK 99519, (907) 243-5525 or (800) 433-9114; Rusts Flying Service, P.O. Box 190325, Anchorage, AK 99519, (907) 243-1595 or (800) 544-2299; or Regal Air, P.O. Box 190702, Anchorage, AK 99579, (907) 243-8535.
Description: Originating near the west side of Little Mount Susitna, south of the Talachulitna River, the Theodore is a small, clear

stream that meanders through mixed forest and lowland brush for some 35 miles to the tidal flats of upper Cook Inlet. It is a fairly productive stream for salmon (as well as trout and charr), with an abundance of holding water. It is ideal for the angler who wants to fish kings and silvers in a small stream setting, apart from crowds, without the expense of a long fly-in.

Salmon fishing is best during and after high tide in the lower river. Later in the season, the upper access points are better as the salmon congregate in dense schools near the spawning grounds on the middle and upper river. The upper stretches of the Theodore also offer some decent trout and Dolly Varden charr action, especially in late summer and fall when the salmon are well into their spawning. Grayling are an occasional bonus. Flyfishing conditions on the upper river are quite good, with lots of rocky runs and cover.

2. LITTLE SUSITNA RIVER SYSTEM

Location: Upper Cook Inlet drainage, Susitna Flats, 15 miles west of Anchorage.

Reference: Anchorage C-6, C-7, C-8, D-6; Tyonek B-1, C-1.

Access: By automobile, there are two major points of access. For the middle river, access is from the town of Houston along the Parks Highway. For the lower river, access is from Knik-Goose Bay Road off the Parks Highway near Wasilla. Rafting or canoeing between access points is popular with anglers. Another option is a boat ride from the Port of Anchorage 12 miles across upper Cook Inlet to the mouth of the river. Extreme caution should be exercised.

Highlights: Excellent road-accessible fishing for silver salmon (in early August), chum salmon (from late July through early August) and pink salmon (in late July); good fishing for king salmon (in early June).

Species: Chum salmon, Dolly Varden, grayling, king salmon, pink salmon, rainbow trout, red salmon, silver salmon.

Regulations: King salmon fishing is closed from July 14 through December 31. For additional restrictions, consult the current Alaska Department of Fish and Game sportfishing regulations or the ADF&G Palmer office, (907) 745-5016.

Facilities: Lodging, guide services, groceries, sporting goods, gas, boat launching and camping are available in Houston. Camping and boat launching also available on the lower river.

Contact: For lodging information and guide services, contact Fishtale

River Guides, HCO 2, Box 7383, Palmer, AK 99645, (907) 376-3687; or Trophy Catch Charters, P.O. Box 245, Palmer, AK 99645, (907) 745-4101.

Description: The Little Susitna is a popular road-fishing stream that meanders through spruce and birch from its origins on the south slopes of the Talkeetna Mountains. It is a moody river. During summer hot spells or rainy periods, its clear waters can easily become high, muddy and difficult to fish, especially on the upper and middle sections of the river where the current is swift. (Beginning and intermediate boaters should stay on the lower river, with its wider water and slower current.) While the river has many sharp bends and twists with some sweepers, most of the Little "Su" is fairly tame. However, its upper reaches are rated Class II to Class III. Rafters can spend two or three days floating the river from the upper or middle access points down to the lower river and Burma Road.

All five species of salmon migrate up the Little Susitna in good numbers and are encountered from Houston downstream, where they hold in the river's many holes, pools and runs. The lower river is worked mostly by boaters fishing the tides, although bankfishing is also possible. Shore fishermen prefer the middle and upper parts of the Little Su which are narrower and concentrate the fishing. The confluence with Nancy Lake Creek is a popular site with many salmon anglers. The upper river also has fairly good rainbow trout, Dolly Varden and grayling action during the summer and fall months when spawning salmon are present.

3. SHIP CREEK

Location: North Cook Inlet drainage, downtown Anchorage.

Reference: Anchorage A-8.

Access: By automobile. Ship Creek is located off 1st Avenue and Loop Road near the Port of Anchorage. Parking is available on both sides of the stream with foot access throughout. Respect private property and please be cautious around inlet mud.

Highlights: Salmon fishing in the heart of Alaska's biggest city. Good fishing for king salmon (throughout June) and silver salmon (from mid-August through early September).

Species: (Chum salmon, Dolly Varden), king salmon, pink salmon, silver salmon.

Regulations: Portions are closed to fishing. King salmon fishing is open from January 1 through July 13. For the latest closures or restrictions, consult the current Alaska Department of Fish and Game sportfishing regulations or the ADF&G Anchorage office, (907) 267-2218.

Facilities: There is parking by the stream and hotels nearby. Groceries, sporting goods and gas are available in Anchorage.

Contact: For fishing information, contact the Alaska Department of Fish and Game Regional Office, Sportfish Division, 333 Raspberry Road, Anchorage, AK 99518; (907) 267-2218. For lodging information, contact the Comfort Inn, 111 West Ship Creek Avenue, Anchorage, AK 99501; (907) 277-6887 or (800) 362-6887.

Description: Ship Creek originates high in the Chugach Mountains and flows west through the greater Anchorage area to Knik Arm. It typically runs clear, but may turn slightly glacial during periods of heavy rains or hot weather. The upper stream sections are wooded with little development. However, surroundings change drastically as the stream nears it terminus in the Port of Anchorage near downtown Anchorage. Salmon fishing takes place in the tidal area of the stream below the Chugach Electric power plant. Although totally lacking the wilderness that is so associated with Alaska, angling with the tide can be quite good during the height of salmon season, particularly in deep holes and runs near the road crossings.

Starting in late spring and continuing into midsummer, a run of wild and hatchery king salmon return in good numbers to Ship Creek. In some years, the action heats up to provide even better catch rates than in the better streams of the Kenai or Susitna. As the king is Alaska's number-one gamefish and this stream is located in the heart of the state's largest city, expect huge crowds. Less attention, however, is paid to an almost equally productive run of silver salmon, which peaks in late summer and continues through most of fall. A fair run of pink salmon are also present during "even" years, in addition to a few chums and Dolly Varden charr.

Ship Creek certainly can't compare to other streams in Alaska, but it makes a very nice diversion if you happen to be in Anchorage with a few hours to kill. Many a visitor has walked from a hotel down to Ship Creek and returned with a 20- to 50-pounder.

4. ALEXANDER CREEK

Location: Lower Susitna River drainage, 25 miles northwest of Anchorage.

Reference: Tyonek B-2, C-2, C-3, D-3.

Access: By floatplane and jet boat. Calm stretches of the river, as well as lakes, are used as landing sites for planes. Boats can be launched from the Port of Anchorage or from Deshka Landing near Willow on the Parks Highway. Floating the river with rafts and canoes is very popular.

Highlights: One of Southcentral's most popular and productive fisheries. Excellent fishing for king salmon (in early June), silver salmon (in early August) and rainbow trout (from June through September). Also good fishing for pink salmon (in late July) and grayling (from May through September).

Species: Chum salmon, Dolly Varden, grayling, king salmon, (northern pike), pink salmon, rainbow trout, red salmon, silver salmon.

Regulations: King salmon fishing is closed from July 14 through December 31. For additional restrictions, consult the current Alaska Department of Fish and Game sportfishing regulations or the ADF&G Palmer office, (907) 745-5016.

Facilities: Lodging, fuel, water and a guide service are available.

Contact: For lodging and guide services, contact Gabbert's Fish Camp, P.O. Box ACR, Alexander Creek, AK 99695; (907) 733-2371. For an air taxi, contact Ketchum Air Service, Pouch O, P.O. Box 190588, Anchorage, AK 99519, (907) 243-5525 or (800) 433-9114; Rusts Flying Service, P.O. Box 190325, Anchorage, AK 99519, (907) 243-1595 or (800) 544-2299; or Regal Air, P.O. Box 190702, Anchorage, AK 99579, (907) 243-8535.

Description: Alexander Creek is one of the most popular and productive waters of its size in Southcentral Alaska, holding large runs of salmon throughout much of the summer and into fall. Access is relatively easy. The creek drains a fairly significant area between the Yentna River and Mount Susitna, running south some 40 miles from its origin at Alexander Lake to join the glacial Susitna River near tidewater. Much of the surrounding area is marshland, contributing significantly to the iron-colored tint of this slow, meandering stream.

Most anglers fly in to the lower river by floatplane, landing on the calm waters near the mouth or on Alexander Lake. Although fishing from the bank is popular on the upper and middle river, most angling on lower Alexander Creek is done from boats. Jet boats can run from the mouth upstream about 18 miles to the confluence with Sucker Creek, a major clearwater tributary, fishing an abundance of good water along the way. One of the best ways to enjoy the Alexander is to float and fish down from the lake in rafts or canoes (an easy four- to five-day trip), with take-out at the mouth.

The creek mouth is the most productive fishing spot. Its confluence with the large glacial Susitna serves as a major holding area for a tremendous number of salmon heading upstream to spawn in the Susitna's other clearwater tributaries. But the Alexander itself has significant runs of king and silver salmon, along with good numbers of red, chum and pink salmon, rainbow trout, Dolly Varden and grayling—even a few northern pike.

5. DESHKA RIVER

Location: Lower Susitna River drainage, 35 miles northwest of Anchorage.

Reference: Talkeetna A-1, A-2, B-1, B-2; Tyonek C-1, D-1, D-2.

Access: Anglers have three access options. One is by floatplane to Neil Lake (just west of the river between Trapper Creek and the "forks") or the mouth of the river. Another is by boat from Deshka Landing south of Willow on the Parks Highway. The last option is the Petersville Road via the Parks Highway, which crosses Kroto and Moose creeks, the two main forks of the Deshka. Floating the river is popular.

Highlights: Excellent fishing for king salmon (in June), silver salmon (in early August), rainbow trout (from June through September) and grayling (from May through September).

Species: Chum salmon, Dolly Varden, grayling, king salmon, (northern pike), pink salmon, rainbow trout, red salmon, silver salmon.

Regulations: King salmon fishing is closed from July 14 through December 31. For additional restrictions, consult the current Alaska Department of Fish and Game sportfishing regulations or the ADF&G Palmer office, (907) 745-5016.

Facilities: Lodging, fuel, water and guide services are available.

Contact: For lodging information, contact Deshka River Lodge, P.O. Box 190355, Anchorage, AK 99519, (907) 243-6813; or Deshka Silver-King Lodge, P.O. Box 1037, Willow, AK 99688, (907) 733-2055. For an air taxi, contact Ketchum Air Service, Pouch O, P.O. Box 190588, Anchorage, AK 99519, (907) 243-5525 or (800) 433-9114; Rusts Flying Service, P.O. Box 190325, Anchorage, AK 99519, (907) 243-1595 or (800) 544-2299; or Regal Air, P.O. Box 190702, Anchorage, AK 99579, (907) 243-8535.

Description: The Deshka River, also known as Kroto Creek, is a major clearwater tributary of the Susitna and a highly productive and popular fishing stream. Flowing approximately 90 miles from its origins south of the Alaska Range near Talkeetna, the slow-moving Deshka empties into the Susitna about eight miles southwest of Willow.

The Deshka River has long been heralded as the number-one producer of king salmon in the Susitna drainage. (This, along with easy access, has made it one of the most heavily fished rivers in Alaska.) Fairly abundant numbers of the other salmon, along with a healthy population of resident rainbow trout and grayling, contribute to its perennial popularity. It can be accessed and fished in several ways. Floatplanes carry anglers to the mouth or drop off rafting parties along the midsection. (The river can also be floated from Petersville Road down, mainly via Moose Creek, with take-out at the Susitna River confluence.) For those with jet boats, the river is navigable to the "forks," where Kroto and Moose creeks join together, about 30 miles upstream from the mouth. Fishing from shore is mostly done on the upper and middle river sections, with the mouth and lower river best fished from a boat or raft.

The confluence of the Deshka and Susitna rivers serves as a resting area for vast schools of salmon migrating farther up the Susitna. Anglers can expect to tangle with all five species of salmon there, in season. Good numbers of rainbow trout and grayling can be found in the upper Deshka River late in the summer and early fall, where conditions are perfect for fly and ultra-light spincasting. Growing numbers of northern pike are also present in parts of the river.

6. LAKE CREEK

Location: Yentna River drainage, 65 miles northwest of Anchorage.

Reference: Talkeetna A-2, A-3, B-3, B-4, C-3, C-4; Tyonek D-3.

Access: By plane, boat or raft. Floatplanes can land at the headwaters at Chelatna Lake, at several other smaller lakes along river (such as Bulchatna Lake) or at the mouth on the Yentna River; wheelplanes can utilize gravel bars. Boaters can access the mouth from the community of Skwentna, which has scheduled air services. Floaters usually put in at Chelatna, with take-out at the mouth.

Highlights: One of Southcentral's finest rivers, with excellent fishing for king salmon (from mid-June through early July); good fishing for silver salmon (from mid-August through early September), rainbow trout and grayling (in May, September and October). Also fair to good fishing for red, chum and pink salmon (from late July through early August) and northern pike (from June through September).

Species: Chum salmon, Dolly Varden, grayling, king salmon, northern pike, pink salmon, rainbow trout, red salmon, silver salmon.

Regulations: King salmon fishing is closed from July 14 through December 31. For additional restrictions, consult the current Alaska Department of Fish and Game sportfishing regulations or the ADF&G Palmer office, (907) 745-5016.

Facilities: Lodging, fuel and water are available.

Contact: For lodging information, contact Riversong Lodge, 2463 Cottonwood Street, Anchorage, AK 99508, (907) 274-2710; or Wilderness Place Lodge, P.O. Box 190711, Anchorage, AK 99519, (907) 248-4337. For an air taxi, contact Ketchum Air Service, Pouch O, P.O. Box 190588, Anchorage, AK 99519, (907) 243-5525 or (800) 433-9114; Rusts Flying Service, P.O. Box 190325, Anchorage, AK 99519, (907) 243-1595 or (800) 544-2299; or Regal Air, P.O. Box 190702, Anchorage, AK 99579, (907) 243-8535.

Description: Lake Creek begins at Chelatna Lake near Kahiltna Glacier at the base of the Alaska Range. It is a fast, clearwater stream that flows south through rocky rapids and canyons some 50 miles to its confluence with the glacial Yentna River. One of the most scenic sportfishing streams in the Susitna River basin, it is also one of the best. Lake Creek offers good to excellent angling for a wide variety of species, including five species of salmon, rainbow trout, grayling and even northern pike. With its whitewater and boulders, Lake Creek is not the easiest water to fish, however, and has its best angling opportunities concentrated in the deep holes, slower runs and mouths of tributary creeks (above and below the canyon in the middle section of the river).

Early in the season, the best fishing is at the confluence of Lake Creek and the Yentna, for bright king salmon holding from their journey upriver (to both Lake Creek and other clear tributaries of the Yentna) and resident rainbow trout and grayling. Later in the season, in the middle and upper sections, salmon fishing continues to be very good. (Lake Creek kings are quite large, some exceeding 50 or even 60 pounds.) August usually brings a fair run of silvers and some lively rainbow trout and grayling. Chelatna Lake at the headwaters even has a population of northern pike.

Perhaps the most popular and exciting way to fish Lake Creek is to put in at Chelatna Lake and float the entire length by raft, down to the mouth at the Yentna. With whitewater varying from Class I to Class III, this is not a river that novice floaters should attempt.

7. TALACHULITNA RIVER

Location: Yentna River drainage, 50 miles northwest of Anchorage.

Reference: Tyonek B-4, C-3, C-4, C-5, D-4, D-5.

Access: By floatplane to the headwaters at Judd Lake, near Hiline Lake at the river's midpoint or the mouth at the Yentna. Boaters can reach the mouth from the community of Skwentna, which is serviced by air. Wheelplanes can also land near the mouth of the "Tal." Floating the river is a popular option to access the best fishing.

Highlights: Southcentral's classic salmon and trout stream, excellent for king salmon (from late June through early July) silver salmon (from late August through early September), rainbow trout (from June through September) and grayling (from June through September). Also good fishing for red and pink salmon (from late July through early August) and chum salmon (from late June through early July).

Species: Chum salmon, Dolly Varden, grayling, king salmon, pink salmon, rainbow trout, red salmon, silver salmon.

Regulations: King salmon fishing is closed from July 14 through December 31; catch-and-release fishing only for rainbow trout. For additional restrictions, consult the current Alaska Department of Fish and Game sportfishing regulations or the ADF&G Palmer office, (907) 745-5016.

Facilities: Private lodges are available along the lower river.

Contact: For lodging and guide services, contact Skwentna Lodge, 8051 Rabbit Creek Road, Anchorage, AK 99516; (907) 345-1702 or (907) 733-2722. For an air taxi, contact Ketchum Air Service, Pouch O, P.O. Box 190588, Anchorage, AK 99519, (907) 243-5525 or (800) 433-9114; Rusts Flying Service, P.O. Box 190325, Anchorage, AK 99519, (907) 243-1595 or (800) 544-2299; or Regal Air, P.O. Box 190702, Anchorage, AK 99579, (907) 243-8535.

Description: One of Alaska's premier fishing locations, the Talachulitna offers some of the finest stream fishing in all of Southcentral Alaska. Located about 60 miles west of Anchorage, the clearwater "Tal" rises from several sources in the highlands above the lower Skwentna, then winds through birch and spruce forests and scenic gorges for some 50 miles before emptying into the swift, glacial tributary of the Susitna.

The Talachulitna has great fishing, seclusion, scenery and exciting floating; it's one of the state's choicest rivers to enjoy by raft, kayak or canoe. The upper section is fairly slow and quite shallow in spots (mostly Class I and Class II). There is an abrupt series of Class

II and III rapids just below the Hiline Lake put-in at mid-river, and the lower river plunges through several high-walled canyons (Class II and Class III) before reaching the Skwentna. Overall, the Tal is definitely not a trip for the novice boater.

Despite the fishing pressure of recent years, the Talachulitna is holding up remarkably well, with strong runs of king and silver salmon, and fairly abundant rainbow trout fishing. In its heyday back in the '50s and '60s, the river was notorious for trophy trout, but nowadays you'll have to work the water pretty hard to turn up a fish of any size. (Rainbows average 12 to 16 inches, and are among the prettiest strains found in Alaska.) The best chances for bigger trout are in the middle and upper river during late summer, where you'll find some decent grayling fishing as well.

For salmon, the mouth of the river and confluences of the tributary creeks (such as Friday and Thursday creeks) have traditionally been the best bets, but the river has an abundance of holding water—pools, riffles and sloughs—for good fishing all the way down. The trip from Judd Lake to the Skwentna makes a perfect seven-day float with plenty of time to fish all the good water.

Guides' tip: The Tal has miles of perfect flyfishing water, with some of Southcentral's best opportunities for dry flyfishing (grayling, rainbows and even, rarely, silver salmon), so come properly geared.

---

8. WILLOW CREEK

Location: Middle Susitna River drainage, 40 miles north of Anchorage.

Reference: Anchorage C-7, C-8, D-6, D-7, D-8; Tyonek D-1.

Access: By automobile. The confluence of Willow Creek and the Susitna River can be reached by a four-mile-long gravel road from the town of Willow. The middle river is intersected by the Parks Highway in Willow. Parts of it can also be reached from the first few miles of Hatcher Pass Road. The upper stream section is accessed by Hatcher Pass Road.

Highlights: Excellent fishing for king salmon (from mid-June through early July), silver salmon (in early August) and pink salmon (from late July through early August). Good fishing for chum salmon (from late July through early August), rainbow trout (in May and September) and grayling (from June through September).

Species: Chum salmon, Dolly Varden, grayling, king salmon, pink salmon, rainbow trout, (red salmon), silver salmon.

Regulations: Unbaited, artificial lures only from September 1 through

May 15. For additional restrictions, consult the current Alaska Department of Fish and Game sportfishing regulations or the ADF&G Palmer office, (907) 745-5016.

Facilities: Camping, gas, groceries, a guide service and a boat launch are available in Willow. Camping is also available at the mouth of the stream.

Contact: For lodging and guide services, contact the Willow Island Resort, P.O. Box 85, Willow, AK 99688; (907) 495-6343. For camping information, contact the Public Lands Information Center, 605 West Fourth Avenue, Suite 105, Anchorage, AK 99501; (907) 271-2737.

Description: Willow Creek is a rocky, clearwater stream that flows swiftly west off the edge of the southern Talkeetna Mountains onto the flatlands of the lower Susitna, near the town of Willow. It is one of the most popular fishing streams in the area, especially for bankfishing, with an abundance of road-accessible holes, runs and pools that can offer decent salmon and trout fishing in season.

Most folks fish the Willow from the road, accessing the river from the Parks Highway or farther up from Hatcher Pass Road. Floating is a popular way of accessing and fishing the creek. Rafts, kayaks and canoes can be launched for short trips from any of the road access points on the upper or middle river. As the Willow is a rapid runoff stream with sweepers, log jams and a high gradient in its upper reaches, floaters should use caution and stay within the middle and lower river sections.

Salmon fishing is the top draw here, with four runs providing substantial action from early summer into fall. Kings are the most sought-after species and can reach a respectable size in the Willow. (Most fish caught are between 15 and 30 pounds, but anglers have a good chance of hooking fish weighing as much as 65 pounds. Kings nudging the 80-pound mark have been taken.) The mouth of the Willow is without a doubt the most popular spot for fishing and draws considerable crowds during the height of the runs. With a little hiking, more adventuresome anglers can find some good fishing for salmon, trout and grayling on the river's middle and upper sections. Spring and fall are very popular and productive for trout on the Willow.

9. SHEEP CREEK

Location: Middle Susitna River drainage, 50 miles north of Anchorage.

Reference: Talkeetna Mountains A-5, A-6; Talkeetna A-1; Tyonek D-1.

Access: By automobile. The middle stretch of Sheep Creek is intersected by the Parks Highway north of Willow. Trails lead up and downstream. The confluence with the Susitna River can be accessed by a gravel road about one mile south of the bridge crossing.

Highlights: Good road-accessible fishing for king salmon (from mid-June through early July), silver salmon (in the first half of August), chum and pink salmon (from late July through early August), rainbow trout (in May and September) and grayling (from June through September).

Species: Chum salmon, Dolly Varden, grayling, king salmon, pink salmon, rainbow trout, (red salmon), silver salmon.

Regulations: Unbaited, artificial lures only from September 1 through May 15. For additional restrictions, consult the current Alaska Department of Fish and Game sportfishing regulations or the ADF&G Anchorage office, (907) 267-2218.

Facilities: Lodging, camping and gas are available at the Parks Highway crossing. Camping and a boat launch are available at the mouth. Groceries and sporting goods can be had on the highway a few miles north of Sheep Creek.

Contact: For fishing information, contact the Alaska Department of Fish and Game Regional Office, Sportfish Division, 333 Raspberry Road, Anchorage, AK 99518; (907) 267-2218. For lodging information, contact the Sheep Creek Lodge, HC 89, Box 406, Willow, AK 99688; (907) 495-6227.

Description: Sheep Creek is a small clearwater tributary of the Susitna that issues from the western edge of the Talkeetna Mountains and flows west some 50 miles before joining the big glacial stream at mid-river. It is a well-used highway angling destination, which offers potentially good salmon fishing, especially for kings.

The creek has an abundance of easy fishing water, especially suited for bankfishing, which is the only real way to work the middle and upper river, but the mouth can also be fished from a boat. Small rafts can also put in at the highway bridge for an easy half-day trip down to the mouth—there are log jams and sweepers, however.

Although fishing is good for four salmon species in season, kings draw the most anglers to the banks of Sheep Creek, as they tend to be slightly above average (up to 40 or 50 pounds, with rare specimens up to 80 pounds a possibility). In spring or late summer and fall, rainbow trout and grayling are best fished in the lower river or upper river. Sheep does has a tendency to become silty and run high during prolonged periods of hot weather or heavy rain.

10. MONTANA CREEK

Location: Middle Susitna River drainage, 60 miles north of Anchorage.

Reference: Talkeetna Mountains A-5, A-6, B-6; Talkeetna A-1.

Access: By automobile. The Parks Highway intersects the lower portion of the creek and provides excellent access to the mouth as well as to trails leading upstream. The upper creek can be reached via a gravel road off the Talkeetna Spur Highway (which connects to the Parks Highway).

Highlights: Excellent road-accessible streamfishing for king salmon (from late June through early July), silver salmon (in early August) and pink salmon (from late July through early August). Good fishing for chum salmon (from late July through early August), rainbow trout (in May and September) and grayling (from June through September).

Species: Chum salmon, Dolly Varden, grayling, king salmon, pink salmon, rainbow trout, (red salmon), silver salmon.

Regulations: Unbaited, artificial lures only from September 1 through May 15. For additional restrictions, consult the current Alaska Department of Fish and Game sportfishing regulations or the ADF&G Anchorage office, (907) 267-2218.

Facilities: Camping is available at a state campground next to the Parks Highway bridge; it tends to be crowded during the height of salmon runs. Gas, groceries, sporting goods and lodging are available a few miles north and south along the highway.

Contact: For fishing information, contact the Alaska Department of Fish and Game Regional Office, Sportfish Division, 333 Raspberry Road, Anchorage, AK 99518; (907) 267-2218. For camping information, contact the Public Lands Information Center, 605 West Fourth Avenue, Suite 105, Anchorage, AK 99501; (907) 271-2737.

Description: Montana Creek is a clear, gravel-bottom, east-side Susitna tributary that comes off the western edge of the Talkeetnas north of Sheep Creek. With headwaters considerably less alpine and glacial than its neighbor (it has three forks that join about 10 miles east of the highway), Montana generally runs quite clear. This, along with its ample productivity as a salmon stream, make it one of the more popular of all Susitna road-fishing streams.

Most angling takes place at the mouth, which is within easy walking distance from the campground beside the Parks Highway bridge. The confluence provides a sanctuary for fish of all species migrating up Montana Creek or continuing up the Susitna to other spawning areas. Anglers concentrating on salmon can also do well in the multitude of runs and holes upstream.

King salmon to 60 or 70 pounds, sometimes even more, are possible, with a good number of fish in the 40-pound range. Silvers, chums and pinks are also abundant from the late summer into fall. And rainbows of 8 to 10 pounds have been taken, mostly from the lower river in spring and fall. Grayling fishing is not too bad on the upper river. Because of its small size, the Montana is strictly a bankfishing stream, but small rafts can be launched from the upper access point and floated to the mouth. (Some portions of the creek are shallow and there is an abundance of sweepers, however.)

11. TALKEETNA RIVER SYSTEM

Location: Middle Susitna River drainage, 80 miles north of Anchorage.

Reference: Talkeetna Mountains A-3, A-4, A-5, B-3, B-4, B-5, B-6, C-4, C-5, C-6.

Access: By automobile, plane, boat and raft. The Talkeetna Spur Highway (from the Parks Highway) ends in the town of Talkeetna and the mouth of the river. Access to the mouths of clearwater tributary streams is by river boat (or raft), and float and wheelplanes can land at several headwater locations. Check with air taxis in Talkeetna before flying in to float or camp along the river, as certain lands have been conveyed to native ownership.

Highlights: One of Southcentral's most significant, highest-quality fisheries; excellent fishing for king salmon (in early July), silver salmon (in mid-August), chum salmon (in early August) and pink salmon (in late July). Also good fishing for red salmon (in late July), rainbow trout (in August and September), Dolly Varden (from July through September) and grayling (from June through September).

Species: Chum salmon, Dolly Varden, grayling, king salmon, pink salmon, rainbow trout, red salmon, silver salmon.

Regulations: King salmon fishing is closed from July 14 through December 31. For additional restrictions, consult the current Alaska Department of Fish and Game sportfishing regulations or the

ADF&G Palmer office, (907) 745-5016.

Facilities: Grocery, sporting goods, gas, lodging, camping, boat launching, and air taxi and guide services are available in Talkeetna.

Contact: For guide services, contact Mahay's Riverboat Service, P.O. Box 705, Talkeetna, AK 99676, (907) 733-2223; or Tri River Charters, P.O. Box 312, Talkeetna, AK 99676, (907) 733-2400. For an air taxi, contact Talkeetna Air Taxi, P.O. Box 73, Talkeetna, AK 99676; (907) 733-2218.

Description: The Talkeetna is a major tributary of the Susitna and one of the most significant fishing rivers in Southcentral Alaska. Since it is a large, glacial, swift wilderness river, the better fishing potential is concentrated in its clearwater tributary streams. The mainstem is fishable, however, barring hot weather and heavy rains. (In spring and fall months, the water usually becomes moderately clear with a greenish tint.)

Due to the size and productivity of this system, the Talkeetna offers superb and varied fishing. All five salmon species fill the river from midsummer into fall, along with rainbow trout, charr and grayling. The best way to sample the hot salmon action—some of the best in the region for kings, chums, silvers and reds—is by boat from the town of Talkeetna, accessing the mouths of some of the clearwater spawning tributaries upstream. This is definitely not a river for novice boaters, however, with its swift currents, rocky shoals and hidden boulders. Jet boats can run way up some of the tributaries (Clear and Prairie creeks for example) for some truly notable fishing for rainbow trout, charr and grayling. Travel by boat on the mainstem above Iron Creek is not advised.

The Talkeetna is also one of the premier whitewater rivers of Alaska. Two long canyons of rapids (Class III and IV) begin below Prairie Creek to challenge even experienced river runners. For floating, most folks put in by floatplane at Murder Lake (below Stephan Lake), or by wheelplane on gravel bars along the upper river (near Yellowjacket Creek), making for a five- to seven-day trip down to the mouth.

Some of the Talkeetna's many hot spots to consider include: Clear Creek for rainbows, king salmon, silver salmon, red salmon, chum salmon and pink salmon (also Dolly Varden and grayling), Larson Creek for red and silver salmon (also pink salmon, rainbow trout, Dolly Varden and grayling), Disappointment Creek for chum salmon (also king salmon, rainbow trout, Dolly Varden and grayling), and Prairie Creek for king salmon (also silver salmon, red salmon, chum salmon, rainbow trout, Dolly Varden and grayling).

Rainbow fishing in the mainstem Talkeetna can be very productive in late September and early October, for fish in the two- to three-pound category.

12. UPPER SUSITNA RIVER SYSTEM

Location: Northwest Talkeetna Mountains drainage, 80 miles north of Anchorage.

Reference: Talkeetna B-1, C-1; Talkeetna Mountains C-1, C-6, D-1, D-2, D-3, D-4, D-5, D-6; Healy A-1, A-2, B-1; Mount Hayes B-6.

Access: By boat from the Parks Highway bridge or the town of Talkeetna, or by train or plane. The Alaska Railroad has regularly scheduled service between Anchorage and Fairbanks, and prearranged stops can be made at Chulitna (a small gravel road leads to upper Indian River and lower Portage Creek) or Gold Creek. Rafters can put in at tributary streams and float downstream to Talkeetna or the Parks Highway bridge.

Highlights: Excellent fishing for king salmon (in early July) and rainbow trout (from July through September). Good fishing for silver salmon (in late August) and grayling (from July through September).

Species: (Chum salmon, Dolly Varden), grayling, king salmon, lake trout, (pink salmon), rainbow trout, (red salmon), silver salmon.

Regulations: King salmon fishing is closed from July 14 through December 31. The upper Susitna is designated as a Trophy Trout Area, and only single hook, artificial lures may be used. For additional restrictions, consult the current Alaska Department of Fish and Game sportfishing regulations or the ADF&G Palmer office, (907) 745-5016.

Facilities: No developed public facilities. Guide services are available in Talkeetna.

Contact: For guide services, contact Mahay's Riverboat Service, P.O. Box 705, Talkeetna, AK 99676, (907) 733-2223; or Tri River Charters, P.O. Box 312, Talkeetna, AK 99676, (907) 733-2400.

Description: The Susitna River is Southcentral Alaska's most significant fish producer. It has its beginnings in the runoff from a series of enormous glaciers in the eastern Alaska Range. From there, it flows swiftly south, then west as it cuts through the edge of the Talkeetnas and south again as it meanders down into the forested lowlands of upper Cook Inlet. Although the upper part of this amazing system is seldom fished, it does have some worthwhile opportunities. (Because of the heavy silt load, sportfishing is mostly limited to clearwater tributaries and sloughs.) The most commonly visited part of the upper Susitna is the section between Devils Canyon—an unrunnable stretch of Class VI whitewater just north of the Talkeetna Mountains—and the confluence of the Chulitna and Talkeetna rivers near the town of Talkeetna. North of Devils Canyon, the upper Susitna is a remote wilderness river, with whitewater, limited access and few sportfishing opportunities. The river below the canyon is much tamer (mostly Class I), heavily braided water with logjams and submerged hazards, but it can be boated, with caution. The scenery is outstanding (great views of Mount McKinley), there are no crowds, and the fishing can be quite good, so it's certainly worth exploring.

Most anglers who visit the upper Susitna do so by powerful jet boats, but some opt to use the railway (with some hiking). Planes can access certain sections, with some careful scouting. But boaters undoubtedly have the best of it, as the upper Susitna has a multitude of small tributary streams and sloughs, with plenty of opportunities for exploring and locating holding salmon and hungry rainbows and grayling.

Fishing for king and silver salmon can be quite good, with the brighter fish available early in the season. Two major clearwater tributaries, the Indian River and Portage Creek, are the top bets and sustain the largest fish populations. Locations and species available include Portage Creek (king salmon, silver salmon, grayling), Whiskers Creek (king salmon, silver salmon, grayling), Lane Creek (king salmon, silver salmon, rainbow trout) and Fourth of July Creek (king salmon, silver salmon, rainbow trout) and Indian River (king salmon, silver salmon, rainbow trout). For those with the yearning (and resources) for some real wilderness angling adventure, there are remote fly-in lakes off the upper river—such as Watana, Clarence, Deadman and Big Lake—that see little pressure and have the potential for truly outstanding wild fishing for lake trout and grayling; the best times are late spring through early summer and fall. Check with air taxi services in Talkeetna for latest conditions.

13. CHULITNA RIVER SYSTEM

Location: Northeast Alaska Range drainage, 75 miles north of Anchorage.
Reference: Talkeetna B-1, C-1, D-1; Talkeetna Mountains D-6; Healy A-5, A-6, B-5, B-6.
Access: By automobile, plane and boat. The Parks Highway between

Anchorage and Fairbanks parallels the river system for most of its length, providing road access. The highway crosses the lower Chulitna mainstem as well as a handful of its clearwater tributaries (also providing boat or raft launch). Small wheelplanes can land on gravel bars along the river.

Highlights: Good, easily accessible fishing for king salmon (from late June through early July), silver salmon (in the second half of August), rainbow trout (from August through September) and grayling (from June through September).

Species: (Chum salmon, Dolly Varden), grayling, king salmon, lake trout, (pink salmon), rainbow trout, red salmon, silver salmon.

Regulations: King salmon fishing is prohibited in all areas of the system, except on the East Fork of Chulitna River. For additional restrictions, consult the current Alaska Department of Fish and Game sportfishing regulations or the ADF&G Palmer office, (907) 745-5016.

Facilities: Food and lodging are available nearby on the Parks Highway.

Contact: For lodging and guide information, contact the Chulitna River Lodge, P.O. Box 13282, Trapper Creek, AK 99688; (907) 733-2521.

Description: The Chulitna River headwaters drain off the towering slopes of the Alaska Range near Denali National Park. Heavily silted from melting glaciers, the mainstem has good fishing conditions only in its clearwater tributaries. (The Middle and East forks both run clear.) The surrounding scenery, with North America's tallest mountains nearby, is quite stirring. Although a major highway bisects the area, the wilderness and some great fishing are only a short hike (or float) away.

Road anglers would do best by starting from the highway access points at the major tributary creeks and hiking up and downstream to find good fishing. The mouths and lower reaches usually have the best salmon fishing, with trout and grayling more concentrated in the upstream stretches during the summer months. The Chulitna can also be fished from rafts or by boat, putting in and taking out at the highway bridges (either the Middle or East forks, the Chulitna River Bridge or Talkeetna). The upper Chulitna above the bridge (milepost 135 of the Parks Highway) should not be attempted by novices, however, as it is very fast, with some serious rapids and other hazards.

Some Chulitna hot spots you should try include the Middle Fork (rainbow trout) and East Fork of the Chulitna River (king salmon, silver salmon, grayling), Honolulu Creek (silver salmon, rainbow trout, grayling), Coal Creek (silver salmon, rainbow trout, grayling),

Little Coal Creek (silver salmon, rainbow trout, grayling), Byers Creek (silver salmon, red salmon, rainbow trout, grayling), Spink Creek (silver salmon, red salmon, rainbow trout, grayling), Troublesome Creek (silver salmon, red salmon, rainbow trout, grayling), Horseshoe Creek (silver salmon, red salmon, rainbow trout, grayling), and Sunny Creek (silver salmon, red salmon, rainbow trout, grayling). King, silver and red salmon are the most sought-after species of summer, while rainbow trout are the primary fish in the fall. Occasionally, lake trout are still taken from Byers, Summit and Miami lakes, although these waters have certainly seen their time.

14. TYONE RIVER SYSTEM

Location: Upper Susitna River drainage, 35 miles northwest of Glennallen, 140 miles northeast of Anchorage.

Reference: Gulkana B-6, C-6.

Access: By automobile, boat and plane. Lake Louise Road, a gravel road heading north from the Glenn Highway between Anchorage and Glennallen, provides access to Lake Louise, the largest lake in the Tyone River drainage. Boat travel is possible from there to all points along the system. Floatplanes can land anywhere in the system and a landing strip is located on the south shore of Lake Louise.

Highlights: Southcentral Alaska's best lake trout waters, with excellent fishing in June, September and October, and abundant opportunities for grayling in June through October.

Species: Lake trout, grayling, northern pike.

Regulations: Burbot fishing is prohibited on Lake Louise. There are size restrictions on lake trout. For additional restrictions, consult the current Alaska Department of Fish and Game sportfishing regulations or the ADF&G Glennallen office, (907) 822-3309.

Facilities: Commercial lodging, a guide service, boat rentals, a boat launch, fuel, a campground, sporting goods and groceries are available in the Lake Louise area.

Contact: For lodging and guide services, contact the Wolverine Lodge, HC 01, Box 1693, Glennallen, AK 99588; (907) 822-3988. For an air taxi, contact Lee's Air Taxi, HC 03, Box 8857, Palmer, AK 99645; (907) 822-3343.

Description: The Tyone River system consists of an extensive complex of lakes and streams in the high plateau country of the upper Susitna, east of the Talkeetna Mountains. Sportfishing opportunities, mostly for grayling and lake trout, are significant, especially in the three largest and deepest lakes—Louise, Susitna and Tyone. These waters are fairly close to the Glenn Highway, a major road between Anchorage and Glennallen. Because of their location and not too difficult access, they see a major share of the state's urban lake fishing effort, but still hold a lot of fine fishing.

The Tyone itself is a slow, meandering river that connects the outlet of Tyone Lake to the silty Susitna River, a distance of about 30 miles. For boaters and fishermen, it is the clear lakes and associated streams—dozens of them—that are of primary interest. Motorboats, canoes, kayaks and inflatables can all be used to access and fish different parts of the system, putting in at the end of Lake Louise Road by car or anywhere between there and the outlet of the Tyone Lake by floatplane. A pick-up by plane can be arranged at any of the lakes or the confluence of Tyone and Susitna rivers.

The major species inhabiting the Tyone River system are grayling, lake trout and burbot (After years of overharvest, burbot are currently off-limits to anglers in Lake Louise.) Lake trout and grayling are still abundant. Lake Louise and Susitna are well known for their trophy lake trout potential, and still boot out a fair share of "lakers" up to 30 pounds each year, despite growing pressure from the nearby urban populations. Like many deep, large lakes, they are best fished right after ice-out in the spring (usually late May or early June in most years) or later, in the fall. Trolling big spoons, bait and plugs is standard practice on these deep waters, but you can do well casting from shore or a skiff at certain times, if you know what you're doing. Check with the local lodges on the Lake Louise for the latest conditions before heading up for fishing. Grayling are found in most of the system's lakes and streams. There are even a few good pike lakes and some spots for rainbow trout fishing, according to locals.

The air taxi services and lodges will be glad to help you find the kind of fishing you're looking for. Since this is wild, big water country with rapidly changing weather and tricky conditions, it's probably best to enlist their services, at least for starters. They can fly or boat you to the best areas of the season and really put you into some truly outstanding fishing, at prices that are reasonable. Two of the best are: Wolverine Lodge at Lake Louise, (907) 822-3988, and Lee's Air Taxi in Glennallen, (907) 822-3343.

REGION 2
KENAI-COOK INLET

This area includes the waters of the Kenai Peninsula and Cook Inlet and contains some of the state's most notable marine and freshwater sportfisheries. The Kenai Peninsula has been characterized as a miniature Alaska, with its immense ice fields, turquoise glacial lakes, sparkling runoff streams, forests, fjords and towering mountains. Its wildlife also mirrors that of the state, with some of the world's largest moose, abundant waterfowl and marine mammals, bears and even caribou. What's more, the Kenai Peninsula and surrounding waters are amply blessed with an amazing fecundity, producing some of Alaska's most abundant and unique fishing opportunities, particularly trophy king salmon and halibut. And best of all, nearly all of it is easy to reach and enjoy by boat, car or a short plane ride.

15. LOWER COOK INLET

Location: Southwest Kenai Peninsula, 100 miles Southwest of Anchorage.

Reference: Kenai A-4, A-5, B-4; Seldovia A-5, A-6, B-6, D-5.

Access: Mostly by boat, although it can be fished by surf-casting. Launches can be made from several points along the Sterling Highway between Ninilchik Village and Anchor Point, the more popular locations being the mouths of the Ninilchik and Anchor rivers, Deep Creek and surrounding beaches, including Whiskey Gulch.

Highlights: Excellent marine inshore fishing for king salmon (from late May through early June and in early July) and halibut (from June through August). Good fishing for silver salmon (in early August and early September), pink salmon (in late July) and Dolly Varden charr (from May through June).

Species: (Chum salmon), Dolly Varden, halibut, king salmon, pink salmon, red salmon, silver salmon, (steelhead).

Regulations: Fishing for halibut is closed from January 1 through January 31; catch-and-release only for steelhead trout. For additional restrictions, consult the current Alaska Department of Fish and Game sportfishing regulations or the ADF&G Soldotna office, (907) 262-9368.

Facilities: Lodging, campgrounds, tackle, groceries, gas and a guide service are available along the Sterling Highway.

Contact: For camping and fishing information, contact the Anchor Angler Tackle Store, P.O. Box 84, Anchor Point, AK 99536; (907) 235-8351. For guide services, contact Alasking Charters, 3507 Willow Place, Apartment C, Anchorage, AK 99517, (907) 243-0564; Reel 'Em Inn, Cook Inlet Charters, P.O. Box 39292, Ninilchik, AK 9963 (in summer), 13641 Venus Way, Anchorage, AK 99515 (in winter), (907) 345-3887; R.W.'s Fishing, P.O. Box 3824, Soldotna, AK 99669, (907) 262-7888 or (800) 478-6900; or Central Charters Booking Agency, 4241 Homer Spit Road, Homer, AK 99603, (907) 235-7847.

Description: Cook Inlet's daunting waters mix the chill gray runoff from melting glaciers with the clear-greenish Pacific Ocean, stirring it with strong tides and unpredictable weather. Some outstanding and unique fishing can be had, however, off the surf-swept beaches and bluffs along the western Kenai Peninsula, in a magnificent Alaska setting. On clear days, the inlet mirrors the snow-capped peaks of Mount Redoubt and Iliamna, two active volcanoes of Alaska's "ring of fire."

The inlet serves as a major migration corridor for countless fish bound for the Kenai Peninsula, streams on the west side of the inlet and the immense Susitna River drainage to the north. Salmon fishing is often fast and furious during the peak of the runs, with trolling being the primary method used by most anglers along the beaches and near stream mouths from Ninilchik south to Anchor Point.

This area is noted for its trophy king salmon and halibut fisheries, with record catches not uncommon. Halibut up to 300 or 350 pounds or more, and kings of 70 to 80 pounds plus, have been caught. (Commercial fisherman have even reported catching fish well over 100 pounds.) There are two runs each of king salmon, silver salmon and red salmon. Although the action is usually best during the early runs, the late runs have larger fish. Red salmon are the most abundant of the three, but due to their reluctance to strike hardware, fishing for them is seldom better than fair. Some of the better locations for salmon in the lower Cook Inlet include Ninilchik River, Deep Creek, Stariski Creek, Anchor Point/River, The Falls, Whiskey Gulch and Happy Valley.

Halibut fishing is outstanding in the summer, with these gargantuan flatfish hitting best at slack high and low tide a few miles offshore on shoals and reefs just about anywhere along the coast of the

Kenai Peninsula. The Barren and Chugach islands around Kennedy Entrance at the mouth of the inlet are good early season bets.

16. KACHEMAK BAY

Location: Southwest Kenai Peninsula, 115 miles southwest of Anchorage.

Reference: Seldovia B-4, B-5, C-3, C-4, C-5, D-3, D-4.

Access: By automobile and boat. The most common point of access is from the town of Homer at the end of the Sterling Highway. The Homer Harbor provides boat launching facilities for anglers wishing to target the fisheries in the bay and adjacent coves. Shorefishing is also possible.

Highlights: Some of the state's best road-accessible marine fishing; excellent for king salmon (from late May through early June), silver salmon (from late August through early September), pink salmon (in the second half of July) and halibut (from mid-June through mid-August). Good fishing for red salmon (in the second half of July) and Dolly Varden charr (in May and June).

Species: Chum salmon, Dolly Varden, halibut, king salmon, pink salmon, red salmon, silver salmon.

Regulations: Halibut fishing is closed from January 1 through January 31. For additional restrictions, consult the current Alaska Department of Fish and Game sportfishing regulations or the ADF&G Soldotna office, (907) 262-9368.

Facilities: Lodging, groceries, gas, a boat rental, a boat launch and guide services are available in the towns of Homer and Seldovia.

Contact: For guide services, contact Cié Jae Charters, P.O. Box 380, Homer, AK 99603, (907) 235-5587; Inlet Charters, P.O. Box 2083, Homer, AK 99603, (800) 770-6126 or (907) 235-6126; or Central Charters Booking Agency, 4241 Homer Spit Road, Homer, AK 99603, (907) 235-7847. For lodging information, contact the Coastal Alaska Wilderness Lodge, P.O. Box 110, Seldovia, AK 99663, (907) 234-7858; or the Lands End Resort, 4786 Homer Spit Road, Homer, AK 99603, (800) 478-0400 or (907) 235-0400.

Description: Beautiful Kachemak Bay, situated on the southern end of the Kenai Peninsula, provides an abundance and variety of fishing in a diverse natural setting, The north side of the bay is dominated by grassy bluffs and long sand beaches, while the south side is more rugged, with mountains, glaciers, deep valleys and hidden coves. With its relatively easy access, renowned fishing and superlative marine environment, Kachemak, along with Resurrection Bay, receives some of the greatest visitor use of any Alaska coastal destination.

The clear-greenish waters are home to both natural and enhanced runs of salmon, in addition to a rich assemblage of shellfish and bottomfish. Well-known hot spots to consider include Homer Spit (king salmon, silver salmon, pink salmon, Dolly Varden) and Bluff Point (king salmon, halibut) on the north side and Halibut Cove/Lagoon (king salmon), Seldovia Bay (king salmon, silver salmon, pink salmon), Tutka Bay/Lagoon (pink salmon), China Poot Bay (red salmon), and Glacier Spit and Gull Island (halibut) on the south side. However, one can do quite well for salmon and charr fishing in or near stream mouths nearly anywhere in the bay and on shoals and reefs in deeper water for halibut and bottomfish. Good trolling for feeder king salmon can be had year-round, with some of the better fishing occurring in spring and fall.

Kachemak Bay is ideal for small craft—such as open skiffs and kayaks—as well as larger sportfishing vessels. It's a short run, about three to four miles straight across from Homer Harbor to the south side, where the majority of good angling occurs. Shorefishing is also productive, particularly in areas (Homer Spit) where enhanced salmon runs occur.

17. UPPER KENAI RIVER SYSTEM

Location: East Cook Inlet drainage, Kenai Peninsula, 50 miles south of Anchorage.

Reference: Seward B-6, B-7, B-8, C-6, C-7, C-8; Kenai B-1.

Access: By automobile and boat. The upper section of the Kenai River and its tributaries are reached via the Sterling and Seward highways from Anchorage. The Sterling Highway parallels the mainstem river most of its length, crossing it in two places. Numerous pulloffs and trails are present. Boats or rafts may be launched from several places to reach more inaccessible areas of the river.

Highlights: Alaska's number-one salmon trout river fishery; excellent for red salmon (in the second half of June and late July through early August). Good fishing for silver salmon (from late August through early September and in the first half of October), rainbow trout (from July through October) and Dolly Varden charr (from July through October).

Species: (Chum salmon), Dolly Varden, grayling, kokanee, lake trout, pink salmon, rainbow trout, red salmon, silver salmon.

Regulations: King salmon fishing is prohibited. For additional restrictions, consult the current Alaska Department of Fish and Game sportfishing regulations or the ADF&G Soldotna office, (907) 262-9368.

Facilities: Lodging, gas, groceries, sporting goods, guide services, campgrounds and boat launching are available along the highway in the Cooper Landing area.

Contact: For guide services, contact the Alaska River Company, P.O. Box 827, Cooper Landing, AK 99572, (907) 595-1226; or the Alaska Trout Fitters, Mile 50 Sterling Highway, Cooper Landing, AK 99572, (907) 595-1557. For lodging information, contact the Kenai Lake Lodge, P.O. Box 828, Cooper Landing, AK 99572; (907) 595-1590.

Description: The lovely upper Kenai River, with its emerald waters, scenic mountains and forests, is one of Alaska's most popular recreation areas. It has a phenomenally productive fishery and a real wilderness character that, despite the high use of recent years, continues to thrill and amaze everyone, newcomers and seasoned Alaskans alike.

Rising from runoff streams and creeks in the Kenai Mountains, the river issues from the outlet of Kenai Lake and flows swiftly west towards Cook Inlet. Most of the river from the lake down is Class I water perfectly suited for drift fishing in boats or rafts. In the last few miles before Skilak Lake, the river enters a canyon with Class III water, which should only be negotiated by experienced boaters.

Like the lower Kenai, the upper river gets two distinct runs of king salmon, silver salmon and red salmon, but is currently closed for king salmon fishing. Silvers are available in August through September and again in October through November. Red salmon appear in abundance during June and again in July and August, creating some of Alaska's best fishing for the species (especially at Russian River—see description on page 408). Another feature unique to the upper Kenai is that it remains ice-free throughout winter—even during temperatures of 20 below or colder—thus creating a small fishery for charr and a winter run of silver salmon. In some years, bright silvers may be taken as late as February near the Kenai Lake outlet.

The upper Kenai also has some of Alaska's best trophy water for rainbow trout and Dolly Varden charr, especially during September and October. Other angling opportunities in the system include Trail Lake (rainbow trout, lake trout, Dolly Varden), Hidden Lake (kokanee, rainbow trout, lake trout, Dolly Varden), Cooper Lake (rainbow trout, Dolly Varden), Vagt Lake (rainbow trout), Grant Lake (rainbow trout), Jean Lake (rainbow trout), Crescent Lake (grayling), Trail River (rainbow trout, Dolly Varden), Quartz Creek (Dolly Varden), Hidden Creek (red salmon, rainbow trout, Dolly Varden), Grant Creek (silver salmon, Dolly Varden), Ptarmigan Creek (rainbow trout, Dolly Varden) and Daves Creek (rainbow trout, Dolly Varden).

Guides' tip: The upper Kenai has some of the best flyfishing opportunities for trophy rainbow trout and Dolly Varden in Southcentral. The main river between Kenai and Skilak lakes is designated a Trophy Trout and Charr Area, with catches up to 10 or 12 pounds not unusual. Autumn is the best time using egg-imitations, flesh flies and attractors, but dry-fly fishing is gaining more recognition with some excellent results during certain parts of the season.

---

18. LOWER KENAI RIVER SYSTEM

Location: East Cook Inlet drainage, Kenai Peninsula, 50 miles southwest of Anchorage.

Reference: Kenai A-1, B-1, B-2, B-3, B-4, C-1, C-2, C-3, C-4.

Access: By automobile and boat. There is extensive access from the Sterling Highway (via Anchorage), which parallels the river more or less from Skilak Lake down to the mouth of the river. There are many pulloffs, gravel roads and trails leading to viable waters in the system. Major points of access include the towns of Sterling, Soldotna and Kenai.

Highlights: Excellent fishing for silver salmon (in the second half of August and from late September through early October), red salmon (in the second half of July) and Dolly Varden charr (from July through October). Good fishing for king salmon (in the first half of June and second half of July) and rainbow trout (from July through October).

Species: (Chum salmon), Dolly Varden, king salmon, lake trout, (northern pike), rainbow trout, red salmon, silver salmon.

Regulations: King salmon fishing is closed from August 1 through December 31, unless otherwise noted. For additional restrictions, consult the current Alaska Department of Fish and Game sportfishing regulations or the ADF&G Soldotna office, (907) 262-9368.

Facilities: Lodging, gas, groceries, sporting goods, guide services, boat rentals and launching, and campgrounds are available in nearby towns.

Contact: For guide services, contact R.W.'s Fishing, P.O. Box 3824,

Soldotna, AK 99669, (907) 262-7888 or (800) 478-6900; Timberline Guide Service, P.O. Box 32, Soldotna, AK 99669, (907) 262-4170 or (907) 561-3037; or Salmon Chaser Charters, P.O. Box 654, Soldotna, AK 99669, (907) 262-9681. For lodging information, contact the Kenai River Lodge, 393 Riverside Drive, Soldotna, AK 99969, (907) 262-4292; or Great Alaska Fish Camp, HC 01, Box 218, Sterling, AK 99672, (907) 262-4515.

Description: The most popular sportfishery in Alaska and perhaps the most famous salmon river in all the world, the bluish-green Kenai is the queen of Alaska's rivers. Easy access, incomparable trophy fishing and abundant salmon runs are the main attractions, especially in the lower river, which begins at glacial Skilak Lake and flows west 50 miles to Cook Inlet, through spruce-cottonwood forests and rolling hills.

Unlike most of the state's rivers, the Kenai receives two distinct waves, or runs, of king, silver and red salmon each year. Early-run king and red salmon invade the river in May and June, with the first silver salmon run during July and August. The second run of kings and reds happens in July and August, while silver salmon numbers peak again in September and October.

Most of all, of course, the Kenai River is noted for its mammoth strain of king salmon. The current International Game Fish Association (IGFA) world record for a sport-caught fish—over 97 pounds—was taken near Soldotna in 1985, and larger kings of over 100 pounds have been sighted. The largest fish each summer invariably go 80 to 95 pounds, with good numbers weighing over 60 and 70 pounds. The Kenai system has also produced numerous world records (IGFA "All Tackle," "line" and "fly rod tippet" classes) for red and pink salmon and Dolly Varden charr, as well as a good share of Alaska's largest trophy rainbows. (See the rainbow trout chapter on page 128.)

The lower Kenai remains partially ice-free in winter, with open-water angling possible from the outlet of Skilak Lake to a few miles downstream. A late run of silver salmon might yield bright fish beyond New Year's and Dolly Varden are almost always present. The late-running salmon also lure many bald eagles to feed on carcasses, providing some rare late winter viewing opportunities. Some good fishing can also be had on several tributary streams and lakes along the lower river.

Local hot spots include the Moose River (king salmon, silver salmon, red salmon, pink salmon, rainbow trout, Dolly Varden),

East Fork of the Moose River (rainbow trout), Killey River (silver salmon, pink salmon, rainbow trout, Dolly Varden), Funny River (silver salmon, pink salmon, rainbow trout, Dolly Varden), Beaver Creek (rainbow trout, Dolly Varden), King County Creek (silver salmon, red salmon, rainbow trout, Dolly Varden), Kelly Lake (rainbow trout), Peterson Lake (rainbow trout), Egumen Lake (rainbow trout), Watson Lake (rainbow trout), Afonas Lake (rainbow trout), Loon Lake (rainbow trout), Grebe Lake (rainbow trout), Longmere Lake (rainbow trout), Scout Lake (landlocked salmon), Sport Lake (rainbow trout), Union Lake (landlocked salmon, rainbow trout) and Arc Lake (landlocked salmon).

Guides' tip: The majority of angling for king and silver salmon takes place on the far lower river below the Soldotna bridge. Both private and guide boats, as well as a few bankfishermen, actively fish the area on the incoming tides using attractor lures with or without salmon roe. Back trolling and drifting are the most popular methods for kings, while anchoring up and still fishing is best for silvers, especially when soaking salmon eggs. The red salmon hug the riverbanks and are most susceptible in the stretch of water from Soldotna bridge upstream to the Killey River. Good numbers of trophy rainbow trout and sea-run Dolly Varden are taken in the first few miles of river from the Skilak Lake outlet to the mouth of the Funny River.

19. RUSSIAN RIVER SYSTEM

Location: East Cook Inlet drainage, Kenai Peninsula, 50 miles south of Anchorage.

Reference: Seward B-8.

Access: By automobile and floatplane. The river is most commonly accessed from the Sterling Highway at Cooper Landing. A trail system allows anglers to access any part of the Russian River from its headwaters at Upper Russian Lake down to the mouth on the Kenai.

Highlights: World-famous, road-accessible salmon locale; excellent for red salmon (in late June and from late July through early August). Good fishing for silver salmon (from late August through early September), rainbow trout (from June through September) and Dolly Varden charr (from August through September).

Species: Dolly Varden, (grayling), king salmon, pink salmon, rainbow trout, red salmon, silver salmon.

Regulations: King salmon fishing is prohibited; catch-and-release fishing only for rainbow trout. For additional restrictions, carefully consult the current Alaska Department of Fish and Game sportfishing regulations or the ADF&G Soldotna office, (907) 262-9368.

Facilities: A forest service campground is located near the mouth of the river. The nearby community of Cooper Landing has lodging, gas, groceries and sporting goods stores. Forest service cabins are available on the Upper and Lower Russian Lakes and on the section of river between the two lakes.

Contact: For lodging information, contact the Kenai Lake Lodge, P.O. Box 828, Cooper Landing, AK 99572; (907) 595-1590. For more information on forest service campgrounds and cabins, contact Chugach National Forest, 201 East 9th Avenue, Anchorage, AK 99501-3698; (907) 271-2500.

Description: The Russian River is a major clearwater tributary of the upper Kenai River that provides a readily accessible, major stream fishery for salmon in Southcentral Alaska. From its headwaters high in the Kenai Mountains, it flows swift and shallow through a narrow valley lined with spruce and cottonwood. Two major lakes are formed along the way—the Upper and Lower Russian. Trails follow the river along its entire length from the upper lake to the Kenai confluence (12 miles), providing for superlative hiking and access to less-visited stretches of water.

The Russian is perhaps the most visited stream of its size in Alaska, drawing anglers with a combination of clearwater sightfishing, easy access and huge schools of salmon (sockeye and silver) that invade every summer. The first of two large runs of red salmon enters the river in June, the second in July and August, followed by a smaller, and much less fished, run of silver salmon in August and September. It's total combat fishing during the peak of the sockeye run, but near-perfect conditions for taking the normally tight-lipped salmon on a fly, so most folks are able to get their limit (three fish).

In late summer and fall, rainbow trout and charr fishing heats up in the lower sections of the Russian near spawning salmon, but it can be good as well in the upper river (from Upper Russian Lake outlet down, for example). The small tributary streams of the lakes are seldom fished, but can also provide good fishing for trout and charr in early summer and fall. Since the Russian River sees an enormous amount of spawning activity in August and September, brown and black bears can be quite common, particularly along the upper river and near the campground. Use caution when fishing and tramping through the brush along the banks, especially in early morning and late evening.

Note: The Russian was one of the first Alaska streams to see successful techniques for flyfishing sockeyes. See the chapter on red salmon on page 64 for details on methods, gear and flies used.

20. KASILOF RIVER SYSTEM

Location: East Cook Inlet drainage, Kenai Peninsula, 75 miles southwest of Anchorage.

Reference: Kenai A-2, A-3, A-4, B-3, B-4.

Access: By automobile, from the Sterling Highway just south of Soldotna. Side roads access the lower river and its confluence with Crooked Creek and the upper river and Tustumena Lake outlet.

Highlights: An immensely popular, road-accessible stream fishery; excellent for king salmon (in the first half of June) and silver salmon (from mid-August through early September). Good fishing for Dolly Varden Charr (from August through September).

Species: (Chum salmon), Dolly Varden, king salmon, lake trout, pink salmon, red salmon, silver salmon, steelhead.

Regulations: King salmon fishing is closed from August 1 through December 31. For additional restrictions, consult the current Alaska Department of Fish and Game sportfishing regulations or the ADF&G Soldotna office, (907) 262-9368.

Facilities: A campground and a boat launch are located on the river. Lodging, guide services and a grocery store are available on the highway nearby.

Contact: For guide services, contact the Timberline Guide Service, P.O. Box 32, Soldotna, AK 99669, (907) 262-4170 or (907) 561-3037; Alasking Charters, 3507 Willow Place, Apartment C, Anchorage, AK 99517, (907) 243-0564; or R.W.'s Fishing, P.O. Box 3824, Soldotna, AK 99669, (800) 478-6900 or (907) 262-7888. For lodging information, contact the Kenai River Lodge, 393 Riverside Drive, Soldotna, AK 99969, (907) 262-4292.

Description: The greenish-gray Kasilof River drains the immense and glacially turbid waters of Tustumena Lake (the Kenai Peninsula's largest lake), at the base of the Kenai Mountains. It provides a fairly significant amount of sportfishing in its lower reaches and clearwater tributaries and is easily accessed from Anchorage. Most of the angling takes place from the Sterling Highway bridge downstream to the confluence with clear Crooked Creek, a major salmon spawning tributary. Fishing is equally productive from the bank or from a raft or driftboat.

The Kasilof is one of the most popular fisheries in all of South-central Alaska during the month of June, when the kings are in heavy. Two runs enter the Kasilof, the first in May and June, the second in July and August. The first run is comprised of both wild and hatchery fish and is by far the stronger of the two. The late run is much weaker in strength, but produces larger fish—up to 60 and 70 pounds or more. Silver salmon show in good numbers in late summer and fall and are targeted primarily at the mouth and lower sections of Crooked Creek. The Kasilof also has the distinction of sustaining the northernmost natural population of steelhead trout in Cook Inlet, as a small run of these flashy fighters returns every fall to spawn in Crooked Creek the following spring.

The Kasilof system, including Tustumena Lake and its tributaries, is one of the leading producers of red salmon in Cook Inlet, but because of its milky nature, it does not have productive sportfishing. However, some really fine fishing can be had for abundant Dolly Varden charr that feed on the smolt and eggs, especially in the fall and spring at the outlet and mouths of the clearwater tributaries along Tustumena Lake. (Accessing by boat is treacherous, due to potentially swamping winds and submerged rocks in the lake and river.) Some fair to good lake trout fishing also occurs near the outlet in spring.

Guides' tip: The extremely turbid waters of the Tustumena and Kasilof River system call for maximum size, flash and color in your lure presentations. Fishing bait, as a teaser or alone, will give you the needed edge in these conditions.

---

21. SWANSON RIVER SYSTEM

Location: Northeast Cook Inlet drainage, Kenai Peninsula, 40 miles southwest of Anchorage.

Reference: Kenai C-2, C-3, D-2, D-3.

Access: By automobile, there are two major points of access. One, on the middle river, lies off Swanson River Road from the Sterling Highway. (This is popular with anglers putting in with canoes to reach the upper river or connecting lakes.) The second, on the lower river where the Swanson dumps into Cook Inlet, can be reached via the Kenai Spur and Sterling highways.

Highlights: Excellent fishing for silver salmon (from mid-August through early September); good fishing for rainbow trout (from June through October) and Dolly Varden charr (from July through October).

Species: Dolly Varden, (king salmon), lake trout, pink salmon, rainbow trout, red salmon, silver salmon.

Regulations: King salmon fishing is prohibited. For additional restrictions, consult the current Alaska Department of Fish and Game sportfishing regulations or the ADF&G Soldotna office, (907) 262-9368.

Facilities: A campground is located at the mouth of the river. Lodging, gas, groceries and sporting goods are available on the road system nearby.

Contact: For fishing information, contact the Alaska Department of Fish and Game, Sportfish Division, P.O. Box 3150, Soldotna, AK 99669; (907) 262-9368. For camping information, contact the Public Lands Information Center, 605 West Fourth Avenue, Suite 105, Anchorage, AK 99501; (907) 271-2737.

Description: The Swanson River is a slow-moving, fairly small river draining a large area of lowland lakes and swamps in the northern Kenai Peninsula. There are over 35 lakes connected to the Swanson system through tiny streams or short portages, many of them having good fishing for rainbow trout, Dolly Varden charr and landlocked silver salmon.

Extremely popular with canoeists, the Swanson River Canoe Route is easily accessed from Swan Lake Road via the Swanson River Road (put-in at Paddle Lake), making for trips lasting from several days to one week. The Swanson can also be accessed at mid-river from the end of Swanson River Road; from there down to the mouth, it is an easy, two-day float and fish trip. Most of the way, the water is flat, but there are some slight rapids near mouth. Take-out is at the Captain Cook Recreation Area, about 36 miles north of the town of Kenai.

Several salmon species spawn in the drainage, but it is the silvers that provide most of the fishing action on the Swanson. These fine fighters can be encountered in large schools throughout the river (especially around the confluences of streams and adjoining lakes) in late summer into fall, but they are best fished on the lower river during incoming tides.

22. PORTAGE AREA RIVER SYSTEMS

Location: Northeast Cook Inlet drainages, Turnagain Arm, 45 miles southeast of Anchorage.

Reference: Seward D-6.

Access: By automobile, via the Seward Highway from Anchorage. The highway crosses the lower river systems near tidewater. Most up-stream access is by boat, equipped with a jet unit, although canoes may be used at times to reach nearby tributaries and sloughs. Hiking is difficult due to dense vegetation. Rafting is possible on Portage Creek from Portage Lake down to the Seward Highway bridge, a four-hour trip.

Highlights: Excellent fishing for silver salmon (from mid-August through mid-September); good fishing for pink salmon (from late July through early August) and Dolly Varden (from July through October).

Species: Chum salmon, Dolly Varden, (king salmon), pink salmon, red salmon, silver salmon.

Regulations: King salmon fishing is prohibited. For additional restrictions, consult the current Alaska Department of Fish and Game sportfishing regulations or the ADF&G Anchorage office, (907) 267-2218.

Facilities: Primitive boat launches are available on the Twentymile and Placer rivers.

Contact: For fishing information, contact the Alaska Department of Fish and Game Regional Office, Sportfish Division, 333 Raspberry Road, Anchorage, AK 99518-1599; (907) 267-2218.

Description: The Portage area at the head of Turnagain Arm has three drainages of glacial origin, the Twentymile, Portage and Placer rivers. They are all within Chugach National Forest. The lower river sections are in open country, with stark reminders of the 1964 earth-quake evidenced in the abundant grey stems of dead spruce trees everywhere. (Once a flourishing forest, the whole area subsided during the quake and flooded with saltwater, killing much of the vegetation.) The setting is spectacular, especially on sunny days, as surrounding mountain peaks display an abundance of greenish-blue glaciers, while the slopes are covered with a thick spruce forest.

The Twentymile River is the larger of the three systems and originates from ice fields around Twentymile Glacier in the Chugach Mountains, running southward to Turnagain Arm. The lower section near the Seward Highway is wide and slow, but becomes quite swift, shallow and braided six to seven miles upstream. The main species in the Twentymile are silver, red and chum salmon and Dolly Varden charr.

Draining out of Portage Lake at the base of world-famous Portage Glacier, Portage Creek flows east to silty Turnagain Arm, fairly fast through most of its length, but particularly so on the upper end.

Good runs of silver, red, chum and pink salmon occur in this drainage along with some Dolly Varden.

Flowing north, the Placer River originates from the Spencer Glacier. The lower river is smooth and slow, yet becomes shallow, fast and braided about 2.5 miles upstream from the highway bridge. Placer is known for its strong late run of silver salmon, some of which may weigh up to 18 pounds. Other species of interest include red salmon and Dolly Varden.

On all three systems, look for clearwater sloughs and stream mouths to target schools of migrating salmon and hungry charr. Keep in mind that many of these hot spots do not have names, but are nonetheless very productive.

23. ANCHOR RIVER

Location: Southeast Cook Inlet drainage, Kenai Peninsula, 115 miles southwest of Anchorage.

Reference: Seldovia C-4, C-5, D-4, D-5.

Access: By automobile. There are several points of lower and middle river access along the Sterling Highway just north of the town of Homer, the most popular being in the vicinity of the town of Anchor Point.

Highlights: Excellent fishing for king salmon (in the first half of June) and Dolly Varden (from July through October). Good fishing for silver salmon (in the second half of August), pink salmon (from late July through early August), steelhead (from late September through October) and rainbow trout (from July through October).

Species: (Chum salmon), Dolly Varden, king salmon, pink salmon, rainbow trout, (red salmon), silver salmon, steelhead.

Regulations: Catch-and-release fishing only for steelhead and rainbow trout. For additional restrictions, consult the current Alaska Department of Fish and Game sportfishing regulations or the ADF&G Soldotna office, (907) 262-9368.

Facilities: A campground, lodging, gas, groceries, sporting goods stores and guide services are available in Anchor Point on the lower river.

Contact: For fishing and guide services, contact the Anchor Angler Tackle Store, P.O. Box 84, Anchor Point, AK 99536; (907) 235-8351. For lodging information, contact the Anchor River Inn, P.O. Box 154, Anchor Point, AK 99556; (907) 235-8531.

Description: The Anchor is a small, highly productive clearwater stream of the southern Kenai Peninsula just north of Kachemak Bay. It is most well known for its runs of steelhead trout—some of the best in Southcentral Alaska—along with outstanding fishing for king and silver salmon. It's close proximity to Anchorage gives it a high amount of seasonal use.

The river begins in a broad valley north of Bald Mountain and flows approximately 34 miles before emptying into Cook Inlet 16 miles northwest of Homer. Shallow and rocky for most of its length, the Anchor is a moody river, turning a chocolaty brown after spells of rain, but usually running clear.

The lower river is open to salmon fishing, and it is especially popular in early summer when the king salmon arrive. The mouth of the river also serves as a launch point for boaters seeking salmon and halibut in the adjoining marine waters. Incoming tides are the best times to fish for fresh runs of salmon (as well as steelhead trout and Dolly Varden in season). The Anchor's steelhead start to appear in late August most years, peaking in numbers by early October. Fishing is good into November, depending on the weather. The fish overwinter in the river, spawn in the spring, and then return to sea. Recent years have seen a rebound of the Anchor's wild steelhead stocks and some excellent fall fishing.

During late summer and fall, the middle and upper river also support high numbers of Dolly Varden, along with some resident rainbows. With a little hiking, anglers can enjoy a measure of solitude and classic stream fishing conditions.

24. ROCKY RIVER

Location: Northwest Gulf of Alaska drainage, Kenai Peninsula, 145 miles southwest of Anchorage.

Reference: Seldovia B-4.

Access: By boat or floatplane to the mouth of the river from the towns of Homer and Seldovia. Hiking upriver is possible. There is floatplane access to the middle river via adjoining Rocky Lake.

Highlights: Excellent fishing for silver salmon (in the first half of September), pink salmon (from late July through early August) and Dolly Varden charr (from July through September). Also good fishing for red salmon (in the first half of August).

Species: Chum salmon, Dolly Varden, pink salmon, red salmon, silver salmon.

Regulations: King salmon fishing is prohibited. For additional restrictions, consult the current Alaska Department of Fish and Game sportfishing regulations or the ADF&G Soldotna office, (907) 262-9368.

Facilities: No developed public facilities.

Contact: For fishing information, contact the Anchor Angler Tackle Store, P.O. Box 84, Anchor Point, AK 99536; (907) 235-8351. For an air taxi, contact Homer Air, P.O. Box 302, Homer, AK 99603; (907) 235-8591. Note: The river is on native lands; a permit is required for camping. For details, contact the Port Graham Native Corporation, P.O. Box 5569, Port Graham, AK 99603-5569; (907) 284-2212.

Description: Rocky River is a small, pristine watershed located on the southern tip of the Kenai Peninsula, just south of Kachemak Bay. Draining out of the Red Mountain area, the river runs a short distance south to Rocky Bay and the Gulf of Alaska. It is beautifully endowed, with thick surrounding forests, an abundance of wildlife, and water that is remarkably clear and deep, creating superb habitat for salmon and charr.

The most productive and popular area to fish on the Rocky is the lower river, working the big schools of anadromous fish that push into the mouth and deep holes with the incoming tides. The middle and upper sections of the river are difficult to reach, except by helicopter or hiking, but they have some great opportunities for anyone willing to do some angling prospecting. A drop-off by floatplane on Big Rocky Lake and a hike up the old, washed-out logging road that runs along the river is a possibility.

One of the best times of the year to visit this small river is autumn (especially September), when trophy-sized sea-run Dolly Varden charr (up to seven or eight pounds) and big silver salmon (over 15 pounds) are taken from the mouth and deep holes.

Note: Since the river is on native lands, a permit is required for camping. For more information, contact the Port Graham Native Corporation at (907) 284-2212.

25. BELUGA RIVER SYSTEM

Location: Northwest Cook Inlet drainage, 30 miles west of Anchorage.

Reference: Tyonek A-3, A-4, B-3, B-4, B-5, B-6, C-5, C-6.

Access: By air from Anchorage. Floatplanes touch down on Beluga and Lower Beluga lakes and the lower river. Boat travel may be possible along sections of river.

Highlights: Good fishing for king salmon (in late June), silver salmon (in early August) and pink salmon (in late July); also rainbow trout (from June through September). Only a short flight from Anchorage.

Species: Dolly Varden, king salmon, pink salmon, rainbow trout, red salmon, silver salmon.

Regulations: King salmon fishing is closed from July 1 through December 31. For additional restrictions, consult the current Alaska Department of Fish and Game sportfishing regulations or the ADF&G Anchorage office, (907) 267-2218.

Facilities: No developed public facilities.

Contact: For fishing information, contact the Alaska Department of Fish and Game Regional Office, Sportfish Division, 333 Raspberry Road, Anchorage, AK 99518-1599; (907) 267-2218. For an air taxi, contact Regal Air, P.O. Box 190702, Anchorage, AK 99519, (907) 243-8535; Ketchum Air Service, P.O. Box 190588, Anchorage, AK 99519, (800) 433-9114 or (907) 243-5525; or Alaska Helicopters, P.O. Box 190283, Anchorage, AK 99519, (907) 243-3404 or (907) 243-1466.

Description: Beluga Lake is a large, silty body of meltwater from two enormous glaciers pouring down the slopes of the Alaska Range north of Mount Spurr. The Beluga River issues from the lake and flows rapidly through a canyon down to the mudflats of Cook Inlet 30 miles away. Though the lake and river are too silty for sportfishing, several clearwater tributary streams support moderate populations of salmon, trout and charr and provide some notable fishing opportunities, a mere 20-minute flight from Anchorage.

   While the upper and lower sections of the Beluga are slower moving and can be accessed by plane, the middle canyon sections are extremely difficult and dangerous to negotiate, even with a powerful boat. Anglers fishing the Beluga should probe the mouths of the clearwater streams for holding salmon (king, silver and sockeye in season), with the best charr and rainbow trout water reached with a little hiking. Some of the best creeks to try are Pretty, Olsen, Drill, Scarp and Coal. Olsen Creek can be accessed at the mouth by small wheelplane. Coal Creek, draining into the lower end of Beluga Lake, has the largest population of salmon and trout and is easily accessed by floatplane. The lake and upper river are among the most dramatically scenic locations in Cook Inlet.

26. CHUITNA RIVER

Location: Northwest Cook Inlet drainage, 40 miles west of Anchorage.

Reference: Tyonek A-4, A-5, B-5.

Access: By plane or helicopter from Anchorage or Kenai. Most anglers access the mouth of the Chuitna by wheelplane, landing on the north side beach. A primitive gravel road network running along the coast provides additional access to the lower river. The upper "Chuit" can be accessed by helicopter. Rafts may be launched from there and floated down to the mouth.

Highlights: Excellent fly-in fishing for king salmon (in the first part of June), silver salmon (in the first part of August) and pink salmon (in the second half of July). Good fishing for rainbow trout (from June through September).

Species: Chum salmon, Dolly Varden, king salmon, pink salmon, rainbow trout, red salmon, silver salmon.

Regulations: King salmon fishing is closed from July 1 through December 31; bait restrictions may apply. For additional restrictions, consult the current Alaska Department of Fish and Game sportfishing regulations or the ADF&G Anchorage office, (907) 267-2218.

Facilities: A commercial lodge and guide services are available on river.

Contact: For fishing information, contact the Alaska Department of Fish and Game Regional Office, Sportfish Division, 333 Raspberry Road, Anchorage, AK 99518-1599; (907) 267-2218. For lodging and guide services, contact the Chuitna River Guides, P.O. Box 82048, Tyonek, AK 99682; (907) 583-2282. For an air taxi, contact Ketchum Air Service, P.O. Box 190588, Anchorage, AK 99519, (800) 433-9114 or (907) 243-5525; or Alaska Helicopters, P.O. Box 190283, Anchorage, AK 99519, (907) 243-3404 or (907) 243-1466.

Description: The Chuitna River is perhaps the most significant westside Cook Inlet salmon and trout stream, well known for outstanding king and silver salmon fishing. It is away from crowds, yet only a short distance from Anchorage by plane. Draining a sizeable, very pretty area of uplands between the Chakachatna and Beluga rivers, it has clear water, with deep holes, swift, rocky runs and canyons, along with several tributaries (such as Lone and Chuit creeks) that offer ideal stream fishing conditions.

The south side of the Chuitna River is private land that is owned by the Tyonek Native Corporation. Permits must be obtained to access this land, so most public use occurs on the north side. The mouth and lower river are the most popular spots for fishing, with the best action during and shortly after the incoming tides. Nearby

Threemile Creek, which you can access by gravel road, also offers outstanding salmon fishing. The middle and upper river contain an abundance of good holding and spawning water, along with decent populations of rainbow trout and Dolly Varden charr in late summer and fall. These sections can be reached partially by a gravel road that runs along the river a ways up from the mouth or by boat or helicopter. (Some fishermen even bring their own all-terrain vehicles or dirt bikes to navigate the gravel road.)

27. CHAKACHATNA-MCARTHUR RIVER SYSTEM

Location: Northwest Cook Inlet drainage, Trading Bay, 65 miles southwest of Anchorage.

Reference: Lime Hills A-1, B-1; Tyonek A-5, A-6, A-7, A-8, B-7, B-8; Kenai D-5.

Access: By helicopter or wheelplane from Anchorage or Kenai. The Chakachatna side of the system may be scouted for wheelplane landing areas—gravel bars—but the McArthur side is accessible only by helicopter.

Highlights: Good fly-in fishing for king salmon (in the last half of June) and silver salmon (in the first half August); just a short flight from Anchorage.

Species: Chum salmon, Dolly Varden, king salmon, pink salmon, red salmon, silver salmon.

Regulations: Consult the current Alaska Department of Fish and Game sportfishing regulations or the ADF&G Soldotna office, (907) 262-9368.

Facilities: No developed public facilities.

Contact: For fishing information, contact the Alaska Department of Fish and Game, Sportfish Division, P.O. Box 3150, Soldotna, AK 99669; (907) 262-9368. For an air taxi, contact Kenai Air, 155 Granite Point Court, Kenai, AK 99611, (907) 283-7561; or Alaska Helicopters, P.O. Box 190283, Anchorage, AK 99519, (907) 243-3404 or (907) 243-1466.

Description: This massive coastal system drains a sizable area of the Alaska Range within Lake Clark National Park. Of glacial origin with heavy silt loads, the rivers' sportfishing is limited to a handful of small, clear tributary streams that provide some concentrated fishing in season, with little pressure. Kings and silvers are the top draw, with some fair to good angling for other salmon (reds, chums and pinks) and Dolly Varden charr. Access is tricky.

The Chakachatna River is somewhat limited in suitable locations to fish. The clear, north fork of Straight Creek is perhaps the best place to try for salmon. Small wheelplanes can land on gravel bars and ridges nearby. McArthur River has a few more streams to choose from, all of them unnamed. The better ones are found on the flats between the two watersheds (west of Noaukta Slough). These clear streams are usually assessed by helicopter and can provide some good fishing, especially for silver salmon during the peak of the runs.

28. KUSTATAN RIVER

Location: Westside Cook Inlet, Redoubt Bay, 60 miles southwest of Anchorage.

Reference: Kenai C-5, D-6; Tyonek A-6.

Access: By floatplane from Anchorage (or Kenai). Boat access is possible along the river.

Highlights: A famous westside salmon stream, with excellent fishing for silver salmon (from August through early September).

Species: (King salmon), Dolly Varden, pink salmon, red salmon, silver salmon.

Regulations: For bag limits and restrictions, consult the current Alaska Department of Fish and Game sportfishing regulations or the ADF&G Soldotna office, (907) 262-9368.

Facilities: Tent camps and guide services are available on the river.

Contact: For an air taxi and guide services, contact Regal Air, P.O. Box 190702, Anchorage, AK 99519, (907) 243-8535; Ketchum Air Service, P.O. Box 190588, Anchorage, AK 99519, (800) 433-9114 or (907) 243-5525; or Rusts Flying Service, P.O. Box 190325, Anchorage, AK 99519, (907) 243-1595.

Description: The Kustatan River of Redoubt Bay is one of the more popular and productive silver salmon streams of Cook Inlet's west side. Although it sees quite a bit of use during the season, it is worth mentioning for its high quality of angling and close proximity to Anchorage.

Access is by small floatplane from Anchorage or Kenai to adjoining lakes along the middle section of river. Most of the fishing is done on the river near the lakes, in small tributary streams or at the mouth (an old gas field road provides access). The upper river, which is most scenic and offers still more good fishing, can be accessed via a small floatplane landing on some small lakes in the hills. Several guide operations are located on the river, and recreational use is growing, so expect company when the action's hot on the Kustatan.

29. BIG RIVER LAKES SYSTEM

Location: Westside Cook Inlet, 60 miles southwest of Anchorage.

Reference: Kenai C-6, C-7, D-6, D-7.

Access: By floatplane from Anchorage.

Highlights: A well-known westside salmon stream, with excellent fishing for red salmon (from mid-June through mid- July) and good fishing for silver salmon (in August).

Species: Dolly Varden, rainbow trout, red salmon, silver salmon.

Regulations: For bag limits and restrictions, consult the current Alaska Department of Fish and Game sportfishing regulations or the ADF&G Soldotna office, (907) 262-9368.

Facilities: A commercial lodge and guide services are available on one of the lakes.

Contact: For lodging and guide services, contact Branham Adventures, P.O. Box 190184, Anchorage, AK 99519; (907) 243-4901. For an air taxi, contact Regal Air, P.O. Box 190702, Anchorage, AK 99519, (907) 243-8535; Ketchum Air Service, P.O. Box 190588, Anchorage, AK 99519, (800) 433-9114 or (907) 243-5525; or Rusts Flying Service, P.O. Box 190325, Anchorage, AK 99519, (907) 243-1595.

Description: The lovely Big River Lakes area across the inlet from Nikiski on the Kenai has been a popular fly-in spot for years, thanks to its abundant salmon fishing in a magnificent, secluded setting. There are four connected lakes, all of glacial origin, nestled above Redoubt Bay. This system forms major habitat for salmon, particularly sockeye. In early summer, hundreds of thousands of feisty reds jam up into the lakes, creating one of Southcentral's most concentrated fishing opportunities.

The lakes are easy to access and the fishing hard to beat, especially in and around the inlet/outlet streams, where sockeyes congregate and aggressively strike a variety of enticements. (Wolverine Creek is designated as flyfishing only—check Alaska Department of Fish and Game regulations.) This is one of the few places in Alaska where bright red salmon can be caught consistently on Pixee spoons. Silver salmon can also be taken later in summer in the mouths of clearwater tributaries along Bachatna Flats, but access is difficult.

There are even some Dolly Varden and a few rainbow trout to be had. The lakes and adjoining streams are also very popular with the brown bears during fishing season, so use caution.

30. CRESCENT RIVER/LAKE

Location: Westside Cook Inlet, 75 miles southwest of Anchorage.

Reference: Kenai B-7, B-8; Lake Clark B-1.

Access: By floatplane from Anchorage. Boat access is possible to the lower river.

Highlights: Another popular and productive westside fishing locale; excellent fishing for red salmon (from late June through July) and good fishing for silver salmon (in August).

Species: Dolly Varden, pink salmon, red salmon, silver salmon.

Regulations: For bag limits and restrictions, consult the current Alaska Department of Fish and Game sportfishing regulations or the ADF&G Soldotna office, (907) 262-9368.

Facilities: No developed public facilities.

Contact: For an air taxi, contact Ketchum Air Service, P.O. Box 190588, Anchorage, AK 99519, (800) 433-9114 or (907) 243-5525; or Kenai Air, 155 Granite Point Court, Kenai, AK 99611, (907) 283-7561.

Description: Scenic Crescent Lake and River is one of the more significant salmon systems for its size in Southcentral Alaska and a popular fly-in fishing location. Glacially tinted a beautiful blue-green, it receives a good run of reds starting in late June, and silvers later in the summer, with some good fishing for Dolly Varden as well. Because it's not too far from Kenai and Anchorage, and has such great fishing for sockeye salmon, it should be considered as an inexpensive alternative to the crowded Russian River and other roadside fisheries.

The most commonly fished parts of the system are the lake outlet (a great spot for camping) and clearwater tributaries, where salmon hold in great concentrations during the peak of the runs. Spring and fall are the best times for Dolly Varden. (Keep in mind that the lake doesn't break up until the middle or last part of June.) Nearby Polly Creek has some good silver salmon fishing and outstanding razor clam digging at low tide. It can be accessed by wheelplane at its mouth.

31. SILVER SALMON CREEK

Location: Westside Cook Inlet, 115 miles southwest of Anchorage.
Reference: Kenai A-8; Seldovia D-8.
Access: By small floatplane from Anchorage.
Highlights: Excellent fishing for silver salmon (in August).
Species: Dolly Varden, pink salmon, red salmon, silver salmon.
Regulations: For bag limits and restrictions, consult the current Alaska
    Department of Fish and Game sportfishing regulations or the
    ADF&G Soldotna office, (907) 262-9368.
Facilities: No developed public facilities.
Contact: For lodging information, contact the Silver Salmon Creek
    Lodge, P.O. Box 3234, Soldotna, AK 99669; (907) 262-4839. For an
    air taxi, contact Ketchum Air Service, P.O. Box 190588, Anchorage,
    AK 99519, (800) 433-9114 or (907) 243-5525; or Kenai Air, 155
    Granite Point Court, Kenai, AK 99611, (907) 283-7561.
Description: Silver Salmon Creek along the lower west side of Cook
    Inlet is worthy of mention as a popular fly-in location for abundant,
    high-quality angling for (what else?) silver salmon in season. Lo-
    cated almost directly across from Ninilchik on the Kenai, this short,
    but extremely productive, drainage is accessed by small floatplane,
    landing in either the small Silver Salmon Lakes nearby or in the nar-
    row tidal lagoon at the mouth (a very tricky landing). Fishing in Au-
    gust and early September can be quite good for bigger silvers than
    are generally encountered elsewhere. The setting is quite magnifi-
    cent, with the deep blue waters of the Pacific absorbing the gray,
    glacial silt of the Inlet.

32. KAMISHAK RIVER

Location: Southwest Cook Inlet, 210 miles southwest of Anchorage.
Reference: Afognak C-6; Mount Katmai C-1, C-2, D-1, D-2;
    Iliamna A-4.
Access: By plane from Homer, Kenai or Anchorage, landing on gravel
    beaches at the mouth of the river.
Highlights: Excellent fishing for silver salmon (from September
    through early October). Good fishing for chum salmon (in July),
    pink salmon (in August) and Dolly Varden charr (from July through
    September).
Species: Chum salmon, Dolly Varden, king salmon, pink salmon,
    (rainbow trout), red salmon, silver salmon.
Regulations: For restrictions, consult the current Alaska Department
    of Fish and Game sportfishing regulations or the ADF&G Soldotna

office, (907) 262-9368.

Facilities: No developed public facilities.

Contact: For an air taxi, contact Homer Air, P.O. Box 302, Homer, AK 99603; (907) 235-8591.

Description: On the west side of lower Cook Inlet across from Kachemak Bay lie some less-visited clearwater streams that offer good seasonal fishing for salmon and charr, along with sweeping coastal scenery and abundant wildlife. The Kamishak River is perhaps the best known of these, and it has been visited regularly over the years by the lodge crowd (particularly those from the Iliamna area), who normally fish it in late summer and fall for silver salmon.

The Kamishak rises in the coastal mountains of Katmai National Park near the headwaters of the Naknek and flows northeast through deep valleys, picking up water from several tributaries (such as the Little Kamishak and Strike Creek) to become a fair-sized river before it spills out on the mudflats of Akumwarvik Bay. The awesome snow-covered peaks of Mount Douglas and nearby volcanic Mount Augustine enhance the rugged splendor of the surroundings, and the world-famous bear habitat of the McNeil River State Game Sanctuary is only eight miles away.

The trick to fishing the Kamishak, as with all these short coastal drainages, is getting in. Floatplane landings are perilous with the tides, and wheelplane access is limited to short gravel bars and beaches. Most of the angling effort occurs on the lower river, fishing the incoming tides for fresh salmon and charr, but there is excellent fishing and some access along the middle section. Since the Kamishak is in an area having some of the world's densest concentrations of brown bears, anglers should be prepared for numerous bear encounters and use extreme caution when wading smaller channels and hiking through the brush.

Guides' tip: The Kamishak (and some nearby drainages) is rumored to have a small run of fall steelhead.

REGION 3
KODIAK-AFOGNAK ISLANDS

Kodiak Island and its associated archipelago (including Afognak, Shuyak and Raspberry islands) is a world unto itself. Most geographers group it with Southwest Alaska, some with Southcentral, but it really is apart from the rest of the state, a unique island complex—the second largest in the U.S. at 3,950 square miles—with its own special character. At the same latitude as Scotland, the big island has similar maritime climate, with more lush vegetation and mountainous terrain. Most people know it for its giant bears, but Kodiak also has one of the richest marine environments on Earth, with abundant wildlife along its coasts and an incredibly prolific fishery. Some of the most productive salmon streams in Alaska are located here, along with Southcentral's best steelhead fishing. A short road system extends from the town of Kodiak out along Chiniak Bay and provides some of the region's best road-fishing opportunities, but for the most part, Kodiak's rugged and remote terrain is accessible by floatplane or boat only.

33. SHUYAK ISLAND

Location: North of Afognak Island, 50 miles north of Kodiak, 200 miles southwest of Anchorage.

Reference: Afognak B-2, C-1, C-2, C-3.

Access: Primarily by floatplane, landing in protected bays and coves of the island such as Big and Neketa bays and Carry Inlet. Inflatable rafts or similar types of craft are ideal for fishing some of the smaller bays, while hiking along the beach to stream mouths may be better in others.

Highlights: Excellent fishing for silver salmon (in the second half of August), pink salmon (from late July through early August) and halibut (from May through September).

Species: Dolly Varden, halibut, king salmon, pink salmon, (red salmon), silver salmon, (steelhead).

Regulations: Halibut fishing is closed from January 1 through 31. For additional regulations, consult the current Alaska Department of Fish and Game sportfishing regulations or the ADF&G Kodiak office, (907) 486-4791.

Facilities: Shuyak Island State Park cabins, commercial lodging and guide services are available.

Contact: For lodging and guide services, contact the Port William Wilderness Lodge, P.O. Box 670556, Chugiak, AK 99567; phone or fax (907) 688-2253. For more information, contact the Public Lands Information Center, 605 West Fourth Avenue, Suite 105, Anchorage, AK 99501, (907) 271-2737; or Alaska State Parks, S.R. Box 3800, Kodiak, AK 99615, (907) 486-6339. For an air taxi, contact Uyak Air Service, P.O. Box 4188, Kodiak, AK 99615, (907) 486-3407; or Sea Hawk Air, P.O. Box 3561, Kodiak, AK 99615, (800) 770-HAWK or (907) 486-8282.

Description: Shuyak Island is a small landmass situated just north of Afognak that is richly endowed with animal life in its many bays, coves, islands, and small lakes and streams. The entire coastline of the island has excellent angling potential for salmon, charr and bottomfish, particularly the northwest shore with its archipelago of reefs, protruding rocks and fish-laden inlets. Angling activity for salmon and sea-run charr is concentrated in bays and inlets with streams. Although the numbers of fish are usually quite small, fishing can be outstanding near the mouths of these spawning streams when the runs are at their peak.

Since much of the best fishing takes place in tidal water, small skiffs, rafts or even kayaks provide the best access. Surf-casting is certainly possible at stream mouths, from points and along beaches. Salmon is the top draw around Shuyak, with some of the choice locations including Neketa, Big and Shangin bays and Carry Inlet. All of these have spawning systems at their heads with small, but highly concentrated runs of silver and pink salmon, as well as fair numbers of Dolly Varden and a sprinkling of reds. A few feeder king salmon may be available in outlying waters, but an angler is most likely to encounter halibut there. These popular flatfish are abundant wherever there is open water with sufficient reef and shoal structure. One of the more promising locations for this species is Shuyak Strait between Shuyak and Afognak islands. Shuyak Island, without a doubt, remains one of the most promising destinations in the entire Kodiak area, with its scenic marine setting and excellent fishing potential.

34. CHINIAK BAY

Location: Northeast Kodiak Island, southeast of Kodiak, 250 miles southwest of Anchorage.

Reference: Kodiak C-1, D-1, D-2.

Access: By boat from the town of Kodiak. The bay is just outside Kodiak and all parts of it are easily accessible by almost any size craft. Outlying areas require larger boats due to rough seas. An extensive road network spans the bay from Spruce Cape to Cape Chiniak with ample locations for launching of small skiffs, rafts or kayaks.

Highlights: Good fishing for king salmon (in May and from August through September), silver salmon (from late August through early September), pink salmon (in the first half of August) and halibut (from June through August).

Species: (Chum salmon), Dolly Varden, halibut, king salmon, pink salmon, (red salmon), silver salmon, (steelhead).

Regulations: Halibut fishing is closed from January 1 through 31. For additional restrictions, consult the current Alaska Department of Fish and Game sportfishing regulations or the ADF&G Kodiak office, (907) 486-4791.

Facilities: Hotels, gas, lodging, boat rentals, boat launches, guide services, sporting goods and groceries are available in Kodiak.

Contact: For guide services, contact the Kodiak Island Charters, P.O. Box 3750, Kodiak, AK 99615; (907) 486-5380. For lodging information, contact Westmark Kodiak, 236 Rezanof Drive West, Kodiak, AK 99615, (907) 486-5712; or Shelikof Lodge, 211 Thorsheim, Kodiak, AK 99615, (907) 486-5657.

Description: Chiniak Bay, near the town of Kodiak and the island's only highway system, is the most popular recreational marine fishery on Kodiak Island. It has numerous islands and lesser bays containing important salmon- and charr-producing streams. Lush, green mountain slopes drop dramatically into the bay's clear blue waters, making for an idyllic Alaska setting.

Despite its easy access and high use, Chiniak Bay manages to hold its own, producing good catches of salmon, charr and bottomfish. Large runs of acrobatic silvers invade the bay every fall, and halibut lurk on reefs and shoals in the deeper waters. Both natural and enhanced populations of king salmon are present, along with sea-run Dolly Varden charr. Fishing from a boat is the best way to enjoy the action, but angling from shore near the mouths of spawning streams can also be productive for salmon and charr. The bay has long been a year-round feeding ground for king salmon, but it was not until quite recently that a fishery developed to catch these dime-bright brutes in the prime of their life. Although not particularly large, about 12 to 20 pounds on average, they are plentiful in the middle and outer parts of Chiniak. Cape Chiniak and Buoy Four are two of the more popular locations. An early summer return of hatchery kings to Mill Bay, just north of Chiniak Bay, provides good action. Pink salmon flood the area in late summer, with the best fishing occurring in bays near the mouths of rivers and creeks. (A few weeks later, schools of silvers flood the same areas.) Halibut are abundant during the summer months and can be best taken from outer bay areas that have the proper depth and structure.

Hot spot locations around Chiniak Bay include Monashka Bay (pink salmon, Dolly Varden), Mill Bay (king salmon, silver salmon), Womens Bay (silver salmon, pink salmon, Dolly Varden), Middle Bay (silver salmon, pink salmon, Dolly Varden), Kalsin Bay (silver salmon, pink salmon, Dolly Varden), Isthmus Bay (pink salmon, Dolly Varden), Long and Woody islands (king salmon, halibut), Pinnacle Rock (king salmon, halibut), Cape Chiniak (king salmon, halibut), Williams Reef (halibut) and Buoy Four (king salmon, halibut).

35. UGAK BAY

Location: Northeast Kodiak Island, 25 miles south of Kodiak, 280 miles southwest of Anchorage.

Reference: Kodiak B-1, B-2, B-3, B-4, C-3.

Access: By plane or car from Kodiak. Float and wheelplanes can land in coves and on beaches around the bay. Two road-accessible locations are Saltery Cove via Saltery Cove Road and Pasagshak Bay via Pasagshak Bay Road through Rezanof Drive West. The road to Saltery Cove is very rough and recommended for four-wheel-drive vehicles only, but the road to Pasagshak is open to all traffic.

Highlights: Good, easily accessible Kodiak fishing for king salmon (from July through August), silver salmon (from late August through early September), pink salmon (from late July through early August), Dolly Varden charr (from May through June) and halibut (from June through August).

Species: Chum salmon, Dolly Varden, halibut, king salmon, pink salmon, (red salmon), silver salmon, (steelhead).

Regulations: Halibut fishing is closed from January 1 through 31. For additional restrictions, consult the current Alaska Department of

Fish and Game sportfishing regulations or the ADF&G Kodiak office, (907) 486-4791.

Facilities: Commercial lodging, a campground and guide services are available.

Contact: For lodging and guide services, contact the Saltery Lake Lodge, 1516 Larch Street, Suite One, Kodiak, AK 99615, (907) 486-5037; or R&R Lodge, P.O. Box 1272, Kodiak, AK 99615, (907) 486-3704. For general information, contact the Kodiak National Wildlife Refuge, 1390 Buskin River Road, Kodiak, AK 99615; (907) 487-2600. For an air taxi, contact Uyak Air Service, P.O. Box 4188, Kodiak, AK 99615, (907) 486-3407; or Sea Hawk Air, P.O. Box 3561, Kodiak, AK 99615, (800) 770-HAWK or (907) 486-8282.

Description: Ugak Bay is a pristine outlet to the Gulf of Alaska, its shores contained within the Kodiak National Wildlife Refuge. A fairly deep, clear bay with a diverse bottom structure accommodating a variety of fish species, Ugak is a popular angling and recreation destination for locals and visitors alike, easily accessible by road or air. The outer bay is surrounded by forested mountains and hills, while the inner bay has deep-cutting valleys and some snow-covered peaks, making for a beautiful setting.

A handful of clearwater streams empty into Ugak, most of them with significant runs of salmon and charr that provide good fishing for boaters and surf-casters alike. Recreational craft like skiffs and kayaks can be launched from beaches or river mouths in Saltery Cove and Pasagshak Bay. (Be aware that strong east winds from the Gulf of Alaska can turn outer Ugak into a whirlpool of whitewater, although its more protected bays and coves are generally calmer and on good weather days are a pleasure to fish.) Large schools of silver and pink salmon traveling close to shore can be seen and targeted, and halibut tend to be on the aggressive side. There is also a developing feeder king salmon fishery in the outer bay. Dolly Varden action is best during late spring and again in late summer, when these sea-run charr forage the points, beaches and stream mouths in search of prey or spawning salmon.

Suggested areas for boaters include Saltery Cove, Portage Bay, Pasagshak Bay and Eagle Harbor for salmon and charr, and the reefs and shoals of their moderately deep waters for bottomfish. Surf-casters do well at the mouths of the Saltery and Pasagshak rivers and the mouths of streams draining into Portage Cove and Eagle Harbor.

36. UYAK BAY

Location: West Kodiak Island, 60 miles west of Kodiak, 285 miles southwest of Anchorage.

Reference: Kodiak B-5, B-6, C-6; Karluk C-1.

Access: By plane from Kodiak or area lodges. Traditional points of access have been Larsen Bay and Amook Bay in the central portion of Uyak Bay. Some lodge operators provide skiffs to fish the better locations around the bay.

Highlights: Excellent fishing for silver salmon (in the second half of August), pink salmon (from late July through early August) and halibut (from June through August); good fishing for king salmon (from July through August) and Dolly Varden (from May through June).

Species: (Chum salmon), Dolly Varden, halibut, king salmon, pink salmon, (red salmon), silver salmon.

Regulations: Halibut fishing is closed from January 1 through 31. For additional restrictions, consult the current Alaska Department of Fish and Game sportfishing regulations or the ADF&G Kodiak office, (907) 486-4791.

Facilities: Commercial lodging, a cabin and guide services are available.

Contact: For lodging and guide services, contact Zachar Bay Lodge, P.O. Box 2609, Kodiak, AK 99615, (907) 486-4120; The Cannery at Zachar Bay, P.O. Box 2609, Kodiak, AK 99615, (907) 486-4120; Zachar Bay Camp, P.O. Box 3911, Kodiak, AK 99615, (907) 486-3008; or Amook Lodge, P.O. Box 111, Larsen Bay, AK 96624, (907) 847-2312. For general information, contact the Kodiak National Wildlife Refuge, 1390 Buskin River Road, Kodiak, AK 99615; (907) 487-2600. For an air taxi, contact Uyak Air Service, P.O. Box 4188, Kodiak, AK 99615, (907) 486-3407; or Sea Hawk Air, P.O. Box 3561, Kodiak, AK 99615, (800) 770-HAWK or (907) 486-8282.

Description: On the west side of Kodiak Island by Shelikof Strait lies Uyak Bay, a long, clear fjord penetrating deeply into the heart of the island. Surrounded by the steep mountain slopes and evergreen forests of the Kodiak National Wildlife Refuge, Uyak is home to abundant marine life—such as fish, waterfowl, seals and whales—and a healthy brown bear population that stalk its beaches and streams in search of food. Some of Kodiak's largest river systems are found in the area, assuring anglers of excellent salmon fishing. Part of Uyak Bay, Larsen Bay has traditionally served as an access point to the ever-popular Karluk River drainage.

The greater bay area between Rocky Point and Cape Kuliuk encompasses 34 streams and rivers, some of which are small and crystal clear, while others are vast, glacial and turbid. Almost without exception, these systems all support fish runs to varying degrees. The best way to explore these numerous prospects is by boat. Surfcasting can be quite productive around the better stream locations, but a boat allows easy access and enables one to probe the deeper water for bottomfish. Salmon, especially silvers and pinks, are abundant throughout much of Uyak, with good numbers of feeder king salmon and Dolly Varden charr also present. Look for halibut and king salmon around reefs, shoals, points, and islands in the outer bay, in moderately deep water. For charr and pinks, target areas around the mouths of clearwater streams. Silver salmon, depending on the time, will be best encountered in deeper, outer waters or in the smaller bays near stream mouths. Spiridon Bay and Zachar Bay receive heavy runs and anglers do very well in and around these areas. For anglers wanting abundant, varied saltwater fishing in an area yet to be fully discovered by the public, Uyak Bay is it.

37. PORTAGE CREEK

Location: North Afognak Island drainage, Perenosa Bay area, 30 miles north of Kodiak, 215 miles southwest of Anchorage.

Reference: Afognak B-2.

Access: By floatplane to the head of Discoverer Bay, a small inlet on the southern end of Perenosa Bay. From there, hike along beach to the mouth and lower sections of stream. Another access option is from Portage Lake, fishing the outlet and hiking downstream.

Highlights: Excellent fishing for silver salmon (from mid-August through early September) and red salmon (second half of June); good fishing for pink salmon (from late July through early August) and Dolly Varden (from June through August).

Species: Dolly Varden, pink salmon, red salmon, silver salmon, steelhead.

Regulations: Spring closure on rainbow and steelhead trout from April 1 through June 14. For additional restrictions, consult the current Alaska Department of Fish and Game sportfishing regulations or the ADF&G Kodiak office, (907) 486-4791.

Facilities: No developed public facilities.

Contact: For an air taxi, contact Uyak Air Service, P.O. Box 4188, Kodiak, AK 99615, (907) 486-3407; or Sea Hawk Air, P.O. Box 3561, Kodiak, AK 99615, (800) 770-HAWK or (907) 486-8282.

Description: Portage Creek is a small, shallow clearwater stream that flows from Portage Lake on northern Afognak Island to Discoverer Bay, two miles away. Since the drainage is quite small, salmon and charr populations are not very large. However, stream conditions are perfect for concentrating fish in shallow runs and pools, while the clear waters make for easy sight-fishing. Flyfishing for silver and red salmon in this creek can be as good as it gets.

The best locations on Portage Creek to fish are the mouth on Discoverer Bay and the lake outlet, where schools of fish tend to herd up. Fish the incoming tides for best results on the lower river, especially for silvers and Dolly Varden. The sockeyes seem more prone to hit once they are concentrated within the confines of the creek. (Sparse flies like a chartreuse Comet or Brassie work well on them.) The creek also has a small fall run of steelhead that begin showing up in September. Check with the Alaska Department of Fish and Game for the latest run conditions before heading down. As this area has quite a few brown bears patrolling during the height of the runs, caution is advised for anglers.

38. PAULS CREEK SYSTEM

Location: North Afognak Island drainage, Perenosa Bay area, 40 miles north of Kodiak, 210 miles southwest of Anchorage.

Reference: Afognak B-1, B-2.

Access: By floatplane to the head of Pauls Bay, a small inlet located on the east side of Perenosa Bay on Afognak Island. Hike from the landing site along the beach to the stream mouth and lower sections. Outlets of Pauls and Laura lakes provide viable access to more remote parts of the system.

Highlights: Some of Afognak's most outstanding stream fishing for silver salmon (from mid-August through early September); also excellent red salmon fishing (in the second half of June) and good pink salmon fishing (from late July through early August).

Species: Dolly Varden, pink salmon, red salmon, silver salmon, steelhead.

Regulations: Spring closure on rainbow and steelhead trout from April 1 through June 14. For additional restrictions, consult the current Alaska Department of Fish and Game sportfishing regulations or the ADF&G Kodiak office, (907) 486-4791.

Facilities: No developed public facilities.

Contact: For an air taxi, contact Uyak Air Service, P.O. Box 4188, Kodiak, AK 99615, (907) 486-3407; or Sea Hawk Air, P.O. Box 3561, Kodiak, AK 99615, (800) 770-HAWK or (907) 486-8282.

Description: Like Portage Creek to the south, Pauls Creek is a rather small, shallow, clear stream. Part of a system of several lakes (including Pauls, Laura and Gretchen), Pauls Creek begins at Gretchen Lake outlet and runs several miles northwest to Laura Lake, then continues about a mile to Pauls Lake. From there, it empties into Pauls Bay, a short distance away.

The Pauls Creek system supports only moderate populations of salmon and charr, so it does not receive much angling effort. Fishing, however, can be excellent at the mouth and surrounding bay area, or in the lake inlets and outlets, during the height of the runs when fish school up and move into the system on incoming tides. Silver salmon fishing is particularly noteworthy in the lower river and outlet of Laura Lake, while reds are best fished in the shallow runs of the creek below Pauls Lake. You'll find hordes of fat sea-run Dollies in the upper parts of the system late in the season. Since the creek system also has a little-fished fall run of steelhead, it's hard to beat overall for varied, small streamfishing in a remote setting.

39. AFOGNAK (LITNIK) RIVER/LAGOON

Location: Southwest Afognak Island drainage, 25 miles northwest of Kodiak, 235 miles southwest of Anchorage.

Reference: Afognak A-3.

Access: By boat or floatplane from Anton Larsen Bay or Kodiak Island to the river mouth. The Afognak Lake outlet is also a popular gateway to the drainage via floatplanes. The main stretch of the river is accessible by four-wheeler road running between the river mouth at the head of Afognak Bay and the Afognak Lake outlet.

Highlights: One of Kodiak-Afognak's best fishing locations. Excellent fishing for silver salmon (from mid-August through early September), red salmon (in mid-June and the second half of July) and pink salmon (from late July through early August).

Species: Dolly Varden, pink salmon, rainbow trout, red salmon, silver salmon, steelhead.

Regulations: Spring closure on rainbow and steelhead trout from April 1 through June 14. For additional restrictions, consult the current Alaska Department of Fish and Game sportfishing regulations or the ADF&G Kodiak office, (907) 486-4791.

Facilities: Commercial lodging and guide services are available.

Contact: For lodging and guide services, contact the Afognak Wilderness Lodge, Seal Bay, AK 99697, (907) 486-6442; or Afognak

Adventures, P.O. Box 1277, Kodiak, AK 99615, (907) 486-6014 or
(800) 770-6014. For an air taxi, contact Uyak Air Service, P.O. Box
4188, Kodiak, AK 99615, (907) 486-3407; or Sea Hawk Air, P.O.
Box 3561, Kodiak, AK 99615, (800) 770-HAWK or (907) 486-8282.

Description: The Afognak or Litnik River is located on the south end
of Afognak Island at Marmot Bay, approximately 25 air miles northwest of the town of Kodiak. Draining the largest body of water on
the island—long and narrow Afognak Lake—the river runs east a
few miles and forms a long lagoon at Afognak Bay. The superb fishing in the crystal-clear waters of the river and lagoon combines with
the magnificent setting and relatively easy access to make this location one of the most fished on the island.

The Afognak is wide and deep, with good pools and runs, making
it excellent for flyfishing. Most of the angling for silver salmon,
however, occurs in the lagoon where coho tend to school up, especially during periods of low water. Access upstream is simplified by
a small road that parallels the river from the mouth to the lake outlet.
The best bet would be to work the lagoon and lower river with the
tide, then move on upstream. The Afognak receives two separate
runs of red salmon, the first during the month of June and the second
in July. Fishing for them is best where they are most concentrated.
The lake outlet is a popular area to try (for silvers as well). The
Afognak also has abundant Dolly Varden charr (best fished in spring
and late summer), some small rainbow trout and even a small fall
run of steelhead that enter the river from September through November. As this is also world-class brown bear country, extreme
caution is advised.

40. MALINA CREEK SYSTEM

Location: Southwest Afognak Island drainage, 35 miles northwest of
Kodiak, 235 miles southwest of Anchorage.

Reference: Afognak A-4.

Access: By floatplane to the stream mouth at Shelikof Strait or outlets
of Upper and Lower Malina lakes. Hike from landing areas to access
all stream sections. Boating to the area is not recommended since
the waters of Shelikof Strait can be turbulent and unpredictable.

Highlights: Excellent fishing for silver salmon (from mid-August
through early September), red salmon (in the second half of June)
and Dolly Varden charr (from June through August); good fishing
for pink salmon (from late July through early August) and some

steelhead trout (from October through November).

Species: Dolly Varden, pink salmon, red salmon, silver salmon, steelhead.

Regulations: Spring closure on rainbow and steelhead trout from April 1 through June 14. For additional restrictions, consult the current Alaska Department of Fish and Game sportfishing regulations or the ADF&G Kodiak office, (907) 486-4791.

Facilities: A small, abandoned cabin on Upper Malina Lake is used by various air taxi operators.

Contact: For an air taxi, contact Uyak Air Service, P.O. Box 4188, Kodiak, AK 99615, (907) 486-3407; or Sea Hawk Air, P.O. Box 3561, Kodiak, AK 99615, (800) 770-HAWK or (907) 486-8282.

Description: Malina Creek and its associated lakes form another productive Afognak system. It drains the hills just west of Afognak Lake and flows west to Shelikof Strait on the southwest side of the island. A small clearwater system, the Malina gets only moderate runs of salmon, trout and charr, but fish tend to concentrate in a few choice locations, making for some abundant angling opportunities in season. At present, fishing pressure is light.

Anglers arrive by floatplane to Lower Malina Lake and hike along the creek, scouting for schools of fish. During incoming tides, the mouth is one of the best places to fish, as is the outlet and inlet of Lower Malina during the peak of the runs. Charr are abundant during summer and most often caught while fishing for other species. Some steelhead trout run the lower creek in late fall, but tend to receive very little attention. The surrounding scenery is outstanding and wildlife is abundant. Brown bears are commonly spotted by the lakes, and the area is also used by elk hunters in fall.

41. UGANIK RIVER SYSTEM

Location: Northwest Kodiak Island drainage, 35 miles west of Kodiak, 270 miles southwest of Anchorage.

Reference: Kodiak C-4, C-5.

Access: By floatplane from Kodiak. Drop-off at the outlet of Uganik Lake, raft to mouth of river, and pick-up in tidal area at the head of the east arm of the Uganik Bay.

Highlights: One of Kodiak's best fishing locations; excellent for silver salmon (from late August through mid-September), red salmon (from late June through early July), pink salmon (from late July through early August) and Dolly Varden charr (year-round).

Species: Chum salmon, Dolly Varden, pink salmon, rainbow trout, red salmon, silver salmon.

Regulations: Spring closure on rainbow and steelhead trout fishing from April 1 through June 14. For additional restrictions, consult the current Alaska Department of Fish and Game sportfishing regulations or the ADF&G Kodiak office, (907) 486-4791.

Facilities: A forest service cabin is available on Uganik Lake.

Contact: For an air taxi, contact Uyak Air Service, P.O. Box 4188, Kodiak, AK 99615, (907) 486-3407; Sea Hawk Air, P.O. Box 3561, Kodiak, AK 99615, (800) 770-HAWK or (907) 486-8282; or Wilderness Air, P.O. Box 768, Kodiak, AK 99615, (907) 486-8101. For general and cabin rental information, contact the Kodiak National Wildlife Refuge, 1390 Buskin River Road, Kodiak, AK 99615; (907) 487-2600.

Description: The Uganik River is situated on the northwest side of Kodiak Island. Gathering water from some of the highest peaks on the central part of the island, its several arms empty into Uganik Lake, from which the river then flows northwest to the east arm of Uganik Bay. The fishing is superb—some of Kodiak's finest—with abundant, huge silver salmon and incredible numbers of Dolly Varden. Some of the largest silvers on Kodiak originate here, with fish regularly caught in the middle and upper teens. There is even potential for cohos over 20 pounds.

The majority of anglers who fish the Uganik system target the lower river between Uganik Lake and Uganik Bay, generally with a raft. It is about a two-hour straight float, but can be extended easily to two days, allowing time to work all the productive stretches of the river. The upper river above Uganik Lake, with its tributaries, is also productive water, but it is more difficult to access. Aside from floating the river, some anglers choose to fish only the lake outlet or the mouth of the river.

The Uganik supports one of the healthiest populations of Dolly Varden charr on Kodiak, along with healthy runs of red and pink salmon. (Fishing for pinks is better on the lower Uganik, while reds and charr can be taken throughout the system.) Some fair rainbow trout fishing is also available in the lake and upper river.

42. LITTLE RIVER LAKES

Location: Northwest Kodiak Island drainage, 50 miles west of Kodiak, 270 miles southwest of Anchorage.

Reference: Kodiak D-5, D-6.

Access: By floatplane from Kodiak or area lodges. Little River Lake is the usual gateway to the drainage.

Highlights: Good fishing for silver salmon (throughout September) and red salmon (throughout June); also steelhead trout (from October through November), and Dolly Varden (from May through October).

Species: Dolly Varden, red salmon, silver salmon, steelhead,

Regulations: Spring closure on rainbow and steelhead trout from April 1 through June 14. For additional restrictions, consult the current Alaska Department of Fish and Game sportfishing regulations or the ADF&G Kodiak office, (907) 486-4791.

Facilities: A forest service cabin is available nearby.

Contact: For an air taxi, contact Uyak Air Service, P.O. Box 4188, Kodiak, AK 99615, (907) 486-3407; or Cub Air, P.O. Box 1616, Kodiak, AK 99615, (907) 486-5851. For general and cabin rental information, contact the Kodiak National Wildlife Refuge, 1390 Buskin River Road, Kodiak, AK 99615; (907) 487-2600.

Description: The Little River Lakes (actually just one large lake with a small extension) are located on a peninsula on the northwest side of Kodiak Island, between Spiridon and Uganik bays. Little River, the outlet stream, is fairly small, clear and fast, with several tributary creeks and forks. Access can be a problem, due to the steep and difficult terrain in parts. For starters, try the lake outlet and the first few miles of river below the lake. Look for schools of silver and red salmon (in season) stacked in the deeper holes and runs. Dolly Varden are abundant on the upper river and the outlet early and late in the season, while steelhead trout can be found during the fall months. Watch for brown bears.

43. BUSKIN RIVER

Location: Northeast Kodiak Island drainage, five miles southwest of Kodiak, 250 miles southwest of Anchorage.

Reference: Kodiak D-2.

Access: By car, there are several access points from the town of Kodiak.

Highlights: One of Kodiak's best road-accessible fisheries. Excellent fishing for pink salmon (from late July through early August) and Dolly Varden charr (in May and from July through October); good fishing for silver salmon (in the second half of September) and red salmon (from late June through mid-July).

Species: Chum salmon, Dolly Varden, king salmon, pink salmon, (rainbow trout), red salmon, silver salmon, (steelhead).

Regulations: King salmon fishing is prohibited, except by emergency order; steelhead trout fishing is also prohibited. Portions of the river (below the first bridge) are closed to salmon from August 1 through September 11. For additional restrictions, consult the current Alaska Department of Fish and Game sportfishing regulations or the ADF&G Kodiak office, (907) 486-4791.

Facilities: Commercial lodging, gas and a campground are available.

Contact: For fishing information, contact the Alaska Department of Fish and Game, Kodiak Office, 211 Mission Road, Kodiak, AK 99615; (907) 486-1880. For lodging and camping information, contact the Buskin River Inn, 1395 Airport Road, Kodiak, AK 99615, (907) 487-2700; or Alaska State Parks, Kodiak District, S.S.R. Box 3800, Kodiak, AK 99615, (907) 486-6339.

Description: The clear-flowing Buskin, located on Chiniak Bay just southwest of the town of Kodiak, is the most popular fishery on the island (supporting nearly half of Kodiak's total sportfishing effort), with easy access and abundant salmon and Dolly Varden charr.

The Buskin system drains a fairly small valley between Pyramid and Erskine mountains and contains a small lake of the same name, located a few miles above Chiniak Bay. The medium-sized river is gravel-bottomed and brushy, with plenty of holding water and good sight-fishing possibilities. Since the Buskin is located along the road system so close to town, it receives its fair share of angling pressure from locals, as well as from outside anglers with limited time or funds to enjoy the Kodiak area.

The Buskin is perhaps best known for its amazing Dolly Varden fishing. Scads of outmigrating fish are typically caught right after break-up (in April and May) on small silver spinners and spoons, while fattened, prime fish enter the river from midsummer through fall and are taken mostly on bright flies and spinners. Some very nice runs of red salmon enter the Buskin in June and July, creating one of Kodiak's most significant, easily accessed sockeye fisheries. Next to the sea-run Dollies, however, silvers are the most sought-after fish, entering the Buskin in mid-August and continuing into September. Because of regulations, the early part of this fishery is restricted to the mouth and lagoon, while later on (in mid-September) it opens up to include the entire river.

In some years, small numbers of king salmon move into the Buskin. These are not native fish, but hatchery kings from Mill Bay (on the northeast side of Kodiak) that have strayed from the release site and seek suitable rearing habitat. Most of these occasional kings are taken near the river mouth on incoming tides.

44. AMERICAN RIVER

Location: Northeast Kodiak Island drainage, 12 miles southwest of Kodiak, 260 miles southwest of Anchorage.

Reference: Kodiak C-2.

Access: By car via Rezanof Drive West, from the town of Kodiak. The road crosses the lower stream with trails leading upstream to productive holes or downstream to the mouth. Just south of the stream crossing, the rough Saltery Cove Road begins and follows the middle and upper river more or less for several miles, crossing in two places.

Highlights: Excellent fishing for silver salmon (in the second half of September), pink salmon (from late July through early August) and Dolly Varden charr (from September through October); good fishing for chum salmon (from late July through early August).

Species: Chum salmon, Dolly Varden, pink salmon, silver salmon.

Regulations: King salmon fishing is prohibited; closed to salmon fishing upstream of the road crossing from August 1 through September 10. For additional restrictions, consult the current Alaska Department of Fish and Game sportfishing regulations or the ADF&G Kodiak office, (907) 486-4791.

Facilities: Commercial lodging, gas and a campground are available.

Contact: For fishing information, contact the Alaska Department of Fish and Game, Kodiak Office, 211 Mission Road, Kodiak, AK 99615; (907) 486-1880. For lodging information, contact the Kalsin Inn Ranch, P.O. Box 1696, Kodiak, AK 99615; (907) 486-2659. For campground information, contact Alaska State Parks, Kodiak District, S.S.R. Box 3800, Kodiak, AK 99615; (907) 486-6339.

Description: The clear American River originates near Center Mountain and runs east through a forested valley to Middle Bay, a small inlet connected to Chiniak Bay. Moderately fast, with good streamfishing conditions, the American has several small tributary creeks and lakes and provides one of the most extensive and popular salmon/charr fisheries on the Kodiak road system.

From midsummer through late fall, the American hosts large runs of silver, chum and pink salmon. The abundance of the smallish humpbacked salmon can be staggering, so much that anglers wishing to target the flashy silvers sometimes delay their fishing until late in the season, when the pinks thin out. The American is also a major spawning ground for sea-run Dollies, which become quite abundant there in the fall. Although the fish are not very large, typically about 10 to 15 inches, their concentrations make for top-notch action. The American is definitely worth checking out if you're fishing the Kodiak road system in late summer or fall.

45. OLDS RIVER SYSTEM

Location: Northeast Kodiak Island drainage, 14 miles south of Kodiak, 265 miles southwest of Anchorage.

Reference: Kodiak C-2.

Access: By car via Rezanof Drive West, from the town of Kodiak. The road crosses the lower river and two tributaries with limited trail access to the river mouth and upstream areas.

Highlights: Excellent fishing for silver salmon (in the second half of September), pink salmon (from late July through early August) and Dolly Varden (from September through October).

Species: Chum salmon, Dolly Varden, pink salmon, (red salmon), silver salmon.

Regulations: King salmon fishing is prohibited; closed to salmon fishing upstream of the road crossing from August 1 through September 11. For additional restrictions, consult the current Alaska Department of Fish and Game sportfishing regulations or the ADF&G Kodiak office, (907) 486-4791.

Facilities: Commercial lodging, gas and a campground are available.

Contact: For fishing information, contact the Alaska Department of Fish and Game, Kodiak Office, 211 Mission Road, Kodiak, AK 99615; (907) 486-1880. For lodging information, contact the Kalsin Inn Ranch, P.O. Box 1696, Kodiak, AK 99615; (907) 486-2659. For campground information, contact the Alaska State Parks, Kodiak District, S.S.R. Box 3800, Kodiak, AK 99615; (907) 486-6339.

Description: Olds River is a road-accessible, clearwater stream draining into Kalsin Bay, on the south side of Chiniak, approximately 25 air miles south and slightly west of Kodiak. Its headwaters originate near Marin Range and there are a few small lakes connected to the system. Like other productive road streams of Chiniak Bay, the Olds receives moderate pressure from local and visiting anglers, but holds up well with especially good fishing for pink and silver salmon, as well as Dolly Varden charr.

Winding through a narrow valley covered with dense forests, the upper and middle sections of the Olds are fairly fast-flowing, while the lower river is slower and wider, especially in its last mile, where a major tributary, Kalsin Creek, joins in from the south. Most people fish salmon in the mouth and lower river, working the incoming tides for bright fish. During low water, conditions are good for sight-fishing.

In addition to great silver and pink salmon runs, the Olds gets a healthy run of spawning Dolly Varden in autumn. These colorful charr brighten up the fishing along the entire river. Like the American, the Olds makes a popular one-day destination for anyone sampling the fishing along the Kodiak road system, with adjacent Kalsin Bay holding some of the more popular and productive salmon and halibut waters in Chiniak Bay.

---

46. PASAGSHAK RIVER SYSTEM

Location: Northeast Kodiak Island drainage, 25 miles south of Kodiak, 275 miles southwest of Anchorage.

Reference: Kodiak B-1.

Access: By car via Rezanof Drive West and Pasagshak Bay Road, from the town of Kodiak. Pasagshak Bay Road briefly parallels a small tributary creek en route to Lake Rose Tead and Pasagshak State Recreation Site near the river's mouth. There are several trails along the river for additional access.

Highlights: Kodiak's best road-accessible coho fishing (in September). Also excellent fishing for pink salmon (from late July through early August); good fishing for red salmon (from late June through early July) and Dolly Varden charr (in May and from July through October).

Species: (Chum salmon), Dolly Varden, (king salmon), pink salmon, red salmon, silver salmon.

Regulations: King salmon fishing is prohibited. For additional restrictions, consult the current Alaska Department of Fish and Game sportfishing regulations or the ADF&G Kodiak office, (907) 486-4791.

Facilities: A campground is available at Pasagshak State Recreation Site.

Contact: For fishing information, contact the Alaska Department of Fish and Game, Kodiak Office, 211 Mission Road, Kodiak, AK 99615; (907) 486-1880. For lodging information, contact the Northland Ranch Resort, P.O. Box 2376, Kodiak, AK 99615; (907) 486-5578. For campground information, contact Alaska State Parks, Kodiak District, S.S.R. Box 3800, Kodiak, AK 99615; (907) 486-6339.

Description: The Pasagshak is one of the most famous and visited

---

streams on the Kodiak road system. With clear, wide waters that are easy to fish, it's one of the most productive systems of its size on the island, with abundant salmon and Dolly Varden charr.

Originating from the south slopes of Marin Range, the headwaters drain into Lake Rose Tead. From there, the river flows only two miles to Ugak Bay. The beach area around the mouth is the hot spot on the Pasagshak, and, as is common on most coastal streams, incoming tides usually bring the best fishing for snappy, bright schools of salmon and charr. Of particular note is the river's trophy silver salmon fishery. Thousands of above-average-sized coho invade the Pasagshak every fall, with ample opportunities for fish weighing in the mid-teens and occasional specimens to 18 and 20 pounds or more. Many diehard anglers still use salmon roe clusters with predictable results, but flies and hardware take a good share of these big Pasagshak silvers.

A strong red salmon run usually occurs in early to midsummer; they're best taken in the shallow, faster sections of the river. Abundant pink salmon usually follow the reds, but they can be caught anywhere, although the mouth is probably the most popular area. Dolly Varden are another Pasagshak highlight. The prime times are during the spring outmigration from Lake Rose Tead right after break-up and again in late summer and fall as the fish return fat, bright and full of fight from the salt of Pasagshak and Ugak bays.

47. SALTERY RIVER

Location: Northeast Kodiak Island drainage, 25 miles south of Kodiak, 275 miles southwest of Anchorage.

Reference: Kodiak C-3.

Access: By car via Rezanof Drive West and Saltery Cove Road, from the town of Kodiak; also by plane from Kodiak, landing at Saltery Cove. Saltery Cove Road is very rough—a four-wheel-drive vehicle is recommended.

Highlights: Excellent fishing for silver salmon (in the second half of September), red salmon (in the first half of July), pink salmon (from late July through early August) and Dolly Varden charr (in May and from July through October).

Species: (Chum salmon), Dolly Varden, pink salmon, rainbow trout, red salmon, silver salmon, (steelhead).

Regulations: Spring closures for rainbow and steelhead trout from April 1 through June 14. For additional restrictions, consult the current Alaska Department of Fish and Game sportfishing regulations or the ADF&G Kodiak office, (907) 486-4791.

Facilities: Commercial lodging is available.

Contact: For lodging and guide services, contact the Saltery Lake Lodge. 1516 Larch Street, Suite One, Kodiak, AK 99615; (907) 486-5037 or (800) 770-5037. For an air taxi, contact Uyak Air Service, P.O. Box 4188, Kodiak, AK 99615, (907) 486-3407; or Sea Hawk Air, P.O. Box 3561, Kodiak, AK 99615, (907) 486-8282.

Description: The Saltery River begins on the south slopes of Center Mountain and flows into Ugak Bay, 25 miles southwest of Kodiak. Accessed via the rough Saltery Cove Road, it is one of the more outstanding Kodiak road streams, noted for superb silver and red salmon fishing and abundant Dolly Varden charr.

The river above Saltery Lake runs swift and straight, but down below it slows considerably and meanders through a flat valley before reaching Saltery Cove. It is beautiful, crystal-clear water, with many deep holes, riffles and runs, and a bottom of fine gravel. Wildlife is abundant in the area and the scenery pleasing. It is fairly remote, even though it lies along the road system, and is highly recommended for first-time Kodiak anglers.

The majority of anglers fish the river's noteworthy silver and red salmon runs. The reds are the first to arrive in early July and spice up the action for flyfishers until August. Next come the silvers. They are hefty fish, many weighing into the teens, which can be caught from tidewater all the way up to the lake outlet. Along with the Buskin and Pasagshak, the Saltery also provides some of the best spring Dolly Varden action along the Kodiak road system, as thousands of fish move out of Saltery Lake on their way to the ocean. This fishery turns on again later in the season (from late summer through fall), as fat Dollies return to the river to feed on salmon eggs and prepare for spawning and overwintering. The upper river, just above the lake, is a major salmon spawning area and one of the best places to find thick schools of voracious charr. Fair to good Dolly fishing can also be enjoyed all summer long in the cove, using narrow silver spoons, herring strips or small diving plugs.

48. KARLUK RIVER SYSTEM

Location: West Kodiak Island drainage, 75 miles southwest of Kodiak, 290 miles southwest of Anchorage.

Reference: Karluk B-1, C-1, C-2; Kodiak B-6.

Access: By floatplane, with three options for fishing access. One is to
fly to the mouth of the river at Karluk Lagoon (a run upstream with
a jet boat is possible). Another is to land in Larsen Bay and make a
two-mile portage to the midsection of the river (aptly named "Portage") and then raft to the mouth. The last possibility is to fly to the
Karluk Lake outlet and float downstream to the Karluk Lagoon or
Portage.

Highlights: Kodiak's ultimate fishing. Excellent for king salmon (from
mid-June through early July), silver salmon (in the second half of
September), red salmon (in mid-June and the second half of July),
pink salmon (from late July through early August), steelhead trout
(from late September through November) and Dolly Varden charr
(from May through November).

Species: (Chum salmon), Dolly Varden, king salmon, pink salmon, red
salmon, silver salmon, steelhead.

Regulations: Spring closures on rainbows and steelhead from April 1
through June 14. For additional restrictions, consult the current
Alaska Department of Fish and Game sportfishing regulations or the
ADF&G Kodiak office, (907) 486-4791.

Facilities: Commercial lodging, guide services and two public cabins
are available.

Contact: For lodging and guide service, contact the Karluk Lodge,
P.O. Box 3, Karluk, AK 99608; (907) 241-2229 or (907) 241-2205.
For an air taxi, contact Uyak Air Service, P.O. Box 4188, Kodiak,
AK 99615, (907) 486-3407; or Sea Hawk Air, P.O. Box 3561,
Kodiak, AK 99615, (907) 486-8282. For more information, contact
the Kodiak National Wildlife Refuge, 1390 Buskin River Road,
Kodiak, AK 99615; (907) 487-2600.

Description: The Karluk River is Kodiak's largest and most productive
drainage. Located about 75 miles southwest of the town of Kodiak,
the 22-mile river is the island's most popular fly-in location, world
famous for its amazing salmon and steelhead runs. It ranks among
the finest fishing streams in Alaska.

The Karluk's extensive mountain headwaters gather at Karluk
Lake, from which the main river flows north to Shelikof Strait. It is
clear, fairly good-sized, with moderate depth and flow—generally
rated Class I water for rafting and kayaking. The upper and middle
river sections run through marshlands and open country in the
Kodiak National Wildlife Refuge, while the lower river cuts a narrow canyon and eventually widens into Karluk Lagoon. Karluk Lake
is situated in a beautiful mountain setting, with nearly a dozen

clearwater tributaries draining deep-cut valleys.

The Karluk is one of the most productive fish systems of its size in all the world, with prolific runs of all five salmon species, particularly sockeye, pink and coho, in addition to Alaska's most significant runs of steelhead north of Yakutat. The Karluk sportfishing season starts in June with the return of the first kings and the beginning of the first of two heavy sockeye runs (the other run starts in July). By late July, pink salmon are well into the lower river, and shortly after, silvers and the first of the fall steelhead begin showing up.

The lagoon and lower river are the most popular areas to target bright salmon early in the season. Later, anglers will usually fly into the midriver, or "Portage," area or float down from the lake to intercept migrating fish. Steelhead fishing is done mostly in late September and October from midriver, where the fish tend to congregate, or the lagoon. The Karluk's abundant Dolly Varden charr provide mostly incidental fishing excitement throughout the season, but they can be targeted in spring, late summer and fall at the lagoon and in tributaries around the lake (like the Thumb River).

The most popular way to sample the action on the Karluk is by raft. The river lends itself perfectly for a leisurely trip of two to five days (depending on the put-in). Most of the river is wide and fairly shallow (one to four feet), with good holding areas noticeably scarce on some sections of the river (especially below Portage). Good campsites and firewood are even harder to find. All in all, however, the Karluk is rated extremely high for its stream conditions, abundant runs, and ease of fishing. It is definitely on the list of Alaska's top 10 fishing rivers.

Note: A land-use permit may be required to fish the Karluk. Check with Koniag Inc., 210 Kashevarof, Suite Six, Kodiak AK 99615, (907) 486-4147, for details.

49. AYAKULIK RIVER SYSTEM

Location: Southwest Kodiak Island drainage, 85 miles southwest of Kodiak, 315 miles southwest of Anchorage.

Reference: Karluk A-1, A-2, B-1, B-2.

Access: By floatplane from Kodiak. Points of entry are limited to the outlet of Red Lake, Red River and the Bear Creek vicinity. Take-outs are normally arranged at the mouth of the river. A few trails are present, particularly around the cabin on Red Lake.

Highlights: Kodiak's best king salmon fishing (in the first half of June). Excellent for silver salmon (throughout September), red salmon (in mid-June and mid-July), pink salmon (from mid-July through early August) and steelhead trout (from October through November); good fishing for Dolly Varden (from June through August).

Species: Chum salmon, Dolly Varden, king salmon, pink salmon, rainbow trout, red salmon, silver salmon, steelhead.

Regulations: Spring closures on rainbow and steelhead are from April 1 through June 14. For additional restrictions, consult the current Alaska Department of Fish and Game sportfishing regulations or the ADF&G Kodiak office, (907) 486-4791.

Facilities: A forest service cabin is located at the outlet of Red Lake. Guide services are available.

Contact: For guide services, contact Kodiak Adventures, P.O. Box 1403, Seward, AK 99664, (907) 373-2285; or Ayakulik Camp, P.O. Box 670071, Chugiak, AK 99567, (907) 696-2484. For an air taxi, contact Uyak Air Service, P.O. Box 4188, Kodiak, AK 99615, (907) 486-3407; or Sea Hawk Air, P.O. Box 3561, Kodiak, AK 99615, (907) 486-8282. For more information, contact the Kodiak National Wildlife Refuge, 1390 Buskin River Road, Kodiak, AK 99615; (907) 487-2600.

Description: The Ayakulik, or Red, River on the southwest corner of the island is generally conceded to have the second best fishing on Kodiak, which says quite a bit, considering the amazing field of rivers its rated among. Like its exalted neighbor, the Karluk, the Ayakulik is blessed with a proliferation of salmon—all five species—as well as abundant charr and steelhead. Considerably smaller than the Karluk, it has much better stream conditions, and it doesn't get anywhere near as much visitation.

The Ayakulik meanders through a shallow valley above Olga Bay, surrounded by rolling green hills, tiny lakes and marshlands. A series of small tributary streams draining the slopes of nearby mountains help shape the river's character, especially Red River, flowing out of Red Lake, which contributes significantly to the Ayakulik sportfishery.

Salmon fishing kicks off on the lower river (below the Red River confluence, near Bear Creek) in early June, starting with king salmon. It trails off in the fall with deep-bodied silvers and steelhead. In between, there is nonstop action for red and pink salmon. The Ayakulik is especially noted for its king salmon fishing, which in many ways outclasses that found on the Karluk (more fish, better flyfishing conditions and less people). The red run has two components, just like on the Karluk; one occurs in June, the other in July. Pink salmon, as most everywhere else on the island, swarm the lower part of Ayakulik in midsummer alongside less numerous chums. Dolly Varden are available most anytime to fill in the brief gaps between salmon runs. The Ayakulik fall steelhead run is about half the size of the Karluk's, but is more spread out along the river, That diffusion, plus the river's smaller size, makes for some outstanding fishing. A small population of rainbow trout lives in Red Lake.

Most folks fish the Ayakulik just below the Red River confluence, near Bear Creek, which is accessible by floatplane. The river makes an excellent float trip of three to five days duration, from the Red Lake or the Red River put-in.

50. AKALURA LAKE/CREEK

Location: South Kodiak Island drainage, 80 miles southwest of Kodiak, 315 miles southwest of Anchorage.

Reference: Karluk A-1.

Access: By floatplane from Kodiak or nearby lodges, landing at the outlet of Akalura Lake or near the creek mouth at Cannery Cove.

Highlights: Excellent fishing for silver salmon (throughout September) and pink salmon (in the second half of July); good fishing for Dolly Varden charr (from June through August).

Species: Dolly Varden, pink salmon, rainbow trout, red salmon, silver salmon.

Regulations: Spring closures for rainbow and steelhead trout from April 1 through June 14. For additional restrictions, consult the current Alaska Department of Fish and Game sportfishing regulations or the ADF&G Kodiak office, (907) 486-4791.

Facilities: No developed public facilities.

Contact: For an air taxi, contact Uyak Air Service, P.O. Box 4188, Kodiak, AK 99615, (907) 486-3407; or Sea Hawk Air, P.O. Box 3561, Kodiak, AK 99615, (907) 486-8282.

Description: Akalura Lake and its adjoining creek is one of the smaller, but productive drainages of Kodiak Island. Located on Olga Bay, just south of Red Lake, Akalura Lake is only 2.5 miles wide and shaped like a triangle. The brushy outlet stream is swift and clear, and empties into Cannery Cove two miles away.

Although not much in size, the Akalura drainage has some concentrated fishing. Silver salmon are thick around the creek mouth during incoming tides in the fall, as are pink salmon and Dolly Varden earlier in the season. A smaller run of red salmon also move into the area in early summer and provide some good flyfishing at the mouth and lake outlet. The lake has some native rainbow trout providing fair fishing in the spring and fall, but the real show at Akalura is the silver salmon fishing. It's a popular spot with the fly-in lodge crowd, who often stop to check the fishing on their way to the Karluk or Ayakulik.

51. DOG SALMON (FRASER) RIVER SYSTEM

Location: South Kodiak Island drainage, 80 miles southwest of Kodiak, 315 miles southwest of Anchorage.

Reference: Karluk A-1, B-1.

Access: By floatplane from Kodiak or any of the area lodges. Access is through the Frazer Lake outlet or the flats at the mouth of the river. Trails lead along upper stretches of Dog Salmon River from outlet. As this is private land, a permit is required to fish here.

Highlights: Kodiak's best chum salmon fishing (from July through early August). Also excellent fishing for red salmon (in the first half of July) and pink salmon (in the second half of July); good silver salmon fishing (in September).

Species: Chum salmon, Dolly Varden, king salmon, pink salmon, red salmon, silver salmon, steelhead.

Regulations: King salmon fishing is prohibited; spring closures for rainbow and steelhead trout are from April 1 through June 14. For additional restrictions, consult the current Alaska Department of Fish and Game sportfishing regulations or the ADF&G Kodiak office, (907) 486-4791.

Facilities: Forest service cabins are available in the Frazer Lake vicinity.

Contact: For an air taxi, contact Uyak Air Service, P.O. Box 4188, Kodiak, AK 99615, (907) 486-3407; or Sea Hawk Air, P.O. Box 3561, Kodiak, AK 99615, (907) 486-8282. For general and cabin rental information, contact the Kodiak National Wildlife Refuge, 1390 Buskin River Road, Kodiak, AK 99615; (907) 487-2600.

Description: Dog Salmon River, also known as Fraser River, drains the second largest lake on the island, Frazer, which is situated between Karluk and Red lakes in the southwest corner of Kodiak. Along with its fabulous neighbor rivers (the Karluk and Ayakulik), the Fraser is one of the island's most productive salmon systems, particularly for sockeye and chum.

The fast and rocky river flows about 11 miles from the lake to the east end of Olga Bay, with a set of falls about a mile below the outlet. On the lower reaches near the mouth, the river slows in an area known as Dog Salmon Flats and the main channel splits. A handful of tributaries, many of them with small lakes at their headwaters, drain into Frazer Lake and the Dog Salmon River. Wildlife, especially bears, is abundant.

True to its name, Dog Salmon River has Kodiak's prime chum salmon fishing. In July, incoming tides push huge numbers of the sea-bright calicos into the river mouth, creating exceptional angling opportunities. Red and pink salmon also return in great numbers to spawn in the drainage, along with a notable silver run. And like so many other productive island streams, the Dog Salmon has a super abundance of Dolly Varden charr—to the point of being a nuisance at times. There are also small numbers of king salmon and steelhead trout, but not enough to support a sportfishery. (Fishing for king salmon is prohibited.)

Many anglers fish the system through Frazer Lake, working the section of river above the falls for silvers and reds. Forest service cabins are available on the north end of the lake and on a small tributary lake west of the outlet.

Note: The land along the creek is private. If you decide to fish there, you'll need to contact Koniag Inc., 210 Kashevarof, Suite Six, Kodiak AK 99615, (907) 486-4147, for a use permit.

52. OLGA LAKE SYSTEM

Location: South Kodiak Island drainage, 90 miles southwest of Kodiak, 325 miles southwest of Anchorage.

Reference: Karluk A-1, A-2.

Access: By floatplane from Kodiak or area lodges. Points of access include the outlet of Upper and Lower Olga lakes as well as the mouth of Olga Creek on Olga Bay.

Highlights: Excellent fishing for silver salmon (in September), red salmon (from late June through early July and in early September) and pink salmon (in the second half of July); good fishing for Dolly Varden (from June through August).

Species: Dolly Varden, pink salmon, rainbow trout, red salmon, silver salmon, (steelhead).

Regulations: Spring closures for rainbow and steelhead trout are from

April 1 through June 14. For additional restrictions, consult the current Alaska Department of Fish and Game sportfishing regulations or the ADF&G Kodiak office, (907) 486-4791.

Facilities: Commercial lodging and a cabin are available.

Contact: For lodging information, contact the Olga Bay Lodge, 321 Maple Street, Kodiak, AK 99615; (907) 486-5373. For an air taxi, contact Uyak Air Service, P.O. Box 4188, Kodiak, AK 99615, (907) 486-3407; or Sea Hawk Air, P.O. Box 3561, Kodiak, AK 99615, (907) 486-8282. For general and cabin rental information, contact the Kodiak National Wildlife Refuge, 1390 Buskin River Road, Kodiak, AK 99615; (907) 487-2600.

Description: The Olga Lakes are located on lower Olga Bay, about 85 miles southwest of Kodiak. Also known as South Olga Lakes or Upper and Lower Olga Lakes, the two bodies of water are connected by a short, wide channel, with Olga Creek, a narrow and slow stream, as the primary outlet to saltwater. Though not a large system, Olga Lakes offers a variety of superb fishing experiences—lake, small stream and tidal water—in fabulous, salmon-rich Olga Bay.

At the mouth, huge schools of red salmon throng beginning in late June and continuing into July, followed by vast numbers of pinks, then silvers later in the fall. (There is another red run in September as well.)

Each tide brings in more fresh, bright salmon, creating opportunities for fishing that can equal the best anywhere on the island. Sea-run Dollies can be taken in the salt off the creek mouth all season and in the river from midsummer on. The outlet of Lower Olga Lake is another prime fishing location for salmon, Dolly Varden charr and even a few rainbows.

Note: Visiting anglers should be aware that area land is privately owned and a trespass permit is required to fish the stream and lakes. Contact Koniag Inc., 210 Kashevarof, Suite Six, Kodiak AK 99615, (907) 486-4147, for a use permit. A fee, which varies with length of stay, is required.

REGION 4
CHUGACH-
PRINCE WILLIAM SOUND

The Chugach subregion, for our purposes, includes the drainages and marine waters along the Gulf of Alaska from the Copper River Delta area to western Prince William Sound. A rich and unexploited coastal paradise, this area has tremendous potential, from some of the mainland's best halibut and silver salmon to cutthroat trout.

53. RESURRECTION BAY

Location: North Gulf Coast, 75 miles south of Anchorage.

Reference: Seward A-7; Blying Sound C-7, D-7.

Access: By car via the Seward Highway, which connects Anchorage to the coastal community of Seward, terminating at the head of Resurrection Bay. Shorefishing is popular around Seward, with the greater fishery occurring in the boat-accessible outer waters of the bay.

Highlights: One of the best road-accessible marine fishing locations in Alaska. Excellent fishing for silver salmon (from mid- through late August), pink salmon (from late July through early August) and halibut (from June through August); also good fishing for king salmon (in the first half of June) and Dolly Varden (from June through July).

Species: Chum salmon, Dolly Varden, halibut, king salmon, pink salmon, red salmon, silver salmon.

Regulations: Ling cod fishing is prohibited. For additional restrictions, consult the current Alaska Department of Fish and Game sportfishing regulations or the ADF&G Soldotna office, (907) 262-9368.

Facilities: Lodging, motels, gas, guide services, boat rentals and a boat launch, groceries and sporting goods are available in Seward.

Contact: For guide services, contact Mariah Charters and Tours, 3812 Katmai Circle, Anchorage, AK 99517-1024, (907) 224-8623 (in summer) or (907) 243-1238 (in winter); Saltwater Safari Company, P.O. Box 241225, Anchorage, AK 99524, (800) 382-1564 or (907) 277-3223; Sablefish Charters, P.O. Box 1588, Seward, AK 99664, (907) 224-3283; or Excellent Adventures, P.O. Box 467, Seward,

AK 99664, (907) 224-2030. For lodging, contact The Breeze Inn, P.O. Box 2147, Seward, AK 99664; (907) 224-5237.

Description: Located at the north end of Blying Sound along coastal Kenai Peninsula, Resurrection Bay is a greenish-clear fjord with several glacial and clearwater streams emptying into it. Although the area does receive its share of bad weather from the Gulf of Alaska, the bay is fairly protected by the surrounding mountain ridges. Thick forests, mountains, snow fields and glaciers make it particularly scenic. Abundant wildlife—sea otters, whales, waterfowl, eagles, even an occasional bear or moose—enhance the overall experience for anglers.

Excellent fishing for enhanced runs of salmon and Dolly Varden charr and halibut, plus easy access and a world-famous silver salmon derby in August make Seward one of Alaska's most-visited destinations. Fishing from shore—docks, beaches, points and stream mouths—is popular and productive, especially during the peak of the runs. (Occasionally, halibut up to 85 pounds or more are even taken by anglers fishing from deep-water docks in front of town.)

Boaters definitely have the edge for accessing the best fishing. During the early part of the season, the outer bay is most productive for salmon, with the rest of the area's waters turning on as summer progresses. Feeder kings and large halibut are taken only in the outer bay area. Trolling bait is the preferred method for kings and silvers, with some mooching, jigging and casting done at times when feeding is concentrated. Look for jumpers and feeding seabirds for sure signs of fish.

Some proven hot spot locations include: the Seward Harbor area (king salmon, silver salmon, pink salmon), the mouths of Lowell Creek (king salmon, pink salmon) and 4th of July Creek (silver salmon, chum salmon, pink salmon); Lowell Point (silver salmon, pink salmon, Dolly Varden) and Tonsina Point (chum salmon, pink salmon, Dolly Varden); Caines and Callisto heads (silver salmon); Thumb Cove (silver salmon, pink salmon), Humpy Cove (silver salmon, pink salmon), Pony Cove (silver salmon), Agnes Cove (silver salmon), Porcupine Cove (silver salmon) and Bulldog Cove (silver salmon); Aialik Cape (king salmon, halibut), Granite Cape (halibut) and Resurrection Cape (halibut); Eldorado Narrows (king salmon, silver salmon); and Rugged Island (king salmon, silver salmon) and Chiswell Island (halibut).

54. VALDEZ ARM

Location: North Prince William Sound, 105 miles east of Anchorage.

Reference: Valdez A-7, A-8; Cordova D-8; Seward D-1.

Access: By car, plane or boat. The town of Valdez is located at the head of Port Valdez and linked to the rest of the state through the Richardson Highway. The outer bay area is reached by plane or boat, while the inner waters can be fished from the road system and boats.

Highlights: Excellent fishing for silver salmon (from late August through early September), pink salmon (in the first half of July) and halibut (from July through September); good fishing for chum salmon (from mid-July through late August) and Dolly Varden charr (from June through July).

Species: Chum salmon, Dolly Varden, halibut, king salmon, pink salmon, (red salmon), silver salmon.

Regulations: Halibut fishing is prohibited from January 1 through 31. For additional restrictions, consult the current Alaska Department of Fish and Game sportfishing regulations or the ADF&G Glennallen office, (907) 822-3309.

Facilities: Lodging, motel, gas, boat rentals, a boat launch, sporting goods, groceries and guide services are available in Valdez.

Contact: For guide services, contact Seaview Charters, P.O. Box 331, Valdez, AK 99686, (907) 835-5115; or Coho Charters, P.O. Box 2198, Valdez, AK 99686, (907) 835-4675. For lodging, contact Totem Inn, P.O. Box 648, Valdez, AK 99686, (907) 835-4443; or Village Inn, P.O. Box 365, Valdez, AK 99686, (907) 835-4445.

Description: Valdez Arm is a long, curved inlet located in northern Prince William Sound. Numerous clearwater and glacial streams draining from the Chugach Mountains greatly influence its physical character and angling. In the greenish-gray, cold waters, all five species of salmon, charr and bottomfish can be taken, but the abundant runs of lure-snapping silver and pink salmon and good-sized halibut draw anglers' attention most. (Valdez is known as the Pink Salmon Capital of the World and has three salmon derbies each summer.) The presence of the Solomon Creek Hatchery across the bay from the town of Valdez considerably enhances the salmon fishing, in some years producing thick concentrations of returning fish and some wild action at the head of the bay. (Silvers have been known to jump into boats and up on docks here.)

Excellent shorefishing for pinks and silvers can be had from beaches, points, docks and creek mouths during the peak of salmon season (in July and August), but the most consistent action is found in areas reached by boats or plane. Halibut fishing is great in the deep waters of the outer bay, particularly in late summer and fall. Feeder king salmon are present in small numbers in spring and early summer, while Dolly Varden charr are usually taken near the mouths of clear rivers and creeks.

Some hot spots to try for various species include Valdez Harbor (silver salmon, pink salmon), Allison Point (silver salmon, chum salmon, pink salmon), the mouth of Gold Creek (silver salmon, pink salmon), Glacier Island (halibut), Port Fidalgo (halibut, silver salmon, chum salmon, pink salmon), Anderson Bay (silver salmon, chum salmon, pink salmon), Jack Bay (halibut, silver salmon, chum salmon, pink salmon, Dolly Varden), Sawmill Bay (chum salmon, pink salmon, Dolly Varden) and Galena Bay (silver salmon, chum salmon, pink salmon, Dolly Varden, halibut).

55. ORCA BAY/INLET

Location: East Prince William Sound, 135 miles southeast of Anchorage.

Reference: Cordova B-5, B-6, B-7; C-5, C-6, C-7, C-8.

Access: By boat or floatplane from the town of Cordova to the better fishing areas. There are also some limited shorefishing opportunities.

Highlights: Excellent fishing for king salmon (in the first half of June), silver salmon (in the second half of August), pink salmon (in the second half of July) and halibut (from June through August); good fishing for Dolly Varden (in May and June).

Species: Chum salmon, Dolly Varden, halibut, king salmon, pink salmon, red salmon, silver salmon.

Regulations: Halibut fishing is prohibited from January 1 through 31. For additional restrictions, consult the current Alaska Department of Fish and Game sportfishing regulations or the ADF&G Anchorage office, (907) 267-2218.

Facilities: Lodging, gas, boat rentals, a boat launch, guide services, sporting goods and groceries are available in the town of Cordova. A 12-by-14-foot forest service cabin is located on Double Bay, Hinchinbrook Island.

Contact: For guide services, contact the Alaska Wilderness Outfitting Company, P.O. Box 1516, Cordova, AK 99574, (907) 424-5552; or Winter King Charters, P.O. Box 14, Cordova, AK 99574, (907) 424-7170. For an air taxi, contact Cordova Air Service, P.O. Box 528, Cordova, AK 99574, (907) 424-7611; or Fishing and Flying, P.O.

Box 2349, Cordova, AK 99574, (907) 424-3324. For lodging, contact the Reluctant Fisherman Inn, P.O. Box 150, Cordova, AK 99574, (907) 424-3272; or Cordova Rose Lodge, P.O. Box 1494, Cordova, AK 99574, (907) 424-7673. For cabin rental information, contact Chugach National Forest, 201 East Ninth Avenue, Suite 206, Anchorage, AK 99501; (907) 271-2500.

Description: Orca Bay and its inlet are situated in eastern Prince William Sound and encompass a number of smaller bays, coves, Hawkins Island and the northeastern corner of Hinchinbrook Island. A multitude of stream and bays, splendid scenery, wildlife and relatively easy access make it one of the more popular coastal fishing areas of Southcentral Alaska.

Access is from the town of Cordova, either by boat (there are hundreds of miles of sheltered coastline) or wheel or floatplane (landing in bays or long gravel beaches near salmon streams). The major species of fish that anglers target are silver and pink salmon, Dolly Varden charr and halibut, though feeder king salmon are becoming increasingly popular in late winter and spring. Several area streams support small populations of cutthroat trout. The better salmon action occurs at the head of bays near spawning streams, the best of them located around Hinchinbrook and Hawkins islands and the northern section of Orca Bay.

The small clearwater streams offer some outstanding spin and flycasting opportunities for salmon, trout and Dolly Varden charr. Halibut are taken in shallow waters during the spring, moving deeper as the season progresses. (They may also be taken in the fall off the mouths of salmon streams in certain areas.) Casting from shore is most frequently done near the town of Cordova, as enhanced runs of king and silver salmon return to locations nearby, but it also works well anywhere concentrations of fish hold close to shore—in the intertidal areas of streams, near points, and at the heads of bays.

The best fishing locations in the Orca Bay area include: Orca Inlet (king salmon, silver salmon, pink salmon, halibut), Hartney Bay (king salmon, silver salmon, pink salmon), Flemming Spit (king salmon, silver salmon) and the mouth of Humpback Creek (pink salmon), outside the town of Cordova; Simpson Bay (silver salmon, pink salmon, halibut), Sheep Bay (silver salmon, pink salmon, halibut) and Port Gravina (silver salmon, pink salmon, halibut), on the northern half of Orca; stream mouths on Hawkins Island-Hawkins Creek (pink salmon, cutthroat trout, Dolly Varden) and Canoe Pas-

sage (pink salmon, cutthroat trout, Dolly Varden); and Anderson
Bay (pink salmon, cutthroat trout, Dolly Varden), Double Bay (pink
salmon, cutthroat trout, Dolly Varden, halibut) and Boswell Bay
(pink salmon, Dolly Varden) on Hinchinbrook Island.

56. WELLS PASSAGE AREA

Location: Northwest Prince William Sound, 65 miles east of Anchorage.
Reference: Anchorage A-2, A-3, A-4, B-2; Seward C-3, C-4, C-5, D-3,
D-4, D-5.
Access: By boat or kayak from the town of Whittier through Passage
Canal or by floatplane from Anchorage.
Highlights: Excellent fishing for silver salmon (in the second half of
August) and pink and chum salmon (in the second half of July).
Also good fishing for Dolly Varden (in May and June) and halibut
(in June and August).
Species: Chum salmon, Dolly Varden, halibut, king salmon, pink
salmon, red salmon, silver salmon.
Regulations: Halibut fishing is prohibited from January 1 through 31.
For additional restrictions, consult the current Alaska Department of
Fish and Game sportfishing regulations or the ADF&G Anchorage
office, (907) 267-2218.
Facilities: Gas, a boat launch and guide services are available in the town
of Whittier. Several forest service cabins are located in the area.
Contact: For lodging information, contact the Sportsman Inn, P.O. Box
688, Whittier, AK 99693; (907) 472-2352. For an air taxi, contact
Rusts Flying Service, P.O. Box 190325, Anchorage, AK 99519,
(800) 544-2299 or (907) 243-1595; or Ketchum Air Service, P.O.
Box 190588, Anchorage, AK 99519, (800) 433-9114 or (907) 243-
5525. For cabin rental information, contact Chugach National Forest, 201 East Ninth Avenue, Suite 206, Anchorage, AK 99501; (907)
271-2500.
Description: For the angler wanting to experience something out of the
ordinary, Wells Passage in the heart of Prince William Sound has
icy blue bays, secluded coves, deserted islands and crystal-clear
streams, with abundant fishing for salmon, charr and bottomfish, as
well as rich ocean fauna and picturesque scenery.

Located in northwest Prince William Sound within Chugach
National Forest (there are several public-use cabins in the vicinity,
at Shrode Lake and Pigot and Paulson bays), the Passage is most
quickly and conveniently accessed by floatplane. But to truly savor
the essence of this special area, you should travel by boat, taking

time to explore and fish the countless bays, coves and stream mouths. (Streams are typically short, shallow and clear. Many drain narrow, jutting peninsulas and islands.)

Pink salmon are by far the most common species. In season, they swarm through the sound in huge schools, invading almost any flowing body of water. Look for schools of bright fish early on in the season to enjoy the best angling for this species. Silver salmon arrive sometime after the pinks and provide superb action when concentrated in bays and coves near their streams of birth, while some red salmon and good numbers of chums and Dolly Varden charr are present in some locations. A hatchery run of king salmon returns to the Esther Island area. Halibut, although usually not of any great size, are also abundant throughout most of the area.

Hot spots to try include: Pigot Bay (chum salmon, pink salmon, halibut), Cochrane Bay (chum salmon, pink salmon, Dolly Varden, halibut) and Long Bay (silver salmon, pink salmon, Dolly Varden); Passage Canal Lagoon (silver salmon, pink salmon), Harrison Lagoon (chum salmon, pink salmon) and Coghill Lagoon (silver salmon, pink salmon, Dolly Varden); and Culross Passage (silver salmon, pink salmon, Dolly Varden) and Esther Passage (king salmon, silver salmon, chum salmon, pink salmon, Dolly Varden).

57. KNIGHT ISLAND PASSAGE

Location: West Prince William Sound, 90 miles southeast of Anchorage.
Reference: Seward A-3, A-4, B-3, B-4, C-2, C-3.
Access: By floatplane or boat from Anchorage, Seward, Whittier or Valdez, to various lagoons, coves, beaches and bays of the area. (Small crafts such as pleasure boats and kayaks can be used in these sheltered waters.)
Highlights: Excellent fishing for pink salmon (in July) and halibut (from June through August); good fishing for silver and red salmon (in the first half of August), chum salmon (in the second half of July) and Dolly Varden (in May and June).
Species: Chum salmon, cutthroat trout, Dolly Varden, halibut, pink salmon, red salmon, silver salmon.
Regulations: Halibut fishing is prohibited from January 1 through 31. For additional restrictions, consult the current Alaska Department of Fish and Game sportfishing regulations or the ADF&G Anchorage office, (907) 267-2218.
Facilities: No developed public facilities.

Contact: For an air taxi, contact Rusts Flying Service, P.O. Box 190325, Anchorage, AK 99519, (800) 544-2299 or (907) 243-1595; or Ketchum Air Service, P.O. Box 190588, Anchorage, AK 99519, (800) 433-9114 or (907) 243-5525.

Description: Like many other areas within Prince William Sound, Knight Island Passage offers some of the finest recreational sportfishing and boating in Southcentral Alaska. Located on the west side of the sound between the eastern Kenai Peninsula and Knight, Chenega, Bainbridge, Evans and Latouche islands, the Passage has dozens of bays, coves, clearwater streams and lakes. It offers a variety of fishing, including four species of salmon, charr and bottomfish, and abundant opportunities to set out pots for crab and shrimp. Thick forests of spruce and an amazing variety of marine animals enhance the overall experience. Protected from strong winds and high seas, the area is ideal for small crafts such as pleasure boats and kayaks.

Although surf-casting can be highly productive in some locations, mooching or trolling for salmon or jigging for halibut from boats are the preferred ways of fishing most of the Passage. Though generally not the size of fish taken from other parts of the state—they average only 15 to 20 pounds—the plentiful halibut of western Prince William Sound are nonetheless worth a try, especially on light tackle. Salmon, although present throughout the passage, are more commonly encountered near spawning streams, so anglers should wisely select bays and coves with streams to maximize their chances for success.

Knight Island Passage hot spots include Main Bay (chum salmon, pink salmon, Dolly Varden, halibut), Ewan Bay (chum salmon, pink salmon, Dolly Varden, halibut), Jackpot Bay (silver salmon, pink salmon, cutthroat trout, Dolly Varden, halibut), Eshamy Bay (silver salmon, chum salmon, pink salmon, Dolly Varden, halibut) and Eshamy Lagoon (silver salmon, red salmon, chum salmon, pink salmon, cutthroat trout, Dolly Varden). Anglers who do a bit of exploring can find many locations that offer great fishing with virtually no pressure.

58. MONTAGUE STRAIT

Location: South Prince William Sound, 100 miles southeast of Anchorage.

Reference: Seward A-1, A-2, A-3, B-1, B-2, B-3, C-2; Blying Sound D-1, D-2, D-3, D-4.

Access: By boat or floatplane from Anchorage, Whittier, Seward or Cordova. (Boats are recommended since the majority of sportfishing in this area is done offshore.) Wheelplane access is also possible along beaches.

Highlights: One of the best marine locations in Prince William Sound; excellent fishing for silver salmon (in the second half of August), pink salmon (in the second half of July) and halibut (from June through August).

Species: (Chum salmon), cutthroat trout, Dolly Varden, halibut, pink salmon, silver salmon.

Regulations: Halibut fishing is prohibited from January 1 through 31. For additional restrictions, consult the current Alaska Department of Fish and Game sportfishing regulations or the ADF&G Anchorage office, (907) 267-2218.

Facilities: Cabins are available on Montague and Green islands.

Contact: For guide services, contact the Saltwater Safari Company, P.O. Box 241225, Anchorage, AK 99524; (800) 382-1564 or (907) 277-3223. For an air taxi, contact Rusts Flying Service, P.O. Box 190325, Anchorage, AK 99519, (800) 544-2299 or (907) 243-1595; or Ketchum Air Service, P.O. Box 190588, Anchorage, AK 99519, (800) 433-9114 or (907) 243-5525. For cabin rental information, contact Chugach National Forest, 201 East Ninth Avenue, Suite 206, Anchorage, AK 99501; (907) 271-2500.

Description: Montague Strait is a long, wide passage located on the southern end of Prince William Sound, between Montague, Knight and Latouche islands. Along with Hinchinbrook Entrance, Montague serves as a major migration corridor for salmon bound for streams deep inside the sound. There are several major bays, ports and harbors, but the strait lacks the abundance of cutting fjords and islands that characterize most of western Prince William Sound, and is more open and susceptible to bad weather.

Montague Strait has long been known for some of the best halibut action in Prince William Sound. The fish there are much larger than those inside the sound, with trophies up to 250 pounds or more not uncommon. Waters near bays containing salmon streams, or around small islands, points and sandy shoals, are favorable locations to find these behemoths. Other bottomfish species like rockfish and ling cod are present as well.

Although large numbers of salmon pass through the strait, there are relatively few streams in the area that contain substantial runs. Creeks there are typically shallow, short and clear, with small numbers of pink and silver salmon and some Dolly Varden. Fair action for cutthroat trout may be had in some streams on Montague Island.

Green and Montague Islands both have 12-by-14-foot forest service cabins available for public use. A boat or some type of watercraft is almost a necessity to access the best fishing, but you can do some fairly productive surf-casting near the mouths of salmon spawning streams, particularly those on the southern half of Montague Island.

Hot spots to explore include Knight Island/Bay of Isles (silver salmon, halibut); Green Island (Dolly Varden, halibut); and Port Chalmers (silver salmon, pink salmon, cutthroat trout, Dolly Varden), Montague Point (halibut), Hanning Bay (pink salmon, Dolly Varden), MacLeod Harbor (pink salmon, Dolly Varden), Cape Cleare (halibut) and San Juan Bay (silver salmon, pink salmon, Dolly Varden) on Montague Island.

---

59. NELLIE MARTIN-PATTON RIVERS

Location: Southeast Montague Island drainage, 120 miles southeast of Anchorage.

Reference: Blying Sound D-1, D-2.

Access: By wheelplane from Seward or Cordova. It is possible to land on the beach area around the mouth of the river and along Patton Bay at low tide. Although the river is within reasonable boating distance, the weather can be hazardous for small craft.

Highlights: One of the best salmon streams in Prince William Sound. Excellent fishing for silver salmon (from late August through early September) and pink salmon (in the second half of July); also good fishing for Dolly Varden charr (in July and August).

Species: (Cutthroat trout), Dolly Varden, pink salmon, (red salmon), silver salmon.

Regulations: Open year-round, all species.

Facilities: A forest service cabin is located on the river.

Contact: For an air taxi, contact Ketchum Air Service, P.O. Box 190588, Anchorage, AK 99519, (800) 433-9114 or (907) 243-5525. For cabin rental information, contact Chugach National Forest, 201 East Ninth Avenue, Suite 206, Anchorage, AK 99501; (907) 271-2500.

Description: The Nellie Martin-Patton rivers of southern Montague Island are popular destinations for fly-in anglers, with some of the best silver salmon fishing in Prince William Sound (abundant runs, with fish up to 18 pounds), along with large numbers of pink salmon and Dolly Varden charr. Crystal clear, with gravel and sand bottoms, long runs and deep pools, the rivers offer great fly and spincasting possibilities.

The mouth and lower sections of both rivers are the most popular and productive areas to fish, especially on the rising tide, but Patton Bay offers good skiff fishing possibilities for silver and pink salmon as well as halibut. Anglers planning a trip to these rivers should allow several days in their schedule for the possibility of bad weather and travel delays. A 12-by-14-foot forest service cabin is available for public use, and is half a mile from the beach.

60. EYAK RIVER/LAKE

Location: Copper River Delta drainage, 150 miles southeast of Anchorage.

Reference: Cordova B-5, C-5.

Access: By car. The main river and lake are accessible from the town of Cordova. Small boats may be launched to fish more remote areas. A well-developed trail system provides foot access to the middle river section as well as to Power Creek, a major tributary emptying into Eyak Lake.

Highlights: Good fishing for silver salmon (in the second half of August) and red salmon (from late June through early July), cutthroat trout (in May) and Dolly Varden charr (in May and August).

Species: Cutthroat trout, Dolly Varden, red salmon, silver salmon.

Regulations: For restrictions, consult the current Alaska Department of Fish and Game sportfishing regulations or the ADF&G Anchorage office, (907) 267-2218.

Facilities: Lodgings, hotel, gas, boat rentals, a boat launch, groceries and sporting goods are available in Cordova. A forest service cabin is located on Power Creek.

Contact: For general, lodging and cabin rental information, contact the Cordova Ranger District, 612 Second Street, Cordova, AK 99574; (907) 424-7661.

Description: The Eyak River is a semi-glacial stream originating from Shephard Glacier in the Chugach Mountains above Cordova. Power Creek drains the valleys of the Heney Range before emptying into

Eyak Lake, from which the smooth flowing river begins. The Eyak flows wide and deep for a short distance, before fanning out onto the flats of the muddy Copper River Delta and then into the Gulf of Alaska.

Due to its easy access (it can be reached via the Copper Highway from Cordova) and good fishing, the Eyak River is one of the more popular and productive locations in the entire Copper River system, with good runs of silver and red salmon. Since it's fairly glacial, anglers do best working the river with extremely bright lures or bait. Although red salmon are present in large numbers in early summer, they can be finicky about lure selection, with best results occurring in areas with large fish concentrations and currents. (For more details, see the sockeye chapter on page 64.) Silvers are much more responsive and provide good action in late summer and fall, while trout and charr make themselves known during their annual migrations to and from the sea.

The lake itself offers some limited possibilities. The outlet is perhaps the best location for fishing on the entire river, but the remainder of the lake is fairly shallow, with deeper channels toward the middle, following the pattern of the Eyak River. Power Creek is also semi-glacial and is the major spawning ground for the Eyak River fish stocks. Salmon fishing is prohibited there, but anglers do very well with Dolly Varden, with some catches of up to four or five pounds. Some cutthroat trout are also taken. The best time to fish is during August and September when the salmon are on the spawning beds.

61. ALAGANIK SLOUGH SYSTEM

Location: Copper River Delta drainage, 165 miles southeast of Anchorage.

Reference: Cordova B-3, B-4.

Access: By car via the Copper River Highway from the town of Cordova. The main road parallels the slough for a few miles, crossing some tributary streams in places, while side roads and trails access other parts of the system, including McKinley Lake. Boat launching is possible to reach more remote sections, while floatplanes can be used to reach the main lake.

Highlights: Excellent fishing for silver salmon (from late August through early September); good fishing for red salmon (from late July through early August), cutthroat trout (from June through September) and Dolly Varden (from July through September).

Species: Cutthroat trout, Dolly Varden, red salmon, silver salmon.

Regulations: King salmon fishing is prohibited. For additional restrictions, consult the current Alaska Department of Fish and Game sportfishing regulations or the ADF&G Anchorage office, (907) 267-2218.

Facilities: Forest service cabins are available on the slough and lake.

Contact: For general and cabin rental information, contact the Cordova Ranger District, 612 Second Street, Cordova, AK 99574; (907) 424-7661.

Description: The Alaganik Slough System consists of an extensive drainage of lakes, clearwater streams and glacial sloughs in the Copper River Delta. Much of the lower system has an abundance of open marshland with slow-moving, semi-glacial water, which is best accessed by boat. However, the upper system has several small, clear creeks and the main channel is fairly wide with thick vegetation around the bank. The Alaganik is influenced by glacial meltwater from area mountains and the silty Copper River.

The majority of sportfishing takes place on Alaganik Slough near the highway and in McKinley Lake and surrounding streams. A 14-by-20-foot forest service cabin is on the lake, tied into an extensive and popular trail system connecting a series of small lakes and the highway (the cabin is two miles from the road). Since Alaganik Slough is so slow, even canoeists can thoroughly enjoy the area by putting in at the highway and paddling upstream to McKinley Lake and the upper system.

The system receives good runs of silver and red salmon, with the best fishing to be had in the middle and upper sections of the slough itself, the outlet of McKinley Lake and the mouths of inlet streams. While silvers can be taken throughout the system, red salmon are usually targeted in areas with at least some current. Cutthroat trout and Dolly Varden are also present, mostly in McKinley Lake and tributary streams. Lake fishing is most productive early in the season. Locations holding concentrations of spawning salmon are the best bets for larger fish in late summer and fall.

For the angler looking to do some hiking or canoeing along with his favorite sport, the Alaganik Slough system is one of the best options around, with miles of trails, abundant, easy water, scenery, wildlife and great fishing.

62. MARTIN RIVER SYSTEM

Location: Copper River Delta drainage, 180 miles southeast of Anchorage.

Reference: Cordova B-1, B-2, B-3.

Access: By plane from the town of Cordova. Floatplanes land on area lakes; wheelplanes use the open country along the mainstem Martin River.

Highlights: Excellent fishing for silver salmon (in the last half of August); good fishing for red salmon (from late June through early July), Dolly Varden (from July through September) and lake trout (from May through October).

Species: (Cutthroat trout), Dolly Varden, lake trout, red salmon, silver salmon, (steelhead).

Regulations: Open year-round, all species.

Facilities: A forest service cabin is located at Martin Lake.

Contact: For general and cabin rental information, contact the Cordova Ranger District, 612 Second Street, Cordova, AK 99574; (907) 424-7661. For an air taxi, contact the Cordova Air Service, P.O. Box 528, Cordova, AK 99574, (907) 424-7611; or Fishing and Flying, P.O. Box 2349, Cordova, AK 99574, (907) 424-3324.

Description: The Martin River system drains a heavily glaciated area of the coastal Chugach Range and empties into the eastern Copper River Delta. The main river is silty, originating from the Martin River Glacier, while the tributary streams and lakes run clear and are ideal for sportfishing. Splendid scenery, abundant wildlife and exciting fishing make it a popular destination.

Considering its size, the system does not support very large numbers of sportfish. Still, the fish are usually concentrated in only a few locations, making for fast action. Most anglers visiting this area stay at the forest service cabin located at the outlet of Martin Lake, as this location has some of the best fishing, but the lower reaches of streams draining into the southern half of the lake are certainly worth a try. Other good fishing locations include the outlet of Little Martin Lake, Tokun Lake and the mouths of clearwater streams and sloughs off the Martin River.

The most sought-after species is the silver salmon. These flashy fighters are present from late summer through early fall, and can be caught with regularity throughout much of the system. The best location is probably the confluence of the Martin River and the small stream draining Martin Lake. The fish school up here and yield superb action, with good conditions for easy spin and flyfishing. Red salmon, difficult to catch, are present in good numbers in some of the tributary streams.

Other species like Dolly Varden and lake trout are present in fishable numbers along with a few cutthroat trout. Large Dollies are taken during the peak of the salmon runs in Martin Lake and its tributaries, while lake trout are taken out of deeper sections of Martin and Tokun lakes. (These lake trout are some of the farthest south- and east-ranging populations of the species in Alaska.)

63. KATALLA RIVER

Location: North Gulf Coast drainage, 190 miles southeast of Anchorage.

Reference: Cordova A-2, B-2.

Access: By small wheelplane from the town of Cordova. There is a rough, short landing strip on the lower river near the mouth with a few trails providing access to other sections of the Katalla.

Highlights: A promising, out-of-the-way salmon and trout stream, with excellent fishing for silver salmon (from late August through early September), pink salmon (from late July through early August) and cutthroat trout (from August through September); good fishing for Dolly Varden (from July through September).

Species: Chum salmon, cutthroat trout, Dolly Varden, (king salmon), pink salmon, (red salmon), silver salmon.

Regulations: Unbaited, artificial lures only from April 15 through June 14. For additional restrictions, consult the current Alaska Department of Fish and Game sportfishing regulations or the ADF&G Anchorage office, (907) 267-2218.

Facilities: No developed public facilities.

Contact: For an air taxi, contact Cordova Air Service, P.O. Box 528, Cordova, AK 99574, (907) 424-7611; or Fishing and Flying, P.O. Box 2349, Cordova, AK 99574, (907) 424-3324.

Description: The Katalla River is perhaps the best prospect of several lesser visited coastal streams found just east of the Copper River Delta. Gathering water from several sources draining the uplands between Bering Lake and the Ragged Mountains, the clear Katalla meanders down through a brushy, wet valley into the gulf at Katalla Bay. The few (mostly hunters) who have fished and explored its reaches report abundant silver salmon, cutthroat trout and Dolly Varden in a totally wild setting.

To fish the Katalla, one must fly by small plane from Cordova, landing on floats in the slough or bay, or by wheelplane to a rough strip along the beach. Fishing spinners and spoons in the mouth and lower river with the tides is certainly one of the better ways to connect with bright salmon, but a hike upstream to check out the pools and small side creeks can yield some delightful flyfishing, especially for Dollies and cutthroats. The best time to fish would be in late summer and fall (from late August through September). Watch out for bears, which are numerous.

The Katalla is definitely worth investigating as one of the more promising gateway streams to the vast unexplored North Gulf Coast beyond the Copper River Delta.

64. BERING RIVER SYSTEM

Location: North Gulf Coast drainage, Controller Bay, 205 miles southeast of Anchorage.

Reference: Cordova A-1, B-1; Bering Glacier B-8.

Access: By plane from Cordova. Floatplanes can land on area lakes (Bering, Charlotte and Kushtaka) or wide, deep sloughs along river; wheelplane landings are possible on gravel bars. Some hiking is required to reach choice fishing spots.

Highlights: A little-visited salmon system with great potential. Good fishing for silver salmon (from mid-August through early September), red salmon (from late June through early July) and Dolly Varden charr (from July through September).

Species: Chum salmon, Dolly Varden, pink salmon, red salmon, silver salmon.

Regulations: Unbaited, artificial lures only from April 15 through June 14. For additional restrictions, consult the current Alaska Department of Fish and Game sportfishing regulations or the ADF&G Anchorage office, (907) 267-2218.

Facilities: No developed public facilities.

Contact: For an air taxi, contact Cordova Air Service, P.O. Box 528, Cordova, AK 99574, (907) 424-7611; or Fishing and Flying, P.O. Box 2349, Cordova, AK 99574, (907) 424-3324.

Description: Bering River is a fair-sized glacial system lying east of the Copper River Delta that, like the Katalla, gets little attention. Originating from the edge of the huge Saint Elias ice fields, the silty Bering flows south to Controller Bay and the Gulf of Alaska. There are several large lakes, a few of which have clearwater streams with habitat for salmon and charr. Along with a number of small holding sloughs and creeks on the east side of the lower river, they hold most of the Bering's sportfish potential.

Anglers flying in to the area from Cordova can land on beaches, lakes and sloughs near holding fish (spotted from the air). Red and silver salmon and Dolly Varden are the species most folks look for. Some of the more promising drainages to scout include Dick Creek (Bering Lake), Shepherd Creek and Stillwater Creek (Kushtaka Lake), although just about any clearwater slough will have salmon potential during the peak of the runs. Bears are quite common, so caution should be used. The Bering system is perfect for anglers with a spirit of adventure and a yearning for some truly unexploited, exciting fishing.

Magnificent scenery, productive coastal streams and easy access are the highlights of Alaska's Southcentral region.

Region 5
Wrangell-Copper River

In the early 1980s, reports of rainbow trout over 20 pounds from a remote location in the rugged Wrangell Mountains focused attention on the vastly underrated sportfishing potential of this scenic corner of the state. Dominated by the huge, glacial Copper River and towering, icy mountains, the Wrangell subregion has much to offer fishermen in its clearer-flowing tributary streams and associated lakes. King and red salmon, grayling, lake trout, some rainbow and even a few steelhead trout are the species highlights for this area.

65. Gulkana River System

Location: Copper River drainage, 165 miles northeast of Anchorage
Reference: Mount Hayes A-3, A-4; Gulkana A-3, A-5, B-3, B-4, B-5, C-4, C-5, C-6, D-4, D-5, D-6.
Access: By car, plane and boat. The Richardson Highway parallels the river more or less from the headwaters down to near the mouth, offering access to the mainstem and some clearwater tributaries. Floatplanes can be used to reach more remote parts of the drainage. Boats, rafts and other craft can be launched from various locations.
Highlights: One of Alaska's premier recreational waters, with excellent fishing for grayling (from May through October). Good fishing for king salmon (from late June through early July) and red salmon (from late June through mid-August); rainbow trout (from July through September) and lake trout (in June and from September through October).
Species: Grayling, king salmon, lake trout, rainbow trout, red salmon, (steelhead).
Regulations: King salmon fishing is closed from July 20 through December 31; catch-and-release fishing only for rainbow and steelhead trout. For additional restrictions, consult the current Alaska Department of Fish and Game sportfishing regulations or the ADF&G Glennallen office, (907) 822-3309.
Facilities: Lodging, camping, gas, groceries, boat launching, sporting goods, cabins and guide services are available in many locations along the road.

Contact: For guide services, contact Ruffitters, P.O. Box 397, Gakona, AK 99586, (907) 822-3168; or the Alaska Wilderness Outfitting Company, P.O. Box 1516, Cordova, AK 99574, (907) 424-5552. For lodging information, contact Paxson Lodge, P.O. Box 3001, Paxson, AK 99737; (907) 822-3330. For an air taxi, contact Gulkana Air Service, P.O. Box 342, Anchorage, AK 99588, (907) 822-5532; or Lee's Air Taxi Service, Glennallen, AK 99585, (907) 822-3343.

Description: The Gulkana River system is an immense clearwater drainage of lakes and streams. It rises at the base of the Alaska Range near the headwaters of the Susitna, then flows south and east approximately 100 miles to join the Copper River. It has two major tributaries, the Middle Fork and the West Fork, short streams that begin in a series of lakes and uplands west of the mainstem river. The most significant sportfishing tributary of the entire Copper River, the Gulkana is one of Alaska's premier recreational waters and has been designated a National Wild and Scenic River.

The river has one of Alaska's most productive and popular grayling fisheries, particularly on the mainstem between Paxson Lake and the West Fork confluence, but also in tributary lakes (Dickey Lake) and streams (Tangle River). Although their average size has suffered from the fishing pressure of recent years, grayling are still quite abundant and easy to catch. The Gulkana is also known for its decent king salmon fishing (from the Middle Fork confluence down) and a prolonged run of red salmon (they're hard to catch, however). Lake trout are found in the large, deep lakes, such as Summit, Paxson and Swede, and fishing can be quite good to outstanding, with some catches of these large lake charr exceeding 30 pounds. The Gulkana also has a few rainbows and some of the northernmost runs of steelhead trout in North America. The best times to fish these elusive fish are in spring and fall in tributaries of the upper Middle Fork and in the mainstem above the West Fork confluence.

There are many ways to fish the Gulkana. Perhaps the most popular and exciting is by raft, canoe or kayak, putting in at either Paxson Lake, Tangle River at milepost 22 of the Denali Highway (with a portage into Dickey Lake), or flying into one of the headwater lakes of the West Fork. The most popular take-out point is Sourdough Campground, at milepost 147.5 of the Richardson Highway. (Almost all powerboat users put in here and fish the stretch upriver to the West Fork confluence.) You can fish further down and take-out where the Richardson Highway intersects the river near Gakona Junction, if you like. The only serious hazards to boaters and floaters are boulders and swift currents (mostly Class II, with some short stretches of Class III to Class IV at the Canyon Rapids on the main-stem and below Dickey Lake on the Middle Fork). For the hiker-angler, there are several cross-country trails that allow access to strategic points along the river system. These include the Swede Lake Trail, beginning at milepost 16 of the Denali Highway, the Meiers Lake Trail, beginning at milepost 169 of the Richardson Highway, and the Haggard Creek Trail, beginning at milepost 161 of the Richardson Highway.

Guides' tip: The hot lure for grayling on the Gulkana is a #2 silver Vibrax spinner. If the grayling act finicky, try a wet fly on the end of the spinner.

66. TAZLINA RIVER SYSTEM

Location: Copper River drainage, 110 miles east of Anchorage.

Reference: Anchorage D-1; Valdez C-6, C-7, C-8, D-6, D-7, D-8; Talkeetna Mountains A-1, A-2; Gulkana A-3, A-4, A-5, A-6.

Access: By car or plane. The Richardson Highway intersects the lower part of the Tazlina River, and the Glenn Highway provides access to clearwater tributaries. Boats and rafts can be launched from the highway crossings. Floatplanes (via Tolsona or Anchorage) can be used to reach more remote fishing areas.

Highlights: Excellent fishing for grayling (from May to October). Good fishing for king and red salmon (in early July) and rainbow trout (from June through September).

Species: Grayling, king salmon, (lake trout), rainbow trout, red salmon, (steelhead).

Regulations: King salmon fishing is prohibited from July 20 through December 31. For additional restrictions, consult the current Alaska Department of Fish and Game sportfishing regulations or the ADF&G Glennallen office, (907) 822-3309.

Facilities: Camping, boat launching, lodging, gas, groceries and guide services are available in Glennallen and surrounding areas.

Contact: For an air taxi and guide services, contact Alaska Air Ventures, P.O. Box 8758, Palmer, AK 99645; (907) 822-3905.

Description: The Tazlina Glacier spills down the northeast slope of the central Chugaches and forms a large, deep body of water at its terminus, Tazlina Lake. From its outlet, the Tazlina River flows east about 60 miles to join the huge Copper River. Although the river and lake are for the most part too silty for sportfishing, the clear tributary lakes and streams offer good to excellent fishing for lake trout, Dolly Varden, grayling and two species of salmon.

There are several ways to sample the fine fishing. Floatplanes offer the quickest and easiest way to reach various choice locations; however, it is possible to launch jet boats from the Richardson Highway bridge and run up the Tazlina River. A few tributary lakes and streams may also be accessed by car from the Glenn Highway. Another option is by raft. Put-ins can be made at the Little Nelchina River on the Glenn Highway with a float down to Tazlina Lake. You can camp and fish at the inlet and fly back, or cross the lake and continue down the Tazlina River to the Richardson Highway bridge. (Be aware of strong winds that can blow off the glacier and make for hazardous conditions—take a small outboard along just in case.) Since the Nelchina and Tazlina rivers are fast, whitewater rivers (possible Class III to Class IV rapids during high-water conditions) and very cold, they definitely should not be attempted by anyone except experienced river runners and only during low water conditions.

Some of the hot spots to try on the Tazlina System include: Kaina Lake (rainbow trout), High Lake (rainbow trout, lake trout, grayling), Moose Lake (rainbow trout, grayling) and Tolsona Lake (rainbow trout, grayling); Mendeltna Creek (grayling), Moose Creek (grayling), Tolsona Creek (grayling) and Kaina Creek (king salmon, red salmon, rainbow trout). The stream mouths are best for salmon in summer. In spring and fall, try for trout and grayling. Some of these streams are major grayling producers and can be phenomenal during the annual spawning migrations in May; use flies and small spinners. A small population of steelhead is reported to spawn on the Tazlina River and a few tributaries.

67. KLUTINA RIVER SYSTEM

Location: Copper River drainage, 140 miles east of Anchorage.
Reference: Valdez B-6, C-5, C-6, C-7, D-4, D-5, D-6.
Access: By car and plane. The major point of access is where the Richardson Highway crosses the lower river near the town of Copper Center, just south of Glennallen. Floatplanes and jet boats are often used to access more remote fishing areas away from the highway.
Highlights: A very popular, road-accessible salmon and trout stream. Good fishing for king salmon (in early July and late July), red salmon (from late June through late July) and Dolly Varden (from July through October).

Species: Dolly Varden, grayling, king salmon, lake trout, red salmon, rainbow trout, (silver salmon, steelhead).

Regulations: King salmon fishing is prohibited from August 11 through December 31. For additional restrictions, consult the current Alaska Department of Fish and Game sportfishing regulations or the ADF&G Glennallen office, (907) 822-3309.

Facilities: Guide services, camping, gas, lodging and groceries are available in Copper Center.

Contact: For guide services, contact Ruffitters, P.O. Box 397, Gakona, AK 99586, (907) 822-3168; or Grove's Klutina River King Salmon Charters, P.O. Box 236, Copper Center, AK 99573, (907) 822-5822.

Description: The Klutina is a glacial river originating from Klutina Lake at the base of the Chugach Range. This greenish-grey river flows northeast 30 miles through rugged and scenic highlands to its confluence with the Copper River. Swift (Class III) and cold, the Klutina offers good to excellent fishing for king and red salmon, Dolly Varden and grayling.

There are three ways to fish the Klutina drainage. One is by road where the Richardson Highway intersects the lower river. Fishing here is mainly from the bank with a limited trail system along the river. An unimproved dirt road leads from the highway to the outlet of Klutina Lake, and makes for a long, rough ride in a four-wheeler. Another option is to launch a jet boat and fish the slower sections of the river, but this is not recommended for novice or intermediate boaters—the current is very strong, and there are numerous hidden rocks and boulders. The third access option is a floatplane to the lake and mouths of clearwater streams.

Fishing from the shore can be very productive along most of the river, particularly for red salmon. (King salmon and Dolly Varden are often taken, too.) Boaters have the most success for kings as the choice locations are more remote. (The Klutina kings are some of the largest in the region, with fish over 50 pounds not uncommon.) There are two runs of these monarchs, one in June and July, another in July and August, but not always distinct. For the most part, Dolly Varden are encountered on the upper river and at the outlet of Klutina Lake, with large specimens up to six or seven pounds possible. Red salmon run continuously from June through September, with a prolonged peak lasting about four or five weeks.

Other less-significant species, such as grayling and lake trout, are taken near the mouths of clearwater streams at times. Spots to try for these, as well as the more abundant species, include Manker and St. Anne creeks and the Mahlo River.

68. TONSINA RIVER SYSTEM

Location: Copper River drainage, 150 miles east of Anchorage.

Reference: Valdez B-3, B-4, B-5, C-2, C-3, C-4, C-5.

Access: By car, plane and boat. The Richardson and Edgerton highways cross the middle and lower river respectively. (Several trails and dirt roads lead away from the roads to points along the river.) More remote locations can be fished by jet boats, rafts or floatplanes (via Tolsona).

Highlights: Good fishing for king salmon (in the first half of July), silver salmon (in September), red salmon (in the second half of July), Dolly Varden charr (in September and October) and grayling (from June through September).

Species: Dolly Varden, grayling, king salmon, lake trout, rainbow trout, red salmon, silver salmon, (steelhead).

Regulations: King salmon fishing is prohibited from July 20 through December 31. For additional restrictions, consult the current Alaska Department of Fish and Game sportfishing regulations or the ADF&G Glennallen office, (907) 822-3309.

Facilities: Guide services and lodging are available along the road system.

Contact: For guide services and lodging information, contact the Upper Tonsina Lodge, P.O. Box 143003, Anchorage, AK 99514; (907) 337-1281, (907) 822-5557 or (800) 822-5584.

Description: The Tonsina drainage is a fairly small system that heads in Tonsina Glacier on the north slope of the Chugach Mountains and flows north and east some 60 miles before emptying into the lower Copper River. A challenging whitewater river, the greenish-gray Tonsina offers some good fishing for salmon, charr and grayling in the slower upper section below the lake and mouths of its clearwater tributary streams.

Although not often fished by any except locals, this river shouldn't be overlooked, as it can offer some quiet and productive fishing. A few faint trails exist for hiking in to the river and tributaries, but probably the most convenient way to access the Tonsina is by jet boat or raft from the highway crossings. You can also fly in to Tonsina Lake and float down, but be advised that the river, particularly the lower sections, can be unnavigable and dangerous during high water. Anglers would be wise to search for slower water or places where clearwater tributaries join the milky Tonsina; it is here that the schools of salmon, charr and grayling tend to congregate.

Some of the best fishing for king salmon, red salmon and grayling occurs at the mouths of streams draining into Tonsina Lake and in the first few miles of river below the outlet, though these species may be taken anywhere on the river in certain holes and runs. One roadside tributary, the Little Tonsina River, has productive angling for a small fall run of silver salmon, as well as Dolly Varden and grayling. Another good spot for salmon is at the mouth of the Tonsina, which may be reached by boat or raft from the Edgerton Highway. Here, the river is slower and wider, ideal holding water for migrating fish. A few steelhead are rumored to spawn in the Tonsina system.

69. TEBAY RIVER SYSTEM

Location: Wrangell Mountains, 200 miles east of Anchorage.

Reference: Valdez A-1, A-2, B-1; McCarthy A-7, A-8.

Access: By floatplane to lakes (Hanagita, Tebay, Summit) from Tolsona or Cordova.

Highlights: Remote, wild watershed with good possibilities for high-quality rainbow trout, grayling and lake trout, along with spectacular scenery and abundant wildlife.

Species: Grayling, king salmon, lake trout, rainbow trout, red salmon, steelhead.

Regulations: Seasonal closures, gear and size restrictions on rainbow trout in parts of watershed. For restrictions, consult the current Alaska Department of Fish and Game sportfishing regulations or the ADF&G Glennallen office, (907) 822-3309.

Facilities: No developed public facilities.

Contact: For an air taxi and guide services, contact the Alaska Wilderness Outfitting Company, P.O. Box 7516, Cordova, AK 99574, (907) 424-5552; or Alaska Air Ventures, P.O. Box 8758, Palmer, AK 99645, (907) 822-3905.

Description: The Tebay River system, in the heart of the Wrangell-Saint Elias Wilderness is a little-visited but esteemed drainage comprised of several high mountain lakes and streams that empty into the silty Chitina River, a major tributary of the Copper. With the area's isolation, magnificent surroundings and wild populations of rainbows, grayling and lake trout, it offers the potential for some of the best angling to be had in Southcentral Alaska.

The river heads at the Tebay Lakes, a fine spot for a fly-in fish camp, with abundant fishing (especially at the connecting outlets) for small to medium-sized rainbows. Six miles below the lower lake outlet, the Tebay is joined by its major tributary, the Hanagita River, which drains a series of small lakes to the east. There are rainbows and grayling in the Hanagita and its tributaries, as well as a few lake trout in the lakes. (A small, fall run of steelhead also spawns in the river below the lakes, but they can be elusive.) The Summit Lake and Bridge Creek drainage, which joins the Tebay from the west about a mile above the Hanagita, also has rainbows and a very interesting history. Originally thought to be barren, Summit Lake produced phenomenal catches of trophy rainbows in the early 1980s, with quite a few fish in the 20-pound (and over) range. The lake was plundered in subsequent years by crowds of fly-in fishermen. Restrictive measures were imposed by the Alaska Department of Fish and Game, but apparently too late to save the trophy fishery. The rainbow fishing there is still good today, though few fish reach any semblance of the size of yesteryear. The best time to fish Summit and the rest of Tebay is in early July or from late August through late September.

ALASKA FISHING
BY REGION:
SOUTHEAST

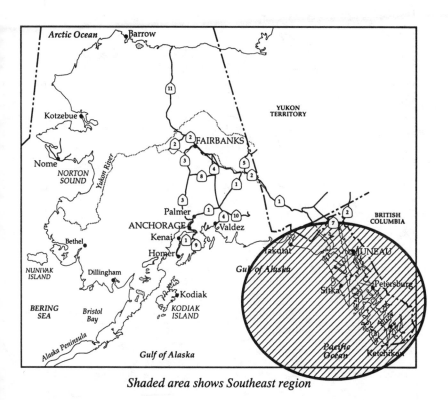

Shaded area shows Southeast region

MAP 6—SOUTHEAST HOTSPOTS

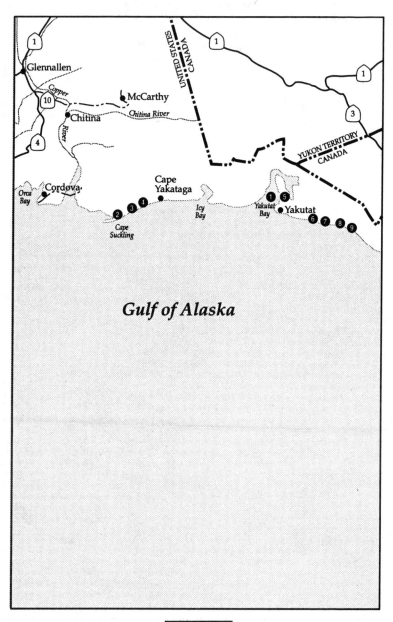

MAP 7—SOUTHEAST HOTSPOTS

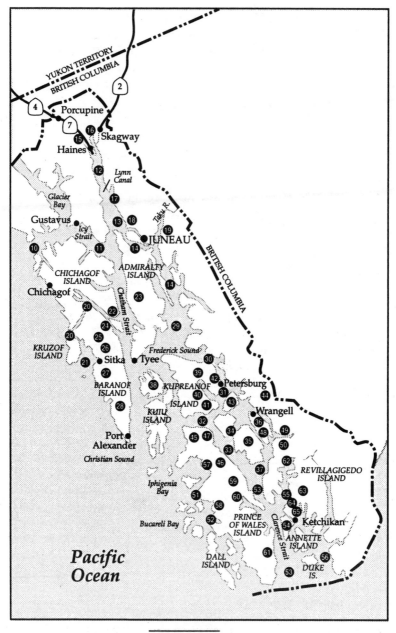

SOUTHEAST HOT SPOTS

SOUTHEAST

Imagine a vacation destination where you spend quiet mornings stalking wild steelhead on small, secluded streams, then, after lunch, boat out to scenic bays and fjords, clip on downriggers and hunt fat feeder kings, or jig for big halibut. At day's end, arms weary, you feast on a cornucopia of delights you've harvested—chunks of batter-dipped halibut, grilled salmon, rockfish, and succulent shrimp and crab pulled fresh from the pot. Later on, around the fire, the next day's anticipation is stoked with talk of exciting adventure, like flights into nearby mountain lakes, where the cutthroat trout and Dolly Varden run thick and hungry, furious to the fly.

Believe it or not, such a place does exist, beyond the realm of anglers' dreams—along the magnificent coastline, islands and sheltered passages that make up the Southeast Panhandle of Alaska. This narrow, 120-mile-wide strip of land wedged between the Pacific and the coast of British Columbia contains, without a doubt, some of the most fabulous country anywhere for sport anglers. Nowhere else in the world can you find such a variety and abundance of world-class opportunities—for steelhead and cutthroat trout, saltwater salmon, halibut, Dolly Varden and others—all within easy reach by boat or plane from a half dozen communities scattered along the coast.

COUNTRY, CLIMATE & CONDITIONS

The Southeast region, like its position on a map of Alaska, is set apart from the rest of the state in its geography, climate and general character. From Dixon Entrance, which divides Canada's Queen Charlotte Islands from their neighboring American counterparts, north in an enormous arc to Icy Cape, the panhandle stretches nearly 600 miles. Within this region lies an impressive and dynamic landscape, shaped by the powerful force of glacial action and uplift of mountains, and nurtured by a benign climate and rich marine environment.

This is the land of temperate rain forests, with most of its coast cloaked in dense stands of hemlock and spruce, including 17-million-acre Tongass National Forest, the largest in the nation. Islands abound, hundreds of them, in a maze of different sizes that includes some of the largest in the U.S., among them Prince of Wales, which ranks third in size behind Kodiak and Hawaii. Even more significant are the countless straits, channels, sounds, narrows, bays and fjords contained within this vast archipelago, for they create a haven for a diversity of marine wildlife, from seabirds to whales to salmon. With its glaciers and abundant rainfall, this coastal paradise is further enhanced with thousands of lakes and streams, most of them containing sportfish of some kind. Much of this area is spectacular wilderness and is a protected in national forests, parks, monuments, wildernesses and preserves.

Southeast's climate is mild, especially compared to the rest of Alaska. Warmed in winter and cooled in summer by the maritime influence of the North Pacific, conditions here can be surprisingly more favorable to outdoor activities than in some locations in the lower 48 states. (Compare the January or July average temperature here with that of Chicago, for instance.) Generally, visitors should come prepared for mild but moist weather, with temperatures in summer ranging from the mid-50s to the upper 60s (with highs in the upper 70s possible) and from the teens to the lower 40s in winter. Areas in the vicinity of large glaciers are subject to strong, cold winds that can sweep down at any time of year. Precipitation is extremely varied within the region (from 30 to over 200 inches a year), but follows the same trend prevalent most elsewhere in Alaska. Late spring and early summer (from May to July) are the driest, sunniest parts of the year, while fall and early winter (from October to January) are the cloudiest and most stormy.

SOUTHEAST FISHING HIGHLIGHTS

As an angling destination, Southeast Alaska has so much to offer that one can only wonder why folks would want to fish anywhere else. For one thing, it has far and away Alaska's most abundant and varied inshore opportunities, with quite a few world-famous salmon and halibut locations. (Communities here actively compete for "the world's best fishing" distinction.) It is also the state's wild steelhead mecca, with hundreds of identified streams containing the species, quite a few of them enjoying world-class distinction. Cutthroat trout and Dolly Varden, similarly, are found throughout the region in hundreds of streams, lakes and ponds, providing added highlights to nearly every fishing excursion, no matter what time of year. Trophy anglers should take special note of the fact that most of the state's largest specimens of silver, chum, steelhead, cutthroat and halibut come from Southeast's waters.

Another of the region's prime features is its milder climate, which has a positive effect on fishing; the season typically begins earlier and continues later than elsewhere in Alaska, with an extended open-water period that allows for fishing in some areas 12 months of the year. (Higher elevation lakes and some locations in northern Southeast ice over much the same as Alaska waters do elsewhere, however.)

ACCESS, SERVICES & COSTS

The region's close proximity to the outside world and its well-developed network of transportation and services adds immeasurably to its appeal as a vacation destination. Major hubs—Juneau, Ketchikan and Sitka—are serviced daily by commercial jetliners linking with West Coast cities. With a limited local road network, access to the better fishing locations is primarily by boat or small plane, with a well-established state ferry route linking many communities. Numerous hiking trails exist throughout Southeast, many of them providing access to prime fishing waters. A very well-known and extensive system of public-use cabins is maintained by the U.S. Forest Service, many of them in popular lake and stream locations, with some skiffs available for fishing. And you'll find a burgeoning visitor services industry to help you make it all happen, with a bewildering array of wilderness lodges, family-style fishing camps, bed and breakfasts, fishing charters, guides, air taxis, boat rentals and even floating hotels offering a world of possibilities for every whim and price range (from $75 dollars to several hundred for a day of fishing).

SOUTHEAST RUN TIMING

Freshwater

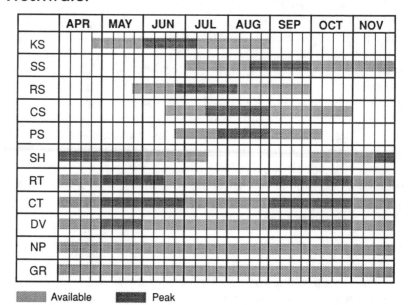

Available   Peak

KS=King Salmon, SS=Silver Salmon, RS=Red Salmon, CS=Chum Salmon, PS=Pink Salmon, SH=Sheefish, RT=Rainbow Trout, CT=Cutthroat Trout, DV=Dolly Varden, NP=Northern Pike, GR=Grayling

Saltwater

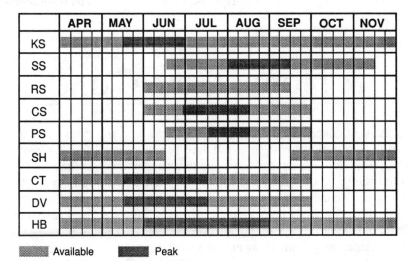

KS=King Salmon, SS=Silver Salmon, RS=Red Salmon, CS=Chum Salmon, PS=Pink Salmon, SH=Sheefish, CT=Cutthroat Trout, DV=Dolly Varden, HB=Halibut

Note: Time periods shown are for bright fish, in the case of salmon entering rivers, or for general availability for resident species. Salmon are present in many systems long after the periods shown, but are usually in spawning/post spawning condition. Peak sportfishing periods for each species are highlighted. Be aware that run timing can vary somewhat from drainage to drainage and generally follows a later trend in waters to the west and north in Alaska. Check with local contacts listed for area run-timing specifics before confirming plans.

REGION 1
YAKUTAT
& NORTH GULF COAST

West of Glacier Bay and Cape Spencer, the wild and stormy North Gulf Coast beckons with some fabulous fishing possibilities. A remote expanse, with enormous glaciers and towering mountains (the Saint Elias Range, with peaks up to 19,850 feet) that drop abruptly to coastal flatlands and deserted beaches, this area, with its short, meandering streams, surprisingly holds some of Alaska's finest steelhead and silver salmon fishing. Except for the area surrounding Yakutat, it receives little visitation, despite its awesome sportfish potential. Access can be difficult and expensive, usually by small plane or boat from Yakutat or Cordova and the weather can be extremely unpredictable and potentially violent. But the species available include locally abundant steelhead, trophy silver salmon, cutthroat and rainbow trout, sockeyes, Dolly Varden, and even some king salmon and halibut. This is truly an unspoiled, unexplored paradise for the adventure angler.

1. YAKUTAT BAY

Location: North Gulf of Alaska, Yakutat area, 350 miles southeast of Anchorage.

Reference: Mount Saint Elias A-4, A-5, C-4, C-5, C-6, C-7, D-4, D-5, D-6.

Access: By boat or car. Boats may be launched from the Yakutat harbor or the mouth of the Situk River. Forest Road 9962 provides vehicle access to the Ocean Cape area.

Highlights: Excellent marine fishing for halibut (from June through August); good fishing for king salmon (in the first half of June), silver salmon (from mid-August through early September) and pink salmon (in the second half of July).

Species: (Chum salmon), Dolly Varden, halibut, king salmon, pink salmon, (red salmon), silver salmon.

Regulations: Closed to halibut fishing from January 1 through 31; closed to lingcod fishing from December 1 through April 30. For additional restrictions, consult the current Alaska Department of Fish and Game regulations or the ADF&G Yakutat office, (907) 747-3222.

Facilities: Lodging, a boat launch, water, fuel and guide services are available in the community of Yakutat.

Contact: For guide services, contact Yakutat Bay and River Charters, P.O. Box 7, Yakutat, AK 99689; (907) 784-3415. For lodging information, contact Blue Heron Inn, P.O. Box 254, Yakutat, AK 99689, (907) 784-3287; or Harlequin Lodge, P.O. Box 162, Yakutat, AK 99689, (907) 784-3341.

Description: Yakutat Bay is located just north of Cape Fairweather, in a spectacular setting. On the west, colossal glaciers (Malaspina, Hubbard and others) spill down from the Saint Elias Mountains, emptying their silty load into the waters of the bay. The east side, however, has small islands, bays and coves and a few streams flowing clear into the green of Yakutat Bay. Bottomfishing is the most popular angling activity here, but in the outer bay and beaches along the coast, there is some very productive but underutilized salmon fishing to be had. In years past, Yakutat was mostly a local fishery, but its appeal is broadening as anglers familiar with the region's salmon and trout streams discover more variety and excitement in nearby marine waters.

Halibut are very plentiful in the Yakutat area; some of the best fishing occurs in the deeper parts of the bay and all along the Gulf Coast from Ocean Cape southward. The shoals and reefs found off points and beaches offer perfect habitat for these huge flatfish, and locals haul in many fish in the 20- to 60-pound range, with occasional catches up to 300 pounds. Although there is good salmon fishing on the east side of the bay and off the mouths of rivers draining into the gulf, this fishery remains underutilized. Some feeder kings are available year-round in area waters, with mature kings taken in early summer prior to entering major spawning systems such as the Situk and Alsek rivers. The Yakutat area streams have some of the finest sportfishing for silver salmon in all Alaska; large schools of these tackle-busters cruise the shorelines near town awaiting the heavy fall rains that push them into freshwater. Pink salmon, cutthroat trout and Dolly Varden are also present in the marine waters of Yakutat and offer fair to good fishing during summer. While enjoying the world-class area stream fisheries for salmon and trout, you might want to give Yakutat Bay a try for some great halibut jigging and salmon trolling.

2. KIKLUKH RIVER

Location: North Gulf of Alaska drainage, 145 miles northwest of Yakutat, 220 miles southeast of Anchorage.

Reference: Bering Glacier A-7, A-8.

Access: By wheelplane from Cordova or Yakutat. Gravel bars next to the river are prime locations to land on the lower sections, but they can be tricky.

Highlights: One of the Gulf Coast's finest, unexploited streamfishing locations for silver salmon (in the first half of September) and cutthroat trout (from June through August).

Species: Cutthroat trout, silver salmon.

Regulations: Unbaited, artificial lures only from November 16 through September 14. For additional restrictions, consult the current Alaska Department of Fish and Game regulations or the ADF&G Yakutat office, (907) 747-3222.

Facilities: Lodging and guide services are available on the river.

Contact: For lodging and guide services, contact Alaska Gulf Coast Adventures, P.O. Box 1849, Cordova, AK 99574; (907) 784-3703 (from spring through fall). For an air taxi, contact Fishing & Flying, P.O. Box 2349, Cordova, AK 99574; (907) 424-3324.

Description: The Kiklukh River, also known as Eightmile Creek, drains a small glacial moraine just northeast of Cape Suckling near Suckling Hills. Meandering through extensive marshland in the upper sections, the lower river area is wooded with gravel beaches at its mouth. The Kiklukh is not large as rivers go, or particularly long, but it has some noteworthy possibilities for salmon and trout for anyone willing to brave the elements and explore a rarely visited area.

Every fall, strong runs of silver salmon enter the Kiklukh from the Gulf Coast. The river's clear, rushing waters and long runs provide perfect conditions for stalking and battling these sea-bright brutes. The last few miles above the mouth are especially noted for ideal flyfishing. Earlier in the season, the Kiklukh River has a good showing of sea-run cutthroat trout in the 10- to 20-inch range.

For a long time, the Kiklukh has been known only to a few locals and serious outsiders. Even today, it remains virtually hidden from most of the angling public. But with its amazing potential, this short river on the edge of the Bering Glacier promises to get the renown it deserves.

3. TSIU RIVER

Location: North Gulf of Alaska drainage, 125 miles northwest of
Yakutat, 235 miles southeast of Anchorage.

Reference: Bering Glacier A-6.

Access: By plane from Cordova or Yakutat. Wheelplanes can land on
gravel beaches and sand dunes next to the river. There is a landing
strip present on the lower river that is used regularly by charter
flights arriving in the area.

Highlights: A premier Gulf Coast silver salmon stream (from late August through mid-September), with good fishing for red salmon
(from late June through early July) and other possibilities.

Species: (Dolly Varden, pink salmon), red salmon, silver salmon, steelhead.

Regulations: Only unbaited, artificial lures may be used from November 16 through September 14. For additional restrictions, consult the
current Alaska Department of Fish and Game regulations or the
ADF&G Yakutat office, (907) 747-3222.

Facilities: Lodging and guide services are available on the river.

Contact: For lodging and guide services, contact the Alaska Wilderness Outfitting Company, P.O. Box 1516, Cordova, AK 99574;
(907) 424-5552. For an air taxi, contact Totem Air, P.O. Box 51,
Yakutat, AK 99689, (907) 784-3563; or Gulf Air, P.O. Box 37,
Yakutat, AK 99689, (907) 784-3240.

Description: The Tsiu is a very small clearwater river in the heart of
Yakataga State Game Refuge, just south of the Bering Glacier. It is
part of an extensive, braided, gravelly drainage that includes the
Tsivat River and at least a dozen tributaries and numerous small
ponds, creating perfect spawning habitat for major runs of silver
salmon. Phenomenally productive for its size, the Tsiu has been
called the "best coho stream in all of Alaska" by both area fishing
guides and biologists.

About two feet deep, the river rushes from upwellings at the
headwaters through an area resembling the Sahara Desert, complete
with sand dunes and very scant vegetation—ideal for flyfishing, yet
certainly not your typical Alaska stream surroundings. The river
slows the last two or three miles and widens considerably as it joins
the Tsivat system and the terrain becomes vegetated. Most anglers
concentrate on this lower section but access and fishing are good
throughout.

The Tsiu River system produces more salmon for its size than
perhaps any other stream in the world—almost 200,000 silvers in a

good year. The run traditionally begins in August, peaks during September, and tapers off in October. At the peak of the influx, these waters can literally "boil" with bright, aggressive coho.

Although much smaller, a run of red salmon earlier in the season provides good action for anglers in the know. Bright yarn and sparse bucktail flies are the most productive enticements to use.

While salmon most occupy the thoughts and energy of anglers visiting the Tsiu, the drainage is host to an as yet "undiscovered" fall run of steelhead trout. Very few have had the chance to participate in this fishery, largely because of the area's unpredictable, and notoriously raw, autumn weather. But indications are that fish up to at least 20 pounds or more are present, presenting a tantalizing challenge for those willing to brave the uncertainties of weather and the area's remoteness.

4. KALIAKH RIVER SYSTEM

Location: North Gulf of Alaska drainage, 115 miles northwest of Yakutat, 245 miles southeast of Anchorage.

Reference: Bering Glacier A-5, A-6.

Access: By plane from Cordova or Yakutat. Wheelplanes can land on gravel bars along or near clearwater streams. A road leads from Cape Yakataga, crosses the mainstem Kaliakh River, and runs up into the foothills with access to a few smaller tributaries.

Highlights: An "undiscovered" Gulf Coast drainage with outstanding possibilities for silver salmon (throughout September) and cutthroat trout (from June through August).

Species: Cutthroat trout, (red salmon), silver salmon.

Regulations: Only unbaited, artificial lures from November 16 through September 14. For additional restrictions, consult the current Alaska Department of Fish and Game regulations or the ADF&G Yakutat office, (907) 747-3222.

Facilities: No developed public facilities.

Contact: For an air taxi, contact Totem Air, P.O. Box 51, Yakutat, AK 99689, (907) 784-3563; or Gulf Air, P.O. Box 37, Yakutat, AK 99689, (907) 784-3240.

Description: The Kaliakh is a fairly large, silt-laden river system originating from the Robinson Mountains and the vast Bering Glacier, east of Cape Suckling. Numerous clearwater tributaries drain into it, providing ideal habitat for sportfish, particularly silver salmon. Of all the watersheds in the Yakutat area, the Kaliakh is probably one of the least fished, due to its remoteness and notorious weather, but it is potentially one of the finest streams around.

Anglers with the time and resources to venture to this isolated drainage will discover awesome silver salmon and sea-run cutthroat trout fishing. Both species are found throughout the Kaliakh and are encountered in the clearer sloughs, backwaters and streams. The Kulthieth River flowing into the midsection of the main river in particular is a hot spot for silvers and is often jammed with these sleek fighters during the peak of the run. (The lower Kulthieth is somewhat glacial, but the middle and upper sections usually run clear and are very fishable.) Cohos arrive here in full force towards the latter half of September, bringing dynamite action.

Another major tributary, the clear Chiuki River, or Stink Creek, is best known for its trophy-sized cutthroat trout. In summer and fall, it is possible to hook "cuts" weighing four and five pounds or more, with silver salmon fishing unparalleled at the mouth during the first part of September.

The Kaliakh River is a true wilderness system, with all the qualities associated with a premier Alaska fishing stream—abundant angling, very little or nonexistent pressure, classic scenery and undisturbed wildlife. Enjoy it while it's still unspoiled and leave it the way you found it.

5. SITUK RIVER SYSTEM

Location: North Gulf of Alaska drainage, five miles east of Yakutat, 375 miles southeast of Anchorage.

Reference: Yakutat B-5, C-4, C-5.

Access: By car or floatplane from Yakutat. Forest Highway 10 crosses the midsection of the river; hiking and tractor trails in the area provide additional access downstream. Gravel roads along the Gulf Coast lead to flats near the mouth of river. Floatplanes can be used for the short hop to Situk, Mountain and Redfield lakes.

Highlights: Northern Southeast's number-one streamfishing location, world famous for steelhead. Excellent angling for king salmon (from mid-June through early July), silver salmon (in the first half of September), red salmon (in the first half of July), pink salmon (from late July through early August) and steelhead trout (from late March through mid-May and October through early December).

Species: Chum salmon, cutthroat trout, Dolly Varden, king salmon, pink salmon, rainbow trout, red salmon, silver salmon, steelhead.

Regulations: Unbaited artificial lures only. For additional restrictions, consult the current Alaska Department of Fish and Game regulations or the ADF&G Yakutat office, (907) 747-3222.

Facilities: Commercial lodging and a boat launch are available. The town of Yakutat, a few miles away, has sporting goods, groceries, guide services, fuel, water and hotels. Forest service cabins are located on Situk Lake and Situk River.

Contact: For lodging and guide services, contact Glacier Bear Lodge, P.O. Box 303, Yakutat, AK 99689, (907) 784-3202; Yakutat Bay and River Charters, P.O. Box 7, Yakutat, AK 99689, (907) 784-3415; Yakutat Lodge, P.O. Box 287, Yakutat, AK 99689, (907) 784-3232; or Blue Heron Inn, P.O. Box 254, Yakutat, AK 99689, (907) 784-3287. For cabin rental information, contact Yakutat Ranger District, P.O. Box 327, Yakutat, AK 99689; (907) 784-3359.

Description: The Situk River of Yakutat certainly isn't lacking notoriety among the world angling fraternity. Small in size, it is a giant of unbelievably productive fishing for a variety of prized sport species, particularly steelhead and salmon. With its easy access, it has been an extremely popular destination for years. Draining three headwater lakes near Russell Fjord in Tongass National Forest, the Situk runs clear, through the wooded Yakutat Forelands into the Gulf of Alaska, some 18 miles away. Small and brushy, it does have some excellent stretches for fly and spincasting, particularly the lower end and outlets of the lakes.

The Situk has become a legend for its abundant spring and fall runs of steelhead trout. These stocks are wild, native fish that offer some of the most exciting fishing available for the species, with runs in good years that jam in like cordwood in some of the better holes. The river receives a major influx of sea-run rainbow in September and October, but the more abundant and spunky spring steelhead (April and May) give the Situk its claim to fame.

Quite a few salmon are also present in the Situk from May into October, providing some of Southeast's best streamfishing. Kings averaging 25 pounds mix with flotillas of red salmon and completely pack certain stretches of the system. Pinks jam in later on, followed by a run of silver salmon that produces some of the highest catch rates in Alaska. Some trophy cohos (20 to 23 pounds) wrestled out of the river from time to time add yet more appeal to this sizzling hot fishery. Cutthroat, rainbow trout and Dolly Varden are taken incidentally, with the best areas to target being the adjoining Situk, Redfield and Mountain lakes.

There are several ways to sample the superb Situk. Most anglers begin by fishing either the mouth or the sections of river up and downstream from the bridge (nine miles out from town). Both these areas are easily accessible by road, and have well-used trails for hiking along the river. A popular option is to rent a boat in town and float and fish down from the bridge, a trip that can be done in one to three days. Yet another possibility is to fly into one of the lakes and camp and fish or float down. (It is very brushy, so be sure to bring a saw and axe.) No matter how you decide to fish it, the Situk is definitely a "must do" river for anyone aspiring to sample some of the very best of Alaska's streamfishing.

6. ITALIO RIVER SYSTEM

Location: North Gulf of Alaska drainage, 25 miles southeast of Yakutat, 380 miles southeast of Anchorage.

Reference: Yakutat B-3, B-4.

Access: By plane from Yakutat. Wheelplanes are traditionally used to access the river, landing on the tidal flats near the mouth. At high tide, boats may enter the mouth. Trails lead upstream. It is also possible to float the river in order to reach otherwise inaccessible areas.

Highlights: Another phenomenal Yakutat area stream, world famous for its silver salmon (from late August through mid-September). Also good fishing for cutthroat (in May and September) and Dolly Varden (from July through September).

Species: (Chum salmon), cutthroat trout, Dolly Varden, (king salmon, pink salmon), rainbow trout, (red salmon), silver salmon, (steelhead).

Regulations: Unbaited, artificial lures only from November 16 through September 14. For additional restrictions, consult the current Alaska Department of Fish and Game regulations or the ADF&G Yakutat office, (907) 747-3222.

Facilities: A forest service cabin is available a few miles from the main river.

Contact: For cabin rental information, contact the Yakutat Ranger District, P.O. Box 327, Yakutat, AK 99689; (907) 784-3359. For an air taxi, contact Totem Air, P.O. Box 51, Yakutat, AK 99689, (907) 784-3563; or Gulf Air, P.O. Box 37, Yakutat, AK 99689, (907) 784-3240.

Description: Draining several lakes at the foot of the Brabazon Range in Tongass National Forest east of Yakutat, the clear-flowing Italio is one of the premier silver salmon streams in Southeast Alaska, with a consistent history of yielding trophy fish (20 pounds or more). Comprised of several branches and tributaries, the river changed its main channel during the giant 1964 earthquake, though little changed in the way of the great fishing. (The forest service cabin was once at the river's edge, but since the quake shifted the river's course, a 3.5-mile hike is required to reach the mainstem Italio.)

There are three main branches of the Italio, which are popularly referred to as the "Middle," the "Old" and the "Little." Sharing much the same headwaters, the Middle and Old branches flow out into the Dangerous River Delta, while Little Italio drains into the lower portion of Akwe River. Silver salmon is the most sought-after and abundant fish species in the system, and runs begin ascending from the Gulf of Alaska in August. The fishing doesn't peak until September, however, when thousands of these powerful salmonids move in following the heavy fall rains. Lasting well into October, the Italio's famous silver run typically yields catches weighing in the mid- to upper teens, with some 20- to 23-pound fish not uncommon.

Dolly Varden are not particularly abundant in the Yakutat subregion, although they are present in good numbers in the Italio, along with some cutthroat trout and even a few rainbow. (There are some rumored steelhead, as well.) The best spots are the upper reaches of the system and in the lakes, with good fishing possible. Next to the Situk River, the Italio with its trophy cohos is the most popular destination in the Yakutat area. Fish it in the fall someday, and you'll understand why.

7. AKWE RIVER SYSTEM

Location: North Gulf of Alaska drainage, 32 miles southeast of Yakutat, 400 miles southeast of Anchorage.

Reference: Yakutat A-3, B-3.

Access: By plane from Yakutat. Wheelplanes often access the river by landing on gravel bars near the mouth or at the confluences with clearwater tributaries. Boats may enter the mouth and run some nine miles upstream through the slough.

Highlights: A lesser-known Gulf Coast stream with good possibilities for silver salmon (from late August through mid-September) and cutthroat trout (from June through August).

Species: (Chum salmon), cutthroat trout, Dolly Varden, (king salmon), red salmon, silver salmon.

Regulations: Unbaited, artificial lures only from November 16 through September 14. For additional restrictions, consult the current Alaska Department of Fish and Game regulations or the ADF&G Yakutat office, (907) 747-3222.

Facilities: A forest service cabin is on nearby Square Lake, a tributary lake to the Ustay River.

Contact: For cabin rental information, contact the Yakutat Ranger District, P.O. Box 327, Yakutat, AK 99689; (907) 784-3359. For an air taxi, contact Totem Air, P.O. Box 51, Yakutat, AK 99689, (907) 784-3563; or Gulf Air, P.O. Box 37, Yakutat, AK 99689, (907) 784-3240.

Description: The glacial, green waters of the Akwe originate from Akwe Lake at the base of the Brabazon Range, east of Yakutat. Since glaciers and snow fields dominate the mountainous terrain at the headwaters, there is a fair amount of silt in the river during the summer months. However, there are several clearwater tributaries anglers can explore for terrific salmon and trout fishing.

Meandering through forests and marshlands toward the coast, the last nine miles of the Akwe widen into a long stillwater slough as it meets the Ustay River, a large glacial tributary. Salmon, trout and charr often use this slough as a feeding and staging area prior to moving upstream, but because of the glacial silt in the water, relatively few anglers fish this section.

A large run of silver salmon are available every fall, along with a sizable population of cutthroat trout and fair numbers of reds (June through July) and Dolly Varden charr. Fishing for both cohos and cutthroats is considered to be excellent, but knowing anglers concentrate on the mouths of clear streams and sloughs to get the best action possible. Around the first of June, before the river begins shedding a lot of silt, a few king salmon can even be picked up on the lower few miles of river.

The Akwe does not produce the number of salmon and other species that neighboring systems do, but it receives much less angling pressure. It can offer outstanding fishing during the height of the season, usually in late summer and fall.

8. EAST ALSEK RIVER

Location: North Gulf of Alaska drainage, 60 miles southeast of Yakutat, 420 miles southeast of Anchorage.

Reference: Yakutat A-1, A-2.

Access: By wheelplane from Yakutat. There is an airstrip at mid-river near the forest service cabin. Also, the lower river near the mouth has gravel beaches ideal for landings. Hiking and tractor trails lead along the river.

Highlights: High-potential Yakutat area stream, with good fishing for king salmon (in the first half of June), silver salmon (from late August through mid-September), red salmon (from late July through early August) and chum salmon (in early August).

Species: Chum salmon, king salmon, (pink salmon), red salmon, silver salmon.

Regulations: Unbaited, artificial lures only from November 16 through September 14. For additional restrictions, consult the current Alaska Department of Fish and Game regulations or the ADF&G Yakutat office, (907) 747-3222.

Facilities: A forest service cabin is available.

Contact: For cabin rental information, contact Yakutat Ranger District, P.O. Box 327, Yakutat, AK 99689; (907) 784-3359. For an air taxi, contact Totem Air, P.O. Box 51, Yakutat, AK 99689, (907) 784-3563; or Gulf Air, P.O. Box 37, Yakutat, AK 99689, (907) 784-3240.

Description: The East Alsek River, or East River, is a short coastal drainage just a few miles south of the vast Alsek River system and located in Glacier Bay National Preserve. Draining into Dry Bay, East Alsek shares a common mouth with the larger Alsek and the clear Doame River. Despite its somewhat reserved appearance, the river contains tremendously productive fish habitat.

Although merely an upwelling of groundwater from the glacial Alsek River, the ice-cold East Alsek pumps out astonishing numbers of red salmon for its size. Only about eight miles long, the river sees returns of some 200,000 of these feisty fighters in a normal year. The run arrives much later—three to four weeks—than usual for the species in the Yakutat area, with above-average-sized fish (seven pounds) available to flyfishermen. If conditions are perfect and anglers hit it just right, they will also catch a small run of kings entering the mouth of the river in early summer, which can provide some good, even excellent, action for a very brief period before moving on up to the glacial Alsek River. The only substantial run of chum salmon around Yakutat is found here as well, with this species particularly abundant on the lower river in late summer. Later in fall, a good run of cohos puts on a finale for this amazing fishery.

A forest service cabin on the west side of East Alsek provides access to the middle and upper sections of the river, and to two smaller tributaries. This is a developing fishery with high potential, especially for flyfishing. It's destined no doubt to become one of the new hot spots in the Yakutat subregion, as the access is relatively easy and inexpensive.

9. DOAME RIVER SYSTEM

Location: North Gulf of Alaska drainage, 65 miles southeast of Yakutat, 425 miles southeast of Anchorage.

Reference: Yakutat A-1.

Access: By plane from Yakutat. Wheelplanes can use gravel bars along the river and beaches near the mouth as landing sites. Upper Doame Lake is suitable for smaller floatplanes, but caution is advised.

Highlights: One of the prettiest rivers in the Yakutat area, with excellent fishing for silver salmon (from late August through mid-September); good fishing for red salmon (from late June through early July) and cutthroat and rainbow trout (from August through September).

Species: (Chum salmon), cutthroat trout, rainbow trout, red salmon, silver salmon.

Regulations: Unbaited, artificial lures only from November 16 through September 14. For additional restrictions, consult the current Alaska Department of Fish and Game regulations or the ADF&G Yakutat office, (907) 747-3222.

Facilities: No developed public facilities.

Contact: For an air taxi, contact Totem Air, P.O. Box 51, Yakutat, AK 99689, (907) 784-3563; or Gulf Air, P.O. Box 37, Yakutat, AK 99689, (907) 784-3240.

Description: The Doame River system consists of a series of small lakes and streams originating from the Deception Hills in Glacier Bay National Park and Preserve, only a few miles south of glacial Alsek River. Meandering through a densely wooded region containing seven lakes, its crystal-blue waters are perfectly suited for angling, especially sight-fishing the river's large schools of salmon as they move upstream from hole to hole. Virtually an untapped fishery, the Doame is destined to become a classic.

Sharing a common outlet with both the East Alsek and Alsek rivers, the Doame receives strong runs of silver and red salmon, along with a few chums. The Doame's sockeyes arrive about a month earlier than those of the East Alsek, and average less in weight. While they are not quite so numerous, they nonetheless present a delightful challenge. Silver salmon fishing on the Doame is much better, with substantial runs. They are available, like the reds, throughout the length of the river from mouth to headwater lakes, and are most abundant during late summer and fall. Some worthwhile fishing for cutthroat and rainbow trout is also reported from the system, primarily in the lakes of the upper drainage, but there have been a few reports of action in the lower river sections as well.

In years past, the Doame has been overshadowed by the spectacular Situk and Italio fisheries nearby. But as more people search out new, uncrowded territory, this "sleeper," like the East Alsek, will gain increasing notoriety for high-quality streamfishing in a remote and very scenic setting.

Southeast is Alaska's saltwater fishing mecca.

REGION 2
JUNEAU-
NORTH TONGASS

The Juneau area encompasses the portion of the Panhandle from Cape Fairweather to Upper Stephens Passage and includes the northern tip of Chichagof and north Admiralty islands, Glacier Bay, Icy Strait and Lynn Canal. All five salmon, some limited steelhead, cutthroat trout, Dolly Varden charr, kokanee and even some rare brook trout and grayling are the species found here.

Along with the Ketchikan area, this is the major saltwater angling hub for Southeast, with some of the finest marine fisheries for salmon and halibut in all of Alaska, if not the world. Most of the effort for salmon occurs as an inside terminal fishery targeting fish bound for important spawning systems like the Taku and Chilkat rivers. Sport anglers do well fishing familiar trolling drags in waters nearby: northern Gastineau Channel along Shelter Island; "The Breadline" from Bridget Cove to Tee Harbor; Berner's Bay in southern Lynn Canal; Auke Bay-Fritz Cove; Taku Inlet and the northern end of Douglas and Admiralty Islands. Occasionally, ventures as far as Icy Strait and Cross Sound are made, often with spectacular results. The productive outer waters of Cross Sound, Chichagof and Glacier Bay are more effectively accessed from local towns like Elfin Cove, Gustavus and Hoonah.

With the most extensive roadside access of any city in Southeast, Juneau has numerous opportunities for both freshwater and saltwater shoreline day fishing, although some locations can be crowded during the peak time of fish abundance. Some of the more popular locations and species are: Cowee, Montana and Auke creeks and surrounding bays for salmon (silver, chum and pink) and Dolly Varden; Gastineau Channel near the Gastineau hatchery for king and coho salmon (a considerable amount of new fishing has been created by hatchery releases); Picnic Cove on north Douglas Island; and Eagle River Beach for Dolly Varden. The area's most significant freshwater fisheries occur at nearby Turner Lake and in the rivers around Haines (such as Chilkat and Chilkoot).

10. CROSS SOUND

Location: North of Chichagof Island, 75 miles west of Juneau, 510 miles southeast of Anchorage.

Reference: Mount Fairweather A-1, A-2, A-3, B-2, B-3.

Access: By boat or floatplane. Boat traffic comes mainly from area communities and sportfishing lodges in Hoonah, Gustavus and Elfin Cove. Floatplanes, however, are used to access these communities and lodges from Juneau or other major population centers in Southeast.

Highlights: An angler's mecca with great marine wildlife viewing, known for its great salmon and halibut opportunities.

Species: Chum salmon, (cutthroat trout), Dolly Varden, halibut, king salmon, pink salmon, (red salmon), silver salmon, (steelhead).

Regulations: For details on halibut and ling cod seasons, consult the current Alaska Department of Fish and Game regulations or the ADF&G Douglas office, (907) 465-4320.

Facilities: Commercial lodging and guide services are available.

Contact: For lodging and guide services, contact Elfin Cove Sportfishing Lodge, Glacier View, Elfin Cove, AK 99825, (907) 697-3131 (in summer) or (206) 228-7092 (in winter); Elfin Cove Charters, P.O. Box 69, Elfin Cove, AK 99825, (800) 323-5346; Tanaku Lodge, General Delivery, Elfin Cove, AK 99825, (907) 239-2205; or Cross Sound Lodge, P.O. Box 85, Elfin Cove, AK 99825, (800) 323-5346. For an air taxi, contact Ward Air, 8991 Yandukin Drive, Juneau, AK 99801, (800) 478-9150 or (907) 789-9150; or Glacier Bay Airways, P.O. Box 1, Gustavus, AK 99826, (907) 697-2249.

Description: Cross Sound is a fairly wide passage between Chichagof Island, Yakobi Island and the Glacier Bay National Park mainland. Several large bays adjoin the sound, and islands of all sizes are scattered along its edges. Brady Glacier, a huge mass of ice dropping into Taylor Bay in the northern part of Cross Sound, contributes to the water's greenish tint.

Much of the area is within the boundaries of Tongass National Forest, and the sound is home to incredible numbers of marine wildlife and fish. Along with Icy Strait to the east, Cross Sound serves as a major migration corridor for the millions of salmon bound for spawning streams throughout northern Southeast Alaska, thus attracting predators such as seals, sea lions, whales, birds and, of course, sport anglers.

Situated on the Alaska Gulf Coast, the area's weather can often be unpredictable and anglers venturing into the sound must be prepared for the unexpected. Aside from that, the fishing in Cross Sound is fantastic for salmon and bottomfish—the sound has been said to host some of the best salt water fisheries in the state. Anglers fish the area mainly by boat, concentrating their efforts on obvious lies and feeding grounds, such as points, tidal rips and narrow passages for salmon, and shoals and reefs for halibut.

Anglers who fish this area come mostly from local communities such as Gustavus and Hoonah, a few from as far away as Juneau, and some from as near as shoreline lodges in Elfin Cove. As is common throughout most of Southeast, the main species targeted are king and silver salmon and halibut. Visitors can expect superb action for these and other salmon and bottomfish species. Feeder kings and halibut are present year-round, but are more frequently caught from spring to fall. Mature, prespawning kings arrive in late spring and early summer (from May through June), offering some of the best action in the region, while larger-than-average silvers (in the second half of August), healthy numbers of ocean-bright chum (in the first half of July) and pink salmon (in the second half of July) provide excitement in late summer. "Barn-door" halibut are active in the sound from spring into fall (from May through September) as concentrations of these flatfish move into shallow water to feed. Fishing is outstanding, with many trophy fish taken and record-size catches possible.

Some of the more popular and proven locations to try in the sound include: Graves Harbor; Yakobi Island—Cape Bingham, Surge Bay; Lisianski Inlet; Port Althorp—Point Lucan, Threemile Island and Elfin Cove; and North Indian Pass—Point Wimbledon.

11. ICY STRAIT

Location: North of Chichagof Island, 35 miles west of Juneau, 525 miles southeast of Anchorage.

Reference: Mount Fairweather A-1, B-1, B-2; Juneau A-3, A-4, A-5, A-6, B-4, B-5, B-6.

Access: By boat and plane. Most anglers access Icy Strait from Juneau by boat, but some choose to use planes and land at the towns of Gustavus or Hoonah and travel by boat from there. Surf-casting is possible, but to reach the better fishing, a boat is recommended.

Highlights: Alaska's number-one marine fishing location, with excellent fishing for king salmon (from mid-May through late June), silver salmon (in the second half of August), pink salmon (in the second half of July) and halibut (from May through September); good fishing for chum salmon (in the first half of July).

Species: Chum salmon, (cutthroat trout), Dolly Varden, halibut, king salmon, pink salmon, (red salmon), silver salmon, (steelhead).

Regulations: For details on halibut and ling cod seasons, consult the current Alaska Department of Fish and Game regulations or the ADF&G Douglas office, (907) 465-4320.

Facilities: Commercial lodging and guide services are available.

Contact: For lodging and guide services, contact the W.T. Fugarwe Lodge, P.O. Box 27, Gustavus, AK 99826, (907) 697-3262; Gustavus Marine Charters, P.O. Box 81, Gustavus, AK 99826, (907) 697-2233; Glacier Bay Lodge, 1500 Metropolitan Park Building, Olive Way at Boren Avenue, Seattle, WA 98101; (907) 697-3221 (in summer) or (206) 624-8551 (in winter); or Hoonah Charters, P.O. Box 384, Hoonah, AK 99829; (907) 945-3334. For an air taxi, contact Ward Air, 8991 Yandukin Drive, Juneau, AK 99801, (800) 478-9150 or (907) 789-9150; or Glacier Bay Airways, P.O. Box 1, Gustavus, AK 99826, (907) 697-2249.

Description: Icy Strait's cold, blue waters split Chichagof Island from the mainland and Chilkat Range, bordering the world-famous Glacier Bay National Park and Wilderness. The strait is 10 to 15 miles wide and 55 miles long, connecting Cross Sound with Chatham Strait. It serves as the largest migrational corridor for mainland-bound salmon in northern Southeast, and is an active feeding ground for halibut and other bottomfish. Area waters teem with a variety of marine animals, particularly whales, birds and seals, attracting substantial numbers of visitors to view and photograph them.

The productivity of these waters is nothing less than phenomenal; Icy Strait is regarded by many—anglers, guides and biologists—as the top saltwater fishing destination in all of Alaska. Millions of salmon pour through the strait bound for inland spawning streams starting in April and continuing to October, with untold numbers of halibut scattered throughout. Most anglers arrive by boats, guided or private, from the Juneau area or the local towns of Hoonah and Gustavus. King and silver salmon and halibut are undoubtedly the favorite target species, with excellent action almost guaranteed. Smaller feeder kings are available year-round, but the larger mainland spawners show up later in the spring and entertain anglers until midsummer. The late summer silver salmon fishing is especially noteworthy, having considerable trophy potential. (The current state record fish of 26 pounds was taken from Icy Strait and several silvers over 20 pounds are caught there every season.)

Halibut are plentiful and better fishing for this species would be hard to find anywhere in the world. Although present year-round, most effort for these behemoths occurs from late spring to early fall when larger fish can be found in moderately shallow water. The current state record holder, a fish of some 440 pounds, was pulled from the bottom here, and flatties over 300 pounds are caught regularly. It is not uncommon to catch 40 to 50 halibut a day from some of the better locations in Icy Strait.

Other species not to be ignored are the chum and pink salmon. A flood of ocean-bright pinks comes through in midsummer and can be caught on virtually every cast. Just before the pinks peak in area waters, huge runs of chums arrive. Chums have never been known to hit anglers' offerings with any vigor, especially in salt water, but with the fish streaming through in concentrated schools the action can be quite hot.

Hot spot locations around Icy Strait are: Chichagof Island—Idaho Inlet, Spasski and Mud bays, Point Adolphus, Burger, Neck and Eagle points, Flynn Cove, Harry Island, Hoonah Island/Gendey Channel and Whitestone Harbor; Point Dundas; South Passage; Lemesurier Island—Willoughby Cove and North Passage; Point Carolus; Glacier Bay—Bartlett Cove, Young Island and Beardslee Entrance; Point Gustavus; Icy Passage; Pleasant Island Reef; Port Frederick—Halibut Island, Crist Point, Point Sophia and The Narrows; Excursion Inlet—Sawmill Bay; Porpoise Islands; Sisters Reef; The Sisters; Spasski Island; Homeshore; Couverden Island/Swanson Harbor; Rocky Island; and Hanus Reef.

12. UPPER LYNN CANAL

Location: Haines/Skagway area, 25 miles northwest of Juneau, 515 miles southeast of Anchorage.

Reference: Skagway A-1, A-2, B-1, B-2.

Access: Primarily by boat from Haines, Skagway or Juneau. The Chilkat and Chilkoot inlets and area waters are fished by boat out of Haines and Skagway, while the southern canal around Berner's Bay is nearer Juneau and is also boat accessible. Shorefishing is possible from the road system in Haines (Mud Bay Road) and Juneau (Juneau Veterans Memorial/Glacier Highway).

Highlights: A very scenic Alaska marine setting, with good fishing for king salmon, silver salmon, pink salmon, Dolly Varden and halibut.

Species: (Chum salmon, cutthroat trout), Dolly Varden, halibut, king salmon, pink salmon, (red salmon), silver salmon, (steelhead).

Regulations: For details on halibut and ling cod seasons, and special restrictions for Chilkat Inlet king salmon, consult the current Alaska Department of Fish and Game regulations or the ADF&G Juneau office, (907) 465-4180.

Facilities: Hotels, gas, lodging, campgrounds, groceries, sporting goods, boat rental and launching and guide services are available in Haines, Skagway and Juneau.

Contact: For guide services, contact Auke Bay Sportfishing Charters, P.O. Box 32744, Juneau, AK 99803, (907) 789-2562 or (907) 789-9783; Islander Charters, P.O. Box 20927, Juneau, AK 99802, (907) 780-4419; or Puffin Charters, 4418 Mint Way, Juneau, AK 99801, (907) 789-0001. For lodging information, contact Captain's Choice Motel, P.O. Box 392, Haines, AK 99827, (800) 247-7153 or (907) 766-3111; or Adlersheim Lodge, P.O. Box 210447, Auke Bay, AK 99821, (907) 780-4778. For an air taxi, contact Ward Air, 8991 Yandukin Drive, Juneau, AK 99801; (800) 478-9150 or (907) 789-9150.

Description: Lynn Canal is situated in a very picturesque part of northern Southeast Alaska, with the snow-clad Chilkat Range in the west, Takshanuk Mountains in the north, and Chilkoot Range and the Coast Mountains in the east. Included in the upper Lynn Canal area are Chilkat, Chilkoot, Lutak and Taiya inlets—four significant fjords within Tongass National Forest—and the coastline south to Berner's Bay. The many glacial rivers and creeks pouring into the north end of Lynn Canal give its water a greenish-grey tint. There are numerous clearwater streams along upper Lynn Canal, however, which receive strong runs of salmon and charr.

Though perhaps not as productive as waters to the west or south, upper Lynn Canal holds some great fishing. There are some year-round feeder kings as well as mature prespawners. Early summer (the first half of June) is the best time to visit as moderate numbers of these popular sportfish migrate through on their way to local rivers. A bit later in the season, about midsummer (from late July through early August), a strong run of pink salmon arrives and keeps anglers busy. Chilkat Inlet and Berner's Bay are the best places to catch these ocean-fresh pinks. Silvers show up in fall (from late August through late September) and are present until the snow flies, with Berner's Bay and Lutak Inlet being the best spots to intercept fish bound for area waters. Although present year-round, halibut are at their best in late summer, with the better catches made in the outer areas of Chilkat Inlet and south along the coast to William Henry and Berner's bays. Sea-run Dolly Varden are present and offer good action in early summer (in June and July) along beaches and points of the Chilkat Peninsula and Berner's Bay.

The upper Lynn Canal is perfect for day trips out of Haines, Skagway or Juneau for the angler short on time or just wanting to sample a little bit of Alaska's renowned fishing.

Hot spots in the canal include: Chilkat Inlet—Letnikof Cove, Glacier and Anchorage points; Chilkoot Inlet—Taiya and Lutak inlets, Skagway Harbor, Portage and Carr's coves; Sullivan Island; Point Sherman; William Henry Bay; and Berner's Bay—Point Saint Mary, Echo Cove and Point Bridget.

13. FAVORITE/SAGINAW CHANNELS

Location: North of Admiralty Island, 25 miles west of Juneau, 550 miles southeast of Anchorage.

Reference: Juneau B-3, C-3.

Access: Primarily by boat from the Juneau area to Shelter Island and "The Breadline." Boat launches are present in several locations between Juneau and Berner's Bay on the Glacier Highway with easy access to both channels. Surf-casting also possible from locations along the highway system.

Highlights: An all-time local favorite, with good fishing for king salmon (in the second half of May), silver salmon (mid-August) and halibut (from June through August).

Species: Chum salmon, cutthroat trout, Dolly Varden, halibut, king salmon, pink salmon, silver salmon.

Regulations: For details on halibut and ling cod seasons, consult the current Alaska Department of Fish and Game regulations or the ADF&G Juneau office, (907) 465-4180.

Facilities: Boat rentals and launching, gas, sporting goods, lodges, hotels, groceries and guide services are available in Juneau, Auke Bay and Dotsons Landing.

Contact: For guide services, contact Auke Bay Sportfishing Charters, P.O. Box 32744, Juneau, AK 99803, (907) 789-2562 or (907) 789-9783; Islander Charters, P.O. Box 20927, Juneau, AK 99802, (907) 780-4419; or Puffin Charters, 4418 Mint Way, Juneau, AK 99801, (907) 789-0001. For lodging information, contact Adlersheim Lodge, P.O. Box 210447, Auke Bay, AK 99821, (907) 780-4778; or Best Western Country Lane Inn, 9300 Glacier Highway, Juneau, AK 99801, (800) 528-1234 or (907) 789-5005.

Description: For several decades, the clear blue waters of Favorite and Saginaw channels have been a major attraction for Juneau area anglers. Between the mainland and Mansfield Peninsula just west of Juneau, nine-mile-long Shelter Island creates the two channels that connect Lynn Canal and Stephens Passage. Untold numbers of migrating and feeding salmon and bottomfish move through every season and are traditionally harvested by both commercial and sportfishing fleets.

The best way to enjoy this fishery is by boat. The west side and south end of Shelter Island and all along the mainland coast of Favorite Channel are top locations for king and silver salmon, while mid-channel islands and reefs are great for halibut. "The Breadline," stretching from Tee Harbor to Benjamin Island along the mainland, is a longtime favorite trolling drag. Feeder kings are available year-round with the better action occurring in late spring and early summer when mature fish arrive. Silvers are abundant in late summer throughout the area. Some of the best fishing is found around Shelter Island, where coho in excess of 20 pounds are taken regularly. Fair numbers of chum and pink salmon and Dolly Varden are present, in addition to a few cutthroat trout. The trout and charr are most often encountered near the mouth of Peterson Creek and at various points and narrows in Favorite and Saginaw channels, while both natural and hatchery-enhanced runs of pinks and chums pass through on their way to Gastineau Channel outside Juneau. Decent numbers of halibut are taken from deeper parts of the channels, with most averaging 15 to 20 pounds and occasional catches over 100 pounds.

Favorite and Saginaw channels are perfect for one-day fishing excursions out of Juneau. Hot spot locations to try are: Favorite Channel—Benjamin, Gull and Aaron islands, Poundstone Rock, Eagle Reef, "The Breadline," Tee Harbor and Point Lena; Lincoln Island—Lincoln Anchorage; North Pass; Shelter Island—Handtrollers Cove, South Shelter and Favorite Reef; Saginaw Channel—Point Retreat, Barlow Point and Barlow Islands.

14. UPPER STEPHENS PASSAGE

Location: North of Admiralty Island, 10 miles south of Juneau, 565 miles southeast of Anchorage.

Reference: Juneau A-1, A-2, A-3, B-1, B-2, B-3; Taku River A-6; Sitka C-1, D-1; Sumdum C-5, C-6, D-5, D-6.

Access: By boat and car to the Douglas Island, Auke Bay and Gastineau Channel area in upper Stephens Passage. Locations along the shores of Admiralty Island and the eastern mainland are strictly for boaters. There are several roads extending out from Juneau that can be used to reach good surf-casting spots, the major ones being Glacier, North Douglas and Douglas highways, Egan Drive and Thane Road.

Highlights: The perfect location for overnight boat trips. Great silver salmon fishing (from late August through late September), with good fishing for king salmon (from late May through mid-July), pink salmon (from mid- through late July), Dolly Varden (in May) and halibut (from mid-June through late August).

Species: Chum salmon, cutthroat trout, Dolly Varden, halibut, king salmon, pink salmon, (red salmon), silver salmon, (steelhead).

Regulations: For details on halibut and ling cod seasons, and special restrictions on Auke Bay Dolly Varden, consult the current Alaska Department of Fish and Game regulations or the ADF&G Juneau office, (907) 465-4180.

Facilities: Hotels, lodges, sporting goods, groceries, gas, boat launches and rentals and guide services are available in and around the greater Juneau area.

Contact: For guide services, contact Auke Bay Sportfishing Charters, P.O. Box 32744, Juneau, AK 99803, (907) 789-2562 or (907) 789-9783; Islander Charters, P.O. Box 20927, Juneau, AK 99802, (907) 780-4419; or Puffin Charters, 4418 Mint Way, Juneau, AK 99801, (907) 789-0001. For lodging information, contact Blueberry Lodge, 9436 North Douglas Highway, Juneau, AK 99801, (907) 463-5886; or Westmark Juneau, 51 West Egan Drive, Juneau, AK 99801, (907) 586-6900 or (800) 544-0970. For an air taxi, contact Ward Air, 8991 Yandukin Drive, Juneau, AK 99801; (907) 789-9150 or (800) 478-9150. For more information, contact Admiralty Island National Monument, P.O. Box 2097, Juneau, AK 99803; (907) 586-8790.

Description: Upper Stephens Passage is a fairly narrow body of water extending from Shelter Island and Favorite and Saginaw channels in the north, to the mouth of Seymour Canal and Windham Bay in the south. The passage parts Admiralty Island from the mainland within Tongass National Forest. It has several large fjords within its domain—Taku Inlet, Port Snettisham, and Tracy and Endicott arms, along with Seymour Canal and several smaller bays and coves. The rugged Coast Mountains are clearly seen in the north, and large glacial rivers pour into the passage from the mainland.

Area fish populations are healthy and strong in Upper Stephens Passage with a mix of natural and hatchery-enhanced runs of salmon returning to its semi-glacial waters. Feeder kings (10 to 15 pounds) are available throughout the year with peak abundance in midsummer, while mature fish (20 to 25 pounds) are at their best in late spring and early summer. The prespawning, wild kings make for Taku River at the head of Taku Inlet; adult hatchery fish are primarily destined for Juneau area release sites. Large hatchery-enhanced runs of silver, chum and pink salmon also flood the upper passage starting in July and continuing until October. Waters adjacent to the Gastineau Hatchery are prime locations to scout for big schools of salmon. Boaters and surf-casters can both enjoy these artificial runs, with offshore areas producing best early in the season and nearshore locations proving better later on. Although chum salmon are only caught incidentally out in the open sea, action can be quite good at the terminal fisheries.

Other species popular with local anglers include Dolly Varden and halibut. Sea-run Dollies are present along beaches and stream mouths through much of spring and summer, and halibut and other bottomfish are taken in deeper parts of the passage all summer long. A few cutthroat trout are also available and usually taken while fishing for charr.

Anglers looking for fast action on short trips are well advised to look into the fisheries of Upper Stephens Passage around Douglas Island outside Juneau. For longer excursions, however, the main passage beyond Taku Inlet is great for wild runs of salmon. There is an abundance of hot spots in this area: Mansfield Peninsula—Piling Point and Colt and Horse islands; Point Louisa; Portland Island; Auke Bay; Cothlan Island; Spuhn Island; Gibby Rock; Douglas Island—Outer, False Outer, Middle and Inner points, Icy Point, White Marker, Marmion Island and Point Hilda; Scull Island; North Admiralty Island—Young Bay, Admiralty and Green coves, Point Young, Stink Creek, Outer Oliver Inlet, False Point Arden and Point Arden; Gastineau Channel—Salmon and Sheep creeks, Dupont and Point Salisbury; Taku Inlet—Point Bishop, Cooper and Greely points and falls; East Admiralty Island—Cove and Station points, Doty Cove and South Island; Circle Point; Slocum Inlet; Grand Island; Suicide Cove; Grave Point; Taku Harbor; Stockade Point; Midway Island; Holkham Bay—Round Islets, Wood Spit; Point Hugh; Seymour Canal—Flaw Point/Mole Harbor and Swan Island; and Windham Bay.

15. CHILKAT RIVER SYSTEM

Location: North Lynn Canal drainage, 85 miles northwest of Juneau, 500 miles southeast of Anchorage.

Reference: Skagway A-2, A-3, B-2, B-3, B-4, C-3, C-4.

Access: By car from Haines or Canada. The Haines Highway parallels much of the middle and lower Chilkat, crossing the river near Wells, and heads up a major tributary, the Klehini River, to the Canadian Border. A few side roads lead to tributary streams and lakes, such as Mosquito Lake. Chilkat Lake is accessible by floatplane from Haines.

Highlights: One of Alaska's special places, noted for fine fall fishing for silver and chum salmon (in the first half of October), spring Dolly Varden (in March and April) and unique, world-famous bald eagle viewing opportunities.

Species: Chum salmon, cutthroat trout, Dolly Varden, halibut, (king salmon), pink salmon, red salmon, silver salmon, (steelhead).

Regulations: Unbaited, artificial lures only from November 16 through September 14; king salmon fishing is prohibited. For additional restrictions, consult the current Alaska Department of Fish and Game regulations or the ADF&G Juneau office, (907) 465-4180.

Facilities: Hotels, lodging, gas, groceries, sporting goods and guide services are available in Haines and at points along the Haines Highway.

Contact: For guide services, contact Don's Fishing, P.O. Box 74, Haines, AK 99827; (907) 766-2272. For lodging information, contact the Captain's Choice Motel, P.O. Box 392, Haines, AK 99827; (907) 766-3111.

Description: The Chilkat River originates high in the Coast Mountains in Canada and flows south to Chilkat Inlet and Lynn Canal. Very braided, it cuts a valley between the Takshanuk and Takhinsha Mountains, and is joined by several major glacial tributaries including the Klehini and Tsirku Rivers. Since the river is glacially fed, the Chilkat runs heavy with silt in the warm summer months, effectively limiting angling opportunities to clearwater tributary lakes and streams. However, during the cooler months of the year, from about mid-September to mid-April, the river runs clear and is very fishable due to the lack of meltwater from the mountains. A large section of the Chilkat River Valley has been designated the "Alaska Chilkat Bald Eagle Preserve." Thousands of these majestic birds gather each fall along the river to feed on a late run of chum and silver salmon.

The prime time to fish the mainstem Chilkat is late fall, particularly in October, as the silt settles and the river clears, revealing a heavy run of chum salmon. Many anglers prefer to target this species near tidewater on the lower river as chances of catching brighter fish are better. An area along the highway by the airport is a favored chum hot spot, but the fish may be taken just about anywhere, upstream to the Tsirku River confluence. Big, bright silvers are available at the same time and are present in small numbers into February. In late winter and early spring, angling for Dolly Varden is a favorite local pastime as overwintering fish begin to actively feed. A very small winter run of steelhead trout spawn in the Chilkat as well.

The outlets of Chilkat and Mosquito lakes are good for fall silvers and fair for reds. Cutthroat trout fishing is great in the lakes, especially after break-up and prior to freeze-up, but fish are present year-round. Pink salmon run in small clearwater streams of the Chilkat in late summer. Stocked grayling may be found in Herman Lake by Klehini River.

For anglers wanting an experience that is out of the ordinary, the Chilkat comes highly recommended. Its great late autumn fishing, easy access, and splendid bald eagle viewing in a magnificent Alaska setting make this location one of a kind.

16. CHILKOOT RIVER SYSTEM

Location: North Lynn Canal drainage, 85 miles northwest of Juneau, 500 miles southeast of Anchorage.

Reference: Skagway B-2, B-3, C-3.

Access: By car, a few miles from Haines. The road parallels the entire lower river and ends at the outlet of Chilkoot Lake. There are pull-offs along the road, with several trails leading to various sections of the river and lake.

Highlights: The most popular river in the Haines area. Good fall fishing for silver salmon (in the first half of October), late summer pink salmon, and spring Dolly Varden (in April and May).

Species: (Chum salmon, cutthroat trout), Dolly Varden, (king salmon), pink salmon, red salmon, silver salmon, (steelhead).

Regulations: Unbaited, artificial lures only from November 16 through September 14; king salmon fishing is prohibited. For additional restrictions, consult the current Alaska Department of Fish and Game regulations or the ADF&G Juneau office, (907) 465-4180.

Facilities: Commercial lodging and a campground are available by the river and lake outlet. The town of Haines a few miles away also has sporting goods, groceries, a hotel and gas.

Contact: For lodging and camping information, contact Captain's Choice Motel, P.O. Box 392, Haines, AK 99827, (907) 766-3111; or Haines Visitor Bureau, P.O. Box 530, Haines, AK 99827; (800) 458-3579 or (907) 766-2234.

Description: The semi-glacial Chilkoot emerges from a series of ice fields high in the Coast Mountains above Haines and flows south to Chilkoot Lake, continuing on to Lutak Inlet. Above Chilkoot Lake, the river is fairly fast and narrow with several tributaries entering the mainstem from the surrounding mountains. The lower river, however, is wider and not as fast, with plenty of deep holes and runs. From the lake down to tidewater, the river is only a little over a mile long; most of the sportfishery takes place there. Boulders and rocks are scattered throughout the Chilkoot, providing excellent fish habitat. There is a state recreation site by the outlet of Chilkoot Lake. This area receives a lot of pressure during the height of the salmon and charr migrations.

Like neighboring Chilkat River, the emerald Chilkoot draws considerable attention from northern Southeast Alaskans, as well as Canadian anglers. The fishing is often very good, with silver and red salmon and Dolly Varden the main targets. Silver salmon are taken all along the lower river from the mouth upstream to and including the outlet of Chilkoot Lake. This late run of coho (in the first half of October) consists of large fish, with many taken in the mid-teens and some specimens of 18 pounds or more. Good numbers of red salmon enter the river in two separate runs, one in June and July, another in August. Action for reds is said to be only fair, as the fish are usually finicky about anglers' offerings, but they have been known to consistently strike red or orange flies and sponge balls. Pink salmon also fill the river in late summer (in the second half of August), and are much easier to catch. Dolly Varden are available year-round, but the best fishing for these sea-run charr occurs in spring (April and May) at the lake outlet as the fish gather in large schools preparing for the annual downstream migration to saltwater. Many charr are caught in late summer and fall after returning from the ocean. Every year, a few stray king salmon show up in the Chilkoot from nearby hatchery release sites.

17. COWEE CREEK

Location: Southeast Lynn Canal drainage, 35 miles northwest of Juneau, 550 miles southeast of Anchorage.

Reference: Juneau C-3.

Access: By car from Juneau. The Glacier Highway crosses the lower section of Glacier Creek. Trails lead to up and downstream areas.

Highlights: The best fishing stream on Juneau's road system, known for salmon and Dolly Varden.

Species: Chum salmon, cutthroat trout, Dolly Varden, pink salmon, silver salmon, steelhead.

Regulations: Unbaited, artificial lures only from November 16 through September 14; king salmon fishing is prohibited. For additional restrictions, consult the current Alaska Department of Fish and Game regulations or the ADF&G Douglas office, (907) 465-4320.

Facilities: No developed public facilities.

Contact: For fishing information, contact the Alaska Department of Fish and Game, Sportfish Division, P.O. Box 240020, Douglas, AK 99824; (907) 465-4320.

Description: Situated close to Juneau, Alaska's capitol, and offering consistent fishing with easy access, Cowee Creek is one of the favorite locations among the local angling community. Healthy runs of three species of salmon and charr are present at various times from early summer to late fall and are primarily targeted close to the highway in the last few miles of water above the ocean. Anglers in the know hit the holes and runs near the mouth during incoming and high tides, and areas further upstream a few hours after the tide. Big schools of fresh salmon can be intercepted at these locations on their way to the spawning grounds higher up in the valley.

A very heavy run of pink salmon (in the second half of July) always draws crowds to this popular stream, but early summer chums (from late June through early July) and fall silvers (in mid-September) are also very popular. Dolly Varden move into the stream during the early part of summer (in June and July) and yield fast action on light tackle. A small spring run of steelhead trout spawns in the creek as well, and a few pan-sized cutthroat trout occasionally add to the creel.

18. MONTANA CREEK

Location: Mainland drainage, Juneau area, 590 miles southeast of Anchorage.

Reference: Juneau B-2, B-3.

Access: By car from Juneau. Mendenhall Loop Road crosses the lower stream section with trails leading up and downstream. Also, Montana Creek Road provides access to reaches of the upper river. From the end of the latter road, a developed trail continues up into the headwaters of Montana Creek.

Highlights: A favorite spot for local fishermen, with good fishing for silver salmon (in the second half of September), chum salmon (in the first half of July), pink salmon (in the second half of July) and Dolly Varden (in July).

Species: Chum salmon, (cutthroat trout), Dolly Varden, (king salmon), pink salmon, (red salmon), silver salmon, (steelhead).

Regulations: Unbaited, artificial lures only; king salmon fishing is prohibited. For additional restrictions, consult the current Alaska Department of Fish and Game regulations or the ADF&G Juneau office, (907) 465-4180.

Facilities: No developed public facilities by stream crossings, but nearby areas have lodging, hotels, sporting goods, groceries and gas.

Contact: For lodging information, contact the Adlersheim Lodge, P.O. Box 210447, Auke Bay, AK 99821, (907) 780-4778; or Best Western Country Lane Inn, 9300 Glacier Highway, Juneau, AK 99801, (800) 528-1234 or (907) 789-5005.

Description: Montana Creek is a small clearwater stream draining out of valleys near Mount Stroller White and McGinnis Mountain, not far from Juneau. It is short, only about 10 miles long, with many riffles and some deep holes and runs. About two miles downstream from the lower access point (Mendenhall Loop Road), the Montana joins the silty Mendenhall River originating from its namesake lake and glacier.

Due to its close proximity to Juneau, the Montana is a popular stream with local anglers. Its clear waters support healthy fish populations with excellent opportunities for salmon and charr. Pink salmon and Dolly Varden are plentiful throughout most stream sections, while small schools of silver and chum salmon are encountered in the deeper parts of the lower Montana. For brighter salmon, try the last few miles of water above the mouth. A few king salmon run the creek in midsummer along with fall steelhead and cutthroat trout.

The Montana is great for anglers who enjoy sight-fishing, as schools of salmon are easily spotted and cast to. For the best possible action, hike in from the road crossings and explore the more remote stream areas. From the upper access point (Montana Creek Road), anglers can scout the shallows for charr among the spawning salmon. For those having some spare time in or around Juneau, Montana Creek is good for a trip lasting a few hours to a day.

19. TURNER LAKE

Location: Mainland lake, east side of Taku Inlet, 22 miles east of Juneau, 585 miles southeast of Anchorage.

Reference: Taku River B-6.

Access: Primarily by a short floatplane hop from Juneau. Most visitors land near the lake outlet or one of the two cabins on the lakeshore. Some anglers, however, choose to access the lake by boat via Taku Inlet, where a trail leads to Turner Lake along the outlet stream.

Highlights: One of northern Southeast's prime trophy cutthroat waters, with good fishing for kokanee (from May through August), pink salmon (in early August) and Dolly Varden (from July through October).

Species: Cutthroat trout, Dolly Varden, kokanee salmon, pink salmon, silver salmon.

Regulations: Unbaited, artificial lures only; catch-and-release fishing only for cutthroat trout. For additional restrictions, consult the current Alaska Department of Fish and Game regulations or the ADF&G Juneau office, (907) 465-4180.

Facilities: Forest service cabins are available at the west and east ends of the lake.

Contact: For cabin rental information, contact the Juneau Ranger District, Tongass National Forest, 8465 Old Dairy Road, Juneau, AK 99803; (907) 586-8800. For an air taxi, contact Ward Air, 8991 Yandukin Drive, Juneau, AK 99801; (800) 478-9150 or (907) 789-9150.

Description: Turner Lake is a deep, clear blue body of water, beautifully situated among tall snow-capped peaks in Tongass National Forest, 22 miles east of Juneau. Bound by steep cliffs with cascading waterfalls, and surrounded with thick stands of spruce, the lake is certainly one of the most scenic angling locations in all of Southeast Alaska.

Turner Lake has long been regarded as one of the premier trophy cutthroat trout waters in all of Alaska. The lake is rich in food sources and supports a sizable population of cutthroat trout, many reaching three to four pounds, and a few as large as five or even more. (The largest recorded fish from Turner was a six-pound, seven-ounce cutthroat.) Most of them are in the 12- to 16-inch range, with enough larger fish present to make a trip to these waters worthwhile. To preserve this remarkable fishing (a three-pound cutthroat may well be 12 years old), Turner Lake has been designated a special "trophy" cutthroat trout water, with only catch-and-release fishing and the use of bait prohibited.

Kokanee, the pan-sized, landlocked sockeye salmon that provide the main forage for the big cutthroats, are abundant in Turner and pursued regularly as sportfish year-round, although the best action occurs in late spring and summer. Dolly Varden provide additional excitement.

Fishing for all species in the lake is still quite good overall, but there are certain times and places to hit for action that is nothing less than red hot. Just after break-up and prior to freeze-up, the salmon and trout bite really peaks, particularly at the lake outlet and vicinity of any of the waterfalls. The outlet stream below the falls is another famous Turner fishing location for good catches of trout, charr and runs of pink and coho salmon. The best times to hit it would be from about midsummer until October, with small spinners and bright attractor flies the best enticements to use. Some good fishing can also be had on the lower stream sections near Taku Inlet.

It's a good idea for anglers to bring a small inflatable raft along to access the deeper parts of the lake for the best trophy fishing, as trolling is the proven method for the big ones; small skiffs are available for use at the forest service cabins. (See the cutthroat chapter on page 156 for more detail on angling techniques.) Plenty of folks, however, do just fine with the smaller fish casting from shore, with an occasional lunker taken near the lake outlet or stream inlets with spinning gear.

REGION 3
SITKA-WEST TONGASS

The Sitka area includes some significant freshwater and marine locations on and around Baranof, Yakobi, western Chichagof and south
Admiralty islands. Important species include king, silver and red
salmon, halibut, steelhead and cutthroat trout and Dolly Varden charr.

Most of the serious salmon effort occurs in salt water, targeting the
productive outer coast, where big king (some of the largest in Southeast) and coho are intercepted on their way to spawning destinations in
Alaska, Canada and beyond. A considerable amount of fishing is done
around Sitka, Salisbury and Nakwasina sounds and Katlian Bay for
salmon and halibut.

Roads leading north and south of town provide access to some seasonally productive shorefishing (Starrigavan Bay) and a few popular
roadside streams (such as Starrigavan Creek and Indian River). Species
most taken are Dolly Varden and silver and pink salmon. Area lakes
(Blue, Beaver and Thimbleberry) offer some fair to good fishing for
rainbow trout, Dollies and even rare brook trout and grayling. More
remote and productive are the prestigious locations of the Sitkoh and
Lake Eva, Port Banks and Mitchell Bay systems.

20. SALISBURY SOUND/PERIL STRAIT

Location: Northwest Baranof Island, 25 miles from Sitka, 570 miles
from Anchorage.

Reference: Sitka B-3, B-4, B-5, B-6, C-3, C-4, C-5, C-6.

Access: By boat and floatplane to Salisbury Sound and Peril Strait;
access by boat is by far the more popular and practical method. Anglers arrive in the area through the protected waters of upper Sitka
Sound and Olga and Neva Straits from Sitka, or by crossing
Chatham Strait into Peril Strait from Angoon on Admiralty Island.

Highlights: A favorite location of Sitka's charter fleet, excellent for
king salmon (from mid-May through mid-June), silver salmon (in
the second half of August) and halibut (from June through August);
good fishing for pink salmon (from late July through early August),
cutthroat trout and Dolly Varden (from May through July).

Species: Chum salmon, cutthroat trout, Dolly Varden, halibut, king salmon, pink salmon, (red salmon), silver salmon, (steelhead).

Regulations: For details on the open season and bag limits for bottom-fish, consult the current Alaska Department of Fish and Game regulations or the ADF&G Sitka office, (907) 747-5355.

Facilities: No developed public facilities, although some lakes in the immediate area do have forest service cabins.

Contact: For guide services, contact Brownie's Charters, 2038 Halibut Point Highway, Sitka, AK 99835, (907) 747-5402; or Sportsman Charters, 821 Charles Street, Sitka, AK 99835, (907) 747-8756. For lodging information, contact Whalers Cove Lodge, P.O. Box 101, Angoon, AK 99820; (800) 423-3123 or (907) 788-3123. For cabin rental information, contact Tongass National Forest, 204 Siginaka Way, Sitka, AK 99835; (907) 747-6671.

Description: Separating the large islands of Chichagof and Baranof is the narrow Peril Strait. Less than a mile wide in places, the strait is an active feeding and migration route for fish bound for Chatham Strait. On the west end is Salisbury Sound, a tremendously productive area between Kruzof and Chichagof islands that offers some of the best saltwater angling in the Sitka area.

There are a number of deep bays, tiny islands, clearwater streams and jutting peninsulas, which are ideal for concentrating anadromous species and bottomfish. On the west side of the strait, in Salisbury Sound, the most sought-after sportfish include king and silver salmon and halibut. These attract considerable attention from local and visiting anglers out of Sitka. The landscape is wild, unruly and very breathtaking; along with the abundant marine wildlife and superb fishing, it makes for a very memorable experience.

King salmon up to 60 or 70 pounds are possible in early summer, while feeder fish are available any time of the year. Behemoth halibut to 300 pounds are present in almost untapped numbers throughout the summer months. In late summer and fall, anglers are busy with the huge coho destined for nearby streams and lakes.

Peril Strait always seems to have some kind of fishing action to offer. Although the big, mature kings are not particularly abundant (like those found in Salisbury Sound), feeders weighing 10 to 25 pounds are common. They are targeted by anglers in the narrower sections, in Hoonah Sound and on the outer edge at Chatham Strait. Two major fish-producing waters drain into Peril Strait: Lake Eva and Sitkoh Creek. Both have good populations of silver, chum and pink salmon, sea-run cutthroat trout and Dolly Varden, as well as other game species. Sitkoh Bay is especially favored for mixed-creel catches.

Salisbury Sound and Peril Strait are perfect marine locations for boating. Their diverse, highly scenic waters and good fishing truly capture the essence of Southeast Alaska.

Hot spots for salmon, trout, charr and halibut include: Fortuna Strait/Klokachef Island; Kruzof Island—Point Kruzof and Kalinin Point; Sinitsin Island; Scraggy Island; Kakul Narrows; Big Island; Baranof Island—Point Kakul, Saint John Baptist Bay, Fish Bay, Pogibishi and Elizabeth points, Outer Rodman Bay and Saook Point/ Bay; Povorotni Island; Chichagof Island—Poison Cove, Sitkoh and Florence bays, Point Craven and Morris Reef.

21. SITKA SOUND

Location: West of Baranof Island, Sitka area, 580 miles southeast of Anchorage.

Reference: Sitka A-4, A-5, A-6, B-5, B-6; Port Alexander D-4, D-5.

Access: By boat or car from Sitka. The best way to reach the more productive fishing areas around the sound is by boat, although surf-casting is possible along Sitka's road system, particularly Halibut Point and Sawmill Creek roads. When the weather cooperates, kayaking is a valid option for access to the inner parts of Sitka Sound.

Highlights: The number-one marine fishery on Baranof Island, one of the best in Southeast. Excellent fishing for king salmon (from mid-May through mid-June), silver salmon (from mid-August through early September), pink salmon (from late July through early August), Dolly Varden (from May through July) and halibut (from June through August); good fishing for chum salmon (from early through mid-August).

Species: Chum salmon, cutthroat trout, Dolly Varden, halibut, king salmon, pink salmon, (red salmon), silver salmon.

Regulations: For details on the open season and bag limits for bottomfish, consult the current Alaska Department of Fish and Game regulations or the ADF&G Sitka office, (907) 747-5355.

Facilities: Commercial lodging, hotels, gas, boat rental and launching, campgrounds, sporting goods, groceries and guide services are available in Sitka.

Contact: For guide services, contact Brownie's Charters, 2038 Halibut Point Highway, Sitka, AK 99835, (907) 747-5402; or Sportsman Charters, 821 Charles Street, Sitka, AK 99835, (907) 747-8756. For lodging information, contact Baranof Sportsman's Vacations, 325 Seward Street, Sitka, AK 99835; (907) 747-4937. For cabin rental information, contact Tongass National Forest, 204 Siginaka Way, Sitka, AK 99835; (907) 747-6671.

Description: Located on the west side of Baranof Island, Sitka Sound has perhaps the most prolific saltwater sportfishing in the area. The sound leads directly to the Pacific Ocean, and boasts one major island, Kruzof, and many smaller islands scattered throughout its waters. Westerly winds can whip the waters into a froth, but on calm days it is one of the most scenic, peaceful bays in Southeast. Smaller, semi-protected bays adjoin the sound, and Mount Edgecumbe, a 3,200-foot volcano on Kruzof Island, adorns the west side across from the town of Sitka. Boating and kayaking are extremely popular with locals and visitors alike. There is prime bottomfish angling in the middle and outer bay areas and unsurpassed action for anadromous species near islands and river mouths closer to Sitka.

The sound's myriad aquatic life attracts feeding fish. Halibut are present year-round, but are larger in size and more numerous during the warmer months. Early and late in the season, the outer waters of the sound produce the best halibut catches, while late summer and early fall see these giants closer to town and in shallower water. Hungry salmon and charr cruise the blue depths of the sound starting in May and continuing into October. All five salmon species are present; king, silver, pink and chum salmon are the most frequently caught.

Immature king salmon weighing 15 to 20 pounds are available any day of the year, but seem to be more numerous from May to September. Mature prespawners bound for mainland rivers and streams are commonly intercepted in early summer and may reach a hefty 70 pounds or more, while trophy coho are another distinct possibility, with some specimens reaching 20 pounds. Dolly Varden are taken off beaches and points around town, with major populations of these sea-run charr inhabiting areas in the northern part of Sitka Sound, such as Nakwasina Sound and Katlian Bay.

Hot spot locations for salmon, charr and halibut in the sound include: Necker Islands—Biorka Channel and Biorka, Legma, Elovoi and Golf islands; Saint Lazaria Island; Vitskari Rocks/Island; Eastern Channel; Sheldon Jackson Hatchery; Silver Bay; Kasiana Island/Western Channel; Middle/Crow Island; Inner Point; Hayward Strait; Magoun Island; Olga Strait; Lisianski Point; Starrigavan Bay; Katlian Bay; Krestof Sound—Halleck, Neva and Whitestone points; and Nakwasina Sound.

22. SITKOH CREEK/LAKE

Location: Southeast Chichagof Island drainage, 35 miles northeast of Sitka, 580 miles southeast of Anchorage.

Reference: Sitka B-3, B-4, C-3.

Access: By plane or boat from Sitka or area lodges. Floatplanes can land on Sitkoh Lake or use the Chatham Seaplane Base in Sitkoh Bay. From the seaplane base, a rough forest road network provides access to the lake. For those accessing through Sitkoh Bay by boat via Peril Strait, a trail begins at the mouth of Sitkoh Creek and leads 4.3 miles along the north side of the stream to a cabin at the Sitkoh Lake outlet.

Highlights: One of northern Southeast's premier steelhead streams, with excellent fishing for pink salmon (from late July through mid-August). Also good fishing for silver salmon (from late August through mid-September), cutthroat trout (from May through June) and Dolly Varden (from July through October).

Species: Chum salmon, cutthroat trout, Dolly Varden, pink salmon, rainbow trout, (red salmon), silver salmon, steelhead.

Regulations: Unbaited, artificial lures only from November 16 through September 14; king and red salmon fishing is prohibited. For additional restrictions, consult the current Alaska Department of Fish and Game regulations or the ADF&G Sitka office, (907) 747-5355.

Facilities: Two forest service cabins are available, one on the west end of Sitkoh Lake, another on the lake's east end.

Contact: For cabin rental information, contact Tongass National Forest, 204 Siginaka Way, Sitka, AK 99835; (907) 747-6671. For an air taxi, contact Ward Air, 8991 Yandukin Drive, Juneau, AK 99801, (907) 789-9150 or (800) 478-9150; Bellair, P.O. Box 371, Sitka, AK 99835, (907) 747-8636; or Mountain Aviation, P.O. Box 875, Sitka, AK 99835, (907) 966-2288.

Description: Sitkoh Lake is nestled in a picturesque valley in the Moore Mountains of Chichagof Island. It is small—only about 2.5 miles long—and drains into Sitkoh Bay through Sitkoh Creek. Thick, rain forest vegetation dominates the landscape with 2,500-foot mountains towering over the lake. The clear and highly productive waters of the drainage have long been a major attraction for salmon and trout enthusiasts, with good chances to spot bears feeding on fish in the stream during late summer and fall.

Sitkoh is among the top producers of sportfish in the Sitka area. Known throughout Southeast for its outstanding steelhead fishing, this drainage has plenty of windfall, and is quite deep in places, but still offers some classic flyfishing. The spring run (from late April through late May) of these large sea-run rainbows (averaging 9 to 11 pounds) receives the most attention, although there is a much smaller late autumn run as well. Additionally, silver and pink salmon are thick in late summer and fall, attracting a fair number of anglers, both the two-legged and furry four-legged kind.

Anglers looking for less robust sport can find an abundance of cutthroat trout and Dolly Varden from the stream mouth at Sitkoh Bay all the way up into the lake. (The area around the mouth of Sitkoh Creek in the bay also offers great fishing for bright silvers, pinks and even a few chums. Halibut are taken in deeper waters further out.) Spring, late summer and fall are particularly good times to try for these species during their annual migrations to and from salt water. The trail from Sitkoh Bay to Sitkoh Lake parallels the whole length of the creek, opening up miles of small stream angling opportunities.

23. MITCHELL BAY SYSTEM

Location: Central Admiralty Island drainage, 50 miles northeast of Sitka, 600 miles southeast of Anchorage.

Reference: Sitka B-1, B-2, C-1, C-2, D-1, D-2.

Access: By floatplane from Sitka or Juneau; by boat from Angoon. Planes can land on any of the lakes in the system or at one of the three canoe portage/trail access sites—Mitchell Bay, Mole Harbor and Windfall Harbor. An extensive canoe route/trail network (part of the Cross Admiralty Canoe Route) connects the system, providing access to almost all lakes and streams in the drainage.

Highlights: The most popular recreation area on Admiralty Island, with excellent fishing for cutthroat trout and good salmon angling.

Species: Chum salmon, cutthroat trout, Dolly Varden, pink salmon, red salmon, silver salmon, (steelhead).

Regulations: Unbaited, artificial lures only from November 16 through September 14; king salmon fishing is prohibited. For additional restrictions, consult the current Alaska Department of Fish and Game regulations or the ADF&G Juneau office, (907) 465-4180.

Facilities: Six forest service cabins and 10 public shelters are available within and around the Mitchell Bay system.

Contact: For lodging information, contact Thayer Lake Lodge, P.O. Box 211614, Auke Bay, AK 99821; (907) 789-5646. For cabin rental information, contact Admiralty Island National Monument,

P.O. Box 2097, Juneau, AK 99803; (907) 586-8790. For an air taxi, contact Ward Air, 8991 Yandukin Drive, Juneau, AK 99801; (907) 789-9150 or (800) 478-9150.

Description: The Mitchell Bay system of Admiralty Island is comprised of a series of beautiful lakes of varying sizes connected by small streams. Ten major lakes, and several smaller ones, offer outstanding cutthroat trout fishing and excellent hiking and canoeing, making the system one of the more attractive recreational destinations in Southeast Alaska.

The more popular locations include Hasselborg Lake, the largest lake in the system, and Distin, Davidsons, Jims, Guerin, Beaver and Alexander lakes, all of which produce exceptional numbers of trout (from May to September), along with some kokanee and charr. Hasselborg Lake contains trophy fish of four to five pounds or heavier, with a few taken out of Jims, Guerin and Distin lakes as well. (See the chapter on cutthroat on page 156 for details on trophy fishing in Southeast lakes.) Fishing can be worthwhile in the small streams during the summer months as well. Hasselborg Creek, draining out of Hasselborg Lake, ties the system to the salt water of Mitchell Bay, and has the most angling potential, with sea-run trout, charr and good runs of salmon. (Starting in July and continuing into October, silver, red, chum and pink salmon move into the stream, with good action reported for all species.)

Hasselborg Creek empties into Salt Lake, a brackish body of water separated from the head of Mitchell Bay only by "The Falls," a narrow chute of water, which is impassable to boaters on low tide. Salmon school in this area before entering the spawning stream. Mitchell Bay itself is a very protected part of Chatham Strait, with its many nooks offering good action for salmon and small halibut. Feeder king salmon are available in the outer bay near Angoon. (It has some very tricky and dangerous tides, so extreme caution is advised if traversing these waters by kayak or small powerboat.)

In addition to a true variety of fishing—lake, stream and salt water—the Mitchell Bay system offers canoeing and/or hiking via the popular, island-traversing Mole Harbor Trail. It is highly recommended for anyone wanting to experience world-famous Admiralty Island in Tongass National Forest.

24. LAKE EVA

Location: North Baranof Island drainage, 20 miles northeast of Sitka, 580 miles southeast of Anchorage.

Reference: Sitka B-4.

Access: By floatplane or boat from Sitka and Angoon. Marine travellers from Sitka must traverse upper Sitka Sound and upper Salisbury Sound into and through Peril Strait, and from Angoon, cross the Chatham Strait into Peril Strait. Drop-offs are usually made by plane near the lake outlet, while boaters moor in Hanus Bay and hike Hanus Bay Trail about a mile to Lake Eva.

Highlights: A well-known, remote Sitka area lake, with a reputation for good spring and fall cutthroat trout and Dolly Varden (from May through June and September through October). Also good salmon fishing for silvers, reds and pinks.

Species: Chum salmon, cutthroat trout, Dolly Varden, pink salmon, red salmon, silver salmon, steelhead.

Regulations: Unbaited, artificial lures only in the lake; king salmon fishing is prohibited. For additional restrictions, consult the current Alaska Department of Fish and Game regulations or the ADF&G Sitka office, (907) 747-5355.

Facilities: A forest service cabin is available on the north shore of Lake Eva. It is wheelchair accessible, with railings and ramps present. Also, a public shelter is found on the southwest shore.

Contact: For cabin rental information, contact Tongass National Forest, 204 Siginaka Way, Sitka, AK 99835; (907) 747-6671. For an air taxi, contact Ward Air, 8991 Yandukin Drive, Juneau, AK 99801; (907) 789-9150.

Description: Lake Eva is situated in a particularly scenic part of Baranof Island. Snow-capped mountains loom to the southwest and the blue waters of narrow Peril Strait lie just a few miles to the north. A small stream drains the lake and pours into Hanus Bay, providing passage for salmon, trout and charr. Although the drainage is not large, it is a very appealing destination due to its scenic location and productive fishing opportunities.

Only about two miles long, Lake Eva offers good opportunities for cutthroat trout and Dolly Varden, and there is a small spring run of steelhead trout. The mouths of inlet streams are concentration areas in fall, as is the lake outlet in spring and early summer. The outlet stream is good during the annual migrational periods and its mouth at Hanus Bay can be productive all summer. Though not of trophy proportions, the fish are nonetheless plentiful and aggressive.

Salmon are popular with anglers visiting the area and can be caught from midsummer on into fall almost anywhere in the drainage. The lake outlet, the outlet stream, and the mouth of the stream at Hanus Bay are all recommended locations for Lake Eva silvers, reds and pinks. Generally, pink salmon are most abundant, but the other salmon species are present in high enough numbers to give an excellent account of themselves. A few chum salmon are always mixed in with the crowd.

The forest service cabin is a popular among a wide range of recreational users. Built for the physically challenged, many elderly and wheelchair-restricted visitors make use of its unique facilities to enjoy the great outdoors. A fishing platform is available, and a public shelter is located at the lake inlet where the Hanus Bay Trail ends.

25. NAKWASINA RIVER

Location: North Baranof Island drainage, 15 miles north of Sitka, 580 miles southeast of Anchorage.

Reference: Sitka A-4, B-4.

Access: By boat from Sitka. Crossing upper Sitka Sound and passing through Nakwasina Sound, marine travellers usually anchor off the river mouth or beach their boats and approach the river on foot.

Highlights: One of Southeast's premier locations for stream Dolly Varden fishing (from July through August), with good fishing for pink salmon (in early August) and silver salmon (from late September through early October).

Species: Chum salmon, Dolly Varden, pink salmon, silver salmon.

Regulations: Unbaited, artificial lures only from November 16 through September 14; king salmon fishing is prohibited. For additional restrictions, consult the current Alaska Department of Fish and Game regulations or the ADF&G Sitka office, (907) 747-5355.

Facilities: No developed public facilities.

Contact: For fishing information, contact the Alaska Department of Fish and Game, 304 Lake Street, Room 103, Sitka, AK 99835; (907) 747-5355.

Description: The Nakwasina River flows into Nakwasina Sound on the upper part of Sitka Sound. Although the upper river sections are fast and rocky, extending high into the surrounding mountains (well over 2,000 feet), the lower section is ideal for angling. A fairly small river, shallow in many places, the Nakwasina is a prime spawning ground for salmon, but most anglers come to this clearwater stream for its healthy run of large sea-run Dolly Varden charr.

Any angler hiking along the river soon discovers why this stream is so popular for Dolly Varden. These bright fish, some as large as eight pounds, enter Nakwasina starting in early summer and are present until fall, offering exceptional flyfishing and spincasting opportunities. The best fishing traditionally coincides with the large return of chum and pink salmon, as Dollies feed heavily on eggs. (Egg pattern flies, attractors and bright spoons and spinners work best, obviously.) A late run of silver salmon, peaking in late October, enters the river, but in the Nakwasina, these fish begin their spawning soon after entering fresh water. Near tidewater or at the river mouth early on in the run is best for some fair to good fishing.

The river's banks are ideal for walking and casting. You can spot-cast toward schools of salmon and pick up the Dolly Varden stacked up behind them, especially in the deep holes on the lower river near salt water. (This is particularly effective on the Nakwasina, with many big fish taken this way.) Anglers focusing on Nakwasina Sound off the river mouth will find superb silver and pink salmon and Dolly Varden fishing. The variety here on the Nakwasina is certainly nothing to write home about, but the top-notch Dolly fishing—some of the best in all of Southeast—more than makes up for it.

26. KATLIAN RIVER

Location: North Baranof Island drainage, 11 miles northeast of Sitka, 585 miles southeast of Anchorage.

Reference: Sitka A-4.

Access: By boat from Sitka. Crossing upper Sitka Sound into Katlian Bay, marine travellers can access the mouth of the Katlian River at high tide. Mooring off the mouth or beaching the boat, the lower river is easily accessible.

Highlights: Another excellent Sitka area stream for big Dolly Varden (from July through August); also good fishing for pink salmon (in early August) and silver salmon (from late September through early October).

Species: Chum salmon, Dolly Varden, pink salmon, silver salmon.

Regulations: Unbaited, artificial lures only from November 16 through September 14; king salmon fishing is prohibited. For additional restrictions, consult the current Alaska Department of Fish and Game regulations or the ADF&G Sitka office, (907) 747-5355.

Facilities: No developed public facilities.

Contact: For fishing information, contact the Alaska Department of Fish and Game, 304 Lake Street, Room 103, Sitka, AK 99835; (907) 747-5355.

Description: The Katlian River is located at the head of Katlian Bay in upper Sitka Sound, where it drains a mountainous, heavily forested region of central Baranof Island. In the east, mountain peaks can be seen towering over 4,600 feet high, bearing ice and snow fields. Although it's not a particularly large river, the Katlian supports good runs of salmon and, one of the main local attractions, a population of trophy sea-run Dolly Varden charr.

Fairly shallow, with lots of riffles and some deeper pools, the Katlian has perfect spawning habitat for salmon. It receives substantial numbers of chums and pinks in August and a smaller showing of silvers peaking in late October. It is common for these fish to stage off the mouth of the river for several days to a couple of weeks before moving into fresh water; they are often in or near spawning condition shortly after entering the river. However, early on in the season it is possible to get fairly bright salmon, especially at or near the mouth. Expect fair to good action for silvers and chums, but hot action for pinks.

Most anglers fish for salmon at the head of Katlian Bay, focusing their attention on the river when Dolly Varden begin entering in fishable numbers around the first of July. It is a popular fishery since many of these charr tend to be on the heavy side; two to four pounds are fairly common, with occasional lunkers up to eight pounds. Look for trophy charr in holes, sloughs or tailouts near spawning salmon on the lower river for best results. Flyfishing conditions on the Katlian are ideal.

27. REDOUBT LAKE

Location: Central Baranof Island drainage, 10 miles south of Sitka, 600 miles southeast of Anchorage.

Reference: Port Alexander D-4.

Access: There are three access options. One is by floatplane from Sitka, a short hop lasting only a few minutes. (Drop-off is usually near the channel connecting the lake to salt water or at a cabin near the lake inlet.) Another way is to hike in via the Redoubt Lake Trail from Silver Bay. The third is by small boat or kayak from Redoubt Bay through the channel into the west end of the lake. Some portaging is required for the latter option; a set of falls must be crossed prior to reaching lake.

Highlights: A very popular Sitka area lake and streamfishing location, with excellent fishing for silver salmon (in the second half of September); also good fishing for sockeye salmon (in the second half of July) and rainbow and cutthroat trout (in May and from September through October).

Species: Chum salmon, Dolly Varden, (king salmon), pink salmon, red salmon, silver salmon.

Regulations: Unbaited, artificial lures only from November 16 through September 14; king salmon fishing is prohibited. For additional restrictions, consult the current Alaska Department of Fish and Game regulations or the ADF&G Sitka office, (907) 747-5355.

Facilities: A forest service cabin is located at the northeastern end of the lake.

Contact: For cabin rental information, contact Tongass National Forest, 204 Siginaka Way, Sitka, AK 99835; (907) 747-6671. For an air taxi, contact Bellair, P.O. Box 371, Sitka, AK 99835, (907) 747-8636; or Mountain Aviation, P.O. Box 875, Sitka, AK 99835, (907) 966-2288.

Description: Redoubt Lake is a clear, narrow, 10-mile-long lake in the heart of Baranof Island. Mountains ranging to 3,500 feet, topped with snow fields, hem the north and south shores, with their steep cliffs dropping almost vertically into the lake. Small streams pour off the forest-clad slopes, creating magnificent waterfalls. This area, considered one of the better spots around Sitka for salmon and trout, receives a fair amount of angling pressure.

Healthy runs of silver and red salmon arrive in the drainage in midsummer and last well into fall. Successful anglers concentrate their efforts in three specific areas: the falls below Redoubt Lake—a temporary barrier for migrating fish, it creates a haven for spin and flycasting, particularly for tackle-busting coho and sockeye salmon; the lake outlet—a very good location, especially for schooling silvers; and the mouth of Redoubt Creek near the forest service cabin.

Resident species, such as rainbow and cutthroat trout, offer very good action, particularly in spring and fall, but can be taken quite readily through the summer in deeper parts of the lake near the inlet and outlet. When the salmon spawn in autumn, target these magnificent gamefish near the inlet stream.

For a combination salmon and trout excursion with a variety of water (intertidal, stream and lake) in the most scenic part of Baranof Island, Redoubt Lake is the top choice of locals and visitors alike.

28. PORT BANKS SYSTEM

Location: Southwest Baranof Island drainage, 35 miles southeast of Sitka, 625 miles southeast of Anchorage.

Reference: Port Alexander C-3.

Access: By plane or boat. Floatplanes traditionally access the area from Sitka by landing either at Port Banks near the mouth of the stream draining Plotnikof Lake, the outlet or inlet of Plotnikof Lake, or the upper end of Davidof Lake. Boaters can reach the system from Sitka via Whale Bay and moor at Port Banks.

Highlights: A famous Sitka area location, with excellent fishing for silver salmon (from late July through late August); good fishing for steelhead (from late April through late May) and rainbow trout (in May and from September through October).

Species: (Chum salmon, pink salmon), rainbow trout, steelhead, silver salmon.

Regulations: Unbaited, artificial lures only from November 16 through September 14; king salmon fishing is prohibited. For additional restrictions, consult the current Alaska Department of Fish and Game regulations or the ADF&G Sitka office, (907) 747-5355.

Facilities: Two forest service cabins are available, one at the inlet of Plotnikof Lake, the other at the inlet of Davidof Lake.

Contact: For cabin rental information, contact Tongass National Forest, 204 Siginaka Way, Sitka, AK 99835; (907) 747-6671. For an air taxi, contact Bellair, P.O. Box 371, Sitka, AK 99835, (907) 747-8636; or Mountain Aviation, P.O. Box 875, Sitka, AK 99835, (907) 966-2288.

Description: Situated within the South Baranof Wilderness, the Port Banks system is indeed one of the more scenic fishing locations on the island. High mountain ridges and snow-covered peaks (some reaching 4,000 feet or higher) surround two larger drainage lakes, Plotnikof and Davidof, providing spectacular views on clear days. This clearwater system is endowed with healthy populations of salmon and trout and is a very popular angling destination during spring and summer.

Quite unique for Southeast sportfisheries, the Port Banks drainage lakes and streams receive a summer run of silver salmon and an extended run of steelhead trout. Starting as early as the Fourth of July and continuing into September, bright cohos enter the system in large numbers, providing outstanding action for anglers taking the time to fish and explore its waters. Although most salmon fishing takes place at the mouth of the stream draining Plotnikof Lake, silvers may be taken just about anywhere within the Port Banks system.

Steelhead are another popular species that receive a fair amount of attention. Considered a spring run, these silvery torpedoes filter into Port Banks beginning in April, with a few ocean-fresh fish still arriving into July. Early in the season, anglers seem to do best near tidewater at Port Banks, while later on (May and June) action peaks at the outlets of Plotnikof and Davidof lakes.

The third major species in the system is rainbow trout. These fine sportfish may be taken from drainage lakes throughout the season with some of the best angling occurring in spring and fall. The autumn months are particularly good as cool temperatures and spawning salmon create perfect feeding (and fishing!) conditions.

Scenic beauty and superb angling make the Port Banks system one of the most well known and highly regarded of the many fine locations in the Sitka area.

REGION 4
PETERSBURG/WRANGELL

The Petersburg/Wrangell area, from Cape Fenshaw to the Cleveland Peninsula, encompasses numerous islands—including Kupreanof, Kuiu, Etolin, Wrangell and Zarembo—along with the Stikine Wilderness on the mainland and a preponderance of straits, channels, sounds and bays. With its abundance of rugged coastline, sheltered waters and dozens of small lakes and streams, this area has significant opportunities for high-quality marine and freshwater fishing, which are probably unequalled for variety anywhere in Southeast.

All five species of salmon occur here. As elsewhere, most of the effort for king and coho takes place primarily in salt water as an intercept fishery, with trolling, mooching and jigging the predominant methods. (The giant Stikine River is far and away the largest spawning destination in the area.) Frederick Sound and Wrangell Narrows, Eastern Passage and Zimovia and Stikine straits are the most frequently fished marine areas. Substantial new opportunities for both king and coho have been created by local hatcheries. Some of the better locations to target these hatchery (and wild stock) fisheries are: Blind Slough, Neets Bay, Earl West Cove, lower Duncan Canal and the mouths of Petersburg and Falls creeks.

A fairly developed road system allows access to many quality locations—both fresh and salt water—within a short hike from the road. Some of the more outstanding of these are: the Thoms Lake and Creek system, 39 miles south of Wrangell (steelhead, red salmon, cutthroat trout, Dolly Varden, silver salmon); Blind River and Blind Slough, 15 miles southeast of Petersburg (king salmon, silver salmon, cutthroat trout, Dolly Varden); Pat Creek and Pat Lake, 11 miles south of Wrangell (king salmon, silver salmon, pink salmon, cutthroat trout, Dolly Varden); the Zimovia and Mitkof Highway shorelines (silver salmon, pink salmon, Dolly Varden, cutthroat trout); and Falls and Ohmer Creeks, south of Petersburg (steelhead, king salmon, silver salmon, Dolly Varden, cutthroat trout).

There are many secluded stream and lake locations within easy reach of a boat or small plane that offer outstanding fishing. Steelhead, cutthroat trout, and Dolly Varden are the main attractions, with some high-quality salmon (silver, pink, chum) and rainbow trout fishing also

530   SOUTHEAST

available in some locations. Petersburg and Kadake creeks, and the Anan, Marten, Swan, Virginia and Eagle Lake systems are a few of the more noteworthy ones.

The U.S. Forest Service maintains 42 public-use cabins in the area, many of them remote. Each accommodates four to six people, and some even come equipped with skiffs. Reservations at some of the more popular locations should be made at least six months in advance.

29. LOWER STEPHENS PASSAGE

Location: Southeast of Admiralty Island, 40 miles from Petersburg, 625 miles southeast of Anchorage.

Reference: Sitka A-1, B-1; Sumdum A-5, A-6, B-4, B-5, B-6, C-5, C-6.

Access: The lower passage is accessible by boat from Petersburg (via Frederick Sound), Juneau or area lodges. Floatplanes often land in protected bays and coves, especially near forest service cabins.

Highlights: A remote marine fishery with little angling pressure but great action. Good fishing for king salmon (from late May through late June), silver salmon (from mid-August through mid-September), pink salmon (from mid-July through mid-August) and halibut (from mid-June through mid-July).

Species: Chum salmon, cutthroat trout, Dolly Varden, halibut, king salmon, pink salmon, (red salmon), silver salmon.

Regulations: For details on the open season for halibut and ling cod, consult the current Alaska Department of Fish and Game regulations or the ADF&G Juneau office, (907) 465-4180.

Facilities: Two forest service cabins are available, one at Church Bite in Gambier Bay, the other at Donkey Bay in Pybus Bay.

Contact: For guide services, contact Real Alaska Adventures, P.O. Box 1124, Petersburg, AK 99833; (907) 772-4121. For cabin rental information, contact Admiralty Island National Monument, P.O. Box 2097, Juneau, AK 99803; (907) 586-8790. For an air taxi, contact Kupreanof Flying Service, P.O. Box 768, Petersburg, AK 99833; (907) 772-3396.

Description: Lower Stephens Passage, between Admiralty Island and the mainland, includes all waters from Gambier Bay and Hobart Bay south to Frederick Strait. Dense rain forests dominate the lower elevations, while snow-capped mountain peaks and glacial valleys decorate the horizon to the east. Although very remote from most recreational boat traffic, a few anglers target the area with overnight trips and are often richly rewarded.

The clear blue waters of Stephens Passage are a major migration corridor and feeding ground for many anadromous and resident species. Many small rivers and streams drain into the passage and adjoining waters, adding excitement to the fishery. Salmon bound for spawning in these and other drainages nearby are effectively intercepted by trolling and mooching along shorelines and small islands. Bottomfish are very abundant during the summer months and most frequently caught by jigging in moderately deep water.

King and silver salmon and halibut are the most sought-after species, with outstanding possibilities for all three in certain locations. Feeder kings are available year-round, with the addition of larger, mature fish in late spring and early summer. (Pybus and Gambier bays are exceptional locations for these monarchs.) When the kings wane in midsummer, the smallest members of the salmon clan, pinks, appear. They are easily taken near the mouths of clearwater streams where they congregate in huge schools. Husky chum salmon are mixed in with the pinks, but expect only fair fishing for them. In late summer, silvers heat up the action in many of the same areas that were most productive for kings. They peak in numbers in fall, and, like the pinks, are taken near or in the mouths of spawning streams.

Sea-run cutthroat trout and Dolly Varden are not abundant here, although some fish may be picked up in small bays and coves with sizable streams at the head of them. The passage is known for its great halibut fishing, however, with the action much more consistent than for salmon. While they are present in great numbers from spring to fall, early summer usually is the best time to catch large fish to 200 pounds or more.

Hot spot locations for salmon, charr and halibut include: Admiralty Island; Point Pybus, Gambier, Price and Elliott islands, and Gambier, Pybus and Little Pybus bays; Hobart Bay/Entrance Island; Point Hobart; Whitney Island; and Cape Fanshaw.

30. EASTERN FREDERICK SOUND

Location: Northeast of Kupreanof Island, Petersburg area, 650 miles southeast of Anchorage.

Reference: Sumdum A-3, A-4, A-5, A-6; Petersburg C-2, C-3, D-2, D-3, D-4.

Access: Primarily by boat from Petersburg or area lodges. It is possible to land floatplanes in some parts of the sound, such as its protected bays and coves. Boat access from Wrangell is via Sumner Strait and Wrangell Narrows, or, if tides permit, Dry Strait on the Stikine River Flats.

Highlights: A traditional local hot spot. Good fishing for king salmon (from late May through late June), silver salmon (from mid-August through mid-September), pink salmon (from late July through early August) and halibut (from June through August).

Species: Chum salmon, cutthroat trout, Dolly Varden, halibut, king salmon, pink salmon, (red salmon), silver salmon, (steelhead).

Regulations: For details on the open season for halibut and ling cod, consult the current Alaska Department of Fish and Game regulations or the ADF&G Ketchikan office, (907) 225-2859.

Facilities: Lodging, groceries, sporting goods, boat rentals and launching, fuel and water are available in Petersburg. Additionally, two forest service cabins are in the area, one on Cascade Creek, another on Spurt Cove in Thomas Bay.

Contact: For guide services, contact Real Alaska Adventures, P.O. Box 1124, Petersburg, AK 99833; (907) 772-4121. For lodging information, contact the Petersburg Chamber of Commerce, P.O. Box 649, Petersburg, AK 99833; (907) 772-3646. For cabin rental information, contact Tongass National Forest, 204 Siginaka Way, Sitka, AK 99835; (907) 747-6671. For an air taxi, contact Kupreanof Flying Service, P.O. Box 768, Petersburg, AK 99833; (907) 772-3396.

Description: Separating Kupreanof and Mitkof islands from the mainland, eastern Frederick Sound includes all waters from Cape Fanshaw and Pinta Point in the west to Stikine River flats in the southeast. It is a breathtaking area of dense coastal forests, deeply incised valleys and enormous tidewater glaciers, which is also blessed with an abundance of fish and marine life.

Seasoned marine boaters, primarily from Petersburg, enjoy a fishery that has been producing good catches of salmon and bottomfish for generations. Today it is still one of the leading sportfish locations in the entire region. King and silver salmon and halibut are by far the most popular of all available species and subject to intense harvest efforts during the summer and fall months.

King salmon, although present year-round, are far more numerous in late spring and early summer as wild runs bound for spawning areas up the Stikine River and hatchery fish returning to release sites in Wrangell Narrows pass through these waters in full force. While they average 15 to 25 pounds, larger fish to 50 or 60 pounds, sometimes more, are frequently taken. By July, as the best king fishing declines, things start to get hot with returning pink salmon. These scrappy fighters are taken in inshore waters everywhere, particularly near and in the mouths of clearwater streams. (Look for numbers of chum salmon, cutthroat trout and Dolly Varden at the same time.) Silvers are the last of the salmon to show and continue to arrive through most of autumn. Many fish are of wild stock origin, with a significant portion being returning hatchery releases.

Halibut fishing is rated as good, with huge flatfish abundant throughout Frederick Sound. Jigging is the most popular angling method, but a fair number are taken incidentally while fishing other species, especially salmon. It is worthwhile to note that the lower southeast section of Frederick Sound may get cloudy with glacial silt in summer. This is due to the heavy discharge from the nearby Stikine River. When the weather cools, the runoff generally subsides completely and the sound becomes clear blue again. Frederick Sound is regarded by most folks as a day-trip fishery, but longer stays are possible by mooring off beaches and stream mouths in protected bays and cove.

Some of the proven hot spot locations in this area for salmon and halibut include: Kupreanof Island; Pinta, Boulder, West, East and Beacon points; Schooner and Portage islands; Cape Strait; and Big Creek.

31. WRANGELL NARROWS/ DUNCAN CANAL

Location: Southeast of Kupreanof Island, Petersburg area, 675 miles southeast of Anchorage.

Reference: Petersburg C-3, C-4, D-3, D-4, D-5.

Access: By boat and floatplane from Petersburg. Boating is by far the most popular method, while floatplanes are able to use protected waters, such as bays and coves, for access. Also, marine travellers from Wrangell can access the narrows and canal via Sumner Strait.

Highlights: One of the best marine fisheries in the Petersburg area. Excellent fishing for king salmon (from late May through late June) and silver salmon (from mid-August through mid-September); also good fishing for chum and pink salmon (from late July through early August) and halibut (from mid-June through mid-July).

Species: Chum salmon, cutthroat trout, Dolly Varden, halibut, king salmon, pink salmon, (red salmon), silver salmon, (steelhead).

Regulations: For details on the open season for halibut and ling cod, consult the current Alaska Department of Fish and Game regulations or the ADF&G Ketchikan office, (907) 225-2859.

Facilities: Lodging, sporting goods, guide service, boat rentals and launching, fuel and water are available in the town of Petersburg. Additionally, there are nine forest service cabins available in the Duncan Canal area: Kah Sheets Bay (one), Bains Cove (one), Beecher Pass (one), Harvey Lake (one), Breiland Slough (one), Castle River/Flats (two) and Saltchuck (two).

Contact: For guide services, contact Real Alaska Adventures, P.O. Box 1124, Petersburg, AK 99833; (907) 772-4121. For lodging information, contact the Petersburg Chamber of Commerce, P.O. Box 649, Petersburg, AK 99833; (907) 772-3646. For cabin rental information, contact Tongass National Forest, 204 Siginaka Way, Sitka, AK 99835; (907) 747-6671. For an air taxi, contact Kupreanof Flying Service, P.O. Box 768, Petersburg, AK 99833; (907) 772-3396.

Description: Wrangell Narrows, separating Mitkof Island from the larger Kupreanof Island, is heralded as one of the most intense marine sportfisheries in southern Southeast. Stretching from Frederick Sound in the north to Sumner Strait in the south, the narrows average only about a mile in width. Cutting deep into the center of Kupreanof Island is Duncan Canal, a fairly long, wide fjord that connects with Wrangell Narrows at Woewodski Island near Sumner Strait. Both serve as major recreational waters for boating and angling and also provide access to streams and cabins in the area.

King salmon are the most favored target of Petersburg anglers. Feeders can be taken consistently every day of the year at the outer ends of Wrangell Narrows and a large hatchery run of these fish returns every season to Blind Slough on Mitkof Island a few miles south of town. An enhanced run of silvers mixed in with wild stocks offers fast action in late summer and fall in the slough and adjoining Blind River, and in varying amounts, throughout the narrows and Duncan Canal as well. Although primarily a boat fishery early in the season, it can be fished with good results by shore anglers later on. Chum and pink salmon are usually caught in areas where large concentrations of these fish occur, such as near the mouths of rivers and streams.

Sea-run cutthroat trout and Dolly Varden are spread throughout the narrows and canal in fair numbers and are usually caught at the mouths of Petersburg, Falls and Duncan Saltchuck creeks, as well as along points and beaches in the vicinity. Halibut fishing predominantly takes place at the north and south ends of the narrows; some smaller fish may be hauled out of deeper parts of Duncan Canal in mid-season.

Visiting anglers are by no means restricted to the Petersburg area for accommodations, as there are quite a few forest service cabins along Duncan Canal.

The main fishing areas for salmon and halibut in Wrangell Narrows and Duncan Canal include: Kupreanof Island–Prolewy, Mountain, Finger and North points; Mitkof Island–Petersburg Harbor, Scow Bay, Danger, Blind and December points, Blind Slough and Point Alexander; Duncan Canal–Whiskey Pass/Butterworth Island, Castle Islands and Saltchuck; and Woody Island.

---

32. UPPER SUMNER STRAIT

Location: North of Prince of Wales and Zarembo islands, south of Kupreanof and Mitkof islands, 25 miles south of Petersburg, 675 miles southeast of Anchorage.

Reference: Petersburg B-2, B-3, B-4, B-5, C-2, C-3, C-4.

Access: By boat from Petersburg (via Wrangell Narrows) and Wrangell. Protected bays and coves in the area provide access opportunities for floatplanes.

Highlights: A longtime favorite area location for salmon and bottomfish. Good fishing for king salmon (from mid-May through mid-June), silver salmon (from early August through early September), pink salmon (from mid-July through early August) and halibut (from June through August).

Species: Chum salmon, cutthroat trout, Dolly Varden, halibut, king salmon, pink salmon, (red salmon), silver salmon, (steelhead).

Regulations: For details on the open season for salmon, halibut and ling cod, consult the current Alaska Department of Fish and Game regulations or the ADF&G Ketchikan office, (907) 225-2859.

Facilities: A forest service cabin is available at the head of Kah Sheets Bay.

Contact: For guide services, contact Real Alaska Adventures, P.O. Box 1124, Petersburg, AK 99833; (907) 772-4121. For cabin rental information, contact Tongass National Forest, 204 Siginaka Way, Sitka, AK 99835; (907) 747-6671. For an air taxi, contact Kupreanof Flying Service, P.O. Box 768, Petersburg, AK 99833; (907) 772-3396.

Description: Upper Sumner Strait is defined here as the area from Stikine River Flats to Point Baker on Prince of Wales Island and Point Barrie on Kupreanof Island. Like certain other straits and passages in Southeast, Sumner is a major migration channel for salmon bound for spawning systems on area islands and the mainland (The Stikine River is probably the major contributing system.) Also, bottomfish use the strait in summer as an active feeding ground. It is common knowledge that some of the best marine sportfishing opportunities in southern Southeast may be found off the strait's beaches, points, reefs, shoals and stream mouths.

King salmon are primarily caught in spring and early summer when mature fish bound for their streams of birth arrive, but persevering anglers can catch smaller, feeder kings on a year-round basis. The waters near Petersburg and Wrangell in particular receive quite a bit of attention from charter fleets. Silver salmon are present in late summer and fall, and can be caught just about anywhere along the shoreline during the height of the run. Pinks, usually not targeted specifically, are fairly abundant. They are most often encountered in mid- to late summer in the vicinity of spawning streams. Some sea-run cutthroat trout and Dolly Varden may be picked up in late spring and summer off the mouths of clearwater streams and adjoining points and beaches.

Bottomfishing is popular during the warmer months, with halibut the obvious favorite. Available throughout the year (except in January, during the statewide closure), early summer is the preferred time to go after huge flatties up to 200 pounds or more. Areas near the eastern end of Sumner Strait are most productive, with fish averaging between 20 and 75 pounds.

Like other straits and passages around the mouth of the glacial Stikine River, the eastern end of Sumner may get silty at times, especially during the warm summer months when runoff peaks. From late fall into spring, however, the entire strait is usually clear blue.

Hot spots for salmon, charr and halibut include: Prince of Wales Island—Point Baker, Merryfield and Red bays and Point Colpoys; The Eye Opener; McArthur Reef; Level Islands; White Rock; Zarembo Island—Vichnefski Rock, Saint John and Baht harbors and Low and Craig points; Kupreanof Island—Outer Kah Sheets Bay/ Lung Island; Mitkof Island—Midway, Wilson and Station islands, Point Alexander, Banana Point, Outer Blind Slough and Point Howe; Vank Island; Two Tree Island; Sokolof Island; Greys Island/ Pass; Rynda Island; Kadin Island; and Liesnoi Island.

33. UPPER CLARENCE STRAIT

Location: East of Prince of Wales Island, southwest of Etolin Island, 50 miles south of Petersburg, 685 miles southeast of Anchorage.

Reference: Petersburg A-2, A-3, A-4, B-3, B-4; Craig D-1, D-2, D-3.

Access: By boat from Wrangell and Petersburg via Wrangell Narrows and Sumner Strait (from Petersburg) or Stikine Strait (Wrangell). Protected bays and coves are sometimes used by floatplanes to access various parts of the strait.

Highlights: Good fishing for king salmon (from mid-May through mid-June), silver salmon (from early August through early September) and halibut (from June through August).

Species: Chum salmon, (cutthroat trout), Dolly Varden, halibut, king salmon, pink salmon, (red salmon), silver salmon, (steelhead).

Regulations: For details on the open season for halibut and ling cod, consult the current Alaska Department of Fish and Game regulations or the ADF&G Ketchikan office, (907) 225-2859.

Facilities: Two forest service cabins are available in the immediate area, Steamer Bay on Etolin Island and Barnes Lake on Prince of Wales Island.

Contact: For lodging and guide services, contact Real Alaska Adventures, P.O. Box 1124, Petersburg, AK 99833, (907) 772-4121; Last Frontier Charters, P.O. Box 19443, Thorne Bay, AK 99919, (907) 828-3989; or the Boardwalk Wilderness Lodge, P.O. Box 19121-BW, Thorne Bay, AK 99919, (907) 828-3918 or (800) 764-3918. For cabin rental information, contact Wrangell Ranger District, Tongass National Forest, P.O. Box 51, Wrangell, AK 99929, (907) 874-2323; or Thorne Bay Ranger District, Tongass National Forest, P.O. Box 1, Ketchikan, AK 99919, (907) 828-3304. For an air taxi, contact Kupreanof Flying Service, P.O. Box 768, Petersburg, AK 99833; (907) 772-3396.

Description: Upper Clarence Strait includes all waters north of a line extending between Narrow Point on Prince of Wales Island and Lemesurier Point on the Cleveland Peninsula. Surrounding land is covered by dense rain forests, with a multitude of wildlife present. Frequented by boaters from the Ketchikan, Petersburg and Wrangell areas, the strait is one of the better marine fisheries in Alaska as it serves as a major migration and feeding corridor for salmon and bottomfish.

The strait is a wonderland of islands, reefs, hidden bays and coves, with clearwater streams that have substantial numbers of anadromous fish species. Two of the more important drainages include Salmon Bay Lake and Sweetwater Lake in the Kashevarof Passage area, but fish destined for spawning rivers in Ernest Sound, Sumner Strait and even the vast Stikine River system flood upper Clarence Strait.

King salmon, always a favorite and always present in the form of immature feeders, are at their best in late spring and early summer, when the large prespawners move to their spawning destinations. Silver salmon is the next most sought-after species, and are usually taken during late summer and fall by trolling and casting in the bays of the strait. Schools of pink salmon may be encountered at times near the mouths of spawning streams as well. You can expect some sea-run cutthroat trout and Dolly Varden when fishing these areas for salmon.

Halibut are common, and are mainly targeted in waters of moderate depth during the summer months, though some fish are present in deeper parts of the strait year-round. Ling cod and rockfish are abundant as well in areas with appropriate bottom structure.

Frequented hot spots for salmon, charr and halibut include: Prince of Wales Island—Point Colpoys, Bay, Ratz and Narrow points, Outer Salmon Bay, Exchange Cove/Island, Thorne Island/Whale Passage, Stevenson Island, Coffman Cove/Island and Ratz Harbor; Rookery Island; Tide Island; Zarembo Island—McNamara Point, Snow Passage and Point Nesbitt; Kashevarof Islands—Bushy, Shrubby and Blashke islands; Rose Rock; Rose Island; Seal Rock; and Key Reef.

34. STIKINE STRAIT

Location: Northeast of Etolin Island, 35 miles south of Petersburg, 700 miles southeast of Anchorage.

Reference: Petersburg A-2, A-3, B-2, B-3.

Access: Primarily by boat from Wrangell, with some traffic also from Petersburg via Wrangell Narrows and Sumner Strait, or, if tides are high enough, through Dry Strait at Stikine River Flats. Floatplanes are generally used only to access the forest service cabin at Steamer Bay.

Highlights: Good fishing for king salmon (from mid-May through mid-June), silver salmon (from early August through early September) and halibut (from June through August).

Species: (Chum salmon, cutthroat trout), Dolly Varden, halibut, king salmon, pink salmon, (red salmon), silver salmon, (steelhead).

Regulations: For details on the open season for halibut and ling cod, consult the current Alaska Department of Fish and Game regulations or the ADF&G Ketchikan office, (907) 225-2859.

Facilities: A forest service cabin is available at Steamer Bay on Etolin Island.

Contact: For guide services, contact Real Alaska Adventures, P.O. Box 1124, Petersburg, AK 99833, (907) 772-4121; or Alaskan Star Charters, P.O. Box 2027, Wrangell, AK 99929, (907) 874-3084. For cabin rental information, contact Wrangell Ranger District, Tongass National Forest, P.O. Box 51, Wrangell, AK 99929; (907) 874-2323. For an air taxi, contact Kupreanof Flying Service, P.O. Box 768, Petersburg, AK 99833; (907) 772-3396.

Description: Stikine Strait separates Zarembo Island from the larger Etolin Island, connecting Sumner and Clarence straits near Wrangell. Serving as one of the main pathways for returning salmon and other species bound for the glacial Stikine River (and other area streams), Stikine Strait is one of the most productive Southeast fishing locations, especially for king and silver salmon and halibut.

Despite the fact that the northern part of the strait may at times carry a silt load from the nearby Stikine River (particularly during the hot summer months), the fishery does yield consistent catches throughout the season. King salmon, present year-round, are primarily taken in late spring and early summer when large prespawners cruise through the area. Following these salmon monarchs, silvers begin to show up in July and are caught into October. Pinks and sea-run Dollies are not particularly abundant in these waters, but they can offer fair action at times when encountered in concentrations near stream mouths.

Halibut fishing is good, with the best catches coming from the north section of Stikine bordering Sumner Strait. Good anglers can find flatties any day of the year (except during the January closure), but most success occurs in early summer when fish are in shallower water. Various other species of bottomfish are available, as well as outstanding crab, clams and abalone in near-shore waters (which are said to be some of the best for the Wrangell and Petersburg area).

Hot spots for salmon and halibut include: Etolin Island—Point Harrington/Steamer Bay, The Bend, Chichagof Pass, Steamer Point and Quiet Harbor; Zarembo Island—Point Nesbitt, Meter Bight, Fritter Cove, South Point and Roosevelt Harbor; Vank Island—Mud Bay and Neal Point; and Woronkofski Island—Elephants Nose, Woronkofski and Reef points, Sunrise Creek, Point Ancon and Drag Island.

35. ZIMOVIA STRAIT

Location: Southwest of Wrangell Island and northeast of Etolin Island, 35 miles southeast of Petersburg, 700 miles southeast of Anchorage.

Reference: Petersburg A-1, A-2, B-1, B-2.

Access: Primarily by boat from Wrangell Harbor, but also from Petersburg via Wrangell Narrows and Sumner Strait, or, if tides permit, through Dry Strait at Stikine River Flats. Zimovia Highway out of Wrangell is used by boaters and shorecasters to fish areas south of town. It is also possible for floatplanes to land in protected waters of the strait.

Highlights: Good fishing for king salmon (from mid-May through mid-June), silver salmon (from early August through early September), red salmon (from mid- through late July), pink salmon (from late July through early August), cutthroat trout and Dolly Varden (from June through August) and halibut (from June through July).

Species: Chum salmon, cutthroat trout, Dolly Varden, halibut, king salmon, pink salmon, red salmon, silver salmon, (steelhead).

Regulations: For details on the open season for halibut and ling cod, consult the current Alaska Department of Fish and Game regulations or the ADF&G Ketchikan office, (907) 225-2859.

Facilities: Commercial lodging, sporting goods, groceries, boat rentals and a boat launch, fuel, water and guide services are available in Wrangell.

Contact: For guide services, contact Real Alaska Adventures, P.O. Box 1124, Petersburg, AK 99833, (907) 772-4121; or Alaskan Star Charters, P.O. Box 2027, Wrangell, AK 99929, (907) 874-3084. For lodging information, contact the City of Wrangell, 205 Brueger Street, Wrangell, AK 99929; (907) 874-2381. For cabin rental information, contact Wrangell Ranger District, Tongass National Forest, P.O. Box 51, Wrangell, AK 99929; (907) 874-2323.

Description: Zimovia Strait lies between the islands of Etolin and Wrangell, south of the town of Wrangell. The rolling green hills and occasional peaks lend scenic contrast to the strait's deep blue waters. With the great fishing and abundant marine wildlife, it is an attractive and very popular recreation area within easy reach of town.

Zimovia is slightly narrower and longer than Stikine Strait. Like the strait, it can get cloudy in its upper end during summer hot spells, due to glacial outwash from the giant Stikine River, but generally it is clear most of the year. King salmon are the most sought-after species here. Feeders can be caught year-round, with the best action from October into May or June, when the big spawners heading for the mainland take over. (Most of the salmon that pass through the strait are headed for clearwater tributaries of the Stikine, with some bound for smaller local streams like Thoms and Pat creeks.) Silver salmon arrive soon after and stay from late summer into fall, with a few fish available into November at the south end of the strait. Very good pink and red salmon, cutthroat trout and Dolly Varden fishing is possible at times at the mouth of Thoms Creek in Thoms Place. Halibut are primarily caught at the outer ends of Zimovia Strait in deeper water, with the best action in early summer.

For easily accessed angling excursions of a few hours up to a day, Zimovia Strait is highly recommended for anyone planning to be in the Wrangell area. Since the strait is fairly protected from most severe weather, kayak and even canoe trips are a possibility.

Good locations for salmon, charr and halibut are: Wrangell Island —Thoms Place, Nemo and Cemetery points, Pat Creek Landing, Bluffs/Shoemaker Bay and Wrangell Harbor; Etolin Island—Olive Cove, Anita Point, Anita Bay and Chichagof Pass; Woronkofski Island—Elephants Nose/Woronkofski Point; and Young Rock.

36. EASTERN PASSAGE

Location: Northeast of Wrangell Island, 35 miles southeast of Petersburg, 700 miles southeast of Anchorage.

Reference: Petersburg B-1, B-2, C-1, C-2; Bradfield Canal A-6, B-6.

Access: Primarily by boat from Wrangell, but also from Petersburg via Wrangell Narrows and Sumner Strait, or, if tides permit, through Dry Strait at Stikine River Flats.

Highlights: Good fishing for king salmon (from mid-May through mid-June), silver salmon (from mid-August through mid-September), pink salmon (from late July through early August), Dolly Varden (from June through August) and halibut (from June through early July).

Species: Chum salmon, Dolly Varden, halibut, king salmon, pink salmon, silver salmon, (steelhead).

Regulations: For details on the open season for salmon, halibut and ling cod, consult the current Alaska Department of Fish and Game regulations or the ADF&G Ketchikan office, (907) 225-2859.

Facilities: A forest service cabin is available on the mainland at Berg Bay.

Contact: For guide services, contact Real Alaska Adventures, P.O. Box 1124, Petersburg, AK 99833, (907) 772-4121; or Alaskan Star Charters, P.O. Box 2027, Wrangell, AK 99929, (907) 874-3084. For cabin rental information, contact Wrangell Ranger District, Tongass National Forest, P.O. Box 51, Wrangell, AK 99929; (907) 874-2323. For an air taxi, contact Kupreanof Flying Service, P.O. Box 768, Petersburg, AK 99833; (907) 772-3396.

Description: Long and narrow Eastern Passage, parting Wrangell Island from the mainland, stretches from Stikine River Flats to Ernest Sound and Bradfield Canal. Part of the Tongass National Forest, the highly scenic surroundings' evergreens, lush valleys and snow-capped mountains—some of which rise up to 5,300 feet—add appeal to the area's great fishing potential. Along with Stikine and Zimovia straits, the passage is one of the main Wrangell destinations for salmon.

Eastern Passage receives substantial numbers of hatchery salmon, as well as wild fish—especially feeder kings. The northern section yields native salmon bound for the glacial Stikine River, while the central portion is more famous for its enhanced runs of king, silver and chum returning to the Earl West Cove Hatchery. Around the southern end, at outer Blake Channel, anglers do well intercepting schools of fish heading for Bradfield Canal drainages.

Mature, prespawning kings are abundant in late spring and early summer, with immature fish scattered throughout year-round. "The Narrows," a half-mile-wide chute separating the passage from Blake Channel, is a major feeder king attraction from November to April, but also holds hatchery salmon later in the season. (A forest service cabin in Berg Bay, only a few miles away, makes a fine point of access.) Large spawner kings up to 40 or 50 pounds are taken in June and July at the south end. Later in the summer anglers begin taking more and more silver salmon as the smaller pinks peak in area waters. Running into October and even November in some locations, these fall coho are right behind the kings in popularity and attract considerable angling attention. Chum salmon, usually only caught incidentally, return in good numbers to the hatchery release site and, along with Dolly Varden, provide fair angling for anyone with a little patience. Halibut are most predictably hooked in moderately deep water around the north and south ends of Eastern Passage and range between 15 and 60 pounds with occasional larger catches.

Area hot spots include: Babbler Point; The Narrows; Wrangell Island—Point Highfield and Earl West Cove; Blake Channel—Blake (Ham) Island.

37. ERNEST SOUND

Location: East of Etolin Island and southeast of Wrangell Island, 65 miles southeast of Petersburg, 730 miles southeast of Anchorage.

Reference: Bradfield Canal A-5, A-6; Petersburg A-1; Ketchikan D-6; Craig C-1, D-1, D-2.

Access: By boat from Wrangell via Zimovia Strait or Ketchikan via Tongass Narrows and Clarence Strait. Some boaters opt to go through Eastern Passage and Blake Channel to access Bradfield Canal on the upper sound. Floatplanes access is also possible, by landing in protected waters such as small bays and coves.

Highlights: Excellent fishing for pink salmon (from mid-July through mid-August); good fishing for king salmon (in June), silver salmon (from late August through mid-September) and halibut (from June through August).

Species: Chum salmon, cutthroat trout, Dolly Varden, halibut, king salmon, pink salmon, (red salmon), silver salmon, (steelhead).

Regulations: For details on the open season for halibut and ling cod, consult the current Alaska Department of Fish and Game regulations or the ADF&G Ketchikan office, (907) 225-2859.

Facilities: Two forest service cabins are available in Bradfield Canal, one at the mouth of Harding River, another at Anan Bay.

Contact: For guide services, contact Alaskan Star Charters, P.O. Box 2027, Wrangell, AK 99929; (907) 874-3084. For cabin rental information, contact Wrangell Ranger District, Tongass National Forest, P.O. Box 51, Wrangell, AK 99929, (907) 874-2323; or Tongass National Forest, Federal Building, Ketchikan, AK 99901, (907) 225-3101. For an air taxi, contact Kupreanof Flying Service, P.O. Box 768, Petersburg, AK 99833; (907) 772-3396.

Description: Ernest Sound is bordered by the Cleveland Peninsula and the mainland in the east and Etolin and Wrangell islands in the west, and includes Bradfield Canal. Situated within Tongass National Forest, the sound is very scenic, with a multitude of bays, coves, and jutting points set among snow-clad mountains and forested valleys. Although it is not mentioned much outside of Petersburg, the sound has great angling potential for a variety of sought-after game species.

The central and outer areas of Ernest Sound are regarded as a highly productive marine fishery for salmon and halibut. Trolling or mooching for king salmon is done year-round, but success rates are much higher in early summer as mature prespawners enter the waters. Some of these monarchs eventually head up a few of the rivers draining into Bradfield Canal, but most continue on to other areas further north.

With a great number of clear rivers and streams flowing into Ernest Sound and connecting waters, angling for the other salmon species is highly productive. Well-known drainages like the Harding and Eagle rivers and Anan Creek are tops on the list. In midsummer, look for schools of dime-bright chum and pink salmon, especially in Bradfield Canal. (Anan Bay receives a tremendous run of pinks, and is regarded as one of the best locations in Southeast for the species. It also has trophy chum salmon up to 20 pounds or more.)

Silver salmon are present from late summer through fall, with a few fresh fish still available in November. The sound is a good area to intercept these battlers, but Bradfield Canal is better, with larger concentrations of fish near the mouths of spawning streams. Halibut are available in deeper parts of the sound, and fair numbers of cutthroat trout and Dolly Varden cruise the shorelines near salmon streams in late spring and early summer.

Some proven hot spot locations around Ernest Sound for salmon, charr and halibut include: Peterson Island; Westerly Island; Easterly Island; Deer Island/Point Peters; Found Island; Wrangell Island—Fools Inlet and Southeast Cove/Thoms Point; and Cleveland Peninsula—Lemesurier, Magnetic, Eaton and Watkins points, Anan Bay, Point Warde, Lemly Rocks, Union and Emerald bays and Cannery Creek.

38. KADAKE CREEK

Location: North Kuiu Island drainage, 45 miles west of Petersburg, 635 miles southeast of Anchorage.
Reference: Petersburg D-6; Port Alexander C-1.
Access: By plane or boat from Petersburg, Wrangell or other area towns. Boaters from Petersburg must go through Frederick Sound and Keku Strait to reach Kadake Bay. From there, access to the mouth of Kadake Creek requires an 18-foot tide. A limited network of forest roads crisscross the northern part of Kuiu Island, providing access to the upper drainage.
Highlights: Good fishing for silver salmon (in the first half of September), chum and pink salmon (from late July through early August), steelhead (from late April through mid-May), cutthroat trout (in May and June) and Dolly Varden (in May and from August through September).
Species: Chum salmon, cutthroat trout, Dolly Varden, pink salmon,

rainbow trout, silver salmon, steelhead.

Regulations: Unbaited, artificial lures only from November 16 through September 14; king salmon fishing is prohibited. For additional restrictions, consult the current Alaska Department of Fish and Game regulations or the ADF&G Ketchikan office, (907) 225-2859.

Facilities: A forest service cabin is available at Kadake Bay at the mouth of Kadake Creek.

Contact: For cabin rental information, contact Tongass National Forest, 204 Siginaka Way, Sitka, AK 99835; (907) 747-6671. For an air taxi, contact Kupreanof Flying Service, P.O. Box 768, Petersburg, AK 99833; (907) 772-3396.

Description: Situated on the northern end of Kuiu Island, Kadake Creek is a fairly small drainage flowing into Kadake Bay and Keku Strait. Due to muskeg in the area, it runs slightly brown in color. The four lakes connected to the stream are small and of little significance to the fishery. The most sought-after species include silver salmon and steelhead and cutthroat trout, which are present in abundance.

Most angling effort takes place on the lower creek sections near the forest service cabin. Visiting anglers usually work the tides at the mouth at Kadake Bay, moving upstream to search for holding fish after the crest of the tide. A big spring run of steelhead and hungry cutthroat trout open the season every year, especially for flyfishing. July and August bring chum and pink salmon into the system. Fishing the tides at the mouth usually produces the most and brightest fish.

Coho invade Kadake beginning in late summer and continuing into October. (Look for in-migrating cutthroats and Dollies along with the salmon, especially around spawning beds.) There are some resident rainbow trout in the upper and middle sections of Kadake Creek, but they are seldom targeted. Also, a very small run of fall steelhead may be present in the latter part of November.

39. DUNCAN SALTCHUCK CREEK

Location: Central Kupreanof Island drainage, 15 miles west of Petersburg, 660 miles southeast of Anchorage.

Reference: Petersburg D-4, D-5.

Access: By plane and boat from Petersburg or Wrangell. From Petersburg, access is via Wrangell Narrows up into Duncan Canal and Saltchuck. (Boaters can access the Saltchuck area and the mouth of the creek only on high tides of at least 17 feet.)

Highlights: Good fishing for silver salmon (in September), steelhead (from late April through mid-May), cutthroat trout (from May through June) and Dolly Varden (in May and from August through September).

Species: Chum salmon, cutthroat trout, Dolly Varden, pink salmon, rainbow trout, silver salmon, steelhead.

Regulations: Unbaited, artificial lures only from November 16 through September 14; king salmon fishing is prohibited. For additional restrictions, consult the current Alaska Department of Fish and Game regulations or the ADF&G Ketchikan office, (907) 225-2859.

Facilities: Two forest service cabins are available at the Saltchuck at the head of Duncan Canal.

Contact: For cabin rental information, contact Tongass National Forest, P.O. Box 309, Petersburg, AK 99833; (907) 772-3871. For an air taxi, contact Kupreanof Flying Service, P.O. Box 768, Petersburg, AK 99833; (907) 772-3396.

Description: Duncan Saltchuck Creek lies at the head of Duncan Canal in the central part of Kupreanof Island. Draining areas of muskeg around the Bohemian Range, it usually has a tannic-brown color, especially after heavy fall rains, but it nonetheless offers productive fishing for salmon, trout and charr in a small stream setting.

Long known for its cutthroat trout, the Saltchuck hosts above average numbers of these fine gamefish in late spring to early summer and again in fall. The last few miles above Duncan Canal is the most popular stretch, and is frequently fished with light spinning and flyfishing gear. Sea-run Dolly Varden are available during the same times with substantial catches being made on egg and attractor pattern flies in the creek and flashy spoons off the mouth.

Steelhead trout bust into the drainage in spring, offering a few weeks of top-notch flyfishing excitement. Most successful anglers fish the tides on the lower creek sections, intercepting these robust sea-run rainbows on their way upstream to spawning areas. Other important species in Duncan Saltchuck include silver salmon and rainbow trout; the lower river and mouth are best for coho, while the upper sections harbor the most rainbow. Additionally, some chum and pink salmon can be enticed into striking flashy hardware right above the mouth in late summer.

The two forest service cabins located on the shore of the Saltchuck make perfect points for staging boat excursions into Duncan Canal or for fishing the lower reaches of the creek.

40. Castle River

Location: South Kupreanof Island drainage, 20 miles southwest of Petersburg, 670 miles southeast of Anchorage.

Reference: Petersburg C-4, C-5.

Access: By floatplane or boat from Petersburg or Wrangell. Boaters from Petersburg arrive via Wrangell Narrows and Duncan Canal, and from Wrangell via Sumner Strait and Duncan Canal. A tide of at least 15 feet is required for floatplanes and 13 feet for boats to access the mouth of river.

Highlights: An important area steelhead and silver salmon stream; good fishing for silver salmon (in the first half of September), chum and pink salmon (from late July through early August), steelhead (from late April through mid-May), rainbow and cutthroat trout (in May and June) and Dolly Varden (in May and from August through September).

Species: Chum salmon, cutthroat trout, Dolly Varden, pink salmon, rainbow trout, silver salmon, steelhead.

Regulations: Unbaited, artificial lures only from November 16 through September 14; king salmon fishing is prohibited. For additional restrictions, consult the current Alaska Department of Fish and Game regulations or the ADF&G Ketchikan office, (907) 225-2859.

Facilities: Two forest service cabins are available near the mouth.

Contact: For cabin rental information, contact Tongass National Forest, P.O. Box 309, Petersburg, AK 99833; (907) 772-3871. For an air taxi, contact Kupreanof Flying Service, P.O. Box 768, Petersburg, AK 99833; (907) 772-3396.

Description: Flowing into west Duncan Canal on Kupreanof Island, Castle River is a tannic-brown stream surrounded by muskeg, rain forests and rolling hills. Small in size, the river is nonetheless one of the most productive streams of the area, known best for silver salmon and steelhead trout.

Most anglers access the drainage at the mouth, then fish and hike upstream. The first major gamefish of the season are spring-run steelhead trout. They are best intercepted early on in the first few miles of the river, fishing the tides. Later on, anglers do better by hiking to holes and runs on the middle Castle. Resident rainbows, as well as sea-run cutthroat trout and Dolly Varden, are also available from spring through fall.

Silver salmon begin running in August and continue until October, and inspire a fair amount of angling effort in the Castle. Chum and pink salmon also show in large numbers, but a little earlier than the coho. As is the case most anywhere, brighter fish are generally taken at the mouth or in the lower river.

There are two forest service cabins with boats in the vicinity, which are ideally situated for anglers intending to fish Castle River and perhaps even do some trolling or jigging in the salt water of Duncan Canal. (Trips to Duncan Saltchuck Creek to the north or the Kah Sheets River to the south are possible by boat.) Because of their popularity, reservations for these cabins should be made early.

41. KAH SHEETS RIVER

Location: South Kupreanof Island drainage, 25 miles southwest of Petersburg, 670 miles southeast of Anchorage.

Reference: Petersburg C-4, C-5.

Access: By boat or floatplane from Petersburg or Wrangell. Boaters from Petersburg go through Wrangell Narrows and lower Duncan Canal to Kah Sheets Bay; those from Wrangell head via Sumner Strait to the bay. (To reach the trailhead at Kah Sheets Bay by boat, a 14-foot tide is required.) The trail leads 2.75 miles to the outlet of Kah Sheets Lake, where floatplane access is possible.

Highlights: One of Southeast's better steelhead and salmon streams; good fishing for silver salmon (in the first half of September), chum and pink salmon (from late July through early August), steelhead (from late April through mid-May), rainbow and cutthroat trout (in May and June) and Dolly Varden (in May and from August through September).

Species: Chum salmon, cutthroat trout, Dolly Varden, pink salmon, rainbow trout, red salmon, silver salmon, steelhead.

Regulations: Unbaited, artificial lures only from November 16 through September 14; king salmon fishing is prohibited. For additional restrictions, consult the current Alaska Department of Fish and Game regulations or the ADF&G Ketchikan office, (907) 225-2859.

Facilities: Two forest service cabins are available, one at the head of Kah Sheets Bay near the mouth of the river, another at the outlet of Kah Sheets Lake.

Contact: For cabin rental information, contact Tongass National Forest, P.O. Box 309, Petersburg, AK 99833; (907) 772-3871. For an air taxi, contact Kupreanof Flying Service, P.O. Box 768, Petersburg, AK 99833; (907) 772-3396.

Description: Kah Sheets River is a lightly tannic-stained stream draining into Kah Sheets Bay and upper Sumner Strait. Only about two miles long, the river is easily fished along its entire length from tidewater to the outlet of Kah Sheets Lake via a well-marked trail. From near and afar, anglers come to experience one of the best streams in southern Southeast for silver salmon and steelhead trout.

Like other drainages on Kupreanof Island, Kah Sheets has a vibrant run of spring steelhead trout. They can be taken anywhere on the river, with the best success reported on incoming tides near the mouth early in the run and in the upper river just below the lake later on. Resident rainbows are found in the lake, giving anglers with canoes or inflatables some action during spring and fall months.Searun cutthroat trout and Dolly Varden are also present in varying numbers throughout the season.

The Kah Sheets also has a reputation for its ballistic coho. Large schools of these fighters enter the river in August and stay into October. They are taken from Kah Sheets Bay clear up into the lake. Earlier trips in midsummer can be productive for hefty chum salmon and spunky pinks. (A small run of reds also occurs, with the best opportunities found in the river's faster flowing stretches.)

Both of the two forest service cabins are ideally situated for excellent access to the best of Kupreanof Island fishing—whether casting for salmon and steelhead in the river, jigging for halibut in the bay, or flyfishing trout and dollies in the lake.

42. PETERSBURG CREEK

Location: Southeast Kupreanof Island drainage, five miles west of Petersburg, 670 miles southeast of Anchorage.

Reference: Petersburg D-4.

Access: Primarily by floatplane or boat from Petersburg or Wrangell. Planes traditionally land on Petersburg Lake. Boaters from nearby Petersburg have two options to access the stream and lake: If tides are higher than 15 feet, boats can reach the creek mouth via Wrangell Narrows, where a trail leads 6.5 miles to Petersburg Lake. Or, if tides don't allow, boaters can moor at a state dock on Wrangell Narrows and take a trail leading 11.5 miles to lake.

Highlights: A tremendously popular and productive Southeast steelhead and salmon stream, with good fishing for silver salmon (in the second half of September), red salmon (in late July), chum and pink salmon (from late July through early August), steelhead (in May), rainbow and cutthroat trout (in May and June) and Dolly Varden (in May and from August through September).

Species: Chum salmon, cutthroat trout, Dolly Varden, pink salmon, rainbow trout, red salmon, silver salmon, steelhead.

Regulations: Unbaited, artificial lures only from November 16 through September 14; king salmon fishing is prohibited. For additional restrictions, consult the current Alaska Department of Fish and Game regulations or the ADF&G Petersburg office, (907) 772-3801.

Facilities: A forest service cabin is available at Petersburg Lake.

Contact: For fishing information, contact the Alaska Department of Fish and Game, Sportfish Division, P.O. Box 667, Petersburg, AK 99833; (907) 772-3801. For cabin rental information, contact Tongass National Forest, P.O. Box 309, Petersburg, AK 99833; (907) 772-3871.

Description: Located on the Lindberg Peninsula of Kupreanof Island, Petersburg Lake and Creek is a very popular recreation area for locals, which gets heavily fished during the height of the salmon and steelhead runs. The lower stream is lined by the crests of Petersburg Mountain and Del Monte Peak, adding considerable scenic appeal. Flowing clear and fairly fast west to Wrangell Narrows across from the town of Petersburg, the creek is perfect for one- or two-day outings to sample some better streamfishing.

As part of the Petersburg Creek-Duncan Saltchuck Wilderness, this area offers some fairly high-quality lake and streamfishing possibilities in combination with short trail excursions. Silver salmon and steelhead trout receive most of the attention on the lower section of the creek, while sea-run cutthroats, Dollies and resident rainbows are taken usually in Petersburg Lake, particularly during the spring and fall months.

Starting in late summer and continuing until late fall, the silvers are pursued with vigor by both spin and flycasters, while spring-run steelhead grab anglers' attention earlier in the season. Petersburg Creek steelies tend toward being some of the largest in Southeast, with a few exceptional fish up to 20 pounds or more possible.

A brief showing of sockeye salmon presents another angling opportunity during the midsummer lull; fish for them from the lake down. During the same period, only running slightly later, the creek often sees good numbers of chums and pinks.

It is a rare delight to find such a productive stream close to a major town. If you have some time to kill in Petersburg, you might as well head over and enjoy some of the good fishing close at hand.

43. OHMER CREEK

Location: South Mitkof Island drainage, 20 miles south of Petersburg, 680 miles southeast of Anchorage.

Reference: Petersburg C-3.

Access: By car from Petersburg. The Mitkof Highway out of town leads along Wrangell Narrows and Blind Slough to a stream crossing and parallels Ohmer Creek for about one mile. Roads can take anglers to other stream sections.

Highlights: Petersburg's top roadside stream, with good fishing for king salmon (from late June through mid-July), silver salmon (in the first half of September), chum and pink salmon (in early August), cutthroat trout (from May through June) and Dolly Varden (in May and from August through September).

Species: Chum salmon, cutthroat trout, Dolly Varden, king salmon, pink salmon, rainbow trout, silver salmon, steelhead.

Regulations: Unbaited, artificial lures only from November 16 through September 14. For additional restrictions, consult the current Alaska Department of Fish and Game regulations or the ADF&G Petersburg office, (907) 772-3801.

Facilities: A campground is available next to the Mitkof Highway, near the mouth of the stream.

Contact: For fishing information, contact the Alaska Department of Fish and Game, Sportfish Division, P.O. Box 667, Petersburg, AK 99833; (907) 772-3801. For camping information, contact the Petersburg Chamber of Commerce, P.O. Box 649, Petersburg, AK 99833; (907) 772-3646.

Description: Ohmer Creek, like the Petersburg drainage, is a heavily fished, local clearwater stream with easy access and good overall fishing. Situated on the mountainous southern end of Mitkof Island, it is a relatively small drainage containing both wild and hatchery stocks of salmon and healthy populations of trout and charr.

One of the more unique features about Ohmer Creek is its run of big king salmon. Although it is hatchery maintained, the fishery is one of few stream locations in Southeast where anglers can legally fish these great sportfish. Present in early and midsummer, the kings add welcome variety to the creek's angling prospects. Silver salmon are popular in fall when a natural run of these spectacular battlers enters the stream in fairly large schools. For both species, local anglers tend to favor the river's lower section, including the mouth, for best fishing.

Other fine species to consider are sea-run cutthroat trout and

Dolly Varden, as they can offer steady action near the road crossing and other spots. Additionally, late summer runs of chums and pinks can add some excitement between the king and silver salmon runs. A small run of native steelhead trout also shows up in spring, with fair fishing to be expected during the peak in May. This creek is certainly a fine possibility, especially if you're ever passing through Petersburg and you have a few hours to spare.

44. STIKINE RIVER SYSTEM

Location: Mainland drainage east of Mitkof Island, 30 miles southeast of Petersburg, 690 miles southeast of Anchorage.

Reference: Bradfield Canal C-6, D-6; Petersburg C-1, C-2, D-1.

Access: By boat or plane from Petersburg and Wrangell. From Petersburg, access is via Frederick and Dry Straits; from Wrangell, access is via Eastern Passage. (To successfully reach the mainstem Stikine River and its clearwater tributaries, a tide of at least 14 feet is necessary to cross the Stikine River Flats.) Small planes are capable of landing in a few locations, if conditions permit.

Highlights: Outstanding fishing possibilities on Southeast's largest river—the mile-wide Stikine. Good fishing for silver salmon (in September), chum and pink salmon (late July through early August), steelhead (from late April through mid-May), rainbow and cutthroat trout (from May through June) and Dolly Varden (in May and from August through September).

Species: Chum salmon, cutthroat trout, Dolly Varden, (king salmon), pink salmon, rainbow trout, red salmon, silver salmon, (steelhead).

Regulations: Unbaited, artificial lures only from November 16 through September 14; king salmon fishing is prohibited. For additional restrictions, consult the current Alaska Department of Fish and Game regulations or the ADF&G Ketchikan office, (907) 225-2859.

Facilities: Five forest service cabins are available in the Stikine River drainage: Red Slough (one), Shakes Slough (two), Figure Eight Lake (one) and Andrew Creek (one).

Contact: For guide services, contact Ellis Inc., P.O. Box 1068, Petersburg, AK 99833; (907) 772-3039. For cabin rental information, contact Tongass National Forest, P.O. Box 309, Petersburg, AK 99833; (907) 772-3871. For an air taxi, contact Kupreanof Flying Service, P.O. Box 768, Petersburg, AK 99833; (907) 772-3396.

Description: The Stikine River is a very large glacial system originating from the snow- and ice-bound Cassiar Mountains in British

Columbia, Canada. The largest transboundary system in Southeast, only the last 30 to 35 miles or so of the river lies within Alaska, fanning out into a huge, sandy delta at the head of Sumner Strait and Frederick Sound just east of Mitkof Island. With a vast number of tributary lakes and clearwater streams, it supports fairly large populations of salmon, charr and trout, and has quite a bit of sportfish potential waiting for anglers with the time to explore its many productive waters.

Since the Stikine is heavily laden with fine silt, most sportfishing takes place at the confluences of clearwater streams and sloughs. The largest and most popular tributary among local anglers is Andrew Creek, on the south bank only a few miles from tidewater. Another, but slightly smaller, stream is nearby Government Creek, situated near the mouth. Both of these receive a fair amount of angling pressure during the height of salmon runs in summer and fall.

Although it has a substantial run of large king salmon (from May through July), the Stikine is currently closed to fishing for the species, with most fish heading unimpeded into major spawning streams in Canada. Good numbers of silvers, chums and pinks along with smaller numbers of reds, however, are present throughout the lower drainage and provide the bulk of angling activity. Dolly Varden are available and seasonally abundant (best in late summer to fall), and there are even occasional cutthroat and rainbow trout taken. (Some may be found in the mainstem Stikine from late fall to early spring, when the river clears for lack of meltwater.) The best areas to fish in the summer are clearwater sloughs and creek mouths. Steelhead are rumored to be available, but elusive; apparently they are concentrated in tributaries farther upriver.

There are quite a few options for adventure angling this impressive drainage. It can be floated by kayak, raft or canoe, with a put-in usually at Telegraph Creek (150 miles above tidewater), which can be accessed via the Cassiar Highway, or at other points along the river by small float or wheelplane. This is ideal as it allows anglers to sample countless opportunities for good angling in tributary creeks, streams, lakes and sloughs on the way down. It is also possible to jet boat upriver from Wrangell and camp and fish or float down. Public-use cabins are available, and there are even some hot springs along the river.

Part of the Stikine-Leconte Wilderness, the river is dramatically scenic, with ice-capped mountain peaks soaring over 4,000 feet, steep gorges and forested valleys and tidewater glaciers. Wildlife is particularly abundant. Anyone willing to explore this huge drainage will most likely not be disappointed, certainly not by the wild, impressive surroundings and the fishing. Since this is a true wilderness river with volatile nature and tidal flats, sandbars and extreme tides on the lower end, the services of a local guide are highly recommended, unless you are a seasoned wilderness traveler.

45. RED LAKE

Location: North Prince of Wales Island drainage, 40 miles southwest of Petersburg, 675 miles southeast of Anchorage.

Reference: Petersburg A-4, B-4.

Access: By floatplane from Petersburg, Wrangell, Klawock, Craig or other area towns, landing at the outlet of Red Lake. Also, limited road access by Prince of Wales Forest Road 5600, from Klawock or Craig via Big Salt Road; Thorne Bay Road, from Thorne Bay, crosses the outlet stream and provides access to the lake.

Highlights: Exceptional scenery and outstanding stream and lake angling possibilities, with good fishing for silver salmon (in the first half of September), red salmon (in late July), chum and pink salmon (from late July through early August), rainbow and cutthroat trout (in June and September) and Dolly Varden (in May and from August through September).

Species: Chum salmon, cutthroat trout, Dolly Varden, pink salmon, rainbow trout, red salmon, silver salmon, steelhead.

Regulations: Unbaited, artificial lures only from November 16 through September 14; king salmon fishing is prohibited. For additional restrictions, consult the current Alaska Department of Fish and Game regulations or the ADF&G Ketchikan office, (907) 225-2859.

Facilities: A forest service cabin is available at Red Lake.

Contact: For cabin rental information, contact Thorne Bay Ranger District, Tongass National Forest, P.O. Box 1, Ketchikan, AK 99919; (907) 828-3304. For an air taxi, contact Kupreanof Flying Service, P.O. Box 768, Petersburg, AK 99833, (907) 772-3396; or Taquan Air, 1007 Water Street, Ketchikan, AK 99901, (907) 225-8800 or (800) 770-8800.

Description: Situated on the northern tip of Prince of Wales Island, Red Lake is fairly small—only two miles long and about a half mile wide—with a small outlet stream connecting it to Red Bay and Sumner Strait. It has a good variety of sportfish, with outstanding fishing at times.

Starting in spring, out-migrating cutthroat trout and Dolly Varden are taken from the lake outlet area and head of Red Bay. Fishing with ultra-light gear is ideal as these fish will go to two or three pounds. Resident rainbows running about the same size are active in all areas of the lake. Additionally, a small spring run of steelhead trout is available, with fair to good fishing in the outlet stream.

After a short break in the spring fishery, decent runs of red, chum and pink salmon begin in mid- to late summer and provide variety and excitement from the lake outlet to tidewater. (Reds are the most sought-after, and may be pursued effectively with sparse bucktail flies in faster flowing, shallow stream sections.) A few weeks later, silver salmon jam the small outlet stream all the way up into the lake, sustaining the fishing action into the fall. As the salmon are running, cutthroat trout and Dolly Varden will move into the drainage from the salt water and begin feeding actively, creating still more angling opportunities.

Although the drainage is accessible by road, many anglers choose to experience Red Lake by flying or boating in to the mouth of the outlet stream.

46. SWEETWATER LAKE SYSTEM

Location: Northeast Prince of Wales Island drainage, 50 miles southwest of Petersburg, 705 miles southeast of Anchorage.

Reference: Craig D-3, D-4; Petersburg A-4.

Access: By floatplane from Petersburg, Wrangell, Klawock, Craig or other area towns and communities, landing on Sweetwater and Galea lakes. A limited forest road system from Klawock, Craig and Thorne Bay provides additional access to the lake, tributaries and forest service cabin.

Highlights: An extensive Prince of Wales drainage, well known for good fishing: silver salmon (from late July through early August and in the second half of September), red salmon (in late July), steelhead (from late April through mid-May), rainbow trout (in May and September), cutthroat trout (from May through June) and Dolly Varden (in May and from August through September).

Species: Chum salmon, cutthroat trout, Dolly Varden, pink salmon, rainbow trout, red salmon, silver salmon, steelhead.

Regulations: Unbaited, artificial lures only from November 16 through September 14; king salmon fishing is prohibited. For additional restrictions, consult the current Alaska Department of Fish and Game regulations or the ADF&G Ketchikan office, (907) 225-2859.

Facilities: Three forest service cabins are available within the system: Sweetwater Lake, Galea Lake and Barnes Lake.

Contact: For cabin rental information, contact Thorne Bay Ranger District, Tongass National Forest, P.O. Box 1, Ketchikan, AK 99919; (907) 828-3304. For an air taxi, contact Kupreanof Flying Service, P.O. Box 768, Petersburg, AK 99833, (907) 772-3396; or Taquan Air, 1007 Water Street, Ketchikan, AK 99901, (907) 225-8800 or (800) 770-8800.

Description: Draining into northern Clarence Strait, the Sweetwater system consists of dozens of lakes and ponds of varying sizes connected by small streams in the interior of Prince of Wales Island. Due to heavy muskeg surrounding much of the drainage, Sweetwater is largely tannic brown. Angling is very good overall, however, with a satisfying variety of species available. With all the good water in this drainage, a visitor can spend weeks exploring and fishing different areas, from headwaters down to the tidal zone. (A well-established canoe route makes it easy.)

The first important gamefish to invade Sweetwater are some spring-run steelhead trout. These flashy fighters are at their best in the outlet stream of Sweetwater Lake—Indian Creek—but can also be encountered in many other flowing waters of the system, including Hatchery and Logjam creeks. Resident rainbow trout are present in the main lake and in its tributaries, along with sea-run cutthroats and Dolly Varden. The lower end of the lakes and inlet streams have traditionally been the hot spots for them, particularly in spring and fall.

Later on in the season, silver and red salmon begin to show in large numbers. Sweetwater has perfect conditions for taking these fine sportfish; anglers do well for them in Indian Creek and the lower sections and the mouths of other large tributaries. While the sockeyes come through in one big push, there are two distinct runs of coho in the system. The first run occurs primarily during July and August, while the second run hits its peak in September and continues into October. Only small numbers of chum and pink salmon show every year, in late summer, with fishing action reported fair for pinks at times.

47. SALMON BAY LAKE

Location: North Prince of Wales Island drainage, 40 miles south of Petersburg, 680 miles southeast of Anchorage.

Reference: Petersburg A-4, B-4.

Access: Primarily by floatplane from Petersburg, Wrangell, Klawock, Craig or other area towns, landing on Salmon Bay Lake. Boat access is possible to the stream outlet, but is not recommended, since only very high tides can allow clear passage through the shallow intertidal areas of Salmon Bay. Once there, a trail leads 1.8 miles to the lake outlet.

Highlights: One of the top area locations for spring and fall fishing. Good fishing for silver salmon (in the first half of September), red salmon (in late July), steelhead (in late November and from late April through mid-May), rainbow trout (in June and September), cutthroat trout (from May through June) and Dolly Varden (in May and from August through September).

Species: Cutthroat trout, Dolly Varden, rainbow trout, red salmon, silver salmon, steelhead.

Regulations: Unbaited, artificial lures only from November 16 through September 14; king salmon fishing is prohibited. For additional restrictions, consult the current Alaska Department of Fish and Game regulations or the ADF&G Ketchikan office, (907) 225-2859.

Facilities: A forest service cabin is available at Salmon Bay Lake.

Contact: For cabin rental information, contact Thorne Bay Ranger District, Tongass National Forest, P.O. Box 1, Ketchikan, AK 99919; (907) 828-3304. For an air taxi, contact Kupreanof Flying Service, P.O. Box 768, Petersburg, AK 99833, (907) 772-3396; or Taquan Air, 1007 Water Street, Ketchikan, AK 99901, (907) 225-8800 or (800) 770-8800.

Description: Draining into upper Clarence Strait through Salmon Bay, the Salmon Bay Lake area offers a well-known mix of good sport-fishing variety. The majority of anglers visiting this drainage do so through Salmon Bay Lake, a body of water about one mile wide and four miles long. There is a forest service cabin at the lake for public use. A trail leads from the lake outlet along the stream towards Salmon Bay.

Red salmon enter the stream and Salmon Bay Lake in midsummer, with most successful anglers concentrating efforts in areas with moderately fast current and shallow depth. Later on, bright coho show up and continue running through most of the fall; along with the red salmon, they are the most sought-after species in the drainage. The Salmon Bay Lake outlet, the deeper holes below in the outlet stream, and the mouth are the best locations to fish this punchy fighter.

Steelhead trout enter the drainage in two distinct runs, one in late fall, another in spring. Both can produce some good fishing action, especially for flycasters, with the spring run probably receiving the most attention. The entire length of the outlet stream offers good fishing during the peak of the runs. Sea-run cutthroat trout and Dolly Varden are also available throughout the drainage. Resident rainbow trout are mostly confined to Salmon Bay Lake, and are best fished in early summer and fall.

As a focal point for fishing and hunting excursions, Salmon Bay Lake is very popular with locals from nearby Petersburg and Wrangell. Parties interested in the forest service cabin are advised to reserve space well ahead of time.

48. THOMS CREEK SYSTEM

Location: South Wrangell Island drainage, 55 miles southeast of Petersburg, 720 miles southeast of Anchorage.

Reference: Petersburg A-1.

Access: There are three ways to access this drainage. The first is by floatplane, landing on Thoms Lake. The second is by car from Wrangell, crossing Thoms Creek and taking a one-mile hike to Thoms Place at the mouth of the stream. The third is by boat from Wrangell, with the option of using a trail from Zimovia Strait to Thoms Lake, or continuing down to Thoms Place and the mouth of Thoms Creek.

Highlights: Wrangell's most productive, road-accessible stream, with good fishing for silver salmon (in the second half of September), red salmon (from late July through early August), chum and pink salmon (from late July through early August), rainbow trout (in May and September), cutthroat trout (from May through June) and Dolly Varden (in May and from August through September).

Species: Chum salmon, cutthroat trout, Dolly Varden, pink salmon, rainbow trout, red salmon, silver salmon, steelhead.

Regulations: Unbaited, artificial lures only from November 16 through September 14; king salmon fishing is prohibited. For additional restrictions, consult the current Alaska Department of Fish and Game regulations or the ADF&G Ketchikan office, (907) 225-2859.

Facilities: A forest service cabin is available on Thoms Lake.

Contact: For cabin rental information, contact Wrangell Ranger District, Tongass National Forest, P.O. Box 51, Wrangell, AK 99929; (907) 874-2323.

Description: The Thoms Creek drainage is a small road-accessible system located on the southern end of Wrangell Island, emptying into Zimovia Strait. Three lakes comprise the heart of the drainage, with Thoms Lake being the largest and most visited. As a fair amount of muskeg is present, the water color is slightly tannic-stained. Easily reached by road from the town of Wrangell, it is a favorite destination among locals, known for its surprisingly good catches of some of the more sought-after gamefish of the region.

Thoms Creek has a reputation for some of the best red salmon fishing in the Petersburg/Wrangell area. Although they don't really return in a very large run, the sockeyes concentrate in dense schools, making for great streamfishing opportunities, particularly flyfishing. The action is usually best on the lower stream near the road crossing and at the mouth (especially during the height of the run). Chums and pinks are also present in fishable numbers and provide some excitement just as the sockeyes begin tapering off. Later in fall, a strong showing of chunky silver salmon puts the capper on the salmon season, with good fishing to be expected from tidewater up to the lakes well into November.

There are some sea-run cutthroat trout and Dolly Varden, with the best fishing generally in spring and fall in Thoms Lake and the lower stream sections. The mouth of Thoms Creek at Thoms Place can also yield some fairly good results during the summer months. Also, Resident rainbow trout are available in Thoms Lake and the upper stream.

Many visiting anglers fish the system from the road crossing, but in recent years it has become increasingly popular to moor a boat at Thoms Place State Marine Park at the mouth of Thoms Creek, then fish the intertidal area for schools of salmon. To get away from the presence of roadside and marine traffic, a stay at the forest service cabin on Thoms Lake is highly recommended.

49. HARDING RIVER

Location: North Bradfield Canal drainage, 70 miles southeast of Petersburg, 730 miles southeast of Anchorage.

Reference: Bradfield Canal A-5, B-5, B-6.

Access: By boat or floatplane, usually from Wrangell, but also as far away as Petersburg and Ketchikan. From Wrangell, boaters reach the Harding River via Eastern Passage and Blake Channel. Boats and planes access the river through its mouth at Bradfield Canal.

Highlights: One of Alaska's best locations for trophy freshwater chum salmon (from late July through early August). Also good fishing for silver salmon (in the second half of September), cutthroat trout (in May and June) and Dolly Varden (in May and from August through September).

Species: Chum salmon, cutthroat trout, Dolly Varden, (king salmon), pink salmon, rainbow trout, silver salmon, steelhead.

Regulations: Unbaited, artificial lures only from November 16 through September 14; king salmon fishing is prohibited. For additional restrictions, consult the current Alaska Department of Fish and Game regulations or the ADF&G Ketchikan office, (907) 225-2859.

Facilities: A forest service cabin is available near the mouth of the river.

Contact: For cabin rental information, contact Tongass National Forest, P.O. Box 309, Petersburg, AK 99833; (907) 772-3871.

For an air taxi, contact Kupreanof Flying Service, P.O. Box 768, Petersburg, AK 99833; (907) 772-3396.

Description: This fairly remote river, located on the north mainland of Bradfield Canal, cuts through a forested valley surrounded by 3,000-foot snow-capped mountain ridges within Tongass National Forest. Its clear waters support strong runs of salmon and healthy populations of trout and charr, which get only moderate pressure from anglers.

Most visitors arrive at the mouth of the river (where a forest service cabin is available). There is a small lake, Fall Lake, several miles upstream, but due to its size (just over one mile long), it can be risky for floatplane landings. The lower Harding is where the best fishing takes place, with anglers concentrating efforts around the tides for best results.

A fall run of silver salmon attracts some attention, but it is the midsummer run of above-average-sized chums for which the Harding is really noted. Although perhaps not equal to the fish taken from the Keta River of Revillagigedo Channel, the Harding does have some trophy fish that weigh as much as 20 pounds or more. A small run of king salmon also enters the river in early summer, but they are currently off-limits to anglers. Pinks are not abundant in this drainage.

As far as other species go, a resident population of rainbows and a spring run of steelhead trout are available, usually offering fair fishing, but better numbers of sea-run cutthroat trout and Dolly Varden are present in early spring and again during the salmon spawning runs in late summer and fall.

50. ANAN CREEK SYSTEM

Location: South Bradfield Canal drainage, 60 miles southeast of Petersburg, 730 miles southeast of Anchorage.

Reference: Bradfield Canal A-5, A-6.

Access: By boat and floatplane primarily from Wrangell, but also from Petersburg and Ketchikan. For boaters, Wrangell is the closest port, and offers access to Anan Bay via Eastern Passage and Blake Channel, crossing Bradfield Canal. Trails lead from Anan Bay to the Anan Lake outlet. Floatplanes regularly fly in to system lakes, such as Anan and Boulder lakes.

Highlights: Outstanding recreational area with excellent fishing for pink salmon (from late July through early August); also good action for silver salmon (in September), steelhead (in the second half of May), rainbow trout (in May and September), cutthroat trout (from May through June) and Dolly Varden (in May and from August through September).

Species: Chum salmon, cutthroat trout, Dolly Varden, pink salmon, rainbow trout, silver salmon, steelhead.

Regulations: Unbaited, artificial lures only from November 16 through September 14; king salmon fishing is prohibited. For additional restrictions, consult the current Alaska Department of Fish and Game regulations or the ADF&G Ketchikan office, (907) 225-2859.

Facilities: A forest service cabin is available at the mouth of Anan Creek in Anan Bay; there is also a public shelter on Anan Creek.

Contact: For cabin rental information, contact Tongass National Forest, P.O. Box 309, Petersburg, AK 99833, (907) 772-3871; or Tongass National Forest, Federal Building, Ketchikan, AK 99901, (907) 225-3101. For an air taxi, contact Kupreanof Flying Service, P.O. Box 768, Petersburg, AK 99833, (907) 772-3396; or Taquan Air, 1007 Water Street, Ketchikan, AK 99901, (907) 225-8800 or (800) 770-8800.

Description: Perhaps best known for its dense bear population, Anan Creek also is an excellent stream for sportfishing. Its clear waters offer a wide variety of species in pleasant forest surroundings, and are fairly accessible by trails from Anan Bay. There are two major lakes in the system—Anan and Boulder—with another dozen smaller lakes spread throughout the drainage. Salmon, trout and charr are relatively abundant, providing anglers with exciting fishing in a small stream setting.

Emptying into Bradfield Canal, the Anan receives a good number of visitors, primarily outdoor enthusiasts and photographers hoping to catch a glimpse of the area's famous bear population. (A platform has been built expressly for the purpose of viewing these creatures in their natural environment.)

The fishing on the Anan is great. A big run of pink salmon enters the creek in late summer, along with a fair showing of chums. Fish on every cast" action is common during the peak of the runs, with the brightest fish taken near salt water. Later on in fall, a run of silvers arrives and continues through October into November. For this species, the lower portion of Anan Creek and the mouth is best, but fish may also be taken out of the Anan and Boulder Lake inlets and outlets as well as the connecting stream.

Little effort is directed toward the spring run of steelhead trout in the system, though fishing can be quite good during some years. Resident rainbow also are found in Anan and Boulder lakes and inlet streams, while sea-run cutthroat trout and Dolly Varden are found throughout the system.

REGION 5
KETCHIKAN-
SOUTH TONGASS

The Ketchikan area, from Dixon Entrance to Ernest Sound, includes the Revillagigedo, Annette, Gravina and Prince of Wales Island complexes, along with part of the Cleveland Peninsula, Behm Canal, Clarence Strait and Misty Fjords National Monument. It has some of Alaska's most significant marine and freshwater fisheries, particularly for salmon, steelhead and cutthroat trout.

This is famous saltwater trolling country—the "Salmon Capitol of the World"—with a major charter fleet working the waters of West Behm Canal, Tongass Narrows and Clarence Strait for king and coho salmon. The extremely productive outside waters are usually targeted for salmon and halibut by area lodges and guides from Prince of Wales (Klawock, Waterfall, Craig, Thorne Bay). Most of the recreational effort, however, occurs near town, from Clover Pass to Mountain Point.

The Ketchikan area is also known for its unique and outstanding freshwater angling opportunities. Southeast's finest lakes (including Naha, Wilson, Humpback and Manzanita) are located here, with Alaska's best trophy cutthroat and kokanee possibilities. Prince of Wales Island, the largest island in Southeast, has abundant, high-quality streamfishing some of the best in Alaska, including world-famous steelhead rivers like the Karta, Klawock and Thorne. An extensive logging road network (over 700 miles) there compromises the wilderness somewhat but also provides access to dozens of previously unreachable locations. Anglers can drive or hike in practically any direction and reach superb fishing for steelhead, cutthroat and rainbow trout, Dolly Varden and silver and red salmon.

The U.S. Forest Service maintains numerous cabins, shelters and some campgrounds in the Ketchikan area, many in remote areas. They are available by advance registration for a reasonable fee. Alaska State Parks also maintains picnic sites and campgrounds along Ketchikan's road system.

51. GULF OF ESQUIBEL

Location: West Prince of Wales Island, 75 miles west of Ketchikan, 700 miles southeast of Anchorage.

Reference: Craig B-5, B-6, C-4, C-5, C-6, D-4, D-5, D-6.

Access: By boat from Klawock, Craig or area lodges via San Cristoval Channel north of San Fernando Island or Portilla Channel east of Lulu Island, a 15- to 20-mile run. Floatplanes can access the gulf by landing in protected bays and coves, such as the Steamboat Bay Seaplane Base on Noyes Island.

Highlights: A traditional local hot spot, among the best in Southeast. Excellent fishing for silver salmon (from late July through mid-September) and halibut (from July through September); good fishing for king salmon (from mid-May through early July) and pink salmon (from mid-July through late August).

Species: (Chum salmon, cutthroat trout), Dolly Varden, halibut, king salmon, pink salmon, (red salmon), silver salmon, (steelhead).

Regulations: For details on the open season for halibut and ling cod, consult the current Alaska Department of Fish and Game regulations or the ADF&G Ketchikan office, (907) 225-2859.

Facilities: Commercial lodging, fuel, water and guide services are available at area islands.

Contact: For guide services, contact Klawock Bay Charters, P.O. Box 145, Klawock, AK 99925; (907) 755-2329. For cabin rental information, contact Craig Ranger District, Tongass National Forest, P.O. Box 500, Craig, AK 99921; (907) 826-3271.

Description: Located on the west side of Prince of Wales Island, the Gulf of Esquibel area, with its heavily wooded islands (Maurelle Islands Wilderness) and abundance of marine life, has long been regarded as a top marine fishing location for salmon and halibut.

Part of Tongass National Forest, Esquibel is an active summer feeding ground for fish bound for watersheds on Prince of Wales Island and the mainland. Very little shorefishing takes place in this area, with most effort expended by boaters from Craig and Klawock. Points of interest include the Heceta and Maurelle islands and, of course, Noyes Island for big feeder kings (50 to 70 pounds possible) and silver and pink salmon. Halibut are caught year-round, although the action is generally better during the summer months in the shallower water surrounding islands and around certain points that have suitable bottom structure. Trophy catches to 350 pounds or more are possible. Other gamefish worth considering include rockfish, ling cod and a multitude of other cod and flounder species. Fair numbers of Dolly Varden can be found off mouths of clearwater streams.

For anglers wanting to spice up their visit, area waters also teem with shrimp and crab, so come prepared to set pots for these tasty shellfish prior to going salmon and halibut fishing. The natural beauty found in and around the Gulf of Esquibel and its vast archipelago of islands is breathtaking.

Some of the more productive locations in the gulf for salmon and halibut include: Noyes Island—Saint Nicholas Point/Channel, Cape Addington, Shaft Rock, Roller and Steamboat bays, and Cape Ulitka; Saint Joseph Island; Sonora Passage; Maurelle Islands—San Lorenzo, Turtle, Sonora, Flotilla, Esquibel and Hendida/Pesquera islands, Hole-In-The-Wall, Anguilla Bay; Saint Phillip Island; Heceta Island—Point Desconocida, Warm Chuck Inlet, Cape Lynch, Gull and Camp islands and Port Alice; Portilla Channel; Point Station Gertrudis; and San Fernando Island—Point Garcia, Hermagos Island and San Cristoval Channel.

52. BUCARELI BAY

Location: West Prince of Wales Island, 65 miles west of Ketchikan, 720 miles southeast of Anchorage.

Reference: Craig A-5, B-3, B-4, B-5, B-6, C-3, C-4.

Access: By boat from Klawock, Craig or area lodges. Floatplanes reach the area by landing in protected bays and coves, such as the privately operated Waterfall Seaplane Base at Point Antonio in Ulloa Channel east of Suemez Island.

Highlights: A favorite saltwater destination of area fishing guides. Excellent fishing for silver salmon (from late July through mid-September) and halibut (from July through September); good fishing for king salmon (from mid-May through early July) and pink salmon (from mid-July through late August).

Species: (Chum salmon, cutthroat trout), Dolly Varden, halibut, king salmon, pink salmon, (red salmon), silver salmon, (steelhead).

Regulations: For details on the open season for halibut and ling cod, consult the current Alaska Department of Fish and Game regulations or the ADF&G Ketchikan office, (907) 225-2859.

Facilities: Commercial lodging, sporting goods, groceries, boat rentals and launching, guide services, gas and water are available in the island towns of Klawock and Craig. A forest service cabin is at Point Amargura on the southern tip of San Fernando Island.

Contact: For guide services, contact Klawock Bay Charters, P.O. Box

145, Klawock, AK 99925; (907) 755-2329. For cabin rental information, contact Craig Ranger District, Tongass National Forest, P.O. Box 500, Craig, AK 99921; (907) 826-3271. For an air taxi, contact Taquan Air, 1007 Water Street, Ketchikan, AK 99901; (907) 225-8800 or (800) 770-8800.

Description: Bucareli Bay is, without a doubt, one of the more scenic and productive saltwater fishing locations on Prince of Wales Island. The bay area includes the ever-popular San Alberto Bay just outside Klawock and Craig and, of course, some of the larger islands, such as Suemez, Baker, Lulu and San Fernando. Some fantastic salmon and halibut angling can be had off points and in bays, passages and channels throughout Bucareli, as area lodges and guides will attest.

Residents from nearby communities report year-round catches of feeder king salmon and some outstanding action for mature prespawners up to 70 pounds in late spring and early summer. Except for a few individuals moving up the Klawock River, there are virtually no king salmon spawning streams on the island; the vast majority of fish are actually heading for mainland locations, and are caught when feeding heavily along the surf-swept coast.

The salmon delivering the hottest action around Bucareli Bay is actually the spunky silver. From late summer into fall, anglers target these flashy fighters as they feed heavily and prepare to enter the area, as well as more distant streams. The best fishing occurs right outside the communities of Klawock and Craig. In between the king and silver runs, good numbers of pink salmon and halibut are up for grabs. Although they are present year-round in the outer bay, midsummer is the best time to target huge flatties up to 200 pounds or more throughout the area.

For a true ocean safari complete with great fishing, lots of marine animals and spectacular coastal scenery, Bucareli Bay delivers. Proven hot spots for salmon and halibut include: Baker Island—Veta and Fortaleza bays, Cape Bartolome, Point Fortaleza, Port San Antonio, Point San Roque, Port Asuncion, Veta/Outer and Granite points, Cape Chirikof and Point Maria; Saint Ignace Island; Port Real Marina; Suemez Island—Cape Felix, Point Rosary, Port Santa Cruz, Cabras and Ridge islands, Port Dolores and Point Verde; Ulloa Channel; Point San Antonio; Joe Island/Cape Flores; Port Estrella; Point Providence; Point Lomas; Port Caldera; San Juan Bautista Island—Diamond Point, Balandra Island and Point Eugenia; Trocadero Bay; Doyle Bay/Culebrina Island; Coronados Island; Port Saint Nicholas; Cape Suspiro; Ursua Channel; San

Fernando Island—Point Colocano, Cruz Pass, Point Amargura, Fern Point and Point Cuerbo; and San Alberto Bay—Fish Egg, Sombrero, Abbess and Ballena islands, San Cristoval Channel, Klawock Inlet and Crab Bay.

53. LOWER CLARENCE STRAIT

Location: East Prince of Wales Island and west of Etolin Island, 20 miles west of Ketchikan, 735 miles southeast of Anchorage.

Reference: Craig A-1, A-2, B-1, B-2, B-3, C-1, C-2, D-1, D-2; Ketchikan A-5, A-6, B-6, C-6; Dixon Entrance C-1, D-1; Prince Rupert D-5, D-6.

Access: By boat or floatplane from Ketchikan, Wrangell and area lodges and towns. Boats run to the specific fishing areas, while floatplanes usually land in protected coves and bays near the mouths of salmon spawning streams.

Highlights: One of Southeast's best marine fishing locations for salmon and bottomfish. Excellent fishing for silver salmon (throughout August), pink salmon (from mid-July through early August) and halibut (from June through August); also good trolling and mooching for king salmon (in June).

Species: Chum salmon, (cutthroat trout), Dolly Varden, halibut, king salmon, pink salmon, (red salmon), silver salmon, (steelhead).

Regulations: For restrictions on bottomfish, consult the current Alaska Department of Fish and Game regulations or the ADF&G Ketchikan office, (907) 225-2859.

Facilities: Commercial lodging and guide services are available in the towns along the strait. Forest service cabins are available at Karta Bay and Trollers Cove (Kasaan Bay), Phocena Rocks (Gravina Island) and Kegan Cove (Moira Sound).

Contact: For guide services, contact Classic Alaska Charters, P.O. Box 6117, Ketchikan, AK 99901, (907) 225-0608; Rock 'N' Rollin' Charter Boat, 11380 Alderwood Street North, Ketchikan, AK 99901, (907) 225-6919 or (800) 876-0925; or Last Frontier Charters, P.O. Box 19443, Thorne Bay, AK 99919, (907) 828-3989. For lodging information, contact Boardwalk Wilderness Lodge, P.O. Box 19121-BW, Thorne Bay, AK 99919, (907) 828-3918 or (800) 764-3918; or Gold Coast Lodge, P.O. Box 9629, Ketchikan, AK 99901, (907) 225-8375 or (800) 333-5992. For cabin rental information, contact Thorne Bay Ranger District, Tongass National Forest, P.O. Box 1, Ketchikan, AK 99919, (907) 828-3304; or Tongass National Forest,

Federal Building, Ketchikan, AK 99901, (907) 225-3101. For an air taxi, contact Taquan Air, 1007 Water Street, Ketchikan, AK 99901, (907) 225-8800 or (800) 770-8800.

Description: The lower Clarence Strait includes all waters south of Thorne Bay and the north tip of the Cleveland Peninsula. Like Icy Strait in the Juneau region, Clarence Strait is a major migration channel and feeding ground for salmon, trout, charr and halibut bound for other locations (the west coast of Prince of Wales Island, Behm Canal, Revillagigedo Island and Ernest Sound). A gorgeous marine haven of fjords, islands, reefs and steep, forest-clad slopes dropping into crystal-clear waters, Clarence is a favorite playground for anglers from Ketchikan and beyond, world famous for having some of the best fishing available in Alaska.

Most angling effort is aimed at the more popular sport species, such as king and silver salmon and halibut, but the strait has good numbers of other salmon and bottomfish species as well. Feeder king salmon are available year-round, as they are most everywhere in Southeast. The better fishing action takes place in early summer when big concentrations of prespawners invade the cool, blue waters of lower Clarence on their way to the mainland. Occasional catches up to 60 and 70 pounds or more have been recorded, with the typical king averaging 15 to 25 pounds.

Silver salmon permeate the strait throughout late summer and into fall, with specimens up to 20 pounds possible. They typically feed heavily early in the season and are targeted mainly by boaters around the traditional holding locations such as point and breakwater beaches. Later, bays, narrows and shorelines in the vicinity of clearwater rivers and streams produce good catches.

Although not the most sought-after salmon, chums and pinks are undoubtedly the most numerous. Ocean-bright pinks, a few of trophy size, provide excellent action on light tackle all along the coast, but primarily near spawning streams. Record-size chums—some between 20 and 30 pounds—have been hoisted from locations near Gravina Island and the mouth of Behm Canal during the months of June and July.

Lower Clarence Strait also offers some of Ketchikan's best action for bottomfish, all summer long, including some flatties that occasionally exceed 300 pounds, as well as rockfish and ling cod.

Hot spot locations to focus on for salmon and halibut are as follows: Thorne Bay; Tolstoi Point; Tolstoi Bay; Cleveland Peninsula—Lemesurier, Niblack and Caamano points, Meyers Chuck and

Ship Island; Grindall Passage; Grindall Island/Approach Point;
Kasaan Bay—Patterson/High islands, Island, Skowl, Baker and
Outer points, Skowl and Twelvemile arms, Saltery Cove and Mills
and Karta bays; Twenty Fathom Bank; Clover Point; Skin Island;
West/South arms; Cholmondeley Sound; Outer Cholmondeley
Sound; Trollers Cove; Chasina Point; South Chasina Point; Windy
Point; Guard Islands; Wedge Islands; Outer Moira Sound—Moira
Rock, Moira Island and Rip Point; Polk Island; Outer Kendrick Bay;
Outer McLean Arm/McLean Point; Stone Rock; Cape Chacon;
Percy Island; Bee Rocks; Hassler Reef; West Rock; and Club Rocks.

54. GRAVINA ISLAND/
TONGASS NARROWS

Location: Southwest of Revillagigedo Island, Ketchikan area, 765
miles southeast of Anchorage.

Reference: Ketchikan A-6, B-5, B-6.

Access: Primarily by boat from Ketchikan. Gravina Island is located
about one mile across Tongass Narrows from Ketchikan. Kayaking
out to and around the island is possible on calm days. Floatplanes
can land in more protected waters on the south-southeast side of
Gravina.

Highlights: An all-time local favorite. Easy access, only minutes away
from Ketchikan, with excellent fishing for silver salmon (from early
August through early September), pink salmon (from early July
through early August); good fishing for king salmon (from late May
through late June), chum salmon (throughout July) and halibut (from
June through August).

Species: Chum salmon, (cutthroat trout), Dolly Varden, halibut, king
salmon, pink salmon, (red salmon), silver salmon, (steelhead).

Regulations: For restrictions on bottomfish, consult the current Alaska
Department of Fish and Game regulations or the ADF&G Ketchikan
office, (907) 225-2859.

Facilities: The town of Ketchikan and other area towns have hotels,
commercial lodging, sporting goods, groceries, guide services, gas,
boat rentals and launching and water. A forest service cabin is
located at Phocena Bay on the southern end of Gravina Island.

Contact: For guide services, contact Classic Alaska Charters, P.O. Box
6117, Ketchikan, AK 99901, (907) 225-0608; Rock 'N' Rollin'
Charter Boat, 11380 Alderwood Street North, Ketchikan, AK 99901,
(907) 225-6919 or (800) 876-0925; Anderson Charters, P.O. Box

7118, Ketchikan, AK 99901, (907) 225-2456; Ken's Charters, P.O. Box 9609, Ketchikan, AK 99901, (907) 225-7290; or Ketchikan Sportfishing, P.O. Box 3212, Ketchikan, AK 99901, (907) 225-7526. For cabin rental information, contact Tongass National Forest, Federal Building, Ketchikan, AK 99901; (907) 225-3101.

Description: Gravina Island lies to the south and west of giant Revillagigedo Island, along fish-rich Clarence Strait. Part of Tongass National Forest, it is heavily wooded with 17 small creeks streaming down its green slopes, most of them with at least one or more sportfish species present. But it is not the streamfishing opportunities that the island is noted for, but rather its phenomenal marine fishery. Its western coastline lies along the path of tens of thousands of salmon bound for rivers, streams and lakes in the region, with good numbers of halibut actively feeding just offshore. Tongass Narrows, along the island's other side, supports both natural and hatchery runs of all five salmon species, as well as native charr and bottomfish.

Trophy-size silver salmon abound in late summer and early fall, with fish in the upper teens not unusual and a 20-pounder always a possibility. Chum salmon of similar size cruise the island's beaches also, particularly on the west side. Pinks are found all around the island, but seem more noticeable in Tongass Narrows where major spawning runs headed for the Ward Lake system and Ketchikan Creek school up in shallow, near-shore areas. King salmon are available as feeder and mature fish, with locals reporting catches throughout the year. (Prespawners are dominant in late spring and early summer.)

Anglers wanting more variety can try for sea-run Dolly Varden along the east side of the island or in Tongass Narrows (Ward Cove), or anywhere a clearwater stream flows into salt water. For bottomfish, the west side of Gravina is a traditional halibut hole, with fish over 100 pounds caught every so often, along with a healthy mix of ling cod, rockfish, and other bottomfish species. Set pots for crab and shrimp in Nichols Passage.

One of the most attractive features about fishing the marine waters around Gravina is the accessibility. Only minutes from the town of Ketchikan, anglers can easily reach some of the state's most productive salmon fishing sites for trolling, mooching and even surfcasting along Tongass Narrows (especially from the shores of Revillagigedo Island).

Local hot spots around the island for salmon, charr and halibut include: Clarence Strait—Vallenar and South Vallenar points, Grant and Nelson coves, Phocena Rocks and Vallenar Bay; Nichols Passage—Gravina, Blank and Bostwick points, Blank and Bostwick inlets, Stomach Bay, Dall Head, Bronaugh and Blank islands and Point McCartey; and Tongass Narrows—Pennock Island, Point Higgins, Mud Bay and Ward Cove.

55. WEST BEHM CANAL

Location: West Revillagigedo Island, 20 miles north of Ketchikan, 750 miles southeast of Anchorage.

Reference: Ketchikan B-6, C-5, C-6, D-5, D-6; Craig C-1.

Access: By boat or floatplane from Ketchikan or area lodges. The western Canal can be reached via Tongass Narrows, and the eastern through the upper sections of Revillagigedo Channel.

Highlights: One of Alaska's premier saltwater fishing locations, renowned for king salmon (in June), silver salmon (from late August to late September) and chum salmon (in the first half of July and the first half of September); also good fishing for halibut (from June through August), pink salmon (from mid-July through mid-August) and spring Dolly Varden (in May and June).

Species: Chum salmon, cutthroat trout, Dolly Varden, halibut, king salmon, pink salmon, (red salmon), silver salmon, (steelhead).

Regulations: For restrictions on salmon and bottomfish, consult the current Alaska Department of Fish and Game regulations or the ADF&G Ketchikan office, (907) 225-2859.

Facilities: Commercial lodging, campgrounds, boat launching and guide services are available, primarily in the west canal area. Forest service cabins are located at Helm Bay, Blind Pass and Anchor Pass.

Contact: For guide services, contact Classic Alaska Charters, P.O. Box 6117, Ketchikan, AK 99901, (907) 225-0608; Rock 'N' Rollin' Charter Boat, 11380 Alderwood Street North, Ketchikan, AK 99901, (907) 225-6919 or (800) 876-0925; Anderson Charters, P.O. Box 7118, Ketchikan, AK 99901, (907) 225-2456; or Ketchikan Sportfishing, P.O. Box 3212, Ketchikan, AK 99901, (907) 225-7526. For lodging information, contact Yes Bay Lodge, 1515 Tongass Avenue, Ketchikan, AK 99901, (907) 225-7906 or (800) 999-0784; or Salmon Falls Resort, P.O. Box 5420-B, Ketchikan, AK 99901, (907) 225-2752 or (800) 247-9059. For cabin rental information, contact Tongass National Forest, Federal Building, Ketchikan, AK 99901, (907) 225-3101. For an air taxi, contact Taquan Air, 1007 Water Street, Ketchikan, AK 99901; (907) 225-8800 or (800) 770-8800.

Description: World-famous Behm Canal completely separates Revillagigedo Island from the mainland. It serves as a conduit for fish bound for numerous area lakes and streams, which include some of Southeast Alaska's most significant spawning systems (such as the Naha River, Wolverine Creek, McDonald Lake and the Chickamin and Unuk rivers). Sportfishing, rated among the best in all of Southeast, is concentrated in the fjords, bays and coves of the outer and upper areas of West Behm Canal (around the southern tip of the Cleveland Peninsula and Bell Island).

Silver salmon regularly grab the limelight as huge (up to 20-plus pounds), aggressive fish make their way through the clear waters of the canal for island and mainland spawning grounds. In some years, the fish are so numerous that anglers can hook dozens in a single day. King salmon fishing is also very productive with the bulk of the catch hauled out of the outer canal near Clarence Strait. Although feeders can be taken year-round, mature prespawners become available during early summer.

If you're looking for a trophy, West Behm Canal is definitely the place to go. Consistent catches of chums between 18 and 25 pounds are reported from the outer and upper canal, with the current state and world record fish (32 pounds) taken from Caamano Point on the Cleveland Peninsula in 1985. July is the best month. Neets Bay is great for hatchery chums in early fall. Trophy pinks are available as well, with typical catches of five or six pounds and up to 10 pounds or more possible.

Halibut fishing is good in the deeper parts of Behm throughout the season, and in a few of the bays near salmon spawning streams in late summer and fall. Rockfish, Dolly Varden, other bottomfish species and even crab are also available.

Hot spots for salmon and halibut in West Behm are as follows: Cleveland Peninsula—Caamano Point, Bond, Outer Smuggler, Helm, Spacious and Yes bays, Helm Point, Wadding Cove and Point Francis; Revillagigedo Island—Point Higgins, Survey, Indian and Chin/Nose/Brow points, Betton Island/Clover Passage, Tatoosh, Back, Grant and Stack islands, Bushy Point/Cove and Naha and Neets bays; Gedney Island; Hassler Island/Pass; Black Island; and Bell Island/Behm Narrows.

Note: The world record steelhead (42 pounds, 3 ounces) was caught in West Behm near Bell Island in 1970, by an eight-year-old boy fishing for salmon.

56. REVILLAGIGEDO CHANNEL

Location: South Revillagigedo Island, 10 miles southeast of Ketchikan, 775 miles southeast of Anchorage.

Reference: Ketchikan A-2, A-3, A-4, A-5, B-2, B-3, B-4, B-5; Prince Rupert D-3, D-4.

Access: By boat from Ketchikan or area lodges. Floatplanes can land in protected bays and coves in the area. Revillagigedo Channel also provides boat access to George and Carroll inlets, Thorne Arm, east Behm Canal, Duke Island and Boca de Quadra.

Highlights: A highly productive intercept fishery, one of the best in southern Southeast, known for silver salmon (from late August through late September), pink salmon (from mid-July through mid-August), king salmon (in June) and halibut (from June through August).

Species: (Chum salmon, cutthroat trout), Dolly Varden, halibut, king salmon, pink salmon, (red salmon), silver salmon, (steelhead).

Regulations: For restrictions on bottomfish, consult the current Alaska Department of Fish and Game regulations or the ADF&G Ketchikan office, (907) 225-2859. Also, observe private property around Annette Island Indian Reservation.

Facilities: Commercial lodging, a boat launch, fuel and water are available at Mountain Point on Revillagigedo Island.

Contact: For guide services, contact Classic Alaska Charters, P.O. Box 6117, Ketchikan, AK 99901, (907) 225-0608; Rock 'N' Rollin' Charter Boat, 11380 Alderwood Street North, Ketchikan, AK 99901, (907) 225-6919 or (800) 876-0925; Anderson Charters, P.O. Box 7118, Ketchikan, AK 99901, (907) 225-2456; Ken's Charters, P.O. Box 9609, Ketchikan, AK 99901, (907) 225-7290; or Ketchikan Sportfishing, P.O. Box 3212, Ketchikan, AK 99901, (907) 225-7526. For lodging information, contact Mink Bay Lodge, 1515 Tongass Avenue, Ketchikan, AK 99901; (907) 225-7906 or (800) 999-0784. For cabin rental information, contact Tongass National Forest, Federal Building, Ketchikan, AK 99901; (907) 225-3101. For an air taxi, contact Taquan Air, 1007 Water Street, Ketchikan, AK 99901; (907) 225-8800 or (800) 770-8800.

Description: Revillagigedo Channel is an important salmon feeding and migration route located south of Revillagigedo Island, between Annette Island and the mainland. The outer channel borders Dixon Entrance near Canada. Anadromous fish heading for mainland rivers and island streams pass through the channel in substantial numbers and are mainly targeted by sportfishing fleets out of Ketchikan.

Salmon and halibut dominate the fishery. Feeder kings weighing between 10 and 40 pounds can be taken year-round in the channel's clear waters, while larger, mature specimens up to 60 or 70 pounds are taken in early summer. (Many of these mature kings are bound for the glacial Chickamin River in east Behm Canal, a major spawning system for southeast Alaska.)

Silver and pink salmon are the most prolific species in Revillagigedo Channel. These fish can be particularly abundant in late summer and fall, and are best targeted fairly close to shore near bays or coastlines with spawning streams. Cohos weighing in the teens are not unusual. Reds and chums run heavy at times, but are taken much less frequently than silvers and pinks by sport anglers. As with many other major saltwater locations in Southeast, Revillagigedo Channel produces some decent halibut fishing at times, with additional opportunities for rockfish, ling cod and even shellfish.

The scenery is fantastic, with inlets cutting far into mainland mountain ranges and islands and an abundance of marine wildlife. (The eastern half of Revillagigedo Channel is part of Misty Fjords National Monument Wilderness.) Although not as popular with recreational users as nearby Clarence Strait or West Behm Canal, the channel has some fabulous sportfishing potential for anglers willing to take the time to explore, particularly the outer Revillagigedo for bottomfish and the mainland bays for salmon. Favorite areas are Mountain Point near Ketchikan and outer East Behm Canal.

The following are known hot spots for salmon and halibut in Revillagigedo Channel: Revillagigedo Island—Mountain Point, Lucky Cove, Cone Island/Point, Herring Bay, California Head, Carroll Point/Ice House Cove and Thorne Arm; Behm Canal—Point Alava, Alava Bay and Point Sykes; Black Island; Slate Island; Quadra Point; White Reef; Kah Shakes Point; Snail Rock; Black Rock; House Rock; Foggy Bay; Foggy Point; Lakekta Point; Humpy Point; Tree Point; Cape Fox/Fox Island; Mary Island; and Duke Island—Duke Point, Kelp Island and East Island.

57. SARKAR RIVER SYSTEM

Location: Northwest Prince of Wales Island drainage, 75 miles northwest of Ketchikan, 695 miles southeast of Anchorage.
Reference: Craig D-4.
Access: By plane, car and boat. Floatplanes land on Sarkar Lake providing access to the public cabin on the north end of the lake, the

lake outlet and tributary streams. Boaters arrive at the mouth of the river from Craig or Klawock via Cristoval Channel, Gulf of Esquibel and Tuxekan Passage. Prince of Wales Island Road from Klawock crosses the Sarkar River, as well as a tributary stream, near the outlet of Sarkar Lake.

Highlights: A great getaway location, offering a variety of fishing. Good fishing for silver salmon (in September), sockeye salmon (in June and July), chum salmon (from late August through early September), pink salmon (in the first half of August), steelhead (from early April through mid-May and late November through late December) and cutthroat and Dolly Varden (from May through June and September through October).

Species: Chum salmon, cutthroat trout, Dolly Varden, pink salmon, (rainbow trout), red salmon, silver salmon, steelhead.

Regulations: Unbaited, artificial lures only from November 16 through September 14; king salmon fishing is prohibited. For additional restrictions, consult the current Alaska Department of Fish and Game regulations or the ADF&G Ketchikan office, (907) 225-2859.

Facilities: A forest service cabin is available at Sarkar Lake.

Contact: For cabin rental information, contact Craig Ranger District, Tongass National Forest, P.O. Box 500, Craig, AK 99921; (907) 826-3271. For an air taxi, contact Taquan Air, 1007 Water Street, Ketchikan, AK 99901; (907) 225-8800 or (800) 770-8800.

Description: The Sarkar River system consists of a network of 19 lakes and ponds of varying sizes and two major tributary streams that drains into El Capitan Passage and Sea Otter Sound. Sarkar Lake, the largest lake in the drainage, is considered the gateway to area fishing and has a forest service cabin available for public use on the north shore. Despite the somewhat brown water, salmon, trout and charr are abundant in the main river and lake, and offer outstanding action from late spring through fall.

Only about 2.5 miles long, the Sarkar River is tidally influenced throughout. The mouth and lower river are more of a lagoon or cove, and serve as a staging area for anadromous species. Some of the better action generally occurs at the road crossing just upstream from the tidal section or in the lake itself, particularly near the mouth of tributary streams. Anglers wise enough to bring a canoe along can navigate throughout much of the system and enjoy some outstanding fishing.

The Sarkar River and its tributaries receive sizable runs of silver, chum and pink salmon, along with fair numbers of reds. Sea-run cutthroat trout and Dolly Varden overwinter in Sarkar Lake and out-migrate in late spring. Flyfishing at times can be superb. Both spring and fall runs of steelhead trout occur in the Sarkar, with some good fishing possible during the height of the runs. In spring, look for these large, ocean-going trout in the deeper holes of tributary streams.

For anglers taking the time to explore Prince of Wales Island, the Sarkar River system is not to be missed. Its diversity of species and water can be challenging, but it has rich rewards.

58. KLAWOCK RIVER

Location: West Prince of Wales Island drainage, 55 miles west of Ketchikan, 725 miles southeast of Anchorage.

Reference: Craig B-3, C-3, C-4.

Access: Floatplanes from Ketchikan can access Klawock Lake or the Klawock Seaplane Base near the mouth of the river. The most popular road access is from Klawock or Craig. The Craig-Klawock-Hollis Road crosses over a narrow portion of Klawock Lagoon and parallels the river more or less from its mouth upstream to the lake outlet and the north shore of the lake.

Highlights: One of the more famous Prince of Wales streams, known for winter steelhead (from late February through early April) and silver salmon (in September); also good fishing for sockeye salmon (in the second half of August), spring and fall Dolly Varden and cutthroat trout (in May, June, September and October).

Species: Chum salmon, cutthroat trout, Dolly Varden, (king salmon), pink salmon, rainbow trout, red salmon, silver salmon, steelhead.

Regulations: Unbaited, artificial lures only from November 16 through September 14. King salmon fishing is prohibited; catch-and-release fishing only for red salmon. For additional restrictions, consult the current Alaska Department of Fish and Game regulations or the ADF&G Ketchikan office, (907) 225-2859.

Facilities: Commercial lodging, gas, water, groceries, sporting goods, boat rentals and a boat launch and guide services are available in the towns of Klawock and Craig, which are a few miles away.

Contact: For lodging information, contact the City of Klawock, P.O. Box 113, Klawock, AK 99925, (907) 755-2261; or the City of Craig, P.O. Box 23, Craig, AK 99921, (907) 826-3275. For cabin rental information, contact Craig Ranger District, Tongass National Forest, P.O. Box 500, Craig, AK 99921; (907) 826-3271. For an air taxi, contact Taquan Air, 1007 Water Street, Ketchikan, AK 99901, (907)

225-8800 or (800) 770-8800; or Kupreanof Flying Service, P.O. Box 768, Petersburg, AK 99833, (907) 772-3396.

Description: Seven-mile-long Klawock Lake is beautifully situated in a valley between Sunny Hay Mountain and Pin Peak near the community of Klawock. The Klawock River heads at the lake and runs approximately two miles west to Klawock Inlet and San Alberto Bay. The light-brown waters are considered to be some of the top salmon and steelhead producers on Prince of Wales Island and receive quite a bit of angling attention during the peak of the runs.

The most sought-after gamefish in the Klawock are silvers and steelhead trout. Silvers run heavy in fall, with some specimens weighing up to 18 pounds, followed by a smaller run of steelhead trout. The sea-run rainbows continue to trickle in throughout the winter months before a sizable showing of spring-run fish arrives sometime around the first of March. A late summer run of red and pink salmon and a fall run of chums also grab anglers' interest. Good trout action may be had in the lake and at the mouth of inlet streams.

The Klawock is very accessible, which makes it even more attractive to anglers looking to save money. The main road in the area provides plenty of parking with an extensive trail system covering the entire north side of the river. Several step falls are present in this short river; successful anglers concentrate their efforts in the areas of lesser gradient between the falls.

As is the case with many streams in Southeast Alaska, the Klawock's salmon and trout seem to be quite sensitive to water levels and often time their entrance into the river accordingly. During much of the summer the Klawock typically runs slow and clear, but once the late summer and fall rains begin and the water rises, fishing really heats up. Look for major influxes of fresh fish to occur after periods of heavy precipitation.

59. THORNE RIVER SYSTEM

Location: East Prince of Wales Island drainage, 45 miles northwest of Ketchikan, 725 miles southeast of Anchorage.

Reference: Craig C-2, C-3, D-2, D-3.

Access: By floatplane, car and boat. The Thorne Bay Road between Thorne Bay and Klawock crosses the lower river two miles from its mouth and parallels the drainage for several miles; it also intersects tributary streams. Floatplanes can access the upper drainage through

Thorne Lake, while the mouth of the Thorne can be reached by boat from Ketchikan.

Highlights: A world-famous Prince of Wales location, noted for outstanding salmon and steelhead, especially silver salmon (from mid-August through early September) and pink salmon (in the first half of August); also good fishing for steelhead trout (from late March through mid-May and late November through late December) and cutthroat trout and Dolly Varden (in May, June, September and October). Also good saltwater fishing.

Species: (Chum salmon), cutthroat trout, Dolly Varden, pink salmon, rainbow trout, red salmon, silver salmon, steelhead.

Regulations: Unbaited, artificial lures only from November 16 through September 14; king salmon fishing is prohibited. For additional restrictions, consult the current Alaska Department of Fish and Game regulations or the ADF&G Ketchikan office, (907) 225-2859.

Facilities: Commercial lodging and a boat launch are available in the Thorne Bay area. A forest service cabin is available at Control Lake on the upper Thorne.

Contact: For lodging and guide services, contact Boardwalk Wilderness Lodge, P.O. Box 19121-BW, Thorne Bay, AK 99919; (907) 828-3918 or (800) 764-3918. For cabin rental information, contact Thorne Bay Ranger District, Tongass National Forest, P.O. Box 1, Ketchikan, AK 99919; (907) 828-3304. For an air taxi, contact Taquan Air, 1007 Water Street, Ketchikan, AK 99901; (907) 225-8800 or (800) 770-8800; or Kupreanof Flying Service, P.O. Box 768, Petersburg, AK 99833, (907) 772-3396.

Description: The largest river system on Prince of Wales Island and a world-famous steelhead location, the Thorne River drains some 28 lakes and ponds of varying size, covering a substantial part of the central island. It's also one of the most accessible prime fishing locations in the Ketchikan area, since a good part of it can be reached by plane, boat, car and foot. Another distinction is that it is one of the few rivers on the island that can be floated.

Draining into Thorne Arm and Clarence Strait on the east side of Prince of Wales, the mainstem and North Fork total about 30 miles in length, and support spring and fall runs of wild steelhead, salmon, cutthroat and rainbow trout and Dolly Varden charr. The fishing season usually kicks off in late March, with the arrival of the first spring steelies, followed by out-migrating schools of cutthroat trout and Dolly Varden in April and May. Summer first brings sockeye, pink and chum, then later silver salmon, which flood the river into the fall months. In late September and October, the action picks up with in-migrating sea-run "cuts" and Dollies and a well-known run of fall steelhead that continues into early winter.

As some anglers have already discovered, the Thorne can be floatfished for most its length. Put-in by floatplane is done at Thorne Lake, with a take-out at the road crossing or the boat launch near Thorne Bay. The distance is approximately eight river miles, or a good one- to two-day float. This is an excellent option, allowing anglers to sample sections of the Thorne that receive little pressure. There is also a canoe route that covers a substantial part of the drainage with a few portages. The trip takes about three days.

Lakes and streams of the upper drainage generally have poor to fair trout and charr fishing, with good numbers of spawning salmon; for this reason, most anglers concentrate their efforts from Thorne Lake down the mainstem to Thorne Bay. For additional variety, try the marine fisheries for salmon and halibut in adjacent Thorne Bay and Clarence Strait.

60. KARTA RIVER SYSTEM

Location: East Prince of Wales Island drainage, 45 miles west of Ketchikan, 730 miles southeast of Anchorage.

Reference: Craig C-2, C-3.

Access: By floatplane or boat from Ketchikan or area lodges. Planes frequently land on Salmon and Karta lakes and in Karta Bay. Boat access from Ketchikan is lengthy—crossing Clarence Strait, up Kasaan Bay to Karta Bay and the mouth of Karta River. A trail leads from the mouth upstream to the lakes.

Highlights: World-famous steelheading in spring and late fall (from late March through early May and late November through late December); also excellent fishing for sockeyes (in the second half of July) and spring and fall Dolly Varden and cutthroat trout. Good fishing for silver salmon (from mid- August through late September) and fall rainbow trout (in September and October) as well.

Species: Chum salmon, cutthroat trout, Dolly Varden, pink salmon, rainbow trout, red salmon, silver salmon, steelhead.

Regulations: Unbaited, artificial lures only from November 16 through September 14; king salmon fishing is prohibited. For additional restrictions, consult the current Alaska Department of Fish and Game regulations or the ADF&G Ketchikan office, (907) 225-2859.

Facilities: There are four forest service cabins available for public use along the Karta River system.

Contact: For cabin rental information, contact Thorne Bay Ranger District, Tongass National Forest, P.O. Box 1, Ketchikan, AK 99919; (907) 828-3304. For an air taxi, contact Taquan Air, 1007 Water Street, Ketchikan, AK 99901; (907) 225-8800 or (800) 770-8800.

Description: The Karta River drainage is one of the most productive systems in southern Southeast Alaska, well known for its abundant steelhead and salmon. Situated 35 miles west of Ketchikan at the head of Kasaan Bay in the central portion of Prince of Wales Island, the 10-mile system drains two major lakes (Karta and Salmon) and several smaller ones. Salmon Lake is the largest and has two forest service cabins (one at McGilvery Creek), while Karta Lake (Little Salmon Lake) has only one cabin. Another cabin is located at the mouth of the river. Part of the Karta River Wilderness, the area also offers excellent hiking in addition to its well-known fishing opportunities. (The U.S. Forest Service has opened up the area considerably by constructing an extensive trail network that takes anglers into the midst of this world-class fishery.)

Starting in early spring and continuing into late fall, the Karta offers consistent, outstanding streamfishing for trout, charr and salmon, especially steelhead and sockeyes. Tens of thousands of bright reds migrate into the system in most years, providing some of Southeast's best flyfishing opportunities for the species. The Karta's steelies come in a spring and fall run. On average, they are larger (10 to 12 pounds) than elsewhere in Southeast, with fair numbers in the mid- to upper teens, and potential for specimens to 20 pounds or more. Spinfishing (with Spin-N-Glos, Okie Drifters, Li'l Corkies, among others) and flies (attractors, egg and forage patterns) are most popular, with April, May and October the best times. Karta anglers also target fairly abundant silver and pink salmon, rainbows and fall and spring runs of sea-run Dolly Varden and cutthroat trout.

Area trails begin at Karta Bay, where boaters can moor their boat at the beach near the first forest service cabin, and extend upstream along the tea-colored river to Karta Lake and the second public-use cabin. The trail then leads to the north shore of Salmon Lake and the third forest service cabin. From there, the trail continues along the lake and up Andersen Creek, a major tributary. The fourth forest service cabin is located at the mouth of McGilvery Creek in the southwest corner of Salmon Lake.

For an angler wishing to sample some of the best freshwater fishing in Southeast Alaska, particularly for steelhead, the Karta River must be given serious consideration. If you are planning on staying in one of the forest service cabins, keep in mind that reservations are at a premium due to the river's growing popularity. Drawings are held in late winter and early spring for reservation dates in the coming summer and fall seasons. (Reserve through the Thorne Bay Ranger District at the address and phone number listed above.)

61. KEGAN RIVER SYSTEM

Location: South Prince of Wales Island drainage, 25 miles southwest of Ketchikan, 765 miles southeast of Anchorage.

Reference: Craig A-1.

Access: From Ketchikan by floatplane or boat. Floatplanes routinely land on Kegan Lake while anglers arrive by boat via Nichols Passage, crossing Clarence Strait into Moira Sound, then Kegan Cove and finally the mouth of the Kegan River. There is a trail leading from Kegan Cove upstream along the river to the outlet of Kegan Lake, about a half-mile hike.

Highlights: A well-known Prince of Wales stream, with good fishing for salmon and steelhead—silver salmon (from mid-August through late September), red salmon (in the second half of July), pink salmon (in the first half of August), steelhead trout (from early April through mid-May), rainbow trout, cutthroat trout and Dolly Varden (from May through June and September through October).

Species: Chum salmon, cutthroat trout, Dolly Varden, pink salmon, rainbow trout, red salmon, silver salmon, steelhead.

Regulations: Unbaited, artificial lures only from November 16 through September 14; king salmon fishing is prohibited. For additional restrictions, consult the current Alaska Department of Fish and Game regulations or the ADF&G Ketchikan office, (907) 225-2859.

Facilities: Two forest service cabins are available, one at Kegan Cove, another 200 yards downstream from Kegan Lake.

Contact: For cabin rental information, contact Thorne Bay Ranger District, Tongass National Forest, P.O. Box 1, Ketchikan, AK 99919; (907) 828-3304. For an air taxi, contact Taquan Air, 1007 Water Street, Ketchikan, AK 99901; (907) 225-8800 or (800) 770-8800.

Description: Situated within Tongass National Forest on south Prince of Wales Island, the Kegan River and Lake area has long been a popular recreation destination. The stream itself is short, less than a mile long, and runs from Kegan Lake to Kegan Cove and salt water on Moira Sound. All of the areas are accessible by foot; a well-developed trail parallels the drainage through an old-growth forest. Since this is a particularly attractive destination known for good fishing for a variety of game species, area cabins reservations are done by lottery drawings from June through September.

The tea-colored waters of the creek and lake host healthy numbers of wild salmon, trout and charr, with additional opportunities for salmon and halibut just off the mouth of Kegan Cove. During the height of the river's runs, anglers can fish the entire length from the outlet of Kegan Lake downstream to Kegan Cove, often with very good results. (Schools of fish often stage in the cove and lake outlet and are very susceptible at such times.)

Good fishing begins in July with reds and pinks, and continues into October with silvers, cutthroats and rainbows. Visitors from local towns and from around the country come to experience the first-class fishing, with a stay in a comfortable cabin only yards away from the action. A spring run of bright steelhead trout also enters the river, peaking in April and May and drawing considerable attention.

Kegan Lake offers good opportunities for cutthroat and charr, with excellent rainbow trout fishing reported at times. A lightweight canoe comes in handy to reach the more inaccessible parts of the drainage and can be carried from nearby cabins to the lake. (On the northeast shore, a tributary stream draining four other lakes in the system, serves as a holding and feeding area; it's a good spot to try.)

62. McDonald Lake System

Location: West Behm Canal drainage, 45 miles north of Ketchikan, 740 miles southeast of Anchorage.

Reference: Ketchikan D-6; Bradfield Canal A-6.

Access: By floatplane or boat from Ketchikan or area lodges. Planes land on McDonald Lake or in Yes Bay at the mouth of Wolverine Creek. Boats arrive via Behm Canal and Yes Bay to the outlet stream. Foot trails lead from there to McDonald Lake.

Highlights: A famous southern Southeast fishing location, especially noted for sockeye salmon (from August through early September). Also excellent fishing for silver salmon (from mid-September through mid-October), Dolly Varden charr (in May, June, September and October); good fishing for pink salmon (from mid-August through early September), steelhead (from mid-April through late May), rainbow trout (in September and October) and cutthroat trout (in May, June, September and October).

Species: Chum salmon, cutthroat trout, Dolly Varden, pink salmon, rainbow trout, red salmon, silver salmon, steelhead.

Regulations: Unbaited, artificial lures only from November 16 through September 14; king salmon fishing is prohibited. For additional restrictions, consult the current Alaska Department of Fish and Game regulations or the ADF&G Ketchikan office, (907) 225-2859.

Facilities: Commercial lodging and a forest service cabin are available at Wolverine Creek and McDonald Lake.

Contact: For lodging information, contact the Yes Bay Lodge, P.O. Box 6440, Ketchikan, AK 99901; (907) 225-7906 or (800) 999-0784. For cabin rental information, contact Tongass National Forest, Federal Building, Ketchikan, AK 99909; (907) 225-3101. For an air taxi, contact Taquan Air, 1007 Water Street, Ketchikan, AK 99901; (907) 225-8800 or (800) 770-8800.

Description: The McDonald Lake system is one of the richest freshwater fisheries in the Ketchikan area, attracting considerable attention from anglers near and far. Situated on the scenic Cleveland Peninsula, the system consists of eight lakes, of which McDonald is the largest. Good to excellent angling for all the popular game species of the region is the norm in McDonald's lakes and streams.

The tinted waters of this drainage are home to distinct, late running stocks of sockeye salmon, which usually enter Wolverine Creek and McDonald Lake two weeks to a month later than in most other area waters. Additionally, the area has a population of trophy pink salmon commonly weighing six to eight pounds, with specimens up to 10 pounds possible.

A healthy run of bright spring steelhead kicks off the fishing season in April, closely followed by an outward migration of searun cutthroat and Dolly Varden, in addition to good spring fishing for resident rainbow trout. Summer brings returning hordes of red, pink and chum salmon. The sockeye run is made up of both wild and hatchery fish. Their sheer numbers often flood Wolverine Creek, creating some of Southeast's best flyfishing conditions for the species. Later in the fall, a late run of large silver salmon keep the action going.

The forest service cabin at McDonald Lake (reservations by lottery only), provides anglers with access to the lake outlet and all of Wolverine Creek via the trail network that extends to Yes Bay. A canoe or inflatable is a definite plus on McDonald Lake, but you can do fairly well just wading and hiking. Wolverine Creek flows rather fast and is quite brushy, making for some challenging flyfishing. From the northern end of McDonald Lake, a trail leads upstream from an abandoned fish hatchery, along Walker Creek, a major system tributary.

63. NAHA RIVER SYSTEM

Location: West Revillagigedo Island drainage, 20 miles northwest of Ketchikan, 765 miles southeast of Anchorage.

Reference: Ketchikan C-5.

Access: By floatplane to lakes (Heckman and Patching) or the mouth at Roosevelt Lagoon from Ketchikan or area lodges. Boats can access Naha Bay and Roosevelt Lagoon from Ketchikan. Trails lead from Roosevelt Lagoon to the river and upstream into the system.

Highlights: One of southern Southeast's premier sportfishing systems, known for its outstanding salmon and trout fishing and unique opportunities for grayling. Excellent angling for pink salmon (in the first half of August) and steelhead trout (from early April through mid-May and late November through late December); good silver salmon (from mid-August through late September), sockeye salmon (in the second half of July), cutthroat trout (in May, June, September and October) and grayling (from May through October).

Species: Chum salmon, cutthroat trout, Dolly Varden, grayling, pink salmon, rainbow trout, red salmon, silver salmon, steelhead.

Regulations: Unbaited, artificial lures only from November 16 through September 14; king salmon fishing is prohibited. For additional restrictions, consult the current Alaska Department of Fish and Game regulations or the ADF&G Ketchikan office, (907) 225-2859.

Facilities: Four forest service cabins are available: Jordan (one), Heckman (two) and Patching lakes (one).

Contact: For cabin rental information, contact Tongass National Forest, Federal Building, Ketchikan, AK 99909; (907) 225-3101. For an air taxi, contact Taquan Air, 1007 Water Street, Ketchikan, AK 99901; (907) 225-8800 or (800) 770-8800.

Description: The Naha River system, like the Karta, is another very significant sportfishing location in southern Southeast. Flowing out of Orton Lake in the central part of Revillagigedo Island, 25 miles northeast of Ketchikan, the Naha is more than 17 miles long and annexes eight small but deep lakes along its way to Naha Bay and Behm Canal. Fishing is good to excellent in both the river and lakes. Silver and red salmon, and steelhead and cutthroat trout are the top draws.

The Naha has a variety of waters for anglers to test their skills on. Tidally influenced Roosevelt Lagoon, a major holding area for migratory fish, is known for its great silver and pink salmon fishing. From the lagoon, a well-developed and popular trail (the Naha River Trail) leads to the river and adjoining lakes, for a variety of superb fishing. Jordan Lake, the first lake in the system, has a forest service cabin along with some of the Naha's best fishing (for cutthroat trout, steelhead, rainbow Dollies and coho). Try the outlet, the mouths of tributary creeks (Emma or others which are unnamed) and the river above and below the lake (for steelhead). Next is Heckman Lake, with two forest service cabins and great trout fishing (try the outlet and Naha River below lake). Beyond Heckman is Patching Lake, the largest, deepest lake in the system, with two cabins. Salmon can't make it up this far because of a barrier waterfall, but cutthroat trout do very well, with trophy fish up to six pounds available in Patching's deep waters. Try the outlet above the falls for small trout; bigger fish are best pursued from a boat or raft. The lake also has a few kokanee and arctic grayling. Further on are Chamberlain, Snow and Orton lakes, all mountain headwater lakes beautifully situated, and offering some of Southeast's rare opportunities for arctic grayling (from stocking done in the 1960s).

Chum and pink are more prevalent in the lower system, while silvers and reds will be scattered throughout the drainage. The best fishing is below the lake outlets, near inlet streams, and in holding areas of the mainstem between lakes.

64. WARD LAKE SYSTEM

Location: Southwest Revillagigedo Island drainage, five miles northwest of Ketchikan, 770 miles southeast of Anchorage.

Reference: Ketchikan B-5, B-6.

Access: By car. The North Tongass Highway crosses Ward Creek just above Ward Cove. Also, Ward Lake Road provides access to Ward Lake with trails continuing to the upper drainage.

Highlights: A great do-it-yourself excursion, with easy access and potentially good fishing for silver salmon (from mid-July through early August), pink salmon (in the first half of August), steelhead trout (from early April through mid-May) and Dolly Varden (in May, June, September and October).

Species: Chum salmon, cutthroat trout, Dolly Varden, pink salmon, rainbow trout, red salmon, silver salmon, steelhead.

Regulations: Unbaited, single-hook, artificial lures only from November 16 through September 14; king salmon fishing is prohibited. For additional restrictions, consult the current Alaska Department of Fish and Game regulations or the ADF&G Ketchikan office, (907) 225-2859.

Facilities: Commercial lodging, fuel, water and a campground are available. The nearby towns of Ward Cove and Ketchikan have additional services, supplies and facilities.

Contact: For lodging information, contact the Ketchikan Chamber of Commerce, P.O. Box 5957, Ketchikan, AK 99901; (907) 225-3185.

Description: The Ward Lake system originates on the north side of Slide Ridge and runs south to Ward Cove and Tongass Narrows. There are four lakes in the system, Ward, Connell, Talbot and Perseverance, all of which are popular with anglers and other recreationists in the Ketchikan area. (Combination hiking and fishing trips are popular in this scenic, heavily forested area.) Clear-flowing Ward Creek is host to significant numbers of salmon, trout and charr, offering good to excellent fishing within a few minutes drive of Ketchikan.

The most abundant and sought-after species are silver and pink salmon, steelhead trout and Dolly Varden charr. These are targeted mostly between April and October, providing a high-yield fishery, comprised of both natural and hatchery fish. The creek's sizable spring run of steelhead migrate in from the salt at roughly the same time overwintering Dollies move out of the system, providing some exciting fishing in April and May. Later on in July, a strong run of coho enters the creek, followed by a much smaller fall run in September and October. (The summer fish are primarily hatchery stock and contribute significantly to area marine fisheries.) A small run of red salmon destined for Ward Lake also offers some fair flyfishing.

The better salmon and steelhead fishing is found at the Ward Lake inlet and in the river above. Since the drainage is in a fairly developed area of Southeast, access is no problem, with ample parking and trails available to anglers. In the upper system, Connell and Talbot lakes are also road/trail accessible, with good opportunities for Dolly Varden and fair numbers of cutthroat trout. Perseverance Lake has a population of stocked brook trout. For an angler with a day or two to kill in the Ketchikan area, the Ward Lake system is highly recommended.

65. KETCHIKAN CREEK SYSTEM

Location: Southwest Revillagigedo Island drainage, Ketchikan area, 775 miles southeast of Anchorage.

Reference: Ketchikan B-5.

Access: By car from downtown Ketchikan. The South Tongass Highway crosses the stream, with trail access to upper stream sections and Ketchikan Lakes.

Highlights: The best city angling in all of Southeast Alaska. Excellent for pink salmon (in the first half of August), with good fishing for king salmon (in July), silver salmon (from mid-August through late September) and some steelhead trout (from early April through mid-May and late November through late December).

Species: Chum salmon, cutthroat trout, Dolly Varden, king salmon, pink salmon, rainbow trout, red salmon, silver salmon, steelhead.

Regulations: Closed to fishing from May 16 through September 14, except by emergency order. This is a heavily regulated urban fishery. For details on restrictions, consult the current Alaska Department of Fish and Game regulations or the ADF&G Ketchikan office, (907) 225-2859.

Facilities: Hotels, commercial lodging, gas, boat rentals and a boat launch, sporting goods, groceries and water are available in Ketchikan.

Contact: For fishing information, contact the Alaska Department of Fish and Game, Sportfish Division, 2030 Sea Level Drive, Suite 205, Ketchikan, AK 99901; (907) 225-2859. For lodging information, contact the Ketchikan Chamber of Commerce, P.O. Box 5957, Ketchikan, AK 99901; (907) 225-3185.

Description: Swift Ketchikan Creek originates from several mountain lakes just north of the town of Ketchikan. (There are four lakes, of which Ketchikan Lake is the largest.) Surrounded by picturesque mountain scenery, with trail access, this extremely popular recreation area at times has impressive fishing for salmon and steelhead, and is worth investigating if you're in the area.

Most of the fishing effort occurs on lower Ketchikan Creek from the mouth at Tongass Narrows upstream a mile. Here, every season, local anglers intercept runs of mixed hatchery and wild stock salmon and trout. Although these waters are heavily regulated and open to angling only by emergency order, fishing, when it occurs, can be quite outstanding.

A hatchery run of king salmon returns to the stream in midsummer, giving anglers a unique fresh water sportfishery for these 15- to

25-pound brutes. The best time is July and early August. A summer run of silvers is also available at the same time and later on, a fall run of wild fish keeps the action going strong until October. Pink salmon, the most abundant species in Ketchikan Creek, are available in August. For variety, anglers can try their flyfishing skills on the creek's steelhead trout, in spring and fall (a smaller run). Dolly Varden show up at roughly the same times.

There are certainly many far superior Southeast locations than Ketchikan Creek for fishing; few, however, can match the easy accessibility of the stream that runs through the middle of Ketchikan. If you've only got a few hours in this Southeast waterfront town, give Ketchikan Creek a try.

Index

M

Mackenzie, Alexander 29
Mackenzie River system 80, 91, 190
MacLeod Harbor 460
Mae West Lake 177
Magnetic Point 545
Magoun Island 519
Mahay's Riverboat Service 395, 396
Mahlo River 472
Main Bay 458
Mainland Lake 513, 514
Makpik Creek 256
Malaspina Glacier 487
Malemute Fork 259
Malina Creek system 76, 98, 114, 155, 376, 434, 435
Malina Lake system 62, 434, 435
Manker Creek 472
Manley, town of 270, 287
Manley Hot Springs 251, 258, 282, 283, 285
Mansfield Lake 187
Mansfield Peninsula 506, 508
Manzanita Bay 166
Manzanita Lake 76, 166, 564
Manzoni Lake 177
Marchant's 318, 319
Marge Lake 177
Mariah Charters and Tours 451
Marin Range 440, 442
Marion Lake 141
Markarka Creek 114
Marmion Island 508
Marmot Bay 434
Marsh Fork 224
Marten Creek 98
Marten Lake 76, 140, 167, 531
Martin Lake 464, 465
Martin River system 61, 76, 114, 376, 464
Mary Island 575
Mat-Su Valley 62, 112, 133, 136, 141
Matanuska Lake 62, 141
Matanuska-Susitna Valleys 177, 375, 381-399
Matcharak Lake 127, 230, 249, 257
Maurelle Islands 565, 566
McArthur Reef 537
McArthur River system 46, 375, 419, 420
McCarthy 474

McDonald Lake system 61, 76, 113, 140, 155, 481, 573, 583, 584, 585
McGilvery Creek 581
McGinnis Mountain 513
McGrath 192, 197, 368, 369
McKinley Lake 76, 114, 167, 462, 463
McKinley, Mount 281, 397
McKinley Village 279
McLean Arm 570
McLean Point 570
McNamara Point 539
McNeil River State Game Sanctuary 424
Meadow Creek confluence 290
Meadows Lake 314
Medfra 289
Meiers Lake 470
Melozitna 260, 287, 288
Melozitna River system 178, 187, 197, 266, 287, 288, 291
Memory Lake 62
Mendeltna Creek 177, 471
Mendenhall Lake and Glacier 513
Mendenhall River 513
Merryfield Bay 537
Mertie Mountains 296
Meshik Lake 338
Meshik River 46, 62, 77, 114, 304, 338, 339
Meter Bight 540
Mexico 145
Meyers Chuck Island 569
Miam Lake system 62
Miami Lake 399
Middle Bay 428, 439
Middle Fork Lake 357
Middle Point 508
Middle Yukon River 266
Middle/Crow Island 519
Midnight Sun Adventures 254
Midway Island 508, 537
Mill Bay 114, 428, 438
Mills Bay 570
Milo, town of 367, 369
Minakokosa Lake 127, 258
Minchumina Lake 187, 281
Mink Bay Lodge 574
Minto Flats 190, 191, 192, 193, 198, 278
Minto Lake 278
Minto River 270
Minto, village of 198

Misheguk Mountain 209, 249
Missouri 181
Missouri River 170
Misty Fjords National Monument 166, 564, 575
Mitchell Bay system 61, 76, 86, 97, 113, 480, 516, 521, 522
Mitkof Island 533, 535, 536, 537, 552, 553, 554
Moira Island 570
Moira Rock 570
Moira Sound 568, 570, 582, 583
Mole Harbor 508, 521
Mole Harbor Trail 522
Monahan Creek 280
Monashka Bay 114, 428
Montague Island 459, 460, 461
Montague Point 460
Montague Strait 61, 376, 459
Montana 170
Montana Creek 46, 61, 62, 87, 97, 98, 113, 141, 375, 393, 394, 480, 499, 513, 514
Monte Lake 127
Monterey, California 50, 80
Moore Mountains 520
Moose Creek 177, 187, 280, 386, 387, 471
Moose Lake 471
Moose River 61, 76, 97, 140, 407, 408
Moraine Creek 142, 329
Morris Reef 518
Mortensen Lagoon 62
Moses Point, town of 237, 238
Mosquito Lake 141, 167, 509, 510
Mother Goose Lake 336
Mount Iliamna 402
Mount Katmai 329
Mount Michelson 223, 224
Mountain Aviation 520, 527, 528
Mountain Lakes 230, 491, 492
Mountain Point 536, 574, 575
Mucha Lake 187, 281
Mud Bay 503, 540, 572
Mud River, Big 290
Mud River, Little 290
Mulchatna Lake 98

Alaska Fishing

APPENDICES

SPECIES QUICK REFERENCE

ARCTIC/DOLLY VARDEN CHARR

Salvelinus malma/alpinus

Alaska common names: Charr, Arctic charr, Dolly Varden, Dolly, trout, salmon-trout, blue or golden fin trout, western brook trout/charr.

Description: Small to moderately large salmonid with silvery/bluish grey to brown back and sides; distinct red, pink or orange spots; whitish underbelly. Ventral fins are yellow to carmine with white edges. The sexually mature fish is dark, olive to brown in color, with orange-red shading on undersides, and vivid spots. Males have pronounced jaw kypes.

Size: Average weight in Alaska is one to two pounds; in western Alaska and especially the northwest part of the state, up to 12 pounds or more.

Meristics: Gill rakers variable 11-32; vertebrae 57-71; pyloric cacae 13-75; lateral line scales 105-152; branchiostegal rays 10-15; dorsal fin 12-16 rays; anal fin 8-15 rays; pelvic fin 8-11 rays.

Range: Coastal, Southeast to Arctic Ocean; inland along major rivers and scattered isolated forms across the state.

Run timing: Spring (April, May, June) and late summer and fall (late August, September).

State record: 19 pounds, 12.5 ounces, Kelly River (Northwest), Ken Ubben, 1991.

Best lures: Spinners—#1 to #6 silver Vibrax, Mepps #0 to #5 (Aglia fluorescent), Black Fury, Comet. Spoons—Krocodile, Dardevle, Fjord, Crippled Herring, HotRod, Pixee. Plugs—Tadpolly (chrome-blue and fluorescent orange), Hot Shot, silver Kwikfish. Other—Spin-N-Glo (red/orange/pink). Flies—Polar Shrimp, Two-Egg Maribou, smolt and fry imitations, Maribou Muddler, Egg-Sucking Leech.

Best waters: Major coastal salmon streams and adjacent saltwater, Southeast to Arctic. Southeast—Nakwasina, Katlian, Chilkoot and Chilkat rivers. South-central—Karluk and Kenai rivers and Kodiak Island. Southwest—Ugashik, Becharof, Iliamna, Naknek lake systems and Togiak and Nushagak rivers. Northwest—Noatak and Wulik rivers. Interior—Chena and Harding lakes. Arctic—Sagavanirktok, Canning and Kongakut rivers.

ARCTIC GRAYLING

Thymallus arcticus

Alaska common names: Grayling, sailfin.

Description: A small, sleek and slender fish. Males are characterized by their huge dorsal fin. Coloration varies from silvery grey to dirty brown to almost black, with spawning individuals darker. Black and purple spots decorate the sides of the fish. The belly is yellowish white. Red and pink markings on dorsal fin are common during spawning period.

Size: Average length is 8 to 14 inches, up to 23 inches and five pounds.

Meristics: Gill rakers 16-23; vertebrae 58-62; pyloric cacae 14-21; lateral line scales 75-103; branchiostegal rays 7-9; dorsal fin 17-25 rays; tail fin 11-15 rays; pelvic fin 10-11 rays; pectoral fin 14-16 rays.

Range: Revillagigedo Island (Southeast) to North Slope (Arctic).

Run timing: Peak is May to September; fish are present year-round.

State record: Four pounds, 13 ounces, Ugashik Narrows (Southwest), Paul Kanitz, 1981.

Best lures: Small spinners (Mepps, Panther Martin, Vibrax) in silver, yellow, gold, blue and black, and dry and wet flies and nymphs.

Best waters: Clearwater highland lakes and streams, tributaries of glacial drainages in Southcentral, Southwest, Northwest, Arctic and Interior. Southcentral—Gulkana and Upper Susitna rivers. Southwest—Becharof River, Tikchik Lakes and Kuskokwim headwaters. Northwest—Pilgrim, Snake and Sinuk rivers. Arctic—Sagavanirktok, Kuparuk and Canning rivers. Interior—Tangle Lakes and Goodpaster River.

CHUM SALMON
Oncorhynchus keta

Alaska common names: Chum, chum salmon, dog, calico, silver salmon (bright fish in some locations in the Interior), silver bright.

Description: A medium-sized salmon with dark metallic-blue back, silvery sides, silver-white on the belly. Minute spotting on the back and dorsal fin. Spawning individuals display vertical markings of red, yellow and black on the sides. Females may have a dark lateral band on the sides. Some fins have whitish tips. Males develop a hooked jaw with several protruding canine teeth.

Size: Average weight is 6 to 10 pounds, up to 20 pounds.

Meristics: Short, smooth gill rakers 16-28; vertebrae 59-71; pyloric cacae 140-249; lateral line scales 124-153; branchiostegal rays 12-16; dorsal fin 10-14 rays; tail fin 13-17 rays; pectoral fin 13-16 rays; pelvic fins 10-11.

Range: Cape Muzon (Southeast) to Point Hope (Northwest).

Run timing: Peak time is July through September; fish are present from May through December.

State record: 32 pounds, Caamano Point (Southeast), Fredrick Thynes, 1985.

Best lures: Flashy spoons—Pixee, Daredevle, Krocodile, Little Cleo. Spinners—Mepps, Vibrax, etc. Flies in silver, gold, green, chartreuse, orange and red.

Best waters: Clearwater rivers and streams in coastal areas; also tributaries of glacial drainages in Southeast, Southcentral, Southwest, Northwest and Interior. Southeast—Behm Canal and Chilkat River. Southcentral—Susitna and Dog Salmon rivers. Southwest—Nushagak, Alagnak and Lower Kuskokwim Bay rivers. Northwest—Unalakleet, Noatak and Kobuk rivers. Interior—Tanana River tributaries, Salcha and Delta rivers.

CUTTHROAT TROUT
Oncorhyncus clarkii

Alaska common names: Coastal cutthroat, cutthroat trout, cut.

Description: A typically trout-like appearance. Sea-run forms have bright silver sides with steel-blue/green back, turning darker, more bronze in freshwater. Spotting is sparse and concentrated on the upper body. Residents range from silver to gold with olive backs and profuse spotting on the body and fins. Colors darken when spawning and some take on a violet hue. The upper jaw extends well beyond the posterior edge of the eye, with small basibranchial teeth at the base of the tongue.

Size: Average length is 10 to 14 inches, up to 26 inches.

Meristics: Gill rakers 14-22; vertebrae 60-64; pyloric cacae 28-56; lateral line scales 115-235; branchiostegal rays 10-12; dorsal fin 8-13; anal fin 11-13 rays; pectoral fin 12-15 rays; pelvic fin 9-11 rays.

Range: Coastal rainforest from Southern Alaska border to Prince William Sound.

Run timing: Residents are available all year; sea-run cutthroat leave fresh water in spring, return in summer through fall. May and September are best.

State record: Eight pounds, six ounces, Wilson Lake (Southeast), Robert Denison, 1977.

Best lures: Red and yellow with gold blade Roostertail spinner ($\frac{1}{16}$- to $\frac{1}{4}$-ounce); silver and gold Kastmaster spoon ($\frac{1}{12}$- to $\frac{1}{4}$-ounce); chartreuse fleck, pumpkin seed, smoke (body colors) Foxee jigs ($\frac{1}{16}$ to $\frac{1}{4}$ ounce); red or pink Pixee spoon ($\frac{1}{8}$ ounce); flies—olive and brown leeches or Woolly Buggers (#6 to #10), smolt patterns and Muddler minnows (#6 to #8); haystack (#10 to #12) Hare's Ear Nymph (#10 to #12); Glo Bugs (#6 to # 8)

Best waters: Coastal streams, lakes and ponds from Ketchikan to eastern Prince William Sound, especially lakes in southern Southeast. Southeast—Florence, Orchard, Wilson, Turner and Hasselborg lakes, and Naha, Karta, Kiklukh and Kaliakh rivers. Southcentral—Katalla and Martin River systems and Hawkins Island streams.

KING SALMON

Oncorhynchus tshawytscha

Alaska common names: King, king salmon, chinook, chinook salmon, feeders (Southeast—immature saltwater).

Description: The largest of Pacific salmon. Purple-blue to black topsides, silver sides, silver-white belly. Irregular black markings on back and dorsal fins, and entire caudal fins. Black gumline in lower jaw. Breeding males are dusky red, copper or brown, with blackish shading, jaw elongated, teeth enlarged. Spawning females are less dramatic.

Size: About 50 to 60 pounds or more. Average is 18 pounds; length is 30 to 36 inches.

Meristics: Gill rakers 16-30; vertebrae 67-75; pyloric cacae 90-240; lateral line scales 130-165; branchiostegals 13-19; dorsal fin 10-14 rays; anal fin 13-19 rays; pectoral fin 14-17 rays; pelvic fin 10-11 rays.

Range: Southeast coastal to Point Hope (Northwest).

Run timing: May through July, with run peaks later to the north of the range; some systems into August.

State/world record: 97 pounds, 4 ounces, Kenai River (Southcentral), 1985, Les Anderson.

Best lures: Large Spin-N-Glo, Vibrax and Teaspoon spinners; Magnum Tadpolly; #3/0 Flashabou, Alaskabou or Fat Freddy streamer flies; also cut or whole herring and salmon eggs.

Best waters: Large coastal river systems and saltwater bays, straits, channels and canals. Southeast—Situk River, Behm Canal, Icy/Clarence Straits, Favorite Channel and Bucareli Bay. Southcentral—Kenai, Susitna and Karluk rivers. Southwest—Nushagak, Naknek and Alagnak rivers. Northwest—Unalakleet, Shaktoolik and Kwiniuk rivers.

LAKE TROUT

Salvelinus namaycush

Alaska common names: Lake trout, laker.

Description: Large lake-dwelling charr. Trout-like, with silver gray or brown back and sides with gold, yellow or white oval spots and vermiculations. Bellies are cream-colored, with lower fins milky, yellow or orange with white borders. Tail fins are deeply forked.

Size: Average weight is three to five pounds, up to 30 pounds or more.
Meristics: Gill rakers 16-26; vertebrae 61-69; pyloric cacae 92-210; lateral line scales 116-138; branchiostegal rays 10-14; dorsal fin 8-10 rays; anal fin 8-10 rays; pelvic fin 8-11 rays; pectoral fin 12-17 rays.
Range: Interior highland lakes, Chugach coastal range to Arctic coastal plain.
Run timing: Spring (May to June) and fall (August to September).
State record: 47 pounds, Clarence Lake (Southcentral), daniel Thorsness, 1970.
Best lures: Spoons and spinners (Vibrax, Mepps, Krokodile, Dardevle, HotRod); also smolt, muddler, leech and attractor pattern streamers.
Best waters: Deep, clear mountain lakes, especially in the Alaska and Brooks ranges, Southcentral to Arctic. Southcentral—Lake Louise-Susitna and Crosswind and Paxson lakes. Southwest—Lake Clark, Tikchik Lakes and Lakes Colville-Grosvenor. Northwest—Walker, Feniak and Selby-Narvak lakes. Arctic—Schraders-Peter, Elusive and Chandler lakes. Interior—Tangle Lakes and Glacier Lake.

NORTHERN PIKE

Esox lucius (linnaeus)

Alaska common names: Pike, northern pike, jackfish, pickerel.
Description: A long, predatory salmonid, with elongated snout and prominent teeth. Green to greenish-gray or brown in color, with a yellow or white belly.
Size: Average four to seven pounds, up to 30 pounds and 50 inches or more.
Meristics: Vertebrae 57-65; no pyloric cacae; lateral line scales 105-150; branchiostegal rays 14-16 each side; dorsal fin 15-25 rays; anal fin 12-22 rays; pectoral fin 14-17 rays; pelvic fin 10-11 rays.
Range: Northern Southeast to the Arctic Slope.
Run timing: Spring (May to June) through fall (October).
State record: 38 pounds, Innoko River (Southwest), Jack Wagner, 1991.
Best lures: Krocodile, Dardevle, silver minnow, red-eye spoons; Marabou jigs, soft baits and plugs—Mr. Twister, Rapala, Flatfish, Jensen minnow, etc.; baitfish and bushy attractor pattern streamers; also whole or strip herring and whitefish.
Best waters: Flatland sloughs and lakes, especially in Interior, Southwest and Northwest. Southwest—Lower Innoko and Holitna River systems. Northwest—Lower Selawik, Noatak and Kobuk rivers and Imuruk basin drainages in the Seward Peninsula. Interior—Minto and Yukon flats, lower Koyukuk and Tanana and Nowitna River drainages. Southcentral—Susitna River valley lakes.

PACIFIC HALIBUT

Hippoglossus stenolepis

Alaska common names: Halibut, flattie.
Description: Dark or dirty brown, with irregular blotches on topside, white or yellowish white on bottom. Somewhat elongated body and small scales. The lateral line extends from head to tail, curving over the pectoral fin. Teeth on both sides of the jaw.
Size: Average 15 to 60 pounds, up to 550 pounds and 100 inches.
Meristics: Vertebrae 49-51; scales cycloid, about 150 along lateral line; dorsal fin 90-106 rays; anal fin 69-80 rays; pectoral fin 19 rays; pelvic fin 6 rays.
Range: Cape Muzon (Southeast) to Bering Strait (Northwest).
Run timing: Peak is May to September; fish are present year-round.
State record: 440 pounds, Icy Strait (Southeast), Joar Savland, 1978.

Best lures: Bait—herring, smelt, salmon head. Large jigs (Krocodile, Sebastes, Vi-Ke, Yohoho), preferably fish imitations.

Best waters: Gravel or sand bottom structure off beaches, around points and islands, and shoals in 30 to 150 feet of water, in Southeast, Southcentral, Southwest and Northwest. Southeast—Icy/Clarence Strait, Sitka Sound, Gulf of Esquibel and Yakutat Bay. Southcentral—Lower Cook Inlet, Resurrection Bay, Montague Island, Valdez Arm and Chiniak Bay.

PINK SALMON

Oncorhynchus gorbuscha

Alaska common names: Pink, pink salmon, humpy, humpback salmon.

Description: A small salmon, steel blue to blue green from head and back, with iridescent silver sides and whitish belly. Oval-shaped black markings on back and tail fin. Spawning individuals are dirty brown on back, sides yellowish-green with slight vertical markings. Males develop distinctive humped back, jaw kype and prominent teeth.

Size: Average weight two to five pounds, up to 10 pounds or more; length is 16 to 22 inches.

Meristics: Gill rakers 24-35; vertebrae 63-72; pyloric cacae 95-224; lateral line scales 145-208; branchiostegal rays 9-15; dorsal fin 10-15 rays; tail fin 13-20 rays; pectoral fin 14-17 rays; anal fin 13-19 rays; pelvic fin 9-11 rays.

Range: Cape Muzon (Southeast) to Point Hope (Northwest).

Run timing: Peak is July through August; fish are present from June through October.

State record: 12 pounds, 9 ounces, Moose River (Southcentral), Steven Lee, 1974.

Best lures: Small spinners (Mepps, Vibrax, Panther Martin) and spoons (Pixee, Krocodile, Little Cleo) in red, orange, green, chartreuse and silver.

Best waters: Lower sections of clearwater rivers and streams, also adjacent saltwater, Southeast to Northwest. Southeast—Wolverine, Anan and Cowee creeks and Situk River. Southcentral—Kenai, Karluk and Susitna (tributary) rivers. Southwest—Alagnak, Nushagak and Anvik rivers. Northwest—Unalakleet and Noatak rivers. Arctic—Colville River system.

RAINBOW/STEELHEAD TROUT

Oncorhynchus mykiss

Alaska common names: Rainbow trout, rainbow, 'bow, 'rainer, steelhead, steelie, metalhead.

Description: A sleek, small to medium-sized salmonid, with greenish or gray topsides in resident forms, silver-gray to steel-blue in lake resident and sea-run fish. Silvery sides with trademark pink or scarlet band along the lateral line in river resident forms, faint or missing in lake resident and sea-run rainbows. Spotted top, sides and tail fin and whitish belly. Tail slightly forked or square in large individuals.

Size: Average two to three pounds for river resident fish; three to five or more for lake resident and sea-run form, up to 15 pounds or more.

Meristics: Gill rakers long 15-22; vertebrae 60-66; pyloric cacae 27-80; lateral line scales 100-155; branchiostegal rays 8-13; dorsal fin 10-12 rays; tail fin 8-12 rays; anal fin 8-2 rays; pectoral fin 11-17 rays.

Range: Coastal Southeast to Kuskokwim Bay (Southwest).

Run timing: Spring (April to June) and fall (September to November).

State/world record: 42 pounds, three ounces, Bell Island (Behm Canal), David White, 1970.

Best lures: Vibrax and Mepps spinners; Pixee and HotRod spoons; Spin-N-Glo and Li'l Corkie drift bobbers; Hot Shot and Tadpolly plugs; smolt, egg and attractor pattern streamers and flies.

Best waters: Clear, swift coastal streams and large lake and river systems, especially Southeast and Southwest. Southeast—Situk, Karta, Klawock and Thorne rivers. Southcentral—Kenai, Anchor and Karluk rivers. Southwest—Naknek and Iliamna Lake systems. Interior—Quartz and Birch lakes and Piledriver Slough.

SHEEFISH
Stenodus leucichthys

Alaska common names: Sheefish, shee, inconnu, cony, Eskimo tarpon, Arctic tarpon.

Description: A long, slender, silvery whitefish with a strong projecting lower jaw. Dorsal body surface is a darker color—metallic-green, blue or light brown. Dorsal and tail fins are dusky; other fins are clear. No spots are present. Both sexes are alike, but larger-sized fish are always female. No coloration differences exist and tubercles are not present at spawning time. Mouths are toothless and fin rays do not possess spines.

Size: Up to 12 pounds for non-anadromous populations; up to 25 pounds or more for anadromous populations.

Meristics: Gill rakers 17-24; vertebrae 63-69; lateral line scales 90-115; dorsal fin 11-19 rays; pectoral fin 14-17 rays; anal fin 14-19 rays; pelvic fin 11-12 rays; head length 30 percent of body length.

Range: Only in Yukon and Kuskokwim rivers and their tributaries and Kobuk and Selawik rivers. Introduced into lakes in Interior Alaska. Not found south of the Alaska Range or 60 degrees north latitude.

Run timing: Break-up to freeze-up (May to October) throughout most of its range. Available through ice in the Kotzebue area and lower Yukon River.

State record: 53 pounds, Pah River (Northwest), Lawrence Hudnall, 1986.

Best lures: Pixee, Dardevle, Krocodile. Flies—fry and smolt imitations, streamers, Egg-Sucking Leech and tube flies.

Best waters: Kobuk and Selawik rivers, Selawik Lake and Hotham Inlet; and Yukon River tributaries including the Rodo, Innoko, Yuki, Melozitna, Nowitna, Koyukuk, Dall, Ray, Porcupine, Kandik, Nation, Seventymile, Chena, Tolovana and Chatanika rivers and Hess and Goldstream creeks. Also Kuskokwim river tributaries including the Aniak, George, Holitna, Tatlawiksuk, Takotna and Middle Fork rivers.

SILVER SALMON
Oncorhynchus kisutch

Alaska common names: Silver, silver salmon, coho, coho salmon.

Description: A medium-sized to large salmon, with steel-blue/green back, brilliant silver sides and a white belly. Similar in appearance to small king salmon, but less robust, with irregular black spots across the back and the upper lobe of the caudal fin (none on the lower lobe) and no dark pigment along the gumline of the lower jaw. Breeding fish are duskier, with green on backs, blackish heads and red/maroon sides. Males have prominent curved jaw kype.

Size: Average six to eight pounds, up to 20 pounds or more.

Meristics: Gill rakers 18-25; vertebrae 61-69; pyloric cacae 45-114; lateral line

---

scales 112-148; branchiostegal rays 11-15; dorsal fin 9-13 rays; tail fin 12-17 rays; pectoral fin 13-16 rays; pelvic fin 9-11 rays.

Range: Coastal Southeast to Point Hope (Northwest, intermittent in northern end of range). Also Yukon and Kuskokwim River drainages in Interior.

Run timing: Late July through November; peak months are August to October through most of their range.

State record: 26 pounds, Icy Strait (Southeast), Andrew Robbins, 1976.

Best lures: #4 to #6 Vibrax spinners; 7/8-ounce Pixee spoon; Hot Shot plugs; Spin-N-Glo; flies—Flash fly, Coho fly, Egg-Sucking Leech; bait—salmon eggs, plug cut or whole herring.

Best waters: Coastal streams and adjacent saltwater, especially northern Southeast, Kodiak, Alaska Peninsula and Kuskokwim Bay. Southeast—Klawock, Thorne, Situk, Italio rivers and McDonald Lake system, Icy Strait, Bucareli Bay and Behm Canal/Clarence Strait. Southcentral—Pasagshak, Karluk, Susitna and Kenai rivers. Southwest—Naknek, Togiak and Kanektok rivers. Northwest—Unalakleet, Shaktoolik and Fish-Niukluk rivers. Interior—Tanana and Nenana rivers and clearwater tributaries (such as Delta Clearwater River and Clear Creek).

SOCKEYE SALMON

Oncorhynchus nerka

Alaska common names: Red, red salmon, sockeye, sockeye salmon.

Description: A medium-sized salmon with a steel-blue/green back and top of head, iridescent silver sides and a whitish belly. No prominent markings on the back or tailfins. Spawning individuals are bright red with greenish black heads, jaw kype and humped backs in males. Females are smaller and less brilliant.

Size: Average weight five to six pounds, up to 12 pounds or more; length is 22 to 28 inches.

Meristics: Gill rakers 30-40 long, serrated first arch; vertebrae 56-67; pyloric caeca 45-115; lateral line scales 120-150; branchiostegals 11-16; dorsal fin 11-16 rays; anal fin 13-18 rays; pectoral fin 11-21 rays; pelvic fin 9-11 rays.

Range: Southeast to Point Hope (Northwest) coastal streams.

Run timing: June through August throughout most of its range.

State record: 16 pounds, Kenai River (Southcentral), Chuck Leach, 1974.

Best lures: Russian River Fly (cohos), Comet, Brassie, Yarn Fly, Sockeye Willie.

Best waters: Freshwater lake and river systems, especially in Southwest to Southeast; in Southeast, also in adjacent saltwater. Southcentral—Russian, Kenai and Karluk rivers. Southwest—Kvichak, Brooks and Alagnak rivers. Southeast—Thoms Creek, McDonald Lake and Karta and Situk rivers.

FLY PATTERNS FOR ALASKA

by Steve Wottlin, René Limeres, Bob Maker and Gunnar Pederson
Illustrations by Mark Whitfield and William Hickman

A dozen basic patterns take roughly 90 percent of the fish caught on flies in Alaska. No set rules exist as far as how these individual patterns should be tied as the design, materials, colors, hooks and other fly factors vary among different anglers and locations. It is far better to understand the generic groups these patterns belong to—what they represent (more or less), why they are effective, and when and how to use them—than to try and memorize the bewildering number and variety of flies used in Alaska.

Forage imitations are the most effective patterns over a wide range of conditions because they mimic important prey species, such as sculpins, smolt and leeches. In a strict sense, this group also includes nymphs, egg patterns and dry flies. Fish these patterns deep—cross current, up or downstream, with a lively strip.

Egg/flesh patterns are flies and streamers tied in colors and shapes to imitate salmon roe on flesh. They are extremely effective in Alaska, especially late in the season when the rivers are pumped full of spawning salmon, and all resident species (such as trout, charr and grayling) are keyed into feeding on loose, drifting roe and the flesh of spawned-out fish. They are best fished on a deep drift or with a very slight strip.

Attractors are a broad, catch-all group of flies that trigger instinctual, aggressive responses in salmon and trout with their bright colors and tantalizing action. Like forage imitations, they can be effective nearly any time and place, and should be fished similarly—deep, with lively action.

Dry flies should be included in every Alaska fisherman's flybox, and their appeal is well known and obvious. Though most of the fishing done for the important sport species in Alaska involves sinking presentations, there is a call for dry flies under certain conditions, outlined in the species chapters in the beginning of this book. (In particular, see the silver salmon, rainbow trout and grayling chapters beginning on pages 48, 128 and 168 respectively.) All dry flies should be fished with floating line and long leaders, although the techniques used for Alaska can depart considerably from classic trout tactics elsewhere.

Specialty patterns is an arbitrary grouping used to describe patterns created for a special set of conditions or species. These can include streamers and flies that work with either forage, egg or attractor appeal or a combination of all three. (The Alaskabou is a perfect example.) Many are gaudy and overstated, but extremely potent in stimulating a strike response.

Use the patterns listed below only as guidelines. Learn the feeding habits and behavior of your favorite species, then experiment and create your own "classics" that are just as effective, less expensive and infinitely more satisfying to use. We've included some specialty patterns and even a few proven favorites of our own.

What follows are the basics—don't leave home without 'em:
(Unless otherwise noted, thread color is black.)

FORAGE IMITATIONS

MUDDLER MINNOW

Species: Charr, chum salmon, cutthroat trout, king salmon, lake trout, rainbow trout, sheefish, silver salmon

Hook: Size 2-8 Streamer

Body: Flat gold tinsel

Tail: Mottle brown turkey quill strip

Head: Spun deer hair, some left unclipped to form hackle

Wing: Brown turkey quill sections over gray squirrel tail

Description: A North American classic, effective in Alaska for rainbows, charr, grayling and salmon. Olive, black, brown and yellow are the most popular colors used. Many variations are possible: maribou, especially white or yellow can be used as a wing before spinning deer hair (for the famous Maribou Muddler); gold tinsel chenille or other colors can be used on the body, and the tail can be dressed up with bright red hackle.

KATMAI SMOLT

Species: Charr, cutthroat trout, lake trout, rainbow trout, sheefish

Hook: Size 2-8 Streamer or Salmon/Steelhead Wet

Body: Light green floss

Butt: Peacock herl

Rib: Peacock herl

Tail: Green hackle or floss

Wing: Green over white bucktail

Throat: Mixed red and blue hackle

Cheeks: Jungle cock or imitation

Description: One of the more complicated smolt patterns, but very effective, developed especially for Alaska by Dan Flanders. A fantastic, early season fly for rainbows and charr during smolt out-migrations.

WOOLLY BUGGER

Species: Charr, cutthroat trout, grayling, king salmon, lake trout, northern pike, rainbow trout, sheefish, silver salmon

Hook: Size 2-8 Streamer, long shank

Body: Chenille, with palmered hackle

Tail: Maribou

Wing: None

Description: A very versatile and popular pattern in Alaska, used mainly for rainbow/steelhead, but also for charr and salmon. The palmered hackle and maribou give it irresistible action, mimicking the movement of a leech, a universal forage species. This fly can be tied in a variety of colors, but purple, black, brown and olive are used most often in Alaska. Tail, body and hackle colors can be mixed.

BUNNY FLY

Species: Charr, chum salmon, cutthroat trout, king salmon, lake trout, northern pike, rainbow trout, sheefish, silver salmon

Hook: Size 1/0-6 Streamer, long shank

Body: Rabbit fur strip in ginger, gray, purple, brown, black
Tail: Rabbit fur strip tied long enough to wrap body
Wing: None
Description: A classic Alaska pattern used heavily for rainbows as a flesh pattern, tied in gray or ginger; or in darker colors, as a forage imitation, mimicking a leech or sculpin to attract a variety of species.

ALEVIN/FRY

Species: Charr, cutthroat trout, grayling, lake trout, rainbow trout
Hook: Size 2-10 Nymph/Streamer Hook, long
Body: Flat tinsel, tinsel chenille or mylar
Tail: Sparse black hackle
Wing: None
Throat: Red maribou, sparse
Eyes: Small silver bead or painted
Description: A very effective spring and early summer pattern, when rainbows, charr and cutthroat are feeding on young salmon. Tie it small and sparse for alevin (just hatched salmon) imitations, larger and dressier for a fry pattern.

EGG-SUCKING LEECH

Species: Charr, cutthroat trout, king salmon, lake trout, northern pike, rainbow trout, sheefish, silver salmon
Hook: Size 2-8 Streamer or Salmon/Steelhead Wet
Body: Purple chenille, with palmered purple hackle
Tail: Purple maribou
Head: Pink chenille tied to resemble egg
Description: Along with Polar Shrimp and Maribou Muddler, one of the all-purpose patterns that should be part of every flyfisher's Alaska survival kit. It's hard to categorize its appeal—forage, egg pattern or attractor? Whatever it is, all Alaska fish, from pike to rainbows, find it irresistible. Other popular variations use sparkle chenille in the body and Krystal Flash in the tail, or black maribou and bright red chenille in the body and head.

EGG/FLESH PATTERNS

GLO BUG

Species: Charr, cutthroat trout, grayling, rainbow trout, sheefish
Hook: Size 2-10 Egg or Glo-Bug Hook
Body: Glo Bug yarn in peach, orange, red, pink
Tail: None
Wing: None
Description: One of the most-fished flies in Alaska, the Glo Bug can be tied in a variety of colors. Because of the food source it so closely imitates, it is extremely effective for rainbow trout and charr, when fished on a dead drift, just like loose spawn.

TWO-EGG SPERM FLY

Species: Charr, cutthroat trout, grayling, rainbow trout, sheefish
Hook: Size 2-8 Salmon Steelhead Wet or Streamer

Body: Tinsel rib over orange or pink chenille (or yarn)
Tail: White bucktail or hackle
Wing: Orange hackle wrapped over white maribou
Description: A very popular and effective egg/flesh fly for rainbow trout and charr, best fished on a dead drift.

ATTRACTORS

POLAR SHRIMP

Species: Charr, chum salmon, cutthroat trout, king salmon, pink salmon, rainbow trout, sheefish, silver salmon
Hook: Size 1/0-8 Salmon/Steelhead Wet
Body: Fluorescent orange chenille
Tail: Orange or red hackle
Wing: White bucktail, calf or fishair
Description: The standard Northwest steelhead pattern for many years, and an excellent all-around fly for Alaska's rainbow/steelhead, charr and salmon. Try a larger version (up to 3/0) for king salmon.

COHO (Russian River)

Species: Charr, red salmon, sheefish, silver salmon
Hook: Size 4 Streamer, long shank
Body: None
Tail: None
Wing: Bright bucktail, two or more colors
Description: A sparsely tied streamer fly that has become the standard for sockeye salmon on the Kenai River and elsewhere. Red over white is the most common combination, but only one of many possibilities. Try others, such as red over orange, red over yellow, green over yellow and purple over pink. Fishair can be substituted for bucktail.

COMET

Species: Charr, chum salmon, cutthroat trout, king salmon, pink salmon, rainbow trout, red salmon, sheefish, silver salmon
Hook: Size 1/0-8 Streamer and Wet Fly
Body: Gold tinsel (oval) or gold mylar
Tail: Orange hackle or bucktail
Wing: Hackle, orange and yellow mixed
Eyes: Gold bead chain
Description: Another classic pattern that works well for all species of salmon in Alaska, especially sockeye. It's got good attractor color and a design that allows it to sink and stay deep where the fish are. Try different colors like chartreuse and pink.

FLASH FLY

Species: Charr, chum salmon, cutthroat trout, king salmon, lake trout, northern pike, pink salmon, rainbow trout, red salmon, sheefish, silver salmon
Hook: Size 1/0-8 Steelhead/Salmon

Body: Wrapped silver tinsel or mylar
Tail: Silver tinsel
Wing: Bright hackle (red, orange, purple) over tinsel
Description: Another classic Alaska attractor pattern for salmon, particularly silvers, which combines a heavy dose of flash and bright color for broad appeal.

ALASKABOU

Species: Charr, chum salmon, king salmon, lake trout, northern pike, rainbow trout, sheefish, silver salmon
Hook: Size: 3/0-6 Salmon/Steelhead Wet or Streamer, forged
Body: None
Tail: None
Thread: Fluorescent orange
Wing: Hackle over dense layers of bright marabou, Flashabou or Krystal Flash in colors of pink, chartreuse, purple or cerise, with optional strands of tinsel or peacock herl
Description: A popular, gaudy pattern that is deadly on Alaska's salmon, particularly kings and silvers. It's usually tied in colors of red, purple, pink and white, but many effective variations are possible. Smaller sizes are good for rainbows, charr and other salmon.

NYMPHS & DRY FLIES
GOLD-RIBBED HARE'S EAR

Species: Charr, cutthroat trout, grayling, rainbow trout
Hook: Size 10-16 Wet Fly and Nymph Hook
Body: Hare's mask fur, dubbed with guard hairs included
Rib: Gold wire
Thorax: Dubbed fur including guard hairs
Tail: Guard hairs from hare's mask
Wing case: Mottle brown turkey feather tied in over thorax
Description: A versatile nymph pattern for Alaska, good in a variety of conditions for trout, charr and grayling.

ELK HAIR CADDIS

Species: Charr, cutthroat trout, grayling, rainbow trout, silver salmon
Hook: Size 10-16 Dry Fly
Body: Dubbed olive poly yarn, with brown palmered hackle
Tail: Elk body hair
Wing: Elk body hair
Description: One of Alaska's most versatile, all-purpose dries, good for rainbows, charr, cutthroat, grayling and even (occasionally) salmon.

BLACK GNAT

Species: Cutthroat trout, grayling, rainbow trout
Hook: Size 10-18 Dry Fly
Body: Black fur, chenille or floss

Wing: Barred black mallard or similar
Hackle: Black
Description: The Black Gnat is another classic dry fly pattern that is useful for a wide variety of surface-feeding conditions. Keep some in your fly box—always!

ADAMS

Species: Charr, grayling, rainbow trout
Hook: Size 10-18 Dry Fly
Body: Dubbed fur
Tail: Mixed gray hackle
Wing: Grizzled hackle tips
Hackle: Mixed gray and brown hackle
Description: A standard dry fly pattern used throughout the world, and a popular fly in Alaska for grayling and rainbows.

SPECIALTY FLIES & OTHER PATTERNS

MOUSE

Species: Charr, lake trout, northern pike, rainbow trout, sheefish, silver salmon
Hook: Size 2-4 Dry Fly long or Nymph/Streamer
Body: Spun deer hair trimmed to shape of mouse
Tail: Deer hair or leather
Wing: None
Description: Alaska's most famous dry fly for rainbows and charr, the Mouse is most effective when fished along stream margins, lake shores and under cutbanks, especially where vole and shrew populations are abundant.

HERRING FLY

Species: Chum salmon, king salmon, northern pike, sheefish, silver salmon
Hook: Double tie, size 5/0 and 4/0 Bait Hook
(Gamakatsu or Mustad)
Body: White Pearlescent Krystal or cactus chenille
Throat: Red Hackle
Wing: Silver Krystal Flash over layers of green, blue then white bucktail, topped with five strands peacock herl, all wing and tail materials tied to just past trailing hook
Tail: Silver Krystal Flash
Head: Optional, painted white or red eye with black pupil
Description: A very important fly for saltwater salmon fishing, also effective in tidal waters and lower river mouths. It can be tied in a variety of color combinations (such as purple/pink/white and red/orange/white).

SOCKEYE WILLIE

Species: Charr, chum salmon, cutthroat trout, rainbow trout, red salmon, silver salmon
Hook: Size 2-4 Streamer Fly
Body: Pearl mylar over fluorescent chartreuse or orange yarn

Wing: Two colors bucktail, chartreuse/white (blue), orange/white
Tail: Fluorescent yarn with unraveled strands of mylar
Thread: Fluorescent orange
Description: A specialty pattern created by Willie Morris for (what else?) the notoriously tight-lipped sockeye salmon of Bristol Bay. It is fast becoming one of the standards for the Kvichak drainage (including Alagnak) and elsewhere. Tie it weighted with lead wire for best results fishing deep.

GREEN BUTT SKUNK

Species: Charr, cutthroat trout, rainbow trout, sheefish
Hook: Size 2-6 Wet Fly or Salmon/Steelhead
Body: Black chenille with fluorescent green or chartreuse butt section
Tail: Red hackle
Ribbing: Flat silver tinsel
Wing: White bucktail
Hackle: Black
Description: One of the standard Northwest steelhead patterns, equally effective on Alaska's wild, sea-run rainbows.

FAT FREDDY

Species: Charr, king salmon, rainbow trout, silver salmon
Hook: 1/0 Mustad 36890 Salmon Fly
Body: Glo Bug yarn wrapped abundantly—orange, pink, peach or chartreuse
Wing: White marabou, strands of silver tinsel/Flashabou
Description: A standard king fly fished on a dead drift, the Fat Freddy will also take charr and rainbows.

OUTRAGEOUS

Species: Charr, chum salmon, king salmon, northern pike, rainbow trout, sheefish, silver salmon
Hook: Size 1/0-4 Mustad 3407 or Tiemco 800S
Body: None
Tail: Paired saddle hackles (red, orange or pink) extending well beyond bend of hook
Wing: Hackle wound over abundant maribou (pink, red, purple or yellow), tied 1/2 hook down from eye; few strands of tinsel, Flashabou (blue or purple) or peacock herl optional
Thread: Red or hot orange nylon wound down throat, Tarpon fly style
Description: The Outrageous is another "super attractor" designed to spark a strike response in salmon, trout and other species when all else fails. This Tarpon fly variation can be tied in a wide range of colors and materials, and is very effective on king and silver salmon and rainbow trout, especially in turbid conditions. Fish it deep, with a lively strip.

MATUKA

Species: Charr, cutthroat trout, rainbow trout, sheefish, silver salmon
Hook: Size 2-8 Salmon/Steelhead Wet or Streamer

Body: Black, brown or purple wool
Wing: Hackle, tied "fixed wing" style
Ribbing: Flat, silver or gold tinsel
Hackle: Neck hackle in black, brown or purple
Description: The classic New Zealand trout pattern, proven on North America's waters under all conditions, and a standard for Alaska rainbows. Fish it deep, like you would a leech or sculpin pattern, with lively, but varied strips. It can be tied weighted to improve sinking characteristics.

D.P. KINGILLER

Species: Charr, chum salmon, king salmon, lake trout, rainbow trout, silver salmon
Hook: Size 1/0-3/0 English Bait Hook or Eagle Claw Kahle Horizontal (with upturned eye)
Body: Sparkle Chenille
Tail & Back Overlay: Pearlescent Flashabou
Wing: None
Eyes: Plastic beads extended from 1/2 inch of 30-pound mono
Description: A sparkle shrimp with a twist, the D.P. Kingiller effectively mimics an important forage species for salmon, with proven results in the lower rivers and tidal waters of Southcentral Alaska. The most popular colors are chartreuse, cerise, and pink. Here's the procedure: Tie the tail and body material in, wrap the body, then bring the excess tail material forward and wrap it with thread as ribbing. Tie in a piece of mono, thread the bead, and then melt the protruding end down to the bead and snub.

MAKER'S ROGUE

Species: Charr, chum salmon, king salmon, rainbow trout, silver salmon
Hook: Size 1/0 Mustad #36890 (Streamer Fly)
Body: Pink Flash Chenille, with palmered red hackle
Tail: Abundant white maribou
Wing: Gold or orange Krystal Flash
Description: A very successful fly for all salmon, especially kings, but will also take rainbows and charr. Fish it on a drift, with sinking line and short leaders.

BLACK FURY

Species: Charr, grayling, rainbow trout
Hook: Size 1/0-8 Salmon/Steelhead Wet or Streamer Fly
Body: Black silk floss with flat silver tinsel ribbing
Tail: Red hackle
Wing: Bright red bucktail over black maribou
Throat: Red hackle
Description: A "most killing fly" for trophy charr and rainbow, proven on the incomparable rivers of western Alaska.

RESOURCES

Statewide Information

For information on sportfish resources in Alaska:
Alaska Department of Fish and Game
P.O. Box 25526, Juneau, Alaska 99802-5526
(907) 465-4112, (907) 465-3088 (fax)

For information on state and national parks, refuges and forests:
Alaska Public Lands Information Center
605 West Fourth Avenue, Suite 105, Anchorage, Alaska 99501-5162
(907) 271-2737

For specific information on Alaska's national forests, including fishing resources and cabin rentals:
U.S. Forest Service Information Center
Centennial Hall
101 Egan Drive, Juneau, Alaska 99801
(907) 586-8751

For information on fisheries on undesignated federal land, Wild and Scenic Rivers and cabin rentals:
Bureau of Land Management
222 West Seventh Avenue, Suite 13, Anchorage, Alaska 99513
(907) 271-5960

Publications

For useful trip planning information, with local information addresses, send for the free "Alaska Vacation Planner" from:
Alaska Division of Tourism
P.O. Box E, Juneau, Alaska 99811-0800
(907) 465-2010

For "The Milepost," a useful guidebook (updated annually) to all roadside attractions along roads and ferries within, to and from Alaska, including fishing:
Alaska Northwest Books
22026 20th Avenue Southeast
P.O. Box 3007, Bothell, WA 98041-3007
(206) 487-6100
(Include $19.95 and $5 postage/handling)

For a member list and directory of better Alaska fishing guides and outfitters:
Alaska Wilderness Recreation and Tourism Association
P.O. Box 1353, Valdez, Alaska 99686
(907) 835-4300

For "The Highway Angler," a comprehensive guidebook to fishing Alaska's roadside waters, with information on over 450 locations:
Alaska Viking Press
2170 Stanford Drive, Anchorage, Alaska 99508
(Include $19.95 and $4 postage/handling)

For "Fly Patterns of Alaska," a color desktop reference of Alaska fly patterns:
Frank Amato Publications
P.O. Box 82112, Portland, Oregon 97282
(503) 653-8108
(Include $19.95 and $3 postage/handling)

For "Alaska Atlas and Gazetteer," a handy atlas of topographic maps and information on the entire state:
Delorme Maps
P.O. Box 298-7000, Freeport, ME 04032
(800) 227-1656, ext. 7000
(Include $19.95 and $3.75 postage/handling)

For an attractive, useful map reference with all-Alaska state record fish locations, best rivers, species, Alaska fish facts, state/world records list (all tackle and line class) and more:
Alaska Hunting and Fishing Map
5140 East 104th Avenue, Anchorage, Alaska 99516
(907) 346-2193
(Include $4.95)

For statewide equipment rentals, including rafts, tents and kayaks:
Alaska Wildwater
P.O. Box 110615, Anchorage, Alaska 99511
(907) 344-8005

For any maps (including USGS and NOAA Nautical and Aeronautical):
The Maps Place
3545 Arctic Boulevard, Anchorage, Alaska 99503
(907) 562-6277

Organizations

For an international organization devoted to promoting the sport of gamefishing, knowledge of species and preservation, and the foremost institution for information on record fishes:
International Game Fish Association
1301 East Atlantic Boulevard, Pompano Beach, Florida 33060
(305) 941-3474
(305) 941-5868 (fax)

For America's leading non-profit coldwater fisheries conservation organization, with over 400 local chapters:
Trout Unlimited
Membership Department
800 Follin Lane Southeast, Suite 250, Vienna, Virginia 22180
(703) 281-1100
($25 annual membership, includes 1-year subscription to *Trout Magazine*)

ABOUT CATCH & RELEASE

Many anglers fish for food while releasing undersized or over-limit fish. As Alaska's fishing population grows, increasing numbers of anglers are fishing our accessible waters and remote areas of the state. Continuation of Alaska's high quality sportfishing will depend upon more anglers choosing to practice catch-and-release.

Tackle

• Use strong line to bring your catch in quickly.
• Fish caught with flies or lures survive more often than fish caught with bait.
• Overly large hooks can damage mouth parts or eyes.
• Small hooks may be taken deeply by fish.
• Use pliers to pinch barbs down.

Landing Your Catch

• Land your fish as carefully and quickly as possible.
• Avoid removing the fish from the water.
• Do not let fish flop in shallow water, over rocks, or on dry land.
• Use nets made with soft or knotless mesh.

Handling Your Catch

• Keep the fish in the water.
• Cradle the fish gently with both hands, one under its belly, one near its tail.
• Keep your fingers out of and away from the gills.
• Use wet cloth gloves or wet your hands when handling the fish.
• Never squeeze the fish.
• If someone is taking your photo with the fish, support the fish in the water.

Removing the Hook

• Remove the hook quickly and gently, keeping the fish underwater.
• Use long-nosed pliers or a hemostat to back the hook out.
• When a fish is hooked deeply, cut the line near the hook.
• Use steel hooks that will quickly rust out: *Avoid using stainless steel hooks.*
• Cut your line rather than injure an active fish.

Reviving Your Catch

• Point your fish into a slow current or gently move it back and forth until its gills are working properly and it maintains its balance.
• When the fish recovers and attempts to swim out of your hands, let it go.
• Large fish may take some time to revive.

Releasing Your Catch

• Land the fish quickly.
• Keep the fish in the water.
• Keep hands away from the gills.
• Handle the fish gently.
• Back the hook out.
• Cut your line if the fish is deeply hooked.
• Support the fish facing into the current until it swims away.
• Keep only the fish you need.

ALASKA FISHING RECORDS

Dolly Varden	Tippet 01 kg (2 lb) Sept. 9, 1993	5.6	Karluk River, Kodiak Island Rocco A. DeLuca
Dolly Varden	Tippet 02 kg (4 lb) Sept. 5, 1993	5.8	Karluk River, Kodiak Island Norman S. Cohen, MD
Dolly Varden	01 kg (2 lb) July 8, 1988	7.3	Noatak River Kenneth T. Alt
Dollly Varden	Tippet 08 kg (16 lb) July 9, 1990	12.0	Wulik River Col. Reeves Lippincott
Dolly Varden	02 kg (4 lb) July 8, 1991	12.1	Sagavanirktok River, Prudhoe Bay George William West
Dolly Varden	Tippet 04 kg (8 lb) July 18, 1992	12.2	Wulik River John A. Holland
Dolly Varden	Tippet 06 kg (12 lb) July 17, 1992	12.12	Wulik River Philip E. Driver
Dolly Varden	04 kg (8 lb) June 16, 1992	13.14	Kivalina River Philip E. Driver
Halibut, Pacific	Tippet 02 kg (4 lb) Sept. 7, 1988	3.12	Chugach Island E.Z. Marchant
Halibut, Pacific	M-01 kg (2 lb) Aug. 2, 1986	25.12	Cook Inlet Rick Townsend
Halibut, Pacific	W-01 kg (2 lb) May 26, 1990	26.0	Cape Muzon Marjorie Cushman
Halibut, Pacific	M-02 kg (4 lb) Sept. 8, 1989	44.0	Elfin Cove Paul Leader
Halibut, Pacific	Tippet 06 kg (12 lb) June 19, 1993	51.6	Chrome Point Lance P. Anderson
Halibut, Pacific	Tippet 08 kg (16 lb) Aug. 27, 1986	59.0	Port Armstrong Tim Dunnagan
Halibut, Pacific	W-02 kg (4 lb) July 25, 1991	70.0	Yasha Island Dorothy A. Loros
Halibut, Pacific	Tippet 10 kg (20 lb) June 18, 1993	70.8	Chrome Point Lindy Keirn
Halibut, Pacific	Tippet 04 kg (8 lb) July 19, 1990	74.0	Port Armstrong Dick DeMars
Halibut, Pacific	W-04 kg (8 lb) Aug. 12, 1988	123.0	Basket Bay, Chichagof Island Susan McCarty Grimes
Halibut, Pacific	W-08 kg (16 lb) Sept. 13, 1986	131.0	Douglas Marsha L. Montag
Halibut, Pacific	W-06 kg (12 lb) June 26, 1989	149.8	Deep Creek, Cook Inlet Jocelyn J. Everette
Halibut, Pacific	M-08 kg (16 lb) May 28, 1989	165.0	Resurrection Bay, Seward Earl D. Cagle
Halibut, Pacific	W-15 kg (30 lb) Aug. 24, 1987	214.4	Gustavus Roxanna M. Andrews

APPENDICES

Halibut Pacific	W-60 kg (130 lb)	237.0	Flat Island, Homer
	Aug. 19, 1988		Brenda K. Hearnsberger
Halibut, Pacific	M-10 kg (20 lb)	242.6	Funter Bay, Juneau
	July 27, 1988		Greg Anderson
Halbut, Pacific	M-04 kg (8 lb)	244.0	Basket Bay, Chichagof Island
	Aug. 18, 1988		Gene Grimes
Halibut, Pacific	W-24 kg (50 lb)	264.0	St. Lazaria Island, Sitka Sound
	Aug. 24, 1986		Elaine M. Loopstra
Halibut, Pacific	M-37 kg (80 lb)	284.6	Gustavus
	June 5, 1987		Anthony C. Manguso
Halibut, Pacific	M-24 kg (50 lb)	344.0	Thomas Bay, Petersburg
	Sept. 13, 1986		Gordon S. Newhouse
Halibut, Pacific	M-15 kg (30 lb)	356.8	Castineau Channel, Juneau
	Nov. 8, 1986		Gregory C. Olsen
Inconnu	Tippet 06 kg (12 lb)	18.0	Pah River
	Aug. 19, 1986		Lawrence E. Hudnall
Inconnu	Tippet 01 kg (2 lb)	21.0	Kobuk River
	Aug. 12, 1987		Lawrence E. Hudnall
Inconnu	Tippet 02 kg (4 lb)	27.8	Kobuk River
	Aug. 14, 1987		Lawrence E. Hudnall
Inconnu	Tippet 08 kg (16 lb)	30.0	Kobuk River
	Aug. 11, 1987		Daniel J. Hudnall
Inconnu	24 kg (50 lb)	32.0	Kobuk River
	Aug. 12, 1987		Daniel J. Hudnall
Inconnu	Tippet 04 kg (8 lb)	33.4	Kobuk River
	Aug. 13, 1987		Lawrence E. Hudnall
Inconnu	15 kg (30 lb)	34.0	Kobuk River
	Aug. 10, 1987		Daniel J. Hudnall
Inconnu	06 kg (12 lb)	35.0	Kobuk River
	Aug. 7, 1987		Daniel J. Hudnall
Inconnu	08 kg (16 lb)	36.0	Kobuk River
	Aug. 7, 1987		Lawrence E. Hudnall
Inconnu	02 kg (4 lb)	38.12	Kobuk River
	Aug. 8, 1987		Lawrence E. Hudnall
Inconnu	04 kg (8 lb)	39.0	Kobuk River
	Aug. 20, 1986		Daniel J. Hudnall
Inconnu	01 kg (2 lb)	41.4	Kobuk River
	Aug. 10, 1987		Lawrence E. Hudnall
Pike, northern	01 kg (2 lb)	23.15	Innoko River
	Aug. 10, 1990		Rick Townsend
Pike, northern	Tippet 02 kg (4 lb)	24.12	Gator Lake
	Aug. 17, 1992		Craig Johnston, MD
Pike, northern	02 kg (4 lb)	25.8	Yukon River
	Aug. 14, 1991		Craig Johnston, MD
Pike, northern	15 kg (30 lb)	34.8	Yukon
	Aug. 10, 1991		Bill Tenney

Salmon, chinook	Tippet 02 kg (4 lb)	29.0	Karluk River, Kodiak Island
	July 11, 1984		Rod Neubert
Salmon, chinook	01 kg (2 lb)	37.9	Kenai River
	May 30, 1994		Raleigh Werking
Salmon, chinook	Tippet 10 kg (20 lb)	48.0	Kenai River
	June 3, 1992		Guido Rahr, III
Salmon, chinook	Tippet 06 kg (12 lb)	56.14	Kenai River
	July 19, 1989		Walter E. Bottelsen
Salmon, chinook	60 kg (130 lb)	63.1	Kenai River
	July 2, 1994		Raleigh Werking
Salmon, chinook	06 kg (12 lb)	67.4	Kenai River, Sterling
	July 31, 1986		Michael J. Fenton
Salmon, chinook	37 kg (80 lb)	71.4	Kenai River
	June 30, 1988		Nathaniel J. Anderson
Salmon, chinook	08 kg (16 lb)	77.8	Kenai River
	July 18, 1985		Jerry Downey
Salmon, chinook	24 kg (50 lb)	81.4	Deep Creek
	July 15, 1985		Dale C. Anderson
Salmon, chum	Tippet 01 kg (2 lb)	13.0	Pah River
	Aug. 18, 1986		Lawrence E. Hudnall
Salmon, chum	Tippet 02 kg (4 lb)	13.9	Baranof Island
	July 28, 1988		Lawrence E. Hudnall
Salmon, chum	01 kg (2 lb)	15.7	Fish Creek
	Aug. 1, 1986		Jeff Trom
Salmon, chum	02 kg (4 lb)	17.5	Fish Creek
	Aug. 1, 1986		Martin Vanderploeg
Salmon, chum	06 kg (12 lb)	19.0	Ketchikan
	July 18, 1987		Lee W. Putman
Salmon, chum	10 kg (20 lb)	25.2	Great Island, Ketchikan
	July 1, 1985		Tracy McLean
Salmon, coho	Tippet 01 kg (2 lb)	15.2	Kenai River
	Jan 23, 1991		Don A. Middleton
Salmon, coho	01 kg (2 lb)	16.1	Kenai River
	Oct. 9, 1988		Pat K. Johnson
Salmon, coho	Tippet 08 kg (16 lb)	16.10	Karluk River, Kodiak
	Sept. 7, 1991		Norman S. Cohen, MD
Salmon, coho	24 kg (50 lb)	17.4	Kenai River
	Sept 14, 1984		Paul W. Pearson
Salmon, coho	Tippet 02 kg (4 lb)	17.13	Karluk River
	Sept. 15, 1990		Burton R. Leed
Salmon, coho	02 kg (4 lb)	18.1	Karluk River
	Sept. 15, 1990		Burton R. Leed
Salmon, coho	Tippet 10 kg (20 lb)	19.4	Karluk River
	Sept. 4, 1992		Burton R. Leed
Salmon, coho	04 kg (8 lb)	19.8	Situk River, Yakutat
	Sept. 20, 1984		Melvin E. Snook

Species	Tippet / Weight	Date	lb	Location / Angler
Salmon, coho	Tippet 04 kg (8 lb)	Sept. 23, 1992	19.9	Kodiak Island / Paul Leader
Salmon, coho	Tippet 06 kg (12 lb)	Sept. 6, 1988	21.0	Karluk River, Kodiak Alaska / Gary R. Dubiel
Salmon, coho	06 kg (12 lb)	Aug. 18, 1984	21.8	Prince William Sound / Robert E. Dolphin
Salmon, pink	Tippet 10 kg (20 lb)	Aug. 3, 1993	3.0	Good News River / Dan Kipnis
Salmon, pink	Tippet 08 kg (16 lb)	July 27, 1990	5.15	Wolverine Creek / Lawrence E. Hudnall
Salmon, pink	Tippet 04 kg (8 lb)	July 23, 1989	6.12	Douglas Island / Andrea U. Warner
Salmon, pink	Tippet 06 kg (12 lb)	July 31, 1985	6.13	Salmon Creeek, Juneau / Bob Garfield
Salmon, pink	02 kg (4 lb)	Aug. 20, 1988	8.9	Kenai River / Pat K. Johnson
Salmon, pink	Tippet 01 kg (2 lb)	July 13, 1984	10.0	Karluk River, Kodiak Island / Rod Neubert
Salmon, pink	01 kg (2 lb)	July 13, 1984	10.4	Karluk River, Kodiak, Island / Rod Neubert
Salmon, pink	03 kg (6 lb)	July 13, 1984	11.8	Karluk River, Kodiak Island / Rod Neubert
Salmon, pink	Tippet 02 kg (4 lb)	July 10, 1984	11.8	Karluk River, Kodiak Island / Rod Neubert
Salmon, sockeye	02 kg (4 lb)	Aug. 14, 1984	10.15	Russian River / Martin Vanderploeg
Salmon, sockeye	Tippet 01 kg (2 lb)	July 29, 1988	11.5	Baranof Island / Lawrence E. Hudnall
Salmon, sockeye	Tippet 02 kg (4 lb)	Aug. 3, 1989	11.8	Prince of Wales Island / Lawrence E. Hudnall
Salmon, sockeye	Tippet 10 kg (20 lb)	July 17, 1992	11.8	Ugashik River / Ted Hartley
Salmon, sockeye	Tippet 04 kg (8 lb)	Sept. 6, 1987	11.12	Kenai River / Galen (Skip) Perry
Salmon, sockeye	03 kg (6 lb)	Aug. 20, 1987	12.2	Russian River / Dale Hallman
Salmon, sockeye	01 kg (2 lb)	Aug. 20, 1987	12.5	Russian River / Martin Vanderploeg
Salmon, sockeye	10 kg (20 lb)	July 3, 1990	13.0	Kenai River / Jesse J. Zalonis
Salmon, sockeye	Tippet 08 kg (16 lb)	July 16, 1993	14.8	Mulchatna River / Alan Haynes
Salmon, sockeye	06 kg (12 lb)	July 17, 1993	14.12	Coktuli River / Warren J. Redmond
Salmon, sockeye	Tippet 06 kg (12 lb)	Aug. 16, 1987	14.3	Russian River / Marcy Yentzer

Dolly Varden	06 kg (12 lb) July 13, 1993	18.9	Kivalina River Richard B. Evans	
Dolly Varden	All-Tackle July 13, 1993	18.9	Mashutuk River Richard B. Evans	
Halibut, Pacific	M-60 kg (130 lb) June 30, 1982	350.0	Homer Vern S. Foster	
Halibut, Pacific	W-37 kg (80 lb) July 5, 1991	368.0	Gustuvus Celia H. Dueitt	
Halibut, Pacific	All-Tackle July 5, 1991	368.0	Gustuvus Celia H. Dueitt	
Inconnu	10 kg (20 lb) Aug. 20, 1986	53.0	Pah River Lawrence E. Hudnell	
Inconnu	All-Tackle Aug. 20, 1986	53.0	Pah River Lawrence E. Hudnell	
Salmon, chinook	15 kg (30 lb) May 17, 1985	97.4	Kenai River Les Anderson	
Salmon, chinook	All-Tackle May 17, 1985	97.4	Kenai River Les Anderson	
Salmon, chum	All-Tackle June 7, 1985	32.0	Behm Canal Fredrick E. Thynes	
Salmon, pink	06 kg (12 lb) Aug. 17, 1974	12.9	Moose & Kenai rivers Steven Alan Lee	
Salmon, sockeye	08 kg (16 lb) June 23, 1983	12.8	Situk River, Yakutat Mike Boswell	
Salmon, sockeye	15 kg (30 lb) Aug. 9, 1987	15.3	Kenai River Stan Roach	
Salmon, sockeye	All-Tackle Aug. 9, 1987	15.3	Kenai River Stan Roach	
Trout, rainbow	All-Tackle June 22, 1970	42.2	Bell Island David Robert White	

ABOUT THE AUTHORS

René Limeres

Wilderness guide and outdoors writer René Limeres spends busy summers leading remote fishing expeditions in Alaska and Russia. René is the creator and publisher of the award-winning *Alaska Hunting and Fishing Calendar,* and former staff editor of *Alaska Outdoors Magazine.* His articles have appeared in *Alaska Magazine, Alaska Outdoors Magazine, Alaska Roadside Salmon Angler's Guide, Alaska Angling Guide* and *Flyfisherman Magazine.* He lives in Anchorage.

Gunnar Pedersen

Gunnar Pedersen developed his passion for fishing as a child in Trondheim, Norway, learning deep-sea fishing along the rugged coast and flyfishing for trout and salmon on the many pristine rivers and lakes. Gunnar is a professional wilderness guide, author of *The Highway Angler,* and a frequent writer for *Alaska Outdoors Magazine.* He has lived in Alaska since 1979.

Thomas Cappiello

Born in Santa Barbara, California, Thomas Cappiello is a lifelong fisherman. He attended Humboldt State University for a B.S in fisheries, and worked in Alaska as a seasonal aid for the U.S. Forest Service while in school. Since graduating, he has worked for the Alaska Department of Fish and Game and the Prince William Sound Aquaculture Corporation, and is currently completing his Master's Degree in fisheries at the University of Alaska-Fairbanks.

Ken Alt

Ken Alt has been involved with the fisheries of western and northern Alaska for nearly 30 years. As a research biologist for the Alaska Department of Fish and Game in the 1960s, Ken did most of the original fish surveys and stream cataloging for a major portion of the state, in addition to pioneering studies of the life history and movements of Alaska sheefish. Retired and living in Fairbanks, Ken now works as a fisheries consultant and still spends considerable time in the field.

Steve Wottlin

Steve Wottlin hails from the Pacific Northwest, where he spent a considerable part of his formative years chasing steelhead and salmon in the region's bays and big rivers. His deep love of fishing and the outdoors prompted a move to Alaska and a stint as a professional wilderness fishing guide. His expertise is vast and respected; he has authored fishing articles for many outdoor publications and is consulted regularly for his knowledge of adventure recreation and flyfishing in Alaska. He currently lives in Anchorage with his wife and works as a teacher.

Gary Souza

Gary Souza has been a confirmed Northwest steelhead addict for years. Raised in California, he "apprenticed" on the coastal streams of his home state and other big rivers of the Northwest and British Columbia before making his pilgrimage to Alaska 10 years ago. Since then, he has spent the majority of every year fishing for trout and salmon in Southeast waters. Gary has conducted steelhead seminars and served as vice-chair of the Tongass Sportfishing Association Chapter of Trout Unlimited for the past three years.

Mark Whitfield

Mark Whitfield's pen and ink talent is a throwback to the great heyday of outdoor literature illustration. His distinct style has been seen in sporting publications like the nationally acclaimed *Alaska Hunting and Fishing Calendar* and *Alaska Outdoors Magazine,* along with dozens of newsletters, brochures and business logos.

Bill Hickman

As an artist, Bill Hickman is remarkably versatile—able to move freely and proficiently through a variety of mediums, from wood carving to computer graphics. His illustrations and designs have enhanced many publications for business, government and the public. Raised in Iowa, Bill came to Alaska over 25 years ago, built a cabin in the woods and raised a family, then surrendered to the easy city life in Anchorage.

ACKNOWLEDGMENTS

In compiling this book, the authors consulted with people from all over the state, many of whom were very generous in their sharing of information. To all who helped in some way with the research and preparation of this project, we offer a heartfelt thanks—especially to the following individuals and organizations:

Perry Mollen, Katmailand
Van Hartley, Branch River Air Service
Chris Goll, Rainbow River Lodge
Paul Allred, Ouzel Expeditions
Tim LaPorte, Iliamna Air Taxi
Phil Bingman, Freshwater Adventures
Gary Benson, Sourdough Oufitters
Mark Leesic, USFWS, Togiak National Wildlife Refuge
Goo Vogt, Alaska Wildwater
The Alaska Resources Library
Robert Farmer, Deshka River Lodge
Bob Plouffe, Wolverine Lodge
Joe Webb, BLM Kobuk District

Special thanks are also in order to all the area biologists with the Alaska Department of Fish and Game, for their help in making this project as accurate as possible:

Andy Hoffman, Barry Stratton, Kelly Hepler, Kevin Delaney and Susie McCarron (Anchorage); Craig Whitmore, Robert Lafferty and Larry Bartlett (Palmer); Dave Nelson, Larry Larsen, Terry Bendock and Dave Athons (Soldotna); Nick Dudiak (Homer); Len Schwarz (Kodiak); Dick Russell (King Salmon); Nicole Szarczi (Glennallen); Jerry Hallberg, Fred DeCiccio and Richard Barnes (Fairbanks); James Parker (Delta Junction); Karen Ogden (Tok); Randy Ericson (Haines); Mark Schwann and Mike Bethers (Juneau); Artwin Schmitt and Robert Dejong (Sitka); Robert Johnson and Gordy Woods (Yakutat); and Glenn Freeman, Steve Hoffman and Dennis Hubbard (Ketchikan).

The authors also wish to express their gratitude to the following individuals for their contributions to this book: Mark Whitfield and Bill Hickman for their outstanding illustrations and graphics; our contributors—Ken Alt, Thomas Cappiello, Steve Wottlin and Gary Souza—for their patience, commitment and material; and finally, all the countless individuals who lent support and encouragement along the way.

ABOUT TROUT UNLIMITED

For over 35 years, Trout Unlimited has been America's leading trout and salmon conservation organization, dedicated to conserving, protecting, and restoring coldwater fisheries and their watersheds. Whether they are planning and building stream improvement projects, working with government to secure fish-friendly legislation, or teaching young people the importance of protecting wild fish and their habitat, TU members are actively engaged in the fight to preserve our precious trout and salmon resources.

Trout Unlimited was born in 1959 when 15 concerned Michigan anglers banded together to ensure the health of trout, their habitat, and the sport of angling. Just two years later, the fledgling conservation organization had won its first victory: Michigan had replaced its indiscriminate stocking of catchable-sized trout with stream improvement programs, fingerling planting, and protective fishing regulations.

Word of the success in Michigan spread quickly and conservation-minded anglers in other states, from Pennsylvania to California, joined together under the Trout Unlimited banner to effect similar change in their trout fisheries. Three decades later, Trout Unlimited is over 70,000 members strong, with more than 430 chapters nationwide.

Trout Unlimited's strength has always rested in its thousands of dedicated volunteers, many of them anglers, committed to conserving trout and salmon for the next generation of fishermen and women. Trout Unlimited's most visible impact has been on the hundreds of streams and rivers nationwide where TU members have spent countless hours restoring trout and salmon habitat. Stream restoration is more than rolling rocks and picking up trash; a typical project often spans years of research, planning and ongoing stream work. Local chapters across the country also survey and research stream ecosystems and fish populations, urge local and state legislators to make environmentally responsible decisions, and organize environmental education programs for people of all ages.

On the national front, TU has been instrumental in enacting important legislation to protect fish and aquatic habitat. Recent legislative victories include the U.S. International Driftnet Fishery Conservation Act, which provides enforcement for the ban on high seas driftnets; legislation to improve fish migration around hydro-power dams; and laws that will strengthen wetlands protection and lay the foundation for removal of two controversial dams in Washington state. In 1993, in response to a TU lawsuit, the California Department of Fish and Game (DFG) agreed to conduct the first-ever environmental impact review of its state hatchery program. The findings of the DFG study will help to reform one of the nation's largest fish hatchery programs and should help fisheries biologists seeking similar reform in other states. In addition, TU is helping to develop responsible habitat management plans for the future through partnerships with state and federal agencies including the U.S. Forest Service and the Bureau of Land Management.

Trout Unlimited's National Resource Board, made up of representatives of TU's volunteer leadership, sets the conservation agenda for TU. Today, protecting trout and salmon requires up-to-the-minute scientific research and active legislative advocacy to back up hands-on habitat restoration. To provide that expertise, and a presence in the nation's capital, Trout Unlimited has built a dedicated national staff of legal and scientific professionals. The national staff, based in Washington, D.C., works at the federal level to influence national environmental policy and carries out TU's national conservation agenda.

There are still many battles to be won to ensure the future of trout and salmon. The threats to the survival of America's coldwater fisheries are many and diverse, but with the perseverance, commitment and dedication of Trout Unlimited volunteers and the expertise of TU's professional staff, we can ensure that the interests of the conservation-minded angler will continue to be represented on all levels. With your help, TU will continue to fight to conserve, protect, and restore trout and salmon and the rivers that are their habitat.

Trout Unlimited: America's Leading Coldwater Fisheries Conservation Organization
Washington, D.C. Headquarters:
1500 Wilson Boulevard, Arlington, VA 22209
Phone: (703) 522-0200 Fax: (703) 284-9400